W9-CQU-458

iOS Games
by Tutorials

SECOND EDITION

By the raywenderlich.com Tutorial Team

Mike Berg, Tom Bradley, Mike Daley, Jacob Gundersen, Kauserali Hafizji,
Matthijs Hollemans, Christopher LaPollo, Rod Strougo, Marin Todorov,
Ray Wenderlich

iOS Games by Tutorials (Second Edition) Updated for Swift 1.2

Mike Berg, Tom Bradley, Mike Daley, Jacob Gundersen, Kauserali Hafizji, Matthijs Hollemans, Christopher LaPollo, Rod Strougo, Marin Todorov, Ray Wenderlich

Copyright ©2015 Razeware LLC.

Notice of Rights

All rights reserved. No part of this book or corresponding materials (such as text, images, or source code) may be reproduced or distributed by any means without prior written permission of the copyright owner.

Notice of Liability

This book and all corresponding materials (such as source code) are provided on an "as is" basis, without warranty of any kind, express or implied, including but not limited to the warranties of merchantability, fitness for a particular purpose, and noninfringement. In no event shall the authors or copyright holders be liable for any claim, damages or other liability, whether in action of contract, tort or otherwise, arising from, out of or in connec- tion with the software or the use or other dealings in the software.

Trademarks

All trademarks and registered trademarks appearing in this book are the property of their respective owners.

ISBN: 978-1-942878-03-2

Table of Contents:

Dedications

"To my wonderful wife and family, who make it possible to do what I do."

-Mike Berg

"To my wonderful wife Sally and my kids, Jessica, Breanna-Lyn and Rhys."

-Tom Bradley

"To my incredible wife Alison and my fantastic kids Caragh, Alex and Matthew. Thanks for all your support and patience :o)"

–Mike Daley

"To my folks. Thanks for your unwavering support."

-Jacob Gundersen

"To my beautiful wife Batul and my parents - Thanks for supporting and believing in me."

-Kauserali Hafizji

"To the crazy ones, the misfits, the rebels and the troublemakers."

–Matthijs Hollemans

"To Darwin and Bram, who amuse, inspire, and encourage me every day, and to Archana, for everything."

-Chris LaPollo

"To my always supportive and understanding wife Agata, and my family. I love you very much."

-Rod Strougo

"To my parents - ever so supportive and loving. To Mirjam."

–Marin Torodov

"To the editors, authors, and translators at raywenderlich.com – it's an honor working (and playing) with such a talented and hard working group. Let's continue making the coolest stuff fun and easy to learn, and helping others (and ourselves) achieve our dreams."

–Ray Wenderlich

Introduction

By Ray Wenderlich

In this book, you will learn how to make iOS games in Swift using Apple's built-in 2D game framework: Sprite Kit. However, this raises a number of questions:

- **Why iOS?** For a game developer, there's no better platform. The development tools are well-designed and easy to learn, and the App Store makes it incredibly simple to distribute your game to a massive audience – and get paid for it!

- **Why Swift?** Swift is an easy language to get started with, especially if you are a beginner to the iOS platform. In addition, we believe Swift is the way of the future for iOS development, so take this as an opportunity to develop your Swift skills early!

- **Why 2D?** As impressive as 3D games may be, 2D games are a lot easier to make. The artwork is far less complicated, and programming is faster and doesn't require as much math. All of this allows you as a developer to focus on creating killer gameplay.

  If you're a beginner, making 2D games is definitely the best way to get started.

  If you're an advanced developer, you can still make a 2D game much faster than a 3D game. Since it's not necessarily the case that you earn more money with 3D games, why not go for the easier win? Plus, some people (like myself) prefer 2D games anyway!

- **Why Sprite Kit?** Sprite Kit is a brand new framework for making 2D games in iOS, introduced in iOS 7. It is presently the best option for making 2D games on iOS, hands down – it's user-friendly, powerful and fully-supported by Apple.

So rest easy – with iOS, 2D games and Sprite Kit, you're making great choices!

Introducing the second edition

It's been a year since we originally wrote *iOS Games by Tutorials*, and we are happy to announce that you are holding a brand new second edition of the book, fully revised for Swift and iOS 8!

We went through each and every chapter of this book and updated all of the games to use Swift (previously Objective-C), to make sure everything works on iOS 8 and the latest version of Xcode, and to use the latest and greatest technologies and API calls where necessary.

Want more details on what's changed in the second edition? Here's the full list.

• Updated all chapters and sample projects to Swift.

• Wrote a new version of our Sprite Kit utility library (SKTUtils) for Swift. Takes advantage of new Swift capabilities such as operator overloading, for even more readable games.

• Updated all games to work on both iPhone and iPad (previously only iPhone), including the new iPhone 6 and iPhone 6 Plus.

• Updated all chapters to be compatible with iOS 8, including using new APIs where possible and adding notes about relevant updates for iOS 8.

• Updated all chapters to be compatible with the latest version of Xcode (6.1 at the time of this update).

• Added additional clarifications and useful notes to many chapters.

• Removed the "AirPlay" chapter. Instead, we added two new chapters: "OS X" and "More OS X", to cover how to port your Sprite Kit games to OS X. We also added new challenges to port the rest of the games in the book to OS X as well.

About this book

If I may say so, this book is something special. Our goal at raywenderlich.com is for this to be the best book on game programming you've ever read.

There are a lot of game programming books out there, and many of them are quite good, so this is a lofty goal! Here's what we've done to try to accomplish it:

- **Learn by making games**: All the books teach the high-level concepts and show code snippets, but many leave you on your own to put together a complete, functioning game. In this book, you will learn by making five games in a variety of genres – games that are actually fun. Our hope is that you can and will reuse techniques or code from these games to make your own games.

- **Learn by challenges**: Every chapter in this book includes some challenges at the end that are designed to help you practice what you've learned. Following a tutorial is one thing, but applying it yourself is quite another. The challenges in this book take off the training wheels and push you to solidify your knowledge by grappling with a problem on your own. (We also provide the answers, of course.) You'll have a blast doing them, too!

- **Focus on polish**: The key to making a hit game is *polish* – adding loads of well-considered details that set your game apart. Because of this, we've put our money where our mouths are and invested in a top-notch artist and sound designer to create resources for the games in this book. We've also included two chapters all about polishing your game with special effects – otherwise known as adding "Juice" – which we think you will love.

- **High-quality tutorials**: Our site is known for its high-quality programming tutorials, and we've put a lot of time and care into the tutorials in this book to make them equally valuable, if not more so. Each chapter has been put through a rigorous multi-stage editing process – resulting in some chapters being rewritten several times! We've strived to ensure that each chapter contains great technical content while also being fun and easy to follow.

After you finish reading this book, please let me know if you think we were successful in meeting these goals. You can email me anytime at ray@raywenderlich.com.

We hope you enjoy the book, and we can't wait to see what games you come up with!

iOS game development: a history

As you will see, it's easy to make games for iOS with SpriteKit – but it wasn't always so. In the early days of iOS, your only option was to make your game with OpenGL ES, which is the lowest-level graphics API available on the platform. OpenGL ES is notoriously difficult to learn, and it was a big barrier to entry for many beginning game developers.

After a while, third-party developers released some game frameworks on top of OpenGL, the most popular of which was called Cocos2D – in fact, several of us wrote a book on the subject! Many of the games at the top of the App Store charts were made with Cocos2D, and many developers can say that Cocos2D was their entry point into the world of game development.

Cocos2D was a great framework, but it wasn't written or supported by Apple. Because of this, there were often problems when new versions of iOS were released, or with integrating other Apple APIs into the system.

To resolve this, with iOS 7 Apple released a brand new framework for making 2D games: Sprite Kit. Its API is very similar to Cocos2D, with similar types for the sprites, actions and scenes that Cocos2D developers know and love, so fans of the older framework will have no trouble getting up to speed. Sprite Kit also has a few extra bells and whistles, like support for playing videos, making shapes and applying special image effects.

The Sprite Kit API is well-designed and easy to use, especially for beginners. Best of all, you can use it knowing that it's fully supported by Apple and heavily optimized to make 2D games on iOS.

From here on out, if you want to make a 2D game on iOS, we definitely recommend you use Sprite Kit rather than other game frameworks. There's one big exception: if you want to make a cross platform game. Sprite Kit is an Apple-only API so it will be more challenging to port your game from Sprite Kit to other platforms than using other options such as Unity or Cocos2D-X.

If you just want to make something simple for iOS only, Sprite Kit is the way to go. So let's get you up to speed with Sprite Kit – the future of 2D games on iOS!

What you need

To follow along with the tutorials in this book, you need the following:

- **A Mac running OS X Mountain Lion or later**. This is so you can install the latest version of the required development tool: Xcode.

- **Xcode 6.3 or later**. Xcode is the main development tool for iOS. You need to use Xcode 6.3 or later in this book, because Xcode 6.3 is the first version of Xcode that supports Swift 1.2 development. You can download the latest version of Xcode for

free from the Mac App Store here:
https://itunes.apple.com/app/xcode/id497799835?mt=12

• **An iPhone or iPod Touch running iOS 8 or later, and a paid membership to the iOS development program [optional].** For most of the chapters in the book, you can run your code on the iOS 8 Simulator that comes with Xcode. However, there are a few chapters later in the book that require a device for testing, like the chapter on using the built-in accelerometer. Also note that Sprite Kit performs better on devices than it does in the Simulator, so your frame rates will appear lower than expected when running your game in the Simulator.

If you don't have the latest version of Xcode installed, be sure to do that before continuing with the book.

Who this book is for

This book is for beginning to advanced iOS developers. Wherever you fall on that spectrum, you will learn a lot from this book!

This book does require some basic knowledge of Swift. If you do not know Swift, you can still follow along with the book because all of the instructions are in step-by-step format. However, there will likely be parts that are confusing due to gaps in your knowledge. Before beginning this book, you might want to go through our *iOS Apprentice* series, which covers the basics of Swift and iOS development:

http://www.raywenderlich.com/store/ios-apprentice

How to use this book

There are two ways to use this book, depending on whether you are a complete beginner to iOS game development or an advanced developer with knowledge of other 2D game frameworks like Cocos2D.

If you are a complete beginner

If you're a complete beginner to iOS game development, the best way to read this book is from cover to cover. We have arranged the chapters to introduce the material in the most logical manner to build up your skills one layer at a time.

However, there are a few exceptions to this. There are several topics (like Core Image filters) that it made sense to include earlier in the book, even though they are on the advanced side.

For every such chapter, we included a note at the beginning suggesting that novice developers might want to skip past the chapter and return to it later, after gaining more experience or upon finding a need for the advanced technique in question.

So, in a nutshell: read through from cover to cover, optionally skipping certain chapters per our suggestions. By the time you're done, you should have a solid basis for making your own 2D iOS games.

If you are an advanced developer

If you're an advanced developer with knowledge of other 2D game frameworks such as Cocos2D, you will have an easier time adapting to Sprite Kit, as the core concepts and syntax will look very familiar.

Our suggestion is to skim through the early chapters and focus more on the later, more advanced chapters, or where you have a particular interest.

We worked hard to make sure there's plenty of interesting material in the book, even if you're a Cocos2D guru. For example, you may find it particularly worthwhile to take a peek at these chapters:

- **Chapter 12, Crop, Video, and Shape Nodes**
- **Chapter 13, Effect Nodes**
- **Chapter 18, Juice Up Your Game, Part 1**
- **Chapter 19, Juice Up Your Game, Part 2**
- **Chapter 28, Making Art for Programmers**

Don't worry – you can jump right into any chapter in the book, because we'll always have a starter project waiting for you!

What's ahead: an overview

iOS Games by Tutorials is split into five sections, moving from beginning to advanced topics. In each section, you will create a complete mini-game, from scratch! The book also includes some bonus chapters at the end that we think you'll enjoy.

Let's take a look at what's ahead!

Section I: Getting started

This section covers the basics of making 2D games with Sprite Kit. These are the most important techniques, the ones you'll use in almost every game you make. By the time you reach the end of this section, you'll be ready to make your own simple game.

Throughout this section you will create an action game called Zombie Conga, where you take the role of a happy-go-lucky zombie who just wants to party!

You will build this game across five chapters, in stages:

1. **Chapter 1, Sprites:** Add your first sprites to the game: the background and the zombie.

2. **Chapter 2, Manual Movement:** Make the zombie follow your touches to move around the screen, and in the process get a crash-course in basic 2D vector math.

3. **Chapter 3, Actions:** Add cats and crazy cat ladies to the game, as well as basic collision detection and gameplay.

4. **Chapter 4, Scenes:** Add a main menu to the game, as well as win and lose scenes.

5. **Chapter 5, Scrolling:** Make the game scroll from left to right and finally, add the conga line itself. (What, we didn't mention the conga line?)

6. **Chapter 6, OS X:** Get Zombie Conga working on the Mac, in just a few simple steps!

Section II: Labels and particle systems

In this section, you'll learn how to add labels to your game to display text and how to create special effects with particle systems, like explosions and star fields.

In the process, you will create a space shooter game called XBlaster, where all of the artwork is ASCII-based!

You will build this game across two chapters, in stages:

7. **Chapter 7, Labels**: Create the player and enemy ships, score, health bar and plasma cannon, all with Sprite Kit labels.

8. **Chapter 8, Particle Systems:** Through the power of particle systems, create a star field background, a propulsion engine for the player ship and yes, explosions.

Section III: Physics and nodes

In this section, you will learn how to use the built-in 2D physics engine included with Sprite Kit to create movement as realistic as that in *Angry Birds* or *Cut the Rope*. You will also learn how to use special types of nodes that allow you to play videos, create shapes and apply image filters in your game.

In the process, you will create a physics puzzle game called Cat Nap, where you take the role of a cat who has had a long day and just wants to go to bed.

You will build this game across five chapters, in stages:

9. **Chapter 9, Beginning Physics**: Before starting on the game itself, create a simple test app to get familiar with the core concepts of the physics engine, such as creating physics bodies and setting properties.

10. **Chapter 10, Intermediate Physics**: Create the first level of the game, pictured above, and learn about debug drawing, physics-based collision detection and creating levels from property list files.

11. **Chapter 11, Advanced Physics:** Add two more levels to the game as you learn about interactive bodies, joints between bodies, complex body shapes and more.

12. **Chapter 12, Crop, Video, and Shape Nodes:** Add some special new blocks to Cat Nap while learning about additional types of nodes that allow you to do some amazing things – like play videos, crop images and create dynamic shapes.

13. **Chapter 13, Effect Nodes**: Wrap up Cat Nap by adding image filters to parts of the game, resulting in some very cool special effects.

Section IV: Tile maps and juice

At the time of writing, Sprite Kit doesn't come packaged with tile map support – but in this section, you're going to learn how to create your own tile map engine! You'll also learn how to take a good game and make it great by adding a ton of special effects and excitement – a.k.a. "juice."

In the process, you will create a tile map-based action game called Pest Control, where you take the role of Arnold, a guy so badass he *never* wears a shirt. Giant bugs have invaded Arnold's town, and he's just the guy to dish out a good smashing.

You will build this game across six chapters, in stages:

14. **Chapter 14, Beginning Tile Maps:** Create the bulk of Pest Control. Write code to create a tile map from a simple text format and add the hero and bug-monsters to the game.

15. **Chapter 15, More Tile Maps:** Add the core gameplay and learn about coordinate conversions and collision detection with tile maps.

16. **Chapter 16, Imported Tile Maps:** Import tile maps into your game that are stored in a popular tile-map format called TMX files, and use an open-source map editor to create your maps.

17. **Chapter 17, Saving and Loading Games:** Implement an autosave feature that stores a player's progress in Pest Control. Also add gameplay features like timers, winning and losing and progressing through multiple levels.

18. **Chapter 18, Juice Up Your Game, Part 1:** Demonstrate how adding simple visual effects can make Pest Control, or any game you write, much more entertaining.

19. **Chapter 19, Juice Up Your Game, Part 2:** Add sounds and even more special effects, because adding fewer effects at this point would be ridiculous.

Section V: Other game APIs

In this section, you'll learn about some APIs other than Sprite Kit that are good to know when making games for iOS. In particular, you will learn how to make user interfaces with UIKit, control movement with the accelerometer, and add Game Center leaderboards, achievements, and multiplayer support into your game.

In the process, you will create a top-down racing game called Circuit Racer, where you take the role of an elite racecar driver out to set a world record. It would be no problem if it weren't for the debris on the track!

You will build this game across six chapters, in stages:

20. **Chapter 20, UIKit**: Integrate Sprite Kit with UIKit to create view controllers for different screens of your game, as well as use standard iOS controls within your main game scene itself (such as creating an on-screen joypad).

21. **Chapter 21, Accelerometer**: Use the accelerometer to move your sprites around the screen!

22. **Chapter 22, More OS X**: You've seen how to port simple Sprite Kit games to OS X, but what about when things get more complicated?

23. **Chapter 23, Game Center Achievements**: Enable Game Center for your game and award the user achievements for accomplishing certain feats.

24. **Chapter 24, Game Center Leaderboards**: Set up various leaderboards for your game and track and report the player's scores.

25. **Chapter 25, Game Center Multiplayer**: Add multiplayer support so players can race against each other in real-time across the Internet!

Bonus chapters

And that's not all – on top of the above, we have some bonus chapters for you!

These bonus chapters come as an optional PDF download, which you can download for free here:

• http://www.raywenderlich.com/store/ios-games-by-tutorials/bonus-chapters

We hope you enjoy the bonus chapters!

26. **Chapter 26, Performance: Texture Atlases**: Take a deep dive into one of the most important aspects in making your game perform well and use less memory: using texture atlases.

27. **Chapter 27, Performance: Tips and Tricks**: Learn how to get the most performance out of your game and gain an understanding of what's fast and what's slow when it comes to making 2D games on iOS.

28. **Chapter 28, Making Art for Programmers**: If you liked the art in these mini-games and want to learn how to either hire an artist or make some art of your own, look no further than this chapter! This chapter guides you through drawing a cute cat in the style of this book with Illustrator.

Book source code and forums

You can get the source code for the book here:

• http://www.raywenderlich.com/store/ios-games-by-tutorials/source-code

Some of the chapters have starter projects or other required resources that are also included, and you'll definitely want to have these on hand as you go through the book.

We've set up an official forum for the book at raywenderlich.com/forums. This is a great place to ask any questions you have about the book or about making games with Sprite Kit, or to submit any errata you may find.

PDF Version

We also have a PDF version of this book available, which can be handy if you ever want to copy/paste code or search for a specific term through the book as you're developing.

And speaking of the PDF version, we have some good news!

Since you purchased the physical copy of this book, you are eligible to buy the PDF version at a significant discount if you would like (if you don't have it already). For more details, see this page:

• http://www.raywenderlich.com/store/ios-games-by-tutorials/upgrade

License

By purchasing *iOS Games by Tutorials*, you acquire the following license:

• You are allowed to use and/or modify the source code provided with *iOS Games by Tutorials* in as many games as you want, with no attribution required.

• You are allowed to use and/or modify all art, music and sound effects that are included with *iOS Games by Tutorials* in as many games as you want, but must include this attribution line somewhere inside your game: "Artwork/sounds: from *iOS Games by Tutorials* book, available at http://www.raywenderlich.com".

• The source code included in *iOS Games by Tutorials* is for your personal use only. You are NOT allowed to distribute or sell the source code in *iOS Games by Tutorials* without prior authorization.

• This book is for your personal use only. You are NOT allowed to sell this book without prior authorization, or distribute it to friends, co-workers or students – they would need to purchase their own copy.

All materials provided with this book are provided on an "as-is" basis, without warranty of any kind, express or implied, including but not limited to the warranties of merchantability, fitness for a particular purpose and non-infringement. In no event shall the authors or copyright holders be liable for any claim, damages or other liability, whether in an action of contract, tort or otherwise, arising from, out of or in connection with the software or the use or other dealings in the software.

All trademarks and registered trademarks appearing in this guide are the property of their respective owners.

Acknowledgements

We would like to thank many people for their assistance in making this book possible:

- **Our families**: For bearing with us during this hectic time as we worked all hours of the night to get this book ready for publication!

- **Everyone at Apple**: For developing an amazing 2D game framework and other helpful APIs for games, for constantly inspiring us to improve our apps and skills, and for making it possible for many developers to have their dream jobs!

- **Ricardo Quesada**: Ricardo is the lead developer of Cocos2D, which got many of us into making games. Sprite Kit seems to draw quite a bit of inspiration from Cocos2D, so Ricardo deserves "mad props" for that as well.

- And most importantly, **the readers of raywenderlich.com and you**! Thank you so much for reading our site and purchasing this book. Your continued readership and support is what makes this all possible!

About the authors

__Harken all genders!__ You may or may not have noticed that all of this book's authors are men. This is unfortunate, and not by design. If you are a woman developing for iOS and are interested in joining the Tutorial Team to write about gaming topics, we'd love to hear from you! ☺

Mike Berg is a full-time game artist who is fortunate enough to work with many indie game developers from all over the world. When he's not manipulating pixel colors, he loves to eat good food, spend time with his family, play games and be happy. You can check out his work at http://www.weheartgames.com.

Tom Bradley has been coding since he was six years old and has over 14 years of industry experience. More recently, he cofounded 71Squared Ltd., known for its Mac-based game development tools, Particle Designer and Glyph Designer. When not in front of the computer or playing with cameras, he can be found spending time with his wife Sally and two children, Jessica and Rhys.

Mike Daley has been developing software for over 25 years. Mike is cofounder of 71Squared Ltd, known for its Mac-based game development tools, Particle Designer and Glyph Designer. When not in front of his computer writing software, he can be with his wife and three children or indulging his other passion, flying light aircraft.

Jake Gundersen is a gamer, maker and programmer. He is cofounder of the educational game company Third Rail Games. He has a particular interest in gaming, image processing and computer graphics. You can find his musings and codings at http://indieambitions.com.

Kauserali Hafizji (a.k.a. Ali) is a developer at heart. He is an avid programmer and loves writing code, even over the weekend. A good read, cool dip in the pool and a hot cheesy meal would be the perfect end to his weekend. You can find Ali on Twitter as @Ali_hafizji.

Matthijs Hollemans is an independent designer and developer who loves to create awesome software for the iPad and iPhone. He also enjoys teaching others to do the same, which is why he wrote the *iOS Apprentice* series of e-books. In his spare time, Matthijs is learning to play jazz piano (it's hard!) and likes to go barefoot running when the sun is out. Check out his blog at http://www.hollance.com.

Chris LaPollo began programming back when a computer with 256 kilobytes of RAM was something to brag about. Now he's an independent developer and contractor focused on making mobile apps and video games. When not staring at computer screens, he's usually relaxing with his wife and kids or climbing up rocks. Contact him on Twitter @ChrisLaPollo.

Rod Strougo began his journey in physics and games way back with an Apple][, writing games in Basic. Rod's career took a diversion, spending 15 years writing software for IBM and AT&T. These days he follows his passion in game development and teaching, providing iOS Training at Big Nerd Ranch and cool secret projects. Originally from Rio de Janeiro, Brazil, he lives in Atlanta, GA with his wife and sons.

Marin Todorov is an independent iOS developer and publisher, with background in various platforms and languages. He has published several books, written about iOS development on his blog, and authored an online game programming course. He loves to read, travel, and write code. Visit his web site: http://www.touch-code-magazine.com

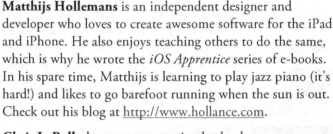

Ray Wenderlich is an iPhone developer, gamer and the founder of Razeware LLC. Ray is passionate about both making apps and teaching others the techniques to make them. He and the Tutorial Team have written a bunch of tutorials about iOS development available at http://www.raywenderlich.com.

About the editors

Chris LaPollo was the tech editor for this book, as well as one of its authors. You may remember him from such places as the the list of authors above. He probably hasn't changed much since then, but if you want an update, feel free to ask @ChrisLaPollo on Twitter.

B.C. Phillips was the editor of this book. He is an independent researcher and editor who splits his time between New York City and the Northern Catskills. He has many interests, but particularly loves cooking, eating, being active, thinking about deep questions and working on his cabin and land in the mountains (even though his iPhone is pretty useless up there).

Toby Stephens has been a software developer for 20 years, working mainly in the financial sector. He is now head of iOS development for inplaymaker, based in the UK. In his spare time, he tinkers with writing iOS games and creating music. You can find him on Twitter as @thetobystephens.

Ray Wenderlich was the final pass editor for this book. He is an iPhone developer, gamer and the founder of Razeware LLC. Ray is passionate about both making apps and teaching others the techniques to make them. He and the Tutorial Team have written a bunch of tutorials about iOS development available at http://www.raywenderlich.com.

About the artists

Mike Berg created all of the artwork in the games for this book. Mike is a full-time game artist who is fortunate enough to work with many indie game developers from all over the world. When he's not manipulating pixel colors, he loves to eat good food, spend time with his family, play games and be happy. You can check out his work at http://www.weheartgames.com.

Vinnie Prabhu created all of the music and sounds for the games in this book. Vinnie is a music composer/software engineer from Northern Virginia who has done music and sound work for concerts, plays and video games. He's also a staff member on OverClocked ReMix, an online community for music and video game fans. You can find Vinnie on Twitter as @palpablevt.

Vicki Wenderlich created many of the illustrations in this book. Vicki discovered a love of digital art five years ago, and has been making app art and digital illustrations ever since. She is passionate about helping people pursue their dreams and makes app art for developers available on her website, http://www.gameartguppy.com.

Section I: Getting Started

This section covers the basics of making 2D games with Sprite Kit. These are the most important techniques, the ones you'll use in almost every game you make. By the time you reach the end of this section, you'll be ready to make your own simple game.

Throughout this section you will create an action game called Zombie Conga, where you take the role of a happy-go-lucky zombie who just wants to party!

Chapter 1: Sprites

By Ray Wenderlich

Now that you know what Sprite Kit is and why you should use it, it's time to try it out for yourself!

The first minigame you will build in this book is called Zombie Conga. Here's what it will look like when you're finished:

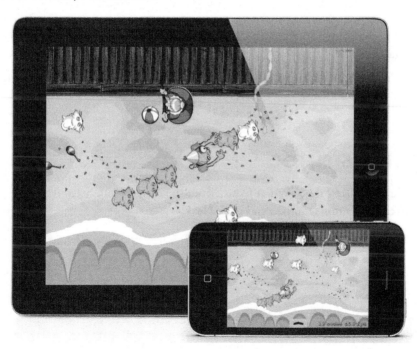

In Zombie Conga, you take the role of a happy-go-lucky zombie who just wants to party!

Luckily, the beach town you occupy has an overly abundant cat population. All you need to do is bite them and they'll join your zombie conga line.

But watch out for crazy cat ladies! These wizened warriors in red dresses won't take kindly to anyone stealing their beloved cats, and will do their best to make the zombie rest in peace—permanently.

You will build this game across the next six chapters, in stages:

1. **Chapter 1, Sprites:** You are here! Get started by adding your first sprites to the game: the background and the zombie.

2. **Chapter 2, Manual Movement:** You'll make the zombie follow your touches around the screen, getting a crash-course in basic 2D vector math in the process.

3. **Chapter 3, Actions:** You'll add cats and crazy cat ladies to the game, as well as some basic collision detection and gameplay.

4. **Chapter 4, Scenes:** You'll add a main menu to the game, as well as win and lose scenes.

5. **Chapter 5, Scrolling:** You'll make the game scroll from left to right, and finally add the conga line itself.

6. **Chapter 6, OS X:** You'll port the game to OS X so you can party on both platforms!

Let's get this conga started!

Getting started

Start Xcode and select **File\New\Project…** from the main menu. Select the **iOS\Application\Game** template and click **Next**.

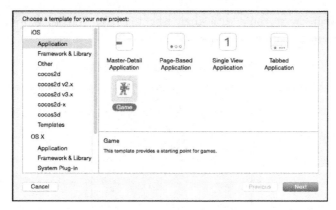

Enter **ZombieConga** for the Product Name, choose **Swift** for Language, **SpriteKit** for Game Technology, **Universal** for Devices and click **Next**.

Select somewhere on your hard drive to save your project and click **Create**. At this point, Xcode will generate a simple Sprite Kit starter project for you.

Take a look at what Sprite Kit made. In Xcode's toolbar, select the **iPhone 6** and click **Play**.

After a brief splash screen, you'll see a single label that says, "Hello, World!" When you click on the screen, a rotating space ship will appear.

In Sprite Kit, a single object called a scene controls each "screen" of your app. A scene is a subclass of Sprite Kit's SKScene class.

Right now this app just has a single scene, GameScene. Open **GameScene.swift** and you'll see the code that displays the label and rotating space ship. It's not important to understand this code quite yet—you're going to remove it all and build up your game one step at a time.

For now, delete everything in **GameScene.swift** and replace it with the following:

```
import SpriteKit

class GameScene: SKScene {
  override func didMoveToView(view: SKView) {
    backgroundColor = SKColor.whiteColor()
  }
}
```

didMoveToView() is the method that Sprite Kit calls before it presents your scene in a view; it's a good place to do some initial setup of your scene's contents. Here, you simply set the background color to white.

Zombie Conga is designed to run in landscape mode, so let's configure the app for this. To do this, select the **ZombieConga** project in the Project Navigator and then select the **ZombieConga** target. Go to the **General** tab and make sure that *only* **Landscape Left** and **Landscape Right** are checked:

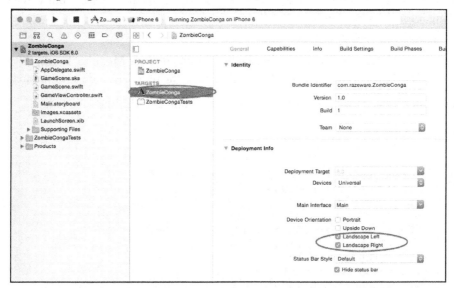

You also need to modify this in one more spot. Open **Supporting File\Info.plist**, and find the **Supported interface orientations (iPad)** entry. Delete the entries for **Portrait (bottom home button)** and **Portrait (top home button)** you see there, so that only the landscape options remain.

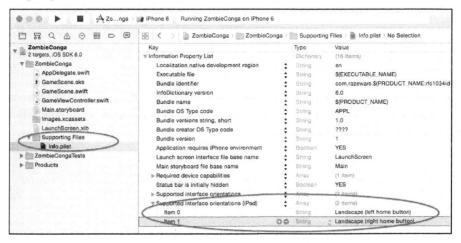

The Sprite Kit template creates a file named **GameScene.sks** automatically. You can edit this file with Xcode's new, built-in Scene Editor to lay out your game scene visually. Think of Scene Editor as a simple Interface Builder for Sprite Kit.

You'll learn all about Scene Editor in Chapter 10, "Intermediate Physics," but you won't be using it for Zombie Conga, as it will be easier (and more instructive) to create the sprites programmatically instead.

So, control-click **GameScene.sks**, select **Delete** and then select **Move to Trash**. Since you're no longer using this file, you'll have to modify the template code appropriately.

Open **GameViewController.swift** and replace the contents with the following:

```swift
import UIKit
import SpriteKit

class GameViewController: UIViewController {
  override func viewDidLoad() {
    super.viewDidLoad()
    let scene =
      GameScene(size:CGSize(width: 2048, height: 1536))
    let skView = self.view as! SKView
    skView.showsFPS = true
    skView.showsNodeCount = true
    skView.ignoresSiblingOrder = true
    scene.scaleMode = .AspectFill
    skView.presentScene(scene)
  }
  override func prefersStatusBarHidden() -> Bool {
    return true
  }
}
```

Previously, the view controller loaded the scene from **GameScene.sks**, but now it creates the scene by calling an initializer on GameScene instead.

Notice that when you create the scene, you pass in a hardcoded size of **2048x1536** and set the scale mode to AspectFill. This leads us into a quick discussion of how this game is designed to work as a universal app.

Universal app support

> **Note**: This section is optional and for those who are especially curious. If you're eager to get coding as soon as possible, feel free to skip to the next section, "Adding the art."

We've designed all the games in this book as universal apps, which means they will work on iPhone and iPad. Also in Chapter 6, "OS X", you will learn how to port it to OS X as well.

The scenes for the games in this book have been designed with a base size of 2048x1536 (or reversed for portrait orientation), with the scale mode set to aspect fill. Aspect fill instructs Sprite Kit to scale the scene's content to fill the entire screen (even if some of the content needs to be cut off).

This results in your scene appearing as-is on the iPad Retina (which has a resolution of 2048x1536), but being scaled/cropped on the iPhone to fit the phone's smaller size and different aspect ratio.

Let's take a look at some examples of how the games will look on different devices in landscape, moving from smallest to largest aspect ratio:

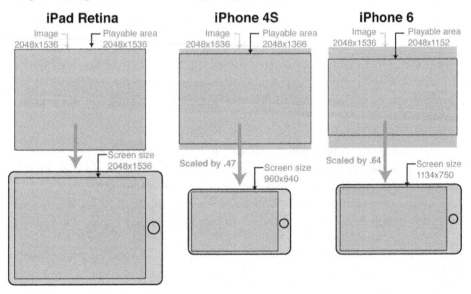

- **iPad Retina [4:3 or 1.33]**: Displayed as-is to fit the 2048x1536 screen size.

- **iPad Non-Retina [4:3 or 1.33]**: Aspect fill will scale a 2048x1536 playable area by 0.5 to fit the 1024x768 screen size.

- **iPhone 4S [3:2 or 1.5]**: Aspect fill will scale a 2048x1366 playable area by 0.47 to fit the 960x640 screen size.

- **iPhone 5 [16:9 or 1.77]**: Aspect fill will scale a 2048x1152 playable area by 0.56 to fit the 1136x640 screen size.

- **iPhone 6 [16:9 or 1.77]**: Aspect fill will scale a 2048x1152 playable area by 0.64 to fit the 1334x750 screen size.

- **iPhone 6 Plus [16:9 or 1.77]**: Aspect fill will scale a 2048x1152 playable area by 0.93 to fit the 1920x1080 screen size.

Since aspect fill will crop the scene on the top and bottom for iPhones, we've designed the games in this book to have a main "playable area" that is guaranteed to be visible on all devices. Basically, the games have a 192-pixel margin on the top/bottom (in landscape) and left/right (in portrait) in which you should avoid putting essential content. We'll show you how to visualize this later in the book.

Note that you need only one set of art for this to work: the art to fit the maximum screen scene (2048x1536). The art will be downscaled on devices other than the iPad Retina.

> **Note:** The con of this approach is that the art will be bigger than necessary for some devices (such as the iPhone 4s), which wastes some texture memory and space. However, the pro is that the game is kept nice and simple and works great on all devices.
>
> An alternate approach would be to add different images for each device, leveraging Apple's built in naming scheme so that it loads the proper sized image for each device (xx.png, xx@2x.png, xx@3x.png, xx~iPad.png, and xx~iPad@2x.png). However, in practice this would complicate your code; you wouldn't be able to use a standard scene size across all devices like you do here.
>
> For this book, we opted to keep things simple, especially since these games have low art requirements.

Adding the art

Next, you need to add the art for the game into the project.

In the resources for this chapter, your images are split into two sets: large background images (**Images**) and smaller game object images (**sprites.atlas**). This split is for performance reasons, as you'll learn in Chapter 26, "Performance: Texture Atlases."

To add these, simply drag the **Images** and **sprites.atlas** folders into your project. Make sure that **Copy items if needed**, **Create Groups**, and the **ZombieConga** target are selected, and click Finish.

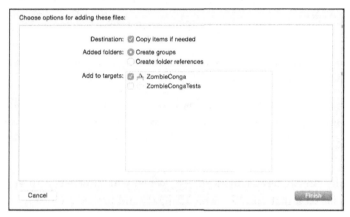

Your project navigator should look like this:

Browse through the art you've added to get familiar with it. Note that as mentioned in the previous sectoin, the art is sized for 2048x1536 scene size.

In particular, look for an image called **background1** in **Images**. This represents the beach town where the game's action takes place—and this is what you're going to use to create your first sprite!

Finishing touches

> **Note:** This is another optional section, as it doesn't have any impact on gameplay; it's just some "nice-to-have" polish that you'd typically want to do for a game. If you want to get straight to coding, feel free to skip to the next section, "Displaying a sprite".

There are two last things you should set up to get this game started on the right foot: configure the launch screen, and an app icon.

The launch screen is what iOS displays when your app is first loading, which usually takes a few seconds. A launch image gives the player the impression that your app is starting quickly—the default black screen, needless to say, does not. For Zombie Conga, you'll show a splash screen with the name of the game.

Your app actually already has a launch screen. When you launched your app earlier, you may have a brief screen that said "Zombie Conga" (and looked a bit ugly, to be frank)!

In iOS 8, your apps have a special **launch screen file**; this is basically a XIB (LaunchScreen.xib in this project) that you can configure to present something to the screen while your app is loading. The advantage of this (over the old method of just displaying an image) is that you can use Auto Layout to have more fine-grained control of how this screen looks on different devices.

Let's try this out. Open **LaunchScreen.xib** and you should see the following:

Select the two labels in this view and delete them. Then, in the Object Library on the right sidebar, drag an image view into the view, so that it fills the entire area:

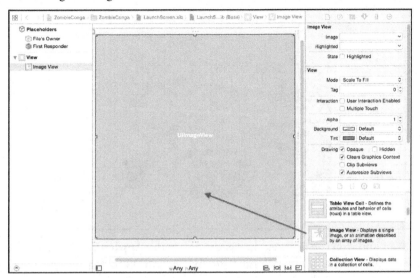

Next you need to set the image view so that it is always the same width and height of it's containing view. To do this, make sure the image view is selected, click the Pin button in the lower right (looks like a tie fighter), click the four light red lines so that it is pinned to each edge, and click **Add 4 Constraints**:

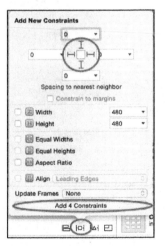

With the image view still selected, make sure the fourth tab on the right is selected (the Attributes Inspector). Set the Image to **MainMenu.png**, and set the **View Mode** to **Aspect Fill**:

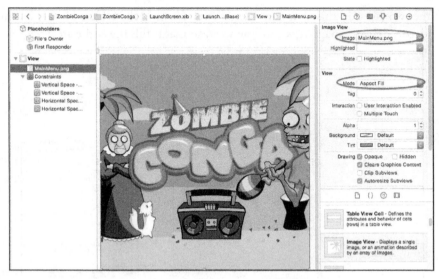

To set up an app icon, open **Images.xcassets**, select the **AppIcon** entry. Then from the resources for this chapter, drag each file from the **Icons\iOS** folder into the appropriate spot, one at a time. You should see the following when you're done:

Finally, select the **Spaceship** entry and hit your delete key to remove it— unfortunately, this is not a game about space zombies! ☺

Build and run your app again. This time, you should see a brief Zombie Conga splash screen:

Which is quickly followed by a (mostly) blank white screen:

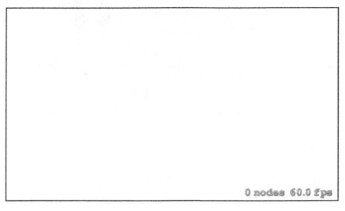

This may not look like much, but you now have a starting point upon which to build your first Sprite Kit game.

Let's move on to the simplest possible task, which also happens to be one of the most important and common tasks when making games: getting an image to appear on the screen.

Displaying a sprite

When making a 2D game, you usually put images on the screen representing your game's various elements: the hero, enemies, bullets and so on. Each of these images is called a **sprite**.

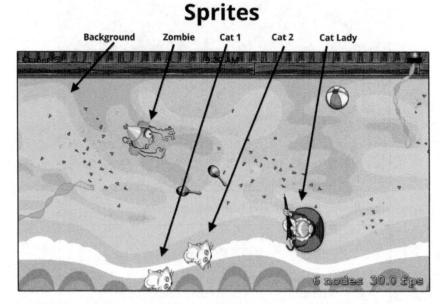

Sprite Kit has a special class called SKSpriteNode that makes it easy to create and work with sprites. This is what you'll use to add all your sprites to the game. Let's give it a try.

Creating a sprite

Open **GameScene.swift** and add this line to didMoveToView(), right after you set the background color:

```
let background = SKSpriteNode(imageNamed: "background1")
```

Note that you don't need to pass the image's extension, as Sprite Kit will automatically determine that for you.

Build and run. Ah, you thought it was simple, but at this point you still see a blank white screen—what gives?

Adding a sprite to the scene

It actually is simple. It's just that a sprite will not show up onscreen until you add it as a child of the scene, or one of the scene's descendent **nodes**.

To do this, add this line of code right after the previous line:

```
addChild(background)
```

You'll learn about nodes and scenes later. For now, build and run again, and you'll see part of the background appear in the bottom left of the screen:

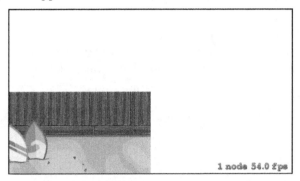

Obviously, that's not quite what you want. To get the background in the correct spot, you have to set its position.

Positioning a sprite

By default, Sprite Kit positions sprites at (0, 0), which in Sprite Kit represents the bottom left. Note that this is different from the UIKit coordinate system in iOS, where (0, 0) represents the top left.

Try positioning the background somewhere else by setting the `position` property. Add this line of code right before calling `addChild(background)`:

```
background.position = CGPoint(x: size.width/2, y: size.height/2)
```

Here you set the background to the center of the screen. Even though this is just one line of code, there are four important things to understand:

1. The type of the `position` property is `CGPoint`, which is a simple structure that has `x` and `y` components:

```
struct CGPoint {
  var x: CGFloat
  var y: CGFloat
}
```

2. You can easily create a new `CGPoint` with the initializer shown above.

3. Since you're writing this code in an `SKScene` subclass, you can access the size of the scene at any time with the `size` property. The `size` property's type is `CGSize`, which is a simple structure like `CGPoint` that has `width` and `height` components.

```
struct CGSize {
  var width: CGFloat
  var height: CGFloat
}
```

4. Note that a sprite's position is within the coordinate space of its parent node, which in this case is the scene itself. You'll learn more about this in Chapter 5, "Scrolling."

Build and run, and now your background is fully visible:

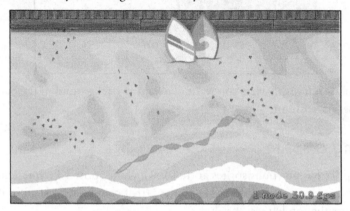

> **Note**: You may notice that you can't see the entire background on iPhone devices—parts of it overlap on the top and bottom. This is by design, so the game works on both iPad and iPhone, as discussed in the Universal App Support section earlier in this chapter.

Setting a sprite's anchor point

When you set the position of the background sprite, you're setting the *center* of the background sprite to that position.

This explains why you could only see the upper half of the sprite earlier. Before you set the position, it defaulted to (0, 0). This placed the center of the sprite at the lower-left corner of the screen, so you could only see the top half.

You can change this behavior by setting a sprite's anchor point. Think of the anchor point as "the spot within a sprite that you pin to a particular position." For example, here is an illustration showing a sprite positioned at the center of the screen, but with different anchor points:

Position: center screen

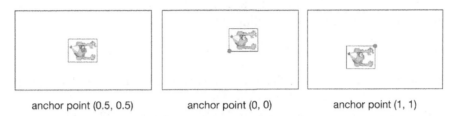

anchor point (0.5, 0.5)   anchor point (0, 0)   anchor point (1, 1)

To see how this works, replace the line that sets the background's position to the center of the screen with the following:

```
background.anchorPoint = CGPointZero
background.position = CGPointZero
```

CGPointZero is a handy shortcut for (0, 0). Here, you set the anchor point of the sprite to (0, 0) to pin the lower-left corner of the sprite to whatever position you set—in this case, also (0, 0).

Build and run, and the image is still in the right spot:

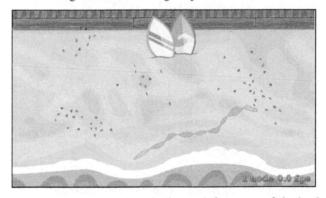

This works because now you are pinning the lower-left corner of the background image to the lower-left corner of the screen.

Here you changed the anchor point of the background for learning purposes. However, usually you can leave the anchor point at its default of (0.5, 0.5), unless you have a specific need to rotate the sprite around a particular point—an example of which is described in the next section.

So, in short: When you set the position of a sprite, by default you are positioning the center of the sprite.

Rotating a sprite

To rotate a sprite, you simply set its zRotation property. Try it out on the background sprite by adding this line right before calling addChild():

```
background.zRotation = CGFloat(M_PI) / 8
```

Rotation values are in radians, which are a method of measuring angles. This example rotates the sprite pi / 8 radians, which is equal to 22.5 degrees. Also notice how you convert M_PI, which is a Double, into a CGFloat. That's because zRotation requires a CGFloat and Swift doesn't automatically convert between types like some other languages do.

> **Note:** I don't know about you, but I find it easier to think about rotations in degrees rather than in radians. Later in the book, you'll create helper routines to convert between degrees and radians.

Build and run, and check out your rotated background sprite:

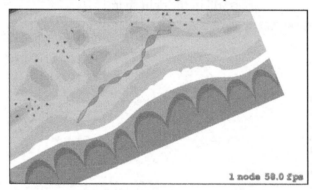

This raises an interesting point. Sprites are rotated about their anchor points. Since you set this sprite's anchor point to (0, 0), it rotates around the bottom-left corner.

> **Note:** Remember that on the iPhone, the bottom-left of this image is actually offscreen! If you're not sure why this is, refer back to the Universal App Support section earlier in this chapter.

Try rotating the sprite around the center instead. Replace the lines that set the position and anchor point with these:

```
background.position = CGPoint(x: size.width/2, y: size.height/2)
background.anchorPoint = CGPoint(x: 0.5, y: 0.5) // default
```

Build and run, and this time the background sprite will have rotated around the center:

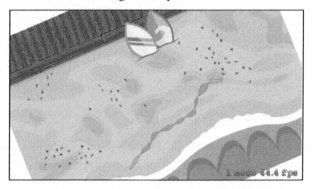

This is all good to know! But for Zombie Conga, you don't want a rotated background, so comment out that line:

```
// background.zRotation = CGFloat(M_PI) / 8
```

If you're wondering when you might want to change the anchor point in a game, imagine you're creating a character's body out of different sprites—one each for the head, torso, left arm, right arm, left leg and right leg:

If you wanted to rotate these body parts at their joints, you'd have to modify the anchor point for each sprite, as shown in the diagram above.

But again, usually you should leave the anchor point at default unless you have a specific need, like the one shown here.

Getting the size of a sprite

Sometimes when you're working with a sprite, you want to know how big it is. A sprite's size defaults to the size of the image. In Sprite Kit, the class representing this image is called a **texture**.

Add these lines after the call to addChild() to get the size of the background and log it to the console:

```
let mySize = background.size
println("Size: \(mySize)")
```

Build and run, and in your console output you should see something like this:

```
Size: (2048.0,1536.0)
```

Sometimes, it's useful to programmatically get the size of a sprite like this instead of hard-coding numbers. Your code will be much more robust and adaptable.

Sprites and nodes

Earlier, you learned that to make a sprite appear onscreen, you need to add it as a child of the scene, or as one of the scene's descendent **nodes**. This section will delve more deeply into the concept of nodes.

Everything that appears on the screen in Sprite Kit derives from a class called SKNode. The scene class (SKScene) derives from SKNode, and the sprite class (SKSpriteNode) also derives from SKNode.

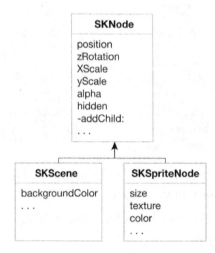

`SKSpriteNode` inherits a lot of its capabilities from `SKNode`. It turns out the position and rotation properties are derived from `SKNode` rather than being particular to `SKSpriteNode`. This means that, just as you can set the position or rotation of a sprite, you can do the same thing with the scene itself or anything else that derives from `SKNode`.

You can think of everything that appears on the screen combined as a graph of nodes, often referred to as a **scene graph**. Here's an example of what such a graph might look like for Zombie Conga if there were one zombie, two cats and one crazy cat lady in the game:

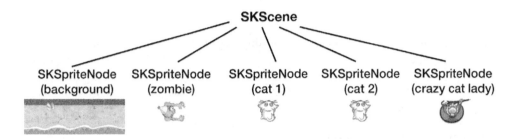

You'll learn more about nodes and the neat things you can do with them in Chapter 5, "Scrolling." For now, you'll add your sprites as direct children of the scene.

Nodes and z position

Every node has a property you can set called `zPosition`, which defaults to 0. Each node draws its child nodes in the order of their z-position, from lowest to highest.

Earlier in this chapter, you added this line to **GameViewController.swift**:

```
skView.ignoresSiblingOrder = true
```

If `ignoresSiblingOrder` is `true`, Sprite Kit makes no guarantees as to the order in which it draws each node's children with the same zPosition. If `ignoresSiblingOrder` is `false`, Sprite Kit will draw each node's children with the same zPosition in the order in which they were added to their parent. In general, it's good to set this property to `true`, because it allows Sprite Kit to perform some optimizations under the hood to make your game run faster.

However, setting this property to `true` can cause problems if you're not careful. For example, if you were to add a zombie to this scene at the same `zPosition` as the background—which would happen if you left them at the default position of 0—Sprite

Kit might draw the background on top of the zombie, covering the zombie from the player's view. And if zombies are scary, just imagine invisible ones!

To fix this, you'll set the background's zPosition to -1. This way, Sprite Kit will draw it before anything else you add to the scene, which will default to a zPosition of 0.

In **GameScene.swift**, add this line right before the call to addChild():

```
background.zPosition = -1
```

Phew! No invisible zombies.

Finishing touches

That's it for this chapter! As you can see, adding a sprite to a scene takes only three or four lines of code:

1. Create the sprite.

2. Position the sprite.

3. (Optionally) Set its z-position.

4. Add it to the scene graph.

Now it's time for you to test your newfound knowledge by adding the zombie to the scene.

Challenges

It's important for you to practice what you've learned on your own, so each chapter in this book has one to three challenges, progressing from easy to hard.

I highly recommend giving all the challenges a try, because while following a step-by-step tutorial is educational, you'll learn a lot more solving a problem by yourself. In addition, each chapter will continue where the previous chapter's challenges left off.

If you get stuck, you can find solutions in the resources for this chapter—but to get the most from this book, try doing these yourself first!

Challenge 1: Adding the zombie

Right now, your game has a nice background, but it's missing the star of the show. You can give your zombie a grand entrance as your first challenge.

Here are a few hints:

- Inside `GameScene`, add a constant property named `zombie` of type `SKSpriteNode`. Initialize it with the image named **zombie1**.

- Inside `didMoveToView()`, position the zombie sprite at (400, 400).

- Also inside `didMoveToView()`, add the zombie to the scene.

If you've got it right, you should see the zombie appear onscreen like so:

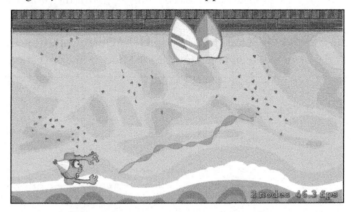

Run your game on the iPad 2 simulator to prove it works there, as well—just with a bigger viewable area!

Challenge 2: Further documentation

This chapter covers everything you need to know about sprites and nodes to keep working on the game.

However, it's good to know where to find more information in case you ever have questions or get stuck. I highly recommend you check out Apple's *SKNode Class Reference* and *SKSpriteNode Class Reference,* as these cover the two classes you'll use most often in Sprite Kit and it's good to have a basic familiarity with the properties and methods they contain.

You can find the references in Xcode by selecting **Help\Documentation and API Reference** from the main menu and searching for SKNode or SKSpriteNode.

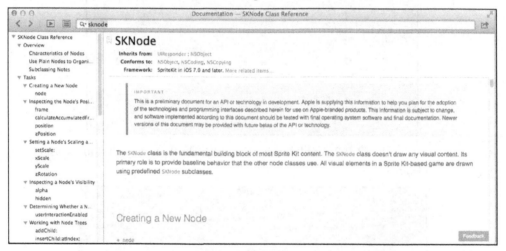

And now for your second challenge: use the information in these docs to double (scale to 2x) the zombie's size. Answer this question: Did you use a method of SKSpriteNode or SKNode to do this?

Chapter 2: Manual Movement

By Ray Wenderlich

If you completed the challenges from the previous chapter, you should now have a rather large zombie on the screen:

> **Note:** If you were unable to complete the challenges or skipped ahead from the previous chapter, don't worry—simply open **ZombieConga-Starter** from this chapter's resources to pick up where the previous chapter left off.

Of course, you want the sprite to move around, not just stand there—this zombie's got an itch to boogie!

There are two ways to make a sprite move in Sprite Kit:

1. As you might have noticed in the previous chapter if you looked at the template code provided by Apple, you can make a sprite move using a concept called **actions**. You'll learn more about actions in the next chapter.

2. You can make a sprite move in the more "classic" way—and that's to set the position manually over time. It's important to learn this way first, because it affords the most control and will help you understand what actions do for you.

However, to set a sprite's position over time, you need a method that the game calls periodically as it runs. This introduces a new topic: the Sprite Kit game loop.

The Sprite Kit game loop

A game works like a flipbook animation. You draw a successive sequence of images, and when you flip through them fast enough, it gives the illusion of movement.

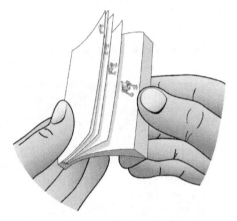

Each individual picture that you draw is called a **frame**. Games typically try to draw frames between 30 to 60 times per second so that the animations feel smooth. This rate of drawing is called the **frame rate**, or specifically **frames per second (FPS)**. By default, Sprite Kit shows you this in the bottom-right corner of your game:

Note: It's handy of Sprite Kit to show your frames per second onscreen by default, because you want to keep an eye on the FPS as you develop your game to make sure your game is performing well. Ideally, you want at least 30 FPS.

You should only pay attention to the FPS display on an actual device, though, as you'll get very different performance on the Simulator.

In particular, your Mac has a faster CPU and way more memory than an iPhone or iPad, but abysmally slow emulated rendering, so you can't count on any accurate performance measurements from your Mac—again, always test performance on a device!

Besides the FPS, Sprite Kit also displays the count of nodes that it rendered in the last pass.

You can remove the FPS and node count from the screen by going into **GameViewController.swift** and setting both `skView.showsFPS` and `skView.showsNodeCount` to `false`.

Behind the scenes, Sprite Kit runs an endless loop, often referred to as the **game loop**, which looks like this:

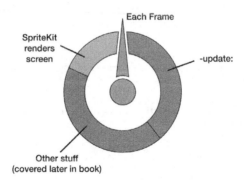

This illustrates that each frame, Sprite Kit does the following:

1. **Calls a method on your scene called** `update()`. This is where you can put code that you want to run every frame—making it the perfect spot for code that updates the position or rotation of your sprites.

2. **Does some other stuff**. You'll revisit the game loop in other chapters, filling in your understanding of the rest of this diagram as you go.

3. **Renders the scene**. Sprite Kit then draws all of the objects that are in your scene graph, issuing OpenGL draw commands for you behind the scenes.

Sprite Kit tries to draw frames as fast as possible, up to 60 FPS. However, if your update() method takes too long, or if Sprite Kit has to draw more sprites than the hardware can handle at one time, the frame rate might decrease.

You'll learn more about ways to resolve performance issues like this in Chapters 25 and 26, "Performance: Texture Atlases" and "Performance: Tips and Tricks," but for now you just need to know two things:

1. **Keep update() fast**. For example, you want to avoid slow algorithms in this method since it's called each frame.

2. **Keep your count of nodes as low as possible**. For example, it's good to remove nodes from the scene graph when they're off screen and you no longer need them.

Now that you know that update() is called each frame and is a good spot to update the positions of your sprites, let's make this zombie move!

Moving the zombie

You're going to implement the zombie movement code in five iterations. This is so you can see some common beginner mistakes and solutions and in the end, understand how movement works step by step.

To start, you'll implement a simple but not ideal method: moving the zombie a fixed amount per frame.

Before you begin, open **GameScene.swift** and comment out the line that sets the zombie to double-sized in didMoveToView():

```
//zombie.setScale(2.0) // SKNode method
```

This line was just a test, so you don't need it anymore. Zombies scare me enough in normal size! :]

Iteration 1: Fixed movement per frame

Inside **GameScene.swift**, add the following method:

```
override func update(currentTime: NSTimeInterval) {
  zombie.position = CGPoint(x: zombie.position.x + 4,
                            y: zombie.position.y)
}
```

Here, you update the position of the zombie to be four more points along the x-axis than last time and keep the same position along the y-axis. This makes the zombie move from left to right.

Build and run, and you'll see the zombie move across the screen:

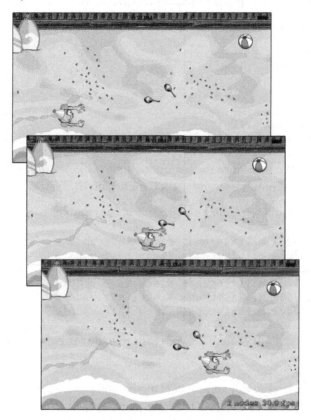

This is great stuff, but you might notice that the movement feels a bit jagged or stuttered. To see why, let's go back to the Sprite Kit game loop.

Remember, Sprite Kit tries to draw frames as quickly as possible. However, there will usually be some variance in the amount of time it takes to draw each frame: sometimes a bit slower, sometimes a bit quicker.

This means the amount of time between calls to your update() loop can vary. To see this yourself, add some code to print out how much time has elapsed since the last update. Add these variables to GameScene's property section, right after the zombie property:

```
var lastUpdateTime: NSTimeInterval = 0
var dt: NSTimeInterval = 0
```

Here, you create properties to keep track of the last time Sprite Kit called update() and the delta time since the last update (often abbreviated as dt).

Then, add these lines to the beginning of update():

```
if lastUpdateTime > 0 {
  dt = currentTime - lastUpdateTime
} else {
  dt = 0
}
lastUpdateTime = currentTime
println("\(dt*1000) milliseconds since last update")
```

Here, you calculate the time since the last call to update() and store that in dt, then log out the time in milliseconds (1 second = 1000 milliseconds).

Build and run, and you'll see something like this in the console:

```
33.4451289963908 milliseconds since last update
16.3537669868674 milliseconds since last update
34.1878019971773 milliseconds since last update
15.6998310121708 milliseconds since last update
33.9883069973439 milliseconds since last update
33.5779220040422 milliseconds since last update
```

As you can see, the amount of time between calls to update() always varies slightly.

> **Note:** Sprite Kit tries to call your update method 60 times a second (every ~16 milliseconds). However, if it takes too long to update and render a frame of your game, Sprite Kit may call your update method less frequently, and the FPS will drop. You can see that here since some frames are taking over 30 milliseconds.
>
> The reason you are seeing such a low FPS is because you are running on the simulator. As mentioned earlier, you can't count on the simulator for accurate performance measurements. If you try running this code on a device, you should see much higher FPS.

> Note that even if your game runs at a smooth 60 FPS, there will still always be some small variance between how often your update method is called. Therefore, you need to take the delta time into account in your calculations - and you will learn how to do that next!

Since you're updating the position of the zombie a fixed amount each frame rather than taking this time variance into consideration, you're likely to wind up with movement that looks jagged or stuttered.

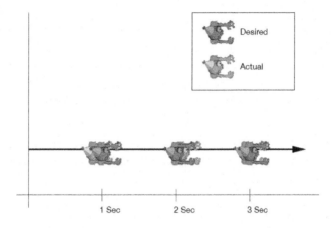

The correct solution is to figure out how far you want the zombie to move per second and then multiply this by the fraction of a second since the last update. Let's give it a shot.

Iteration 2: Velocity multiplied by delta time

Start by adding this property to the top of `GameScene`, right after `dt`:

```
let zombieMovePointsPerSec: CGFloat = 480.0
```

You're saying that in one second, the zombie should move 480 points (about 1/4 of the scene width). You set the type to `CGFloat`, because you'll be using this value in calculations with other `CGFloats` inside a `CGPoint`.

Right after that line, add one more property:

```
var velocity = CGPointZero
```

So far, you've used `CGPoints` to represent positions. However, it's also quite common and handy to use `CGPoints` to represent **2D vectors**.

A 2D vector represents a **direction** and a **length**:

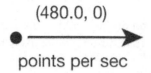

(480.0, 0)

points per sec

The diagram above shows an example of a 2D vector you might use to represent the zombie's movement. You can see that the orientation of the arrow shows the **direction** in which the zombie should move, while the arrow's **length** indicates how far the zombie should move in a second. The direction and length together represent the zombie's **velocity** – you can think of it as how far (and in what direction) the zombie should move in 1 second.

However, note that the velocity has no set position. After all, you should be able to make the zombie move in that direction, at that speed, no matter where the zombie starts.

Try this out by adding the following new method:

```
func moveSprite(sprite: SKSpriteNode, velocity: CGPoint) {
  // 1
  let amountToMove = CGPoint(x: velocity.x * CGFloat(dt),
                             y: velocity.y * CGFloat(dt))
  println("Amount to move: \(amountToMove)")
  // 2
  sprite.position = CGPoint(
    x: sprite.position.x + amountToMove.x,
    y: sprite.position.y + amountToMove.y)
}
```

You've refactored the code into a reusable method that takes the sprite to be moved and a velocity vector by which to move it. Let's go over this line by line:

1. Velocity is in points per second, and you need to figure out how many points to move the zombie this frame. To determine that, this section multiplies the points per second by the fraction of seconds since the last update. You now have a point representing the zombie's position (which you can also think of as a vector from the origin to the zombie's position) and a vector representing the distance and direction to move the zombie this frame:

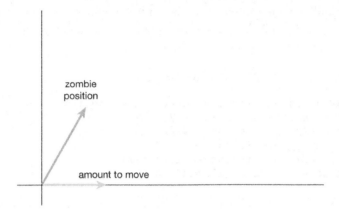

2. To determine the zombie's new position, just add the vector to the point:

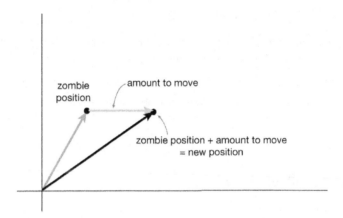

You can visualize this with the diagram above, but in code you simply add the x- and y-components of the point and the vector together.

> **Note:** To learn more about vectors, check out this great guide:
> http://www.mathsisfun.com/algebra/vectors.html.

Finally, inside update(), replace the line that sets the zombie's position with the following:

```
moveSprite(zombie,
           velocity: CGPoint(x: zombieMovePointsPerSec, y: 0))
```

Build and run, and now the zombie moves much more smoothly across the screen. Look at the console log, and you'll also see that the zombie is now moving a different amount of points each frame, based on how much time has elapsed.

```
0.0 milliseconds since last update
Amount to move: (0.0,0.0)
47.8530780237634 milliseconds since last update
Amount to move: (11.4847387257032,0.0)
33.3498929976486 milliseconds since last update
Amount to move: (8.00397431943566,0.0)
34.2196339915972 milliseconds since last update
Amount to move: (8.21271215798333,0.0)
```

If your zombie's movement still looks jittery, be sure to try it on a device instead of on the Simulator, which has different performance characteristics.

Iteration 3: Moving toward touches

So far, so good, but now you'll make the zombie move toward whatever spot the player touches. After all, everyone knows zombies are attracted to noise!

Your goal is for the zombie to move toward the point the player taps and keep moving even after passing the tap location, until the player taps another location to draw his attention.

There are four steps to make this work—let's cover them one at a time.

Step 1: Find the offset vector

First, you need to figure out the offset between the location of the player's tap and the location of the zombie. You can get this by simply subtracting the zombie's position from the tap position.

Subtracting points and vectors is similar to adding them, but instead of adding the x- and y- components, you—that's right—subtract them! :]

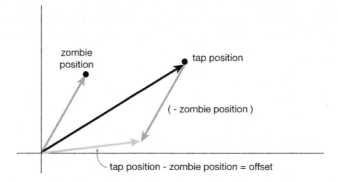

This diagram illustrates that if you subtract the zombie position from the tap position, you get a vector that shows the offset amount. If you move the offset vector so it begins from the zombie's position, you can see this even more clearly:

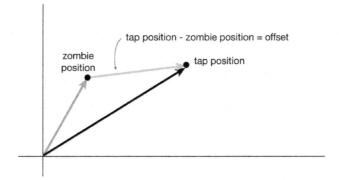

By subtracting these two positions, you get something with a direction and a length. Call this the offset vector.

Try it out by adding the following method:

```
func moveZombieToward(location: CGPoint) {
  let offset = CGPoint(x: location.x - zombie.position.x,
                       y: location.y - zombie.position.y)
}
```

This is just the beginning; you're not done writing this method.

Step 2: Find the length of the offset vector

Now you need to figure out the length of the offset vector, a piece of information you'll need in Step 3.

Think of the offset vector as the hypotenuse of a right triangle, where the lengths of the other two sides of the triangle are defined by the x- and y- components of the vector:

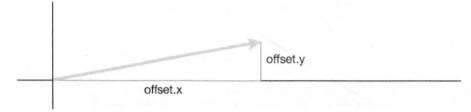

You want to find the length of the hypotenuse. To do this, you can use the Pythagorean theorem. You may remember this simple formula from geometry—it says the length of the hypotenuse is equal to the square root of the sum of the squares of the two sides.

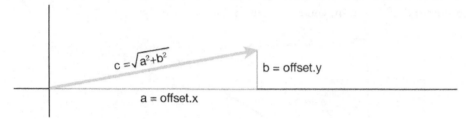

Put this theory into practice. Add the following line to the bottom of `moveZombieToward()`:

```
let length = sqrt(
  Double(offset.x * offset.x + offset.y * offset.y))
```

You're not done yet!

Step 3: Make the offset vector a set length

Currently, you have an offset vector where:

• The **direction** of the vector points toward where the zombie should go.

• The **length** of the vector is the length of the line between the zombie's current position and the tap location.

What you want is a velocity vector where:

• The **direction** points toward where the zombie should go.

• The **length** is `zombieMovePointsPerSec` (the constant you defined earlier, 480 points per second).

So, you're halfway there—your vector points in the right direction, but isn't the right length. How do you make a vector pointing in the same direction as the offset vector, but of a certain length?

The first step is to convert the offset vector into a **unit vector**, which means a vector of length 1. According to geometry, you can do this by simply dividing the offset vector's x- and y- components by the offset vector's length.

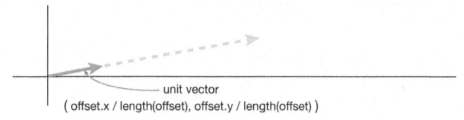

unit vector
(offset.x / length(offset), offset.y / length(offset))

This process of converting a vector into a unit vector is called **normalizing** a vector.

Once you have this unit vector, which you know is of length 1, it's easy to multiply it by zombieMovePointsPerSec to make it the exact length you want.

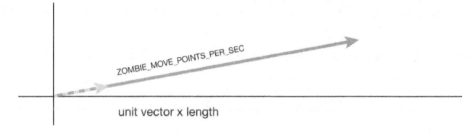

unit vector x length

Give it a try. Add the following lines to the bottom of moveZombieToward():

```
let direction = CGPoint(x: offset.x / CGFloat(length),
                        y: offset.y / CGFloat(length))
velocity = CGPoint(x: direction.x * zombieMovePointsPerSec,
                   y: direction.y * zombieMovePointsPerSec)
```

Now you've got a velocity vector with the correct direction and length.

There's only one step left!

Step 4: Hook up to touch events

In Sprite Kit, to get notifications of touch events on a node, you simply need to set that node's userInteractionEnabled property to true and then override that node's

touchesBegan(withEvent:), touchesMoved(withEvent:) and/or
touchesEnded(withEvent:) methods. Unlike other SKNode objects, SKScene's
userInteractionEnabled property is set to true by default.

To see this in action, implement these touch handling methods for GameScene, as
follows:

```
func sceneTouched(touchLocation:CGPoint) {
  moveZombieToward(touchLocation)
}

override func touchesBegan(touches: Set<NSObject>,
  withEvent event: UIEvent) {
  let touch = touches.first as! UITouch
  let touchLocation = touch.locationInNode(self)
  sceneTouched(touchLocation)
}

override func touchesMoved(touches: Set<NSObject>,
  withEvent event: UIEvent) {
  let touch = touches.first as! UITouch
  let touchLocation = touch.locationInNode(self)
  sceneTouched(touchLocation)
}
```

Finally, inside update(), edit the call to moveSprite() so it passes in velocity (based
on the touch) instead of the preset amount:

```
moveSprite(zombie, velocity: velocity)
```

That's it! Build and run, and now the zombie will chase your taps. Just don't get too
close—he's hungry!

> **Note**: You can also use gesture recognizers with Sprite Kit if you'd like. They can be especially handy if you're trying to implement complicated gestures, such as pinching or rotating.
>
> You can add the gesture recognizer to `view` in `didMoveToView()`, and you can use `SKScene`'s `convertPointFromView()` and `SKNode`'s `convertPoint(toNode:)` methods to get the touch in the coordinate space you need.
>
> For a demonstration of this, see the sample code for this chapter, where I've included a commented-out demonstration of gesture recognizers for you. Since it does the same thing as the touch handlers you implemented, comment out your touch handlers when you run with the gesture recognizers if you want to be sure the gestures are working.

Iteration 4: Bounds checking

As you played the latest version of the game, you might have noticed that the zombie happily runs straight off the screen if you let him. While I admire his enthusiasm, in Zombie Conga you'd like him to stay on the screen at all times, bouncing off an edge if he hits one.

Here's the basic idea: You need to check if the newly calculated position is beyond any of the screen edges and make the zombie bounce away, if so. To do this, add this new method:

```
func boundsCheckZombie() {
  let bottomLeft = CGPointZero
  let topRight = CGPoint(x: size.width, y: size.height)

  if zombie.position.x <= bottomLeft.x {
    zombie.position.x = bottomLeft.x
    velocity.x = -velocity.x
  }
  if zombie.position.x >= topRight.x {
    zombie.position.x = topRight.x
    velocity.x = -velocity.x
  }
  if zombie.position.y <= bottomLeft.y {
    zombie.position.y = bottomLeft.y
    velocity.y = -velocity.y
  }
  if zombie.position.y >= topRight.y {
```

```
        zombie.position.y = topRight.y
        velocity.y = -velocity.y
    }
}
```

First, you make constants for the bottom-left and top-right coordinates of the scene.

Then, you check the zombie's position to see if it's beyond or at any of the screen edges. If it is, you clamp the position and reverse the appropriate velocity component to make the zombie bounce in the opposite direction.

Now call your new method at the end of `update()`:

```
boundsCheckZombie()
```

Build and run, and now you have a zombie bouncing around the screen. I told you he was ready to party!

Iteration 5: Playable area

Run the game on your iPhone 5 Simulator and move your zombie toward the top of the screen. Notice that your zombie moves off-screen before he bounces back!

Run the game on the iPad Simulator, and you'll see the game works as expected. Does this give you a clue as to what's going on?

Recall from the Universal App Support section in Chapter 1 that Zombie Conga has been designed with a 4:3 aspect ratio (2048x1536). However, you want to support up to a 16:9 aspect ratio (1136x640), which is what the iPhone 5, 6, and 6 Plus uses.

Let's take a look at what happens with a 16:9 device. Since you've configured the scene to use aspect fill, Sprite Kit first calculates the largest 16:9 rectangle that fits within the 2048x1536 space: 2048x1152. It then centers that rectangle, and scales it to fit the actual screen size: a scale of 0.64 to fit the iPhone 6 1134x750 screen size, for example.

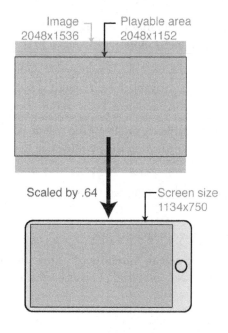

This means on 16:9 devices, there are 192-point gaps at the top and bottom of the scene that won't be visible (1536-1152=384. 384/2=192). Hence, you should avoid critical gameplay in those areas—such as letting the zombie move in those gaps.

Let's solve this problem. First, add a new property to `GameScene` to store the playable rectangle:

```
let playableRect: CGRect
```

Then, add this initializer to set the value appropriately:

```
override init(size: CGSize) {
  let maxAspectRatio:CGFloat = 16.0/9.0 // 1
  let playableHeight = size.width / maxAspectRatio // 2
  let playableMargin = (size.height-playableHeight)/2.0 // 3
  playableRect = CGRect(x: 0, y: playableMargin,
                        width: size.width,
                        height: playableHeight) // 4
  super.init(size: size) // 5
}

required init(coder aDecoder: NSCoder) {
  fatalError("init(coder:) has not been implemented") // 6
}
```

Line by line, here's what this code does:

1. Zombie Conga supports aspect ratios from 3:2 (1.33) to 16:9 (1.77). This makes a constant for the max aspect ratio supported: 16:9 (1.77).

2. With aspect fit, regardless of aspect ratio the playable width will always be equal to the scene width. To calculate the playable height, you divide the scene width by the max aspect ratio.

3. You want to center the playable rectangle on the screen, so you determine the margin on the top and bottom by subtracting the playable height from the scene height and dividing the result by 2.

4. You put it all together to make a centered rectangle on the screen, with the max aspect ratio.

5. You call the initializer of the superclass.

6. Whenever you override the default initializer of a Sprite Kit node, you must also override the required `NSCoder` initializer. This is used when you are loading a scene

from the scene editor. Since you are not using the scene editor in this game, you simply add a placeholder implementation that logs an error for now.

To help visualize this, add a helper method to draw this playable rectangle to the screen:

```
func debugDrawPlayableArea() {
  let shape = SKShapeNode()
  let path = CGPathCreateMutable()
  CGPathAddRect(path, nil, playableRect)
  shape.path = path
  shape.strokeColor = SKColor.redColor()
  shape.lineWidth = 4.0
  addChild(shape)
}
```

Don't worry about how this works at the moment; you'll learn all about **SKShapeNodes** in Chapter 12, "Crop, Video and Shape Nodes." For now, just consider this a black box that draws the debug rectangle to the screen.

Next, call this method at the end of **didMoveToView()**:

```
debugDrawPlayableArea()
```

And finally, modify the first two lines in **boundsCheckZombie()** to take into consideration the y-values in **playableRect**:

```
let bottomLeft = CGPoint(x: 0,
                         y: CGRectGetMinY(playableRect))
let topRight = CGPoint(x: size.width,
                       y: CGRectGetMaxY(playableRect))
```

Build and run, and you'll see the zombie now bounces correctly, according to the playable rectangle (drawn in red and matched to the corners of the screen):

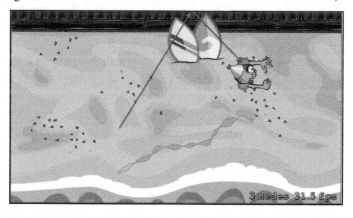

Then build and run on an iPad simulator, and you'll see the zombie bounces correctly there, as well, according to the playable rectangle:

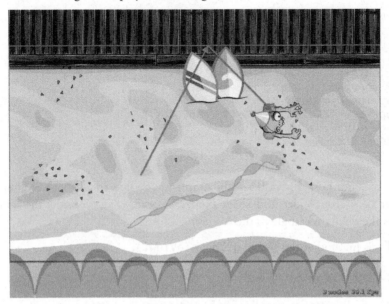

Notice that the playable area outlined in red is exactly what you see on the iPhone device, which has the largest supported aspect ratio, 16:9.

Now that you have a playable rectangle, you simply need to make sure the rest of the gameplay takes place in this box—and your zombie can party everywhere!

Note: An alternate method would be to restrict the zombie's movement based on the visible area of the current device. In other words, you could let the zombie move all the way to the edges of the iPad, rather than restricting him to the minimum playable area.

However, this would make the game easier on the iPad, as there'd be more space to avoid enemies. For Zombie Conga, we think it's more important to have the same difficulty across all devices, so we're keeping the core gameplay in the guaranteed playable area.

Rotating the zombie

The zombie is moving nicely, but he always faces the same direction. Granted, he is undead, but this zombie is on the curious side and would like to turn to see where he's going!

You already have a vector that includes the direction the zombie is facing: `velocity`. You just need to find the angle to rotate to get the zombie to face in that direction.

Once again, think of the direction vector as the hypotenuse of a right triangle. You want to find the angle:

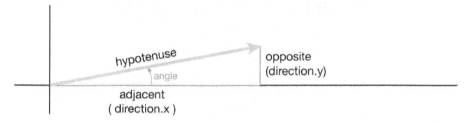

You may remember from trigonometry the mnemonic SOH CAH TOA, where the last part stands for:

```
tan(angle) = opposite / adjacent
```

Since you have the lengths of the opposite and adjacent sides, you can rewrite the above formula as follows to get the angle of rotation:

```
angle = arctan(opposite / adjacent)
```

If none of this trigonometry rings any bells, don't worry. Just think of it as a formula that you type in to get the angle—that's all you need to know.

Try it out by adding the following new method:

```
func rotateSprite(sprite: SKSpriteNode, direction: CGPoint) {
    sprite.zRotation = CGFloat(
      atan2(Double(direction.y), Double(direction.x)))
}
```

This uses the equation from above. It includes a bunch of casting because `CGFloat` is defined as a `Double` on 64-bit machines and a `Float` on 32-bit machines.

This works because the zombie image faces to the right. If the zombie image were instead facing toward the top of the screen, you'd have to add an additional rotation to compensate because an angle of 0 points to the right.

Now call this new method at the end of `update`:

```
rotateSprite(zombie, direction: velocity)
```

Build and run, and the zombie rotates to face the direction he's moving:

Congratulations, you've given your zombie life! The sprite moves smoothly, bounces off the edges of the screen and rotates on both iPhone and iPad—a great start to a game.

But you're not done yet—it's time for you to try some of this stuff on your own to make sure you've got it down!

Challenges

This chapter has three challenges, and they're particularly important ones. Performing these challenges will give you useful practice with vector math and introduce new math utilities you'll use throughout the rest of the book.

As always, if you get stuck, you can find solutions in the resources for this chapter—but give it your best shot first!

Challenge 1: Math utilities

As you've no doubt noticed while working on this game, you frequently have to perform calculations on points and vectors: adding and subtracting points, finding lengths and so on. You've also been doing a lot of casting between `CGFloat` and `Double`.

So far in this chapter, you've done this all yourself inline. That's a fine way of doing things, but it can get tedious and repetitive in practice. It's also error-prone.

Create a new file with the **iOS\Source\Swift File** template and name it **MyUtils**. Then replace the contents of **MyUtils.swift** with the following:

```swift
import Foundation
import CoreGraphics

func + (left: CGPoint, right: CGPoint) -> CGPoint {
  return CGPoint(x: left.x + right.x, y: left.y + right.y)
}

func += (inout left: CGPoint, right: CGPoint) {
  left = left + right
}
```

In Swift, you can make operators like +, –, * and / work on any type you want. Here, you make them work on `CGPoint` (sometimes in combination with `CGFloat`).

Now you can add points like this (don't add this anywhere, this is just an example):

```swift
let testPoint1 = CGPoint(x: 100, y: 100)
let testPoint2 = CGPoint(x: 50, y: 50)
let testPoint3 = testPoint1 + testPoint2
```

Let's override operators for subtraction, multiplication, and division on `CGPoints` as well. Add this code to the end of **MyUtils.swift**:

```swift
func - (left: CGPoint, right: CGPoint) -> CGPoint {
  return CGPoint(x: left.x - right.x, y: left.y - right.y)
}
func -= (inout left: CGPoint, right: CGPoint) {
  left = left - right
}
func * (left: CGPoint, right: CGPoint) -> CGPoint {
  return CGPoint(x: left.x * right.x, y: left.y * right.y)
}
func *= (inout left: CGPoint, right: CGPoint) {
  left = left * right
}
func * (point: CGPoint, scalar: CGFloat) -> CGPoint {
  return CGPoint(x: point.x * scalar, y: point.y * scalar)
}
func *= (inout point: CGPoint, scalar: CGFloat) {
  point = point * scalar
}
```

```
func / (left: CGPoint, right: CGPoint) -> CGPoint {
  return CGPoint(x: left.x / right.x, y: left.y / right.y)
}
func /= (inout left: CGPoint, right: CGPoint) {
  left = left / right
}
func / (point: CGPoint, scalar: CGFloat) -> CGPoint {
  return CGPoint(x: point.x / scalar, y: point.y / scalar)
}
func /= (inout point: CGPoint, scalar: CGFloat) {
  point = point / scalar
}
```

Now you can subtract, multiply, or divide a `CGPoint` by another `CGPoint`. You can also multiply and divide points by scalar `CGFloat` values like this (again don't add this anywhere, this is just an example):

```
let testPoint5 = testPoint1 * 2
let testPoint6 = testPoint1 / 10
```

Finally, add a class extension on `CGPoint` with a few helper methods:

```
#if !(arch(x86_64) || arch(arm64))
func atan2(y: CGFloat, x: CGFloat) -> CGFloat {
  return CGFloat(atan2f(Float(y), Float(x)))
}

func sqrt(a: CGFloat) -> CGFloat {
  return CGFloat(sqrtf(Float(a)))
}
#endif

extension CGPoint {

  func length() -> CGFloat {
    return sqrt(x*x + y*y)
  }

  func normalized() -> CGPoint {
    return self / length()
  }

  var angle: CGFloat {
    return atan2(y, x)
  }
}
```

The #if/#endif block is true when the app is running on 32-bit architecture. In this case, CGFloat is the same size as Float, so this code makes versions of atan2 and sqrt that accept CGFloat/Float values (rather than the default of Double), allowing you to use atan2 and sqrt with CGFloats, regardless of the device's architecture.

Next, the class extension adds some handy methods to get the length of the point, return a normalized version of the point (i.e., length 1) and get the angle of the point.

Using these helper functions will make your code a lot more concise and clean. For example, look at moveSprite(velocity:):

```
func moveSprite(sprite: SKSpriteNode, velocity: CGPoint) {
  let amountToMove = CGPoint(x: velocity.x * CGFloat(dt),
                             y: velocity.y * CGFloat(dt))
  println("Amount to move: \(amountToMove)")
  sprite.position = CGPoint(
    x: sprite.position.x + amountToMove.x,
    y: sprite.position.y + amountToMove.y)
}
```

Simplify the first line by multiplying velocity and dt with the * operator, and avoid the cast. Also, simplify the final line by adding the sprite's position and amount to move with the += operator.

Your end result should look like this:

```
func moveSprite(sprite: SKSpriteNode, velocity: CGPoint) {
  let amountToMove = velocity * CGFloat(dt)
  println("Amount to move: \(amountToMove)")
  sprite.position += amountToMove
}
```

Your challenge is to modify the rest of Zombie Conga to use this new helper code and verify that the game still works as expected. When you're done, you should have the following calls, including the two mentioned already:

- += operator: 1 call

- – operator: 1 call

- * operator: 2 calls

- angle: 1 call

You should also notice when you're done that your code is a lot cleaner and easier to understand. In future chapters, you'll use a math library we made that's very similar to this.

Challenge 2: Stop that zombie!

In Zombie Conga, when you tap the screen, the zombie moves toward that point—but then continues beyond it.

That's the behavior you want for Zombie Conga, but in another game, you might want the zombie to stop where you tap. Your challenge is to modify the game to do this.

Here are a few hints for one possible implementation:

- Create an optional property called `lastTouchLocation` and update it whenever the player touches the scene.

- Inside `update()`, check the distance between the last touch location and the zombie's position. If that remaining distance is less than or equal to the amount the zombie will move this frame (`zombieMovePointsPerSec * dt`), then set the zombie's position to the last touch location and the velocity to zero. Otherwise, call `moveSprite(velocity:)` and `rotateSprite(direction:)` like normal. `boundsCheckZombie()` should always occur.

- To do this, use the – operator once and call `length()` once using the helper code from the previous challenge.

Challenge 3: Smooth moves

Currently, the zombie immediately rotates to face where you tap. This can be a bit jarring—it would be nicer if the zombie rotated smoothly over time to face the new direction.

To do this, you need two new helper routines. Add these to the bottom of **MyUtils.swift** (to type π, use Option-p):

```swift
let π = CGFloat(M_PI)

func shortestAngleBetween(angle1: CGFloat,
                          angle2: CGFloat) -> CGFloat {
  let twoπ = π * 2.0
  var angle = (angle2 - angle1) % twoπ
  if (angle >= π) {
    angle = angle - twoπ
  }
  if (angle <= -π) {
    angle = angle + twoπ
  }
```

```
    return angle
}

extension CGFloat {
  func sign() -> CGFloat {
    return (self >= 0.0) ? 1.0 : -1.0
  }
}
```

`sign()` returns a 1 if the `CGFloat` is greater than or equal to 0; otherwise it returns -1.

`shortestAngleBetween()` returns the shortest angle between two angles. It's not as simple as subtracting the two angles, for two reasons:

1. Angles "wrap around" after 360 degrees (2 * M_PI). In other words, 30 degrees and 390 degrees represent the same angle.

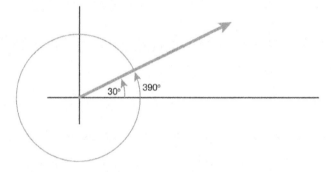

2. Sometimes the shortest way to rotate between two angles is to go left, and other times to go right. For example, if you start at 0 degrees and want to turn to 270 degrees, it's shorter to turn -90 degrees than 270 degrees. You don't want your zombie turning the long way around—he may be undead, but he's not stupid!

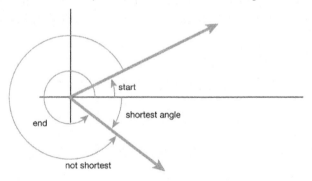

So this routine finds the difference between the two angles, chops off any amount greater than 360 degrees and then decides if it's faster to go right or left.

Your challenge is to modify `rotateSprite(direction:)` to take and use a new parameter: the number of radians the zombie should rotate per second.

Define the constant as follows:

```
let zombieRotateRadiansPerSec:CGFloat = 4.0 * π
```

And modify the method signature as follows:

```
func rotateSprite(sprite: SKSpriteNode, direction: CGPoint,
                  rotateRadiansPerSec: CGFloat) {
  // Your code here!
}
```

Here are a few hints for implementing this method:

- Use `shortestAngleBetween()` to find the distance between the current angle and the target angle. Call this `shortest`.

- Figure out the amount to rotate this frame based on `rotateRadiansPerSec` and `dt`. Call this `amtToRotate`.

- If the absolute value of `shortest` is less than the `amtToRotate`, use that instead.

- Add `amountToRotate` to the sprite's `zRotation`—but multiply it by `sign()` first, so that you rotate in the correct direction.

- Don't forget to update the call to rotate the sprite in `update()` to use the new parameter.

If you've completed all three of these challenges, great work! You really understand moving and rotating sprites, using the "classic" approach of updating the values yourself over time.

Ah, but the classic, while essential to understand, always gives way to the modern. In the next chapter, you'll learn how Sprite Kit can make some of these common tasks much easier, through the magic of actions!

Chapter 3: Actions

By Ray Wenderlich

So far, you've learned how to move and rotate Sprite Kit nodes—a node being anything that appears onscreen—by manually setting their position and rotation over time.

This do-it-yourself approach works and is quite powerful, but Sprite Kit provides an easier way to move sprites incrementally: **actions**.

Actions allow you to do things like rotate, scale or change a sprite's position over time—with just one line of code! You can also chain actions together to create movement combinations quite easily.

In this chapter, you'll learn all about Sprite Kit actions as you add enemies, collectibles and basic gameplay logic to your game.

You'll see how actions can simplify your game-coding life, and by the time you've finished this chapter, Zombie Conga will be action-packed!

> **Note:** This chapter begins where the previous chapter's Challenge 3 left off. If you were unable to complete the challenges or skipped ahead from an earlier chapter, don't worry—you can simply open **ZombieConga-Starter** from this chapter's resources to begin in the right place.

Move action

Right now, your zombie's "life" is a bit too carefree. Let's add action to this game by introducing enemies to dodge: crazy cat ladies!

Open **GameScene.swift** and create the start of a new method to spawn an enemy:

```
func spawnEnemy() {
  let enemy = SKSpriteNode(imageNamed: "enemy")
  enemy.position = CGPoint(x: size.width + enemy.size.width/2,
                          y: size.height/2)
  addChild(enemy)
}
```

This code should be a review from the previous two chapters: You create a sprite and position it at the vertical center of the screen, just out of view to the right.

Now you'd like to move the enemy from the right of the screen to the left. If you were to do this manually, you might update the enemy's position each frame according to a velocity.

No need to trouble yourself with that this time! Simply add these two lines of code to the bottom of spawnEnemy():

```
let actionMove = SKAction.moveTo(
  CGPoint(x: -enemy.size.width/2, y: enemy.position.y),
  duration: 2.0)
enemy.runAction(actionMove)
```

To create an action in Sprite Kit, you call one of several static constructors on the SKAction class, such as the one you see here, moveTo(duration:). This particular constructor returns an action that moves a sprite to a specified position over a specified duration (in seconds).

Here, you set up the action to move the enemy along the x-axis at whatever speed is necessary to take it from its current position to just off the left side of the screen in two seconds.

Once you've created an action, you need to run it. You can run an action on any SKNode by calling runAction(), as you did in the above code.

Give it a try! For now, call this method inside didMoveToView(), right after calling addChild(zombie):

```
spawnEnemy()
```

Build and run, and you should see the crazy cat lady race across the screen:

Not bad for just two lines of code, eh? You could have even done it with a single line of code if you didn't need to use the `actionMove` constant for anything else.

Here you saw an example of `moveTo(duration:)`, but there are a few other move action variants:

- `moveToX(duration:)` and `moveToY(duration:)`. These allow you to specify a change in only the x- or y-position; the other is assumed to remain the same. You could have used `moveToX(duration:)` in the example above to save a bit of typing.

- `moveByX(y:duration:)`. The "move to" actions move the sprite to a particular point, but sometimes it's convenient to move a sprite as an offset from its current position, wherever that may be. You could've used `moveByX(y:duration:)` in the example above, passing –(`size.width` + `enemy.size.width`) for x and 0 for y.

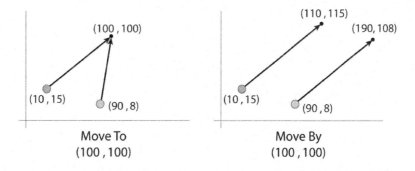

You'll see this pattern of "[action] to" and "[action] by" variants for other action types, as well. In general, you can use whichever of these is more convenient for you—but keep in mind that if either works, the "[action] by" actions are preferable because they are reversible. For more on this topic, keep reading.

> **Note:** You may be used to extending classes to implement new functionality. However, there is no way to extend the SKAction class. The *only* way to create an SKAction is via one of its static constructor methods.
>
> In this chapter, you'll learn about specific methods that allow you to create SKActions that run custom code, and you'll learn how to combine SKActions to create complex behaviors. Using these two techniques, you should be able to accomplish your goals without subclasses.

Sequence action

The real power of actions lies in how easily you can chain them together. For example, say you want the cat lady to move in a V: down toward the bottom of the screen, then up to the goal position.

To do this, replace the lines that create and run the move action in spawnEnemy() with the following:

```
// 1
let actionMidMove = SKAction.moveTo(
  CGPoint(x: size.width/2,
          y: CGRectGetMinY(playableRect) + enemy.size.height/2),
  duration: 1.0)
// 2
let actionMove = SKAction.moveTo(
  CGPoint(x: -enemy.size.width/2, y: enemy.position.y),
  duration:1.0)
// 3
let sequence = SKAction.sequence([actionMidMove, actionMove])
// 4
enemy.runAction(sequence)
```

Let's go over this line by line:

1. Here you create a new move action, just like you did before, except this time it represents the "mid-point" of the action—the bottom middle of the playable rectangle.

2. This is the same move action as before, except you've decreased the duration to 1.0, since it will now represent moving only half the distance: from the bottom of the V, off-screen to the left.

3. Here's the new sequence action! As you can see, it's incredibly simple—you use the `sequence:` constructor and pass in an `Array` of actions. The sequence action will run one action after another.

4. You call `runAction()` in the same way as before, but pass in the sequence action this time.

That's it! Build and run, and you'll see the crazy cat lady "bounce" off the bottom of the playable rectangle:

The sequence action is one of the most useful and commonly used actions—chaining actions together is just so powerful! You'll be using the sequence action many times in this chapter and throughout the rest of this book.

Wait for duration action

The wait for duration action does exactly what you'd expect: It makes the sprite wait for a period of time, during which the sprite does nothing.

"What's the point of that?" you may be wondering. Well, wait for duration actions only truly become interesting when combined with a sequence action.

For example, let's make the cat lady briefly pause when she reaches the bottom of the V-shape. To do this, simply replace the line in `spawnEnemy()` that creates `sequence` with the following lines:

```
let wait = SKAction.waitForDuration(0.25)
let sequence = SKAction.sequence(
  [actionMidMove, wait, actionMove])
```

To create a wait for duration action, call waitForDuration() with the amount of time to wait in seconds. Then, simply insert it into the sequence of actions where you want the delay to occur.

Build and run, and now the cat lady will briefly pause at the bottom of the V:

Run block action

At times, you'll want to run your own block of code in a sequence of actions. For example, say you want to log out a message when the cat lady reaches the bottom of the V.

To do this, simply replace the line in spawnEnemy() that creates sequence with the following lines:

```
let logMessage = SKAction.runBlock() {
  println("Reached bottom!")
}
let sequence = SKAction.sequence(
  [actionMidMove, logMessage, wait, actionMove])
```

To create a block action, simply call runBlock() and pass in a block of code to execute.

Build and run, and when the cat lady reaches the bottom of the V, you should see the following in the console:

```
Reached bottom!
```

> **Note:** If your project still includes the `println` statements from earlier chapters, now would be a great time to remove them. Otherwise, you'll have to search your console for the above log statement—it's doubtful you'll notice it within the sea of messages scrolling by.
>
> While you're at it, you should remove any comments as well, to keep your project nice and clean.

Of course, you can do far more than log a message here—since it's an arbitrary code block, you can do anything you want!

You should be aware of one more action related to running blocks of code:

- `runBlock(queue:)` allows you to run the block of code on an arbitrary dispatch queue instead of in the main Sprite Kit event loop. You'll learn more about this in Chapter 27, "Performance: Tips and Tricks."

Reversed actions

Let's say you want to make the cat lady go back the way she came: After she moves in a V to the left, she should move in a V back to the right.

One way to do this would be, after she goes off-screen to the left, having her run the existing `actionMidMove` action to go back to the middle, and creating a new `moveTo(duration:)` action to send her back to the start position.

But Sprite Kit gives you a better option. You can reverse certain actions in Sprite Kit simply by calling `reversedAction()` on them. This results in a new action that is the opposite of the original action.

For example, if you run a `moveByX(y:duration:)` action, you can run the reverse of that action to go back the other way:

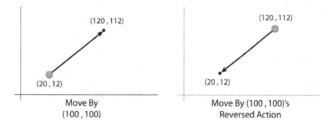

Not all actions are reversible—for example, moveTo(duration:) is not. To find out if
an action is reversible, look it up in the SKAction class reference, which indicates it
plainly:

```
+ moveByX:y:duration:

Creates an action that moves a node relative to its current position.

Declaration

SWIFT
class func moveByX(_ deltaX: CGFloat,
                y deltaY: CGFloat,
          duration sec: NSTimeInterval) -> SKAction!

OBJECTIVE-C
+ (SKAction *)moveByX:(CGFloat)deltaX
                    y:(CGFloat)deltaY
             duration:(NSTimeInterval)sec

Parameters

deltaX    The x-value, in points, to add to the node's position.

deltaY    The y-value, in points, to add to the node's position.

   sec    The duration of the animation.

Return Value
A new move action.

Discussion
When the action executes, the node's position property animates from its current position to its new position.

This action is reversible; the reverse is created as if the following code were executed:

    [SKAction moveByX: -deltaX y: -deltaY duration: sec];
```

Let's try this out. First, replace the declarations of actionMidMove and actionMove in
spawnEnemy() with the following code:

```
let actionMidMove = SKAction.moveByX(
  -size.width/2-enemy.size.width/2,
  y: -CGRectGetHeight(playableRect)/2 + enemy.size.height/2,
  duration: 1.0)
let actionMove = SKAction.moveByX(
  -size.width/2-enemy.size.width/2,
  y: CGRectGetHeight(playableRect)/2 - enemy.size.height/2,
  duration: 1.0)
```

Here, you switch the `moveTo(duration:)` actions to the related `moveByX(y:duration:)` variant, since that is reversible.

Now replace the line in `spawnEnemy()` that creates `sequence` with the following lines:

```
let reverseMid = actionMidMove.reversedAction()
let reverseMove = actionMove.reversedAction()
let sequence = SKAction.sequence([
  actionMidMove, logMessage, wait, actionMove,
  reverseMove, logMessage, wait, reverseMid
])
```

First, you switch the `moveTo(duration:)` actions to the related `moveByX(y:duration:)` variant, since that is reversible.

Then, you create the reverse of those actions by calling `reversedAction()` on each, and insert them into the sequence.

Build and run, and now the cat lady will go one way, then back the other:

> **Note:** If you try to reverse an action that is *not* reversible, then it will return the same action.

Because sequence actions are also reversible, you can simplify the above code as follows. **Remove** the lines where you create the reversed actions and replace the sequence creation with the following lines:

```
let halfSequence = SKAction.sequence(
  [actionMidMove, logMessage, wait, actionMove])
let sequence = SKAction.sequence(
  [halfSequence, halfSequence.reversedAction()])
```

This simply creates a sequence of actions that moves the sprite one way, and then reverses the sequence to go back the other way.

Astute observers may have noticed that the first half of sequence logs a message as soon as it reaches the bottom of the screen, but on the way back, the message isn't logged until after the sprite has waited at the bottom for one second.

This is because the reversed sequence is the exact opposite of the original, unlike how you wrote the first version. Later in this chapter, you'll read about the group action, which you could use to fix this.

Repeat action

So far, so good, but what if you want the cat lady to repeat this sequence multiple times? Of course, there's an action for that!

You can repeat an action a certain number of times using repeatAction(count:), or an endless number of times using repeatActionForever().

Let's go with the endless variant. Replace the line that runs your action in spawnEnemy() with the following two lines:

```
let repeat = SKAction.repeatActionForever(sequence)
enemy.runAction(repeat)
```

Here, you create an action that repeats the sequence of other actions endlessly, and run that repeat action on the enemy.

Build and run, and now your cat lady will continuously bounce back and forth. I told you she's crazy!

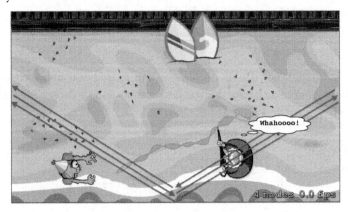

Congratulations! You now understand many useful types of actions:

• Move actions

• Sequence actions

• Wait for duration actions

• Run block actions

• Reversing actions

• Repeat actions

Next, you're going to put all of these together in a new and interesting way to make cat ladies spawn periodically, so your zombie can never get too comfortable.

Periodic spawning

Right now, the game spawns a single cat lady at launch. To prepare for periodic spawning, you'll revert the spawnEnemy() code to the original version that simply moves the cat lady from right to left. You'll also introduce some random variance so the cat lady doesn't always spawn at the same y-position.

First things first: You need a helper method to generate a random number within a range of values. Add this new method to **MyUtils.swift**, alongside the other math utilities you added in the challenges in the previous chapter:

```
extension CGFloat {
  static func random() -> CGFloat {
    return CGFloat(Float(arc4random()) / Float(UInt32.max))
  }

  static func random(#min: CGFloat, max: CGFloat) -> CGFloat {
    assert(min < max)
    return CGFloat.random() * (max - min) + min
  }
}
```

This extends CGFloat to add two new methods: the first gives a random number between 0 and 1, and the second gives a random number between specified minimum and maximum values.

It's not important for you to understand these methods beyond that. But if you're really curious, you can read the note below.

> **Note:** random() calls arc4random(), which gives you a random integer between
> 0 and the largest value possible to store with an unsigned 32-bit integer,
> represented by UInt32.max. If you divide that number by UInt32.max, you get a
> float between 0 and 1.
>
> Here's how random(min:max:) works. If you multiply the result of random()
> (remember, a float between 0 and 1) by the range of values (max – min), you'll get
> a float between 0 and the range. If you add to that the min value, you'll get a float
> between min and max. Voilà, job done!

Next, head back to **GameScene.swift** and replace the current version of spawnEnemy()
with the following:

```
func spawnEnemy() {
  let enemy = SKSpriteNode(imageNamed: "enemy")
  enemy.position = CGPoint(
    x: size.width + enemy.size.width/2,
    y: CGFloat.random(
      min: CGRectGetMinY(playableRect) + enemy.size.height/2,
      max: CGRectGetMaxY(playableRect) - enemy.size.height/2))
  addChild(enemy)

  let actionMove =
    SKAction.moveToX(-enemy.size.width/2, duration: 2.0)
  enemy.runAction(actionMove)
}
```

You've modified the fixed y-position to be a random value between the bottom and top
of the playable rectangle, and you've reverted the movement back to the original
implementation. Well, the moveToX(duration:) variant of the original
implementation, anyway.

Now it's time for some action. Inside didMoveToView(), replace the call to
spawnEnemy() with the following:

```
runAction(SKAction.repeatActionForever(
  SKAction.sequence([SKAction.runBlock(spawnEnemy),
                     SKAction.waitForDuration(2.0)])))
```

This is an example of chaining actions together inline instead of creating separate
variables for each. You create a sequence of calling spawnEnemy() and waiting two
seconds, and repeat this sequence forever.

Note that you're running the action on the scene itself. This works because the scene is a node, and any node can run actions.

> **Note:** You can pass spawnEnemy directly as an argument to runBlock(), because a function with no arguments and no return value has the same type as the argument to runBlock(). Handy, eh?

Build and run, and the crazy cat ladies will spawn endlessly, at varying positions:

Remove from parent action

If you keep the game running for a while, there's a problem.

You can't see it, but there are a big army of cat ladies off-screen to the left. This is you never removed the cat ladies from the scene after they are finished moving.

A never-ending list of nodes in a game is not a good thing. This node army will eventually consume all of the memory on the device, and at that point, the OS will automatically terminate your app, which from a user's perspective will look like your app crashed.

You'll learn more about performance strategies in Chapter 25, "Performance Tips and Tricks," but for now a good rule of thumb is, "If you don't need it anymore, remove it."

And as you may have guessed, there's an action for that, too! When you no longer need a node and want to remove it from the scene, you can either call removeFromParent() directly or use the remove from parent action.

Give this a try. Replace the call to runAction() inside spawnEnemy() with the following:

```
let actionRemove = SKAction.removeFromParent()
enemy.runAction(SKAction.sequence([actionMove, actionRemove]))
```

Build and run, and now your nodes should be cleaned up properly. Ah—much better!

> **Note:** The removeFromParent() action removes the node that's running that action from its parent. This raises a question: What happens to actions after you run them? Calling runAction() stores a strong reference to the action you give it, so won't that slowly eat up your memory?
>
> The answer is no. Sprite Kit nodes do you the favor of automatically removing their references to actions when the actions finish running. So you can tell a node to run an action and then forget about it, feeling confident that you haven't leaked any memory.

Animation action

This one is super useful, because animations add a lot of polish and fun to your game.

To run an animation action, you first need to gather a list of images called **textures** that make up the frames of the animation. A sprite has a texture assigned to it, but you can always swap out the texture with a different one at runtime by setting the texture property on the sprite.

In fact, this is what animations do for you: automatically swap out your sprite's textures over time, with a slight delay between each.

Zombie Conga already includes some animation frames for the zombie. As you can see below, you have four textures to use as frames to show the zombie walking:

zombie1.png   zombie2.png   zombie3.png   zombie4.png

You want to play the frames in this order:

  1   2   3   4   3   2

You can then repeat this endlessly for a continuous walk animation.

Give it a shot. First, create a property for the zombie animation action:

```
let zombieAnimation: SKAction
```

Then, add the following code to `init(size:)`, right before the call to `super.init(size:)`:

```
// 1
var textures:[SKTexture] = []
// 2
for i in 1...4 {
  textures.append(SKTexture(imageNamed: "zombie\(i)"))
}
// 3
textures.append(textures[2])
textures.append(textures[1])

// 4
zombieAnimation = SKAction.animateWithTextures(textures,
timePerFrame: 0.1)
```

Let's go over this one section at a time:

1. You create an array that will store all of the textures to run in the animation.

2. The animation frames are named **zombie1.png**, **zombie2.png**, **zombie3.png**, and **zombie4.png**. This makes it easy to fashion a loop that creates a string for each image name and then makes a texture object from each name using the `SKTexture(imageNamed:)` initializer.

   The first `for` loop adds frames 1 to 4, which is most of the "forward walk."

3. This adds frames 3 and 2 to the list (remember, the textures array is 0 based). In total, the textures array now contains the frames in this order: 1, 2, 3, 4, 3, 2. The idea is you will loop this over and over for a continuous animation.

4. Once you have the array of textures, running the animation is easy—you just create and run an action with `animateWithTextures(timePerFrame:)`.

Finally, add this line to `didMoveToView()`, just after calling `addChild(zombie)`:

```
zombie.runAction(SKAction.repeatActionForever(zombieAnimation))
```

This runs the action wrapped in a repeat forever action. This will seamlessly cycle through the frames 1,2,3,4,3,2,1,2,3,4,3,2,1,2....

Build and run, and now your zombie will strut in style!

Stopping action

Your zombie's off to a good start, but there's one annoying thing: When the zombie stops moving, his animation keeps running. Ideally, you'd like to stop the animation when the zombie stops moving.

In Sprite Kit, whenever you run an action, you can give the action a key simply by using a variant of `runAction()` called `runAction(withKey:)`. This is handy because then you can stop the action by calling `removeActionForKey()`.

Give it a shot by adding these two new methods:

```
func startZombieAnimation() {
  if zombie.actionForKey("animation") == nil {
    zombie.runAction(
      SKAction.repeatActionForever(zombieAnimation),
      withKey: "animation")
  }
}

func stopZombieAnimation() {
  zombie.removeActionForKey("animation")
}
```

The first method starts the zombie animation. It runs the animation as before, except it tags it with a key called "animation".

Also note that the method first uses `actionForKey()` to make sure there isn't already an action running with the key "animation"; if there is, the method doesn't bother running another one.

The second method stops the zombie animation by removing the action with the key "animation".

Now, go to `didMoveToView()` and comment out the line that ran the action there:

```
//zombie.runAction(
//   SKAction.repeatActionForever(zombieAnimation))
```

Call `startZombieAnimation()` at the beginning of `moveZombieToward()`:

```
startZombieAnimation()
```

And call `stopZombieAnimation()` inside `update()`, right after the line of code that sets `velocity = CGPointZero`:

```
stopZombieAnimation()
```

Build and run, and now your zombie will only move when he should!

Scale action

You have an animated zombie and some crazy cat ladies, but the game is missing one very important element: cats! Remember, the player's goal is to gather as many cats as she can into the zombie's conga line.

In Zombie Conga, the cats won't move from right to left like the cat ladies do—instead, they'll appear at random locations on the screen and remain stationary. Rather than have them appear instantly, which would be jarring, you'll start them at a scale of 0 and grow them to a scale of 1 over time. This will make the cats appear to "pop in" to the game.

To implement this, add the following new method:

```
func spawnCat() {
  // 1
  let cat = SKSpriteNode(imageNamed: "cat")
  cat.position = CGPoint(
    x: CGFloat.random(min: CGRectGetMinX(playableRect),
```

```
                    max: CGRectGetMaxX(playableRect)),
      y: CGFloat.random(min: CGRectGetMinY(playableRect),
                    max: CGRectGetMaxY(playableRect)))
  cat.setScale(0)
  addChild(cat)
  // 2
  let appear = SKAction.scaleTo(1.0, duration: 0.5)
  let wait = SKAction.waitForDuration(10.0)
  let disappear = SKAction.scaleTo(0, duration: 0.5)
  let removeFromParent = SKAction.removeFromParent()
  let actions = [appear, wait, disappear, removeFromParent]
  cat.runAction(SKAction.sequence(actions))
}
```

Let's go over each section:

1. You create a cat at a random spot inside the playable rectangle. You set the cat's scale to 0, which makes the cat effectively invisible.

2. You create an action to scale the cat up to normal size by calling `scaleTo(duration:)`. This action is not reversible, so you also create a similar action to scale the cat back down to 0. In sequence, the cat appears, waits for a bit, disappears and is then removed from the parent.

You want the cats to spawn continuously from the start of the game, so add the following inside `didMoveToView()`, just after the line that spawns the enemies:

```
runAction(SKAction.repeatActionForever(
  SKAction.sequence([SKAction.runBlock(spawnCat),
                     SKAction.waitForDuration(1.0)])))
```

This is very similar to the way you spawned the enemies. You run a sequence that calls `spawnCat()`, waits for one second and then repeats.

Build and run, and you'll see cats pop in and out of the game:

You should be aware of a few variants of the scale action:

- `scaleXTo(duration:)`, `scaleYTo(duration:)` and `scaleXTo(y:duration:)`: These allow you to scale just the x-axis or y-axis of a node independently, which you can use to stretch or squash a node.

- `scaleBy(duration:)`: The "by" variant of scaling, which multiples the passed-in scale by the current node's scale. For example, if the current scale of a node is 1.0 and you scale it by 2.0, it is now at 2x. If you scale it by 2.0 again, it is now at 4x. Note that you could not use `scaleBy(duration:)` in the previous example, because anything multiplied by 0 is still 0!

- `scaleXBy(y:duration:)`: Another "by" variant, but this one allows you to scale x and y independently.

Rotate action

The cats in this game should be appealing enough that the player wants to pick them up, but right now they're just sitting motionless.

Let's give them some charm by making them wiggle back and forth while they sit.

To do this, you need the rotate action. To use it, you call the `rotateByAngle(duration:)` constructor, passing in the angle (in radians) by which to rotate.

Replace the declaration of the `wait` action in `spawnCat()` with the following:

```
cat.zRotation = -π / 16.0
let leftWiggle = SKAction.rotateByAngle(π/8.0, duration: 0.5)
let rightWiggle = leftWiggle.reversedAction()
let fullWiggle = SKAction.sequence([leftWiggle, rightWiggle])
let wiggleWait = SKAction.repeatAction(fullWiggle, count: 10)
```

Then, replace the `wait` action with `wiggleWait` inside the declaration of the `actions` array, as shown below:

```
let actions = [appear, wiggleWait, disappear, removeFromParent]
```

Rotations go counterclockwise in Sprite Kit, so negative rotations go clockwise. First, you rotate the `cat` clockwise by 1/16 of π (11.25 degrees) by setting its `zRotation` to –π/16. The user won't see this because at this point, the cat's scale is still 0.

Then you create `leftWiggle`, which rotates counterclockwise by 22.5 degrees over a period of 0.5 seconds. And since the cat starts out rotated clockwise by 11.25 degrees, this results in the cat being rotated counter-clockwise by 11.25 degrees.

Since this is a "by" variant, it is reversible, so you use `reversedAction()` to create `rightWiggle`, which simply rotates back the other way to where the cat started.

You create a `fullWiggle` by rotating left and then right. Now the cat has wiggled left and right and is back to its start position. This "full wiggle" takes one second total, so in `wiggleWait` you repeat this 10 times to have a 10-second wiggle duration.

Build and run, and now your cats look like they've had some catnip!

Group action

So far, you know how to run actions one after another in sequence, but what if you want to run two actions at exactly the same time? For example, in Zombie Conga, you want to make the cat scale up and down slightly as he's wiggling.

For this sort of multitasking, you can use what's called the group action. It works in a similar way to the sequence action, where you pass in a list of actions. However, instead of running them one at a time, a group action runs them all at once.

Let's try this out. Replace the declaration of the `wiggleWait` action in `spawnCat()` with the following:

```
let scaleUp = SKAction.scaleBy(1.2, duration: 0.25)
let scaleDown = scaleUp.reversedAction()
let fullScale = SKAction.sequence(
  [scaleUp, scaleDown, scaleUp, scaleDown])
let group = SKAction.group([fullScale, fullWiggle])
let groupWait = SKAction.repeatAction(group, count: 10)
```

This code creates a sequence similar to that of the wiggle sequence, except it scales up and down instead of wiggling left and right.

It then sets up a group action to run the wiggling and scaling at the same time. To use a group action, you simply provide it with the list of actions that should run at the same time.

Now replace the `wiggleWait` action with `groupWait` inside the declaration of the `actions` array, as shown below:

```
let actions = [appear, groupWait, disappear, removeFromParent]
```

Build and run, and your cats will bounce with excitement:

Note: The duration of a group action is equal to the longest duration of any of the actions it contains. So if you include an action that takes one second and

> another that takes 10 seconds, both actions will begin to run at the same time, and after one second, the first action will be complete. The group action will continue to execute for nine more seconds until the other action is complete.

Collision detection

You've got a zombie, you've got cats, you've even got crazy cat ladies—but you don't have a way to detect when they collide.

There are multiple ways to detect collisions in Sprite Kit, including using the built-in physics engine, as you'll learn in Chapter 10, "Intermediate Physics." In this chapter, you'll take the simplest and easiest approach: bounding-box collision detection.

There are three basic ideas you'll use to implement this:

1. You need a way of getting all of the cats and cat ladies in a scene into lists so that you can check for collisions one-by-one. An easy solution is to give nodes a name when you create them, allowing you to use `enumerateChildNodesWithName(usingBlock:)` on the scene to find all of the nodes with a certain name.

2. Once you have the lists of cats and cat ladies, you can loop through them to check for collisions. Each node has a `frame` property that gives you a rectangle representing the node's location onscreen.

3. If you have the frame for either a cat or a cat lady, and the frame for the zombie, you can use the built-in method `CGRectIntersectsRect()` to see if they collide.

Let's give this a shot. First, set the name for each node. Inside `spawnEnemy()`, right after creating the enemy sprite, add this line:

```
enemy.name = "enemy"
```

Similarly, inside `spawnCat()`, right after creating the cat sprite, add this line:

```
cat.name = "cat"
```

Then add these new methods to the file:

```
func zombieHitCat(cat: SKSpriteNode) {
  cat.removeFromParent()
}
```

```
func zombieHitEnemy(enemy: SKSpriteNode) {
  enemy.removeFromParent()
}

func checkCollisions() {
  var hitCats: [SKSpriteNode] = []
  enumerateChildNodesWithName("cat") { node, _ in
    let cat = node as! SKSpriteNode
    if CGRectIntersectsRect(cat.frame, self.zombie.frame) {
      hitCats.append(cat)
    }
  }
  for cat in hitCats {
    zombieHitCat(cat)
  }

  var hitEnemies: [SKSpriteNode] = []
  enumerateChildNodesWithName("enemy") { node, _ in
    let enemy = node as! SKSpriteNode
    if CGRectIntersectsRect(
      CGRectInset(node.frame, 20, 20), self.zombie.frame) {
      hitEnemies.append(enemy)
    }
  }
  for enemy in hitEnemies {
    zombieHitEnemy(enemy)
  }
}
```

Here, you enumerate through any child of the scene that has the name "cat" or "enemy" and cast it to an SKSpriteNode, since you know it's a sprite node if it has that name.

You then check if the frame of the cat or enemy intersects with the frame of the zombie. If there is an intersection, you simply add the cat or enemy to an array to keep track of it. After you finish enumerating the nodes, you loop through the hitCats and hitEnemies arrays and call a method that removes the cat or enemy from the scene.

Note that you don't remove the nodes from within the enumeration. It's unsafe to remove a node while enumerating over a list of them, and doing so can crash your app.

Also, notice that you do a little trick for the cat lady. Remember that the frame of a sprite is the sprite's entire image, including transparent space:

That means it would "count" as a hit if the zombie went into the area of transparent space at the top of the cat lady image. Totally unfair!

To resolve this, you shrink the bounding box a little bit by using CGRectInset(). It's not a perfect solution, but it's a start. You'll learn a better way to do this in Chapter 11, "Advanced Physics."

Add the following call to your collision detection method at the end of update():

```
checkCollisions()
```

Build and run, and now when you collide with a cat or enemy, it disappears from the scene. It's your first small step toward the zombie apocalypse!

The Sprite Kit game loop, round 2

There is a slight problem with the way you're detecting collisions, and it's related to Sprite Kit's game loop.

Earlier, you learned that during Sprite Kit's game loop, the update() method gets called, then some "other stuff" occurs, and finally Sprite Kit renders the screen:

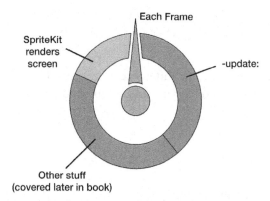

Well, one of the things in the "other stuff" section is the evaluation of the actions you've been learning in this chapter:

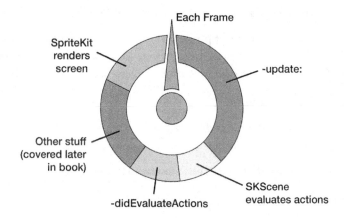

Herein lies the problem with the way you're currently detecting collisions. You check for collisions at the end of the update() loop, but Sprite Kit doesn't evaluate the actions until *after* this update() loop. Therefore, your collision detection code is always one frame behind!

As you can see in your new event loop diagram, it would be much better to perform collision detection after Sprite Kit evaluates the actions and all the sprites are in their new spots. So comment out the call at the end of update():

```
//checkCollisions()
```

And implement `didEvaluateActions()` as follows:

```
override func didEvaluateActions() {
  checkCollisions()
}
```

You probably won't notice much of a difference in this case, because the frame rate is so fast, it's hard to tell it was behind. But it could be quite noticeable in other games, so it's best to do things properly.

Sound action

The last type of action you'll learn about in this chapter also happens to be one of the most fun—it's the action that plays sound effects!

Using the `playSoundFileNamed(waitForCompletion:)` action, it takes just one line of code to play a sound effect with Sprite Kit. The node on which you run this action doesn't matter, so typically you'll run it as an action on the scene itself.

First, you need to add sounds to your project. In the resources for this chapter, find the folder named **Sounds** and drag it into your project. Make sure that **Copy items if needed**, **Create Groups** and the **ZombieConga** target are selected, and click **Finish**.

Now for the code. Add this line to the end of `zombieHitCat()`:

```
runAction(SKAction.playSoundFileNamed("hitCat.wav",
  waitForCompletion: false))
```

Then add this line to the end of `zombieHitEnemy()`:

```
runAction(SKAction.playSoundFileNamed("hitCatLady.wav",
  waitForCompletion: false))
```

Here, you play the appropriate sound action for each type of collision. Build and run, move the zombie around and enjoy the sounds of the smash-up!

Sharing actions

In the previous section, perhaps you noticed a slight pause the first time the sound plays. This can occur when the sound system is initialized. The solution to this problem also demonstrates one of the most powerful features of Sprite Kit's actions: sharing.

The `SKAction` object does not actually maintain any state itself, and that allows you to do something cool: reuse actions on any number of nodes simultaneously! For example, the action you create to move the cat ladies across the screen looks something like this:

```
let actionMove =
  SKAction.moveToX(-enemy.size.width/2, duration: 2.0)
```

But you create this action for every cat lady. Instead, you could create an `SKAction` property, store this action in it and then use that property wherever you are currently using `actionMove`.

In fact, you could modify Zombie Conga so it reuses most of the actions you've created so far. This would reduce the amount of memory your system uses, but that's a performance improvement you probably don't need to make in such a simple game. You'll learn more about things like this in Chapter 27, "Performance: Tips and Tricks."

But how does this relate to the sound delay?

The application is loading the sound the first time you create an action that uses it. So to prevent the sound delay, you can create the actions in advance and then use them when necessary.

Create the following properties:

```
let catCollisionSound: SKAction = SKAction.playSoundFileNamed(
  "hitCat.wav", waitForCompletion: false)
let enemyCollisionSound: SKAction = SKAction.playSoundFileNamed(
  "hitCatLady.wav", waitForCompletion: false)
```

These properties hold shared instances of the sound actions you want to run.

Finally, replace the line that plays the sound in `zombieHitCat()` with the following:

```
runAction(catCollisionSound)
```

And replace the line that plays the sound in `zombieHitEnemy()` with the following:

```
runAction(enemyCollisionSound)
```

Now you are reusing the same sound actions for all collisions rather than creating a new one for each collision.

Build and run again. You should no longer experience any pauses before the sound effects play.

As for music, stay tuned (no pun intended!)—you'll learn about that in the next chapter, where you'll wrap up the core gameplay by adding a win/lose scene to the game.

But before you move on, be sure to get some practice with actions by trying out the challenges for this chapter!

Challenges

This chapter has three challenges, and as usual, they progress from easiest to hardest.

Be sure to do these challenges. As a Sprite Kit developer, you'll be using actions all the time, so it's important to practice with them before moving further.

As always, if you get stuck, you can find solutions in the resources for this chapter—but give it your best shot first!

Challenge 1: The ActionsCatalog demo

This chapter covers the most important actions in Sprite Kit, but it doesn't cover all of them. To help you get a solid understanding of all the actions available to you, I've created a little demo called ActionsCatalog, which you can find in the resources for this chapter.

Open the project in Xcode and build and run. You'll see something like the following:

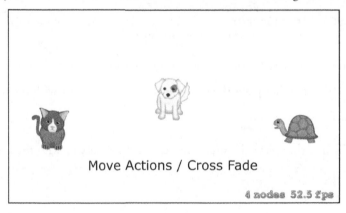

Each scene in the app demonstrates a particular set of actions, shown as the part of the label before the backslash. This first example demonstrates the various move actions.

Each time you tap the screen, you'll see a new set of actions. As the scenes transition, you'll also see different transition effects, shown as the part of the label after the backslash.

Your challenge is to flip through each of these demos, then take a look at the code to answer the following questions:

1. What action constructor would you use to make a sprite follow a certain pre-defined path?

2. What action constructor would you use to make a sprite 50% transparent, regardless of what its current transparency settings are?

3. What are "custom actions" and how do they work at a high level?

You can check your answers in a comment at the top of **GameScene.swift** in the solution project for this chapter.

Challenge 2: An invincible zombie

Currently, when an enemy hits the zombie, it destroys the enemy. This is a sneaky way of avoiding the problematic scenario of the enemy colliding with the zombie multiple times in a row as it moves through the zombie, which would result in the squish sound effect playing just as many times in rapid succession.

Usually in a video game, you resolve this problem by making the player sprite invincible for a few seconds after getting hit, so the player has time to get his or her bearings.

Your challenge is to modify the game to do just this. When the zombie collides with a cat lady, he should become temporarily invincible instead of destroying the cat lady.

While the zombie is invincible, he should blink. To do this, you can use the custom blink action that is included in ActionsCatalog. Here's the code for your convenience:

```
let blinkTimes = 10.0
let duration = 3.0
let blinkAction = SKAction.customActionWithDuration(duration) {
  node, elapsedTime in
  let slice = duration / blinkTimes
  let remainder = Double(elapsedTime) % slice
  node.hidden = remainder > slice / 2
}
```

If you'd like a detailed explanation of this method, see the comment in the solution for the previous challenge.

Here are some hints for solving this challenge:

• You should create a variable property to track whether or not the zombie is invincible.

• If the zombie is invincible, you shouldn't bother enumerating the scene's cat ladies.

• If the zombie collides with a cat lady, don't remove the cat lady from the scene. Instead, set the zombie as invincible. Next, run a sequence of actions where you first make the zombie blink 10 times over three seconds, then run the block of code as described below.

• The block of code should set hidden to false on the zombie (making sure he's visible at the end no matter what) and set the zombie as no longer invincible.

Challenge 3: The conga train

This game is called Zombie Conga, but there's no conga line to be seen just yet!

Your challenge is to fix that. You'll modify the game so that when the zombie collides with a cat, instead of disappearing, the cat joins your conga line!

In the process of doing this, you'll get more practice with actions, and you'll also review the vector math material you learned in the last chapter. Yes, that stuff still comes in handy when working with actions!

Here are the steps to implement this challenge:

1. Create a constant CGFloat property to keep track of the cat's move points per second. Set it to 480.0.

2. Set the zombie's zPosition to 100. This makes the zombie appear on top of the other sprites. Larger z values are "out of the screen" and smaller values are "into the screen," and the default value is 0.

3. When the zombie collides with a cat, don't remove the cat from the scene. Instead, do the following:

   a. Set the cat's name to "train" (instead of "cat").

   b. Stop all actions currently running on the cat by calling removeAllActions().

   c. Set the scale to 1 and the rotation of the cat to 0.

   d. Run an action to make the cat turn green over 0.2 seconds. If you're not sure what action to use for this, check out ActionsCatalog.

4. Make a new method called moveTrain. The basic idea for this method is that every so often, you make each cat move toward the current position of the previous cat. This creates a conga line effect!

   Use the following template:

```
func moveTrain() {
  var targetPosition = zombie.position

  enumerateChildNodesWithName("train") {
    node, _ in
    if !node.hasActions() {
      let actionDuration = 0.3
      let offset = // a
      let direction = // b
      let amountToMovePerSec = // c
      let amountToMove = // d
      let moveAction = // e
      node.runAction(moveAction)
    }
    targetPosition = node.position
  }
}
```

You need to fill in **a through d** by using the CGPoint operator overloads and utility functions you created last chapter, and **e** by creating the appropriate action. Here are some hints:

   a. You need to figure out the offset between the cat's current position and the target position.

   b. You need to figure out a unit vector pointing in the direction of the offset.

    c. You need to get a vector pointing in the direction of the offset, but with a length of the cat's move points per second. This represents the amount and direction the cat should move in a second.

    d. You need to get a fraction of the `amountToMovePerSec` vector, based on the `actionDuration`. This represents the offset the cat should move over the next `actionDuration` seconds. Note you'll need to cast `actionDuration` to a `CGFloat`.

    e. You should move the cat a relative amount based on the `amountToMove`.

5. Call `moveTrain` at the end of `update()`.

And that's it—who said you couldn't herd cats? If you got this working, you've truly made this game live up to its name: Zombie Conga!

Chapter 4: Scenes

By Ray Wenderlich

Zombie Conga is beginning to look like a real game—it has character movement, enemies, sounds, animation, collision detection—and if you finished the challenges from last chapter, even its namesake conga line!

However, right now all the action takes place in a single **scene** of the game: the default GameScene created for you by the Sprite Kit project template.

In Sprite Kit, you don't have to place everything within the same scene. Instead, you can create multiple unique scenes, one for each "screen" of the app, much like how view controllers work in iOS development.

In this short chapter, you'll add two new scenes: one for when the player wins or loses the game and another for the main menu. You'll also learn a bit about using the cool transitions you saw in the ActionsCatalog demo from last chapter's Challenge 1.

But first, you need to wrap up some gameplay logic so you can detect when the player should win or lose the game. Let's get started!

> **Note:** This chapter begins where the previous chapter's Challenge 3 left off. If you
> were unable to complete the challenges or skipped ahead from an earlier chapter,
> don't worry—you can simply open **ZombieConga-Starter** from this chapter's
> resources to begin in the right place.

Win and lose conditions

Here's how the player will win or lose Zombie Conga:

• **Win Condition**: If the player creates a conga line of 30 cats or more, the player wins!

• **Lose Condition**: The player will start with five lives. If the player spends all of his or
  her lives, the player loses.

Right now, when a crazy cat lady collides with the zombie, nothing bad happens—
there's only a sound. To make this game challenging, you'll change this so collisions with
a cat lady result in the following effects:

1. The zombie loses a life.

2. The zombie loses two cats from his conga line.

Let's make it so. Inside **GameScene.swift**, add a new property to keep track of the
zombie's lives and another to keep track of whether the game is over:

```
var lives = 5
var gameOver = false
```

Next, add this new helper method to make the zombie lose two cats from his conga line:

```
func loseCats() {
  // 1
  var loseCount = 0
  enumerateChildNodesWithName("train") { node, stop in
    // 2
    var randomSpot = node.position
    randomSpot.x += CGFloat.random(min: -100, max: 100)
    randomSpot.y += CGFloat.random(min: -100, max: 100)
    // 3
    node.name = ""
    node.runAction(
      SKAction.sequence([
        SKAction.group([
```

```
            SKAction.rotateByAngle(π*4, duration: 1.0),
            SKAction.moveTo(randomSpot, duration: 1.0),
            SKAction.scaleTo(0, duration: 1.0)
          ]),
          SKAction.removeFromParent()
       ]))
    // 4
    loseCount++
    if loseCount >= 2 {
      stop.memory = true
    }
  }
}
```

Let's go over this section by section:

1. Here, you set up a variable to track the number of cats you've removed from the conga line so far, then you enumerate through the conga line.

2. You find a random offset from the cat's current position.

3. You run a little animation to make the cat move toward the random spot, spinning around and scaling to 0 along the way. Finally, the animation removes the cat from the scene. You also set the cat's name to an empty string so it's no longer considered a normal cat or a cat in the conga line.

4. You update the variable that is tracking the number of cats you've removed from the conga line. Once you've removed two or more, you set the `stop` Boolean to `true`, which causes Sprite Kit to stop enumerating the conga line.

Now that you have this helper method, call it in `zombieHitEnemy()`, right after playing the enemy collision sound:

```
loseCats()
lives--
```

You're ready to add the code that checks if the player should win or lose. Begin with the lose condition. Add this to the end of `update()`:

```
if lives <= 0 && !gameOver {
  gameOver = true
  println("You lose!")
}
```

Here, you check if the player's remaining lives number 0 or less and make sure the game isn't over already. If both of these conditions are met, you set the game to be over and log out a message.

To check for the win condition, you'll make a few modifications to moveTrain(). First, add this variable at the beginning of the method:

```
var trainCount = 0
```

You'll use trainCount to keep track of the number of cats in the train. Increment this counter with the following line inside the enumerateChildNodesWithName() block, *before* the call to hasActions():

```
trainCount++
```

Finally, add this code at the end of moveTrain():

```
if trainCount >= 30 && !gameOver {
   gameOver = true
   println("You win!")
}
```

Here, you check if there are more than 30 cats in the train and make sure the game isn't over already. If both of these conditions are met, you set the game to be over and log out a message.

Build and run, and see if you can collect 30 cats.

When you do, you'll see the following message in the console:

```
You win!
```

That's great, but when the player wins the game, you want something a bit more dramatic to happen. Let's create a proper game over scene.

Creating a new scene

To create a new scene, you simply create a new class that derives from SKScene. You can then implement init(size:), update(), touchesBegan(withEvent:) or any of the other methods you overrode in GameScene to implement the behavior you want.

For now, you're going to keep things simple with a bare-bones new scene. In Xcode's main menu, select **File\New\File...**, select the **iOS\Source\Swift File** template and click **Next**.

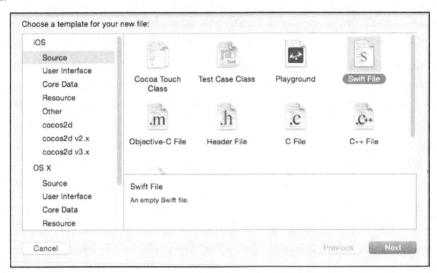

Enter **GameOverScene** for **Save As**, make sure the **ZombieConga** target is checked and click **Create**.

Open **GameOverScene.swift** and replace its contents with some bare-bones code for the new class:

```
import Foundation
import SpriteKit

class GameOverScene: SKScene {
}
```

With this, you've created an empty class, derived from SKScene, which defaults to a blank screen when presented. Later in this chapter, you'll return to this scene to add artwork and logic.

Now, how do you get to this new scene from your original scene?

Transitioning to a scene

There are three steps to transition from one scene to another:

1. **Create the new scene**. First, you create an instance of the new scene itself. Typically, you'd use the default `init(size:)` initializer, although you can always choose to create your own custom initializer if you want to be able to pass in extra parameters. Later in this chapter, you'll do just that.

2. **Create a transition object**. Next, you create a transition object to specify the type of animation you'd like to use to display the new scene. For example, there are crossfade transitions, flip transitions, door-opening transitions and many more.

3. **Call the SKView's presentScene(transition:) method**. In iOS, `SKView` is the `UIView` that displays Sprite Kit content on the screen. You can get access to this via a property on the scene: `view`. You can then call `presentScene(transition:)` to animate to the passed-in scene (created in step 1) with the passed-in transition (created in step 2).

Let's give this a try. Open **GameScene.swift** and add the following lines in `moveTrain()`, right after the code that logs "You Win!" to the console:

```
// 1
let gameOverScene = GameOverScene(size: size)
gameOverScene.scaleMode = scaleMode
// 2
let reveal = SKTransition.flipHorizontalWithDuration(0.5)
// 3
view?.presentScene(gameOverScene, transition: reveal)
```

These three lines correspond exactly to the three steps above.

Notice that after creating the game over scene, you set its scale mode to the same as the current scene's scale mode to make sure the new scene behaves the same way across different devices.

Also notice that to create a transition, there are various constructors on `SKTransition`, just as there are various constructors for actions on `SKAction`. Here, you choose a flip horizontal animation, which flips up the scene into view from the bottom of the screen. For a demo of all the transitions, refer to ActionsCatalog, as discussed in the previous chapter's challenges.

Now add the exact same lines as above to `update()`, right after the code that logs "You lose!" to the console.

Build and run, and either win or lose the game. Feel free to cheat and change the number of cats to win to less than 30—after all, you're the developer!

Whether you win or lose, when you do, you'll see the scene transition to a new blank scene:

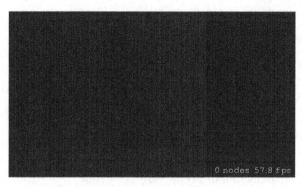

That's really all there is to scene transitions! Now that you have a new scene, you can do whatever you like in it, just as you did in GameScene.

For Zombie Conga, you'll modify this new scene to show either a "You Win" or a "You Lose" background. To make this possible, you need to create a custom scene initializer to pass in either the win or lose condition.

Creating a custom scene initializer

Open **GameOverScene.swift** and modify GameOverScene as follows:

```
class GameOverScene: SKScene {
  let won:Bool

  init(size: CGSize, won: Bool) {
    self.won = won
    super.init(size: size)
  }

  required init(coder aDecoder: NSCoder) {
    fatalError("init(coder:) has not been implemented")
  }
}
```

Here, you add a custom initializer that takes just one extra parameter: a Boolean that should be true if the player won and false if the player lost. You store this value in a property named won.

Next, implement `didMoveToView()` to configure the scene when it is added to the view hierarchy:

```
override func didMoveToView(view: SKView) {

  var background: SKSpriteNode
  if (won) {
    background = SKSpriteNode(imageNamed: "YouWin")
    runAction(SKAction.sequence([
      SKAction.waitForDuration(0.1),
      SKAction.playSoundFileNamed("win.wav",
        waitForCompletion: false)
    ]))
  } else {
    background = SKSpriteNode(imageNamed: "YouLose")
    runAction(SKAction.sequence([
      SKAction.waitForDuration(0.1),
      SKAction.playSoundFileNamed("lose.wav",
        waitForCompletion: false)
    ]))
  }

  background.position =
    CGPoint(x: self.size.width/2, y: self.size.height/2)
  self.addChild(background)

  // More here...
}
```

This looks at the won Boolean and chooses the proper background image to set and sound effect to play.

In Zombie Conga, you want to display the game over scene for a few seconds and then automatically transition back to the main scene. To do this, add these lines of code right after the "More here…" comment:

```
let wait = SKAction.waitForDuration(3.0)
let block = SKAction.runBlock {
  let myScene = GameScene(size: self.size)
  myScene.scaleMode = self.scaleMode
  let reveal = SKTransition.flipHorizontalWithDuration(0.5)
  self.view?.presentScene(myScene, transition: reveal)
}
self.runAction(SKAction.sequence([wait, block]))
```

By now, this is all be review for you. The code runs a sequence of actions on the scene, first waiting for three seconds and then calling a block of code. The block of code creates a new instance of `GameScene` and transitions to that with a flip animation.

One last step: You need to modify your code in `GameScene` to use this new custom initializer. Open **GameScene.swift** and inside `update()`, change the line that creates the `GameOverScene` to indicate that this is the lose condition:

```
let gameOverScene = GameOverScene(size: size, won: false)
```

Inside `moveTrain()`, change the same line, but indicate that this is the win condition:

```
let gameOverScene = GameOverScene(size: size, won: true)
```

Build and run, and play until you win the game. When you do, you'll see the win scene, which will then flip back to a new game after a few seconds:

Now that your game is close to done, it's a good time to turn off the debug drawing for the playable rectangle. Comment out this line in `didMoveToView()`:

```
//debugDrawPlayableArea()
```

Gratuitous music

You almost have a complete game, but you're missing one thing: awesome background music!

Luckily, we've got you covered. Open **MyUtils.swift** and add the following to the bottom of the file:

```
import AVFoundation

var backgroundMusicPlayer: AVAudioPlayer!

func playBackgroundMusic(filename: String) {
  let url = NSBundle.mainBundle().URLForResource(
    filename, withExtension: nil)
  if (url == nil) {
    println("Could not find file: \(filename)")
    return
  }

  var error: NSError? = nil
  backgroundMusicPlayer =
    AVAudioPlayer(contentsOfURL: url, error: &error)
  if backgroundMusicPlayer == nil {
    println("Could not create audio player: \(error!)")
    return
  }

  backgroundMusicPlayer.numberOfLoops = -1
  backgroundMusicPlayer.prepareToPlay()
  backgroundMusicPlayer.play()
}
```

There is no built-in way to play background music in Sprite Kit itself, so you'll have to fall back on other iOS APIs to do it. One easy way to play music in iOS is to use the AVAudioPlayer class inside the AVFoundation framework. The above helper code uses an AVAudioPlayer to play some background music endlessly.

Back in **GameScene.swift**, try it out by adding this line to the top of didMoveToView():

```
playBackgroundMusic("backgroundMusic.mp3")
```

Here, you make the game play the background music when the scene first loads.

Finally, you need to stop the background music when the player switches scenes, so they can hear the "you win" or "you lose" sound effects. To do this, add this line right after the "You Win!" log line in moveTrain():

```
backgroundMusicPlayer.stop()
```

Also add that same line right after the "You Lose!" log line in update().

Build and run, and enjoy your groovy tunes!

Challenges

This was a short and sweet chapter, and the challenges will be equally so. You've just one challenge this time: to add a main menu scene to the game.

As always, if you get stuck, you can find the solution in the resources for this chapter—but give it your best shot first!

Challenge 1: Main menu scene

Usually, it's best to start a game with an opening or main menu scene, rather than throw the player right into the middle of the action. The main menu often includes options to start a new game, continue a game, access game options and so on.

Zombie Conga's main menu scene will be very simple: It will show an image and allow the player to tap to continue straight to a new game. This will effectively be the same as the splash screen, except it will allow the player more time to get their bearings.

Your challenge is to implement a main menu scene that shows the **MainMenu.png** image as a background and transitions upon screen tap to the main action scene, using a "doorway" transition over 1.5 seconds.

Here are a few hints for how to accomplish this:

- Create a new class that derives from `SKScene` named `MainMenuScene`.

- Implement `didMoveToView()` on `MainMenuScene` to display **MainMenu.png** in the center of the scene.

- Inside **GameViewController.swift**, edit `viewDidLoad()` to make it start with `MainMenuScene` instead of `GameScene`.

- Build and run, and make sure the main menu image appears. So far, so good!

- Finally, implement `touchesBegan(_:withEvent:)` in `MainMenuScene` to call a helper method, `sceneTapped()`. `sceneTapped()` should transition to `GameScene` using a "doorway" transition over 1.5 seconds.

If you've gotten this working, congratulations! You now have a firm understanding of how to create and transition between multiple scenes in Sprite Kit.

Chapter 5: Scrolling

By Ray Wenderlich

So far, the background in Zombie Conga is stationary. In contrast, many games have large scrolling worlds, like the original *Super Mario Bros.*:

The red box shows what you can see on the screen, but the level continues beyond to the right. As the player moves to the right, you can think of the background as moving to the left:

Typically in these kinds of games, the player, enemies and power-ups are considered children of the "background layer." To scroll the game, you simply move the background layer from right to left, and its children move with it.

Of course, the children can move within the background layer as well – for example, in the *Super Mario Bros.* level above, the mushroom power-up, Goomba enemies and Mario all move around within the background layer's space.

In this chapter, you're going to modify Zombie Conga so that the level endlessly scrolls from right to left. In the process, you'll learn more about nodes, children and coordinate spaces. Let's get scrolling!

> **Note:** This chapter begins where the previous chapter's Challenge 1 left off. If you were unable to complete the challenge or skipped ahead from an earlier chapter, don't worry—you can simply open **ZombieConga-Starter** from this chapter's resources to begin in the right place.

A scrolling background

As you may remember from Chapter 2, you are using a background named **background1** that is the same size as the scene itself. Your project contains a second background named **background2** that's designed to be placed to the right of background1, like so:

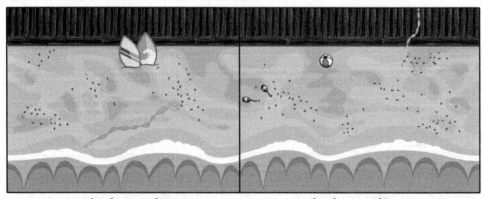

background1   **background2**

Your first task is simple: combine these two background images into a single node so you can easily scroll them both at the same time.

To do this, open **GameScene.swift** and add this new method:

```
func backgroundNode() -> SKSpriteNode {
  // 1
  let backgroundNode = SKSpriteNode()
  backgroundNode.anchorPoint = CGPointZero
  backgroundNode.name = "background"
  // 2
  let background1 = SKSpriteNode(imageNamed: "background1")
  background1.anchorPoint = CGPointZero
  background1.position = CGPoint(x: 0, y: 0)
  backgroundNode.addChild(background1)
  // 3
  let background2 = SKSpriteNode(imageNamed: "background2")
  background2.anchorPoint = CGPointZero
  background2.position =
    CGPoint(x: background1.size.width, y: 0)
  backgroundNode.addChild(background2)
  // 4
  backgroundNode.size = CGSize(
    width: background1.size.width + background2.size.width,
    height: background1.size.height)
  return backgroundNode
}
```

Let's go over this section by section:

1. You create a new SKNode to contain both background sprites as children. In this case, instead of using SKNode directly, you use an SKSpriteNode with no texture. This is so you can conveniently set the size property on the SKSpriteNode to the combined size of the background images.

2. You create an SKSpriteNode for the first background image and pin the bottom-left of the sprite to the bottom-left of backgroundNode.

3. You create an SKSpriteNode for the second background image and pin the bottom-left of the sprite to the bottom right of background1 inside backgroundNode.

4. You set the size of the backgroundNode based on the size of the two background images.

Next, replace the code in `didMoveToView()` that creates the background sprite with the following:

```
let background = backgroundNode()
background.anchorPoint = CGPointZero
background.position = CGPointZero
background.name = "background"
addChild(background)
```

This simply creates the background using your new helper method rather than creating it based on just a single background image.

Also note that previously, you had the background centered on the screen. Here, you pin the lower-left corner to the lower-left of the scene instead.

Changing the anchor point to the lower-left like this will make it easier to calculate positions when the time comes. You also name the background "background" so that you can find it readily.

Finally, your goal is to make this background scroll from right to left. To do this, add a property for the background's scrolling speed:

```
let backgroundMovePointsPerSec: CGFloat = 200.0
```

Next, add this helper method to move the background:

```
func moveBackground() {
  enumerateChildNodesWithName("background") { node, _ in
    let background = node as! SKSpriteNode
    let backgroundVelocity =
      CGPoint(x: -self.backgroundMovePointsPerSec, y: 0)
    let amountToMove = backgroundVelocity * CGFloat(self.dt)
    background.position += amountToMove
  }
}
```

This finds any child with the "background" name and moves it to the left according to the velocity. If you are unsure how the above lines of code work, refer back to Chapter 3, "Manual Movement."

Finally, call this new method inside `update()`, right after the call to `moveTrain()`:

```
moveBackground()
```

Build and run, and now you have a scrolling background:

There's one big problem, though. After the background runs out, you're left with empty space:

An endlessly scrolling background

The most efficient way to fix this is to make two background nodes instead of one and lay them side by side:

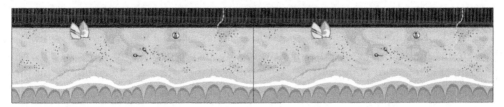

Then, as you scroll both images from right to left, once one of the images goes off-screen, you simply reposition it to the right:

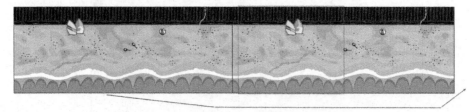

Let's see how this works. Replace the code in didMoveToView(): that creates the background node with the following:

```
for i in 0...1 {
  let background = backgroundNode()
  background.anchorPoint = CGPointZero
  background.position =
    CGPoint(x: CGFloat(i)*background.size.width, y: 0)
  background.name = "background"
  addChild(background)
}
```

Also, if you still have the lines that get and log the background's size, comment them out.

The above wraps the code in a for loop that creates two copies of the background, then sets the position so the second copy begins after the first ends.

Next, add the following code in moveBackground(), inside the enumerateChildNodesWithName() block, after the code that sets the background's position:

```
if background.position.x <= -background.size.width {
  background.position = CGPoint(
    x: background.position.x + background.size.width*2,
    y: background.position.y)
}
```

This checks if the background node's x-position is less than the negative width of the background node. In other words, since the sprite's anchor point is the lower-left, if the position of that anchor point is the negative width of the background node, it means the background node is fully off-screen.

In that case, the code simply moves the background node to the right by double the width of the background. Since there are two background nodes, this places the first node immediately to the right of the second.

Build and run, and now you have an endlessly looping background!

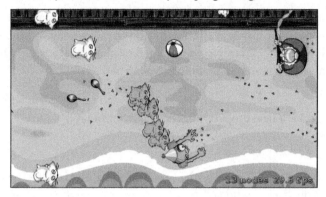

Moving to layers

As you play the game, you'll notice that the behavior of the cats now seems a little strange—even for cats!

Since the cats are supposed to remain in the same spots until picked up by the zombie, they should be moving to the left as the background moves to the left.

In other words, the cats should be children of the background so that they move along with it. This raises an issue: There are two different background sprites, but a node can only have a single parent. What should you do?

The solution is to create an empty node that you'll treat as the "background layer." To this, you'll add the background sprites, cats and other children—the zombie and crazy cat ladies. Then, with each frame you can update the position of the background layer and all its children will move with it.

> **Note:** You might wonder if you could just move the position of the scene itself from right to left, since everything is already a child of the scene. However, in Sprite Kit, changing the position of the scene has no effect.
>
> It's best practice to create a separate layer anyway, as you're doing here. That way, you can easily position sprites at fixed points on the screen, even if the rest of the scene is scrolling—if, for example, you wanted to make a Heads-Up Display (HUD) to show the zombie's remaining lives.

Give this a try. Create a new property for the background layer node:

```
let backgroundLayer = SKNode()
```

Then create the backgroundLayer at the very beginning of didMoveToView(), before the code that sets the background color:

```
backgroundLayer.zPosition = -1
addChild(backgroundLayer)
```

Note that you set the zPosition of the backgroundLayer to -1. This ensures that the backgroundLayer shows up underneath everything else in your scene.

Now, every place you add something as a child of the scene, you should add it as a child of the backgroundLayer instead. There are four cases:

1. In didMoveToView(), when adding the zombie sprite:

```
backgroundLayer.addChild(zombie)
```

2. In didMoveToView(), when adding the background sprites:

```
backgroundLayer.addChild(background)
```

3. In spawnEnemy(), when adding the enemy sprite:

```
backgroundLayer.addChild(enemy)
```

4. In spawnCat(), when adding the cat sprite:

```
backgroundLayer.addChild(cat)
```

You also have to fix the code that enumerates child nodes of the scene, now that the nodes have been made children of the background layer instead. Modify the line that

enumerates the cats in `checkCollisions()` so it calls
`enumerateChildNodesWithName()` on `backgroundLayer`. Do this by adding
"`backgroundLayer.`" to the start of the line, like this:

```
backgroundLayer.enumerateChildNodesWithName("cat") { node, _ in
```

Now modify three more lines the same way:

1. The line in `checkCollisions()` that enumerates the enemies:

```
backgroundLayer.enumerateChildNodesWithName("enemy") {
  node, _ in
```

2. The line that enumerates the conga line in `moveTrain()`:

```
backgroundLayer.enumerateChildNodesWithName("train") {
  node, _ in
```

3. And the line that enumerates the conga line in `loseCats()`:

```
backgroundLayer.enumerateChildNodesWithName("train") {
  node, stop in
```

Finally, modify `moveBackground()` so it moves the position of `backgroundLayer`
rather than the individual background sprites themselves:

```
func moveBackground() {
  let backgroundVelocity =
    CGPoint(x: -backgroundMovePointsPerSec, y: 0)
  let amountToMove = backgroundVelocity * CGFloat(dt)
  backgroundLayer.position += amountToMove

  backgroundLayer.enumerateChildNodesWithName("background") {
    node, _ in
    let background = node as SKSpriteNode
    if background.position.x <= -background.size.width {
      background.position = CGPoint(
        x: background.position.x + background.size.width*2,
        y: background.position.y)
    }
  }
}
```

Build and run. At first it looks all right, but then… oh no, everything goes flying off the
screen!

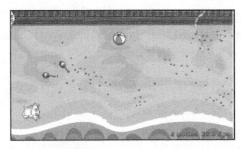

Something is very wrong here! And it's because you're comparing coordinate system apples to oranges.

Coordinate systems

Recall what you learned in Chapter 2: A sprite's position is within the coordinate space of its parent node, which up until this chapter was the scene itself.

You've switched the sprites to be children of the background layer, so their positions are now within the coordinate space of that layer.

For example, when the level begins, the zombie is at position (400, 400) in both the screen coordinate system, where (0, 0) represents the bottom-left of the screen, and in the background layer coordinate system, where (0, 0) represents the bottom-left of the background layer.

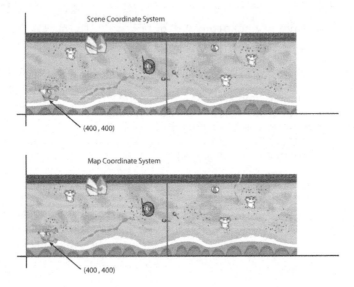

Here, the red box indicates what's currently visible on the screen. At first, the positions correspond.

The problem begins when you start moving the background layer to the left. Now the two coordinate systems don't match:

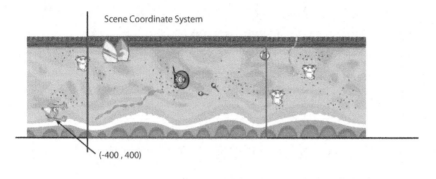

Scene Coordinate System

(-400 , 400)

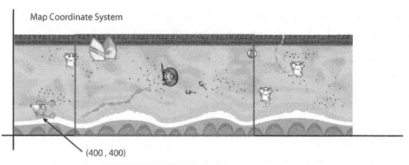

Map Coordinate System

(400 , 400)

Again, the red box indicates what's visible on the screen.

As you can see, after moving the background layer 800 points to the left, the zombie is at (-400, 400) in scene coordinates, but is still at (400, 400) in map coordinates. His position now depends on which coordinate system you are using!

Currently, you have a bunch of code that attempts to compare apples (scene coordinates) to oranges (background layer coordinates). Your goal is to make sure you're comparing apples to apples instead, by converting one set of coordinates to the other.

Let's fix these one at a time, starting with boundary checking for the player.

Fixing the bounds checking

Take a look at this snippet from boundsCheckZombie() (below are only the lines relevant to this discussion):

```
let bottomLeft = CGPoint(x: 0, y: CGRectGetMinY(playableRect))
let topRight =
  CGPoint(x: size.width, y: CGRectGetMaxY(playableRect))

if zombie.position.x <= bottomLeft.x {
  zombie.position.x = bottomLeft.x
  velocity.x = -velocity.x
}
```

This is trying to compare background layer coordinates (zombie.position) to scene coordinates (such as CGPoint(x:0, y: CGRectGetMinY(playableRect))), which won't work.

Luckily, this is easy to fix—just convert the scene coordinates to background layer coordinates, so that you're comparing the same coordinate types.

To do this, replace the lines that set the bottomLeft and topRight points with the following:

```
let bottomLeft = backgroundLayer.convertPoint(
  CGPoint(x: 0, y: CGRectGetMinY(playableRect)),
  fromNode: self)
let topRight = backgroundLayer.convertPoint(
  CGPoint(x: size.width, y: CGRectGetMaxY(playableRect)),
  fromNode: self)
```

To convert points from one coordinate system to another, you use convertPoint(fromNode:). Here's how it works:

• You pass the node that has the coordinate space you want to convert *from* in the fromNode: parameter. In this case, you're dealing with a scene coordinate, so you pass in the scene here (self).

• You pass the point you want to convert as the first parameter.

• The node that has the coordinate space you want to convert *to* is the object on which you call this method. In this case, you want to convert to the background layer's coordinate space.

Build and run, and you'll see you've correctly prevented your zombie from flying off the screen:

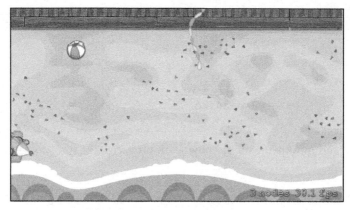

As you play around, though, you'll notice that the touch behavior no longer works properly—once the background scrolls far enough to the left, the app feels unresponsive. Let's fix this next.

Fixing the touches

Take a look at touchesBegan(withEvent:):

```
override func touchesBegan(touches: NSSet,
                           withEvent event:  UIEvent) {
  let touch = touches.anyObject() as UITouch
  let touchLocation = touch.locationInNode(self)
  sceneTouched(touchLocation)
}
```

This method gets the touch location by using touch.locationInNode(self), which gives the location of the zombie in scene coordinates. Instead, you want the location of the zombie in background layer coordinates.

To fix this, simply replace self with backgroundLayer in the line referenced above, like so:

```
let touchLocation = touch.locationInNode(backgroundLayer)
```

Repeat this for the other touch method, as well—touchesMoved(withEvent:).

Also, since the background is continuously scrolling, this game will now work a lot better if you disable the code that stops the zombie once he reaches the target point. To fix this, comment out the relevant code in update(), as shown below:

```
/*if (diff.length() <= zombieMovePointsPerSec * dt) {
```

```
    zombie.position = lastTouchLocation!
    velocity = CGPointZero
    stopZombieAnimation()
} else {*/
    moveSprite(zombie, velocity: velocity)
    rotateSprite(zombie, direction: velocity,
                rotateRadiansPerSec: zombieRotateRadiansPerSec)
//}
```

Build and run, and movement should now work properly.

> **Note:** You'll notice that the zombie moves more slowly to the right. That's because his speed is relative to the background layer, and since the background layer is scrolling to the left, the zombie has to use up some of his velocity to keep up with the scrolling!
>
> I like this behavior for Zombie Conga because it feels more realistic, so I left it this way. However, if you want a different behavior for your game, you could make the zombie a direct child of the scene to give him independent movement.

As you play around, you'll find other problems. First, the cats and enemies still don't handle the scrolling very well, but you'll fix those as challenges later. A more pressing issue is that the background no longer scrolls continuously. I bet you can guess why—yep, coordinate systems again!

Fixing the background scrolling

So that the background will once more repeat endlessly, you need to modify `moveBackground()`. First, add the following line just after the line that creates `background` inside the `enumerateChildNodesWithName()` block:

```
let backgroundScreenPos = self.backgroundLayer.convertPoint(
    background.position, toNode: self)
```

Then, change the line right below the one you just added—the `if` statement—so it checks against the value you just calculated, like this:

```
if backgroundScreenPos.x <= -background.size.width {
```

The problem was that you were again comparing apples (background layer coordinates) to oranges (scene coordinates). Here, you convert the background layer coordinates to scene coordinates so that they're the same.

Notice that this time, instead of using `convertPoint(fromNode:)`, you are using `convertPoint(toNode:)`. Here's how this variant works:

- You pass the node that has the coordinate space you want to convert *to* in the `toNode:` parameter. In this case, you want to convert these coordinates to scene coordinates, so you pass in the scene (`self`).

- You pass the point you want to convert as the first parameter.

- The node that has the coordinate space you want to convert *from* is the object on which you call this method. In this case, you want to convert it from the background layer coordinate space.

Build and run, and the background will scroll endlessly again.

> **Note:** There's one more thing to keep in mind when scrolling. For most games this won't be a factor, but in some cases, you may encounter rounding errors as your background's position moves farther and farther away from (0,0).
>
> These rounding errors can start to introduce errors in your display when items need to line up perfectly. If you find yourself in such a situation, you'll want to periodically move your background back to (0,0). When doing so, you'll need to adjust the positions of all child nodes to compensate.
>
> For example, if your player node is at (100, 50) and your background is at (-100, 0), moving the background to the right by 100 would bring it to (0, 0) but would require you to compensate by moving your player to the left by 100 to go to (0, 50). Of course, to see these rounding errors, you'll need to be working with values much farther away from the origin than the ones shown here.

w00t, you're almost done—the only things left to fix are the cats and the enemies!

And those are your final challenges. Once completed, you will have fulfilled your work with the mobile version of Zombie Conga. In the next chapter, you'll learn how to port it to OS X so you can play it on your Mac! After that, you'll be ready to move on to your next minigame—where you'll learn all about game physics.

Challenges

This is your final set of challenges for the iOS version of Zombie Conga—your game is 99% complete, so don't leave it hanging! All you have to do is fix the cats and enemies to work with the new scrolling behavior.

As always, if you get stuck, you can find the solutions in the resources for this chapter—but give it your best shot first!

Challenge 1: Fixing the cats

Currently, the cats spawn correctly at the beginning of the level, but seem to no longer appear on the screen after the background scrolls. Take a look at the line that sets a new cat's position in spawnCat():

```
cat.position = CGPoint(
  x: CGFloat.random(min: CGRectGetMinX(playableRect),
                    max: CGRectGetMaxX(playableRect)),
  y: CGFloat.random(min: CGRectGetMinY(playableRect),
                    max: CGRectGetMaxY(playableRect)))
```

Can you deduce what's apples to oranges here?

Since this is the easy challenge, I'll tell you: The code above is trying to place the position of the cat using scene coordinates, but it should be using background layer coordinates.

Your challenge is to fix this by converting the scene coordinates to background layer coordinates.

Here are some hints:

• Create a new CGPoint called catScenePos and set it to the same random value that the current code uses.

• Then use convertPoint(fromNode:) to convert this point from scene coordinates to background layer coordinates.

Build and run, and now the cats should always spawn!

Challenge 2: Fixing the enemies

Your next challenge is to fix the enemy spawning behavior. There are currently two problems:

1. A with the cats, enemies appear to stop spawning after a while due to a coordinate conversion problem.

2. Once you fix the first problem, you'll see enemies appear to spawn faster and faster over time.

Here are some hints to get you started:

• The solution to the first problem is very similar to the solution to Challenge 1, above.

• There are two ways to solve the second problem. You can either do another coordinate conversion, or you can change the action type that you use to move the enemies.

If you've made it this far, a huge congratulations—you've completed your first Sprite Kit minigame from scratch! Think of all you've learned to do:

• Add sprites to a game.

• Move them around manually.

• Move them around with actions.

• Create multiple scenes in a game.

• Make a scrolling game and convert between coordinate systems.

Believe it or not, this knowledge is sufficient to make 90% of Sprite Kit games. The rest is just icing on the cake! ☺

Chapter 6: OS X

By Ray Wenderlich

Over the last five chapters, you built a complete game called Zombie Conga that is fully functional on both the iPhone and iPad.

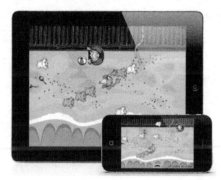

Wouldn't it be great if the game could work on OS X, as well?

Good news! There are only a few simple steps to get your Sprite Kit games to work on OS X. This chapter will show you how.

> **Note:** This chapter begins where the previous chapter's Challenge 2 left off. If you were unable to complete the challenges or skipped ahead from an earlier chapter, don't worry—you can simply open **ZombieConga-Starter** from this chapter's resources to begin in the right place.

Adding an OS X target

Projects in Xcode consist of multiple targets. Each target builds a binary with a subset of the files in the project, with different configuration settings.

Select **ZombieConga** in the project navigator, and you'll see it already contains two targets (click the circled icon to expand this view if you don't see it already):

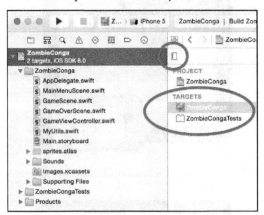

The first target, **ZombieConga**, builds the universal iOS app. The second target, **ZombieCongaTests**, builds the unit tests for the game, which you currently aren't using.

> **Note**: Unit tests are pieces of code you write to test the rest of your program. This is beyond the scope of this book, but if you'd like to learn more check out our *iOS by Tutorials* series, which has several chapters on unit testing.

To add an OS X app to this Xcode project, you simply need a new target.

To get one, go to **File\New\Target...**, select **OS X\Application\Game** and click **Next**.

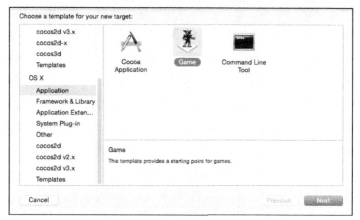

For **ProductName** enter **ZombieCongaMac**, for **Language** choose **Swift** and for **Game Technology** choose **SpriteKit**, then click **Finish**.

At this point, you'll see a new group in your project navigator called **ZombieCongaMac** containing OS X-specific files:

Let's see what this target template looks like. Up in the top navigation bar, switch to the **ZombieCongaMac** target and build and run:

You should see a "Hello, world!" scene where, like the one you saw way back in Chapter 1, you can click to make rotating space ships:

Your goal is to make this OS X target show your Zombie Conga scene instead of this placeholder scene. The first step is to make sure your Zombie Conga code is part of both the iOS and OS X targets.

Sharing files across targets

There is some code in your project that is target-specific (such as **AppDelegate.swift** and **GameViewController.swift**), but most of the code you want to share across both the iOS and OS X targets.

Creating a group for the shared code will help you visualize what's common among the targets. To do this, select your **ZombieConga** project, select **File\New\Group** and name the group **Shared**.

Then, drag the following files and folders from your **ZombieConga** group into the **Shared** group:

- The **Sounds** group

- The **Images** group

- The **sprites.atlas** folder

- **GameScene.swift**

- **GameOverScene.swift**

- **MainMenuScene.swift**

- **MyUtils.swift**

- **Images.xcassets**

When you're done, your project navigator should look something like this:

You've done this simply to keep things organized; the grouping does not affect which targets include these files. To begin adding these files to your OS X target, select **sprites.atlas** and make sure the File Inspector is open (**View\Utilities\Show File Inspector**). In the **Target Membership** section, check **ZombieCongaMac**:

Now repeat this for the rest of the files in the Shared group. As a shortcut, you can do this for all of the files at once by selecting them and then checking **ZombieCongaMac**— just be sure to select the files *inside* the Sounds and Images groups and not the Sounds and Images groups themselves, or it won't work.

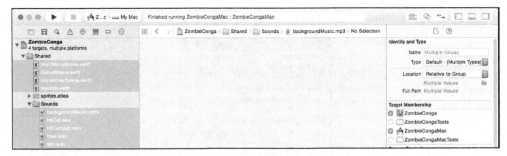

You need to do one more thing. OS X uses different icon sizes than iOS, so you need to add new icons to Images.xcassets. Open **Images.xcassets** and select the **AppIcon** entry. In the **Attributes Inspector** (the third tab), click the checkbox next to **Mac** for **All Sizes**:

You will see new boxes appear at the bottom of the area with all the icons into which you can drag icons.

In the resources for this chapter, find a folder named **OS X Icons**. Drag each icon from this folder into the appropriate spot in the **AppIcon** window. For example, put **Icon16.png** into the **16pt 1x** slot, and put **Icon32.png** into the **16px 2x** slot *and* the **32 px 1x slot**. When you're done, your icons should look like the following:

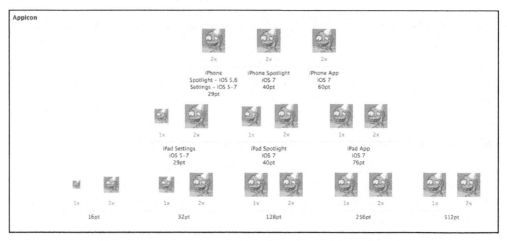

There's one final change you should make in this step. Since you are sharing the versions of **GameScene.swift** and **Images.xcassets** in the Shared folder, delete the versions of **GameScene.swift** and **Images.xcassets** in the **ZombieCongaMac** folder (i.e., the default ones the template created for you). In the popup that appears, select **Move to Trash**.

Your OS X target now includes the required resources, but if you try to compile your project, you'll see a bunch of errors. This is because you have to make two changes for the OS X target: accepting mouse events, and fixing up the game's initialization.

Touch events vs. mouse events

One major difference between iOS and OS X Sprite Kit development is in the handling of user input. On iOS, the user touches the screen, but on OS X, the user manipulates a mouse.

Because of this, you can't override methods like `touchesBegan(withEvent:)` on OS X. Instead, you need to use the mouse equivalents like `mouseDown(theEvent:)`.

Let's give this a shot. Open **MainMenuScene.swift** and replace `touchesBegan(withEvent:)` with the following:

```
#if os(iOS)
  override func touchesBegan(touches: Set<NSObject>,
    withEvent event: UIEvent) {
    sceneTapped()
  }
#else
  override func mouseDown(theEvent: NSEvent) {
```

```
        sceneTapped()
    }
  #endif
```

Here, you use `#if os(iOS)` to check if the code is compiled for an iOS target and if so, include the same `touchesBegan(withEvent:)` method as before.

If the code is compiled for an OS X target, you use `mouseDown(theEvent:)` instead, calling the `sceneTapped()` helper just the same as you do in the other case.

Now repeat this for the game scene. Open **GameScene.swift** and wrap the existing touch methods—`touchesBegan(withEvent:)` and `touchesMoved(withEvent:)`—inside an OS-specific conditional block, with OS X mouse-handling methods inside the `#else` block, as follows:

```
#if os(iOS)
  . . . existing touch methods here . . .
#else
  override func mouseDown(theEvent: NSEvent) {
    let touchLocation = theEvent.locationInNode(backgroundLayer)
    sceneTouched(touchLocation)
  }

  override func mouseDragged(theEvent: NSEvent) {
    let touchLocation = theEvent.locationInNode(backgroundLayer)
    sceneTouched(touchLocation)
  }
#endif
```

Here, you follow a similar pattern as before. Note that `mouseDragged(theEvent:)` is the equivalent of `touchesMoved(withEvent:)`, and an `NSEvent` has a `locationInNode()` method, just like a `UITouch` does.

You're almost done! There's one final thing you must do for this to run: update **AppDelegate.swift**.

Updating AppDelegate

AppDelegate.swift currently contains placeholder code to load the game scene from GameScene.sks. But you want to load the initial scene from MainMenuScene.swift instead, so you need to fix this.

First, delete **GameScene.sks** from your **ZombieCongaMac** group and select **Move to Trash**.

Then, open **AppDelegate.swift** inside the **ZombieCongaMac** group and replace its contents with the following:

```swift
import Cocoa
import SpriteKit

@NSApplicationMain
class AppDelegate: NSObject, NSApplicationDelegate {

  @IBOutlet var window: NSWindow?
  @IBOutlet var skView: SKView?

  func applicationDidFinishLaunching(
    aNotification: NSNotification) {

    let scene = MainMenuScene(
      size: CGSize(width: 2048, height: 1536))
    scene.scaleMode = .AspectFill
    self.skView!.presentScene(scene)
    self.skView!.ignoresSiblingOrder = true
    self.skView!.showsFPS = true
    self.skView!.showsNodeCount = true
  }

  func applicationShouldTerminateAfterLastWindowClosed(
    sender: NSApplication) -> Bool {
    return true;
  }
}
```

This code is very similar to what you set up in GameViewController.swift for the iOS version. It creates a new main menu scene with an initial size (the 2048x1536 size for which the game is designed), sets the scale mode to aspect fill and presents the scene.

With that, you're done! Build and run, and enjoy your OS X game!

Challenges

Your game works on iPhone, iPad and Mac, but there are a few final changes you'd probably want to make before you submit it to the App Store. In these challenges, you'll try them for yourself!

Challenge 1: Fixing the app name

Apple would probably reject Zombie Conga if you uploaded it to the App Store as-is. This is because Apple requires the name of the app and all its windows and menu bar items to be the same as the App Store app name (which would be "Zombie Conga" in this case). However, Zombie Conga lists ZombieCongaMac instead!

Your challenge is to fix this. You'll have to change the name in several places:

• The **Bundle name** in **Supporting Files\Info.plist** in the **ZombieCongaMac** group

• One of the menus inside **MainMenu.xib**

• The main window's title inside **MainMenu.xib**

Challenge 2: Window sizes and aspect fit

By default, you can resize windows on OS X apps. For the most part, this is no problem for Zombie Conga, since you've set up the game to work on a variety of aspect ratios and have activated aspect fill on the scene.

However, if you try to resize the window to a size larger than the max aspect ratio (the iPhone 5's 16:9), strange things will occur:

You can fix this in one of two ways:

1. By using aspect fit instead of aspect fill; or

2. By preventing the user from resizing the window.

Your challenge is to try both ways and choose which you prefer for Zombie Conga.

For the first fix, simply change the scale mode from aspect fill to aspect fit in the OS X version. Hint: You need to change just one line of code to do this! Build and run, resize the window and you'll see the game simply adds black bars when necessary to fit within the available space.

For the second fix, change the scale mode back to aspect fill. Then in **MainMenu.xib**, select the main window, uncheck the **Resize** checkbox in the Attributes Inspector and set the **Window Size** to **1024x768** in the Size Inspector (the same 1.333 aspect ratio as the 2048x1536 scene size, just half the size). Build and run, and notice you can't resize the window anymore, even if you go fullscreen—it's always the specified size.

Now, which do you like best for your game? There's no right answer— you're the game designer, after all! ☺

Section II: Labels and Particle Systems

In this section, you'll learn how to add labels to your game to display text and how to create special effects with particle systems, like explosions and star fields.

In the process, you will create a space shooter game called XBlaster, where all of the artwork is ASCII-based!

Chapter 7: Labels

Chapter 8: Particle Systems

Chapter 7: Labels

By Mike Daley & Tom Bradley

It's often useful in games to display text to keep your player informed. There is little point going into battle with an enemy boss if you don't know how much health you have left or how many bullets are in your weapon of choice!

In this chapter, you'll learn how to display fonts and text within your games. Specifically, you'll create a unique space shooter game called XBlaster. It will be a space shooter with a twist: *all* of the graphics you use will be made from text—yes, you read that right, text!

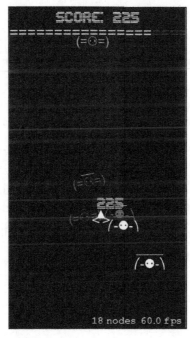

In this chapter, you won't build XBlaster from the ground up as you did with Zombie Conga. Instead, you'll focus on the functionality related to text and fonts.

This is because covering the gameplay logic would repeat too much information covered in the previous chapters. We want to keep this chapter short and focused on the subject at hand—fonts and text—so you have time and energy to continue with the rest of the book, which contains a lot of awesome information you'll want to know.

By the time you're done this chapter, you'll have a thorough understanding of fonts and text in Sprite Kit—and you'll have the honor of bringing ASCII art back to the modern era!

Built-in fonts and font families

In iOS, fonts are broken into sets called "families." A font "family" consists of variants of the same font—such as lighter or heavier versions of the font—which may be useful in different situations.

For example, the "Thonburi" font family contains three fonts:

1. **Thonburi-Light**: A thin/light version of the font.

2. **Thonburi**: A standard version of the font.

3. **Thonburi-Bold**: A bold version of the font.

Some font families have even more variants—the "Avenir" family has 12!

iOS 8 ships with a number of built-in font families and fonts, so before you start using labels, you need to know what's available to you. To find this out, you'll create a simple Sprite Kit project that lets you see these different fonts at a glance.

Create a new project in Xcode by selecting **File\New\Project…** from the main menu. Select the **iOS\Application\Game** template and click **Next**.

Enter **AvailableFonts** for the Product Name, select **Swift** as the language and **SpriteKit** as the Game Technology, choose **Universal** for Devices and then click **Next**.

Select a location on your hard drive to store the project and click **Create**. You now have a simple Sprite Kit project open in Xcode that you will use to list out the font families and fonts you can play with.

You want this app to run in portrait mode, so select the **AvailableFonts** project in the Project Navigator and then select the **AvailableFonts** target. Go to the **General** tab, check Portrait and uncheck all other orientations.

Just like in Zombie Conga, you will be creating this scene programmatically (not using the scene editor). To do this, select **GameScene.sks** and delete it from your project. Then open **GameViewController.swift** and replace the contents with the following:

```swift
import UIKit
import SpriteKit

class GameViewController: UIViewController {
  override func viewDidLoad() {
    super.viewDidLoad()
    let scene = GameScene(size:CGSize(width: 768, height: 1024))
    let skView = self.view as SKView
    skView.showsFPS = true
    skView.showsNodeCount = true
    skView.ignoresSiblingOrder = true
    scene.scaleMode = .AspectFill
    skView.presentScene(scene)

  override func prefersStatusBarHidden() -> Bool  {
    return true
  }
}
```

This is the same code you used in Zombie Conga; it simply creates and presents GameScene to the screen.

Let's code that next. Open **GameScene.swift** and replace its contents with the following:

```swift
import UIKit
import SpriteKit

class GameScene: SKScene {

  var familyIdx: Int = 0

  required init?(coder aDecoder: NSCoder) {
    super.init(coder: aDecoder)
  }

  override init(size: CGSize) {
    super.init(size: size)
    showCurrentFamily()
  }
```

```
func showCurrentFamily() {
  //TODO: Coming Soon...
}

override func touchesBegan(touches: Set<NSObject>,
  withEvent event: UIEvent) {
  familyIdx++
  if familyIdx >= UIFont.familyNames().count {
    familyIdx = 0
  }
  showCurrentFamily()
}
}
```

You begin by displaying the font family with index 0. Every time the user taps, you advance to display the next font family name. Notice you can get a list of the built-in font family names in iOS 8 by calling `UIFont.familyNames()`.

The code to display the fonts in the current font family will be in `showCurrentFamily()`, so implement that now by placing the following code inside that method:

```
// 1
removeAllChildren()

// 2
let familyName = UIFont.familyNames()[familyIdx] as! String
println("Family: \(familyName)")

// 3
let fontNames =
  UIFont.fontNamesForFamilyName(familyName) as! [String]

// 4
for (idx, fontName) in enumerate(fontNames) {
  let label = SKLabelNode(fontNamed: fontName)
  label.text = fontName
  label.position = CGPoint(
    x: size.width / 2,
    y: (size.height * (CGFloat(idx+1))) /
      (CGFloat(fontNames.count)+1))
  label.fontSize = 25
  label.verticalAlignmentMode = .Center
  addChild(label)
}
```

Let's go over this section by section:

1. You remove all of the children from the scene so that you start with a blank slate.

2. You get the current family name based on the index that the user increments with each tap. You also log out the family name, in case you're curious.

3. UIFont has another helper method to get the names of the fonts within a family, called fontNamesForFamilyName(). You call this here and store the results.

4. You then loop through the block and create a label using each font, with text showing the name of that font. Since labels are the subject of this chapter, let's go over this section in more detail.

Creating a label

Creating a label is easy—you simply call SKLabelNode(fontNamed:) and pass in the name of the font:

```
SKLabelNode(fontNamed: fontName)
```

The most important property to set is the text, which is what you want the font to display.

```
label.text = fontName
```

You also usually want to set the font size.

```
label.fontSize = 25
```

Finally, just as with any other node, you should position it and add it as a child of another node, the scene itself in this case.

```
label.position = yourPosition
addChild(label)
```

Don't worry too much about the math you're using here to position the labels or your use of verticalAlignmentMode—that's just some magic to space the labels evenly up and down the screen. You'll learn more about alignment later in this chapter.

Build and run, and now every time you tap the screen, you'll see a different built-in font family:

Tap through to get an idea of what's available to you. This app will be a handy reference in the future when you're wondering what font would be the perfect match for your game.

Loading custom fonts

While the list of built-in fonts is large, there will be times you want to use fonts that aren't included by default. The minigame you'll start in this chapter, for instance, is going to be a little retro, so it would be great to use a font that has a retro, pixelated look.

None of the fonts included by default are going to meet your needs. Luckily for you, Apple has made it super simple to use a **True Type Font** (TTF) in your project.

First, you need to find the font you want to use. One excellent source of fonts is http://www.dafont.com. Open your browser of choice and enter the URL. You'll see there's a large selection of categories from which to choose, including one called **Pixel/Bitmap**.

Click on that category and you'll see a huge list of fonts with example text. Some people could spend hours looking through these fonts just for fun, so take as much time as you like to see what's available.

Now that you're back, the font you're going to use is called **Edit Undo Line** by Brian Kent (username Ænigma). Type that name into the search bar on the **dafont.com** website. A preview for that font will appear:

This nice, retro looking font is a perfect fit for the minigame you're creating. Click the **Download** button. Once the download is complete, unzip the package and find the file named **edunline.ttf**. This is the file you need for this project, so place it somewhere safe. The resources for this chapter also includes a copy of this font in case you have trouble downloading it.

> **Note:** It's important to check the license for any fonts you want to use in your project. Some fonts require you to have permission or a license before you can use them, so checking now could save a lot of heartache and cost later on.
>
> You'll see that the Edit Undo Line Font you're using is marked as **Free** just above the download button, but always check the license information included in the downloaded zip file. In this case, you'll see the font uses the Creative Commons Attribution Share Alike license, which you can read about here:
>
> http://creativecommons.org/licenses/by-sa/3.0/

Now that you have your font, create a new project by selecting **File\New\Project...** from the main menu, just as you did earlier. Select the **iOS\Application\Game** template and click **Next**.

Enter **XBlaster** for the Product Name, choose **Swift** for Language, **SpriteKit** as the Game Technology and **Universal** for Devices, then click **Next**. Select a location on your hard drive to store the project and click **Create**. This is the project you'll use throughout the rest of this chapter to build the minigame.

Unlike Zombie Conga, you want XBlaster to run in portrait mode instead of landscape. So select the **XBlaster** project in the Project Navigator and then select the **XBlaster** target. Go to the **General** tab and uncheck Landscape Left and Landscape Right so that only **Portrait** is checked.

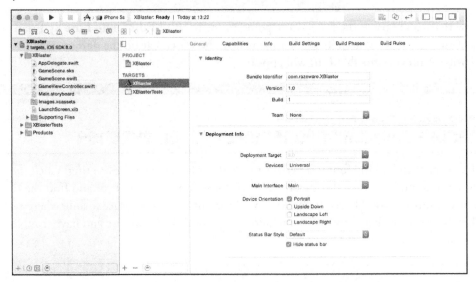

Next, you need to add **Edit Undo Line Fonts** to the project. Click on the **Info** tab at the top of the target settings and you'll see the **Custom iOS Target Properties**. Click on the last entry in the list, called **Bundle versions string, short**, and you'll see plus (+) and minus (-) buttons appear next to that title.

Click the plus button and a new entry will appear in the table with a drop-down list of options:

In the drop-down box, type **Fonts**, making sure to use a capital **F**. The first option that comes up will be **Fonts provided by application**. Hit **Return** to select that option and then hit **Return** again to add that entry to the list. This will create an entry with a type of array that allows you to add any number of custom fonts to your project.

Click the triangle to the left of the new entry to expand it and double-click inside the value field. Inside the textbox that appears, type **edunline.ttf**. This is the name of the font file you downloaded and that you're going to use in the game. Be sure to spell it correctly or else your app won't be able to load it later.

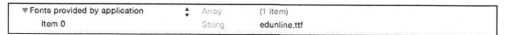

The last step is to copy the actual font file into the project. In the project navigator in Xcode, right-click on the **XBlaster** group and choose **New Group**. Name the newly-created group **Resources**. Use the same technique to create a group named **Fonts** inside the **Resources** group.

Drag the **edunline.ttf** file you downloaded earlier into the new **Fonts** group. Make sure to tick **Copy items if needed** and to select **XBlaster** in the **Add to targets** panel, and click **Finish**.

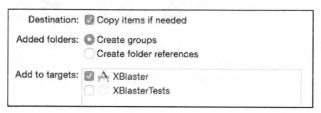

Now to try out this font!

Open **GameScene.swift** and you'll see the template code that places the "Hello, World!" label on the screen along with the rotating spaceships. Replace the contents of the file with the following:

```
import SpriteKit
```

```swift
class GameScene: SKScene {

    override func didMoveToView(view: SKView) {
        let myLabel = SKLabelNode(fontNamed:"Edit Undo Line BRK")
        myLabel.text = "Hello, World!"
        myLabel.fontSize = 40
        myLabel.position = CGPoint(x:CGRectGetMidX(self.frame),
            y:CGRectGetMidY(self.frame))
        self.addChild(myLabel)
    }
}
```

This simply creates a label using the new font you added to the project. Note that you use the full name of the font itself, not the name of the TTF file. You can get the full name of the font by installing the font under OS X and using the Font Book application.

There's one item left: To get this game started on the right foot, you should set up an app icon.

Open **Images.xassets** and select the **AppIcon** entry. Then, in the resources for this chapter, drag each of the files from the **AppIcon** folder into the appropriate area on the right. You should see the following when you're done:

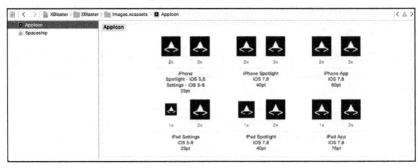

Build and run, and you'll see **Hello, World!** displayed in the center of the screen in the new font:

Wow, I suddenly feel a lot older! ☺

Alignment modes

So far, you know you can place a label by setting its position—but how can you control the placement of the text in relation to the position?

Unlike SKSpriteNode, SKLabelNode doesn't have an anchorPoint property. In its place, you can use the verticalAlignmentMode and horizontalAlignmentMode properties.

The verticalAlignmentMode controls the text's placement vertically in relation to the label's position, and the horizontalAlignmentMode controls the text's placement horizontally in relation to the label's position. You can see this visually in the diagram below:

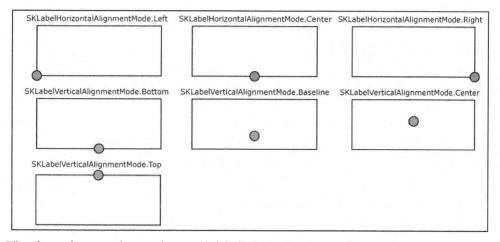

The above diagram shows where each label's bounding box will be rendered in relation to the label's position, represented by the red and blue points, for the different alignment modes. There are two things worth noting here:

- SKLabelNode's default alignment modes are Center for horizontal and Baseline for vertical.

- Baseline uses the actual font's baseline, which you can think of as the "line" on which you would draw a font if you were writing on ruled paper. For example, the tails of letters such as **g** and **y** will hang below the position defined.

Let's try this out. Add the following to didMoveToView() after the code that sets myLabel.position:

```
myLabel.horizontalAlignmentMode = .Right
```

Build and run the app, and you'll see that the label now sits on the left-hand side of the screen.

This is because you are now aligning the right side of the text to the label's position, which is the center of the screen. Similarly, if you were to change the `horizontalAlignmentMode` to `Left`, the label would sit on the right-hand side of the screen.

Play around with the different alignment modes using this text to get a feel for how they work. In your games, simply choose the alignment that makes it easiest for you to position your text where you want it.

Introducing SKTUtils

In the first few chapters of this book, while you were working on Zombie Conga, you created some handy extensions to allow you to do things like add or subtract two `CGPoints` by using the + or − operators.

Rather than make you continuously re-add these extensions in each minigame, we've gathered them together into a little library called `SKTUtils`.

In this section, you are going to add `SKTUtils` to your project so you can make use of these methods in the rest of the chapter. Let's go!

You can find `SKTUtils` in the root folder for this book. Drag the entire **SKTUtils** folder into the project navigator in Xcode. Make sure **Copy items if needed**, **Create Groups** and the **XBlaster target** are all checked. Click **Finish**.

Take a minute to peek around the contents of the library. It should look quite familiar, with a few additions and tweaks.

```
XBlaster > SKTUtils > CGPoint+Extensions.swift > No Selection

XBlaster
2 targets, iOS SDK 8.0          35   * Given an angle in radians, creates a vector of length 1.0 and returns the
  SKTUtils                      36   * result as a new CGPoint. An angle of 0 is assumed to point to the right.
    CGFloat+Extensions.swift    37   */
    CGPoint+Extensions.swift    38   init(angle: CGFloat) {
    CGVector+Extensions.swift   39     return self.init(x: cos(angle), y: sin(angle))
    Int+Extensions.swift        40   }
    SKAction+Extensions.swift   41
    SKAction+SpecialEffects.swift 42   /**
    SKColor+Extensions.swift    43   * Adds (dx, dy) to the point.
    SKNode+Extensions.swift     44   */
    SKTAudio.swift              45   mutating func offset(#dx: CGFloat, dy: CGFloat) -> CGPoint {
    SKTEffects.swift           46     x += dx
    SKTTimingFunctions.swift    47     y += dy
    Vector3.swift              48     return self
  Resources                    49   }
  XBlaster                     50
  XBlasterTests                51   /**
  Products                     52   * Returns the length (magnitude) of the vector described by the CGPoint.
                               53   */
                               54   func length() -> CGFloat {
                               55     return sqrt(x*x + y*y)
                               56   }
                               57
```

Now every class in your project has access to these timesaving math functions.

Making a scene

Now that you have `SKUtils` included in your project, as well as a good understanding of how to create and position a label with a custom font, let's crack on with building your minigame.

When you create a project using the Game template in Xcode, it creates a default scene file for you called **GameScene.sks**. For XBlaster, you're going to be generating all the graphics using labels, so delete **GameScene.sks**.

Open **GameViewController.swift** and replace the contents with the following:

```swift
import UIKit
import SpriteKit

class GameViewController: UIViewController {

  override func viewDidLoad() {
    super.viewDidLoad()
    let scene = GameScene(size: CGSize(width: 768,
      height: 1024))
    let skView = self.view as SKView
    skView.showsFPS = true
    skView.showsNodeCount = true
    skView.ignoresSiblingOrder = true
    scene.scaleMode = .AspectFill
```

```
      skView.presentScene(scene)
   }

   override func prefersStatusBarHidden() -> Bool {
      return true
   }
}
```

This is the same code you've seen several times before - it creates an instance of `GameScene` and presents it as the current scene. There's one difference though – you change the scene's size from 1024x768 to 768x1024, because XBlaster is going to run in portrait mode.

Layer by layer

This chapter will give you plenty of practice using labels, as everything rendered in this game will start life as a label.

As you saw in Chapter 5, "Scrolling," it's a good idea to build your scene using a number of different layers, where a layer is usually a plain **SKNode**. This makes it easier to move everything in a layer at once or to place items in one layer above or below another layer.

For the work you're going to do in this chapter, you need layers for the following:

• The heads up display or HUD, which will show the player's score and health;

• The player's ship.

In one of the challenges, you'll add a layer for bullets, and in another, you'll take a peek at the final project, with gameplay added, that includes additional layers for both the bullets and enemy ships.

For now, just add the two you need right away. Open **GameScene.swift** and add the following properties:

```
let playerLayerNode = SKNode()
let hudLayerNode = SKNode()
```

You're going to access these layers frequently, so it will be convenient to have references to them.

Now create a new method called `setupSceneLayers()`:

```
func setupSceneLayers() {
```

```
    playerLayerNode.zPosition = 50
    hudLayerNode.zPosition = 100

    addChild(playerLayerNode)
    addChild(hudLayerNode)
}
```

This method simply sets the zPositions for your scene's layers and adds them to the scene.

The specific zPositions you use here aren't important, but their relative order is. You want to render the player node behind the HUD layer, so you make sure the HUD's zPosition is larger than the player's. By giving a nice bit of space between values, you have more room to go back and add other layers later if you'd like.

Now add two new properties:

```
let playableRect: CGRect
let hudHeight: CGFloat = 90
```

Like Zombie Conga, all the games in this book will be universal and work on any device. In Chapter 1, you implemented this by defining a playable rectangle to contain all the game action so that the difficulty was the same across devices. You're going to do the same thing for XBlaster.

Note that hudHeight defines the height of the HUD which you will create in the next section.

Now add a couple of new methods. The required init(coder:) which is the designated initializer and also the init(size:), as follows:

```
    required init(coder aDecoder: NSCoder) {
      fatalError("init(coder:) has not been implemented")
    }

    override init(size: CGSize) {
      // Calculate playable margin
      let maxAspectRatio: CGFloat = 16.0/9.0 //iPhone 5"
      let maxAspectRatioWidth = size.height / maxAspectRatio
      let playableMargin = (size.width-maxAspectRatioWidth) / 2.0
      playableRect = CGRect(x: playableMargin, y: 0,
        width: maxAspectRatioWidth,
        height: size.height - hudHeight)

      super.init(size: size)
```

```
    setupSceneLayers()
}
```

This calculates the playable area that is guaranteed to be visible across all supported devices, and then calls setupSceneLayers() after the scene is created so that the layers you're using all get set up. It's good to place functions like this in their own methods, as it keeps the configuration functions easy to read and extend.

Now remove didMoveToView() entirely, as you have all of your initialization code inside init(size:).

Build and run the app. All you'll see is a dark grey screen, because as yet there is nothing in the layers to render—but not for long!

Creating the HUD

With the layers set up, you can move on to adding the always-important HUD. XBlaster's HUD will be comprised of the player's score and health displayed on a black background. You're about to get a lot of practice with labels and positioning!

Start by adding the following new method:

```
func setUpUI() {
  let backgroundSize =
    CGSize(width: size.width, height:hudHeight)
  let backgroundColor = SKColor.blackColor()
  let hudBarBackground =
    SKSpriteNode(color: backgroundColor, size: backgroundSize)
  hudBarBackground.position =
    CGPoint(x:0, y: size.height – hudHeight)
  hudBarBackground.anchorPoint = CGPointZero
  hudLayerNode.addChild(hudBarBackground)
}
```

This code draws a colored background for the HUD using an SKSpriteNode.

Here you use an SKSpriteNode in a different way than you've seen in the past. To create an SKSpriteNode, you don't have to pass in the name of an image; you can alternatively pass in a color and a size. This is useful if you're trying to quickly prototype a game, or if you're trying to draw a simple colored background like you're doing here.

Next, add the following line at the end of init(size:):

```
setUpUI()
```

Build and run the app, and you'll see a subtle black box at the top of the screen. This forms the basis of XBlaster's main HUD.

In the next few sections, you'll flesh this out by adding the score label, making it "pop" and finally, by adding a player health label.

Adding a score label

Let's add the label that will display the player's score. First, add a new constant to the class called `scoreLabel`:

```
let scoreLabel = SKLabelNode(fontNamed: "Edit Undo Line BRK")
```

This creates a new label using the custom font you added to the project earlier.

Next, add the following code to the end of `setUpUI()`:

```
// 1
scoreLabel.fontSize = 50
scoreLabel.text = "Score: 0"
scoreLabel.name = "scoreLabel"
// 2
scoreLabel.verticalAlignmentMode = .Center
// 3
scoreLabel.position = CGPoint(
  x: size.width / 2,
  y: size.height - scoreLabel.frame.size.height + 3)
// 4
hudLayerNode.addChild(scoreLabel)
```

Let's run through this in detail:

1. You set the properties on the label to define its size, text and name. The name is useful should you want to access this node later.

2. You set the vertical alignment so the text will render with its vertical center at the label's position.

3. You then set the position by calculating half the width of the screen for the x-position and then the height of the screen minus the height of the label node for the y-position, adding 3 to make it look just right.

4. Finally, you add the label as a child of the HUD layer.

Build and run the app, and you'll see the dark background bar for the HUD along with the score label:

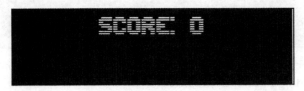

Actions and labels

Since `SKLabelNode` derives from `SKNode`, you can run actions on labels just as you can on any other node.

Try this out by creating an action to run on the score label every time the score changes. Open **GameScene.swift** and add the following property:

```
var scoreFlashAction: SKAction!
```

Then add this code to the end of `setUpUI()`:

```
scoreFlashAction = SKAction.sequence([
  SKAction.scaleTo(1.5, duration: 0.1),
  SKAction.scaleTo(1.0, duration: 0.1)])
scoreLabel.runAction(
  SKAction.repeatAction(scoreFlashAction, count: 20))
```

This is a simple action that scales the node to 1.5 times its size over 0.1 seconds and then scales it back to 1.0 over 0.1 seconds. Running this action on the score label will give the score a nice little pop when it changes, adding some juice to an otherwise plain label.

The second line is a quick test to bounce the score label 20 times on startup so you can make sure it's working. It will be a bit of overkill right now, but later you'll use this action more appropriately.

Build and run, and enjoy your juiced up label!

Displaying the player's health

The last element of your HUD is a label for the player's health. Instead of displaying health as a word followed by a number, as you did with the score, you're going to illustrate it graphically, as a meter—still using text!

Add the following constants to the class:

```
let healthBarString: NSString = "======================="
let playerHealthLabel =
  SKLabelNode(fontNamed: "Arial")
```

`healthBarString` holds the string used to render the health bar when the player's health is at 100%. Later, the game will perform a simple calculation to work out how much of that string to display based on the player's current health.

Then, add the following code for the player's health meter to the end of `setUpUI()`:

```
// 1
let playerHealthBackgroundLabel =
  SKLabelNode(fontNamed: "Arial")
playerHealthBackgroundLabel.name = "playerHealthBackground"
playerHealthBackgroundLabel.fontColor = SKColor.darkGrayColor()
playerHealthBackgroundLabel.fontSize = 50
playerHealthBackgroundLabel.text = healthBarString as String
// 2
playerHealthBackgroundLabel.horizontalAlignmentMode = .Left
playerHealthBackgroundLabel.verticalAlignmentMode = .Top
playerHealthBackgroundLabel.position = CGPoint(
  x: CGRectGetMinX(playableRect),
  y: size.height - CGFloat(hudHeight) +
    playerHealthBackgroundLabel.frame.size.height)
hudLayerNode.addChild(playerHealthBackgroundLabel)
// 3
playerHealthLabel.name = "playerHealthLabel"
playerHealthLabel.fontColor = SKColor.greenColor()
playerHealthLabel.fontSize = 50
playerHealthLabel.text =
  healthBarString.substringToIndex(20*75/100)
playerHealthLabel.horizontalAlignmentMode = .Left
playerHealthLabel.verticalAlignmentMode = .Top
playerHealthLabel.position = CGPoint(
  x: CGRectGetMinX(playableRect),
  y: size.height - CGFloat(hudHeight) +
playerHealthLabel.frame.size.height)
hudLayerNode.addChild(playerHealthLabel)
```

This looks like a lot of code, but it's really just setting up a couple of labels. Let's look at the steps a little closer.

1. You use the `playerHealthBackground` label to render a dark version of the player's health meter that will be revealed as the player's health goes down. This simply enhances the appearance of the health meter. Since you're not going to change this label, you won't need access to it, so you don't bother defining this label as an instance variable or property.

2. You set the label's alignment so that horizontally, the position represents the left-hand edge of the label, while vertically it represents the top of the label. You calculate the x-position to be at the very left of the screen and you calculate the y-position based on the heights of the background bar and the label.

3. You're going to draw `playerHealthLabel` over the top of the background label. You set it up as a property, because the label's properties will change during gameplay and referencing like this makes that easy. The length of `healthBarString` is 50 characters, so to test your new meter, you set `playerHealthLabel.text` to a substring of `healthBarString` that is 75% of the full length. Everything else about this label matches the background label. You'll set the color later, in `update()`.

Build and run the app, and underneath the score label you'll see a line of green equals sign (=) characters representing the player's health:

Nice! You've got a score label that can animate and a meter you can use to display the player's health. But something is missing... Ah, yes, the player! :]

Inheritance-based game architecture

So far in this book, all of the code for your minigames has been inside a single class—the scene's class.

Although this works for extremely simple games like Zombie Conga, it can rapidly result in a large file with spaghetti code!

In this chapter, to keep your code nicely organized, you'll use inheritance-based game architecture. This means that you'll create a base class to contain common code that is the same across different game objects in your game (such as bullets, enemy ships, or the player ship), and then subclass that base class for each type of game object.

> **Note:** Inheritance-based game architecture works well for many games of simple-to medium-level complexity, and it's easy and straightforward to develop.
>
> As your games get more complex, you might want to investigate alternatives such as component-based game architecture. To learn more about component-based game architecture, check out this post:
>
> http://www.raywenderlich.com/24878/introduction-to-component-based-architecture-in-games

Let's begin by creating the class that will contain the common code used by all the entities in the game.

Right-click on the **XBlaster** group in Xcode and choose **New Group**. Name the group **Entities**. Create a new file in this group by right-clicking on the group and choosing **New File...** from the popup menu.

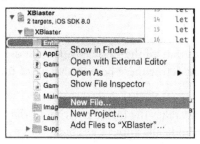

From the template selection panel, select **iOS/Source/Swift File** and click **Next**. Enter **Entity.swift** in the Save As field, make sure the **XBlaster** target is selected and click **Create**.

This class will act as the base class for all the entities in the game, including the player's ship, bullets and the enemy ships. You will never create an instance of this class; other classes, such as `PlayerShip`, will inherit from it.

Open **Entity.swift** and replace its content with the following:

```
import SpriteKit

class Entity : SKSpriteNode {
  // 1
  var direction = CGPointZero
  var health = 100.0
```

```
    var maxHealth = 100.0

    required init?(coder aDecoder: NSCoder) {
      super.init(coder: aDecoder)
    }
    // 2
    init(position: CGPoint, texture: SKTexture) {
      super.init(texture: texture, color: SKColor.whiteColor(),
 size: texture.size())
      self.position = position
    }
    //3
    class func generateTexture() -> SKTexture? {
      // Overridden by subclasses
      return nil
    }
    // 4
    func update(delta: NSTimeInterval) {
      // Overridden by subclasses
    }
  }
```

Let's go through this in detail:

1. There are a few properties that all the game entities will use, such as direction of travel and current health, so you define these here so that all of the subclasses will inherit them.

2. The initializer for this class takes the initial position of the entity along with the entity's texture. This method calls super.init(texture:color:size:) to get the SKSpriteNode created.

3. Since this chapter is all about labels, you're going to use labels to represent *all* of the objects in this game: the player's ships, the bullets and the enemies. However, it would be inefficient to use labels directly, as behind the scenes, Sprite Kit would need to generate a new texture every time you create a new object.

   It's much more efficient to generate the texture for a type of ship once and then reuse that texture multiple times. generateTexture() is a class method that will do just that.

4. The entities in XBlaster may need to perform actions during each game loop, so subclasses can override this method to perform those actions, such as AI.

With the base entity class in place, you can create the player's ship—and that means more playing with ASCII art!

Generating a texture from a node

To create the player's ship, you're going to generate a texture from several
SKLabelNodes.

Create a new **Swift File** called **PlayerShip.swift** inside the **Entities** group and replace
the contents of that file with the following:

```
import SpriteKit

class PlayerShip: Entity {

  required init?(coder aDecoder: NSCoder) {
    super.init(coder: aDecoder)
  }

  init(entityPosition: CGPoint) {
    let entityTexture = PlayerShip.generateTexture()!
    super.init(position: entityPosition, texture: entityTexture)
    name = "playerShip"
  }
}
```

PlayerShip's init(entityPosition:) calls the generateTexture() class method to
generate the player's texture and uses that texture, along with the position, to call the
super class's init(position:texture:). It also sets the object's name, which is a good
practice because it makes it easy to search for the node in your scene using
enumerateChildNodesWithName() or childNodeWithName().

Remember that Entity returns nil from its implementation of generateTexture(),
so add the following implementation of the method for PlayerShip:

```
override class func generateTexture() -> SKTexture? {
  // 1
  struct SharedTexture {
    static var texture = SKTexture()
    static var onceToken: dispatch_once_t = 0
  }

  dispatch_once(&SharedTexture.onceToken, {
    // 2
    let mainShip = SKLabelNode(fontNamed: "Arial")
    mainShip.name = "mainship"
    mainShip.fontSize = 40
    mainShip.fontColor = SKColor.whiteColor()
```

```
    mainShip.text = "▲"
    // 3
    let wings = SKLabelNode(fontNamed: "Arial")
    wings.name = "wings"
    wings.fontSize = 40
    wings.text = "< >"
    wings.fontColor = SKColor.whiteColor()
    wings.position = CGPoint(x: 1, y: 7)
    // 4
    wings.zRotation = CGFloat(180).degreesToRadians()

    mainShip.addChild(wings)
    // 5
    let textureView = SKView()
    SharedTexture.texture =
      textureView.textureFromNode(mainShip)
    SharedTexture.texture.filteringMode = .Nearest
    })

  return SharedTexture.texture
}
```

This is an important method, so let's go over it section by section:

1. While the game will have only one instance of PlayerShip, you're generating the texture in such a way that there is only ever one texture, regardless of how many instances of PlayerShip there are. For this reason, you create a static texture variable and use a call to dispatch_once to guarantee that the code inside its block is only ever run once.

2. You create an SKLabelNode with a size and color and set the text to the shape of the main hull of the player's ship. Note that the text for the hull is a special triangle-shaped character. You may wonder how to type this!

The characters you have available to use depend on the font you specify when setting up the label. If you want to access special characters, you can go to **Edit\Special Characters…** or use the shortcut **CTRL + CMD + SPACE**. This displays a popup from which you can select the special characters you want:

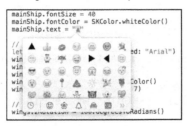

Note that the character you choose will look slightly different based on the font you use to render the text. The Arial font is usually a good font to start with, as it contains a large number of characters in different languages—that's why you use it for this SKLabelNode instead of the custom font.

3. You create another SKLabelNode to represent the wings of the player's ship. You then adjust the position to place the wings correctly on the ship's main hull. This position is in node space.

4. To finish the wings, you rotate the node 180 degrees using an extension from SKTUtils that converts degrees to radians.

5. This part is the key to this method, in that it creates a new SKView that you use to render to a texture with textureFromNode(). You pass in the mainShip node and end up with a texture you can use for the PlayerShip.

Again, the above process ensures that you need only a single texture for all instances of this object, which helps with performance. Although there will only be one player ship, you can use this same technique for classes where there will be many copies, such as bullets or enemies.

Now that you've created the player's ship, you need to add it to the scene. Open **GameScene.swift** and add the following property:

```
var playerShip: PlayerShip!
```

Now add a new method called setupEntities():

```
func setupEntities() {
  playerShip = PlayerShip(
    entityPosition: CGPoint(x: size.width / 2, y: 100))
  playerLayerNode.addChild(playerShip)
}
```

This creates an instance of PlayerShip and positions it in the center of the screen horizontally and 100 points up from the bottom of the screen. It then adds the PlayerShip instance to the playerLayerNode.

Add a call to this new method at the end of init(size:):

```
setupEntities()
```

Build and run the app, and you'll see the result of all your hard work: a cool-looking spaceship hovering in the middle of the screen.

I bet you never thought of using labels in quite this way! :]

Moving the player

Once you've calmed down from the excitement of seeing your player's ship rendered onscreen, there's one last thing to do before you try out some of this on your own in the challenges. Although this isn't specifically about fonts or text, you can't just leave the player's ship sitting there, doing nothing—it's time to get that ship moving!

Rather than put some kind of virtual D-Pad onscreen, you'll allow the player to simply slide his or her finger around the screen to move the ship.

Add the following variables in **GameScene.swift**, which you'll use to track the distance the player's finger moves per game update:

```
var deltaPoint = CGPointZero
```

Now you need to capture the player's touches, so add the following methods:

```
override func touchesMoved(touches: Set<NSObject>,
                               withEvent event: UIEvent) {
  let touch = touches.first as! UITouch
  let currentPoint = touch.locationInNode(self)
  let previousTouchLocation =
    touch.previousLocationInNode(self)
  deltaPoint = currentPoint - previousTouchLocation
}
```

touchesMoved(withEvent:) sets the currentPoint variable to the current position of the player's finger onscreen. It then calculates the difference between the current point and the previous point and stores it in deltaPoint.

Inside touchesEnded(withEvent:) and touchesCancelled(withEvent:), the code simply sets deltaPoint to a zero point, as the player has now removed her finger from the screen.

If you run the app now, you're won't notice much of a difference. Although you are capturing touches and calculating the delta, you aren't using this information anywhere. This is where update() comes in.

In previous chapters, you've seen how the scene's update() is called once per frame, allowing you to update your game's logic. This is the perfect place for code that will update the position of the player's ship based on the player's input.

Implement an update() method as follows:

```
override func update(currentTime: NSTimeInterval) {
  // 1
  var newPoint:CGPoint = playerShip.position + deltaPoint
  // 2
  newPoint.x.clamp(
    CGRectGetMinX(playableRect), CGRectGetMaxX(playableRect))
  newPoint.y.clamp(
    CGRectGetMinY(playableRect),CGRectGetMaxY(playableRect))
  // 3
  playerShip.position = newPoint
  deltaPoint = CGPointZero
}
```

1. First, you calculate the new position of the ship by adding the deltaPoint updated in the touch methods.

2. You use another extension from SKTUtils, named clamp, to ensure the ship cannot be moved off the edge of the screen. There is nothing more annoying than losing your ship to the depths of space and not being able to retrieve it!

3. You update the position of the player's ship with the new position. You also reset the delta point back to zero, since you've already moved the ship this amount.

Build and run the app, and move your finger around the screen. You'll see that the player's ship now moves relative to the movements of your finger—hooray!

Bitmap font labels

Throughout this chapter you have been learning about how to use SKLabelNode to create dynamic labels within Sprite Kit. Before we finish this chapter I wanted to leave a quick note about another type of label called a **bitmap font label**.

Sprite Kit does not use bitmap font labels by default. Instead, it creates SKLabelNodes by using only the information that is held within a TTF font file. This allows you, the developer, to use any characters that a particular font supports and set the color and size. The drawback is this method does not allow you to have more elaborate styles like colored outlines, gradients, image fills, or shadows.

If you want to use these more fancy effects, you should use bitmap fonts. The idea is you use an external tool to take a TTF font and apply style effects such as outlines, fills and shadows. Such a tool will then generate two files, a texture atlas that contains an image for each of the characters you've selected, and a control file. The control file identifies the location of each character within the texture atlas, its size and its kerning, or information about how it should be positioned relative to other characters.

Because each character is, in fact, an image, you can create fonts that are as elaborate as you like. Each character gets drawn to the screen as a sprite and is therefore really fast too.

There are a number of tools available, both free and paid, that help you design bitmap fonts for use in games. Some of these already have support for Sprite Kit. Because Sprite Kit doesn't directly support the concept of a bitmap font, you'll need to use an external library or specially written classes that can process the information generated by these tools and then render labels to the screen as needed.

One such tool is Glyph Designer (written by myself and Tom, the author of the next chapter). Glyph Designer is a Mac app that allows you to take a TTF font, apply effects and then generate the output described above.

We also provide a library for use on OS X and iOS that allows you to use fonts generated in Glyph Designer within Sprite Kit. This library exposes a class called `SSBitmapFont` that takes the output from Glyph Designer and lets you use it to generate `SSBitmapFontLabelNode`s the same way you generate `SKLabelNode`s in Sprite Kit.

If you are curious to try this out, inside the resources for this chapter you'll find a project called **BitmapFont** that demonstrates how to use our library to draw fonts created in Glyph Designer. You can also learn more at the following URL:

- https://71squared.zendesk.com/hc/en-us/articles/200037472-Using-Glyph-Designer-with-Sprite-Kit

Challenges

And with that, it's time for you to try out some of your newfound knowledge!

But first, an important note.

This chapter focuses on labels, and as such, you've been building a label-based game. But because of this focus, there's still a lot to do to complete the game, such as adding a weapon to the player's ship, introducing enemies and enabling both the enemies and the player to take damage and die.

Rather than having you type out all this code yourself (which is not related to labels), we think it is more important that you keep focused on the main topic of each chapter (such as labels in this chapter, and particles in the next). Therefore, we are going to provide you a starter project in Challenge 2 that has the non-relevant gameplay added.

We realize some of you like to type out each and every line of the game yourself. Don't worry – in all the rest of the games in this book, you will do exactly that! We are just providing you a shortcut for this particular game so you can have enough energy to keep going through the rest of the book – there's some very cool stuff ahead we want you to get to like game physics, making your games "juicy", UIKit integration, Game Center, and more.

Since we are providing you with an updated project with some extra code added in Challenge #2, it will be a bit harder than usual since you might not understand how all of the code works yet. If you have trouble don't worry – just skip this challenge for now – you can return to this challenge after you finish the rest of the book, and you should find it much more clear.

As always, if you get stuck you can find the solutions in the resources for this chapter—but give it your best shot first!

Challenge 1: The plasma cannon

Your first challenge is to add something rather important: a plasma cannon. No self-respecting space fighter goes into battle without a big gun!

Here are a few hints:

• Create a new class that derives from `Entity` named `Bullet`.

• Implement `init(entityPosition:)` similarly to the way you did for `PlayerShip`, except set the name to **bullet**.

• Implement `generateTexture()` similarly to the way you did for `PlayerShip`, except use a new character of your choosing for the bullet! You probably only need one label unless you're getting fancy.

• Add the following properties to **GameScene.swift**:

```
var bulletInterval: NSTimeInterval = 0
var lastUpdateTime: NSTimeInterval = 0
var dt: NSTimeInterval = 0
```

• Then, add the following code to the bottom of `update()`:

```
if lastUpdateTime > 0 {
  dt = currentTime - lastUpdateTime
} else {
  dt = 0
}
lastUpdateTime = currentTime

bulletInterval += dt
if bulletInterval > 0.15 {
  bulletInterval = 0

  // 1: Create Bullet
  // 2: Add to scene
  // 3: Sequence: Move up screen, remove from parent
}
```

• Implement comment #1 to create a new instance of your `Bullet` class using your new constructor and the player ship's position.

- Implement comment #2 to add the new bullet to the scene. Create a new layer called `bulletLayerNode` inside `setupSceneLayers()` with a `zPosition` value of 25, which will place it below the player's ship. Don't forget to create a variable for the `bulletLayerNode` just as for the other layer nodes.

- Implement comment #3 to run a sequence of actions. The first action in the sequence should move the bullet along the y-axis a distance equal to the height of the screen over one second. The second action in the sequence should remove the bullet from its parent.

Build and run, and if all goes well, you should have a ship shooting plasma bullets made from labels!

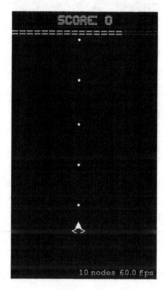

Challenge 2: A moving score label

Note: As mentioned earlier, this challenge is more difficult than other challenges, as we are providing you with a starter project with some additional gameplay added so you can stay focused on the main topic of this chapter.

Remember - if you have any troubles, skip past this challenge and return to it later, it will become clear by the end of the book!

Find **Challenge 2 – Starter** in the resources for this chapter and open the project in Xcode. You will see that it includes gameplay—again, this is so you can remain focused on the subject of this chapter. The biggest change: The game now has enemies to fight!

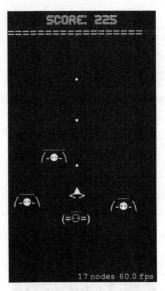

Feel free to take a look through the project. Not everything will make sense yet as it's using some concepts we haven't covered yet – but you should be able to get at least a high level idea about what's going on.

Your challenge is to add one more feature to this game involving labels. It's often cool in a game to show informational labels near where an event of interest occurs—for example, showing the HP damage the player caused an enemy right near the enemy.

In this game, you'll add a score label that appears when the player destroys a ship. You should add this label to the screen at the location the enemy was killed and slide it up the screen slowly while fading it out.

Here are some hints:

- Add a new SKLabelNode property to **Enemy.swift** called scoreLabel using the Thirteen Pixel Fonts.

- Inside **Enemy.swift**, create a new static SKAction called scoreLabelAction to go along with the other static vars.

- Inside loadSharedAssets(), create the scoreLabelAction. It should run a sequence of two groups.

- The first group is the "label appears" effect. It should scale to 1 over 0 seconds (resetting the scale to 1), fade out over 0 seconds (resetting the alpha to 0), fade in over 0.5 seconds (the "real" fade) and move 20 points up along the y-axis over 0.5 seconds.

- The second group is the "label disappears" effect. It should move by 40 points along the y-axis over 1 second and fade out over 1 second.

- Inside `init(entityPosition:texture:playableRect:)`, set up the `scoreLabel` with 50 font size, R=0.5, G=1.0, B=1.0, Alpha=1.0 and the text displaying the `score` field formatted as a string.

- Inside `collidedWith(body:contact:)`, inside the clause where the enemy's health is less than or equal to 0, set the score label to the enemy's current position. Also, if the label is not already in the scene by checking its `parent`, add it to the `mainScene`'s `hudLayerNode`. Finally, remove all actions on the label and run the `scoreLabelAction` you created earlier.

If the code looks good, build and run, and when you destroy an enemy ship, you should see something like the following:

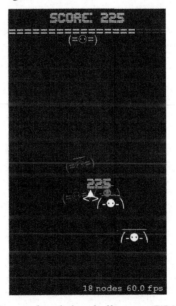

If you've made it this far and completed the challenges, CONGRATULATIONS, you have achieved a great deal in this chapter. Now it's time for some explosions—and remember not to look back!

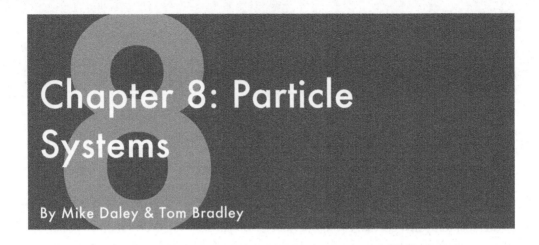

Chapter 8: Particle Systems

By Mike Daley & Tom Bradley

Nothing spices up your game quite like a particle system.

Particle systems, such as this awesome explosion, are an easy way to create a wide range of special effects in your game. Here are just a few of the things you can simulate with a particle system:

smoke	water	fog
star fields	snow	rain
fire	explosions	magical potions
sparks	blood	bubbles

And this is just the beginning! It's impossible to imagine all you could do with a particle system, and it pays to be creative. For instance, how could you easily simulate subatomic particles emanating from a rip in the space-time continuum? By using a particle system, of course!

What else makes particle systems so great? To achieve a special effect like the explosion above without a particle system, you'd have to make a traditional frame-by-frame animation, which would require many images taking up significant texture space and memory. With a particle system, the special effects are generated by one small texture and a configuration file, greatly reducing the memory requirements and allowing real-time editing.

In this chapter, you'll get hands-on experience with particle systems by adding special effects to the XBlaster game you created in the previous chapter. You'll learn how to create particle systems programmatically, as well as by using the built-in Xcode editor.

Here's how your XBlaster project will look after you've completed this chapter:

Quite an improvement, eh? That's the power of particle systems!

Note: This chapter begins where the previous chapter's Challenge 2 left off. If you were unable to complete the challenges or skipped ahead from an earlier chapter, don't worry—you can simply open **XBlaster-Starter** from this chapter's resources to begin in the right place.

How does a particle system work?

Before you dive into coding, let's consider how a particle system works—both in theory, and with Sprite Kit specifically.

Particle systems in theory

A single particle in Sprite Kit is simply two triangles drawn together to create a square or quad. This quad is then textured, colored and rendered to the screen. For example, here's a raindrop depicted as a particle:

During each frame, the particle system looks at each individual particle it owns and advances it according to the system's configuration. For example, the configuration might say, "Move each particle between 2-10 pixels toward the bottom of the screen." You can see the effects of this configuration in the following diagram:

Frame 1	Frame 2	Frame 3
• • •		

A particle system will typically create a cache of particles when it's initialized, known as the **particle pool**. When it's time for a new particle to be born, the particle system will obtain an available particle from its particle pool. It will set the initial values of the new particle and then add it to the rendering queue.

When a particle has reached the end of its life, the system will remove it from the render queue and return it to the particle pool to be used at a later time.

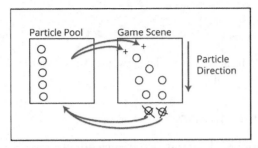

That's the high-level view of a particle system—now let's turn to the nitty-gritty of how it works in Sprite Kit.

Particle systems in practice

Sprite Kit makes it incredibly easy to create and use particle systems. It contains a special node called SKEmitterNode, the sole purpose of which is to make particle systems and render them as quickly as possible.

This section will give you a quick overview of how to use particle systems in Sprite Kit. Just read through for now without doing anything in Xcode – you'll try it out for yourself in the rest of the chapter.

To use a SKEmitterNode programmatically, you simply declare an instance of the node and set up its properties, like this:

```
let rainTexture = SKTexture(imageNamed: "rainDrop.png")
let emitterNode = SKEmitterNode()

emitterNode.particleTexture = rainTexture
emitterNode.particleBirthRate = 80.0
emitterNode.particleColor = SKColor.whiteColor()
emitterNode.particleSpeed = -450
emitterNode.particleSpeedRange = 150
emitterNode.particleLifetime = 2.0
emitterNode.particleScale = 0.2
emitterNode.particleAlpha = 0.75
emitterNode.particleAlphaRange = 0.5
emitterNode.particleColorBlendFactor = 1
emitterNode.particleScale = 0.2
emitterNode.particleScaleRange = 0.5
emitterNode.position = CGPoint(
  x: CGRectGetWidth(frame) / 2, y: CGRectGetHeight(frame) + 10)
emitterNode.particlePositionRange =
  CGVector(dx: CGRectGetMaxX(frame), dy: 0)
addChild(emitterNode)
```

Don't worry yet about what these properties mean—you'll learn about them later in this chapter. To see the effects this code produces, open and run the **Rain** project included in the resources for this chapter.

You can also use Xcode's built-in editor to visually create and configure a particle system:

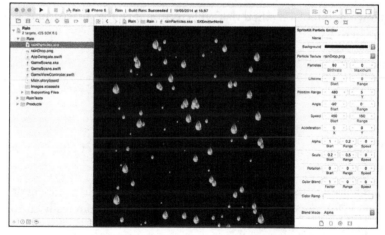

To do this, you simply create a new file with the **iOS\Resource\SpriteKit Particle File** template, which will give you an **.sks** file that you can edit with the built-in particle system editor. Then in code, you create an `SKEmitterNode` with the file, like this:

```swift
let rainEmitter = SKEmitterNode(fileNamed: "rain.sks")
rainEmitter.position = CGPoint(x: 100, y: 100)
addChild(rainEmitter)
```

This visual editor is super-convenient, because you can visualize the particle system in real-time as you tweak its properties. This makes it quick and easy to get exactly the effects you want.

In this chapter, you'll practice creating an SKEmitterNode programmatically, as well as using the visual editor. Let's have a play!

Programmatic particle systems

Every space shooter needs a star field moving majestically in the background, and a particle system is perfect for that!

In this section, you'll get your first taste of particle systems by programmatically creating a star field simulation. Creating it programmatically will help you better understand what's going on behind the scenes, as well as how to tweak settings on a particle system to make it dynamic—that is, so it reacts to events in the game.

Open **XBlaster-Starter project** and make sure the project builds and runs successfully. Your star field simulation is going to sit beneath everything in your scene, so open **GameScene.swift** to begin setting up your star field.

Add the following stub of a method that will create and configure a particle system based on a few parameters:

```
func starfieldEmitterNode(
    #speed: CGFloat, lifetime: CGFloat, scale: CGFloat,
    birthRate: CGFloat, color: SKColor) -> SKEmitterNode {
    // more to come
}
```

Xcode will now report an error, because this method does not yet return a value. But you aren't finished, so don't worry about that for now.

Sprite Kit renders every particle displayed onscreen using a single texture attached to the particle system. This texture can be anything you wish, so you can really customize the look of your particle system.

Your star field needs a texture that looks like a star, so let's borrow one of the techniques you learned in the previous chapter and generate a texture from an SKLabelNode.

Add the following in
starfieldEmitterNode(speed:lifetime:scale:birthRate:color:):

```
let star = SKLabelNode(fontNamed: "Helvetica")
star.fontSize = 80.0
star.text = "✦"

let textureView = SKView()
let texture = textureView.textureFromNode(star)
texture.filteringMode = .Nearest
```

The code above will be familiar from the previous chapter. It creates an SKLabelNode using the built-in Helvetica font and sets its size and text values. You are using the star symbol from the Helvetica font, which should fit in nicely with your star field.

> **Note**: As a reminder, you can add the star character by going to **Edit\Special Characters...** or using the shortcut **CTRL + CMD + SPACE**. This displays a popup from which you can select the special characters you want:

```
func starfieldEmitterNode(
    #speed: CGFloat, lifetime: CGFloat, scale: CGFloat,
    birthRate: CGFloat, color: SKColor) -> SKEmitterNode {

  let star = SKLabelNode(fontNamed: "Helvetica")
  star.fontSize = 80.0
  star.text = "✦"

  let textureView =
  let texture = te⟩                              e(star)
  texture.filtering

}
```

You then turn this SKLabelNode into a usable texture using an SKView. You set the filtering mode to Nearest to get clean edges on the characters.

Now that you have a texture, you can create the actual particle system. Add the following code below the lines you just added:

```
let emitterNode = SKEmitterNode()
emitterNode.particleTexture = texture
emitterNode.particleBirthRate = birthRate
emitterNode.particleColor = color
emitterNode.particleLifetime = lifetime
emitterNode.particleSpeed = speed
emitterNode.particleScale = scale
emitterNode.particleColorBlendFactor = 1
emitterNode.position =
```

```
    CGPoint(x: CGRectGetMidX(frame), y: CGRectGetMaxY(frame))
  emitterNode.particlePositionRange =
    CGVector(dx: CGRectGetMaxX(frame), dy: 0)
  return emitterNode
```

This is a convenience method that makes it easy to create a particle emitter. You simply call this method and specify the values you want to use inside the SKEmitterNode.

In the method, you first create a brand new SKEmitterNode. Then you set several properties on the emitter using the values that were passed into starfieldEmitterNode(speed:lifetime:scale:birthRate:color:):

- particleTexture is the texture to use for each particle and probably the most important property to set. The default value is nil and if you don't set a texture, emitter uses a colored rectangle to draw the particle. If you provide a non-nil value, the emitter will use that texture to draw the particles and color them based on other SKEmitterNode settings.

- particleBirthRate is the rate at which the emitter generates the particles in particles per second. It defaults to 0.0. If you leave the birth rate as 0.0, the emitter generates NO particles. In the following example, you're going to set the birth rate to 1 particle per second.

- particleColor is the color that the emitter blends with the particle texture using the particleColorBlendFactor (see below). The default value for this property is SKColor.clearColor(). In the following example, you're going to set this to SKColor.lightGrayColor().

- particleLifetime is the duration in seconds each particle is active. The default value is 0.0, and if you don't change this, the emitter generates NO particles. In the following example, you're going to calculate this to a value that allows each particle to live long enough to move from the top of the screen to the bottom.

- particleSpeed is the initial speed for a new particle in points per second. The default value is 0.0. In the following example, you're going to set this to -24, causing the particles to move down the screen 24 points per second.

- particleScale is the scale at which the emitter renders each particle. The default value is 1, which means the emitter renders the texture for each particle at the texture's full size. Values greater than 1 scale up the particle texture while values less than 1 scale it down. In the following example, you're going to set the scale to 0.2 (20%) the original size of the texture you use.

- `particleColorBlendFactor` is the amount of color the emitter applies to the texture when rendering each particle. It defaults to 0, which means the emitter uses the color of the texture and blends none of the color specified in `particleColor` with the texture. A value greater than 1 blends the texture color with the `particleColor` using the `particleBlendMode` defined. In the following example, you're going to set the blend factor to 1 to fully blend `particleColor` with the texture color.

- `position` is the starting point of every new particle within the parent node's coordinate system. The default is (0.0, 0.0). In the method you just added, you set the x-position to the center of the screen and the y-position to the very top of the screen.

- `particlePositionRange` is the maximum distance from the starting point at which that the emitter generates particles. It defaults to (0.0, 0.0), meaning the emitter generates all particles on the starting point. In the method you just added, you set the x-position range to the width of the screen, causing the emitter to generate each particle's x-position randomly across the width of the screen.

There are many other properties you can set on an `SKEmitterNode`, which you'll learn about later in this chapter, but these are all you need for the star field.

Now that you have a method that can create and configure a particle system, add one to your scene to see what it looks like. Add the following code to `setupSceneLayers()`:

```
let starfieldNode = SKNode()
starfieldNode.name = "starfieldNode"
starfieldNode.addChild(starfieldEmitterNode(
  speed: -48, lifetime: size.height / 23, scale: 0.2,
  birthRate: 1, color: SKColor.lightGrayColor()))
addChild(starfieldNode)
```

You create an `SKNode` to hold your star field, add a particle system to it and then add the `starfieldNode` to your scene. Notice that when you calculate the lifetime of the particles, you divide the window height by 23 rather than by 24, the speed of the particles. This causes the particles to live long enough to move completely off the bottom of the screen before disappearing. If you divided the height by 24, you would see particles vanishing when only half their height had moved past the bottom of the screen.

Build and run the game. Wait, why don't you see the particle system? Well, play the game for 30 seconds or so, and you'll begin to see particles fall from the top of the screen.

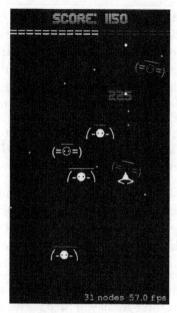

It's a good start, but the delay before the particles begin appearing is quite annoying. You can fix that!

Advancing a particle simulation

You've set up your particle system to make one particle appear every second and move slowly down the screen. You want the entire screen to be populated with stars, but it takes time to generate enough stars and move them down the screen, so you have to wait for your star field.

Basically, you want to "fast forward" the particle system a bit before the game starts. Fortunately, SKEmitterNode exposes a method called advanceSimulationTime() that allows you to advance the emitter to a future point in time. Cool!

Go back to starfieldEmitterNode(speed:lifetime:scale:birthRate:color:) and add the following line after you configure the emitter, just above the return statement:

```
emitterNode.advanceSimulationTime(NSTimeInterval(lifetime))
```

Remember that each particle lives for an amount of time (in seconds) represented by the lifetime variable. Therefore, after lifetime seconds, the first star particle will have finished moving to the bottom of the screen and will be destroyed. Other particles generated after the first will be at various stages in their lifetimes, filling the screen from top to bottom.

This is the earliest possible moment when the star field fully fills the screen, and thus the perfect moment to fast-forward your simulation to. Build and run the game again, and it will look much better:

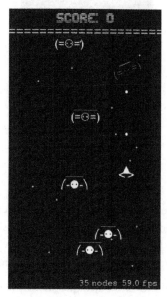

Great! Any time you want to advance a particle system to a point beyond its initial state, you'll find this method handy.

More basic particle system properties

As mentioned earlier, there are many more properties on a particle system beyond the ones you've set so far. Let's play around with a few and then briefly describe all the others for your reference.

One of the most useful properties is the `emissionAngle`. This controls the direction in which particles are emitted, beginning at the default 6 o'clock position (straight down), which is 0, and moving clockwise.

To see what this looks like, add the following line to the bottom of `starfieldEmitterNode(speed:lifetime:scale:birthRate:color:)`, just before the call to advance the simulation time:

```
emitterNode.emissionAngle = CGFloat(M_PI_4)
```

This sets the emission angle to 45 degrees. Build and run, and you'll see the stars now emit at an angle of 45 degrees toward the left-hand edge of the screen:

Controlling the emission angle is useful when you want to create effects like fountains or geysers, where the water should move up the screen before slowing and falling back down the screen, as if affected by gravity. In combination with the emissionAngleRange property, it's also super helpful when creating explosions.

For XBlaster, you want the stars to move straight down the screen, so delete the line you just added.

Another property you should know about is particleAction. This is a normal SKAction that will run on every particle in the system. Give it a shot by adding the following line to the bottom of starfieldEmitterNode(speed:lifetime:scale:birthRate:color:), before the call to advance the simulation time:

```
emitterNode.particleAction =
  SKAction.repeatActionForever(SKAction.sequence([
    SKAction.rotateByAngle(CGFloat(-M_PI_4), duration: 1),
    SKAction.rotateByAngle(CGFloat(M_PI_4), duration: 1)]))
```

This code makes the stars rotate back and forth as they move down the screen.

You'll find particleActions useful for adding additional effects to your particle systems that the built-in engine doesn't enable you to do. You could use the example shown above to simulate leaves falling from a tree and rotating back and forth as they fall to the ground.

> **Note:** Be careful when using particle actions in conjunction with `advanceSimulationTime()`. This method does not run any attached actions while advancing the particle system, so you could end up with unexpected results. Also consider that running actions on a large number of particles could adversely affect your game's performance.

There are a number of other core particle system properties beyond these. Here's a reference of what's available:

- `particleZPosition`: The starting z-position for each particle. It defaults to 0.

- `particleBlendMode`: The blend mode used when rendering particles. Possible values are:

  a. `Alpha`: Multiplies the alpha component of the source texture with red, green and blue components and then adds them to the pixel values in the destination buffer.

  b. `Add`: Adds the pixel values of the source texture to the pixel values in the destination buffer.

  c. `Multiply`: Multiplies the pixel values of the source texture with the pixel values in the destination buffer.

  d. `MultiplyX2`: Multiplies the pixel values of the source texture with the pixel values in the destination buffer, and doubles the result.

  e. `Replace`: Simply copies the values of the source texture into the destination buffer.

  f. `Screen`: Divides the pixel values of the source texture by the pixel values in the destination buffer.

  g. `Subtract`: Subtracts the pixel values of the source texture from the pixel values in the destination buffer.

- `particleColorRed/Green/Blue/AlphaSpeed`: The rate at which each color component changes per second, per particle. It defaults to 0.

- `particleColorBlendFactorSpeed`: The rate at which the blend factor changes per second. It defaults to 0.

- `xAcceleration`: The amount of x-acceleration to apply to the velocity of each particle. It defaults to 0.

- yAcceleration: The amount of y-acceleration to apply to the velocity of each particle. It defaults to 0.

- numParticlesToEmit: The number of particles the emitter should emit before stopping. It defaults to 0, meaning there is no limit. This is a useful property when creating an explosion, as you can set a high birth rate to initially generate a large number of particles, but as soon as the emitter reaches the numParticlesToEmit value, particle emission will stop, while the particles already emitted will continue to move as defined.

- particleRotation: The starting rotation to apply to each particle. It defaults to 0.

- particleRotationSpeed: The rate at which the amount of rotation should change in 1 second. It defaults to 0.

- particleSize: The initial size of each particle. It defaults to CGSizeZero, causing the particle to use the assigned texture size as its initial size.

- particleScaleSpeed: The rate at which to modify the particle's scale in 1 second. It defaults to 0.

- particleAlpha: The initial alpha value of each pixel. It defaults to 1.

- particleAlphaSpeed: The rate at which to modify the particle's alpha in 1 second. It defaults to 0.

- targetNode: This allows particles to be rendered as if they belong to another node. This is an important property that allows you to create some unique effects, so this chapter covers it in more detail below.

Range properties

There is another set of properties on SKEmitterNode designed to allow you to add random variance to a related property. You've seen an example of this already, when you used particlePositionRange to set random variance for the position property so stars would spawn randomly across the screen.

Let's take a look at other range properties by adding variation to the speed of the stars. Right now, the stars are the same size and move together, as though they're all on the same plane. That's not very convincing for the depths of space!

Add this line to starfieldEmitterNode(speed:lifetime:scale:birthRate:color:), before the call to advance the simulation time:

```
emitterNode.particleSpeedRange = 16.0
```

The `particleSpeedRange` represents a random variance from the starting speed for each particle. It defaults to 0, meaning no variance. Here you set it to 16, so now the speed will vary randomly by plus or minus half the range value.

Build and run the game again, and you'll observe each particle moving at a different pace:

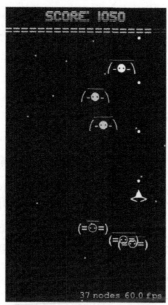

Just as you can modify the speed of a particle by a random value, you can add random variance to other properties, as well:

- `particleZPositionRange`: This randomly determines the initial z-position of each particle and may vary by plus or minus half the range value. It defaults to 0.

- `particleColorRed/Green/Blue/AlphaRange`: This creates each particle with random red/green/blue/alpha component values, according to the range. It defaults to 0.

- `particleColorBlendFactorRange`: This randomizes the initial blend factor of each particle. It defaults to 0.

- `particlePositionRange`: This starts every particle in a random position. It defaults to (0.0, 0.0), meaning all particles originate from the same position.

- `emissionAngleRange`: Use this to randomize the angle at which new particles are emitted. It defaults to 0.

- `particleLifetimeRange`: Use this to randomize the lifetime of each particle, meaning some particles will live longer than other particles.

- `particleRotationRange`: Use this to randomize the initial rotation of each particle. It defaults to 0.

- `particleScaleRange`: Use this to randomize the initial scale, according to range. It defaults to 0.

- `particleAlphaRange`: Use this to randomize the amount of alpha applied to each particle. It defaults to 1.

Keyframe properties

There are four properties on `SKEmitterNode` left to discuss, and they all use a very cool technique: key framing.

Instead of simply varying the property between a single value and a random range, the idea with key frames is to change a property to several specific values over time.

For example, there is a keyframe property on `SKEmitterNode` called `particleColorSequence` (its type is `SKKeyframeSequence`):

```
var particleColorSequence: SKKeyframeSequence!
```

To use a keyframe property, you first initialize it and then add one or more keyframes. Each keyframe has two properties:

- `time`: The time the keyframe occurs within the lifetime of the particle. This is a value in the range of 0 (the moment the particle is created) to 1 (the moment the particle is destroyed). For example, if the lifetime of a particle is 10 seconds and you specify 0.25 for `time`, the keyframe would occur at 2.5 seconds.

- `value`: The value the property takes when this keyframe occurs. `particleColorSequence` expects an `SKColor` instance for the value, such as `SKColor.yellowColor()`. Other properties may expect different types of values (more on that later).

Let's give this a shot and use the `particleColorSequence` to make the stars "twinkle" between white and yellow periodically. Add this code to `starfieldEmitterNode(speed:lifetime:scale:birthRate:color:)`, right before the call to advance the simulation time:

```
//1
let twinkles = 20
let colorSequence = SKKeyframeSequence(capacity: twinkles*2)
//2
let twinkleTime = 1.0/CGFloat(twinkles)
for i in 0..<twinkles {
  //3
  colorSequence.addKeyframeValue(
    SKColor.whiteColor(),time: CGFloat(i)*2 * twinkleTime/2)
  colorSequence.addKeyframeValue(
    SKColor.yellowColor(), time: (CGFloat(i)*2+1)*twinkleTime/2)
}
//4
emitterNode.particleColorSequence = colorSequence
```

Let's go over this section in detail:

1. You're going to make the stars twinkle 20 times. Each twinkle is two keyframes, one where the star is white and one where the star is yellow, so you create a keyframe sequence with a capacity of 40 keyframes.

2. Since there will be 20 twinkles, each twinkle will take $1/20^{th}$ of the particle's lifetime. You then start a loop to create the keyframes for each twinkle.

3. As mentioned in step 1, each twinkle consists of two keyframes: one where the star is white and one where the star is yellow. Here you specify the time to begin and end each keyframe, based on the index of the loop. Each keyframe takes $1/40^{th}$ of the particle's lifetime.

4. Finally, you set the `particleColorSequence` to the keyframe sequence you just created. Note that by setting a keyframe property, you are overriding the non-keyframe variants: in this case, `particleColor`, `particleColorAlphaRange`, `particleColorRedRange`, `particleColorGreenRange`, `particleColorBlueRange`, `particleColorAlphaSpeed`, `particleColorRedSpeed`, `particleColorGreenSpeed` and `particleColorBlueSpeed`.

Build and run, and enjoy your twinkling stars:

Keyframe sequences are powerful. In this example, you only alternate between two colors, but you could use multiple colors at different times to create some very cool effects!

There are four other properties that support keyframe sequences:

• `particleColorBlendFactorSequence`: This allows you to accurately control the blend factor applied to each particle during its lifetime.

• `particleScaleSequence`: Using this sequence allows you to scale each particle up and down multiple times during its lifetime.

• `particleAlphaSequence`: This sequence gives you full control over each particle's alpha channel during its lifetime.

• `particleRotationSequence`: This sequence gives you full control over each particle's rotation value during its lifetime.

There are two important properties on `SKKeyframeSequence`. These are the `interpolationMode` and `repeatMode`.

The `interpolationMode` property specifies how to calculate the values for times between keyframes. The available `SKInterpolationMode` values are:

• `Linear`: This mode calculates the interpolation values linearly.

- **Spline:** This mode calculates the interpolation values using a spline. This gives the effect of easing at the start and end of a keyframe sequence. If you were to scale a particle with this mode, then the scale change would begin slowly, pick up speed and then slow down until coming to the end of the sequence, providing a smooth transition.

- **Step:** The time values between keyframes are not interpolated when using this mode. The value is simply calculated as that of the most recent keyframe.

The `repeatMode` property specifies how to calculate values if they are outside the keyframes defined in the sequence. It's possible to define keyframes from 0.0 all the way to 1.0, but you don't have to. You could have a keyframe that runs from 0.25 to 0.75. In that case, the `repeatMode` property defines what values to use from 0.0 to 0.25 and from 0.75 to 1.0. The available `SKRepeatMode` values are:

- **Clamp:** This mode clamps the value to the range of time values found in the sequence. If, for example, the last keyframe in a sequence had a time of 0.5, any time from 0.5 to 1.0 would return the last keyframe value.

- **Loop:** This mode causes the sequence to loop. If, for example, the last keyframe in a sequence had a time value of 0.5, any time from 0.5 to 1.0 would return the same value as from 0.0 to 0.5.

Parallax scrolling with particle systems

To improve your star field even more, you're going to add a second layer of stars that are smaller in size and slower-moving. This will create a 3D-like effect and is commonly known as **parallax scrolling**.

Go back to `setupSceneLayers()` and add a second particle system to the `starfieldNode`. Add this code to the end of the method:

```
var emitterNode = starfieldEmitterNode(
  speed: -32, lifetime: size.height / 10, scale: 0.14,
  birthRate: 2, color: SKColor.grayColor())
emitterNode.zPosition = -10
starfieldNode.addChild(emitterNode)
```

In this emitter node, the particles will be slower and smaller, but there will be more of them. Notice that you set `emitterNode`'s `zPosition` to `-10` so that it will appear behind the first particle system you added.

Build and run to partake of the nifty illusion you've just created:

Why stop there? Now create a third layer, adjusting the properties further to simulate even more distant stars. Add the following to the end of setupSceneLayers():

```
emitterNode = starfieldEmitterNode(
  speed: -20, lifetime: size.height / 5, scale: 0.1,
  birthRate: 5, color: SKColor.darkGrayColor())
starfieldNode.addChild(emitterNode)
```

Build and run once more and peer into the depths of space:

There you have it—you built an impressive star field using particle systems and the parallax scrolling technique. You also applied what you learned in the previous chapter by using an SKLabelNode as a texture.

Visual particle systems

Your ship looks a little naked floating through space, especially with those fancy stars in the background. Let's upgrade its engine to a state-of-the-art plasma propulsion system. First off, this requires an introduction to Apple's SKS file.

Creating an SKS file

Adding particle systems programmatically is not your only option. Sprite Kit also supports an Xcode file type called an SKS file. This file allows you to store all the necessary settings for a particle system in a single file as part of your project, so you can take advantage of the built-in Xcode editor as well as easy loading and saving via NSCoding.

Let's create a new group to hold all of your particle systems. Highlight the **XBlaster** group in the project tree and select **File\New\Group** to add a new group. Call this group **Particles** and press enter to confirm.

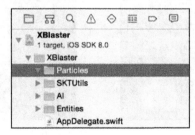

With the **Particles** group highlighted, select **File\New\File...** from the main menu. Select **iOS\Resource\SpriteKit Particle File**.

Click **Next** and on the next screen, you'll see a drop-down that contains a number of different particle templates.

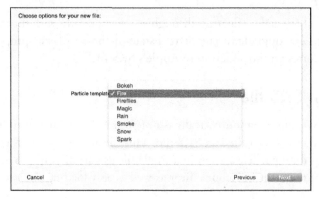

These templates give you a starting point from which to create your own particles. The items in the list are common particle configurations that you can adapt to your own needs. The following images show you what each of these templates looks like.

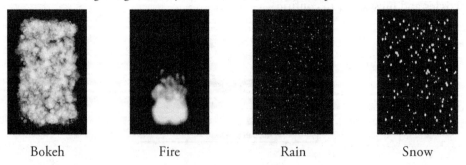

Bokeh   Fire   Rain   Snow

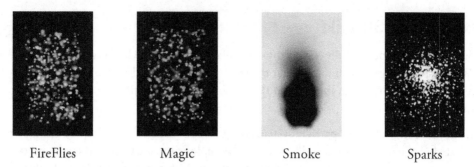

FireFlies   Magic   Smoke   Sparks

You could use any of these templates to get started on the ship's engine effect, but fire is the closest to an engine flame, so select the **Fire** template from the list.

Click **Next** once more, enter **engine** for the file name (Xcode will automatically add the file extension), ensure the **XBlaster** target is selected and click **Create**.

Note: Notice that when you add your first particle file to a project, Xcode automatically adds a second file, **spark.png**, alongside it. This image file is the default texture for all particle templates built into Xcode, apart from one: the Bokeh template has its own default image called **bokeh.png**.

You don't have to use this texture for your particle system. If you want to use your own texture, simply add it to the project and select the SKS file. In the utilities bar on the right, select the third tab (the SKNode inspector), and you can then choose your alternative texture file:

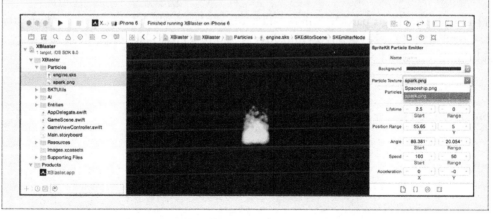

Loading an SKS file

The SKEmitterNode is fully NSCoding-compliant, making the loading process simple. NSCoding is an Apple technology that makes it easy to save and load objects from an archive. To find out more about NSCoding, take a look at Chapter 17, "Saving and Loading Games."

When you edit and save a particle system using Xcode, your SKS file will be updated and included in the application bundle, ready to be deployed to a device. To load a particle system in code, simply initialize an SKEmitterNode with the name of the SKS file.

Before you start tweaking any of the particle system's values, let's get the default particle system you made with the template loaded and rendering in the game.

Open **PlayerShip.swift** and add the following method:

```
func createEngine() {
  let engineEmitter = SKEmitterNode(fileNamed: "engine.sks")

  engineEmitter.position = CGPoint(x: 1, y: -4)
  engineEmitter.name = "engineEmitter"
  addChild(engineEmitter)
}
```

First, you create an SKEmitterNode given the filename of the SKS file you created. Next, you position the particle emitter just below your ship, give it a name and add it to the ship node. Note that the position will be relative to the ship's position, which is why −4 is "just below the ship," no matter where the ship happens to be.

That's it for loading a particle emitter and adding it to a node, but now you need to call createEngine(). PlayerShip's initializer would be a great place to do this. Add the following to the end of init(entityPosition:):

```
createEngine()
```

Build, run and give it a whirl.

Mayday—Mayday—Mayday—Fire detected aboard ship!

That's not quite the look you were after, so this is a good opportunity to learn how to edit your particle system using the built-in Xcode editor.

The Xcode particle editor

Not all properties of an SKEmitterNode are configurable through Xcode's built-in particle editor, such as the sequence properties for scale, blend factor and alpha, but the most important ones are. To access the editor, highlight the **engine.sks** file in the project navigator and ensure the inspector is visible on the right and set to the third tab (the SKNode inspector):

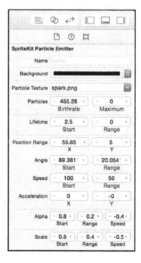

Play around with the settings in the inspector to change how the particle system behaves. Notice the **Particle Texture** property? It's set to use the default texture file, **spark.png**.

The first property for you to change is the color. The engine is supposed to be a state-of-the-art plasma propulsion drive and the flame effect doesn't cut it—not to mention there is no air in space, so you wouldn't get a flame anyway!

Locate the **Color Ramp** property in the editor and click on the color stop at the left of the color selection panel. This will display a standard OS X color picker. Change the color in the picker and watch the color of the particles change.

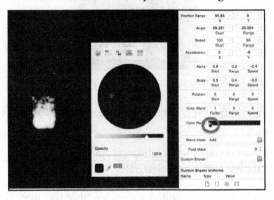

For the plasma engine, you want to set the color to a dark pink/purple. Select the **Color Sliders** tab and make sure that the drop-down shows **RGB Sliders**. Now enter **188** for the red value, **26** for green and **107** for blue, making sure the Opacity slider is at **100%**:

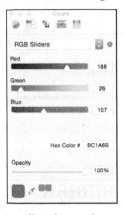

The Color Ramp in the editor is actually editing the emitter's `particleColorSequence`. Double-click toward the end of the color well to add a new color stop. The color will match that of the nearest color stop to its left.

With the new color stop selected, change the opacity of the color to **0%**. You will now have a pink flame in the emitter editor.

You could continue to add colors to the Color Ramp and the particles would transition smoothly from one color to the next over their lifetime.

With the color set, you can now start to edit the shape, speed and position of the emitter. Perform the steps in the table below.

Change the **Particles Birthrate** to **1000** with a **Maximum** of **0**. This causes the emitter to generate 1000 particles per second. To optimize performance, you want to keep the number of particles as low as possible to get the effect you want. Even though 1000 seems high, 1000 particles per second * 0.1 seconds lifetime per particle means only about 100 particles will be onscreen at a time.	
Change the **Lifetime Start** to **0.1** with a **Range** of **0.4**. This reduces the amount of time particles are alive, which reduces the length of the plasma trail.	
Change the **Position Range X** to **8** and **Y** to **0**. This causes the position of the particles on the x-axis to range from -4 to 4.	
Change **Angle** to **-90** with a **Range** of **0**. This causes the particles to be emitted down the screen rather than up.	
Change **Speed Start** to **300** with a **Range** of **10**. This makes the default speed of the particles 300 with a range of 10, so the speed will be between 295 and 305.	

Change **Scale Start** to **0.25** with a **Range** of **0** and a **Speed** of **-0.3**. This scales the texture to 25% of its original size and reduces that scale by 0.3 per second.

After all that hard work, you should now see a plasma trail fit for any state-of-the-art propulsion system.

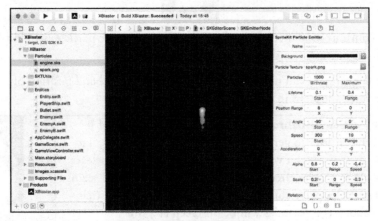

Give it another build and run to see how it's looking. Woo-hoo! You've upgraded the ship's engine and it looks like it's ready for a fight!

Play once particle systems

So far, you've made particle systems that run continuously, like the star field effect and the ship's engine. Next, you're going to make a particle system designed for a one-time explosion.

Specifically, let's have a little fun and ignite an enemy ship's plasma core when it dies instead of just making the ship disappear from the screen.

Highlight the **Particles** group and select **File\New\File...** from the main menu. Select **iOS\Resource\SpriteKit Particle File**. Select **Spark** from the list of templates and press **Next**.

In the save dialogue, call the file **enemyDeath**, make sure the **XBlaster target is selected,** then press **Create**.

You now have a new particle file that you can start to edit. Select **enemyDeath.sks** to bring up the editor and change the configuration of the emitter by following these steps:

Change **Particles Birthrate** to **10000** particles per second with a **Maximum** of **1000**. Setting the maximum will cause the emitter to spit out 1000 particles at a time (last time you had 0 for unlimited). This particle system will only run once, as the emitter will stop emitting particles once it has emitted the maximum number. You want this particular explosion to look substantial. Given that the particles are very small, rendering 1000 particles, even on a mobile device, should not cause any problems. If performance is an issue, then you can reduce the maximum.	
Change **Lifetime Start** to **0.5** and **Range** to **3**. This reduces the overall lifetime of the particles, getting you closer to the explosion effect you're after. The result will look fairly similar to that of the previous step.	
Change **Position Range X** to **0** and **Y** to **0**. You want all the particles to originate from the same point in this example.	You will not see any noticable difference at this point.

Change **Angle Start** to **0** and **Range** to **360**. For an explosion in space, you want particles to be ejected in all directions.	You will not see much noticable difference at this point.
Change **Speed Start** to **100** and **Range** to **20**. With a small range on the speed, you end up with a ring of particles that gets larger. That's more like the kind of impressive explosions you see in space films.	
Change **Acceleration X** to **0** and **Y** to **0**. This stops the particles from being pulled to the bottom of the screen. You're beginning to see a much more convincing explosion effect now.	
Change **Scale Start** to **0.1**, **Range** to **0.0** and **Speed** to **0.0**. This scales the texture to 10% of its original size and keeps it that size over the lifetime of the particle.	
Change the **Color Ramp** color stop to **white** with **100% opacity**.	Color Ramp
Add a new color stop to the **Color Ramp** and set **Red** to **255**, **Green** to **128** and **Blue** to **0**. Position this color stop very close to the first, so the color changes very quickly from bright white to orange.	Color Ramp
Add a third color stop to **Color Ramp** and set the color to **white** with **0%** opacity. This causes the explosion to fade out while getting brighter over time for a cool effect.	Color Ramp

Nice! You now have an impressive explosion you can use when an enemy ship dies.

To add the explosion to the game, you'll create a new layer in **GameScene.swift** for the explosion emitters. This will allow you to add particle emitters to their own layer that isn't attached to the enemy ships.

Why is this necessary? If you attached an emitter to an enemy ship, it would move with the ship, which isn't what you want. Adding the emitter to its own node means you can move the ship around and the explosion will stay where it is, just as it should be. You'll see another method for detaching an emitter's particles from the emitter node in the next section.

Open **GameScene.swift** and add the following constant:

```
let particleLayerNode = SKNode()
```

Next, you need to add it to the scene. Add the following code to `setupSceneLayers()`:

```
particleLayerNode.zPosition = 10
addChild(particleLayerNode)
```

You position this layer below the scene's other layers but above the star field particle emitters. This ensures things like the score popups appear above the explosions, but the stars still appear in the distance.

With the new layer in place, you can add the explosion emitter. You're going to use this emitter when an enemy dies, so the `Enemy` class is the perfect place to load up the emitter file, allowing each enemy to run its own particle emitter when it bites the dust.

Inside **Enemy.swift**, add a property to initialize the particle emitter:

```
let deathEmitter:SKEmitterNode = SKEmitterNode(fileNamed:
"enemyDeath.sks")
```

All that's left to do now is run the emitter when the enemy dies. Every time a bullet collides with an enemy, `didBeginContact()` in the scene calls `collidedWith(body:contact:)`. In that method, you reduce the enemy's health until it has none left and set its dead status to true.

With this in mind, add the following code to `collidedWith(body:contact:)`, *after* displaying the score label:

```
deathEmitter.position = position
if deathEmitter.parent == nil {
  mainScene.particleLayerNode.addChild(deathEmitter)
}
deathEmitter.resetSimulation()
```

You set the position of the death emitter in the same way you set the position of the score label in the last chapter. Next, you add your emitter to `mainScene`'s `particleLayerNode` if it hasn't already been added.

Finally, you call `resetSimulation()` on the death emitter. This handy method completely resets the running state of the emitter and starts it off again, which is great for effects like this that you want to start from the beginning each time, play once and then be done with.

Build and run the game, and when an enemy dies, you'll see your satisfying explosion as the enemy's plasma coils overload and the ship is blown into smithereens.

Targeted particle systems

In the previous section, you added the particle emitter node to a layer in the main scene called `particleLayerNode`, allowing you to set display a particle emitter explosion that won't follow the enemy ship when you reset its position to the top of the screen.

You can achieve this same result using the `targetNode` property of `SKEmitterNode`. The `targetNode` property lets you to define a node other than the `SKEmitterNode` that should influence the emitter particles while they are alive.

When a particle is first created, its properties are calculated based on those of the emitter node, but after that and throughout its lifetime, the particle is affected by the properties of the node which has been defined as the `targetNode`.

By default, `targetNode` is set to nil, which means that all particles generated by an emitter are treated as children of that emitter. In that circumstance, a particle's properties continue to be affected by the emitter node's properties.

Currently, the plasma trail from the back of the player's ship is static—that is, as you move the ship around, the trail continues to flow straight out from the ship. To improve the look of this, you'll use the `targetNode` property to add the engine's particles to `GameScene`'s `particleLayerNode`.

Open **PlayerShip.swift** and add the following code to the end of `createEngine()`:

```
var mainScene = scene as! GameScene
engineEmitter.targetNode = mainScene.particleLayerNode
```

This simply sets the engine emitter's `targetNode` to the `particleLayerNode` in the main scene.

Your app will crash if you run it right now. That's because `PlayerShip` calls `createEngine()` during initialization, but its `scene` property will be `nil` until after it has been initialized and added to the scene's node hierarchy.

That means you need to refactor this a bit. **Remove** the call to `createEngine()` in `init(entityPosition:)`. Then, open **GameScene.swift** and add the following method call *after* you add `playerShip` to `playerLayerNode` in `setupEntities()`:

```
playerShip.createEngine()
```

Now build and run, and as you move the player's ship around, you'll see that the engine trail behaves much more dynamically.

Just one more thing before you go!

Gratuitous music and sound effects

You can't leave before adding catchy music and sound effects to wrap up the game! Sound may not travel through space, but you want your players to hear your fancy new explosion, right?

In the resources for this chapter, find a folder named **Sounds**. Drag it into your project, make sure **Copy items if needed** and **Create groups** are selected, the **XBlaster** targets is checked, and click **Finish**.

Open **GameScene.swift** and add these two constants:

```
let laserSound = SKAction.playSoundFileNamed("laser.wav",
  waitForCompletion: false)
let explodeSound = SKAction.playSoundFileNamed("explode.wav",
  waitForCompletion: false)
```

Then, add these lines to the end of init(size:):

```
SKTAudio.sharedInstance().playBackgroundMusic("bgMusic.mp3")
```

Then add these two methods:

```
func playExplodeSound() {
  runAction(explodeSound)
}

func playLaserSound() {
  runAction(laserSound)
}
```

Call `playLaserSound()` in `update()`, right before running the action on the bullet:

```
playLaserSound()
```

And to play the explosion sound, open **Enemy.swift** and add this line in `collidedWith(body:contact:)`, right after resetting the death emitter:

```
mainScene.playExplodeSound()
```

Also, call this in **PlayerShip.swift** at the top of `collidedWith(body:contact:)`:

```
var mainScene = scene as! GameScene
mainScene.playExplodeSound()
```

Adding this code to **PlayerShip.swift** without any conditional code will ensure the game plays the explode sound every time the player's ship collides with an enemy ship.

Build and run, and enjoy your new game!

And that's it—believe it or not, you've learned almost everything there is to know about particle systems in Sprite Kit!

Throughout this chapter, you've learned how to add awesome visual effects to your game. You've also learned, by experience, the coolest thing about particle systems: the ease with which you can create so many different effects by changing just a few properties.

Now it's time to try out your newfound knowledge with a few fun challenges!

Challenges

Particle systems can be a lot of fun—with the built-in particle editor, it's a breeze to mess around and see what you can create.

This chapter contains two challenges: one to give you practice creating your own particle system in the built-in editor, and a second to see if you can add it to the game.

If you get stuck, you can find the solutions in the resources for this chapter—but give yourself a chance to succeed first!

Challenge 1: Create a venting plasma effect

Your first challenge is to create a new particle effect to depict plasma venting from the player's ship. Now, while I've never actually seen venting plasma, I've watched way too much Syfy channel to know the kind of effect you are looking for is this:

To kick things off, you should create a new particle file resource using the **Spark** template. That template already has particles moving in all directions, so it's a good place to start.

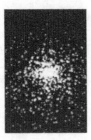

You'll want to review the following properties to turn the Spark template into the effect you're after:

- **Particle birthrate**: You should decrease this from the defaults.

- **Position range:** You should make this have no variance.

- **Speed:** You should decrease this from the defaults.

- **Scale:** You should slightly increase this from the defaults.

- **Color Ramp:** You should make this a 50% transparent green going to fully transparent.

Using what you've learned in this chapter, you should be able to adjust the properties above to achieve the venting plasma effect. If you get stuck you, can check out the finished particle system inside **XBlaster – Challenge 1** in the resources for this chapter.

Challenge 2: Add your new effect to the game

Your second challenge is to take the venting plasma effect you created in challenge 1 and add it to the game. To make this a little more interesting, the venting plasma should only appear on the player's ship when its health is 30% or less.

Here are some hints:

1. Add a new SKEmitterNode constant to **PlayerShip.swift** called ventingPlasma. Set this constant to an instance of SKEmitterNode initialized with the file named **ventingPlasma.sks**.

2. Inside init(entityPosition:), make sure to hide the new emitter by setting its hidden property to true. Also add it as a child.

3. At the end of collidedWith(body:contact:), set the emitter's hidden property to the result of the expression health > 30.

Once you've made the necessary changes, build and run the project and let the player's ship take some knocks. Once the player's health drops to less than or equal to 30%, the player's ship should start venting plasma:

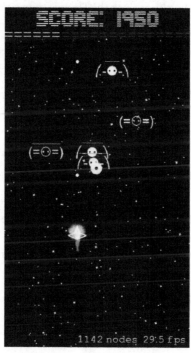

I'm sure you agree that adding particle effects to XBlaster has made a significant difference to the game. It feels more dynamic with the explosions, engine and leaking plasma. Having made it this far, you've earned the right to sit in the Captain's chair and command all the particle systems at your disposal.

Challenge 3: Make the game run on OS X

Your final challenge is to port XBlaster to the Mac. You've already learned how to make Sprite Kit apps work on OS X in Chapter 6, so refer back to that chapter if you get stuck. Here are some hints:

- You need a new target for the OS X version of the game, named **XBlasterMac**.

- It's a good idea to put all the shared code and resources into a new **Shared** group. The only things that are not shared between the iOS and OS X versions are the storyboard and launch file, the MainMenu.xib, the AppDelegate.swift and GameViewController.swift source files, and Info.plist.

- All the files from the Shared group should be added to the **XBlasterMac** target.

- The **XBlasterMac** target should not use the GameScene.swift and Images.xcassets from the template but the shared ones. You can also remove GameScene.sks.

- The OS X icons should be added to the asset catalog. You can find the icon images in the Resources folder for this chapter.

- Place the touchesBegan() method in **GameScene.swift** into an #if os(iOS) block and add a mouseDown() method to handle clicks on OS X.

- Change **AppDelegate.swift** so that it doesn't load the scene from GameScene.sks but instantiates it programmatically, just like GameViewController.swift does it. A scene size of 1536 by 2048 points looks just right.

- On iOS we added a line to the info.plist file telling the game about our custom font. We need to do the same for OS X but the key to add to the info.plist file is different. The key your after is "Application fonts resource path" and should be set to an empty string. Using an empty string causes the game to search its root folder for custom fonts.

It's quite a few steps, but now you've got XBlaster running on the Mac!

Section III: Physics and Nodes

In this section, you will learn how to use the built-in 2D physics engine included with Sprite Kit to create movement as realistic as that in *Angry Birds* or *Cut the Rope*. You will also learn how to use special types of nodes that allow you to play videos, create shapes and apply image filters in your game.

In the process, you will create a physics puzzle game called Cat Nap, where you take the role of a cat who has had a long day and just wants to go to bed.

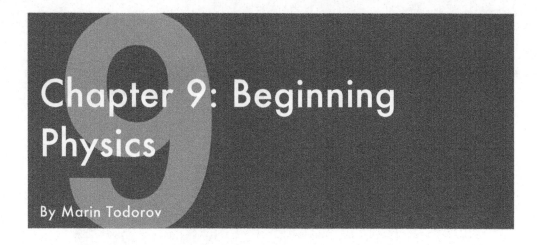

Chapter 9: Beginning Physics

By Marin Todorov

So far, you have learned how to move sprites around by manual positioning, or by running actions. But what if you want to simulate real-life behavior, like bouncing a ball against a wobbly pillar, making a chain of dominos fall down, or making a house of cards collapse?

You could accomplish the above with a bunch of math, but there's an easier way. Sprite Kit contains a powerful and easy to use physics engine that you can use to easily make objects move in a realistic way.

By using a physics engine, you can accomplish effects like you see in many popular iOS games:

- **Angry Birds**: Uses a physics engine to simulate what happens when the bird collides with the tower of bricks.

- **Tiny Wings**: Uses a physics engine to simulate the bird riding the hills and flying into the air.

- **Cut the Rope**: Uses a physics engine to simulate the movement of the ropes and the gravity affecting the candy.

Physics engines are great when combined with touch controls, because they make your game seem realistic, dynamic – and like you see in Angry Birds, sometimes destructive!

If you like this kind of reckless behavior and you want to know how to build your own physics-based game, you're in for a treat.

In this chapter, you'll get started with Sprite Kit physics by making a little test project. You'll add a few physics shapes with different properties, and add tiny sand particles that flow around them in a cool and dynamic manner.

Since this will be your sandbox physics project the best way to get started is by getting on a playground. And I don't mean an actual playground (you are probably a bit too big to fit those swing seats anyway) but an Xcode playground – a new feature introduced in Xcode 6, which is just perfect for learning and experimenting.

After you learn the basics of the Sprite Kit physics engine you will continue learning through two more chapters and build upon this foundational knowledge to create your own physics-enabled game with touch controls, realistic movement, and yes – being reckless (with cats)!

Sprite Kit physics

Under the hood, Sprite Kit uses a library called Box2D. This library performs all the physics calculations. Box2D is a great open source physics library – it's full featured, fast and powerful. In fact, it's already used in a lot of popular games on the iPhone, Android,

BlackBerry, Nintendo DS, Wii, OSX and Windows – so it's nice to see it as part of Sprite Kit.

However, Box2D has two main drawbacks for iOS developers: it is written in C++ and it could stand to be more user-friendly, especially to beginning developers.

Apple doesn't expose Box2D directly – instead, it abstracts it behind its own API in Sprite Kit. In fact, Box2D is walled so well that Apple could choose to change the physics engine in a later version of iOS and you wouldn't know a thing.

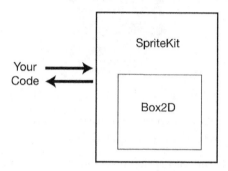

Long story short – in Sprite Kit, you get access to all the power of a super-popular engine, but through a friendly, polished Apple-style API.

Physics bodies

In order for the physics engine to control the movement of one of your sprites, you have to create a **physics body** for your sprite. You can think of a physics body as a rough boundary for your sprite that is used for collision detection.

The illustration below shows what a physics body for a sprite might look like. Note that the shape of the physics body does not need to match the boundaries of the sprite exactly. Usually, you choose a simpler shape so the collision detection algorithms can run faster.

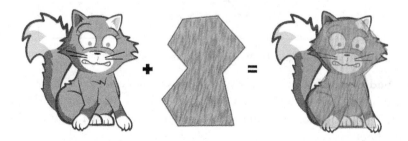

In Sprite Kit you can actually tell the physics engine to detect the shape of your sprite by ignoring all transparent parts of the image. This is a good strategy if you really want real life collision between the objects in your game. For example for the cat image above the automatically detected physics body based on transparency will look something like that:

"Excellent!" you might be thinking already "I'll just use that all the time"

Think twice just there. It takes **much more** processing power to calculate the physics for such complex shapes as poor cat above compared to a rectangle or a simpler shape.

Once you set physics body for your sprite, it will move similarly to how it would in real life – it will fall with gravity, be affected by impulses and forces, and move in response to collisions with other objects.

You can adjust the nature of your physics bodies, such as how heavy or bouncy they are. You can also alter the laws of the whole simulated world – for example, you can decrease the gravity so a ball would bounce back off the ground higher and will go further. On the image below two balls are thrown and bounce for a while –the red one in normal Earth gravity, the blue one in low gravity (for example on the Moon):

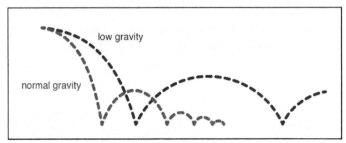

There are few things you should know about physics bodies:

• **Physics bodies are rigid**. In other words, physics bodies can't get squished or deformed under pressure, and do not change shape as a consequence of the physics simulation. For example, you cannot simulate a squishy ball that deforms as it rolls along the floor.

- **Complex physics bodies cost performance** It does look very convenient to just use the alpha mask of your images as the physics body but this feature should be used only when really necessary. If you have many shapes on screen colliding with each other – try using alpha mask only for your main character or 2 – 3 main characters and set the rest to rectangle shapes or circles.

- **Physics bodies are moved by forces or impulses**. Physics bodies are moved by applying forces or impulses. Impulses adjust the object's momentum immediately (such as the transfer of energy when two physics bodies collide), while forces affect the object gradually over time (such as gravity moving a physics body). You can apply your own forces or impulses to physics bodies as well – for example, you might use an impulse to simulate firing a bullet from a gun, but a force to simulate launching a rocket. You'll learn more about forces and impulses later in this chapter.

The great thing about Sprite Kit is that it makes all of these features, and many more, incredibly easy to use. In Apple's typical manner, most of the configuration is fully pre-defined. This means a blank Sprite Kit project already includes life-like physics with absolutely no setup.

Getting started

Let's learn about Sprite Kit physics in the best way possible – by experimenting in real time inside an Xcode playground.

Start Xcode and you will see its initial dialogue, which offers you to start working by using several different approaches (one of them is by creating a new playground). Click on **Get Started with a Playground**.

In the next dialogue enter as Name **SpriteKitPhysicsTest** and (very important) select as Platform **OSX**.

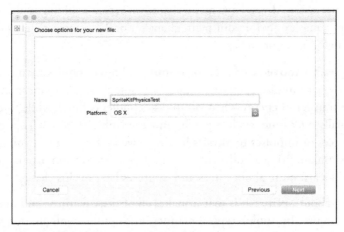

Click **Next** and select a location on your disc to save the Playground.

Alternatively, if you have previously disabled the startup dialogue, select **File\New\File...** from the main menu. Select the **OS X\Source\Playground** template and click **Next**.

> **Note:** You probably wonder why do you have to create an OS X Playground. SpriteKit itself is truly multiplatform – it works equally great on both iOS and OSX. However at the time of editing this chapter for Xcode 6.1 Playgrounds still have some problems with the combination of iOS and SpriteKit. Hopefully that will be fixed in an upcoming version of Xcode.

Enter **SpriteKitPhysicsTest** for file name and click **Create**.

No matter which of the two approaches you use to create the Playground, as soon as you click **Create** Xcode will create a new empty playground and start you off by importing the **Cocoa** framework at the top of the source code so you can use all the data types, classes and structures you are used to work with in your OS X projects.

> **Note**: If you create an iOS playground you will have a code line that imports `UIKit` instead of `Cocoa`. But as said in order to use SpriteKit for the time being you need to use an OSX Playground.

The empty playground window should look like this:

I can imagine you must be having an odd feeling right now. You have the absolute right to be tiny bit confused at first by the look of that Xcode window.

Let's have a look at some key differences in the Xcode interface compared to what you are used to when working with Xcode projects and learn a bit more about how to experiment in a playground.

> **Note:** If you are already familiar with working in playgrounds you can skip the next section.

Your first playground

In the previous chapters you have been working with Xcode projects. Projects usually include many source files, resources, storyboards, game scenes, and so forth. A playground on the other hand is just a single file with an extension **.playground** which allows you to experiment with your code in real time.

Let's have a look at your empty playground window again and spot some key areas:

On the left hand side you have a code editor (1) and on the right hand side there's an output area (2). That's all. As you type in more code Xcode executes it and every line of code that declares a constant, variable, or calls a function - produces the resulting value as text to the right.

Change "Hello, playground" to "Sprite Kit rulez!" and you will see immediately this change also in the output area. You can experiment with anything you want, but right now give the code below a try:

```
let number = 0.4
var string = "Sprite Kit is #\(5-4)"
let reversed = Array(1...5).reverse()

var j = 0
for i in 1..<10 {
    j += i*2
}
```

As soon as you paste in or enter the code you will see the output area update accordingly and neatly align the output of every line against the corresponding code in the editor.

Let's inspect few key features of the output area and then you will have enough basic skills to move on to playing with Sprite Kit and physics.

The first simple line of code produces output you already expect (code line and output below):

```
let number = 0.4
0.4
```

Besides static values (and to prove the code really gets executed in real time) you can also see the output of an expression; look at the output of the second line:

```
var string = "Sprite Kit is #\(5-4)"
"Sprite Kit is #1"
```

Note that the output is wrapped in quotes to show you that the data type of that output is a String. The next example shows you the output of an even more elaborate code:

```
Array(1...5).reverse()
[5, 4, 3, 2, 1]
```

The code creates a new array containing Int elements with values from 1 to 5 and it reverses the order of the elements in the array. This time you do not assign the value to any variable or constant.

When you just put in an expression like that on a code line by itself Xcode will evaluate it and send the result to the output area. This is incredibly useful for debugging purposes – you do not have to use a separate log function, just write a variable name or an expression and you will immediately see its value on the right.

The final example produces a somewhat surprising output – the text "9 times":

```
var j = 0
for i in 1..<10 {
    j += i*2
}
(9 times)
```

Considering everything you learned so far – this output is to be expected. The output is aligned to the code so even the line j += i*2 is executed 9 times in the loop it still can produce only a single line of text.

The line tells you how many times the loop ran, but this is far from what is actually useful to you – to see the values of the variables while the loop runs.

No fear – a playground is smarter than that. Hover with your mouse cursor over the text (**9 times**). You should see an extra button appear and a little tip:

Click on the (+) button and you will see the history of the value of your expression over the 9 iterations of the loop show up directly under the line of code where you calculate the value of j. You can click on the points representing the loop iterations to see the value of your tracked expression in a little popup.

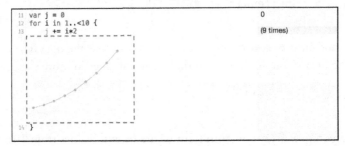

Congratulations! You now have basic knowledge how to use a playground in Xcode. Now comes the interesting part – conducting physics experiments in an Xcode playground.

Creating a Sprite Kit Playground

Delete any code you have in your playground and put these imports at the top:

```
import Cocoa
import SpriteKit
import XCPlayground
```

These will import the basic Cocoa classes, the Sprite Kit framework, and a very handy framework called XCPlayground that will help you visualize your Sprite Kit scene right inside the playground window.

You already know how to create a new game scene so let's do that first.

Make sure that Xcode's Assistant Editor is open – it usually stays in the right hand side of the window. If you followed the instructions from the last section - you still have the

Assistant Editor open and it's showing an empty graph for the (currently) non-existing expression "j += i*2"; click the close button on that graph panel to remove it.

Any time you want to show the Assistant Editor you can do that from Xcode's main menu by choosing **View/Assistant Editor/Show Assistant Editor**.

Now add the following to your playground's source code:

```
let sceneView = SKView(frame:
  CGRect(x: 0, y: 0, width: 480, height: 320))
let scene = SKScene(size: CGSize(width: 480, height: 320))
sceneView.showsFPS = true
sceneView.presentScene(scene)

XCPShowView("My Scene", sceneView)
```

This code is surely already familiar to your eyes, though you have never seen it in such context. Let's have a look at what you achieve above.

You create a new **SKView** view instance and give it frame of size 480 by 320 pixels, then you create an empty default **SKScene** instance and give it the same size. This is what the code in your view controller has been doing for you in the previous chapters of this book.

Finally you tell the **SKView** to present the scene and then there is… one more thing :] You call the function **XCPShowView** (from the **XCPlayground** framework) and pass it a string title and your view.

What **XCPShowView** does is very, very handy:

1. First and foremost – it tells Xcode not to abort executing your playground as soon as it runs trough the source code. In a game prototype you'd like things to keep running, right? So in this case the playground will keep running for the default duration of 30 seconds every time you change the source code.

2. Renders the current state of the SKView (or any other view you pass in) in the Assistant Editor.

3. When rendering the view the Assistant Editor will also record the view over time so you can rewind, fast forward, and skim trough the recorded session.

From Xcode's main menu select View/Assistant Editor/Show Assistant Editor. This will open the Assistant Editor on the right hand side of Xcode's window and you will see your game scene:

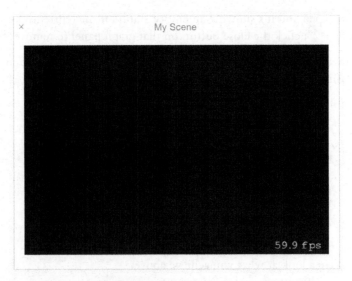

You (might) notice the frame rate label flickering as it renders different rates – this shows you that the scene is actually rendered live. Wait until the 30 seconds of execution time are finished and then drag the little knob on the timeline at the bottom of the window left and right – you are dragging trough the recorded session, how cool is that?

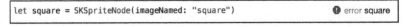

Unfortunately playing with a black empty game scene is not so much fun. Fortunately – that's not so hard to change! You have now a nice blank slate. Your next step is to add sprites into the scene to work with.

Add this code to the playground to create a new sprite with the image **square.png**:

```
let square = SKSpriteNode(imageNamed: "square")
```

This will result in an error showing up in the output area:

You will also notice that under your scene preview in the Assistant Editor there's an extra capture panel called **Console Output**:

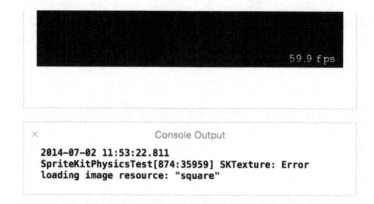

Sprite Kit tells you that it could not find an image called **square.png** to use as the sprite texture. And Sprite Kit has right to complain this time – you did not add any assets to your playground.

Select from Xcode's main menu **View/Navigators/Show Project Navigator** and have a look at the file structure of your playground:

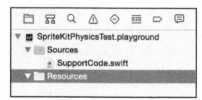

The playground contains two folders. The former "**Sources**" contains Swift code you want to pre-compile and make available to your playground code. "Resouces" contains any assets you want to use from your playground code.

In the **Assets** folder of the book for this chapter, you will find a folder called **Shapes** that includes all the artwork you need for this physics test.

Grab all files inside **Shapes** and drop them in the **Resources** folder in your playground:

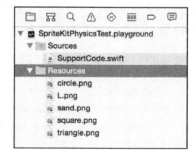

Good job! Now switch back to Xcode and have a look at the Assistant Editor (you might need to close and re-open the playground file if you get an error message from Xcode) – the console output panel has disappeared. All is well.

> **Note:** You still might see an error in the output area of the playground, but as long as you don't see it in the Assistant Editor you should not worry.

Now you can go on with your Sprite Kit code. Add this code chunk at the end of file:

```
square.position = CGPoint(x: scene.size.width * 0.25, y:
scene.size.height * 0.50)

let circle = SKSpriteNode(imageNamed: "circle")
circle.position = CGPoint(x: scene.size.width * 0.50, y:
scene.size.height * 0.50)

let triangle = SKSpriteNode(imageNamed: "triangle")
triangle.position = CGPoint(x: scene.size.width * 0.75, y:
scene.size.height * 0.50)
```

This code creates three constants: `square`, `circle`, and `triangle`. All of them are sprite nodes and you initialize them with the textures **square.png**, **circle.png**, and finally **triangle.png**.

> **Note**: Again - you might keep seeing faux errors in the output area. Keep ignoring them.

Note that at this point you can see in the output area that the 3 sprites are created successfully but you still can't see them on screen. You need to add them to your scene:

```
scene.addChild(square)
scene.addChild(circle)
scene.addChild(triangle)
```

This creates three sprites in the center of the screen – a square, a circle and a triangle. Check them out:

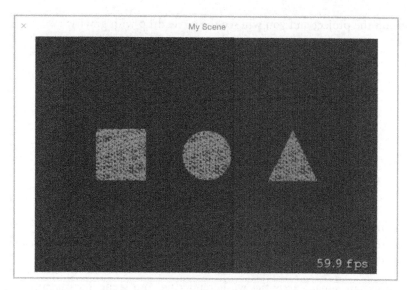

So far, this is review of creating sprites and positioning them manually on screen from what you learned in the previous chapters. It's time to introduce something new – let's make these objects physics-controlled!

Circle bodies

Remember two things from earlier in this chapter:

1. In order for the physics engine to control the movement of one of your sprites, you have to create a **physics body** for your sprite.

2. You can think of a physics body as a rough boundary for your sprite that is used for collision detection.

Let's try this out by attaching a physics body the circle. Add:

```
circle.physicsBody = SKPhysicsBody(circleOfRadius:
circle.size.width/2)
```

Since the `circle` sprite uses an image shaped like a circle, you want to create a physics body of roughly the same shape. `SKPhysicsBody` has a convenience init method `SKPhysicsBody(circleRadius:)` that creates a circle-shaped body.

Believe it or not, thanks to Sprite Kit's pre-configured physics simulation, you are all done!

Build and run the project and you will see the circle drop with gravity:

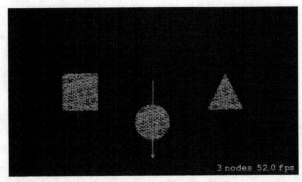

But wait a minute – the circle keeps going off-screen and disappears! Not to speak that by the time the scene is rendered the circle is almost out of the screen – you can't see much falling happen.

Since Xcode executes many activities while rendering your scene like capturing value output and recording, the first couple of seconds are a bit bumpy- that's why you can't enjoy fully your physics experiment.

But there's an easy way to fix that – let's turn off gravity at the start of your scene and turn it on few seconds later. Yes – you heard me right – let's turn off gravity :]

Skim trough your Swift code and find the line where you call `presentScene()` on your `SKView`. Just before this line add this code to turn off gravity by default:

```
scene.physicsWorld.gravity = CGVector(dx: 0, dy: 0)
```

Your scene has a property `physicsWorld`, which represents the basic physics setup of your game. When you alter the `gravity` vector of your physics world you change how bodies interact, how strong they bounce off of each other, etc.

As soon as you enter the code to reset gravity to a zero vector you will see that now the circle stays at its initial position without falling down. So far, so good.

Now you are going to create a little helper function called `delay`. Since you will write it once and not need to re-compile it each time the playground executes you can put it aside in that extra "**Sources**" folder you discovered previously.

Open Sources/SupportCode.swift and add inside:

```
import Foundation

func delay(#seconds: Double, completion:()->()) {
```

```
    let popTime = dispatch_time(DISPATCH_TIME_NOW,
        Int64( Double(NSEC_PER_SEC) * seconds ))

    dispatch_after(popTime,
        dispatch_get_global_queue(DISPATCH_QUEUE_PRIORITY_LOW, 0)) {
        completion()
    }
}
```

You will need to delay code execution throughout this chapter so it's a good thing to have it handy and short.

Open back the playground by clicking on **SpriteKitPhysicsTest.playground** in the Project Navigator.

Now you can scroll back down to the end of the code and add this to re-instantiate gravity 2 seconds after the scene is created:

```
delay(seconds: 2.0) {
    scene.physicsWorld.gravity = CGVector(dx: 0, dy: -9.8)
}
```

Keep this piece of code at the bottom of the file – from now on when I say "add this and this code" – add the relevant code just above the call to `delay(seconds…)`.

In the Assistant Editor you can observe your scene appearing on screen and shortly after that - the circle shape falling under the pull of gravity.

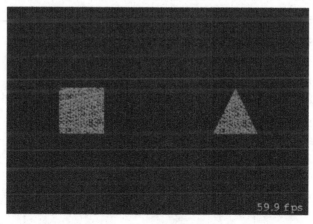

However – that's still not exactly what you want! For this demo, you want the circle to stop when it hits the bottom of the screen and stay there.

Luckily, Sprite Kit provides an easy way to do this by using something called an edge loop body.

Edge loop bodies

To add a boundary for the scene (something you need to do in almost all your physics based games), add this line of code:

```
scene.physicsBody = SKPhysicsBody(edgeLoopFromRect: scene.frame)
```

First, notice you are setting the physics body for the scene itself. Any Sprite Kit node can have a physics body, and a scene is a node too!

Next, notice you are creating a different type of body this time – an edge loop body, rather than a circle body. These two types of bodies have a major difference:

• The circle body is a **dynamic** physics body (i.e. it moves). It is solid, has mass and can collide with any other type of physics body. The physics simulation can apply various forces to move volume-based bodies.

• The edge loop body is a **static** physics body (i.e. it does not move). As the name implies, an edge loop only defines the edges of a shape. It does not have mass, cannot collide with other edge loop bodies and it is never moved by the physics simulation. Other objects can be inside or outside of the edges.

The most common use for an edge loop is to define collision areas to describe your game's boundaries, ground, walls, trigger areas or any other type of unmoving collision space.

Since you want to restrict bodies so that they can only move within the screen boundaries, you create the scene's physics body to be an edge loop with the scene's frame CGRect:

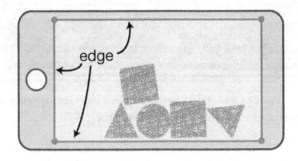

Build and run to see how this works. Now the ball stops when it hits the bottom of the screen, and even bounces just a little bit:

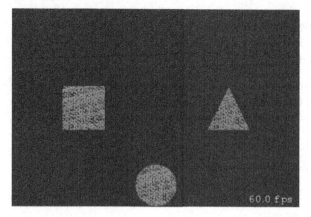

Rectangle bodies

Next let's add the physics body for the square sprite. Add the following line to the end of your code:

```
square.physicsBody = SKPhysicsBody(rectangleOfSize:
square.frame.size)
```

You can see that creating a rectangle-based physics body is very similar to creating a circle body. The only difference is that instead of passing in the radius of the circle, you pass in a `CGSize` representing the width and height of the rectangle.

Build and run, and now the square will fall down to the bottom of the scene too:

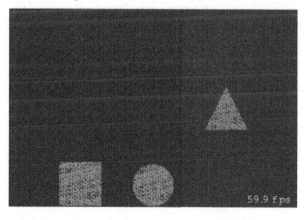

Custom shaped bodies

So far you've some very simple shapes – a circle and a square. This is great if your sprite is similar to these basic forms, but what if your shape is more complicated? For example, there is no built-in triangle shape.

Luckily, Sprite Kit provides a way for you to create arbitrarily shaped bodies, by giving Sprite Kit a **Core Graphics path** that defines the boundary of the body. The easiest way to understand how this works is by looking at an example – so let's try this out with the triangle shape.

Add the following code:

```
var trianglePath = CGPathCreateMutable()

CGPathMoveToPoint(trianglePath, nil, -triangle.size.width/2, -
triangle.size.height/2)
CGPathAddLineToPoint(trianglePath, nil, triangle.size.width/2, -
triangle.size.height/2)
CGPathAddLineToPoint(trianglePath, nil, 0,
triangle.size.height/2)
CGPathAddLineToPoint(trianglePath, nil, -triangle.size.width/2,
-triangle.size.height/2)

triangle.physicsBody = SKPhysicsBody(polygonFromPath:
trianglePath)
```

Let's go through this step-by-step:

1. First you create a new `CGMutablePathRef`, which you will use to draw the triangle.

2. You move your virtual "pen" to the starting point where you want to draw by using `CGPathMoveToPoint()`. Note that the coordinates are relative to the sprite's anchor point, which is by default its center.

3. You then draw three lines to the three corners of the triangle by calling `CGPathAddLineToPoint()`.

4. You create the body by passing the `trianglePath` to `SKPhysicsBod(polygonFromPath:)`.

Build and run the project, and now all of the objects will fall down:

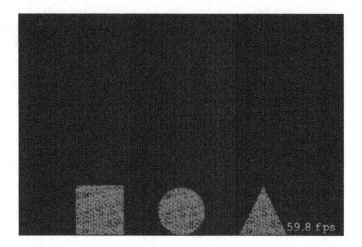

Visualizing the bodies

Each of the three objects now has a physics body that matches its shape, but right now you can't prove that the physics bodies are indeed different for each sprite.

Before adding the code for this section add one more utility function to make your code shorter and easier to read. Open **Sources/SupportCode.swift** and add:

```
func random(#min: CGFloat, #max: CGFloat) -> CGFloat {
  return CGFloat(Float(arc4random()) / Float(0xFFFFFFFF)) * (max
- min) + min
}
```

Back in the playground let's pour some particles over the objects to observe their true physical shapes. Add this function to your playground:

```
func spawnSand() {
  let sand: SKSpriteNode = SKSpriteNode(imageNamed: "sand")
  sand.position = CGPoint(
    x: random(min:0, max:scene.size.width),
    y: scene.size.height - sand.size.height)

  sand.physicsBody = SKPhysicsBody(circleOfRadius:
    sand.size.width/2)
  sand.name = "sand"
  scene.addChild(sand)
}
```

In this function, you make a small circular body (just like you did before) out of the texture called **sand.png** and you position the sprite in a random location at the top of the screen. You also give the sprite the name **sand** for easier access to it later on.

Let's add 100 of these sand particles and see what happens! Modify your call to `delay(seconds:, completion:)` at the bottom of the file to look like this (new code is highlighted):

```
delay(seconds: 2.0) {
  scene.physicsWorld.gravity = CGVector(dx: 0, dy: -9.8)

  scene.runAction(
    SKAction.repeatAction(
      SKAction.sequence([
        SKAction.runBlock(spawnSand),
        SKAction.waitForDuration(0.01)
      ]),
    count: 100)
  )
}
```

Finally some (SK) action! :]

You create a sequence of actions that calls `spawnSand` and then waits for 0.01 seconds. Then you execute the sequence 100 times on the scene instance.

When the scene starts rendering in the Assistant Editor you should see small particles – the "sand" – rain down and fill in the spaces between the three bodies on the ground:

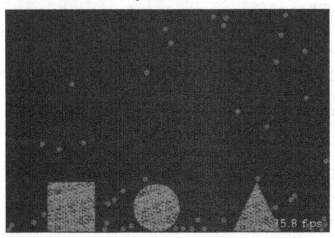

You can observe nicely how the sand bounces from the shapes, finally proving that they indeed have differently shaped bodies.

Doesn't that look great? Wait for the "rain" to end; the scene settles down to something like this:

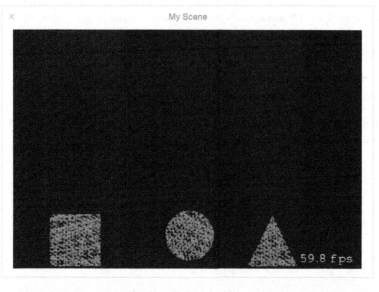

After 30 seconds of execution you can scrub the recording knob left and right to observe some really hilarious action of the sand going up and down and bouncing off and towards the shapes.

Have some fun with that – you deserved it!

Note: At this point you might see Xcode complain that `spawnSand` is not defined like so:

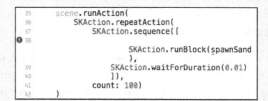

In case this bothers you move the piece of code that calls delay and enables gravity to the bottom of the playground or to the Sources folder.

Bodies with complex shapes

The code to create `CGPath` instances is not very easy to read, especially after it's been a while since you wrote it. Additionally – imagine you have a very complex body shape to create; it's going to be a long and cumbersome process to create the path for it by code.

While it is very handy to know how to create custom paths and bodies out of them, there is a much easier way to handle complex shapes – let's have a look!

There's one more shape you are going to add to your scene – it does look a bit like a rotated capital letter L:

Considering the code you wrote to define a triangular path you probably already realize that the shape above will be painful to put together in code.

Let's use the image alpha transparency to create the physics body for the sprite. Add to your code:

```
let l = SKSpriteNode(imageNamed:"L")
l.position = CGPoint(x: scene.size.width * 0.5,
  y: scene.size.height * 0.75)
l.physicsBody = SKPhysicsBody(texture: l.texture, size: l.size)
scene.addChild(l)
```

The convenience init `SKPhysicsBody(texture:, size:)` is the one that takes the burden off your shoulders and automatically detects the shape of your sprite. It takes two parameters – an `SKTexture` and a `CGSize`.

In the example above you use the image of the sprite to generate the physics body for that sprite – but you are not restricted to always using the same texture. If your sprite's image has a very complex shape, you can also use a different texture image with a rough outline of your sprite to improve the performance of your game.

If you adjust the `size` parameter of `SKPhysicsBody(texture:, size:)` you can also control how big the created body would be.

Look at the scene now – you will see that the L shape automatically got physics body following its outline. It conveniently falls on the circle shape for a stronger visual effect:

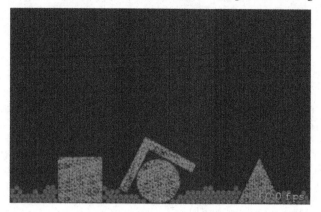

I am sure that you already wonder how would you debug a real game scene with many complex shapes – you can't always have particles raining over your game objects!

Apple to the rescue!

The Sprite Kit physics engine provides a very convenient feature – an API that enables physics debug output into your live scene. You can see the outlines of your objects, the joints between them, the physics constraints you create, and more.

Find the line in your code that enables the frame counter label `sceneView.showsFPS = true` and add below:

```
sceneView.showsPhysics = true
```

As soon as the scene starts rendering anew you will notice the shapes of all your bodies drawn in a bright blue color:

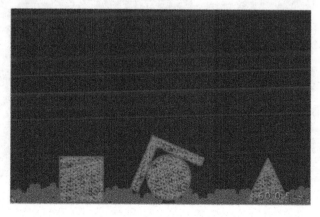

Besides the outlines of the shapes and the sand particles you would notice also four little circles in the four corners of the scene – these are the joints of the edge loop body.

Thanks to this feature you can do some really serious debugging of your physics setup.

Physics body properties

There's more to physics bodies than just collision detection. A physics body also has several properties you can set, such as how slippery, bouncy, or heavy the object is.

To see how body's properties affect the game physics, let's adjust the properties for the sand. Right now the sand falls down as if it is very heavy – much like granular rock. What about if the pieces were made out of soft, elastic rubber?

Add the following line to spawnSand():

```
sand.physicsBody!.restitution = 1.0
```

The restitution property describes how much energy the body retains when it bounces off of another body. Basically it's a fancy way of saying "bounciness".

Values can range from 0.0 (the body does not bounce at all) to 1.0 (the body bounces with the same force with which it started the collision). The default value is 0.2.

Oh my! The balls go crazy:

> **Note**: Sprite Kit sets all properties of physics bodies to *reasonable* values by default. An object's default weight is based on how big it looks on screen; restitution and friction are set to values matching the material of most everyday objects, and so forth.
>
> One more thing: while valid values for `restitution` must be from 0 to 1, the compiler won't complain if you supply values outside of that range. However, think about what it means to have a value greater than 1, for example. The body would actually end a collision with *more* energy than it had initially. That's not realistic behavior and it would quickly break your physics simulation, as the values grow too large for the physics engine to calculate accurately. It's not something I'd recommend in a real app, but give it a try if you want for fun.

Next, let's make the particles much more dense, so they are effectively heavier than the other shapes. Provided how bouncy they are, it should be an interesting sight!

Add this line to the end of `spawnSand()`:

```
sand.physicsBody!.density = 20.0
```

Density is defines as mass per unit volume – in other words, the higher the density of an object is and the bigger it is, the heavier it will be. Density defaults to 1.0, so here you are setting the sand as being 20x as dense as usual.

This results in the sand being heavier than the other shapes – the other shapes behave as-if they are styrofoam. You should end up with something like this on the screen after the simulation settles down:

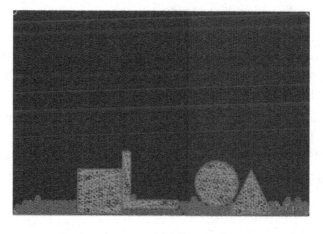

The red particles now literally throw their considerable weight around and push the bigger (but lighter) blue shapes aside. When you control the physics, size doesn't necessarily have to matter!

Here's a quick tour of the rest of the properties on a physics body:

- **friction**: This sets how "slippery" an object is. Values can range from 0.0 (the body slides smoothly along surfaces like an ice cube) to 1.0 (the body is quickly stopped while sliding along surfaces). The default value is 0.2.

- **dynamic**: Sometimes you want to use physics bodies for collision detection, but move the node yourself with manual movement or actions. If this is what you want, simply set dynamic to `false`, and the physics engine will ignore all forces and impulses on the physics body and let you move the node yourself.

- **usesPreciseCollisionDetection**: By default, Sprite Kit does not perform precise collision detection, because it's faster to avoid doing this unless absolutely necessary. However, this has a side effect in that if an object is moving very quickly (like a bullet), it might pass through another object. If this ever occurs, you should try turning this flag on to enable more accurate collision detection.

- **allowsRotation**: Sometimes you might have a sprite that you want the physics engine to simulate, but never rotate. If this is the case, simply set this flag to `false`.

- **linearDamping** and **angularDamping**: These values affect how much the linear velocity (translation) or angular velocity (rotation) decreases over time. Values can range from 0.0 (the speed never decreases) to 1.0 (the speed decreases immediately). The default value is 0.1.

- **affectedByGravity**: All objects default as affected by gravity, but you can set this off for a body simply by setting this to `false`.

- **resting**: The physics engine has an optimization where objects that haven't moved in a while are flagged as 'resting' so the physics engine does not have to perform calculations on them any more. If you ever need to "wake up" a resting object manually, simply set this flag to `false`.

- **mass and area**: These are automatically calculated for you based on the shape and density of the physics body. However, if you ever need to manually override these values, they are here for you.

- **node**: The physics body has a handy pointer back to the `SKNode` it belongs to.

- **categoryBitMask**, **collisionBitMask**, **contactBitMask**, and **joints**: You will learn all about these in Chapter 9, "Intermediate Physics" and Chapter 10, "Advanced Physics."

Applying an impulse

To wrap up with this introduction to physics in Sprite Kit, you're going to add some special effects to your app. Every now and then you'll apply an impulse to the particles – making them jump up like so:

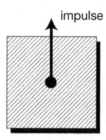

The effect will look like a seismic shock, which just throws everything in the air. Remember that impulses adjust an object's momentum immediately, like a bullet firing from a gun.

To test this out, add this new method to your playground:

```
func shake() {
  scene.enumerateChildNodesWithName("sand") { node, _ in
    node.physicsBody!.applyImpulse(
      CGVector(dx: 0, dy: random(min: 20, max: 40))
    )
  }
}
```

This function loops over all nodes in your scene having the name **sand** and applies an impulse to each of them. You apply an upwards impulse by having the x component always equal to zero, and having a random positive y component between 20 and 40.

You create the impulse as a `CGVector`, which is just like a `CGPoint`, but named so that it's more clear it's used as a vector instead of a point. You then apply the impulse to the anchor point of each particle. Since the strengths of the impulses are random, the shake effect will look pretty natural.

You need to call the function before you see everything jump up. Find the call to delay(seconds:, completion:) at the bottom of the file and add a line to the closure (change highlighted below):

```
delay(seconds: 2.0) {
  scene.physicsWorld.gravity = CGVector(dx: 0, dy: -9.8)

  scene.runAction(
    SKAction.repeatAction(
      SKAction.sequence([
        SKAction.runBlock(spawnSand),
        SKAction.waitForDuration(0.01)
      ]),
      count: 100)
  )

  delay(seconds: 8, shake)
}
```

You call shake() after 8 seconds have passed – this is to give time to the scene to settle down so you can observe the seismic shock.

It's a bit odd that the shapes do not jump by themselves but are rather "lifted" by the sand particles. Add this code to your shake() function to make them jump too:

```
scene.enumerateChildNodesWithName("shape") { node, _ in
  node.physicsBody!.applyImpulse(
    CGVector(dx: random(min:20, max:60),
             dy: random(min:20, max:60))
    )
}

delay(seconds: 3, shake)
```

First you loop through all shapes and apply a random vector impulse to each of them, then you call delay(seconds:, completion:) and tell it to call shake() again in three seconds.

Don't forget to replay those shakes back and forth using the scrubber – it's pretty funny!

You have now covered the basics of the physics engine in Sprite Kit, and you are almost ready to put these concepts to use in a real game. But first, it's time to push yourself to prove all that you've learned so far!

Challenges

This chapter has three challenges that will get you ready to create your first physics game. You'll learn about forces, and create a dynamic sprite with collision detection.

As always, if you get stuck you can find the solutions in the resources for this chapter – but do give it your best shot first!

Challenge 1: Porting your code from a playground into an Xcode project

The ultimate goal of developing some code or a demo in a playground is to one happy day take this code and use it in a real project. In this challenge you will port your playground code to an Xcode project that you can run on your iPhone.

Create a new Xcode project and as a project template select **iOS/Application/Game**. Enter any name you want and for language select **Swift** and for Game Technology **SpriteKit**.

Don't forget to import the image assets from the **Shapes** folder as you did for the playground earlier.

Now transfer all your code from the playground to your Xcode project – all scene code you can add to the `GameScene` class that Xcode created automatically for you. This task is a bit tedious since you will have to remove all references to the variable scene.

If you feel a bit put off by the manual labor – look into the book resources for this chapter. You will find the folder **SpriteKitPhysicsTest-Challenge1** – the solution is inside.

If you feel up to the challenge, here are few more tips you will appreciate along the way:

1. As mentioned earlier on iOS you do not need to release the triangle path, actually releasing it will cause the app to crash. So you can make your code multiplatform by adding a check if you are running on OS X like so:

```
#if os(OSX)
CGPathRelease(trianglePath)
#endif
```

2. The default Sprite Kit template loads the scene from an **.sks** file. You still did not learn about using the Scene Editor so you will have to ignore that feature for the time being. Instead of the default code that creates the scene just create one yourself:

```
let scene = GameScene(size: CGSizeMake(480, 320))
```

3. It will help if you set the project orientation to Landscape right away.

When you finish porting your code run the app in the iPhone Simulator to check if everything is working as expected:

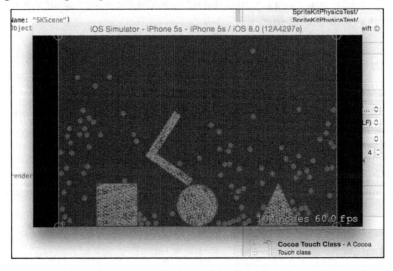

As an extra effort for this challenge – remove the periodic calls to shake() and invoke that function when the user taps the screen. That makes the scene interactive and more fun to play with!

Challenge 2: Forces

So far you've learned how to make the sand move immediately when you tap by applying an impulse. But what if you wanted to make objects move more gradually over time?

In this challenge, your goal is to simulate a very windy day that will blow your objects back and forth across the screen. Here are some guidelines on how to accomplish this:

First add these private instance variables:

```
var dt: NSTimeInterval = 0
var lastUpdateTime: NSTimeInterval = 0
var windForce: CGVector = CGVector(dx: 0, dy: 0)
var blowing: Bool = false
var timeUntilSwitchingDirection: NSTimeInterval = 0
```

Finally add this stub implementation of update:

```
override func update(currentTime: NSTimeInterval) {
  //1
  if lastUpdateTime > 0 {
    dt = currentTime - lastUpdateTime
  } else {
    dt = 0
  }
  lastUpdateTime = currentTime

  //2
  timeUntilSwitchingDirection -= dt

  if timeUntilSwitchingDirection < 0 {
    timeUntilSwitchingDirection = random(min: 1, max: 5)
    windForce = CGVector(dx: 0, dy: 0) //3 - Replace me!
  }

  //4 - Do something here!
}
```

Let's go over this section-by-section:

1. This is the same code from Zombie Conga that determines how much time has elapsed since the last frame.

2. This keeps track of how much time until the wind direction should switch (a random time between 1-5 seconds). Once the time elapses, it resets the time and sets the wind force.

3. Right now the wind forces is set to be (0, 0). Modify this to be between -50 and 50 along the x-axis, and 0 along the y-axis.

4. In section 4, apply this force to all nodes in the scene (both the sand and the shape objects). Similarly to `applyImpulse(impulse:)` physics bodies have an `applyForce(force:)` method.

Note that the difference between applying forces and impulses is that forces are something you apply every frame while the force is active, but impulses are something you fire once and only once.

If you get this working, you should see the objects slide back and forth across the screen as the wind direction changes:

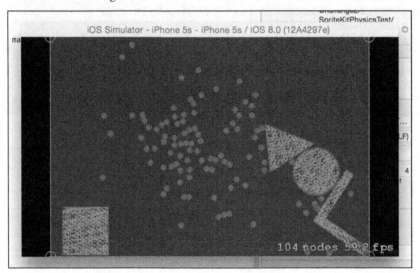

Challenge 3: Kinematic Bodies

In your games you might have some sprites you want to move with manual movement or custom actions, and others you want the physics engine to move. However, you still want collision detection to work even with sprites you move yourself.

As you learned earlier in this chapter, you can accomplish this by setting the `dynamic` flag on a physics body to `false`. Bodies that you move yourself (but that still have collision detection) are sometimes called **kinematic bodies**.

Here your challenge is to try this out for yourself, by making the circle sprite move wherever you tap. Here are a few hints:

• Set the `dynamic` property of the circle's physics body to `false` (after creating it).

• Inside `touchesBegan:withEvent:`, choose a single touch from the set and get the touch's location in the scene. You can use the same method you did in Zombie Conga to do this.

• Remove all actions from the circle, and then run a move to action to move the circle to the touch location.

If you get this working, you should see that everything is affected by the gravity, wind, and impulses except for the circle. However, the objects still collide with the circle as usual:

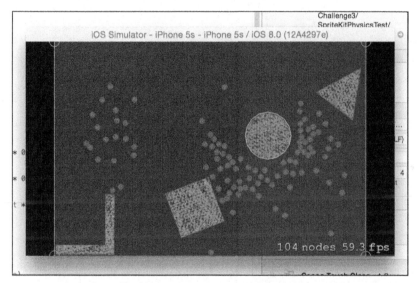

You probably noticed that the outline of the circle is now in green color – this shows you that this body is not dynamic, but kinematic one. Move the circle around by touching in different places on screen – the effect is pretty cool!

If you made it through all three of these challenges, congratulations! You now have a firm grasp of the most important concepts of the Sprite Kit physics engine, and you are now 100% ready to put these concepts to use in a physics-enabled game.

Over the next few chapters, you'll create a puzzle game that features a lazy cat, trampolines and, of course, out-of-this-world physics. Meow!

Chapter 10: Intermediate Physics

By Marin Todorov

In the last chapter, you got started with Sprite Kit physics by making a test project inside a playground. You learned how to create shapes, customize physics properties and even apply forces and impulses.

In this chapter, you'll begin to build the third minigame in this book: a puzzle game called Cat Nap. Here's what it will look like when you're finished:

In Cat Nap, you take the role of a cat who's had a long day and just wants to go to bed.

However, a thoughtless human has cluttered the cat's bed with scrap materials from their home renovation, preventing the cat from falling asleep! Of course, the cat sits on top of the scrap anyway undaunted.

Your job is to destroy the blocks by tapping them so the cat can comfortably fall into place. However, if you cause the cat to fall on the floor or tip onto his side, he'll wake up and get really cranky.

The puzzle is to destroy the blocks in the correct order so that the cat falls straight down. One wrong choice and—face the Wrath of Kitteh!

You'll build this game across the next four chapters, in stages:

1. **Chapter 9, Intermediate Physics**: You are here! You'll begin by creating the first level of the game, which is pictured above. You'll learn about physics-based collision detection and creating levels in Xcode's Scene Editor.

2. **Chapter 10, Advanced Physics:** You'll add two more levels to the game as you learn about interactive bodies, joints between bodies, composed bodies and more.

3. **Chapter 11, Crop, Video, and Shape Nodes:** You'll add special new blocks to Cat Nap while learning about additional types of nodes that allow you to do amazing things—like play videos, crop images and create dynamic shapes.

4. **Chapter 12, Effect Nodes and Core Image:** You'll wrap up Cat Nap by adding image filters to parts of the game, resulting in cool special effects.

Let's get started—there's nothing worse (or perhaps funnier[1]) than an impatient cat!

Getting Started

Start Xcode and select **File\New\Project...** from the main menu. Select the **iOS\Application\Game** template and click **Next**.

---

[1] http://www.youtube.com/watch?v=70wuAWxOEZA

Enter **CatNap** for the Product Name, **Swift** for Language, **Sprite Kit** for Game Technology and **Universal** for Devices. Click **Next**. Choose somewhere on your hard drive to save your project and click **Create**.

You want this app to run in landscape rather than portrait mode, so just as you did in Chapter 1, "Sprites," select the **CatNap** project in the project navigator and then select the **CatNap** target. Go to the **General** tab and ensure the only device orientation checked is **Landscape Left**.

You also need to modify this in one more spot. Open **Supporting Files\Info.plist**, and find the **Supported interface orientations (iPad)** entry. Delete the entries for **Portrait (bottom home button)** and **Portrait (top home button)** you see there, so that only the landscape options remain.

To get this game started on the right foot (or should we say paw), you should set up an app icon.

To set up an app icon, select **Images.xassets** in the project navigator on the left, and then select the **AppIcon** entry. Then, in the resources for this chapter, drag all of the files from the **Icons** sub-folder into the area on the right. You might need to drag a few individual files until Xcode matches all required icons. You should see the following when you're done:

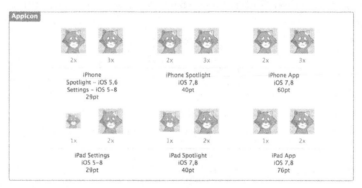

There's one final step. Open **GameViewController.swift** and modify the line that sets skView.ignoresSiblingOrder from true to false:

```
skView.ignoresSiblingOrder = false
```

This makes it so nodes with the same zPosition are drawn in the order in which they are added to the scene, which will make developing this game a bit simpler. Note that there is a performance cost incurred by setting this to false, but for a simple game like this it is no problem.

Build and run the project on the iPhone Simulator. You'll see the "Hello, World!" message nicely positioned in the center of the screen in landscape mode.

Introducing texture atlases

Before you can add sprites to the scene, you need sprite images, right? In the resources for this chapter, find the **Resources** folder, which includes all the images, sounds and other files you need for Cat Nap. Drag this folder into your project and make sure that **Copy items if needed**, **Create groups**, and the **CatNap** target are all checked.

At this point, you should see folders for the backgrounds, sounds and sprites in your project navigator:

You might also notice something about the way Xcode imported these files. The folder containing the sprites, **sprites.atlas**, is blue—what's that about?

In Sprite Kit, if you import a folder that ends with the extension **.atlas**, Sprite Kit will automatically pack all of the sprites in that folder into a special image called a **texture atlas**, also known as a **sprite sheet**. The texture atlas for Cat Nap looks something like this:

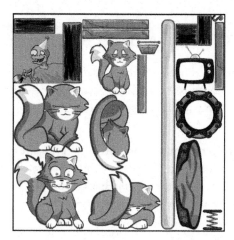

You'll learn more about sprite sheets in Chapter 26, "Performance: Texture Atlases." For now, you just need to know three things about texture atlases:

1. It's good practice to put your images into texture atlases. This will make your game run faster and use less memory.

2. Generally, you want to keep large images (like backgrounds) outside of texture atlases. Texture atlases are best for packing a bunch of small images together. This is why Cat Nap has one folder for backgrounds and another for sprites.

3. To put a set of images in a texture atlas, simply put the sprites in a folder that ends in **.atlas** and import them into your project. Then, create sprites the same way you usually would if the sprites were in individual files—Sprite Kit takes care of the rest behind the scenes!

> **Note:** Want to see how Xcode generates texture atlases for your app? Open Terminal, switch to Cat Nap's art directory and run this command:
>
> ```
> /Applications/Xcode.app/Contents/Developer/Tools/../usr/bi
> n/TextureAtlas sprites.atlas ~/Desktop/
> ```
>
> Xcode will then generate a directory called **sprites.atlasc** on your desktop that contains two image files (one with normal art and one with retina art) as well as a property list that describes where each sprite is in the images. Cool!

You've finished setting up your project—back to physics!

Getting started with Scene Editor

Cat Nap is a puzzle game based on levels that the player needs to solve one after the other. This is the perfect reason to learn to use Scene Editor—the very purpose of that built-in Xcode tool is to help you design levels without having to write everything in code.

The default Sprite Kit project template contains a level file already. Look in the project navigator for CatNap and you'll see a file called **GameScene.sks**. Select the file and you'll see a new editor panel that shows a gray background:

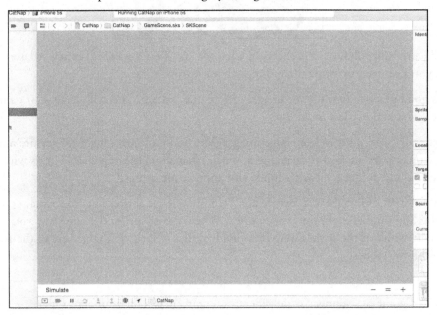

Click the minus (–) button in the bottom-right corner several times until you see a yellow rectangle appear. This is the boundary of your level scene. The default size for a new scene is 1024 x 768 pixels.

Since you are working on a universal game you will need to handle resolutions much bigger than 1024 x 768. For example the iPhone6 Plus has an effective pixel resolution of 1920 x 1080. iPad Mini with Retina display has a 2048 x 1536 pixel resolution.

For CatNap you are going to use 2048 x 1536 and let Sprite Kit to downscale the images for all devices with a smaller screen resolution. Let's resize the scene right now.

Open the **Assistant Editor** and select the **SKNode Inspector tab** then enter the new dimensions of the scene in:

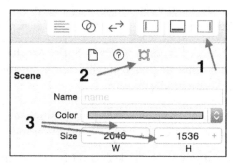

Now the scene has the proper size for all devices.

The Object Library

Make sure the Assistant Editor on the right-hand side is open. If it's not already open, click **View\Assistant Editor\Show Assistant Editor**.

In the Assistant Editor, select the **Object Library**:

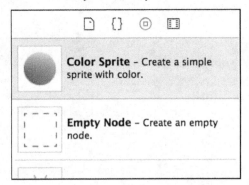

The Object Library shows you a list of objects you can drop onto your scene and configure via Xcode's Assistant Editor. When you load the scene file in your game, those objects will appear in their correct positions with the properties you set for them in Scene Editor. That's much better than writing code to position and adjust every game object one by one, isn't it?

Some of the objects you can use are:

• **Color Sprite:** This is the object you use to put sprites onscreen and the one you'll use the most throughout this chapter and the next. Do you remember physics bodies from the previous chapter? You can configure those on your sprites with no code, just with a few clicks in Scene Editor.

• **Shape Node:** These are special types of nodes in Sprite Kit that allow you to easily draw squares, circles, and other shapes. You will learn more about these in Chapter 12, "Crop, Video, and Shape Nodes."

• **Label:** You already know how to create labels programmatically, but with the Scene Editor you can create them by simply dragging and dropping.

• **Emitter:** Similarly, you can place a particle emitter in your scene and tell it which particle file in your project to load and display—all inside Scene Editor.

• **Light:** You can place a light node in your scene for a spotlight effect and have your scene objects cast shadows. We won't be covering lights in this book, but it's here if you need it.

The best thing about Scene Editor is that it's not only an editor—it also serves as a simulator. You can easily preview the scenes you edit without needing to run the app, as you'll see shortly.

Adding and positioning sprites

Make sure you see the yellow frame of your scene and that it fits into the editor window. Drag and drop a **Color Sprite** object into the editor area.

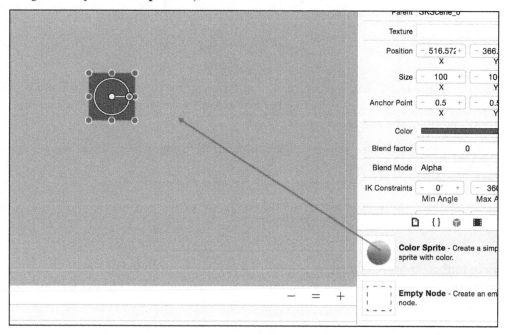

With the sprite selected (it is by default when you create a new one), you can see on the right-hand side all the properties you can control. Make sure you have the last tab on the right open, like so:

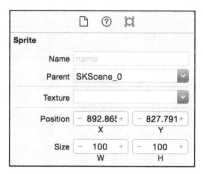

You might recognize a lot of these properties—you have used many of them programmatically in your Zombie Conga project. Let's have a quick look.

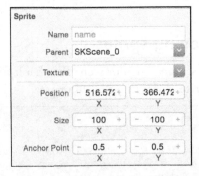

You can set the sprite's name, parent node and the image file that Sprite Kit will use as the texture. In addition, you can set (either by hand or by dragging with the mouse) the sprite's position, size and also its anchor point.

Further down in the same panel, you'll see the controls to adjust the sprite's scale, z-axis position and z-axis rotation:

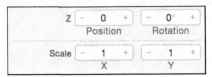

Even further down, you'll find more properties to experiment with, but what's important for this chapter is the section almost at the bottom called **Physics Definition**:

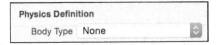

Currently, your sprite doesn't have a physics body and is therefore not taking part in a physics simulation. But you can easily change the type of the sprite's physics body to a rectangle or circle, or tell Sprite Kit to use the alpha mask of the texture image:

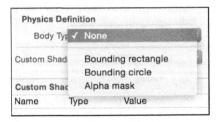

For now, keep the body type as **None**. You'll look at physics bodies in more detail in just a bit. In the meantime, let's begin designing Cat Nap's first level.

Select the sprite you just added to your scene, and on the right-hand side in the Assistant Editor, set its properties to the following values:

* **background.png** for **Texture**;

* **1024** for **Position X**; and

* **768** for **Position Y**.

This should start you off nicely with the level's background image:

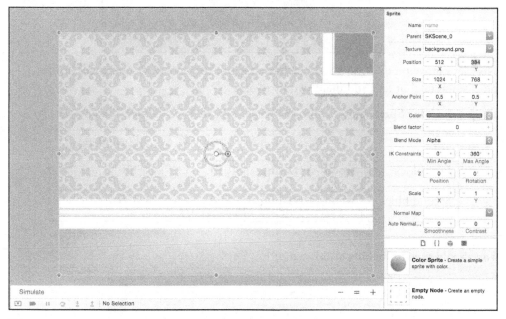

That was easy!

Next, you're going to add the cat bed to the scene. Drag another **Color Sprite** onto the scene and set its properties as follows:

* **cat_bed.png** for **Texture**;

* **1024** for **Position X**; and

* **272** for **Position Y**.

This will position the cat bed nicely a bit off the bottom of the scene.

Now let's move on to those wood blocks that get in the cat's way. There will be four blocks in total, but let's add them two by two.

Drop two **Color Sprite** objects onto the scene. Edit their properties like so:

	Texture	Position X	Position Y
First block	**wood_vert1.png**	1024	330
Second block	**wood_vert1.png**	1264	330

You should now be looking at this setup:

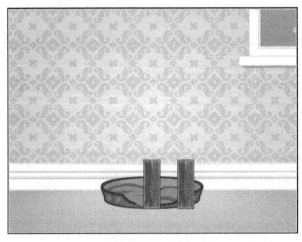

I hope you already appreciate how much easier it is to set objects onscreen via the Scene Editor instead of through code! However, I'm sure you also feel good knowing what goes on behind the scenes. Plus, you've still got a lot of coding to do in this project—just wait! :]

Now add the horizontal blocks. Drop two more **Color Sprite** objects onto the scene and adjust their properties like in the table below:

	Texture	Position X	Position Y
Third block	**wood_horiz1.png**	**1050**	**580**
Fourth block	**wood_horiz1.png**	**1050**	**740**

The scene continues to develop—all the obstacles are there now and you're missing only your main character:

Drop one last **Color Sprite** object onto the scene. This will be the cat. Edit it as follows:

	Texture	Position X	Position Y
Cat	**cat_sleepy.png**	1024	1036

Your scene for this level is now complete:

Build and run, and you'll see that your scene appears on the screen (along with the "Hello, World" label from the template code):

These are the basic skills you need to use Scene Editor to create levels for your games. You'll learn even more about Scene Editor later, but first, let's throw down some code.

Connecting sprites to variables

Next you need to connect the sprites you created in the scene editor to variables, so you can access the sprites in code. For those familiar with UIKit development, this is somewhat like connecting views in your Storyboard to outlets.

Open **GameScene.swift** and replace the contents of the file with the following:

```
import SpriteKit

class GameScene: SKScene {

  var bedNode: SKSpriteNode!
  var catNode: SKSpriteNode!

}
```

catNode and bedNode are the cat and cat bed sprite nodes, respectively. You're going to connect these to the sprites you created via Scene Editor in a moment.

First, override the scene's didMoveToView() to do some additional scene initialization. Just as you did for Zombie Conga, you need to set the scene's playable area—when you're finished developing Cat Nap, it will be an awesome iPhone, iPad and OS X game.

Add the following code inside the GameScene class:

```
override func didMoveToView(view: SKView) {
  // Calculate playable margin
  let maxAspectRatio: CGFloat = 16.0/9.0 // iPhone 5
  let maxAspectRatioHeight = size.width / maxAspectRatio
  let playableMargin: CGFloat =
    (size.height - maxAspectRatioHeight)/2
  let playableRect = CGRect(x: 0, y: playableMargin,
    width: size.width, height: size.height-playableMargin*2)

  physicsBody = SKPhysicsBody(edgeLoopFromRect: playableRect)
}
```

As for Zombie Conga, you begin with the aspect ratio of the iPhone 5 screen and then define the frame of the playable area based on the current scene size.

Since Cat Nap is a physics-based game, you set the detected playable frame as the edge loop for the scene. That's all there is to it—Sprite Kit will now automatically confine your game objects within the area you designate for the gameplay.

Next, connect those cat and bed variables to the corresponding sprites in your scene.

Open **GameScene.sks** and select the cat sprite. In the Assistant Editor, enter **cat** in the Name field. Then select the cat bed and enter **bed** in the Name field.

Next, switch back to **GameScene.swift** and add this to didMoveToView(view:):

```
bedNode = childNodeWithName("bed") as! SKSpriteNode
catNode = childNodeWithName("cat") as! SKSpriteNode
```

childNodeWithName() is a method you call on your scene that looks through its children and gives you back the first node with the required name. Here, you look up the bed and cat sprite based on the name you set in the Scene Editor.

> **Note:** You can set multiple child nodes to have the same name—that's an easy way to group nodes, as you learned in the previous chapter. If you have more than one child node with the same name, instead of using childNodeWithName() you should use enumerateChildNodesWithName(usingBlock:).

Now you have a reference to each sprite, so you can modify them in code. To test this out, add the following two lines to the end of didMoveToView(view:):

```
bedNode.setScale(1.5)
catNode.setScale(1.5)
```

Build and run, and you'll see giganto-cat!

Now that you've proved you can modify the sprites in code, comment out those two lines to revert back to normal (sorry about that, giganto-cat):

```
//bedNode.setScale(1.5)
//catNode.setScale(1.5)
```

Adding physics

You already know from the previous chapter that for the physics engine to kick in, you need to create physics bodies for your sprites. In this section, you're going to learn three different ways to do that.

Using simple shape bodies in Scene Editor

Looking at your scene as it is now, you can't help but notice that those wooden blocks would make perfect use of physics bodies with rectangular shapes.

You already know how to create rectangular bodies in code, so let's look at how to do it in Scene Editor.

First, select the four block sprites in your scene. Hold the **Cmd** key on your keyboard and click on each block until you have them all selected.

In the **Physics Definition** section in the Assistant Editor, change the selection for **Body Type** to **Bounding Rectangle**. This will open a section with additional properties, allowing you to control most aspects of a physics body. You read about each of these properties in the last chapter.

The default property values look about right for your wood blocks: the bodies will be **dynamic**, can **rotate** when falling and are **affected by gravity**. The Mass field says **Multiple Values** because Sprite Kit assigned a different mass to each of the wooden blocks based on its size.

That's all you need to do to set up the blocks' physics bodies. You will notice that now the blocks are outlined in blue to indicate their physics bodies:

There's one last thing to do: Select all four wooden blocks again, scroll to the top of the Assistant Editor and enter **block** in the Name field. Now you can easily enumerate all the blocks in the scene.

Simulating the scene

Let's quickly explore another feature of Scene Editor.

You already know about the (–) and (+) buttons at the bottom-right of the Scene Editor window. But there's also another button on the left side of that same panel that you haven't yet tried.

Click the **Simulate** button and watch what happens:

Scene Editor instantly simulates the scene! How cool is that?

In Scene Editor, you can simulate a scene easily without going through the hassle of running the complete game, greatly speeding the process of designing and testing multiple levels. The simulation will run all your physics, particle emitters, fields and more.

Now click the same button, which at present says **Edit,** and you'll return to editing mode.

Creating simple bodies from code

What if you want a physics body to be smaller than a node's bounding rectangle or bounding circle? That's also easy to do. Let's see if you can apply your skills from the last chapter in Cat Nap.

The cat bed itself won't participate in the physics simulation, instead remaining static on the ground and exempt from collisions with other bodies in the scene.

The cat bed will still have a physics body, though, because you need to detect when the cat falls on the bed. So the bed needs a small, non-interactive body for the purpose of detecting contacts.

Since you've already connected your `bedNode` instance variable to the bed sprite, it's a matter of creating the body in code, and you already posses that skill.

Switch to **GameScene.swift** and add the following to `didMoveToView(view:)`:

```
let bedBodySize = CGSize(width: 40, height: 30)
bedNode.physicsBody = SKPhysicsBody(
   rectangleOfSize: bedBodySize)
bedNode.physicsBody!.dynamic = false
```

As you learned in the previous chapter, a sprite's physics body doesn't necessarily have to match the sprite's size or shape. For the cat bed, you want the physics body to be much smaller than the sprite, because you only want the cat to fall happily asleep when he hits the exact center of the bed. Cats are known to be picky, after all!

For this purpose, you first create a `CGSize` that is 40 by 30 points, and then you initialize a rectangular body with that size for the bed.

Since you never want the cat bed to move, you set its `dynamic` property to `false`. This makes the body static, which allows the physics engine to optimize its calculations because it can ignore any forces applied to this object.

> **Note**: Notice how you need to force unwrap the physicsBody property – it's an *Optional* property so you need to use ! when you are sure there is a body attached to the sprite, or ? if you don't know that.

Open **GameViewController.swift** and add the following line inside viewDidLoad(), just after the code that declares skView:

```
skView.showsPhysics = true
```

Build and run the project in the iPhone Simulator. You'll see your scene come alive:

Look at the little rectangle toward the bottom of the screen—that's the physics body of the cat bed! It's green so that you remember it's not a dynamic physics body.

I'm sure you also noticed that your carefully built obstacle tower appeared messed up. That happened because the bed body pushed aside your central wooden block. To fix this, you'll need to set the block bodies and the bed body so that they don't collide with each other, something you'll learn how to do a bit later.

Using custom bodies

Let's move to the last object in the game scene—your main character.

Looking at the cat sprite, you can instantly guess that a rectangular or a circular body won't do for it. From the last chapter, you know you can create a physics body based on the sprite image itself. Let's give that a try.

Open **GameScene.sks** and select the cat sprite. Then for **Body Type**, select **Alpha Mask**. Sprite Kit generates quite a detailed body shape for your cat, shown as a blue outline around the cat:

This is impressive, but not optimal—such a detailed shape costs a lot for the physics engine. The alpha mask body type works well for simpler bodies, but for a complex shape like your cat, it's just not worth it.

In addition, the automatically-generated cat body can't stand on its own. The cat's big, fluffy tail gives considerable weight to the left side of the sprite, while the paws sticking out from its body detract from its stability. Consequently, the cat keeps rolling over and off the blocks. Not good!

Luckily, you can fix this from code.

Select the cat sprite and set its **Body Type** to **None**. Then, open **GameScene.swift** and add this code to didMoveToView(view:):

```
let catBodyTexture = SKTexture(imageNamed: "cat_body")
catNode.physicsBody =
  SKPhysicsBody(texture: catBodyTexture, size: catNode.size)
```

First, you create a new texture object out of an image called **cat_body.png.** Open **cat_body.png** (you can find that image in the project navigator along with the other project assets) and you'll see it's a rough outline of your cat image:

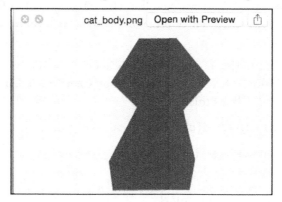

This shape doesn't include the cat's tail and it doesn't follow the outline of the paws (using a flat bottom edge instead)—the problems you had with the automatically-generated shape.

Next, you just create a body for the cat sprite using an SKPhysicsBody instance and the appropriate texture and size. You're already familiar with how to do this from the previous chapter.

Build and run the game again, and check out the debug drawing of the cat's body—and this time, it stays where it should. Excellent work!

Now that your first level is set up, let's get the player in the mood for puzzles by turning on some soothing and delightful background music.

Gratuitous background music

Just as you did in Chapter 7, "Labels," you'll integrate the SKTUtils library so you can easily play background music. Some of the other methods will come in handy in the next chapter, as well.

You can find SKTUtils in the root folder for this book. Drag the entire **SKTUtils** folder into the project navigator in Xcode. Make sure **Copy items if needed** and the **CatNap target** are both checked. Click **Finish**.

Finally, add this code to didMoveToView() to start the music:

```
SKTAudio.sharedInstance().playBackgroundMusic(
    "backgroundMusic.mp3")
```

Build and run, and enjoy the happy tune!

Controlling your bodies

So far, you know how to create physics bodies for sprites and let the physics engine do its thing.

But in Cat Nap, you want a bit more control than that:

• **Categorizing bodies.** You want to keep the cat bed from colliding with the blocks, and vice versa. To do this, you'll need a way to categorize bodies and set up collision flags.

• **Finding bodies.** You want to enable the player to destroy a block by tapping it. To do this, you'll need a way to find a body at a given point.

• **Detecting collisions between bodies**. You want to detect when the cat hits the cat bed, so he can get his beauty sleep. To do this, you'll need a way to detect collisions.

You'll investigate these areas over the next three sections. By the time you're done, you'll have implemented the most important parts of the minigame!

Categorizing bodies

Sprite Kit's default behavior is for all physics bodies to collide with all other physics bodies. If two objects are occupying the same point (like the bottom-right brick and the cat bed), the physics engine will automatically move one of them aside.

The good news is, you can override this default behavior and specify whether two physics bodies collide with each other.

There are two steps to do this:

1. **Define the categories**. The first step is to define categories of physics bodies—for example, block bodies, cat bodies and cat bed bodies.

   In Sprite Kit, you define those categories using a **bit mask**, which is a way of using a 32-bit integer as a set of 32 individual flags you can turn on or off. This means, at most, you can have 32 unique object categories in your app—so choose your categories wisely!

2. **Set the category bit mask**. Once you have your set of categories, you specify what categories each physics body belongs (a physics body can belong to more than one category) to by setting its category bit mask.

3. **Set the collision bit mask**. You also need to specify the collision bit mask for each physics body. This controls which categories of bodies it should collide with.

Let's start with step 1 and define the categories for Cat Nap. Still in **GameScene.swift**, add the category constants **inside** the GameScene class, preferably at the top, just under the class keyword:

```
struct PhysicsCategory {
  static let None:  UInt32 = 0
  static let Cat:   UInt32 = 0b1   // 1
  static let Block: UInt32 = 0b10  // 2
  static let Bed:   UInt32 = 0b100 // 4
}
```

This way, you can comfortably access body categories like PhysicsCategory.Cat and PhysicsCategory.Bed, and if you want to use them outside of your GameScene class, you can do so by using the form GameScene.PhysicsCategory.Cat.

You've probably already spotted that each of the categories turns on another bit:

	Decimal	Binary
PhysicsCategory.None	0	00000000
PhysicsCategory.Cat	1	00000001
PhysicsCategory.Block	2	00000010
PhysicsCategory.Bed	4	00000100

This is very handy (and very fast for the physics engine to calculate) when you want to specify that the cat should collide with all block bodies and the bed. You can then say the collision bitmask for the cat is `PhysicsCategory.Block |`
`PhysicsCategory.Bed` (read as "block OR bed"), which produces the logical OR of the two values:

	Decimal	Binary
`PhysicsCategory.Block	PhysicsCategory.Bed`	6	00000110

> **Note**: If you are not quite at ease with binary arithmetic, you can read more about bitwise operations here:
>
> http://en.wikipedia.org/wiki/Bitwise_operation

Let's move to steps 2 and 3 and set the category and collision bit masks for each object, starting with the blocks.

Go back to **GameScene.sks** and **select the four wooden blocks** as you did earlier. Have a look at the current **Category Mask** and **Collision Mask**.

Both are set to the biggest integer value possible, thus making all bodies collide with all other bodies. If you convert the default value of 4294967295 to binary, you'll see that it has all bits turned on and therefore, it collides with all other objects:

4294967295 =	11111111111111111111111111111111

It's time to implement custom collisions. Edit the blocks' properties like so:

- For **Category Mask**, enter the value of `PhysicsCategory.Block`, which is **2**;

- For **Collision Mask**, enter the bitwise OR value of `PhysicsCategory.Cat | PhysicsCategory.Block`, which is **3**.

> **Note**: Just put the decimal values in the boxes—that is, for the Collision Mask, enter **3**.

Here, you set each block's body to be of the `PhysicsCategory.Block` category, and you set all of the blocks to collide with both the cat and other blocks.

Next, set up the bed. You create this body from code, so go back to **GameScene.swift** and add the following to the end of `didMoveToView()`:

```
bedNode.physicsBody!.categoryBitMask = PhysicsCategory.Bed
bedNode.physicsBody!.collisionBitMask = PhysicsCategory.None
```

With the code above, you set the category of the bed body and then set its collision mask to `PhysicsCategory.None`—you don't want the bed to collide with any other game objects.

At this point, you've set up both the wooden blocks and the cat bed with the proper categories and collision masks. Build and run the game one more time:

Just as expected, you see a block right in front of the bed's body without either body pushing the other away. Nice!

Finally, set up the cat. Since you create the physics body for your cat sprite in code, you also have to set the category and collision mask in **GameScene.swift**. Add this to didMoveToView():

```
catNode.physicsBody!.categoryBitMask = PhysicsCategory.Cat
catNode.physicsBody!.collisionBitMask = PhysicsCategory.Block
```

The cat has its own category, PhysicsCategory.Cat, and is set to collide only with blocks.

> **Note:** A physics body's collisionBitMask value specifies which categories of objects should affect the movement of *that* body when those two bodies collide. But remember, you set the bed's dynamic property to false, which already ensures that no forces will ever affect the bed. So there's no need to set the bed's collisionBitMask.
>
> Generally, there is never a reason to set the collisionBitMask for an object with its dynamic property set to false. Likewise, edge loop bodies are always treated as if their dynamic property is false, even if it isn't. So there is never a reason to set the collisionBitMask for an edge loop, either.

Now you know how to make a group of bodies pass through some bodies and collide with others.

You'll find this technique useful for many types of games. For example, in some games you want players on the same team to pass through each other, but collide with enemies from the other team.

Finding bodies

Often in games, you want to find out what physics bodies are at a given point. Sprite Kit provides a method on the physics world called enumerateBodiesAtPoint(usingBlock:) that does exactly that:

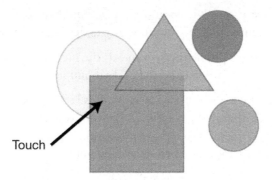

Touch

There's also a similar method, which might be more interesting for your own projects, called enumerateBodiesInRect(usingBlock:).

In Cat Nap, you're going to use nodeAtPoint() to find the first body occupying the point tapped by the user. This method will be fine for Cat Nap, because the objects the user can tap won't really overlap, so you don't need to do an enumeration—you can simply grab and use the first node.

Add the following new method to GameScene:

```
func sceneTouched(location: CGPoint) {
  //1
  let targetNode = self.nodeAtPoint(location)
  //2
  if targetNode.physicsBody == nil {
    return
  }
  //3
  if targetNode.physicsBody!.categoryBitMask ==
    PhysicsCategory.Block {

    targetNode.removeFromParent()
    //4
    runAction(SKAction.playSoundFileNamed("pop.mp3",
      waitForCompletion: false))

    return
  }
}
```

This method checks if the tapped object is a block and destroys it if so. Let's go over it section by section:

1. You get the first node at the given location, if any. nodeAtPoint() returns an optional **SKNode** because there might not be any nodes at the given point.

2. If the node doesn't have a physics body, you exit the method. This will generally be the case if the player taps anywhere on the background image.

3. Since all destructible bodies are of the category PhysicsCategory.Block, it's easy to determine whether to destroy the current body. If so, you use the node's removeFromParent() method to remove it from the scene, which will also remove the node's physics body from the physics world of your scene.

4. As a final touch (a horrible pun, intended!), you make the blocks *pop* by playing **pop.mp3**.

Now add this method, which calls sceneTouched() whenever the user taps the screen:

```
override func touchesBegan(touches: Set<NSObject>,
                           withEvent event: UIEvent) {
  let touch: UITouch = touches.first as! UITouch
  sceneTouched(touch.locationInNode(self))
}
```

You get the position of the touch in the scene, the same as you did for Zombie Conga, and then pass the location of the touch to sceneTouched() for handling.

Build and run the project, and now you can tap blocks to destroy them:

Try destroying the blocks in different orders. The following illustration shows one way to correctly land the cat in the cat bed and one way to send him tumbling! Since you haven't added any win/lose capability yet, you'll have to restart the game after each try.

Detecting collisions between bodies

Very often in games, you'd like to know if certain bodies are in contact. Two or more bodies can "touch" or pass through each other, depending upon whether or not they're set to collide. In both cases, they are in contact:

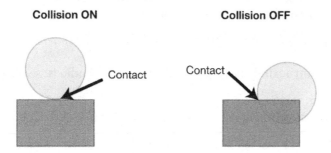

In Cat Nap, you want to know whether certain pairs of bodies touch:

1. If the **cat touches the floor**, it means it's on the ground but out of its bed, so the player fails the level.

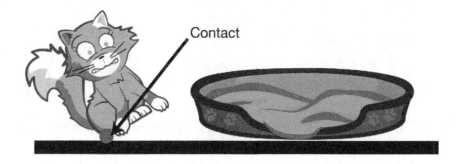

2. If the **cat touches the bed**, it means it landed successfully on the bed, so the player solved the level.

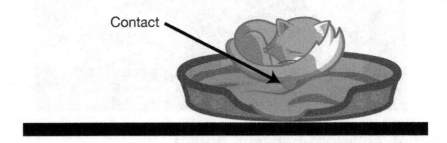

Contact

Sprite Kit makes it easy for you to receive a callback when two physics bodies make contact. The first step is to implement the SKPhysicsContactDelegate methods. In Cat Nap, you'll implement these methods in GameScene.

Scroll to the top of **GameScene.swift** and add the SKPhysicsContactDelegate protocol to the class declaration line so it looks like this:

```
class GameScene: SKScene, SKPhysicsContactDelegate {
```

The SKPhysicsContactDelegate protocol defines two methods you can implement in GameScene:

• didBeginContact() will tell you when two bodies first make contact.

• didEndContact() will tell you when two bodies end their contact.

The diagram below shows how these methods would be called for the case of two bodies passing through each other:

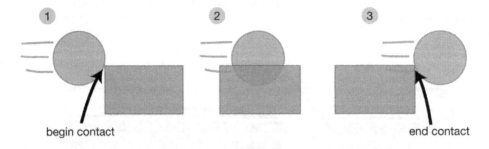

begin contact   end contact

You'll most often be interested in didBeginContact(), because much of your game logic will occur when two objects touch.

However, there are times you'll want to know when objects stop touching. For example, you may want to use the physics engine to test when a player is within a trigger area. Perhaps entering the area sounds an alarm, while leaving the area silences it. In a case such as this, you'll need to implement `didEndContact()`, as well.

Let's try this out. First, you need to add a new category constant for the edges of the screen, since you want to be able to detect when the cat collides with the floor. To do this, scroll to the top of **GameScene.swift** and add this new `PhysicsCategory` value:

```
static let Edge:  UInt32 = 0b1000 // 8
```

Then, find this line inside `didMoveToView()`:

```
physicsBody = SKPhysicsBody(edgeLoopFromRect: playableRect)
```

And just below it, add the following:

```
physicsWorld.contactDelegate = self
physicsBody!.categoryBitMask = PhysicsCategory.Edge
```

First, you set `GameScene` as the contact delegate of the scene's physics world. Then, you assign `PhysicsCategory.Edge` as the body's category.

Build and run to see the results of your actions so far.

Hmm… that's not right. All the blocks fall through the edge! And just seconds ago, the project worked fine!

Let me pinpoint the problem for you right away: The world edge now has a category (`PhysicsCategory.Edge`) but the blocks aren't set to collide with it. Therefore, they fall through the floor. Meanwhile, the cat bed's `dynamic` property is set to `NO`, so it can't move at all.

Fix that now. Open **GameScene.sks** in Scene Editor and select the four wooden blocks as you did before. Then, change the Collision Mask for their bodies from 3 to **11**.

	Decimal	Binary
`PhysicsCategory.Block | PhysicsCategory.Cat` `| PhysicsCategory.Edge`	11	00001110

Build and run the game now, and you'll see the familiar scene setup. But try popping all the blocks out of the cat's way, and you'll see the cat fall through the bottom of the screen and disappear. Goodbye, Kitty!

By now, you can probably figure out such a problem in a jiff. The cat doesn't collide with the scene's edge loop, of course!

Go back to **GameScene.swift** and change the line where you set the cat's collision mask so that the cat also collides with the scene boundaries:

```
catNode.physicsBody!.collisionBitMask = PhysicsCategory.Block |
    PhysicsCategory.Edge
```

This ought to keep him onscreen. Build and run the project again, and everything will appear (and behave!) as normal.

Now for the new stuff... You've learned to use the `categoryBitMask` to set what categories a physics body belongs to, and the `collisionBitMask` to set what categories a physics bodies collides with. Well, there's another bit mask: `contactTestBitMask`. You can probably guess from its name what it does.

You can use `contactTestBitMask` to detect contact between a physics body and designated categories of objects. Once you've set this up, Sprite Kit will call your physics contact delegate methods at the appropriate time.

You want to receive callbacks when the cat makes contact with either the edge loop body or the bed body, so add this line to the end of `didMoveToView()`:

```
catNode.physicsBody!.contactTestBitMask = PhysicsCategory.Bed |
  PhysicsCategory.Edge
```

That's all the configuring you need. Every time the cat body makes contact with either the bed body or the edge loop body, you'll get a message.

Now to handle those contact messages, add this contact delegate protocol method to your class:

```
func didBeginContact(contact: SKPhysicsContact) {
  let collision: UInt32 = contact.bodyA.categoryBitMask |
    contact.bodyB.categoryBitMask

  if collision == PhysicsCategory.Cat | PhysicsCategory.Bed {
    println("SUCCESS")
  } else if collision ==
      PhysicsCategory.Cat | PhysicsCategory.Edge {
    println("FAIL")
  }
}
```

Have a look at the parameter this method receives. It's of class `SKPhysicsContact` and tells you a lot about the contacting bodies:

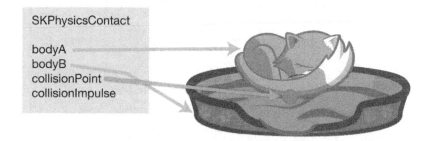

There is no way to guarantee a particular object will be in `bodyA` or `bodyB`. There are various ways you can find out, such as by checking the body's category or for some property of the body's node.

But this simple game contains only four categories (so far), which correspond to the integer values 1, 2, 4, 8. That makes it simple to check for contact combinations—just use bitwise OR as you did to define collision and contact bitmasks.

Categories	2-Category Combinations
Cat: 1	Cat (1) | Block (2) = 3
Block: 2	Block (2) | Block (2) = 2
Bed: 4	Cat (1) | Bed (4) = 5
Edge: 8	... other combinations

> **Note**: If you feel the ground loosening under your feet when you read about comparing bitmasks and such, consider reading this short but informative article: http://en.wikipedia.org/wiki/Mask_(computing).

Inside your implementation of `didBeginContact()`, you first add the categories of the two bodies that collided and store the result in `collision`. The two `if` statements check `collision` for the combinations of bodies in which you are interested:

• If the two contacting bodies are the cat and the bed, print out "SUCCESS".

• If the two contacting bodies are the cat and the edge, print out "FAIL".

Build and run, and lose on purpose. You should see the "FAIL" message print out several times in the console, as shown below:

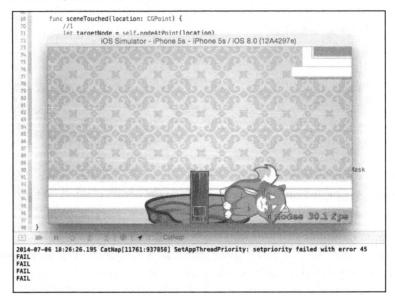

> **Note**: When the cat falls on the ground, you see several FAIL messages. That's because the cat bounces off the ground just a tiny bit by default, so it ends up making contact with the ground more than once. You'll fix this later.

Finishing touches

You're almost there—you already know when the player should win or lose, so you just need to do something about it!

There are three steps remaining:

• Add an in-game message;

• Handle losing; and

• Handle winning.

Adding an in-game message

First, add this new category value to the `PhysicsCategory` structure in **GameScene.swift**:

```
static let Label: UInt32 = 0b10000 // 16
```

Then, add a new method to show messages on the screen—with the help of the physics engine.

```
func inGameMessage(text:String) {
  //1
  let label: SKLabelNode = SKLabelNode(
    fontNamed: "AvenirNext-Regular")
  label.text = text
  label.fontSize = 128.0
  label.color = SKColor.whiteColor()
  //2
  label.position = CGPoint(x: frame.size.width/2,
                           y: frame.size.height/2)

  label.physicsBody = SKPhysicsBody(circleOfRadius: 10)
  label.physicsBody!.collisionBitMask = PhysicsCategory.Edge
  label.physicsBody!.categoryBitMask = PhysicsCategory.Label
  label.physicsBody!.contactTestBitMask = PhysicsCategory.Edge
```

```
    label.physicsBody!.restitution = 0.7
    //3
    addChild(label)
    //4
    runAction(SKAction.sequence([
      SKAction.waitForDuration(3),
      SKAction.removeFromParent()
      ]))
  }
```

Let's go over this step by step:

1. In step one, you create a Sprite Kit label node just as you learned to do in Chapter 7, "Labels."

2. You then add a physics body to the label and set it to collide with the edge of the screen. You also make it pretty bouncy. Note that you can add a physics body to any kind of node, not just sprite nodes!

3. You add the label to the scene.

4. Finally, you run a sequence action, which waits for a bit and then removes the label from the screen.

The effect of invoking this method is an onscreen label that falls down and bounces a bit before it disappears.

Now you're going to add a method to help you restart the current level. You'll simply call presentScene() again on the SKView of your game and it will reload the whole scene.

Add the newGame() method to your scene class:

```
func newGame() {
  view!.presentScene(GameScene(fileNamed:"GameScene"))
}
```

In just one line of code, you:

1. Create a new instance of GameScene out of **GameScene.sks** by using the init(fileNamed:) initializer.

2. Pass the new GameScene instance to presentScene(), which removes the current, used scene and shows the new and shiny scene.

With all the helper methods in place, you can continue implementing lose and win sequences.

Handling losing

Begin with losing. Add the initial version of the `lose` method:

```
func lose() {
  //1
  catNode.physicsBody!.contactTestBitMask = PhysicsCategory.None
  catNode.texture = SKTexture(imageNamed: "cat_awake")
  //2
  SKTAudio.sharedInstance().pauseBackgroundMusic()
  runAction(SKAction.playSoundFileNamed("lose.mp3",
    waitForCompletion: false))
  //3
  inGameMessage("Try again...")
  //4
  runAction(SKAction.sequence([
    SKAction.waitForDuration(5),
    SKAction.runBlock(newGame)
  ]))
}
```

Let's go over this section by section:

1. You disable further contact detection by setting `catNode`'s `contactTestBitMask` to `PhysicsCategory.None`. This fixes the problem you saw earlier where you received multiple contact messages. Then, you change `catNode`'s texture to the awakened kitty.

2. You play a fun sound effect when the player loses. To make the effect more prominent, you pause the in-game music by calling `pauseBackgroundMusic()` on `SKTAudio`. Then, you run an action to play the effect on the scene.

3. You spawn a new in-game message that says, "Try again..." to keep your players motivated. :]

4. Finally, you wait for five seconds and restart the level.

That's it for now—head to `didBeginContact()` and replace `println("FAIL")` with:

```
lose()
```

Now you have a working fail sequence. Give it a try.

The five-second delay after the player fails is just enough time for the player to witness the raging cat animation and the onscreen message.

When the level restarts, things don't look exactly the same as when you first started the game:

Ah! You tried to be too smart.

There's an extra line in the `viewDidLoad()` of your `GameViewController` class that sets the scene scale mode. To make the scene stretch properly after it's reloaded, you'll have to implement this in `newGame()`, as well.

Replace the `newGame()` method with the following:

```
func newGame() {
  let scene = GameScene(fileNamed:"GameScene")
  scene.scaleMode = .AspectFill
  view!.presentScene(scene)
}
```

Build and run again, and do your best to lose again. This time around, no matter how many times you lose the game, the level always shows up just right:

Handling winning

Now it would only be fair to add a success sequence, right? Add this new method to your scene class:

```
func win() {
  //1
  catNode.physicsBody = nil
  //2
  let curlY = bedNode.position.y + catNode.size.height/3
  let curlPoint = CGPoint(x: bedNode.position.x, y: curlY)
  //3
  catNode.runAction(SKAction.group([
    SKAction.moveTo(curlPoint, duration: 0.66),
    SKAction.rotateToAngle(0, duration: 0.5)]))
  //4
  inGameMessage("Nice job!")
  //5
  runAction(SKAction.sequence([SKAction.waitForDuration(5),
                               SKAction.runBlock(newGame)]))
  //6
  catNode.runAction(SKAction.animateWithTextures([
    SKTexture(imageNamed: "cat_curlup1"),
    SKTexture(imageNamed: "cat_curlup2"),
    SKTexture(imageNamed: "cat_curlup3")], timePerFrame: 0.25))
  //7
  SKTAudio.sharedInstance().pauseBackgroundMusic()
  runAction(SKAction.playSoundFileNamed("win.mp3",
    waitForCompletion: false))
}
```

There's a lot of code here, but luckily, it's mostly review. Let's go over it step by step:

1. First, you set the `physicsBody` of the cat to `nil` so that the physics simulation no longer affects `catNode`.

2. You want to animate the cat *onto* the bed, so you calculate the proper y-coordinate for the cat to settle down upon, and use that with `bedNode`'s x-coordinate as the target.

3. You run an action on `catNode` to move the cat to the target position, while rotating it to zero degrees to ensure it's nice and straight.

4. You show a success message onscreen.

5. You restart the level. This part is identical to the `lose` method.

6. You animate the cat so he curls up in happiness, using the same technique you learned in Zombie Conga.

7. Finally, you stop the background music and play the winning tune included with the chapter's resources.

As a last step, in `didBeginContact()`, find the line `println("SUCCESS")` and replace it with:

```
win()
```

Build and run the project now, and you have a winning sequence in place—in both senses of the word:

Believe it or not, you've completed another minigame! And this time, your game also has a complete physics simulation in it. Congratulations!

Don't be sad that your game has only one level. You'll continue to work on Cat Nap in the next chapter, adding two more levels and some crazy features before you're done.

Make sure you aren't rushing through these chapters. You are learning a lot of new concepts and APIs, so iterating over what you learn is the key to retaining it.

That's one reason why the challenges at the end of each chapter are your best friends. If you feel confident about everything you've covered so far in Cat Nap, why not take on the ones below?

Challenges

This chapter introduced a lot of new APIs, so in case you get stuck, the solutions are in the resources folder for this chapter. But have faith in yourself—you can do it!

Challenge 1: Count the bounces

Think about that in-game message that you show when the player wins or loses the level. Your challenge is to fine-tune when it disappears from the scene.

More specifically, your challenge is to count the number of times the label bounces off the bottom margin of the screen and kill the message on exactly the fourth bounce. Working through this will teach you more about **SKNode**s and custom actions during contact detection. Base your solution on the fact that you can attach an arbitrary object to any node in the scene.

You can attach an object to a node by storing it in **SKNode**'s `userData` property, which is an **NSMutableDictionary**. Count the bounces and store the count in an `Int`, then attach the `Int` to the label sprite.

Your solution should follow this guide:

- Delete (or comment) the code that removes the label after a timeout.

- Implement a new condition in `didBeginContact()` that checks for a contact between the edge and the label.

- Add the proper contact bitmasks to the contacting bodies.

- Remember, there's no way to guarantee whether the label's body will be in `bodyA` or `bodyB`. So check the category bit mask to figure out which body is the label's body, and get a reference to that physics body's node (i.e., the label). Hint: physics bodies have a property called `node` that points back to the Sprite Kit node for that body.

- Check to see if the label's userData dictionary is nil. If it is, create a new mutable dictionary with a single entry with the key bounceCount and the value of 1 as an Int. If userData isn't nil, look up the bounceCount entry and increment the number.

- Please note that userData is of the precise type NSMutableDictionary. That means, when you create a new dictionary to store in userData, you'll have to do it like so to match the required data type:

```
labelNode.userData = NSMutableDictionary(object: 1 as Int,
forKey: "bounceCount")
```

- If the number of bounces equals 4, kill the label—that is, remove it from its parent node.

This exercise should get you on the right path to implementing more complicated contact handlers. Imagine the possibilities—all the custom actions that you could make happen in a game depending on how many times two bodies touch, or how many bodies of one category touch the edge, and so forth.

Chapter 11: Advanced Physics

By Marin Todorov

In the last chapter, you saw how easy it is to create responsive game worlds with Sprite Kit, especially when using Scene Editor. By now, you're a champion of creating sprites and physics bodies and configuring them to interact under simulated physics.

But perhaps you're already thinking in bigger terms. So far, you only can move shapes letting gravity, forces and impulses affect them. But what if you want to constrain the movement of shapes with respect to other shapes—for example maybe you want to pin a hat to the top of the cat's head that can rotate slightly back and forth based on physics? Dr. Seuss would be proud!

In this chapter, you'll learn how to do things like this by adding two new levels to Cat Nap—three if you successfully complete the chapter's challenge! By the time you're done, you'll have brought your knowledge of Sprite Kit physics to an advanced level and will be able to apply this newfound force in your own apps.

The Sprite Kit game loop, round 3

To get you back on track with Cat Nap, you're going to add one last touch to Level 1: a smarter failure detection system.

Specifically, you want to detect whether the cat is leaning to either side by more than 25 degrees. If he is, you want to wake up the cat, at which point the player should fail the level.

To achieve this, you'll check the position of the cat every frame, after the physics engine does its job. But in order to do this, you have to understand a bit more about the Sprite Kit game loop.

Back in the third chapter of this book, you learned that the Sprite Kit game loop looks something like this:

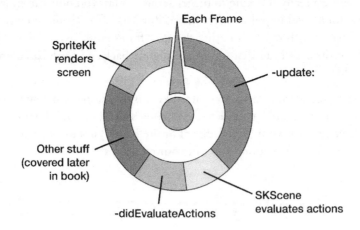

Now it's time to introduce the next piece of the game loop: simulating physics.

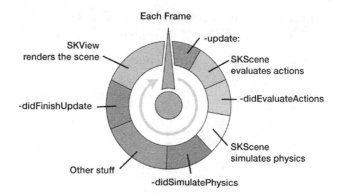

After executing `update()` and evaluating the sprite actions, and just before rendering the sprites onscreen, Sprite Kit performs the physics simulation and moves the sprites and bodies accordingly. After this occurs, you have a chance to perform any code you might like by implementing `didSimulatePhysics()`. This is the perfect spot to check to see if the cat is tilting too much!

To do this, you'll use a function from `SKTUtils`, the library of helper methods you added to the project in the previous chapter. In particular, you'll use a handy method that converts degrees to radians.

Inside **GameScene.swift**, implement `didSimulatePhysics()` as follows:

```
override func didSimulatePhysics() {
  if let body = catNode.physicsBody {
    if body.contactTestBitMask != PhysicsCategory.None &&
       fabs(catNode.zRotation) > CGFloat(45).degreesToRadians() {
      lose()
    }
  }
}
```

Here you perform three tests:

1. **Does the cat node have a body?** You check to see if `catNode` has a physics body using Swift's standard `if let` statement.

2. **Is the cat still active?** To determine this, you check whether the cat's `contactTestBitMask` is set. Remember, you disable the cat's contact bitmask when the player completes the level.

3. **Is the cat tilted too much?** Specifically, is the absolute value of the cat's `zRotation` property more than the radian equivalent of 45 degrees?

When all three of these conditions are true, then you call lose() right away, because obviously the cat is falling over and should wake up immediately!

Build and run, then fail the level on purpose. The cat wakes up while it's still in the air, before it even touches the ground.

This is a bit more realistic behavior, as it's hard to sleep when you're 45 degrees vertical! Although I admit, I probably could have done that in my college days.

Introducing level 2

So far, you've been working on a game with a single game scene. Cat Nap, however, is a level-based puzzle game, so you need a way to present different levels onscreen.

In this section of the chapter, you're going to give the game the ability to present different levels, and you'll add a second level right away. Level 2 will feature new interactive physics objects, like springs, ropes and hooks.

Except, for this game, you'll call the springs "catapults"!

Fortunately for the cat, this level will have just one catapult. Here's how the level will look when you've finished:

Notice that catapult just underneath the cat and the hook on the ceiling. This looks rather nefarious, but I promise no animals will be harmed in the making of this game.

To win the level, the player first needs to tap the catapult. This will launch the cat upward, where he will be caught by the hook, and the player can then destroy the blocks before releasing the cat. The player can then tap the hook to release the cat, who can then descend safely to the bed with no blocks obstructing the path.

On the other hand, if the player destroys the blocks and then taps the catapult, the cat won't rise high enough for the hook to catch him, causing the player to lose the level.

Loading levels

Lucky for you, you are actually already loading levels in your game!

You have a single level so far, and the level file is called **GameScene.sks.** You load it and show it onscreen, then you implement the game logic in your GameScene class.

What you need to do is create more **.sks** files for each of Cat Nap's levels and then load and display them one after the other onscreen—provided the player solves them successfully.

First of all, to avoid confusion, rename GameScene.sks to **Level1.sks**.

Next, you need to add a factory method on your GameScene class that takes a level number and creates a scene by loading the corresponding **.sks** file from the game bundle.

Add the following property and class function to `GameScene`:

```
//1
var currentLevel: Int = 0
//2
class func level(levelNum: Int) -> GameScene? {
  let scene = GameScene(fileNamed: "Level\(levelNum)")
  scene.currentLevel = levelNum
  scene.scaleMode = .AspectFill
  return scene
}
```

`currentLevel` is the property that will hold the current level's number. The class method `level()` takes in a number and calls `GameScene(fileNamed:)`. If the level file is successfully loaded, you set the current level number on the scene and make it scale correctly.

Now you should make a few changes to your project. Open **GameViewController.swift** and find the following line in `viewDidLoad()`:

```
if let scene = GameScene.unarchiveFromFile("GameScene") as?
GameScene {
```

Replace it with:

```
if let scene = GameScene.level(1) {
```

That's much nicer on the eye, isn't it?

Now open **GameScene.swift** and find `newGame()`. You can improve it with the new factory method as well, so replace the complete method body with simply:

```
view!.presentScene(GameScene.level(currentLevel))
```

Build and run, and make sure the game works as usual. Good work - now you can focus on building Level 2.

Scene Editor, round 2

After doing so much in code, it'll be nice to use Scene Editor again.

From Xcode's menu, select **File\New\File...**, then **iOS\Resource\SpriteKit Scene** and click **Next**.

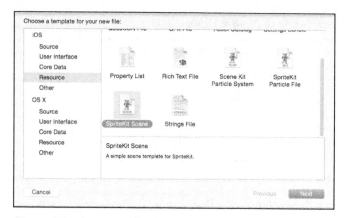

Name the new file **Level2.**sks and click **Create**.

As soon as you save the file, Xcode opens it in Scene Editor. Zoom out until you see the yellow border:

With the Scene Editor skills you already possess from the last chapter, it shouldn't be too much work to set up the scene.

First of all resize the scene to 2048 x 1536:

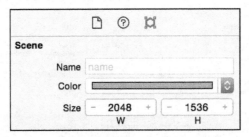

Next add six Color Sprite objects to the scene and set their properties as follows:

Texture	Name	Position (X, Y)	Body Type	Category Mask	Collision Mask
background.png		1024, 768	None		
cat_bed.png	bed	1024, 272	None		
cat_sleepy.png	cat	1024, 890	None		
wood_horiz1.png	block	1024, 260	Bounding Rectangle	2	43
wood_horiz1.png	block	1024, 424	Bounding Rectangle	2	43
spring.png	spring	1024, 588	Bounding Rectangle	32	11

Whoa, that's a lot of objects! Most of the setup you're doing is recreating what you have in Level 1—a background image, a cat, a cat bed and some blocks.

In this level, you also add a sprite for the spring and set its category to 32. You'll add this category to your code a bit later.

Give the level a try. Head to **GameViewController.swift** and replace this:

```
if let scene = GameScene.level(1) {
```

With this:

```
if let scene = GameScene.level(2) {
```

Now you can start the game from the second level, rather than having to solve Level 1 just to test Level 2. You're allowed to cheat in your own game!

Build and run the project, and you'll see the initial setup for your new level:

You'll see the cat passes straight through the spring. This is because your existing code doesn't yet know about your new spring objects.

Catapults

Since catapults are a new category of objects for your game, you also need a new method to set them up on the scene. The code will be almost identical to the code that adds the blocks onscreen, so I won't spell out all the details, and you can move through this part quickly.

First, open **GameScene.swift** and add a new category bitmask to `PhysicsCategory` for the new body types:

```
static let Spring:UInt32 = 0b100000 // 32
```

For the catapult bodies, you'll use the new body category constant, `PhysicsCategory.Spring`.

To make the cat to sit on top of the catapult, you need to enable collisions between them. Change the line in `didMoveToView()` that sets the cat's `collisionBitMask` to include `PhysicsCategory.Spring`, like so:

```
catNode.physicsBody!.collisionBitMask = PhysicsCategory.Block |
    PhysicsCategory.Edge | PhysicsCategory.Spring
```

Now your catapult should behave. Build and run the game, and check it out.

One small change in code – one big step for sleepy cats!

Next, let's make the catapult hurl that kitty when the player taps on the spring sprite. It's actually quite easy—if the player taps on the catapult, you'll apply an impulse to the spring (which will bounce the cat as well, if the cat is on top of the spring). Scroll to sceneTouched() and add the following code at the bottom of the method:

```
if targetNode.physicsBody!.categoryBitMask ==
  PhysicsCategory.Spring {

  let spring = targetNode as! SKSpriteNode
  spring.physicsBody!.applyImpulse(CGVector(dx: 0, dy: 190),
    atPoint: CGPoint(x: spring.size.width/2,
                     y: spring.size.height))

  targetNode.runAction(SKAction.sequence([
    SKAction.waitForDuration(1),
    SKAction.removeFromParent()]))

  return
}
```

If the tapped body is a catapult, you cast it to type SKSpriteNode and store it in the spring variable. Then, you apply an impulse to its body using applyImpulse(atPoint:), similar to what you did in Chapter 8 on the sand particles. Finally, you remove the catapult after a delay of one second and play a sound effect.

Build and run the game again, and tap on the catapult:

You have liftoff!

Right now, when catapulted, the kitty just makes a flip in the air and lands on its head. That's why you need to add the swinging from the ceiling hook that you saw in the beginning of the chapter showing how the completed level 2 will look like.

When catapulted the kitty will jump in the air, catch on the hook, and than jump down straight in its bed. Mrrow!

Joints: An overview

In Sprite Kit, joints allow you to constrain the positions of two bodies relative to each other. Let's consider what practical uses you might find in a game for the five different types of joints that Sprite Kit offers.

Fixed joint

A fixed joint gives you the ability to fix two physics bodies together. Imagine you have two objects and you nail them to each other with a number of big, rusty nails. The two objects are fixed together, so if you take one of them and throw it, the other one will fly with it. Fixed!

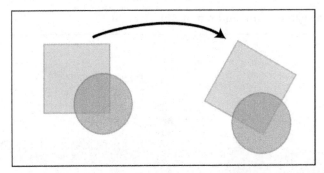

Often, you want an object to be immoveable. Just fix it to the scene edge loop and you are ready to go. Other times, you want a complex object that the player can destroy into pieces. Just fix the parts together and remove the joints when you want the body to fall apart.

Limit joint

A limit joint sets the maximum distance two objects can be from each other. The two bodies can be closer than that distance, but not farther apart. You can imagine the limit joint as a soft but strong rope that connects two objects. On the diagram below, the ball is connected to the square via a limit joint—it can bounce around, but can never move farther away than the length of the limit joint:

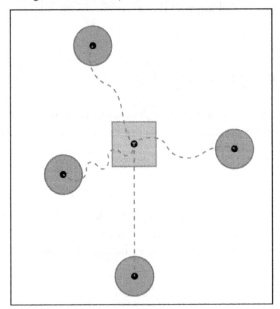

For example, this can be useful to make sure that different players always stay within a fixed range of each other in multiplayer games.

Spring joint

A spring joint acts much like a limit joint, but the connection between the two bodies is also elastic, much like if the two bodies were connected by a spring. As with the limit joint, this joint is useful to simulate rope connections, especially ropes made of elastic. If you have a game about bungee jumping, the spring joint will be of great help!

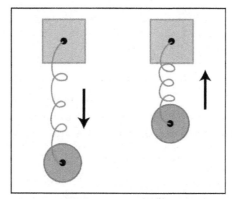

Pin joint

A pin joint fixes two objects around a certain point, the anchor of the joint. This allows both to rotate freely around this point—if they don't collide, of course. You can imagine the pin joint as a big screw that keeps two objects tightly together, but still allows them to rotate:

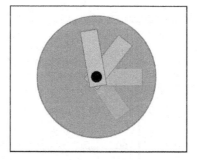

If you were to build a clock, you'd use a pin joint to fix the hands to the dial, or if you were to build a physics body for an airplane, you'd use a pin joint to attach the propeller to the plane's nose.

Sliding joint

A sliding joint fixes two bodies on an axis along which they can freely slide; you can further define the minimum and maximum distances the two bodies can be from each other while sliding along the axis.

The two connected bodies act as though they are moving on a rail and there's a limit on their distance from each other:

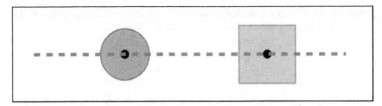

You can use the sliding joint for complex interactive bodies, like a crane with a control cabin on top and a robotic arm, both hanging on the crane's jib—the cabin and the robotic arm being the two bodies that slide along the crane's jib axis.

> **Note:** You can apply more than one joint to a physics body if you'd like. For example, you could use a pin joint to attach a clock face to its hour hand, and add a second pin joint to connect the clock face with its minute hand.

Using joints in your hook object

Consider this blueprint for the hook object that you're going to create and attach to the ceiling:

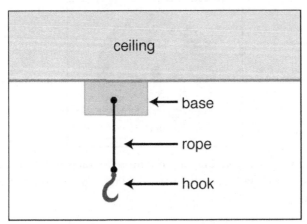

You'll have one body (the base) fixed to the ceiling, another body that will be the hook itself, and finally, you'll have the rope that "connects" them together.

To make this structure work, you'll use joints, of course. Specifically, you'll use two types of joints:

1. **A fixed joint** to fix the base to the ceiling.

2. **A spring joint** to connect the hook to the base.

The easiest way to learn how to use joints is to try them out for yourself—so let's get started by attaching the base to the ceiling.

Fixed joint

First you need to add the relevant sprites in Scene Editor. Open **Level2.sks** and add two color sprites, configured as follows:

Texture	Name	Position (X, Y)	Body Type	Category Mask	Collision Mask
wood_horiz1.png		1024, 1466			
hook_base.png	hookBase	1024, 1350	Bounding Rectangle	[Default]	[Default]

hookBase is the node that the hook and its rope will be attached to. The base itself is going to be fixed on the ceiling by a joint to the scene edge body.

You might wonder what is the purpose of the wood block – it does not even have a physics body! Let's look at how the playable area looks like on an iPhone and an iPad:

On a 4" screen iPhone the scene cuts out somewhere just before the top edge of the hook base – it looks like the hook base is built into the ceiling. But on an iPad (remember that the screen aspect ratio is different?) you can see more of the scene and if it wasn't for the wood piece on top it would look like the hook base just floats in the air.

So the wood chunk doesn't play any other than just a visual role in the level – further on an iPhone it's out of the screen bounds so the player does not even see it.

Next you can continue with the code to make the hook swing. You need a way to access all its parts so add the following properties in **GameScene.swift**:

```
var hookBaseNode: SKSpriteNode!
var hookNode: SKSpriteNode!
var hookJoint: SKPhysicsJoint!
var ropeNode: SKSpriteNode!
```

You'll use these properties to store references to the three nodes and the joint that will make up the hook construction plan described earlier. You don't need to create a property for the joint that connects the hook to the base, because you won't ever need to modify it after you create it.

Set up the hook's base by adding the following method:

```
func addHook() {
  hookBaseNode = childNodeWithName("hookBase") as? SKSpriteNode
  if hookBaseNode == nil {
      return
  }

  let ceilingFix =
    SKPhysicsJointFixed.jointWithBodyA(hookBaseNode.physicsBody,
        bodyB: physicsBody, anchor: CGPointZero)
  physicsWorld.addJoint(ceilingFix)
}
```

This connects your `hookBaseNode` variable with the appropriate sprite in the scene file. Notice the method returns if the scene doesn't have a node named `hookBase`. That will be important when your player tries to load other levels that don't use the hook object.

Then you use `SKPhysicsJointFixed`'s factory method to create a joint instance between the `hookBaseNode`'s body and the scene's own body, which is the edge loop. You also give the joint an anchor point, which tells the scene at what location to create the connection between the two bodies.

You always specify the anchor point in scene coordinates. When you attach a body to the scene's body, you can safely pass any value as the anchor point, so you use ({0, 0}). Also note that the sprites you're joining must already be added as children of the scene before you create the joint.

Finally, you add the joint to the scene's physics world. Now these two bodies are connected until death do them part—or until you remove that joint.

> **Note:** When creating a fixed joint, the two bodies don't actually need to be touching—each body simply maintains its relative position from the anchor point.
>
> Also, note that you could get this same behavior more simply without using a joint at all. Instead, you could make the physics body static, either by unchecking the **Dynamic** field in the Scene Editor or by setting the `physicsBody`'s `dynamic` property to `false`. This would actually be more efficient for the physics engine, but you're using a fixed joint here for learning purposes.

Now call this new method at the end of `didMoveToView()`:

```
addHook()
```

Build and run the game, and you'll see the hook base fixed soundly to the top of the screen:

Look at that line going from the bottom-left corner to the top of the scene—this is the debug physics drawing representing the joint you just created. It indicates that there is a joint connecting the scene itself (with a position of (`0, 0`)) to the hook.

So far, so good. Let's see how to create other types of joints, as this is a heavily-used concept in physics-based games.

Spring joint

You need one more body category for the hook, so add this new value to the
`PhysicsCategory`:

```
static let Hook:  UInt32 = 0b1000000 // 64
```

Next, add the following lines to the end of `addHook()` to add the hook sprite:

```
hookNode = SKSpriteNode(imageNamed: "hook")
hookNode.position = CGPoint(x: hookBaseNode.position.x,
                            y: hookBaseNode.position.y - 100)

hookNode.physicsBody =
  SKPhysicsBody(circleOfRadius: hookNode.size.width/2)
hookNode.physicsBody!.categoryBitMask = PhysicsCategory.Hook
hookNode.physicsBody!.contactTestBitMask = PhysicsCategory.Cat
hookNode.physicsBody!.collisionBitMask = PhysicsCategory.None

addChild(hookNode)
```

You create a sprite as usual, set its position and create a physics body for it. Then, you set
the category bitmask to `PhysicsCategory.Hook` and instruct the physics world to
detect contacts between the hook and the cat.

The hook doesn't need to collide with any other objects. You will implement some
custom behavior for it that default Sprite Kit physics doesn't provide.

You position the hook sprite just under the ceiling base, as the distance between the base
and the hook is precisely the length of the rope that will hold them together.

Now, create a spring joint to connect the hook and its ceiling holder together by adding
this to `addHook()`:

```
let ropeJoint =
  SKPhysicsJointSpring.jointWithBodyA(hookBaseNode.physicsBody,
    bodyB: hookNode.physicsBody,
    anchorA: hookBaseNode.position,
    anchorB:
      CGPoint(x: hookNode.position.x,
              y: hookNode.position.y+hookNode.size.height/2))
physicsWorld.addJoint(ropeJoint)
```

Using a factory method similar to the one you just used for the ceiling joint, you connect
`hookNode`'s body and `hookBaseNode`'s body with a spring joint. You also specify the

precise points (in the scene's coordinate system) where the rope connects to the two bodies.

Build and run the game now. If all is well, you'll see your hook hanging in the air just under the ceiling:

The rope joint works fine, but there's no rope sprite for the player to see. It's almost as if the poor cat's house is haunted—now he'll never get any sleep!

The Sprite Kit game loop, round 4

At long last, it's time to introduce the final missing piece of the Sprite Kit game loop: constraints!

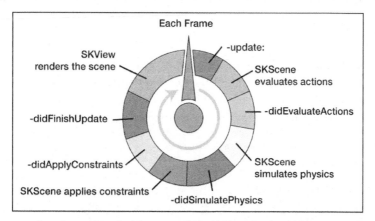

As you can see, after Sprite Kit finishes simulating physics, it performs one last step: applying something called "constraints" to the scene (and notifying your scene that this has occurred). Let's take a look at how this works.

Constraints: An overview

Constraints are a handy new feature of Sprite Kit introduced in iOS 8 that allow you to easily ensure certain relationships are true regarding the position and rotation of sprites in your game.

The best way to understand constraints is to see this in action. Add the following code to the end of `didMoveToView()`:

```
let rotationConstraint =
  SKConstraint.zRotation(
    SKRange(lowerLimit: -π/4, upperLimit: π/4))
catNode.constraints = [rotationConstraint]
```

There are two steps to using constraints:

1. **Create the constraint**. This example creates a constraint that limits z rotation from -45° to 45°, and applies it to the cat node.

2. **Add the constraint to a node**. To add the constraint to a node, simply add the constraint into the constraints array on the node.

> **Note**: To type π in your source code hold the **Alt** key on your keyboard and press **P**. π is just a constant defined in SKTUtils, you can press Cmd and click on it in Xcode to jump to its definition. If you prefer that you could use `CGFloat(M_PI)` instead.

After Sprite Kit finishes simulating the physics, it runs through each node's constraints and updates the position and rotation of the node so that the constraint stays true. Build and run to see this in action:

As you can see, even though the physics simulation sometimes determines that according to gravity the cat should fall over beyond 45°, during the constraint phase of the game loop Sprite Kit updates the cat's rotation to 45° so the constraint stays true.

This was just a test, so comment out the previous code:

```
//let rotationConstraint =
//SKConstraint.zRotation(
//  SKRange(lowerLimit: −π/4, upperLimit: π/4))
//catNode.constraints = [rotationConstraint]
```

You could also add constraints to:

• Limit a sprite so it stays within a certain rectangle

• Make a turret in your game point toward where it's shooting

• Constrain a sprite's movement along the x-axis

• Limit the rotation of a sprite to always be within a certain range

Note that constraints and joints are two different things: constraints work on any node whether they have a physics body or not, while joints require physics bodies. In your games, you can choose the best tool for the job—often you will find yourself using both.

After this crash course in constraints, you're ready to use a real constraint in your Cat Nap game. Let's finish building the hook object by adding the final piece: the rope.

Implementing a rope with a constraint

In this section, you're going to position a rope sprite on the screen, based on the position coordinates that the physics simulation calculates for the hook and the hook base.

Scroll to the middle of the body of **addHook()** and find this line:

```
hookNode = SKSpriteNode(imageNamed: "hook")
```

Just above it, add the rope sprite node so the rope will appear under the hook sprite:

```
ropeNode = SKSpriteNode(imageNamed: "rope")
ropeNode.anchorPoint = CGPoint(x: 0, y: 0.5)
ropeNode.zRotation = CGFloat(270).degreesToRadians()
ropeNode.position = hookBaseNode.position
addChild(ropeNode)
```

As usual, you add a new sprite from an atlas texture and set its position in the scene. This time, let's highlight few details:

- The rope image is horizontal, so here you rotate the rope 270° so that it is vertical.

- You don't create a physics body for the rope, because you don't want it to collide or make contact with other bodies.

- Finally, to make the rope sprite swing like a pendulum, you set its anchor point to one of its ends, effectively pinning it to the scene on that end.

Now that you have the rope in your scene, let's position the hook so that it is placed exactly at the end of the rope.

Change the line of code that sets hookNode's position in addHook() to place it relative to the rope's width (you use width because the rope image is horizontal), like this:

```
hookNode.position = CGPoint(
  x: hookBaseNode.position.x,
  y: hookBaseNode.position.y - ropeNode.size.width )
```

Now you're going to use a constraint to make sure the rope is always oriented toward the hook sprite, which makes it appear that the rope is connected to the hook.

Add the following code at the end of addHook():

```
let range = SKRange(lowerLimit: 0.0, upperLimit: 0.0)
let orientConstraint =
  SKConstraint.orientToNode(hookNode, offset: range)
ropeNode.constraints = [orientConstraint]
```

SKConstraint.orientToNode(offset:) produces a constraint object that automatically changes the zRotation of the node to which it's being applied so that the node always points toward another "target" node.

You can also provide an offset range to the constraint if you don't want to orient the node with perfect precision. Since you want the end of the rope and the hook to be tightly connected, you provide a zero range for the constraint.

Finally, you set the orientConstraint as the sole constraint for the ropeNode.

One last step: there's nothing making the hook move at the moment, so add this line so you can see the constraint in action:

```
hookNode.physicsBody!.applyImpulse(CGVector(dx: 50, dy: 0))
```

This applies an impulse to the hook node so that swings around its base. Build and run the game again, and check out your moving customized level-object:

Remember that there are two things going on here to make this behavior work:

- You set up a **joint** connecting the hook to the base. This makes it so the hook is always a certain distance away from the base, so that it appears to "swing" around the base.

- You set up a **constraint** making the rope always orient itself toward the hook. This makes the rope appear to follow the hook.

Together, this makes for a pretty sweet effect!

Note: The previous edition of this book instructed readers to manually orient the rope inside the scene's `update()` method. On every invocation of `update()`, the code calculated the angle between the base and hook sprites and set this angle for the `zRotation` of the rope.

This is still a perfectly valid strategy, but since Sprite Kit now has built-in constraints that can handle this for you, this edition uses the new approach. In your games, choose whichever is easiest for you.

There's one thing I should mention to keep my conscience clear: Right now, the rope is represented by just one sprite. That means your rope is more like a rod.

If you'd like to create an object that better resembles a rope, you could create several shorter sprite segments and connect them to each other, as shown below:

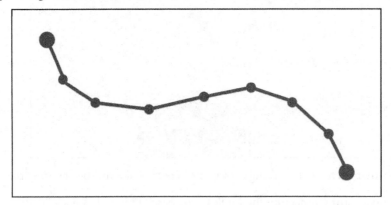

In this case, you might want to create physics bodies for each rope segment and connect them to each other with pin joints.

More constraints

So far, you have seen examples of the `zRotation()` and `orientToNode(offset:)` constraints.

There are a number of other types of constraints you can create in Sprite Kit beyond these. Here's a reference of what's available:

- `positionX()`, `positionY()`, and `positionX(y:)`: These allow you to restrict the position of a sprite within a certain range on the x-axis, y-axis, or both. For example, this can be useful to restrict the movement of a sprite within a certain rectangle on the screen.

- `orientToPoint(offset:)` and `orientToPoint(inNode:offset:)`: Just like you can make a sprite orient itself to another sprite (like you made the rope orient itself toward the hook), you can make a sprite always orient itself toward a certain point as well. This could be useful to make a turret point toward where the user taps for example.

- `distance(toNode:)`, `distance(toPoint:)`, and `distance(toPoint:inNode)`: These allow you to ensure that two nodes (or a node and a point) are are always within a certain distance of each other. This is similar to a limit joint, except that it works on any node, whether or not it has a physics body.

Creating and removing joints dynamically

You need to make a few final touches to get the whole cat-hooking process to work: You need to check for hook-to-cat contact and create and remove a joint to fix the cat to the rope dynamically.

Add this to the end of `didBeginContact()`:

```
if collision == PhysicsCategory.Cat | PhysicsCategory.Hook {
  catNode.physicsBody!.velocity = CGVector(dx: 0, dy: 0)
  catNode.physicsBody!.angularVelocity = 0

  let pinPoint = CGPoint(
    x: hookNode.position.x,
    y: hookNode.position.y + hookNode.size.height/2)

  hookJoint = SKPhysicsJointFixed.jointWithBodyA(contact.bodyA,
    bodyB: contact.bodyB, anchor: pinPoint)
  physicsWorld.addJoint(hookJoint)
}
```

First, you alter the physics simulation manually a bit. You intervene in Sprite Kit's business and force a velocity and angular velocity of zero on the cat's body. You do this to calm him down in mid-air when he's about to get hooked, because otherwise the cat might swing for a time on the hook, and you don't want to make the player wait too long before their next move.

The important point here is that you can manually alter the physics simulation. How great is that? Don't be afraid to do this—making the game fun is your top priority.

Next, you get all the data for the new dynamic joint instance from your `SKPhysicsContact` object: the two bodies and the point where they touched. Using this data, you create a new `SKPhysicsJointFixed` and add it to the world.

You also have to make `didSimulatePhysics()` respect the fact that the kitty is "hooked," so that rotating to angles more than the margin of 45 degrees is okay with the game. Scroll to that method and wrap the call to `lose()` inside an `if` check (new code is highlighted below):

```
if hookJoint == nil {
  lose()
}
```

Now when the cat swings on the hook, he won't wake up. Build and run the game again, and play around!

When the cat hangs from the ceiling, you can safely destroy the blocks over the cat bed. But you're still missing one thing—the cat needs to jump off the hook and into the bed. To make that happen, you need to remove the joint you just added.

Add the following method to `GameScene`:

```
func releaseHook() {
  catNode.zRotation = 0
  hookNode.physicsBody!.contactTestBitMask =
PhysicsCategory.None
  physicsWorld.removeJoint(hookJoint)
  hookJoint = nil
}
```

First, you set the `zRotation` of the cat to zero, so it won't accidentally wake up when unhooked.

Removing the hook joint is as easy as calling `removeJoint` on your physics world object. Finally, you set `hookJoint` to `nil` because you won't need it any more.

Now call this method when the player taps the cat. Inside `sceneTouched()`, add this at the end:

```
if targetNode.physicsBody?.categoryBitMask ==
PhysicsCategory.Cat
  && hookJoint != nil {
  releaseHook()
}
```

If the player taps the cat and there's a living `hookJoint` object, you invoke `releaseHook()`. That's all!

Build and run the game again, and try to land the cat on the bed. You probably don't need this advice, but: tap on the catapult, tap on all the blocks and then tap the cat to solve the level:

Creating joints dynamically is a fun and powerful technique—I hope to see you use it a lot in your own games!

Compound shapes

It's time to move onto the third and final level of Cat Nap.

In this level, you'll tackle another concept in game physics, one related to body complexity. With this in mind, have a look at the completed Level 3 and try to guess what's new compared to the previous levels:

You guessed right if you said that in Level 3, one of the blocks has a more complicated shape than your average wooden block. Perhaps you also noticed that the shape is broken into two sub-shapes, and wondered why it was done that way instead constructed as a polygon shape, as you did in the challenge in Chapter 9.

Sometimes in games, for reasons related to game logic, you need an object that's more complex than a single image with a physics body. To better understand the problem, consider a physics game in which the player drives a car:

The car is a complex shape and you might be tempted to have a single texture and a single body for it. But if you make the wheels separate bodies, pinned to the car, you could rotate them as the car moves!

And did you notice that in the image above, the car is heading straight toward a land mine? If you constructed your car of numerous physics bodies, you could easily simulate an explosion by detaching all the parts of the car and sending them flying into the air when the front wheel runs over the mine. You would apply an impulse to each of the parts, much as you did to the sand particles in Chapter 9. Bam!

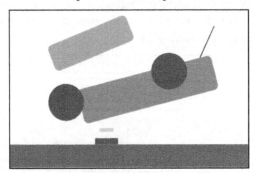

Let's try building a simple compound body for the next level of Cat Nap.

Just as before, replace the starting level in **GameViewController.swift**:

```
if let scene = GameScene.level(3) {
```

Designing the third level

Creating the third level of Cat Nap in Scene Editor will be much the same process as what you did earlier for Level 2.

Select the **Shared** group in the Project Navigator. From Xcode's menu, select **File\New\File...** and then **iOS\Resource\SpriteKit Scene**. Save the file as **Level3.sks**.

You will be rewarded, as usual, with the sight of an empty game scene. First of all resize the scene to a size of 2048 x 1536 pixels. Add the following Color Sprite objects to it:

Texture	Name	Position (X, Y)	Body Type	Category Mask	Collision Mask
background.png		1024, 768	None		
cat_bed.png	bed	1024, 272	None		
cat_sleepy.png	cat	1024, 980	None		
wood_square.png	block	946, 276	Bounding Rectangle	2	11
wood_square.png	block	946, 464	Bounding Rectangle	2	11
wood_vert2.png	block	754, 310	Bounding Rectangle	2	11
wood_vert2.png	block	754, 552	Bounding Rectangle	2	11
rock_L_vert.png	stone	1282, 434	None		
rock_L_horizontal.png	stone	1042, 714	None		

This is the complete Level 3 setup. Build and run the game to see what you have so far.

The level in its current state doesn't look too good. The cat falls through the stone L block as if it were not in the scene at all. And no wonder – you did not set any bodies for the two blocks that build the L shaped block. This is because in the next section you will learn how to create a complex body that matches the shape of the new stone block.

Making compound objects

You already placed the two stone pieces on the scene in Scene Editor. In your scene code you will create a new empty node and then you will move the two stone pieces from the scene into this new node. Then you will create bodies matching the two stones and create a compound body out of them for their parent node.

First, create a new method in `GameScene` called `makeCompoundNode()`:

```
func makeCompoundNode() {
  let compoundNode = SKNode()
  compoundNode.name = "compoundNode"
}
```

You start by simply creating a new empty `SKNode` and giving it a name. Later on you will be able to identify this node by its name.

Now you will go on according to the plan and grab all stone piece nodes, move them into the new compound node, and create bodies for them. Append to the newly created method:

```
var bodies:[SKPhysicsBody]  = [SKPhysicsBody]()

enumerateChildNodesWithName("stone") {node, _ in
  node.removeFromParent()
  compoundNode.addChild(node)
```

```
    let body = SKPhysicsBody(rectangleOfSize: node.frame.size,
      center: node.position)
    bodies.append(body)
  }
```

First you create a new empty array of SKPhysicsBody objects. You go on by enumerating all nodes in the scene whose name is "*stone*" (in your case they are only two, but there could easily be more if you add them in Scene Editor).

You remove each "*stone*" node from the scene by calling on it removeFromParent() and immediately afterwards you add the node as a child of compoundNode.

So far so good – the only thing left is to create a body for each of the nodes. Still in the block enumerating the matching nodes you create an SKPhysicsBody with the size and position of the current stone block.

This is the first time you use SKPhysicsBody(rectangleOfSize:, center:) to create bodies – so far you always had the body of your nodes centered in the sprite, but this time you also want to position the bodies. By just providing as the center parameter the position of the stone sprite you will position the physics bodies the same way that the sprites are laid out.

Finally you add each body to the bodies array.

It's time to create the compound physics body and add the compound node to the scene.

Add these final lines to the makeCompoundNode() method:

```
compoundNode.physicsBody = SKPhysicsBody(bodies: bodies)

compoundNode.physicsBody!.collisionBitMask =
PhysicsCategory.Edge | PhysicsCategory.Cat |
PhysicsCategory.Block
addChild(compoundNode)
```

You create the compoundNode's physics body by using the convenience initializer SKPhysicsBody(bodies:), which takes in an array of bodies and fixes them together in a rigid structure.

You set the proper collision bitmask and add the compound node to the scene.

I'm sure you are already itching to see the result. Scroll to didMoveToView() and at the very bottom of the method body add:

```
makeCompoundNode()
```

Build and run the game, and behold the stone L!

That was easy, wasn't it? Destroy one of the **wooden** blocks on the left to see that the two stone pieces now behave as one solid body:

Victory! You have a compound body in your scene.

If you try to solve the level however, you will quickly notice a little problem that didn't exist just moments ago – when you tap one of the square wood blocks they don't disappear.

You will have to debug this problem because right now the level is impossible to solve!

Scroll to the method `sceneTouched()` and below the first line where you define the `targetNode` add:

```
println(targetNode)
```

This will print the tapped node information in the console and hopefully will help you understand where the current problem lies.

Run the game again and tap one of the square blocks then check the Output console in Xcode. You will see something similar to this:

It looks like the compoundNode **covers** the rest of the blocks! When you add children to compoundNode it grows its frame to accommodate these child nodes and therefore its actual frame looks something like this:

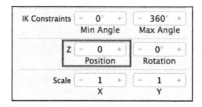

nodeAtPoint() returns the node at a given point with the highest position on the screen. Since you added compoundNode last to the scene – it is above all other nodes. Luckily you can easily reposition the key nodes in the scene so that compoundNode will be behind the other blocks.

First open **Level3.sks** and in Scene Editor select the background image node. In the Inspector on the right hand side of the Xcode window find the **Z Position** field:

Click few times the "-" button until you set the value to **-3**. This will send the background image to the back of the scene. Next select the Cat Bed node and set its Z Position to **-2**.

You should see no visible change in Scene Editor but now all nodes have Z Position equal to 0 and the background and the cat bed respectively -3 and -2, which will send them behind all blocks and the cat. The lower the Z Position value the more to the back is the node.

Now you can easily insert the compound node in between the background and the rest of the blocks by, you guessed it, setting its Z Position to **-1**.

Open **GameScene.swift** and find the line: `let compoundNode = SKNode()`. Just below that line set the node's Z Position:

```
compoundNode.zPosition = -1
```

This should successfully order the nodes so that you can tap on all wooden blocks. You should run the game right now and give that a try!

The game works just as before – that's nice. Even nicer, of course, it will be if you can tap and destroy the stone block and solve the level! Right now the rock is just indestructible!

Scroll **to the top of** `sceneTouched(location:)` and add this code under the line `let targetNode = self.nodeAtPoint(location)` to check for taps on the compound node:

```
if targetNode.parent?.name == "compoundNode" {
  targetNode.parent!.removeFromParent()
}
```

You check if the parent of the tapped node has name of "*compoundNode*" and if so you remove the parent from the scene. Since the building parts of the L shape are the last to be added to the node tree they are the ones to catch the taps – you remove all parts by just removing the compound node (and automatically all its children with their physics bodies).

You can give the game another go and finally solve the level:

Level progression

You have worked on one level at a time, so you've been manually specifying which level to load. However, that won't work for players—they expect to proceed to the next level after winning!

This is quite easy to implement. Begin by setting the game to load Level 1 when started. Change the line that loads the scene in **GameViewController.swift** so it looks like this:

```
if let scene = GameScene.level(1) {
```

Then in **GameScene.swift**, add the following code at the beginning of win():

```
if (currentLevel < 3) {
  currentLevel++
}
```

Now, every time the player completes a level, they'll move on to the next one. Finally, to raise the stakes, add this to the beginning of lose():

```
if (currentLevel > 1) {
  currentLevel--
}
```

That'll certainly make the player think twice before tapping a block!

Challenges

By now, you've come a long way toward mastering physics in Sprite Kit.

And because I'm so confident of your skills, I've prepared a challenge for you that will require a solid understanding of everything you've done in the last three chapters—and will ask even more of you!

Challenge 1: Add one more level to Cat Nap

Your challenge is to develop an entirely new level by yourself. If you do everything just right, the finished level will look like this:

As you can see, this time, besides blocks, there's also a seesaw between the poor cat and its bed. This cat sure has a hard life.

And yes—it's a real seesaw; it rotates around its base and is fully interactive. And you developed it all by yourself! Er, sorry—you *will* develop it all by yourself.

I'll just lay down the main points and you can take it from there. Here are the objects to place in **Level4.sks**:

Texture	Name	Position (X, Y)	Body Type	Category Mask	Collision Mask
background.png		1024, 768	None		
cat_bed.png	bed	1024, 272	None		
cat_sleepy.png	cat	1024, 944	None		
wood_square.png	block	1024, 626	Bounding Rectangle	2	11
wood_square.png	block	1024, 266	Bounding Rectangle	2	11
wood_square.png	seesawBase	514, 448	Bounding Rectangle	Uncheck Dynamic 0	0
ice.png	seesaw	518, 440	Bounding Rectangle	2	3

Once you've placed these objects, the scene should look something like this:

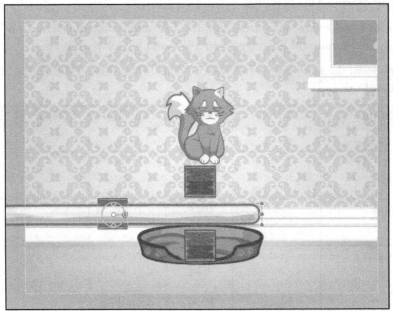

There's not much left to do from here—I'll assume you've done everything perfectly so far!

With this additional level, you need to change the `if` check you added at the top of `win()`. Instead of checking for three levels, you need to check for four.

Build and run the game to see what happens. You can destroy the wood blocks, but the seesaw does not really work and you cannot complete the level:

You'll need to fix the seesaw board to its base on the wall. Do that by creating a pin joint that will anchor the center of the board to the center of the base, and allow the board to rotate around that anchor, like so:

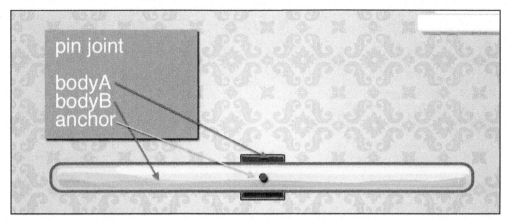

You can create a pin joint in two different ways. First, try using `SKPhysicsJointPin.jointWithBodyA(bodyB:anchor:)` to create it in code to make sure you understand it. You'll need to find the node by name and use it to create the joint.

After that, you can remove that code and do the much simpler thing: Check the **Pinned** checkbox in the Scene Editor, in the seesaw's **Physics Definition** section. This creates a pin joint that connects the node to the scene at the node's anchor point.

That should get there! Try solving the level yourself—I'm not going to give you any other tip besides the fact that the order in which you destroy the blocks matters!

Although you are now done with physics, you are not done with Cat Nap yet! Stay tuned for the next two chapters, where you'll learn about the four remaining types of nodes in Sprite Kit that you haven't seen yet. In the process, you'll make this poor cat's life even more difficult! ☺

Chapter 12: Crop, Video, and Shape Nodes

By Jacob Gundersen

You learned in the very first chapter of this book that everything appearing onscreen in Sprite Kit derives from a class called SKNode. So far, you've used four types of SKNodes:

1. **SKSpriteNode**: This node displays images. You learned about this in Chapter 1, "Sprites," and have used it in every chapter since.

2. **SKScene**: This node represents a "screen" in your app and usually contains a bunch of other nodes. You learned about this in Chapter 4, "Scenes."

3. **SKLabelNode**: This node displays text. You learned about this in Chapter 7, "Labels."

4. **SKEmitterNode**: This node displays particle systems. You learned about this in Chapter 8, "Particle Systems."

There are four advanced types of nodes that you haven't learned about yet. In this chapter, you'll use three of them:

5. **SKCropNode**: This node allows you to apply a mask to a node or node tree, effectively "cropping" its children to display only a certain region.

6. **SKVideoNode**: This node allows you to easily play video files right from within your games.

7. **SKShapeNode**: This node draws a shape (with a stroke, fill and glow color) from a CGPath path. You briefly touched on this when drawing the playable rectangle in Chapte 2, "Manual Movement", but we'll go into more detail here.

Then in the next chapter, you'll learn to use the final node type:

8. **SKEffectNode**: This node applies a Core Image filter—responsible for post-processing special effects—to its children.

These four nodes let you create cool and unique effects in your games that would be quite difficult to accomplish in other game frameworks, so it's well worth it to learn about them.

Make no mistake! As you'll see, these nodes are powerful weapons in your game development arsenal. But with great power comes... Well, you know the rest. These nodes all require greater resources. When using them, it's important to keep an eye on performance, because you may find that your brilliant game only runs on the latest hardware.

Over the next two chapters, you'll get hands-on experience with these nodes by adding them to Cat Nap. By the time you're done, you'll be able to create effects like these:

Cropping   Videos   Shapes

Before you start, make sure that Cat Nap is configured to start at level 1 in **GameViewController.swift**'s `viewDidLoad()`:

```
let scene = GameScene.level(1)
```

> **Note:** This chapter begins where the previous chapter's Challenge 1 left off. If you were unable to complete the challenges or skipped ahead from an earlier chapter, don't worry—you can simply open **CatNap-Starter** from this chapter's resources to begin in the right place.

Crop nodes

Let's say you want to put this picture:

Inside this picture frame:

Should be easy, right? Just draw the picture and then draw the photo frame on top. To do this, add the following method to the bottom of **GameScene.swift**:

```swift
func createPhotoFrameAtPosition(position: CGPoint) {
  let photoFrame = SKSpriteNode(imageNamed: "picture-frame")
  photoFrame.name = "PhotoFrameNode"
  photoFrame.position = position

  let pictureNode = SKSpriteNode(imageNamed: "picture")
  pictureNode.name = "PictureNode"
  pictureNode.position = position
  addChild(pictureNode)
  addChild(photoFrame)
}
```

This should be review—you simply create SKSpriteNodes for the picture and the frame and add them to the scene. You give names to the nodes so you can easily look them up later in the chapter.

Now call this new method at the end of didMoveToView():

```swift
createPhotoFrameAtPosition(CGPointMake(250, 820))
```

Build and run, and you'll see the following:

As you can see, the zombie bleeds outside the photo frame—and everybody knows zombies don't bleed! Hmm, this isn't as easy as it first seemed.

Wouldn't it be cool if you could dynamically crop this picture so only the parts inside the photo frame showed up? Enter SKCropNode.

Using crop nodes

To use a crop node, you need to do three things:

1. **Create the crop node**. This is as simple as calling SKCropNode().

2. **Add child nodes** to display. The children should be the things you want to crop. In this example, you would want to add the zombie picture sprite node as a child of the crop node.

3. **Set a mask node**. This is a node indicating which portions of the child nodes should be drawn to the screen. Any parts of the mask that are transparent will make the corresponding parts of the child node transparent, and only the remaining parts will appear onscreen.

   For this example, let's say you have an image of a white circle that matches the "open area" of the picture frame (with the non-white area transparent). All you'd need to do is create an SKSpriteNode using this image, and set it as the crop node's mask node.

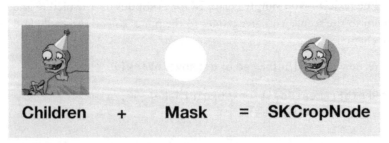

4. **Add it to the scene.** As usual, the last step is to add the crop node to the scene.

And that's it! Once you add the crop node to the scene, it will apply the mask to its children, so only the parts that aren't transparent will show through.

Let's try this out. Replace the contents of `createPhotoFrameAtPosition()` with the following:

```
// 1
let photoFrame = SKSpriteNode(imageNamed: "picture-frame")
photoFrame.name = "PhotoFrameNode"
photoFrame.position = position

let pictureNode = SKSpriteNode(imageNamed: "picture")
pictureNode.name = "PictureNode"

// 2
let maskNode = SKSpriteNode(imageNamed: "picture-frame-mask")
maskNode.name = "Mask"

// 3
let cropNode = SKCropNode()
cropNode.addChild(pictureNode)
cropNode.maskNode = maskNode
photoFrame.addChild(cropNode)
addChild(photoFrame)
```

There are just three steps here:

1. This part is the same as what you had earlier, but for one difference: You no longer set the position of the picture node. This is because you'll be adding it as a child of the crop node, and you want it centered at the crop node's position.

2. You load an image I've prepared for you that indicates the region of the zombie picture that you want to show through. This image is white at the center of the photo frame and transparent otherwise.

> **Note:** It doesn't matter what color you use for the mask node—just the transparency matters.

3. Finally, you create the crop node following the three steps you learned above. Note that you add the crop node as a child of the photo frame. This is so all parts of the picture frame (border, crop node, mask and children) can be positioned or moved by a single node—the `photoFrame`. This will make some code later in this chapter easier to write.

Build and run, and check out your picture now:

Ah, much better—this house is looking more homey already!

Dynamic cropping

You might be thinking to yourself that you could have saved several lines of code if you'd just cropped the source image in Photoshop:

That would work in this case, but there are many times it would not:

- **Different shapes**. What if you wanted to put this zombie picture in a series of picture frames, each with a different shape? You'd have to save another version of the zombie image for each picture frame, which would waste memory and storage, plus be an all-around pain.

- **Dynamic images**. What if the image you wanted to put in the frame came from a dynamic source, like from a web server or the user's photo library? You couldn't pre-crop that in Photoshop.

So to show you the real power of crop nodes, you'll take on the second of these cases—you'll modify Cat Nap to allow the user to choose their own picture to display in the picture frame.

Detect tap on node

You want to let the user select a photo when they tap on the picture frame, so the first thing you need to do is write code for that.

You already have code in `sceneTouched()` that looks through all of the nodes and detects if any of them are at the current touch point. It makes sense to leverage that same code. You'll also add a physics body to the photo frame, so it can be part of the level.

To do this, add the following code to the end of `createPhotoFrameAtPosition()`:

```
photoFrame.physicsBody = SKPhysicsBody(
  circleOfRadius: ((photoFrame.size.width * 0.975) / 2.0))
photoFrame.physicsBody!.categoryBitMask = PhysicsCategory.Block
photoFrame.physicsBody!.collisionBitMask =
  PhysicsCategory.Block | PhysicsCategory.Cat |
    PhysicsCategory.Edge
```

This code should look familiar—it's the same code you used to create bodies that are already in the game.

You use a radius that's slightly smaller than the radius of the sprite itself. This is a little trick to make the game look better—it makes the borders of the photo frame sprite seem to overlap other sprites slightly, as if it's "sinking in." This is a personal preference of mine.

Now that you have a physics body for the photo frame, change the first line of `sceneTouched()`, which looks like this:

```
let targetNode = self.nodeAtPoint(location)
```

To this:

```
var targetNode = self.nodeAtPoint(location)

let nodes = self.nodesAtPoint(location) as! [SKNode]
for node in nodes {
  if let nodeName = node.name {
    if nodeName == "PhotoFrameNode" {
      println("Picture tapped!")
    }
  }
}
```

You first change `targetNode` from a constant to a variable, which will be important later when you need to modify `targetNode`. Because the photo frame node contains several nodes as children, tapping on it doesn't reliably return the parent node, as you want it to. So here, you iterate through all the nodes and check each one for the right name, "PhotoFrameNode". You then log to the console so you can verify that it's working.

Build and run, and you'll notice the picture frame drops to the ground. It has a physics body, so now it's under the control of the physics simulation. Tap the photo, and you'll see this message in the console log:

```
Picture tapped!
```

Note that this actually lets you tap outside of the picture frame and still see the picture tapped message, because the picture frame's size includes its transparent pixels.

Displaying the image picker

Next, you want to display the image picker when the user taps the photo. iOS comes with a built-in view controller for this: `UIImagePickerController`.

However, usually you display view controllers from inside another view controller, and your game code is running inside a scene class. You could pass a reference to the `GameViewController` to the `GameScene` class, but there's a more elegant way that won't tie the classes so tightly together.

You're going to create a protocol for a delegate you can add to a `GameScene`. The delegate will have a method to request a `UIImagePickerController`. The `GameViewController` class will implement this protocol and set itself as the scene's delegate. When the user chooses an image, the `GameViewController` will then call a method on `GameScene` that changes the image in the photo node.

Start with the delegate protocol. Add this code to **GameScene.swift**, after the `import SpriteKit` statement:

```
protocol ImageCaptureDelegate {
  func requestImagePicker()
}
```

Then, add these properties to `GameScene`:

```
var imageCaptureDelegate: ImageCaptureDelegate?
var photoChanged: Bool = false
```

The first variable is the delegate object, so you can set up the relationship between the `GameScene` object and the `GameViewController` object (which will be in charge of presenting the image picker).

The second variable is a Boolean that keeps track of whether or not the player has changed the picture. Once the picture has been changed, a second tap will remove the photo frame from the level.

Next, add the function that will change the image in the photo frame:

```
func changePhotoTexture(texture: SKTexture) {
  let photoNode =
    childNodeWithName("//PictureNode") as! SKSpriteNode
  photoNode.texture = texture
  photoChanged = true
}
```

This is pretty simple. You'll pass an SKTexture object to the function. The only thing you need to do is get a reference to the picture node object—not the photo frame, but the SKSpriteNode that holds the image within the frame, labeled PictureNode. When you pass // in front of a string, childNodeWithName() will search through the entire scene graph to find the named node.

After setting the node's texture to the passed-in texture, you set photoChanged to true so that the next time the player touches the frame, it will remove itself from the scene.

In **GameViewController.swift**, change the class declaration to include all the following delegate protocols:

```
class GameViewController: UIViewController,
  ImageCaptureDelegate, UIImagePickerControllerDelegate,
  UINavigationControllerDelegate
```

Xcode will now report an error stating GameViewController does not conform to the ImageCaptureDelegate protocol. Correct this by adding the following method:

```
func requestImagePicker() {
  let imagePickerControlller = UIImagePickerController()
  imagePickerControlller.delegate = self
  presentViewController(
    imagePickerControlller, animated: true, completion: nil)
}
```

This code is simple. You create the UIImagePickerController object, set the GameViewController object as the delegate and call presentViewController(animated:completion:). Setting the delegate allows you to handle the callback after the user chooses an image from their album. Add that method next:

```
func imagePickerController(picker: UIImagePickerController,
  didFinishPickingMediaWithInfo info: [NSObject:AnyObject]) {
  //1
  let image =
```

```
    info[UIImagePickerControllerOriginalImage] as! UIImage
    //2
  picker.dismissViewControllerAnimated(true, completion: {
    //3
    let imageTexture = SKTexture(image: image)
    //4
    let skView = self.view as! SKView
    let gameScene = skView.scene as! GameScene
    //place core image code here
    //5
    gameScene.changePhotoTexture(imageTexture)
    })
  }
```

Let's go over this one part at a time:

1. This delegate method receives a `Dictionary` in which one of the keys is `UIImagePickerControllerOriginalImage`. The value for this key is a `UIImage` object containing the chosen photo.

2. The `UIImagePickerController` has to be told to dismiss itself and takes a block callback.

3. Here, you create a texture from a `UIImage`. `SKTexture(image:)` works with `UIImage` objects in iOS and `NSImage` objects in OS X. You can also initialize an `SKTexture` using its `SKTexture(CGImage:)` initializer, passing a `CGImage` from a `UIImage`'s `CGImage` property.

   At the end of the day, `CGImage`, `UIImage`, `NSImage` and `SKTexture` are all different object wrappers (each with their own uses) around a buffer of memory containing pixel information. It's usually easy to move from one type to another.

4. The next two lines get a reference to the `GameScene` object.

5. Finally, you call `changePhotoTexture()` on `gameScene`.

Next, you'll set the scene's `ImageCaptureDelegate`. Add the following line inside `viewDidLoad()`, just before the line that presents the scene in the view:

```
scene.imageCaptureDelegate = self
```

Now that you have all the pieces in place, open **GameScene.swift** and find the "Picture tapped!" log line in `sceneTouched()`. Replace that with the following:

```
//1
targetNode = node
```

```
//2
if !photoChanged {
  //3
  imageCaptureDelegate?.requestImagePicker()
  return
}
```

1. First, you set the `targetNode` variable to the photo frame node, which you'll need in order to remove the frame from the scene after a user taps on it.

2. Next, you check the status of `photoChanged`. If `photoChanged` is `true`, you skip the next few lines of code and run the existing routine that removes the photo frame.

3. Here, you call the `requestImagePicker` delegate method. You are relying on optional chaining. If the delegate isn't set, the method isn't called. Then, you bail out of `sceneTouched()` to avoid removing the node.

You need to add one more thing to get the `UIImagePickerController` to work. The controller only works in portrait orientation, but right now, this game only runs in landscape mode. You have to add support for portrait orientation somewhere in the app so it can show the `UIImagePickerController`.

Open **AppDelegate.swift** and add this method:

```
func application(application: UIApplication,
  supportedInterfaceOrientationsForWindow window: UIWindow?)
    -> Int
{
  return
    Int(UIInterfaceOrientationMask.AllButUpsideDown.rawValue)
}
```

Build and run now. Tap on the photo frame, and it will launch the picker:

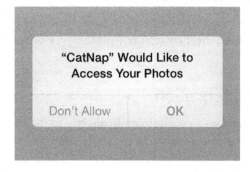

Tap OK. Pick a photo from your album, and you should see it appear in the photo frame.

However, you may notice a problem. When you rotate the game to portrait, it will resize and adjust. You don't want it to do that, but you still need to support portrait mode in the `appDelegate` for the `UIImagePickerController`.

Fortunately, there's a simple fix. Replace the contents of `supportedInterfaceOrientations` in **GameViewController.swift** with the following:

```
return Int(UIInterfaceOrientationMask.Landscape.rawValue)
```

Now the picker is presented in portrait, but the game view won't rotate to portrait.

At this point, you have a custom image cropped to fit inside the photo frame—pretty cool, eh? Now that you have this new feature working, let's integrate it properly into the game.

Interlude: Level integration

Right now, you're adding your new photo node directly to the scene no matter what. This means it will show up in every level of the game, often messing up the puzzles and making some impossible!

Let's fix this by treating the photo node just the same as the other types of blocks: loadable from Scene Kit files.

In the resources for this chapter, you'll find several new CatNap levels that I created for you (**Level5-7.sks**). Add these files to your project.

To create and configure these new kinds of nodes, you need to make some modifications to the code that loads the level files. Inside **GameViewController.swift**, find the line in `viewDidLoad()` that sets the current level and change it to 5:

```
let scene = GameScene.level(5)
```

Level 5 has a node included that just has the photo frame. You'll create a method to add a crop node, a mask node and a child node to the existing photo frame in the Sprite Kit file. You'll then add a method that checks for nodes named `PhotoFrameNode` in the current scene.

Add the following method inside **GameScene.swift**:

```
func addPhotoToFrame(photoFrame: SKSpriteNode) {
  let pictureNode = SKSpriteNode(imageNamed: "picture")
  pictureNode.name = "PictureNode"

  let maskNode = SKSpriteNode(imageNamed: "picture-frame-mask")
  maskNode.name = "Mask"

  let cropNode = SKCropNode()
  cropNode.addChild(pictureNode)
  cropNode.maskNode = maskNode
  photoFrame.addChild(cropNode)

  photoFrame.physicsBody = SKPhysicsBody(
    circleOfRadius: ((photoFrame.size.width * 0.975) / 2.0))
  photoFrame.physicsBody!.categoryBitMask =
    PhysicsCategory.Block
  photoFrame.physicsBody!.collisionBitMask =
    PhysicsCategory.Block | PhysicsCategory.Cat |
      PhysicsCategory.Edge
}
```

This method takes an existing `SKSpriteNode`, one that will be loaded from the .sks file. It sets up the crop node similarly to the way you did in `createPhotoFrameAtPosition()`, but it doesn't need to position `photoFrame`, nor does it need to add it to the scene, because those things were configured in the Scene Editor.

Next, you need a function that checks for nodes that need to have this method called on them. You already have this line of code in didMoveToView():

```
createPhotoFrameAtPosition(CGPointMake(250, 820))
```

Replace that line with this:

```
enumerateChildNodesWithName("PhotoFrameNode") {node, _ in
  self.addPhotoToFrame(node as! SKSpriteNode)
}
```

This will find all the nodes that have PhotoFrameNode as their name property. Then, for each one, it calls the method to add the crop, mask and content nodes to the photo frame. This structure allows you to add features and characteristics to your nodes, but still use Xcode's Scene Editor to position and lay out nodes.

Now change the first line of win to this:

```
if currentLevel < 5 {
```

This change ensures you'll return to this level if you fail to clear it while playing and the game kicks you back to Level 4.

Build and run. You should see Level 5 and have a round photo frame block in your scene:

This level makes for a nice challenge—you have to time the sliding and destruction of the blocks just right to land the cat in the bed. You can change the picture to your own image just for fun. :]

There's one last change you need to make before moving on. You set the imageCaptureDelegate if you start the level from the GameViewController class, but what if you move from level to level? You still need to set the delegate in that case. Replace the contents of newGame() in GameScene with the following:

```
func newGame() {
  if let newScene = GameScene.level(currentLevel) {
    newScene.imageCaptureDelegate = imageCaptureDelegate
    newScene.scaleMode = scaleMode
    view!.presentScene(newScene)
  }
}
```

This sets the delegate on the next scene (which is the following scene if you win and the previous scene if you lose) to the same delegate as the current scene. That should do it for the crop node.

But this is just the beginning of what you can do with crop nodes! Let's take a look at one last thing.

Different types of mask nodes

One of the coolest things about SKCropNode is that the maskNode can be any kind of node—not just an SKSpriteNode!

To see what I mean, open **GameScene.swift** and add the following code at the beginning of didMoveToView():

```
let backgroundDesat =
  SKSpriteNode(imageNamed: "background-desat")
let label = SKLabelNode(fontNamed: "Zapfino")
label.text = "Cat Nap"
label.fontSize = 296

let cropNode = SKCropNode()
cropNode.addChild(backgroundDesat)
cropNode.maskNode = label

if let background = childNodeWithName("Background") {
  background.addChild(cropNode)
}
```

This project includes a second version of the background named **background-desat.png**, which I've "de-saturated" to be slightly grayer. In the code above, you create a label that says "Cat Nap" and use a crop node on the de-saturated background, with the label as its mask.

Then, you get a reference to the existing background node—the one loaded in the .sks file—and add the crop node to the background node.

Build and run, and you'll see the following:

Neat, right? I'm sure you can come up with all kinds of creative ways to use SKCropNode in your own games.

Now that you've seen how great a mask node can be, I want you to comment out that code you just added. Why? Did you try to play through the level?

You may have noticed you can no longer tap a block to remove it. This is because you're receiving that new, de-saturated node as the target touched node, instead of the blocks. You could use the enumeration methods to sort this out, but for now, it's easier to simply remove that extra node.

Video nodes

Video nodes allow you to easily play video content right within your game. They work just like other nodes, so you can move them, scale them, rotate them, apply physics forces (and collisions) to them and much more!

SKVideoNode supports the following types of video files (from the AVFoundation Constants Reference):

- Quicktime Movies (.mov, .qt)
- MPEG4 (.mp4)
- Apple MPEG4 (.m4v)
- 3GP Format (.3gp, .3gpp)

In this section, you'll create a TV that plays the trailer for this book, which, of course, features Cat Nap. If you've ever had cats, you know they can be pretty vain! :]

Using video nodes

To use a video node, you need to do three things:

1. **Create an SKVideoNode**. The first step is to create an instance of SKVideoNode. You can either simply pass in the URL of the video to play or initialize it with an AVPlayer (more on that later).

2. **Call play**. When you're ready to play the video, just call the play method.

3. **Add it to the scene.** As usual, the last step is to add the video node to the scene.

That's all that's required—it's pretty simple stuff. Here are a few optional steps you might sometimes want to do:

• **Create an AVPlayer**. When you create an SKVideoNode, you can optionally pass in an AVPlayer, which is a class in AVFoundation introduced in iOS 5 that makes it nice and easy to play video.

This is great if you want more control over the video. It allows you to control the playback rate so you can play a video at half or double speed, create a seamless video loop, jump to specific locations in the video and much more.

• **Mask the video**. Sometimes, you'll want the video to play within a certain boundary, like the inside of a TV sprite. Yes, you can use SKCropNode to crop videos, too!

Let's try this out by adding a TV to Cat Nap. It won't be a flat-screen, our poor cat can't afford that – it's just an old-style CRT TV.

Since implementing the TV will be slightly more complicated than creating the photo frame, you're going to create a separate class to contain all its code.

In Xcode's main menu, select **File\New\File…**, select the **iOS\Source\Swift File** template and click **Next**. Enter **OldTVNode.swift** for Save As. Finally, make sure the **CatNap** target is checked and click **Create**.

First, import a few additional frameworks inside **OldTVNode.swift**:

```
import AVFoundation
import SpriteKit
```

Next, declare a new class with the following lines of code:

```
class OldTVNode : SKSpriteNode {
}
```

Then, add a couple of properties:

```
let player: AVPlayer
let videoNode: SKVideoNode
```

The AVPlayer is for finer control of the video playback. The video node will play video.

Similar to the photo frame, the root object of the TV hierarchy will be a sprite node with the TV image. It will have a crop node as a child, which in turn will have the video node as a child.

SKSpriteNode has a required initializer that you must implement, init(coder:). Sprite Kit uses this when it loads a node from an SKS file or from an archive you create in code, like the ones you'll create in Chapter 17, "Saving and Loading Games."

However, you cannot currently set a node in the Scene Editor in Xcode to a custom subclass, so you won't be able to add an OldTVNode there directly. Instead, you'll add a placeholder sprite in the Scene Editor and then replace it with an OldTVNode in code.

That means you won't need init(coder:) in this class, but the method is still required. Therefore, add the following code to satisfy the compiler:

```
required init(coder: NSCoder) {
  fatalError("NSCoding not supported")
}
```

If this initializer is called, it will simply throw an error and log that the NSCoding protocol is not supported for this class. That's OK, because Cat Nap won't ever call this method.

To create your objects, you'll use an initializer that takes a CGRect so that you can pass the position and size of the block in from the Sprite Kit scene file, kind of like you did with the photo frame block. The difference is that here, you'll replace an existing node in the scene with a new node instead of adding children to the existing node.

Add the following implementation of this new initializer method:

```
init(frame: CGRect) {
  //1
  let filePath = NSBundle.mainBundle().pathForResource(
    "BookTrailer", ofType: "m4v")
  let fileURL = NSURL(fileURLWithPath: filePath!)
  //2
  player = AVPlayer.playerWithURL(fileURL) as! AVPlayer
  videoNode = SKVideoNode(AVPlayer: player)
  //3
  let cropNode = SKCropNode()
  let maskNode = SKSpriteNode(imageNamed: "tv-mask")
  cropNode.maskNode = maskNode
  cropNode.addChild(videoNode)
  //4
  let rect = CGRectInset(frame, frame.size.width * 0.15,
                         frame.size.height * 0.24)
  videoNode.size = rect.size
  videoNode.position = CGPoint(x: -frame.size.width * 0.1,
                               y: -frame.size.height * 0.06)
  //5
  let texture = SKTexture(imageNamed: "tv")
  super.init(texture: texture, color: nil, size: texture.size())
  //6
  self.name = "TVNode"
  self.addChild(cropNode)
  //7
  self.position = CGPoint(x: CGRectGetMidX(frame),
                          y: CGRectGetMidY(frame))
  self.size = frame.size
  //8
  player.volume = 0.0
  videoNode.play()
}
```

Let's go over this section by section:

1. First, you set up a file URL for the video file you're going to play. I've included a trailer for this book as a video file.

2. Next, you initialize the AVPlayer with the fileURL and the SKVideoNode with the AVPlayer.

3. Here, you set up a crop node, add the `maskNode` and add the `videoNode` as a child of the crop node.

4. In these lines, you set up the size and position of the `videoNode`. Because the screen is oddly shaped and a bit off-center, I determined these values through trial and error.

5. Next, you need to call the superclass initializer. You have to use the designated initializer, which for `SKSpriteNode` is `init(texture:color:size:)`. To do this, you need an `SKTexture`. The next two lines create a texture object and call the superclass initializer.

6. You give the node the name "`TVNode`" so you can look it up later. You also add the `cropNode` to the main node (the TV).

7. You use the frame `CGRect` that you pass into the method to position and size the node.

8. Finally, you turn the volume down on the video so it doesn't compete with the game's music, and you call `play()` on `videoNode`.

It's time to test your new node type. First, add the following to **GameScene.swift,** at the end of `didMoveToView()`:

```
let tvNode = OldTVNode(frame: CGRectMake(20, 500, 300, 300))
addChild(tvNode)
```

This code simply creates an instance of the TV node and adds it to the scene. Build and run, and up on the wall, you should see a TV node with the trailer for the book playing:

It's amazing to be able to play videos so easily like this. There are many creative uses for video nodes in your own games, from special effects to intro sequences to tutorials and more—your imagination is the only limit!

Interlude: Level integration

Just like last time, now that you've got the node working, you need to integrate the logic that creates levels from the property lists.

First, you should add a physics body to the TV node. Add this code to **OldTVNode.swift**, inside `init(frame:)` before the call to `videoNode.play()`:

```
self.physicsBody = SKPhysicsBody(
  rectangleOfSize: CGRectInset(frame, 2, 2).size)
self.physicsBody!.categoryBitMask =
  PhysicsCategory.Block
self.physicsBody!.collisionBitMask =
  PhysicsCategory.Block | PhysicsCategory.Cat |
  PhysicsCategory.Edge
```

This code should look familiar, as it's similar to that for the other physics bodies you've created. You need to move the `PhysicsCategory` struct outside the `GameScene` class in order for other classes to be able to use it. So, cut this entire block of code:

```
struct PhysicsCategory {
  static let None:  UInt32 = 0
  static let Cat:   UInt32 = 0b1    // 1
  static let Block: UInt32 = 0b10   // 2
  static let Bed:   UInt32 = 0b100  // 4
  static let Edge:  UInt32 = 0b1000 // 8
  static let Label: UInt32 = 0b10000 // 16
  static let Spring:UInt32 = 0b100000 // 32
  static let Hook:  UInt32 = 0b1000000 // 64
}
```

Paste it into the section (in **GameScene.swift**) before this line:

```
class GameScene: SKScene, SKPhysicsContactDelegate {
```

When you've done that, the compiler warnings in **OldTVNode.swift** will go away.

Now it's time to load the TV node based on the SKS file. Back in **GameScene.swift**, replace the following lines in `didMoveToView()`:

```
let tvNode = OldTVNode(frame: CGRectMake(20, 500, 300, 300))
addChild(tvNode)
```

With these:

```
let tvNodes = (children as! [SKNode]).filter ({node in
```

```
    return node.name == .Some("TVNode")
})

for node in tvNodes {
  let tvNode = OldTVNode(frame: node.frame)
  self.addChild(tvNode)
  node.removeFromParent()
}
```

Unlike how you set up the photo frame, here `OldTVNode` constructs the entire node tree in one class. So, you need to remove the existing `SKSpriteNode` created by the `SKScene` class and replace it with the entirely realized node graph created by the `OldTVNode` initializer.

I've set up **level6.sks** to contain the TV block in the level, so let's switch the game to start on that level. Find the line in `viewDidLoad()` in **GameViewController** that initializes the `GameScene` and change the 5 to a 6, like this:

```
let scene = GameScene.level(6)
```

Likewise, change the first line of `win()` in **GameScene.swift** to compare against 6 instead of 5, like this:

```
if currentLevel < 6 {
```

Build and run, and you'll have a new level that uses your TV node!

Your level is loads as you'd expect, but touching the TV doesn't remove it from the level. As with the photo frame node, you have to iterate through the nodes to find the right one.

Inside `sceneTouched()`, find the following `if` statement:

```
if nodeName == "PhotoFrameNode" {
```

And replace it with this:

```
if nodeName == "PhotoFrameNode" || nodeName == "TVNode" {
```

This simply checks for TV nodes in addition to photo frame nodes.

Then, find the following line, which should be right after the line you just added:

```
targetNode = node
```

And add this code right after it:

```
if nodeName == "TVNode" {
  break
}
```

You don't want to run the `imagePickerDelegate` logic when the user taps a TV node, so once the `targetNode` is set, you break out of the loop if it's a TV node.

Build and run again, and now you should be able to remove the TV with a tap.

Controlling video playback

That's all you'll do with video nodes in this chapter, but before you move on, I wanted to mention a few other things you can do with video nodes.

Of course, if you want to play or pause your video, you simply call the `play` or `pause` methods on the video node, respectively. Unfortunately, that's all the control you have from `SKVideoNode` directly—to do more, you have to go one level deeper and use the methods on `AVPlayer`.

The good news is that `AVPlayer` has just about everything you might need. It contains methods to increase the play rate, seek to a spot in the video, perform a callback when the video ends and much more. For further details, see Apple's official AVPlayer Class Reference.

Let's move on to the last type of special node for this chapter!

Shape nodes

A shape node allows you to easily draw a shape in your game, such as a line, rectangle, or even an arbitrary Core Graphics path.

Shapes nodes are great for when you need to visualize something quickly or create dynamic shapes in your game based on user input or randomness, rather than pre-rendered graphics.

You've actually been using shape nodes ever since Chapter 2, "Manual Movement", to visualize the playable area in your games:

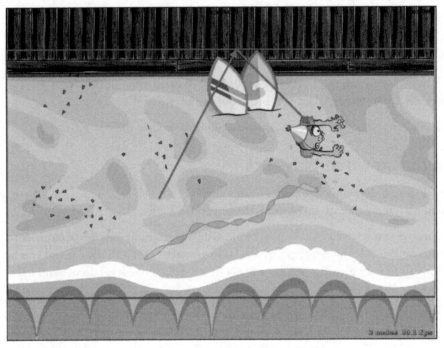

In this section, you'll go deeper and learn more things you can do with shape nodes. In particular, you'll add a new type, the "wonky block", to your game. Wonky blocks will vary slightly each time you run the level, by using random numbers to create shapes that are somewhat, but not completely, rectangular.

This means the levels, too, will be slightly different each time you play the game. Some levels might not even be solvable—but hey, cats have nine lives for a reason!

Using shape nodes

To use a shape node, you need to do four things:

1. **Create an SKShapeNode**. This is as simple as calling `SKShapeNode()`.

2. **Create a path**. The most important part of creating an `SKShapeNode` is to set the path that defines the shape. There are a number of ways to do this. For example, you can use Core Graphics, which is a C API, or you can use the higher-level `UIBezierPath` (`NSBezierPath` on OS X). In this chapter, you'll use Core Graphics.

3. **Set properties (optional)**. An `SKShapeNode` has properties to control the stroke color and width, the fill color and the glow around the stroke.

4. **Add it to the scene.** As usual, the last step is to add the shape node to the scene.

There is also an `SKShapeNode` square you can add to an `SKScene` using Xcode's Scene Editor. You can control all the properties of the shape node by using the IB Interface. The only thing you can't edit is the shape (or path) of the shape node. Apple may correct that in a future version of Xcode.

Let's give shapes nodes a try by implementing the new wonky blocks in Cat Nap.

First, you'll create a couple of helper methods to make the code more usable. The idea is you'll choose a target position, and then make a helper method that will return a position some small random distance away from the target position.

Grey circle = 15% of height and 15% width of box
This is the random zone; point can end up anywhere within the grey circle.

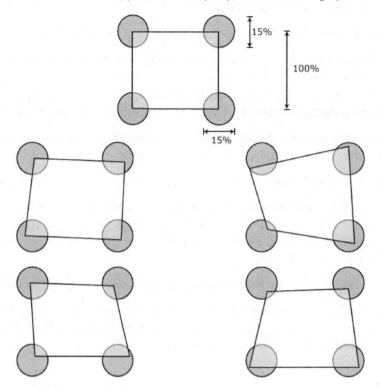

First, add a method to **GameScene.swift** that takes in a CGPoint and CGSize and returns a randomized point:

```
func adjustedPoint(inputPoint: CGPoint, inputSize: CGSize)
  -> CGPoint {
  //1
  let width = inputSize.width * 0.15
  let height = inputSize.height * 0.15
  //2
  let xMove = width * CGFloat.random() - width / 2.0
  let yMove = height * CGFloat.random() - height / 2.0
  //3
  let move = CGPoint(x: xMove, y: yMove)
  //4
  return inputPoint + move
}
```

Let's go quickly through these sections:

1. You find the maximum height and width of the deviation (15% of width or height) and store them in the variables width and height.

2. You multiply a random number between 0.0 and 1.0 by the width or height and then subtract half the input width or height. You do the subtraction to create a movement range that's centered between positive and negative movement. The ultimate range of the point's movement is between -0.075 * and 0.075 *, width or height.

3. Here, you create a CGPoint that contains the movement amount.

4. Finally, you add that random movement amount to the input point. You now have a random output point.

Now that you've got helper methods, you're ready to add the method that creates a wonky block. This method will be long, so you'll add it in two parts. First add the following code:

```
func makeWonkyBlockFromShapeNode(shapeNode: SKShapeNode)
  -> SKShapeNode {
  //1
  let newShapeNode = SKShapeNode()
  //2
  let originalRect = shapeNode.frame
  //3
  var leftTop = CGPoint(x: CGRectGetMinX(originalRect),
                        y: CGRectGetMaxY(originalRect))
  var leftBottom = originalRect.origin
  var rightBottom = CGPoint(x: CGRectGetMaxX(originalRect),
                            y: CGRectGetMinY(originalRect))
  var rightTop = CGPoint(x: CGRectGetMaxX(originalRect),
                         y: CGRectGetMaxY(originalRect))
  //4
  let size = originalRect.size
  leftTop = adjustedPoint(leftTop, inputSize: size)
  leftBottom = adjustedPoint(leftBottom, inputSize: size)
  rightBottom = adjustedPoint(rightBottom, inputSize: size)
  rightTop = adjustedPoint(rightTop, inputSize: size)
}
```

Here's what this method does so far:

1. First, you allocate a new SKShapeNode. As with the TV node, you'll be replacing the entire node with a new, configured shape node. But you can use the existing frame to size and position the new node so it matches what you set up in the editor.

2. In this step, you store the frame of the passed-in SKShapeNode in a new variable. This is mostly to make the next few lines easier to write, as you'll be referencing this frame many times.

3. Here you calculate the points at the four corners of the existing rectangle. You'll use these points to randomly adjust the shape of the node.

4. In this step, you pass each of the four corners into adjustedPoint() to get randomized versions of the points.

Now that you have the locations calculated for the corners of the block, add the following code to complete the method:

```
//5
let bezierPath = CGPathCreateMutable()
CGPathMoveToPoint(bezierPath, nil, leftTop.x, leftTop.y)
CGPathAddLineToPoint(
  bezierPath, nil, leftBottom.x, leftBottom.y)
CGPathAddLineToPoint(
  bezierPath, nil, rightBottom.x, rightBottom.y)
CGPathAddLineToPoint(bezierPath, nil, rightTop.x, rightTop.y)
//6
CGPathCloseSubpath(bezierPath)
//7
newShapeNode.path = bezierPath
//8
leftTop -= CGPoint(x: -2, y: 2)
leftBottom -= CGPoint(x: -2, y: -2)
rightBottom -= CGPoint(x: 2, y: -2)
rightTop -= CGPoint(x: 2, y: 2)
//9
let physicsBodyPath = CGPathCreateMutable()
CGPathMoveToPoint(physicsBodyPath, nil, leftTop.x, leftTop.y)
CGPathAddLineToPoint(
  physicsBodyPath, nil, leftBottom.x, leftBottom.y)
CGPathAddLineToPoint(
  physicsBodyPath, nil, rightBottom.x, rightBottom.y)
CGPathAddLineToPoint(
  physicsBodyPath, nil, rightTop.x, rightTop.y)
//10
CGPathCloseSubpath(physicsBodyPath)
//11
newShapeNode.physicsBody =
  SKPhysicsBody(polygonFromPath: physicsBodyPath)
newShapeNode.physicsBody!.categoryBitMask =
  PhysicsCategory.Block
newShapeNode.physicsBody!.collisionBitMask =
  PhysicsCategory.Block | PhysicsCategory.Cat |
```

```
    PhysicsCategory.Edge
//12
newShapeNode.lineWidth = 1.0
newShapeNode.fillColor =
  SKColor(red: 0.73, green: 0.73, blue: 1.0, alpha: 1.0)
newShapeNode.strokeColor =
  SKColor(red: 0.165, green: 0.165, blue: 0.0, alpha: 1.0)
newShapeNode.glowWidth = 1.0
//13
return newShapeNode
```

Here's what this code does:

5. You use a `CGPath` to construct a shape, first calling `CGPathCreateMutable()` to instantiate the new path object.

   `CGPathMoveToPoint()` moves a cursor to a point without doing any drawing, while `CGPathAddLineToPoint()` moves from the current point to a new point and adds a line between the two points.

6. To finish a `CGPath` (to make it a complete, fillable volume), you need to call `CGPathCloseSubpath()`. This will add a new line from the last point to the first.

   In addition to these methods, `CGPath` also has methods to create rectangles, circles and Bezier curves (that's when it gets really fun).

7. This is where you set the shape of the `SKShapeNode` to the shape defined by your `CGPath`.

   Here, you use Core Graphics to define the path. Pre-swift Core Graphics was a C API that was a little more cumbersome to use than the Objective-C counterparts, UIBezierPath (on iOS) and NSBezierPath (on Mac). However, with Swift, the C API isn't much harder to use (Core Foundation memory is managed for you in Swift) and it has the benefit of being cross-platform, so it will run on iOS and Mac without any messy `#if` statements.

8. Next, you want to shrink the points a little to make a physics body path that's slightly smaller than the shape node itself.

9. Here you create a new path, but this one is slightly inset from the one you just created. It defines the physics body shape.

10. Here, you create the `SKPhysicsBody` from the path. It uses the same physics attributes as the other bodies you created.

11. You now set the `SKShapeNode` attributes that control appearance. `lineWidth` specifies the stroke's width, `strokeColor` its color and `glowWidth` specifies a glow width around the stroke. `fillColor` specifies the color of the shape's fill.

12. Finally, you return the configured `SKShapeNode`.

> **Note:** The requirements for a polygon physics body are as follows:
>
> It must be a convex polygon—none of its corners can point inward.
>
> It must have a counterclockwise winding.
>
> It must not intersect itself—that is, none of its lines can cross.

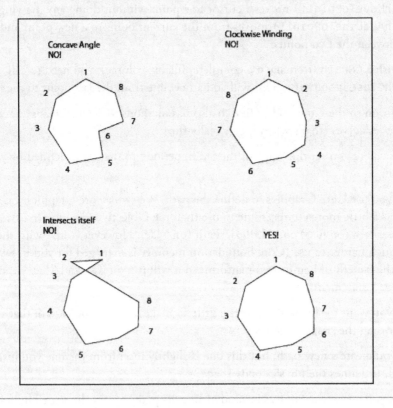

Now that you have a new block type, add it to the process that loads blocks from the Scene Kit file. You'll do this similarly to how you replaced the TV node.

Add the following code to the end of `didMoveView()`:

```
let shapeNodes = (children as! [SKNode]).filter ({node in
  return node.name == .Some("Shape")
})
for node in shapeNodes {
  let shapeNode =
    makeWonkyBlockFromShapeNode(node as! SKShapeNode)
  addChild(shapeNode)
  node.removeFromParent()
}
```

This simply gets all the children named **"Shape"** and loops through them. For each node, it adds a new wonky node in its place and then removes the original from the scene.

To test this, change the `GameScene.level(6)` in **GameViewController.swift** to this:

```
let scene = GameScene.level(7)
```

Back in **GameScene.swift**, change the first line of `win()` to this:

```
if currentLevel < 7 {
```

Build and run now.

Level 7 is full of wonky blocks! Each time you replay this level, you'll get a slightly different puzzle. Some of them may not be solvable, but that's what you get with wonky blocks!

Note: At the time of writing, my testing shows that you cannot use an SKShapeNode as a maskNode for an SKCropNode. Using just a path works, but if you fill the path, it doesn't act as a mask.

There's one work-around I've found and tested that will help in a limited capacity. You can make an SKShapeNode a child of an SKEffectNode (which you'll learn about in the next chapter) and set the SKEffectNode's shouldRasterize property to true. This will draw the shape into the SKEffectNode's buffer (without any filter, because you don't have to set the filter property or the shouldEnableEffects property). Then, setting the SKEffectNode as the maskNode property on the SKClipNode will clip that node's children to the shape drawn by the path.

This solution is limited. To update the shape, you must repeat the entire process, which is even more expensive than using the SKShapeNode on its own.

Another quick note about using SKEffectNodes: If you don't need to change the shape of your SKShapeNodes often, this is actually a good way to save on performance. Using an SKEffectNode (with a shape node) without a filter will result in much better performance than using an SKShapeNode directly. Once the shape node is rendered into the effect node, it's much more like an SKSpriteNode—the image data is cached and can be drawn very quickly. Of course, if you want to change the shape, you have to update the SKEffectNode (by setting the shouldRasterize property back to false).

There's one last thing I'd like to show you. As of iOS 8, there's a new feature where instead of filling a shape node with a color, you can fill it with a texture instead! However, at the time of writing this chapter you cannot use a texture that's in a texture atlas; it must be a normal image added to your project.

In the resources for this chapter, you'll find a file named **wood_texture.png**. Drag this file into your project's **Images** folder, and then add this line to the end of makeWonkyBlockFromShapeNode() before the return statement:

```
newShapeNode.fillTexture = SKTexture(imageNamed: "wood_texture")
```

Build and run and you should see the following:

Ahh, much better! You can also set the stroke of a shape node as a texture if you'd like.

That's it for the new block types! At this point, you've learned seven of the eight types of SKNodes available in Sprite Kit. Before you move on to the final type of SKNode, take a break to play around a bit more with video nodes!

Challenge

There's just one challenge for you in this chapter, and that is to make a video loop endlessly.

As always, if you get stuck, you can find the solution in the resources for this chapter— but give it your best shot first!

Challenge 1: Endless looping

Because video files are quite large, in your game you might want to use a small video file and loop it endlessly. You can do this by setting up a key-value observer on the AVPlayer's AVPlayerItemDidPlayToEndTimeNotification key. When the observer receives that notification, you set the video to start over.

I've provided another video in the starter project called **loop.mov**. This is a 16-second video whose end frame matches seamlessly with its beginning frame, allowing you to play that video for as long as you want.

Your challenge is to modify **OldTVNode.swift** to play this video file endlessly. What follows are a few hints for how to do this.

AVPlayer has a property called actionAtItemEnd. This stores an enum that tells the AVPlayer what it should do when the currently playing item has ended. AVPlayer's default behavior is to stop the video. You want to change `actionAtItemEnd` to `AVPlayerActionAtItemEndNone` so it won't stop the video.

Instead, you want to call `self.player.seekToTime(kCMTimeZero)` to reset the playback to the very beginning of the video. This should happen without any noticeable jitter in playback.

Here's what that code should look like:

```
player.actionAtItemEnd = .None
notificationCenter.addObserverForName(
  AVPlayerItemDidPlayToEndTimeNotification,
  object: nil, queue: mainQueue) { _ in
  self.player.seekToTime(kCMTimeZero)
}
```

All of this code can be efficiently placed in the `OldTVNode` class. You'll need to load Level 6 or add a node named "`TVNode`" to another level to see it in action.

The `kCMTimeZero` constant is part of the Core Media framework, so you'll need to import that framework to use this code.

Once you've got it working, you should see something like this:

That's just a taste of what you can do with `AVPlayer`—there are many other handy methods in there if you find you ever need them.

And with that, you've made it to the end of the chapter! Stay tuned for the last Cat Nap chapter, where you'll learn how to add special effects to your game using Core Image filters.

Chapter 13: Effect Nodes

By Jacob Gundersen

So far, you've learned about seven types of nodes in Sprite Kit.

In this chapter, you'll learn about the eight and last type of node: SKEffectNode.

An SKEffectNode allows you to apply special effects to its children nodes. For example, you could use it to modify a sprite's vibrance, hue or exposure, blur the sprite, or convert it to black and white.

These special effects are created with a technology introduced in iOS 5 called Core Image. Core Image allows you to perform many of the functions that custom shaders would usually perform. However, effect nodes have the benefit of being much easier to use than writing OpenGL and GLSL code!

Sprite Kit provides three ways to use Core Image to do image processing, of which SKEffectNode is just one of the options:

1. **SKTexture**. This class has a method called textureByApplyingCIFilter(CIFilter?) that takes the texture object and creates a new texture by processing it with the provided filter.

2. **SKEffectNode**. All the children of this node will be rendered and post-processed by the provided Core Image filter chain. This could be the entire scene or some child node tree.

3. **SKTransition**. This class has a method called SKTransition(CIFilter:duration:). You can write a custom CIFilter subclass that takes in two input images (the previous scene and the one to which you want to transition) and use whatever combination of filters you wish to create a transition effect. This could be as simple as a fade, but you can do more complex things.

In this chapter, you'll get hands-on experience using Core Image in all three of these ways by adding a lot of special effects to Cat Nap, such as this "old projector" effect:

Using effect nodes and Core Image is a great way to make your game stand out with a unique appearance. So let's dive in and make this game look funky!

More about Core Image

Core Image is an image processing framework available on OS X and iOS. It provides a number of predefined filters that you can use to do anything from altering the brightness or contrast of an image, to combining multiple images, to applying a 3D transformation.

Core Image has a number of classes available in its API. However, in the context of Sprite Kit, you'll only use one main filter class, `CIFilter`. `CIFilter` has a class method that creates a `CIFilter` subclass called `filterWithName()`. This method returns a subclass for a given filter name, such as `CISepiaTone`, `CIBloom`, `CIGaussianBlur` and many more.

Each filter has a set of parameters that you can alter from their default values so as to customize the filter's effects. This can range from changing the center point of the effect, to changing the intensity, to changing the color of the filter.

This chapter will explain the basics of using Core Image as you go along, but to learn more, check out the four chapters on Core Image in our books *iOS 5 by Tutorials* and *iOS 6 by Tutorials*, which delve much deeper into the subject.

Performance notes

Using Core Image to process a node may require a lot of processing power. The resources required to process an image depends on the pixel size of the image. As a rule of thumb, the bigger the image you want to filter, the more processing power it will take.

The processing power required also depends on the complexity of the filter or filter chain. A Gaussian blur, for example, is a particularly expensive filter because it has to calculate each pixel using inputs from the pixels that surround it.

Throughout this chapter, I'll make note of the performance issues and limitations of using Core Image filters. In most cases, you won't be able to process the entire scene each frame on older hardware—the iPhone 4 is particularly slow, as it has an older GPU.

Long story short, Core Image and effect nodes can be expensive, so use them with care and keep performance in mind.

Filtering a texture

To get started, you're going to try out the first of the three ways to use Core Image in Sprite Kit: filtering a texture.

Specifically, you're going to apply a sepia filter to the image that you chose to place in your photo frame in the last chapter. A sepia filter makes an image look yellowed and old.

Go to **GameViewController.swift** and replace the line that calls changePhotoTexture() in imagePickerController(didFinishPickingMediaWithInfo:), just below the comment that reads "//place core image code here":

```
//1
let sepia = CIFilter(name: "CISepiaTone")
//2
sepia.setValue(0.8, forKey: "inputIntensity")
```

```
//3
let filteredTexture =
  imageTexture.textureByApplyingCIFilter(sepia)
//4
gameScene.changePhotoTexture(filteredTexture)
```

Let's review this line by line:

1. To create a CIFilter, you call CIFilter(name:) and supply a string that is the name of the filter. In this case, "CISepiaTone" is the name of the filter.

   You always use this method to create a Core Image filter from the built-in set of filters.

2. To set a parameter on a CIFilter, you call setValue(forKey:) and supply a valid value (it can be a raw number, NSNumber, CIVector, CIImage, CIColor, etc.) and key name.

3. Finally, you apply the filter to the image texture by calling textureByApplyingCIFilter() and passing in the filter you just created. This returns to you a new, modified texture.

4. Then, you call the method that passes the texture to the GameScene.

To test this, you need to switch back to Level 5, because that's the level that has the photo frame node. Change currentLevel back to 5 in viewDidLoad() in **GameViewController.swift**:

```
let scene = GameScene.level(5)
```

Build and run now. If you tap on the photo frame, it will present the photo picker as before, but now when you choose a photo, it will insert it into the frame with a sepia filter applied.

> **Performance Note:** The CISepiaTone filter is fairly lightweight as filters go. Even if it weren't, this operation would work just fine on any device that supports Sprite Kit.
>
> That's because in this example, you only apply the filter once, so even if it takes a while to process, you only take a one-time performance hit, rather than getting hit each frame.
>
> The app then saves the result as the texture for the photo node. In fact, it replaces the previous texture—the node no longer has a reference to the image the way it was before you applied the filter. Only the sepia version remains.

Applying a filter to a texture when you first create a node is a great way to reuse an image. For example, you could use the CIHueAdjust filter to create differently-colored enemies from the same original image.

There's a challenge at the end of this chapter where you'll do exactly that.

Exploring available filters

You may be wondering how I knew to put "CISepiaFilter" for the filter name and that it takes "inputIntensity" as a parameter. You might also be wondering what other filter types are available on iOS.

Core Image provides over 125 filters for iOS and even more for OS X. Fortunately, there are built-in methods you can use to determine which filters are available on the current platform and the parameters they accept.

To try this out, open **GameViewController.swift** and add the following code to viewDidLoad():

```
let ciFilters =
  CIFilter.filterNamesInCategory(kCICategoryBuiltIn)
for filterName in ciFilters {
  println(ciFilters.count)
  println(filterName)
  let filter = CIFilter(name: filterName as! String)
  println(filter.attributes())
}
```

filterNamesInCategory() returns an array of all the names of the filters in that category. The constant kCICategoryBuiltIn will return a list of all the filters available on the platform on which you're running, in this case iOS.

In the above code, you use the String name of the filter to create an instance of that filter. You can then call the attributes method, which returns an NSDictionary containing the attributes of that filter. These include the name of the filter, the input parameters the filter accepts and information about each input parameter: acceptable range, data type, UISlider values and so on.

Build and run, and you'll see a list of filters in the console that looks something like this:

```
127
CIAccordionFoldTransition
[CIAttributeFilterDisplayName: Accordion Fold Transition, inputBottomHeight: {
    CIAttributeClass = NSNumber;
    CIAttributeDefault = 0;
    CIAttributeMin = 0;
    CIAttributeType = CIAttributeTypeDistance;
}, inputTargetImage: {
    CIAttributeClass = CIImage;
    CIAttributeType = CIAttributeTypeImage;
}, inputNumberOfFolds: {
    CIAttributeClass = NSNumber;
    CIAttributeDefault = 3;
    CIAttributeMax = 50;
    CIAttributeMin = 1;
    CIAttributeSliderMax = 10;
    CIAttributeSliderMin = 1;
    CIAttributeType = CIAttributeTypeScalar;
}, inputImage: {
    CIAttributeClass = CIImage;
    CIAttributeType = CIAttributeTypeImage;
}, CIAttributeFilterCategories: (
    CICategoryTransition,
    CICategoryVideo,
    CICategoryStillImage,
    CICategoryBuiltIn
), CIAttributeFilterName: CIAccordionFoldTransition, inputTime: {
    CIAttributeClass = NSNumber;
    CIAttributeDefault = 0;
    CIAttributeIdentity = 0;
    CIAttributeMin = 0;
    CIAttributeSliderMax = 1;
    CIAttributeSliderMin = 0;
    CIAttributeType = CIAttributeTypeTime;
}, inputFoldShadowAmount: {
    CIAttributeClass = NSNumber;
    CIAttributeDefault = "0.1";
    CIAttributeMax = 1;
    CIAttributeMin = 0;
    CIAttributeSliderMax = 1;
    CIAttributeSliderMin = 0;
    CIAttributeType = CIAttributeTypeScalar;
}]
127
CIAdditionCompositing
[CIAttributeFilterDisplayName: Addition, inputBackgroundImage: {
    CIAttributeClass = CIImage;
    CIAttributeType = CIAttributeTypeImage;
}, inputImage: {
```

For example, search through the console log you'll find a filter named CIBloom. It has three attributes:

1. **inputImage**: The input image—almost all filters have this. Sprite Kit will set this property for you, and you will only need to set it yourself if you create a filter chain.

2. **inputIntensity**: A number ranging from 0-1 that represents how strong the bloom effect should be.

3. **inputRadius**: A number ranging from 0-100 that represents the radius of the bloom effect.

Apple has a Core Image Filter Reference in the developer docs that has a comprehensive list of filters and better explanations on their usage and function. However, this API is a more up-to-date reference. A few of the available filters aren't up on the developer site yet, and a few filters have different names in the API than in the developer portal.

Even the API is not always accurate. I've found some of the listed default minimum and maximum values returned by the API to be wrong, or I've been able to use values outside the returned minimum and maximum values.

When you're done perusing all the great filters available, comment out the code you just added in `viewDidLoad()`. Printing that much text to the console every time you start a new level is taxing and it may prevent the transitions you'll add a little later from working.

Filtering an effect node

Next, you're going to try out the second of the three ways to use Core Image in Sprite Kit: filtering an `SKEffectNode`.

Remember that an `SKEffectNode` will apply its Core Image effect to all of its child nodes. So you could create an `SKEffectNode` and add the cat sprite as a child, and it would apply the Core Image effect to just the cat.

But what if you want to apply an effect to the entire scene? It turns out that `SKScene` is a subclass of `SKEffectNode`, so you can simply set a Core Image filter on the scene itself to filter the entire scene!

> Note: At the time of this writing, setting a `filter` property on `SKScene` while setting `shouldEnableEffects` to `true` doesn't work. This will probably be fixed in a future update.

In this section, you're going to add an "Old Timey" effect to the background node. But to accomplish this effect, you're going to need more than one simple filter—you're going to need to chain multiple filters together, one after another.

And to do that, you need to understand how to use filter chains.

Filter chains

A filter chain is just what it sounds like: a way to tell Core Image to efficiently run a sequence of filters on an input image.

There are a number of ways to construct a filter chain when using Core Image. However, if you're using Sprite Kit, you need to contain your filter chain in a CIFilter subclass. This is because every method in Sprite Kit takes only a single CIFilter object as a parameter.

So to create a filter chain in Sprite Kit, you need to perform these steps:

1. Create a subclass of CIFilter for your filter chain.

2. Make sure your CIFilter has an inputImage property.

3. Override setDefaults to initialize any parameters you may need.

4. Override outputImage to create the chain of filters. You basically chain the input image from the user to the input of filter A, then the output of filter A to the input of filter B, and so on—returning the final result.

Let's try this out by creating the "Old Timey" filter chain!

The Old Timey filter chain

The "Old Timey" filter chain will make your game look like it's being run on an old projector. It will work by applying the following effects, in order:

1. **Color controls effect**: First, the filter will use a color controls effect to turn the scene black and white, and make it randomly flicker from bright to dark.

2. **Vignette effect**: Then, the filter will use a vignette effect to darken the edges of the scene so it looks like a worn photo.

3. **Affine Transform Effect**: Finally, the filter will use an affine transform effect to move the image around a bit randomly to make it seem like a shaky camera.

Remember, the first step is to create a subclass of `CIFilter` for the filter chain, so let's do that now.

In Xcode's main menu, select **File\New\File…**, select the **iOS\Source\Swift File** template and click **Next**. Enter **OldTimeyFilter**, make sure the **CatNap** target is checked and click **Create**.

First, you need to import Core Image and set up the new class, so add this code to **OldTimeyFilter.swift**:

```
import CoreImage

class OldTimeyFilter : CIFilter {
}
```

Next, add a property to store the input image:

```
var inputImage: CIImage?
```

In the case of your `CIFilter` subclass, you're going to set all your parameters in `outputImage`, so you don't need to do the third step (implementing `setDefaults`).

That means you're onto the fourth and last step—implementing `outputImage`. All the important stuff goes here, so let's build this up one step at a time.

You'll utilize some C source code in this step, which you can find in the resources for this chapter. The file contains a C implementation of the Perlin noise algorithm, which you can think of as "smooth noise." This algorithm is commonly used to generate 2D textures like clouds or dirt, and when you visualize it, it looks something like this:

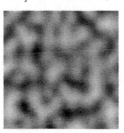

> **Note**: For more information than you may want to know about Perlin noise, see here: http://webstaff.itn.liu.se/~stegu/TNM022-2005/perlinnoiselinks/perlin-noise-math-faq.html

Drag **perlin.c** from the resources for this chapter into your project. When the following popup appears, click **Yes**:

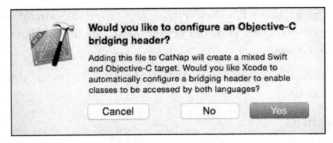

In order to use Objective-C or C code from Swift, you have to import the functions you want to use in a special bridging header. Clicking yes on this dialog creates an empty bridging header for you – you just hve to add the declaration for the perlin noise function you want to call from Swift.

Open **CatNap-Bridging-Header.h** and add the following line:

```
float noise2(float vec[2]);
```

Now you can use the Perlin noise function from the C file in Swift. To use it, add the following to **OldTimeyFilter.swift**:

```
override var outputImage:CIImage? {
  get {
    let time = CFAbsoluteTimeGetCurrent()
    let first = sin(time / 15.0) * 100.0
    let second = sin(time / 2.0) * 25.0

    let v1: [Float] = [Float(first), 1.5]
    let v2: [Float] = [Float(second), 1.5]

    let randVal1 = noise2(UnsafeMutablePointer(v1))
    let randVal2 = noise2(UnsafeMutablePointer(v2))
}
```

You are overriding an existing property on the CIFilter superclass called `outputImage`.

The Perlin noise function `noise2` takes as input two floats that represent the x- and y-coordinates, and returns to you the value of the noise at those coordinates. Here you're always passing 1.5 for the y-coordinate and changing the x-coordinate each frame.

Remember that the Perlin noise algorithm generates random (but smoothly-changing) values over time, so you'll get a random value that you can then pass to your Core Image filters as input, like brightness and intensity of the vignette.

You may wonder how I came up with the values for the x-coordinates to the Perlin noise function: v1 and v2. Here are a few notes on that:

• CFAbsoluteTimeGetCurrent() returns a value that is the system clock in seconds. This becomes an input value you use to drive the random noise values. You could have set up your own variable to keep track of the time since program execution, but this built-in method works just fine.

• Putting this time value into the sin function will return a value between 1.0 and -1.0 that will cycle smoothly over time. By dividing time by 15 in the first float, you make the cycle take 15 times as long. Multiplying by 100 scales up the resulting value.

• I chose the exact values 15 and 100 through trial and error.

You can pass Swift float array values as C pointers by encasing them in UnsafeMutablePointer().

Next, add some code to the end of outputImage to create the first filter:

```
let colorControls = CIFilter(name: "CIColorControls")
colorControls.setValue(0.0, forKey: "inputSaturation")
colorControls.setValue(randVal2 * 0.2,
                       forKey: "inputBrightness")
```

This creates the first filter in the chain, CIColorControls. This filter has three parameters you can use to adjust the image: brightness, contrast and saturation. First, you set the saturation to 0.0. This takes a color image and turns it black and white.

Next, you scale the randVal2 value and use that as the inputBrightness. You can set the brightness value between -1.0 and 1.0, with 0.0 meaning no change. randVal2 will return a random value between 0.0 and 1.0, so by multiplying it by 0.2, you'll set the brightness to a random value between 0.0 and 0.2.

It's time for the second filter. Add this code to the bottom of outputImage:

```
let vignette = CIFilter(name: "CIVignette")
vignette.setValue(0.2 + randVal2, forKey: "inputRadius")
vignette.setValue(randVal2 * 0.2 + 0.8,
                  forKey: "inputIntensity")
```

The vignette filter adds a vignette effect to the image, which darkens the edges of the image. You set both the size and intensity of the vignette based on randVal2. This causes the vignette to change size and darken based on the changes in randVal2, simulating the look of aged film.

There's still one more filter left to add. Add this code to the bottom of `outputImage`:

```
//1
var transform =
  CGAffineTransformMakeTranslation(
    CGFloat(0.0), CGFloat(randVal1 * 45.0))
//2
colorControls.setValue(inputImage, forKey: kCIInputImageKey)
//3
vignette.setValue(colorControls.outputImage,
                  forKey: kCIInputImageKey)
return vignette.outputImage.imageByApplyingTransform(transform)
```

In this last section, you are doing a number of things:

1. First, you create a `CGAffineTransform` with a call to `CGAffineTransformMakeTranslation`. A translation is a transform that moves the position of an element. You can also create transforms that rotate or scale an object, and you can combine transformations, as well.

   You pass in the `randVal1` noise result and multiply it by 45.0 (chosen, again, through trial and error) in the y-dimension.

   You'll use this transform in the last step.

2. Here, you start chaining filters together. On the first filter, you set the `privateInputImage` as the `inputImage` property of the first filter (`colorControls`).

> **Note:** In Core Image, you have a number of framework-defined strings you can use for the keys. `kCIInputImageKey` is equivalent to `inputImage`.

3. On all the subsequent filters, you set the `outputImage` property of one filter to the `inputImage` key of the next one. This is how you construct `CIFilter` chains—by connecting the `outputImage` from one filter to the `inputImage` of the next filter.

   Finally, you return the `outputImage` of the final filter, but on that `CIImage` object, you call one more function, `imageByApplyingTransform(CGAffineTransform)`. This applies the transform matrix created earlier to the current output of the vignette filter, returning a `CIImage` property.

Applying a filter to a node

Switch to **GameScene.swift**. You'll set the filter to operate on the background image. Add the following code to the end of `didMoveToView()`:

```
//1
let effectNode = SKEffectNode()
effectNode.shouldEnableEffects = true
//2
effectNode.filter = OldTimeyFilter()
//3
let backgroundNode = childNodeWithName("Background")
backgroundNode!.removeFromParent()
effectNode.addChild(backgroundNode!)
//4
backgroundNode!.setScale(0.975)
backgroundNode!.position = CGPoint(x: size.width / 2.0,
  y: size.height / 2.0)
//5
effectNode.zPosition = -1
addChild(effectNode)
```

Here's what you're doing:

1. First, you instantiate a new instance of an `SKEffectNode` and set its `shouldEnableEffects` to true. This property makes it easy to turn the filter on and off on an `SKEffectNode`. Filtering a node, especially a full-screen node, can be expensive.

2. Then, you create your `OldTimeyFilter` and set it on `effectNode`.

3. You'll be applying the effect to the background image. For you to do this, the background sprite node needs to be a child of the effect node. Here you get a reference to the background node by its name, and then you remove it from the scene and add it as a child of the effect node.

4. These two lines are a workaround for a current bug in the framework. As of the time of writing, you cannot use an `SKSpriteNode` that's larger than 2007 points wide as the child of an `SKEffectNode.` Hopefully this will be fixed in a future release.

   By scaling the node down to 97.5% of its size (2048 to 1996), it will show up in the effect node. (To see what I mean, remove the lines that scale it down, no background!).

   The only problem is that the background image fills the screen at normal size and it will have blank border spaces around the edges. To fix that, you reposition the smaller node in the center and you change the size of the entire scene. I'll show you how to change the scene size next.

> Note: Related to this bug, the iPhone 6+ won't render the background unless you scale it to `.65`. This would require a major refactoring of all the nodes in order to make the scaling work, so you won't fix it in this case. Just keep in mind that rendering Core Image with a full screen size image has limitations and needs to be tested on all devices.

5. Here, you set `effectNode`'s `zPosition` to make sure it shows up in the background, and you add it to the scene.

Now, you need to change the size of the `SKScene` by adding a new line to the very beginning of `viewDidLoad()`:

```
size = CGSize(width: 1996.0, height: 1467.0)
```

The code that changes the scene size needs to go at the beginning of the method, because some of the other code in `didMoveToView` relies on the scene size. Changing the size 'zooms in' on the scene so that the empty border left by shrinking the background isn't visible.

There's another property on `SKEffectNode` called `shouldRasterize`. This property is set to `false` by default. When set to `true`, it will apply the filter and save the contents to a buffer, rather than re-applying the filter each frame.

If you're filtering a large node or using a complex filter chain, this can be very helpful. Applying a complex image filter 30 or 60 times a second is sometimes too much for good performance. If the node doesn't change every frame, you can avoid the overhead by setting `shouldRasterize` to `true` until the node needs updating.

> **Note:** This filter chain has three different filters in it and you're applying it to the entire screen. On an iPhone 4S, this filter will reduce the frames per second to about 38, which isn't ideal.
>
> If you need to support these devices, you probably want to find a way to run this filter chain periodically in your game, rather than every frame. To save on processing resources, you can set the `shouldRasterize` property to `true`, as explained above.

By switching that flag on and off every other frame, you only have to apply the expensive filter half the time. If the game runs at 60 FPS, the screen refreshes 30 times per second. However, the game can still accept user input at 60 FPS.

Alternatively, if you're applying a filter to a subtree of the scene and those elements don't change every frame, you can set the filter to run only after a change has been registered, further saving resources.

Build and run now. You should have a game that looks like it's running from an old projector:

That was a lot of work, but the result is worth it!

Note: At this point, if you're running on the Simulator or on an older device, your FPS has dropped a bit. That's no surprise, as full-screen Core Image effects with multiple filters can be very expensive!

This lower frame rate also creates an interesting problem: When the cat collides with the bed, the game sends the win method. Similarly, when the cat collides with the floor, the game sends the lose method. It's possible with a low frame rate for the game to call both collisions at once (since the physics simulation might need to process an unexpectedly long amount of time), meaning your player would both win and lose the game simultaneously!

If you'd like to resolve this, simply add a Boolean property to the class called `gameOver`. Initialize its value to `false` and then set it to `true` whenever the player wins or loses. Finally, check to make sure `gameOver` is `false` before letting the player win or lose in the future.

Filtering transitions

You already learned about the `SKTransition` class in Chapter 4, "Scenes." Remember, this is the class you can use to run special effects to transition between scenes, like a door-opening or a flip effects.

But what if the built-in transitions aren't enough and you want to create one of your own? Well, you can do this with the third and final way to use Core Image in Sprite Kit: filtering transitions.

`SKTransition` has an initializer named `init(CIFilter:duration:)`. You can pass a specially-constructed `CIFilter` object to this method, along with a duration, and the method will use the filter to create the transition effect.

To use a `CIFilter` subclass in an `SKTransition`, the `CIFilter` subclass needs to have two parameters for `CIImage` input images: `inputImage` and `inputTargetImage`. It also needs to have an `inputTime` property.

The `inputTime` property will be passed in at render time, and ranges from 0.0 to 1.0 for the duration time passed into the method. For example, if the duration of the transition is 0.8 seconds, after 0.4 seconds in the transition, the `inputTime` property will have a value of 0.5.

You can use the value of `inputTime` to determine where you are in the transition. Then you can create an `outputImage` based on this time location.

To illustrate this point, you're going to create a very simple fade transition.

The first step is to add a normal transition to Cap Nap. Inside **GameScene.swift**, replace the last line of `newGame()` with these two lines:

```
let transition = SKTransition.flipVerticalWithDuration(0.5)
view!.presentScene(newScene, transition: transition)
```

Build and run. Play through a level and witness your new transition in action!

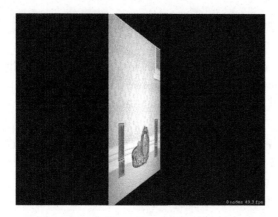

> **Note**: If you have trouble seeing the transition, make sure you run the code on an actual device rather than the Simulator, and that you use a relatively new device like an iPhone 5. Remember, Core Image filters are expensive and might not perform well on older hardware.

Creating a custom transition

It's time to create a custom `CIFilter` to make a custom transition.

This custom transition will perform a simple fade from one scene's image to the next, and it will also rotate the scene as it does so.

In Xcode's main menu, select **File\New\File...**, select the **iOS\Source\Swift File** template and click **Next**. Name the file **CustomTransitionFilter.swift**, make sure the **CatNap** target is checked and click **Create**.

First, import Core Image and create your class. Add this code:

```
import CoreImage

class CustomTransitionFilter: CIFilter {
}
```

Next, add the following properties to **CustomTransitionFilter.swift**:

```
var inputImage: CIImage?
var inputTargetImage: CIImage?
var inputTime: NSNumber?
```

inputTime must be an NSNumber because that's the class Sprite Kit will use to set the parameter.

Sprite Kit will automatically set these properties when you set this filter on an SKTransition. inputImage will be the source scene, inputTargetImage will be the destination scene and inputTime will always range from 0.0 to 1.0.

That last part may be confusing. Regardless of how much time you pass the duration parameter when you call init(CIFilter:duration:), inside the CIFilter subclass that value is scaled to a value between 0.0 and 1.0. For example, if you pass a transition duration of 0.75 seconds, halfway through the transition, or at .375 seconds into the transition, inputTime will be 0.5:

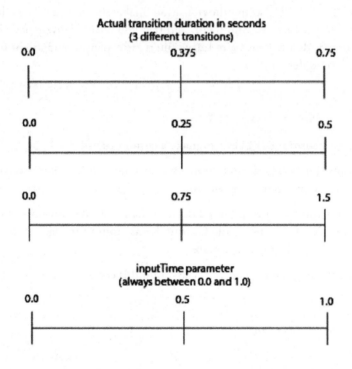

Now add the following method to **CustomTransitionFilter.swift**:

```
override var outputImage:CIImage? {
  get {
  //1
  if inputTime == nil {
```

```
      return nil;
    }
    if inputTargetImage == nil {
      return nil;
    }
    if inputImage == nil {
      return nil;
    }
    //2
    let color = CIFilter(name: "CIConstantColorGenerator")
    color.setValue(
      CIColor(red: 1.0, green: 1.0, blue: 1.0,
      alpha: CGFloat(inputTime!.floatValue)),
      forKey: "inputColor")
    //3
    let blendWithMask = CIFilter(name: "CIBlendWithAlphaMask")
    blendWithMask.setValue(color.outputImage,
      forKey: "inputMaskImage")
    blendWithMask.setValue(inputImage,
      forKey: "inputBackgroundImage")
    blendWithMask.setValue(inputTargetImage,
      forKey: "inputImage")
    //4
    let transform = CGAffineTransformMakeRotation(
      CGFloat(inputTime!) * 3.14 * 4.0)
    //5
    return

 blendWithMask.outputImage.imageByApplyingTransform(transform)
    }
}
```

This filter is not so complicated when you break it down into steps:

1. The first step is to check the status of your conditionals so you don't crash when you force-unwrap them.

2. The first filter you create in the chain is called `CIConstantColorGenerator`. There is a class of `CIFilters` called generators that don't require an input image. Other generators include linear and radial gradients, noise and checkerboards.

The constant color generator outputs a single color. In this case, you need to create an alpha mask that ranges from 0.0 to 1.0. The color doesn't matter as much as the last parameter for the alpha argument. Here, you pass in `inputTime!.floatValue`. First you unwrap the `NSValue` optional and then you get the `floatValue` from it. You need to convert it to a `CGFloat` to use it in the `CIColor` constructor.

3. The second filter blends the source and destination scenes according to the alpha mask.

For any given pixel, the filter interpolates between the `inputImage` and the `inputBackgroundImage` based on the alpha value of the pixel in the `inputMaskImage`. When the alpha value is 0.0, the `inputBackgroundImage` is fully displayed; in this case, since `inputBackgroundImage` is set to the `inputImage` property of your `CIFilter` subclass, or the source scene. When the alpha pixel value is 1.0, the image displayed is the `inputImage`, which in this case is the `inputTargetImage` or destination scene image.

4. Here, you use `CGAffineTransformMakeRotation` to create a transformation matrix that will spin the image twice.

5. Finally, you return the result of calling `imageByApplyingTransform()` on the `outputImage` of the `blendWithMask` filter.

That's it for this filter. As the value in `inputTime` moves from 0.0 to 1.0, the filter masks more and more of the image from the original scene, and you'll see more and more of the target scene. As the time increments, the scene will also spin, making two rotations, as 3.14 is half a rotation.

Back in **GameScene.swift**, replace the current scene transition in `newGame()` with your new custom transition filter:

```
let transition = SKTransition(
  CIFilter: CustomTransitionFilter(), duration: 1.0)
```

Build and run now, and enjoy your simple fade transition.

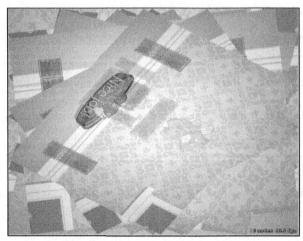

At this point, you've experienced using Core Image in all three of the ways available in Sprite Kit: filtering textures, filtering an SKEffectNode and filtering transitions.

But before you bid farewell to Cat Nap for good, why not practice what you just learned by adding a special effect to the game on your own? The cat will love you for it. :]

Challenges

You have one challenge in this chapter, designed to give you more practice using SKEffectNode. In it, you'll learn a little about using color manipulations on a sprite.

As always, if you get stuck, you can find the solution in the resources for this chapter—but give it your best shot first!

Challenge 1: A colorful resurrection

Remember the zombie from Zombie Conga? Well, he's about to rise from the grave!

In the resources for this chapter, you'll find a starter project called **ZombieCongaHue Starter**. Open it in Xcode and build and run, and you'll see that your favorite zombie has returned!

Take a look through the code. It's very similar to the Zombie Conga project, but there are two main differences:

1. The zombie moves around automatically, bouncing off walls. Maybe the crazy cat ladies wore off on him!

2. This time, the zombie is made up of two images: one sprite for the zombie itself and a child sprite for the zombie's hat. I'll explain why this is this later on.

   However, note that both the zombie and the hat are added as children of the main scene, and their position and rotation are updated so they always stay in sync.

Your challenge is to adjust the hue of the zombie to be a random color. This is a handy technique if you want to have different types of enemies in your game, but not have them all look exactly the same.

This brings us to the reason why the zombie's hat is a different sprite. Often, you want to adjust some parts of a sprite's color, but keep other parts unchanged. By making the hat a different sprite, you can apply a filter to the zombie sprite but the hat can rest on top, unchanged.

To adjust the zombie's color, you need to apply a `CIHueAdjust` filter to the zombie. The goal is that whenever you tap the screen, you update the `CIFilter` to make the zombie—but not the zombie's hat—switch to a new color.

Here are some hints for how to do this:

1. Create properties for an `SKEffectNode` and a `CIFilter`.

2. Initialize the `SKEffectNode` and instead of adding the `zombie` to `self`, add it to the `SKEffectNode`. Then, add the `SKEffectNode` to `self`.

3. Initialize the `CIHueAdjust` filter and set the default value `inputAngle` to 0. This means no hue adjustment. The input angle parameter rotates the color of the sprite fully (returning to the original color) every 2π rotations, so values of 0.0, 2π and -2π all mean no change in hue. π is halfway around the color wheel, so that value will create a visible shift in color.

4. Set the `filter` property of the effect node to your filter and set the `shouldEnableEffects` parameter to `true`.

5. Now, in `touchesBegan(withEvent:)`, set the filter's `inputAngle` property to a random value between 0.0 and 2π.

Each time you tap the screen, the zombie will change color, but his hat will remain the same:

You may wonder why you bothered doing this when you could have simply set the color property on the zombie. See for yourself by commenting out the lines in touchesBegan(withEvent:) that update the filter's inputAngle value, replacing them with the following:

```
zombie.color =
  SKColor(red: 1.0, green: 0.0, blue: 0.5, alpha: 1.0)
zombie.colorBlendFactor = 1.0
```

Build and run, and notice how the zombie looks when you tap:

Setting the color changes the color of the entire zombie, while varying the hue results in some nice variance between different parts of the zombie, and generally looks better. So what you've learned in challenge is definitely a neat technique to have in your tool belt!

Now bring out your shotgun and put this zombie to rest—permanently. It's time to move on to a new game about a badass with an attitude facing off again a whole lot of giant bugs.

Challenge 2: OS X

You learned how to port a Sprite Kit game to OS X in Chapter 6, so this should be mostly a reminder. However, there are a few issues specific to the content in **CatNap**. Here's a list of things that you'll need to do:

- Add a new target for the Mac version of the game. Name it **CatNapMac**.
- Move all the shared code to a Shared folder. This will include most of the source files (perlin.c, don't forget it), with the exception of the **AppDelegate.swift** and the **GameViewController.swift** files.
- You're new target will have a new **Images.xcassets** container. Use it to set up the icons for the Mac version. The icon files are included in the **Resources/Icons/Mac** folder.
- You need to add all the images, sounds, videos, and altas folders to the CatNapMac target
- You need to set the Objective-C Bridging Header in the CatNapMac target to be the same file you use in the CatNap target, **CatNap-Bridging-Header.h**.
- Change the `GameScene` loading line in **AppDelegate.swift** (in the Mac target) from `unarchiveFromFile()` to `level()`.
- Add `self.skView!.showsPhysics = true` if you want SpriteKit to draw lines around the physics bodies as it does in the iOS target.
- Place the `touchesBegan()` method in **GameScene.swift** into an `#if os(iOS)` block and add a `mouseDown()` method in `#elseif` to handle clicks on OS X. Call `sceneTouched(theEvent.locationInNode(self))` from `mouseDown` like you do in `touchesBegan`.
- SpriteKit in OS X has some bugs with the CoreImage integration. SKEffectNode doesn't work as of this time of writing. The only parts currently using an SKEffectNode are the lines in didMoveToView() in GameScene. Wrap the lines that makes filters the background image with an OldTimeyFilter filter in an #if os(iOS)/#endif macro.

- For those classes that import CoreImage, on OS X Core Image isn't a separate framework, it's part of AppKit, so you must import AppKit.

- One last issue you need to address is level 5's replace photo code. On iOS, you use a `UIImagePicker` to select a photo to replace the zombie head. Mac has no such class. So, instead (and there is more than one way to do this), I suggest using an `NSOpenPanel` to navigate and pick an image file from the user's hard drive.

- You need to set the `AppDelegate` class as implementing the `ImageCaptureDelegate` protocol and set the scene's `imageCaptureDelegate` property to the `AppDelegate` classs.

- You should implement the `requestImagePicker` method in `AppDelegate`. This method will be called when the user clicks on the zombie photo frame sprite.

- In that method, use an `NSOpenPanel`. `NSOpenPanel` has a way to restrict the files selectable by type, called `allowedFileTypes`. You can set that array property to `NSImage`'s class method, `imageTypes()`. That method will supply an array of all the files supported by `NSImage`.

- `NSOpenPanel` has a method that opens the panel and executes a completion block when the panel is closed. You can use this completion block to either do nothing (if the user clicked cancel) or call `GameScene`'s `changePhotoTexture` method with the new texture from the file selected.

`NSOpenPanel` can be referenced inside the completion block to check whether the URL property has a value (it's an optional property). If a file is selected, you use the URL to instantiate an `NSImage`, and use the `NSImage` to instantiate an `SKTexture` to pass to the `changePhotoTexture` property.

Section IV: Tile Maps and Juice

At the time of writing, Sprite Kit doesn't come packaged with tile map support – but in this section, you're going to learn how to create your own tile map engine! You'll also learn how to take a good game and make it great by adding a ton of special effects and excitement – a.k.a. "juice."

In the process, you will create a tile map-based action game called Pest Control, where you take the role of Arnold, a guy so badass he *never* wears a shirt. Giant bugs have invaded Arnold's town, and he's just the guy to dish out a good smashing.

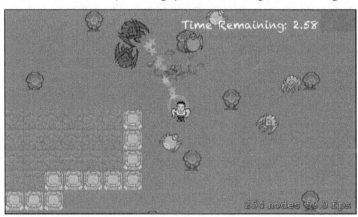

Chapter 14: Beginning Tile Maps

Chapter 15: More Tile Maps

Chapter 16: Imported Tile Maps

Chapter 17: Saving and Loading Games

Chapter 18: Juice Up Your Game, Part 1

Chapter 19: Juice Up Your Game, Part 2

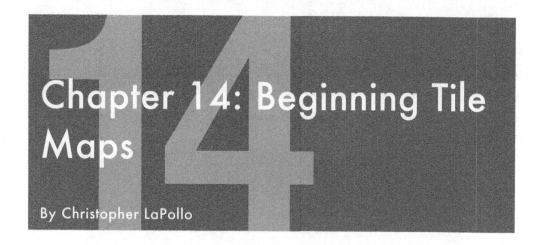

Chapter 14: Beginning Tile Maps

By Christopher LaPollo

From the first days of computers, developers have had to find ways to get more performance out of limited CPU cycles, RAM and disk space. Video game makers discovered one trick early on: building up level backgrounds by combining and repeating smaller images, referred to as **tiles**. You've seen tiles in countless games, like *Mega Man*, *Contra*, *Super Mario Bros.* and *The Legend of Zelda*.

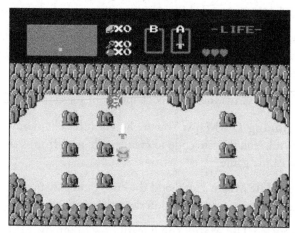

For indie iOS developers, tile maps are a great choice for a number of reasons:

• **Improved performance**. Tile maps require less memory and processing time than many alternative methods. This is particularly important for iOS, since mobile processing power is quite limited compared to PCs or consoles.

• **Reduced art costs**. With tile maps, a small set of tiles can make many large levels, allowing you to make the most of an often limited art budget.

- **Reduced time to market**. Tile maps are quite simple to create and work with, allowing you to quickly produce and iterate upon levels.

Over the next few chapters, you'll create a new minigame: Pest Control. Here's what it will look like when you're finished:

In Pest Control, your player takes the role of Arnold, a guy so badass he *never* wears a shirt. Arnold's town has been invaded by giant bugs in need of a good smashing.

Pest Control uses very simple pixel art. Each of its animations consists of only two frames and its backgrounds are plain. This is by design, to show you what you can accomplish with relatively basic art.

You'll build Pest Control across the next six chapters, in stages:

1. **Chapter 14, Beginning Tile Maps:** You are here! In this chapter, you'll create the bulk of Pest Control. You'll write code to create a tile map from a simple text format and add the hero to the game.

2. **Chapter 15, More Tile Maps:** You'll add the core gameplay in this chapter and learn about coordinate conversions and collision detection with tile maps.

3. **Chapter 16, Imported Tile Maps:** You'll learn how to import tile maps that are stored in a popular tile-map format called TMX files, and you'll use an open-source map editor to create your maps.

4. **Chapter 17, Saving and Loading Games:** You'll learn how to implement an autosave feature that stores a player's progress in Pest Control. You'll also add gameplay features like timers, winning and losing, and progressing through multiple levels.

5. Chapter 18, Juice Up Your Game, Part 1: You'll learn how adding simple visual effects can make Pest Control, or any game you write, more entertaining.

6. Chapter 19, Juice Up Your Game, Part 2: You'll add sounds and even more effects, because adding fewer effects at this point would be ridiculous.

Controlling pests takes a lot of work, so let's get started.

Getting started

Start Xcode and select **File\New\Project…** from the main menu. Select the **iOS\Application\Game** template and click **Next**.

Enter **PestControl** for the Product Name, choose **Swift** for Language, choose **SpriteKit** for Game Technology, choose **Universal** for Devices, and click **Next**.

Choose somewhere on your hard drive to save your project and click **Create**.

Inside your new project, modify the **PestControl** target to support only **Landscape Left** and **Landscape Right**.

While you're there, make sure **Hide status bar** is checked, because you don't want players distracted by the time while they're supposed to be playing your game.

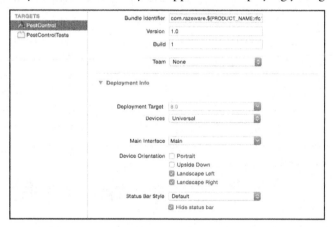

You also need to modify this in one more spot. Open **Supporting File\Info.plist**, and find the **Supported interface orientations (iPad)** entry. Delete the entries for **Portrait (bottom home button)** and **Portrait (top home button)** you see there, so that only the landscape options remain.

Pest Control won't be using SKS files, so select **GameScene.sks**, delete it from the project and select **Move to Trash**.

You also need to modify the template code that loads the scene. Open **GameViewController.swift** and replace its viewDidLoad() with the following:

```
override func viewDidLoad() {
  super.viewDidLoad()
  let scene = GameScene(size:CGSize(width: 1024, height: 768))
  let skView = view as! SKView
  skView.showsFPS = true
  skView.showsNodeCount = true
  skView.ignoresSiblingOrder = true
  scene.scaleMode = .AspectFill
  skView.presentScene(scene)
}
```

This is the same code you've used in earlier games like Zombie Conga, so there's no need to go over it again.

You'll want access to the math functions in your old friend SKTUtils, so drag the **SKTUtils** folder from the book's resources into your project. Make sure **Copy items if needed**, **Create groups**, and the **PestControl** target are all checked.

Swift files within the same project can access each other freely, so you can now use anything from the SKTUtils folder you just imported.

Finally, just to keep things official-looking, set up the app's icon. Open **Images.xassets** and select the **AppIcon** entry. Open the Attributes Inspector (**View\Utilities\Show Attributes Inspector**), and make sure that both the **iPhone** and **iPad** sections have **iOS 7.0 and Later Sizes** checked. Make sure the **iPhone** section has **iOS 8.0 and Later Sizes** checked, too. Then, in the resources for this chapter, drag each file from the **Icons\iOS** folder into its appropriate spot. You should see the following when you're done:

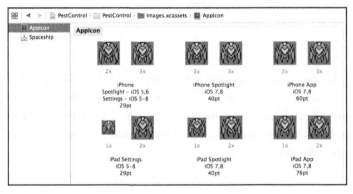

Import resources

The next step is to import the resources you need for Pest Control. To do this, drag the **Resources** folder from this chapter's resources into your project. Make sure **Copy items if needed**, **Create groups** and the **PestControl** target are all checked.

The **Resources** folder you just added includes two subfolders, **Levels** and **Art**:

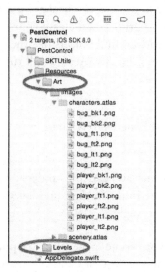

Levels contains configuration data that you can ignore for now. **Art** currently contains another folder, named **Images**, and you'll add even more resources there in later chapters.

Images contains folders named **scenery.atlas** and **characters.atlas**. As you learned in Chapter 10 of this book, Xcode automatically creates a texture atlas from the images inside any folder whose name ends with **.atlas**. Xcode might create more than one texture atlas per folder if there are too many images to fit within its size constraints.

There aren't many images in Pest Control, so they could all easily fit into a single texture atlas. But to demonstrate some additional Sprite Kit features, I've divided the images into two groups:

- Those images you'll use to create the map are stored in **scenery.atlas**. For this folder, Xcode will create a texture atlas named **scenery**.

- Those images that make up the player and bug animations are stored in **characters.atlas**. For this folder, Xcode will create a texture atlas named **characters**.

With the project created and its resources in place, let's make a map.

Map-building with tiles

In most games, the background art takes up the most screen space. That means it threatens to take up most of your art budget and dominate the space in your app's bundle, too.

In this section, you'll see how you can create a background using only a few simple images, repeated and laid out in a grid. You'll create your scene using multiple layers: one for the bugs, a second for background objects like the grass and water and a third for some special decorations, the trees. Finally, Arnold will run around on top of these layers.

> **Note:** There are a number of benefits to separating your scene into multiple layers.
>
> First, it keeps your code cleaner and easier to understand. For example, if you know the background tiles are in the background layer and the bugs are in the bug layer, you can code accordingly.
>
> Second, multiple layers in your scene make it easy to put tiles in front of or behind other layers. For example, in Pest Control, the tree tiles will be partially transparent so you can see the grass behind them. You could also do even fancier things, like have another layer on top of the bug layer so bugs could hide behind a bush, or use multiple background layers to implement parallax scrolling.
>
> Third, multiple layers can result in better performance. Sprite Kit attempts to speed up its rendering by drawing as much as it can with a single texture atlas before loading a different texture atlas into the GPU. It's actually more complicated than that, but one way you can drastically improve rendering performance is to organize your sprite nodes by texture atlas.
>
> Put another way, your game might run really slowly if you mix texture atlases within a single node and its children. In fact, even if all the sprites in a node use the same texture atlas, you may still need to put them on different layers if they are treated differently in some other way—like if they all don't use the same blend mode. For more information, see Chapter 26, "Performance: Texture Atlases."

OK, before Arnold can rid his town of its bug infestation, you need to build him a town filled with bugs. Start things off with the background layer.

Tile layers

Go to **File\New\File…**, choose the **iOS\Source\Swift File** template and click **Next**. Name your file **TileMapLayer**, be sure the **PestControl** target is checked and click **Finish**.

Open **TileMapLayer.swift** and replace its contents with the following:

```
import SpriteKit

class TileMapLayer : SKNode {
  let tileSize: CGSize
  var atlas: SKTextureAtlas?

  required init?(coder aDecoder: NSCoder) {
    fatalError("NSCoding not supported")
  }

  init(tileSize: CGSize)
  {
    self.tileSize = tileSize

    super.init()
  }
}
```

Importing the SpriteKit module gives you access to all of its classes. You're making TileMapLayer extend SKNode so you can add instances of this class directly to your scene.

You add two properties to TileMapLayer—tileSize and atlas—and you define the initial version of TileMapLayer's designated initializer. Right now, it only initializes the tileSize constant with the given value and calls super.init(). You'll add more to this method later, but this is enough to keep the compiler happy for now.

tileSize describes the width and height of this layer's tiles, measured in points. You'll use this to position tiles in the map, and the math you'll use to do so only works if every tile in the grid is the same size. If your app needs to support multiple tile sizes, group them into different TileMapLayer objects.

atlas will hold the optional SKTextureAtlas you'll use to create this node's sprites. SKTextureAtlas class provides direct access to the texture atlases Xcode generates for you. It only has a few methods, but as you'll soon see, there are benefits in using it to create your sprites.

You declare `atlas` as optional because you'll create layers without an atlas in Chapter 16, "Imported Tile Maps." Rather than change your code later to work without an atlas, you're planning for it now.

Creating tiles

In this chapter, you're going to create tile maps using simple text files. For now, you'll only support two tile types: grass and walls. You'll put the 'o' character wherever you want grass to appear, and the 'x' character wherever you want a wall. I chose these two characters just because I like the way they look.

For example, the following line:

```
@"xoooooooooooooooox"
```

Will be converted into a sequence of 1 wall tile, 16 grass tiles and 1 wall tile, like this:

You need a method that takes a character and returns the right kind of tile for that character. For the wall and grass tiles, you will simply create an `SKSpriteNode` with the appropriate image set.

To do this, add the following new method to `TileMapLayer`:

```
func nodeForCode(tileCode: Character) -> SKNode? {
  // 1
  if atlas == nil {
    return nil
  }
  // 2
  var tile: SKNode?
  switch tileCode {
    case "x":
      tile = SKSpriteNode(texture: atlas!.textureNamed("wall"))

    case "o":
      tile = SKSpriteNode(texture:atlas!.textureNamed("grass1"))

    default:
      println("Unknown tile code \(tileCode)")
  }
  // 3
```

```
    if let sprite = tile as? SKSpriteNode {
      sprite.blendMode = .Replace
    }
    return tile
}
```

This is the heart of your operation. Or the brains. Maybe the guts? It's definitely something important. This method takes a character and returns an appropriate SKNode for it. You declare nodeForCode() to return an optional value because it may not recognize the given tile code, and in that case returns nil rather than a default tile.

There are three things to note here:

1. You return nil immediately if atlas is nil. The rest of the code in this method assumes atlas exists, but in Chapter 16, you'll add another method for creating tiles that doesn't rely on the texture atlas.

2. You use a switch statement to create the correct sprite based on the value of tileCode. For now, it only supports two characters, x and o, used to create wall and grass tiles, respectively. But you'll be adding more tile types to this statement throughout this chapter.

   Note that here you're creating your SKSpriteNodes in a different way than you have in previous chapters. Instead of calling SKSpriteNode(imageNamed:), you call SKSpriteNode(texture:), passing in textures retrieved by name from atlas. I'll cover this in more detail below.

3. You check to see if tile currently points to an SKSpriteNode. This ensures you don't try to access SKSpriteNode methods on nodes of other types, or on non-existent objects in cases where tile is nil because of an unrecognized tile code.

   If tile is an SKSpriteNode, you set its blendMode property to Replace. By default, Sprite Kit uses a blend mode of Alpha, which supports combining a sprite's pixels with whatever pixels are below it. This is necessary when layering sprites that contain transparent pixels. But most of your images are background tiles that you know don't have transparent pixels, so setting the blend mode this way allows Sprite Kit to speed up its rendering by ignoring the pixels below this sprite. Later, when you add sprites that include transparency, you'll make sure their blend modes remain set to the default mode.

Now—back to why you're creating sprites with SKSpriteNode(texture:) in this method. There are two potential benefits to creating SKSpriteNodes this way, instead of with the image-name-based method you've been using.

1. **You control the source texture**. When you call `textureNamed()` on an
   `SKTextureAtlas`, Sprite Kit knows exactly where to find the texture. If you call
   `SKSpriteNode(imageNamed:)` or `SKTexture(imageNamed:)`, Sprite Kit first
   searches your app's bundle for an image file with that name; if it can't find one, it
   searches your app's texture atlases.

   If your app contains multiple files with the same name, each in a different atlas, then
   Sprite Kit will simply pick one. For example, maybe you have multiple atlases
   arranged by map area, but each contains a different image named tree.png.

   `textureNamed()` is called on a specific atlas, so Sprite Kit bypasses that search and
   returns the correct texture immediately. This means you can have image files with the
   same name in different atlases, allowing you to name your images descriptively
   without worrying about file names in other atlases.

2. **Increased performance.** Because you specify the texture the image comes from
   directly, Sprite Kit doesn't have to search for it. This makes finding images this way a
   tiny bit faster. To be clear, I'm not touting this as a performance optimization tip—
   it's doubtful your app's overall performance will be noticeably different either way.
   However, it's worth mentioning to give you a better idea of what's going on behind
   the scenes. The *real* performance increase comes from `SKTextureAtlas`'s ability to
   share objects efficiently, but I'll come back to that later.

Still inside **TileMapLayer.swift**, add the following method that initializes a
`TileMapLayer` from some strings:

```
convenience init(atlasName: String, tileSize: CGSize,
                 tileCodes: [String]) {
  self.init(tileSize: tileSize)

  atlas = SKTextureAtlas(named: atlasName)

  for row in 0..<tileCodes.count {
    let line = tileCodes[row]
    for (col, code) in enumerate(line) {
      if let tile = nodeForCode(code) {
        // add tiles here
      }
    }
  }
}
```

The code above defines a convenience initializer for a `TileMapLayer` object. You already
know what `tileSize` is for, but take a look at the other two parameters:

- `atlasName` is the name of a texture atlas created by Xcode, in which it will find images for this layer's tiles. As previously mentioned, Pest Control will have two atlases: **scenery** and **characters**. The way you'll implement the game, each `TileMapLayer` will only use images from a single atlas. In Chapter 16, "Imported Tile Maps", you'll create layers without this limitation.

- `tileCodes` is an array of `Strings`. This array defines the layout of the map itself, where each string represents a row of tiles on the map, and each of the string's characters represents a single tile in that row. You create a tile for each character using `nodeForCode()`, which you just added.

`init(atlasName:tileSize:tileCodes:)` first calls the designated initializer you created earlier to perform any required set up, passing it `tileSize`. It then assigns `atlas` an `SKTextureAtlas` to access the texture atlas named in `atlasName`. Finally, it loops through `tileCodes` to build sprites for the tiles.

Notice you check to see if `nodeForCode()` returns `nil`. That's because you defined `nodeForCode()` to return an optional value, but you only want to use the returned value if it's actually an object. A good way to do this is to use optional binding to test if the object contains a value and assign it to a temporary variable if so, as you see here.

Positioning tiles

Once you create a sprite, you need to position it correctly in the map. Add the following method to calculate a tile's x- and y-positions, based on its row and column in the tile grid:

```
func positionForRow(row: Int, col: Int) -> CGPoint {
  let x = CGFloat(col) * tileSize.width + tileSize.width / 2
  let y = CGFloat(row) * tileSize.height + tileSize.height / 2
  return CGPoint(x: x, y: y)
}
```

This isn't complicated. (It's also not completely correct, but you'll fix it soon.) Take a look at this diagram and the explanation that follows to see how you find the position for a tile:

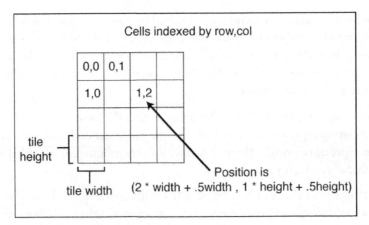

Rows count from top to bottom and columns count from left to right. So you multiply col by the tile width to find its x-position, and you multiply row by the tile height to find its y-position. You add half the tile's width and height to those x- and y-values, because you're calculating the tile's center point.

Inside `init(atlasNamed:tileSize:tileCodes:)`, replace the comment that reads "add tiles here" with the following:

```
tile.position = positionForRow(row, col: col)
addChild(tile)
```

The code above sets the tile's position and adds it to the layer.

Almost done! You just need to create your new `TileMapLayer` object to see it in action.

Your first map

Open **GameScene.swift** and remove the methods `GameScene` currently contains—those were provided by the iOS Game template, but you'll implement each one as you need it.

To keep things neat, you'll organize your scene initialization code into several methods. Add the first one to `GameScene` now, named `createScenery()`:

```
func createScenery() -> TileMapLayer {
  return TileMapLayer(atlasName: "scenery",
                      tileSize: CGSize(width: 32, height: 32),
                      tileCodes: ["xxxxxxxxxxxxxxxxxx",
                                  "x0000000000000000x",
                                  "x0000000000000000x",
                                  "x0000000000000000x",
                                  "x0000000000000000x",
```

```
                                 "X000000000X000000X",
                                 "X000000000X000000X",
                                 "X00000XXXXX000000X",
                                 "X00000X0000000000X",
                                 "XXXXXXXXXXXXXXXXXX"])
  }
```

This is really only one line of code. It returns a new `TileMapLayer` that creates tiles from the texture atlas named **scenery**, all of which are 32 points wide and tall. It defines a grid made of xs and os that is 18 tiles wide and 10 tiles high.

Because you already know that x translates to a `wall` tile and o translates to `grass`, you can imagine what the map will look like just by glancing at this grid of characters. But you can do better than that! So add the following method to create your map and add it to the scene:

```
override func didMoveToView(view: SKView) {
  addChild(createScenery())
}
```

You've already learned about `didMoveToView()`, so you know it's a good place to initialize your scene. Here you simply call `createScenery()` and add the `TileMapLayer` it returns to the scene.

Build and run in the **iPhone 5s Simulator**.

Note: It's important to use a four-inch simulator or device throughout the next few sections. Otherwise, the screenshots and explanations will not match exactly what you see. You'll be able to use any size device a bit later.

When you run, you should see the following:

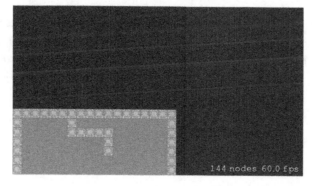

Hmm. That doesn't seem right. You made a tile map that is 18 tiles wide by 10 tiles high, and since each tile should be 32x32 points, you might expect your map to fill the entire view on an iPhone 5s. However, the tiles seem too small, and some of them are completely off-screen!

Scale mode revisisted

The problem is in `GameViewController`'s `viewDidLoad()`, where you initialized the scene with a size of 1024x768 and used a `scaleMode` of `AspectFill`. It's the same code you used in earlier games to support multiple device sizes, but it isn't what you want for Pest Control.

Why not? Well, why are the tiles so small? You defined the scene to be 1024x768 points, but you only specified 320x576 points' worth of tiles. When Sprite Kit scales your scene using the `AspectFill` scale mode, you end up with tiles that look too small, along with a lot of empty space.

That explains the sizing issue, but what about the missing tiles? As you learned in the very first chapter of this book, the settings you used here result in Sprite Kit cropping off 96 points from both the top and bottom of your scene for iPhone 4" devices. However, you placed the tiles starting at (0, 0), so the bottom 96 points' worth of tiles, or three rows, are below the edge of the screen.

Pest Control's gameplay will allow the scene to scroll both horizontally and vertically. That means there's no need to scale it to fit the screen. Instead, you'll set it up so that the level is always the same size, and the device determines how much of the level the player can see at once.

Open **GameViewController.swift** and find `viewDidLoad()`. Change the line that sets `scene`'s `scaleMode` property to the following:

```
scene.scaleMode = .ResizeFill
```

This tells Sprite Kit to resize the scene's dimensions to match those of its view but to leave the scene's contents unscaled. That is, your 32x32-point tiles will now take up 32x32 points, no matter what device you're using. However, you'll see more tiles at once on a larger device like an iPad than you will on a smaller device like an iPhone.

> **Note:** As a side effect of this new scale mode, you'll need to make sure you create levels that are large enough to fill an iPad. For example, with 32x32-point tiles, your levels should be at least 32 tiles wide by 24 tiles tall.

Run the app, and now you should see this:

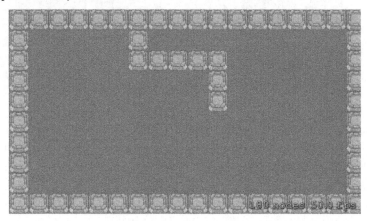

Much better. Your scene isn't filling the screen because Sprite Kit resized the scene to fit the device size exactly, placing the origin in the lower-left corner. And your tiles are sized correctly, too, so the 10 rows you defined fill the screen exactly. (There are a few pixels cut off on the right because 18 tiles are slightly wider than the iPhone 5s screen.)

> **Note:** Sprite Kit calls a method on your scene named `didChangeSize()` whenever the scene's size changes, and even sometimes when it doesn't. One day, you might write a game that needs to support multiple sizes at runtime—for example, if it supports both portrait and landscape modes. In such a case, implement this method to update anything in your scene that depends on the screen size, such as the placement of UI elements.

The tiles are sized correctly now, but there's something about them that's still bugging me. See what I did there, with the bugging?

Filtering modes

If you look very closely, you'll see the tiles are a bit blurry, when they should appear with a sharp pixel-art style.

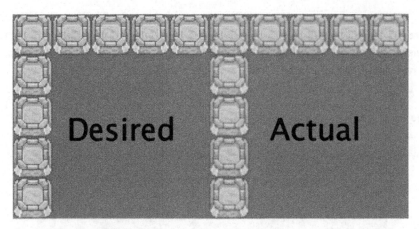

You are displaying the tiles as 32x32 points so that Pest Control shows the same number of tiles on both Retina and non-Retina displays. However, the image you're using for the tile is actually 32x32 *pixels*, so on Retina devices, it gets scaled by 2 to account for the display's double-pixel density. But why is it blurry?

By default, Sprite Kit produces scaled images that are antialiased, or smooth. To achieve this result, it blends pixel colors in such a way that sharp lines are often lost. This looks great for a lot of art, but Pest Control uses pixel art, which is meant to show the stark outlines of individual pixels.

Fortunately, there's a simple way to fix this. Open **TileMapLayer.swift** and add the following line to nodeWithCode(), immediately after the line that sets sprites's blendMode property:

```
sprite.texture?.filteringMode = .Nearest
```

Run again, and now you'll see your map in all its pixelated glory!

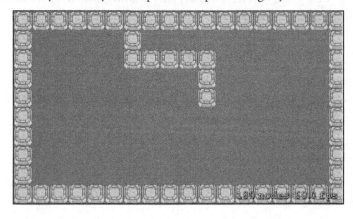

Upside-down maps

Looks good now, right? Not quite.

You may not have noticed, but if you compare the image with the grid you defined in `createScenery()`, you'll find that the map is upside down!

The problem lies in your implementation of `positionForRow(col:)` in **TileMapLayer.swift**.

You built the tile map using standard array syntax, counting left to right, top to bottom. But remember that in Sprite Kit's coordinate system, y-values move *up* the screen as they increase. So tile coordinate (0,0) is at the upper-left of your grid, but your math will place that tile at the lower-left of your screen.

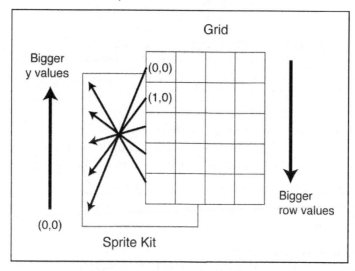

To fix this, you need to adjust the y-positions of all your tiles. Instead of counting up from (0,0), you want to count down from the top of the map.

To do so, you'll need access to a couple more pieces of information about your tile map. Open **TileMapLayer.swift** and add the following properties:

```
let gridSize: CGSize
let layerSize: CGSize
```

As soon as you add those lines, Xcode starts indicating you have an error in your class. That's because you haven't provided values for these properties in your designated initializer. You'll take care of that soon, but first, here's what these properties are for:

- `gridSize` returns the width and height of the grid, measured in tiles. For example, this map will be 18x10 tiles.

- `layerSize` returns the layer's width and height, measured in points. Conceptually, it's `gridSize * tileSize`. For example, this map will be 576x320 points.

Now replace `TileMapLayer`'s `init(tileSize:)` with this new method that has three parameters:

```
init(tileSize: CGSize, gridSize: CGSize,
     layerSize: CGSize? = nil) {
  self.tileSize = tileSize
  self.gridSize = gridSize
  if layerSize != nil {
    self.layerSize = layerSize!
  } else {
    self.layerSize =
      CGSize(width: tileSize.width * gridSize.width,
             height: tileSize.height * gridSize.height)
  }
  super.init()
}
```

This new initializer uses `tileSize` just like the old method did, and handles `gridSize` similarly. However, notice that `layerSize` is declared optional and has a default value of `nil`. This allows you to call this method with or without the `layerSize` parameter.

As such, if `layerSize` is a non-nil value, the method uses it to initialize `self.layerSize`. If not, it calculates an appropriate size based on the values of `tileSize` and `gridSize`.

Now you have another compiler error to correct. Replace the first line of `init(atlasName:tileSize:tileCodes:)` with the following:

```
self.init(tileSize: tileSize,
          gridSize: CGSize(width: count(tileCodes[0]),
                           height: tileCodes.count))
```

Here you replace the call to match the designated initializer's new signature. Notice how it doesn't include the `layerSize` parameter. Instead, it takes advantage of the default `layerSize` value of `nil`.

You assign `gridSize`'s `width` using the number of characters in the first string in `tileCodes`, and you use the number of items in `tileCodes` for the `height`.

> **Note:** `TileMapLayer` assumes every item in `tileCodes` is the same size, but to keep things short, it doesn't include any error checking. So make sure your strings are sized properly, or you may experience errors.

Now, change the last line of `positionForRow(col:)` to the following:

```
return CGPoint(x: x, y: layerSize.height - y)
```

This subtracts from the layer's height the y-value you already calculated, effectively flipping the map's (x,y) coordinates, making the method return higher y-values for higher row values.

Build and run. Here's what you'll get:

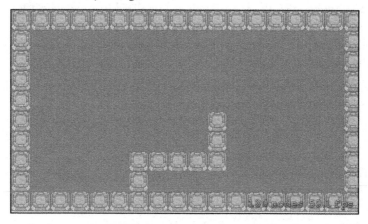

OK, your map displays correctly! Notice, though, that the tiles along the right edge are cut off, while on the left edge, they're intact. Wouldn't you feel better if the map were centered?

Centering the scene

It's not hard to center your scene. However, as you add more and more nodes, moving things around becomes problematic, so you'll refactor the scene a bit while you're at it.

Instead of adding nodes directly to the scene, you'll add them all to a single node like you did in Chapter 5, "Scrolling." This will allow you to move everything in your scene by moving just that node. Later, you'll add UI elements like labels directly to the scene, so you can move the map while the labels remain in place.

Open **GameScene.swift** and add the following properties:

```
var worldNode: SKNode!
var backgroundLayer: TileMapLayer!
```

worldNode is the single node that will contain all the scene's elements. backgroundLayer will store the TileMapLayer returned from createScenery().

Notice how you declare each of these properties as an implicitly unwrapped optional. You're making them implicitly unwrapped because you'll be using them a lot and you know they'll never be nil once they've been initialized. This solution is nicer than muddying your code with a bunch of worldNode!'s everywhere.

Why not make them constants? Ideally, you would, but that's not always easy to do. In this case, you're going to assign these values by calling methods in GameScene, but you can't call any GameScene methods until you've initialized its superclass. Of course, you can't initialize its superclass until you've assigned values to all of GameScene's constants and non-optional properties, which you want to use methods to do, which you can't because of the initialization order rules. And round and round we go.

As soon as you add those properties, Xcode reports an error that GameScene has no initializers. Swift: always looking out for you.

Add the following initializers to GameScene:

```
required init?(coder aDecoder: NSCoder) {
  fatalError("NSCoding not supported")
}

override init(size: CGSize) {
  super.init(size: size)
}
```

These methods don't actually set the properties you just added, but it's enough to hush up the compiler. You'll add more to the latter method later.

Now add the following method:

```
func createWorld() {
  backgroundLayer = createScenery()

  worldNode = SKNode()
  worldNode.addChild(backgroundLayer)
  addChild(worldNode)

  anchorPoint = CGPointMake(0.5, 0.5)
```

```
    worldNode.position =
        CGPointMake(-backgroundLayer.layerSize.width / 2,
                    -backgroundLayer.layerSize.height / 2)
}
```

Much like `createScenery()`, this method organizes some of your scene's setup. It assigns the `TileMapLayer` returned from `createScenery()` to `backgroundLayer`. It creates `worldNode`, adds `backgroundLayer` as a child of `worldNode` and adds `worldNode` to the scene.

Finally, the method changes the scene's `anchorPoint` to (0.5,0.5) and sets `worldNode`'s position. These two lines are what actually center the scene:

1. The new `anchorPoint` value moves the scene's origin—point (0,0)—to the center of the screen.

2. Then, you move the `worldNode` down and to the left. Remember, though: The way you positioned your tiles, (0,0) in the layer is the lower-left corner of the map. By moving the map in a negative direction by half its width and half its height, the map's center is now at the scene's origin.

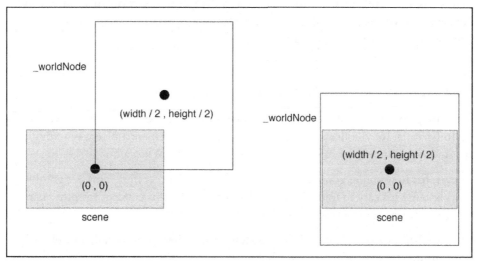

Inside `didMoveToView()`, replace this line:

```
addChild(createScenery())
```

With this one:

```
createWorld()
```

Build. Run. Centered. Yay!

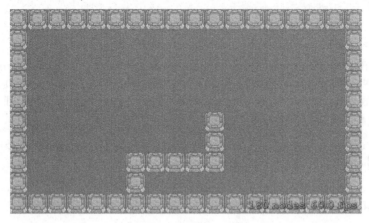

You finally have your map onscreen exactly as intended. But your hero in Pest Control is a cardio nut—he's going to need a bit more running space.

> **Note:** As you continue with this chapter and the rest of Pest Control, you can run using any size simulator or device. However, if you want your view to match what you see in the screenshots, use an iPhone 5 or 5s.

Loading layers from text files

Hard-coding your levels, like you're doing now in `createScenery()`, isn't a very good idea. In Chapter 16, you'll see how to load TMX files, which are a nice way to define tile maps since you can use a third-party tool to draw your maps visually.

However, for now you're going to simply load levels from text files. This is a good way to start because it's easy to understand, and you can reuse this concept for other bare-bones level editing tools in your own games.

In the **Levels** folder you imported (inside **Resources**), there is a file called **level-1-background.txt**. Here are its first few lines:

```
scenery
32x32
XXXXXXXXXXXXXXXXXXXXXXXXXXXXXXXXX
X0000000000000000000000wwwwwwwwwwX
X0000000000000000000000wwwwwwwwwwX
```

It simply contains the same type of information you've been providing to TileMapLayer's `init(atlasNamed:tileSize:tileCodes:)`: an atlas name, tile size and rows of characters representing tiles.

The **Levels** folder you imported earlier includes a file named **TileMapLayerLoader.swift**. This file includes a single helper function I wrote for you named `tileMapLayerFromFileNamed()`, which uses the contents of a text file formatted like the one shown above to initialize and return a new `TileMapLayer`.

Open **TileMapLayerLoader.swift** and remove each of the two lines that include "REMOVE THIS LINE." These were included to temporarily comment out `tileMapLayerFromFileNamed()`. Otherwise, you would have been stuck with compiler errors as soon as you imported the chapter's resources.

This code is straightforward and well commented, so its contents are not discussed here. However, please look it over to make sure you understand it.

> **Note:** There is one thing you do need to know about `tileMapLayerFromFileNamed()` if you use it to load layer data files you've edited yourself. It's written in the same style as the rest of Pest Control, in that it lacks production-level error checking. If it loads a file that includes any empty lines where the rows of tile characters should appear—including any blank lines at the end of the file—it will produce gaps in the tile map.
>
> If you ever run your game and see an extra row's worth of space at the bottom of the map, you probably pressed return/enter at the end of the last row of characters in your layer data file.

Inside **GameScene.swift**, replace the contents of `createScenery()` with the following call to load the level defined in **level-1-background.txt**:

```
return tileMapLayerFromFileNamed("level-1-background.txt")
```

Xcode should immediately indicate an error. That's because `tileMapLayerFromFileNamed()` returns an optional `TileMapLayer`, whereas you declared `createScenery()` to return a non-optional value.

Fix this error by changing `createScenery()`'s return type to `TileMapLayer?`, as shown below:

```
func createScenery() -> TileMapLayer? {
```

Run the app, and you should see this:

What are those dark areas? Look in your console, and you should see a bunch of statements similar to these:

```
Unknown tile code w
Unknown tile code =
```

That's just because level-1-background.txt contains a couple of characters your project doesn't yet support. I wanted you to see what happens when your level contains an unsupported character, in case you try to extend this app and run into this situation.

Open **TileMapLayer.swift** and add support for these new characters by adding the following case statements to the switch statement in nodeForCode():

```
case "w":
  tile = SKSpriteNode(texture: atlas!.textureNamed("water1"))

case "=":
  tile = SKSpriteNode(texture: atlas!.textureNamed("stone"))
```

Run again, and you should no longer have those dark areas.

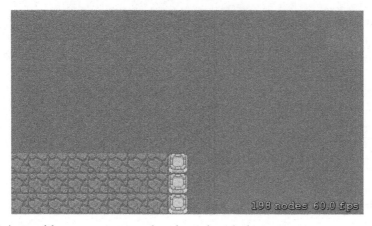

But wouldn't you like to move around and see the whole map?

Moving the camera

In Pest Control, you'll keep the camera focused on your pest-smashing hero as he runs around the map. As you learned in Chapter 5, "Scrolling", you can implement scrolling by moving the scene's nodes. This effectively simulates a moving camera.

Your scene's nodes are all children of worldNode, so you'll find the player sprite's position in worldNode and place the center of the screen on top of it. Astute readers will note there is no player sprite yet—all in due time.

You won't be able to simply center the view on the player's position, however, because if he's too close to the edge of the map, the camera will appear to move over too far and expose the black nothingness that lies beyond. This means you'll have to do some math to enforce limits on the camera.

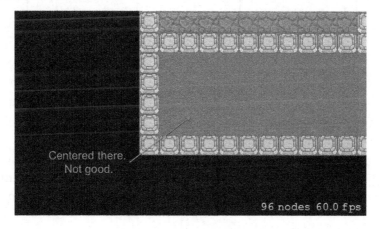

Open **GameScene.swift** and add this method:

```swift
func centerViewOn(centerOn: CGPoint) {
  let x = centerOn.x.clamped(
    size.width / 2,
    backgroundLayer.layerSize.width - size.width / 2)
  let y = centerOn.y.clamped(
    size.height / 2,
    backgroundLayer.layerSize.height - size.height / 2)

  worldNode.position = CGPoint(x: -x, y: -y)
}
```

There's a bit of math to explain here, so let's review this in detail.

The scene's size defines the limits for how close to the map's edge the center can be. For example, if the scene is 320 points tall, the scene's origin is 160 points from the top and bottom of it. That means you don't want to center on any point less than 160 or more than the map's height minus 160.

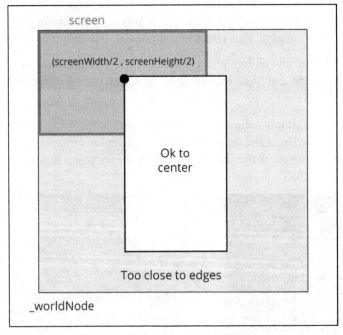

The first two lines determine the best x- and y-values that satisfy the above constraints. You use `CGFloat`'s `clamped` method to choose either the coordinate from `centerOn` or the minimum/maximum allowed value, if `centerOn`'s value is outside the allowable range. The allowable sizes are based on `backgroundLayer`'s dimensions, because it's assumed the background layer defines the largest area that you want visible in the level.

> **Note:** `clamped` is defined in the `CGFloat` extension in **CGFloat+Extensions.swift**, which you imported as part of `SKUtils`.

Finally, you negate the values and use those to position `worldNode`. Remember how you originally centered the map by negating half its width and height? Here you're doing the same thing, except you aren't centering over the center of the map, but rather over the position you just calculated.

To see it in action, add this method to center the view on a touch location (or replace the existing `touchesBegan(withEvent:)` if you still have it from the template):

```
override func touchesBegan(touches: Set<NSObject>,
                          withEvent event: UIEvent) {
  let touch = touches.first as! UITouch
  centerViewOn(touch.locationInNode(worldNode))
}
```

Build and run. Tap the screen, and notice how the map moves so that the point you tapped is as close to the screen's center as possible, without ever revealing anything beyond the map's edges.

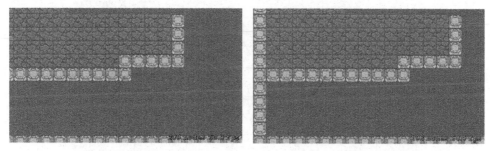

Take a look around the map. You'll see some walls, some water and a lot of grass. Maybe too much grass. You're about to learn a tip for making your maps look less repetitive.

Randomizing the tiles

There are several ways you could improve this tile map. For example, the boundaries between the water and grass tiles are pretty blocky. You could use special tiles along these transition points to show a more gradual, pleasing border between the two tile types.

However, placing such tiles manually can be time consuming, and implementing logic so your app can choose appropriate boundary tiles automatically is a bit too complicated for this chapter. The open-source tool you use in Chapter 16, "Imported Tile Maps," does support this sort of behavior, but even using the tool to do it is too complicated to explain in this book.

Keeping it simple, though, doesn't mean you can't mix it up a little. One trick is to return one of several different images for a type rather than always returning the same image.

Open **TileMapLayer.swift** and replace the `case` statements in `nodeForCode()` that create the grass and water tiles with these:

```
case "o":
  tile = SKSpriteNode(texture: atlas!.textureNamed(
    CGFloat.random() < 0.1 ? "grass2" : "grass1"))
case "w":
  tile = SKSpriteNode(texture: atlas!.textureNamed(
    CGFloat.random() < 0.1 ? "water2" : "water1"))
```

These simply choose a different grass or water tile about 10 percent of the time.

Build and run, and now the large areas of grass or water have a bit more visual interest. And as an added bonus, your map will look slightly different every time you play.

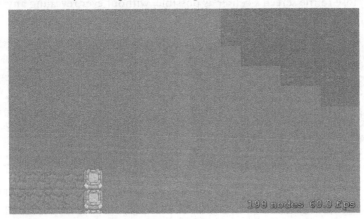

You've defined a nice, peaceful map. But it's a bit desolate. Hey, who's that I hear banging on the door?

Adding and moving the player

The hero of Pest Control is a badass named Arnold who can't stand idly by while giant bugs roam free across his land. In fact, he can't stand still at all, and he's more than willing to destroy everything he sees in pursuit of a world free of giant bugs.

When the player taps the screen, Arnold will start running and either bounce off or run straight through anything he comes across. There's no stopping this guy once he gets going. Speaking of which, let's get going with some code.

Go to **File\New\File…**, choose the **iOS\Source\Swift File** template and click **Next**. Name your file **Player**, be sure the **PestControl** target is checked and click **Create**.

Open **Player.swift** and replace its contents with the following:

```swift
import SpriteKit

class Player : SKNode {
  let sprite: SKSpriteNode

  required init?(coder aDecoder: NSCoder!) {
    fatalError("NSCoding not supported")
  }

  override init() {
    let atlas = SKTextureAtlas(named: "characters")
    let texture = atlas.textureNamed("player_ft1")
    texture.filteringMode = .Nearest

    sprite = SKSpriteNode(texture: texture)

    super.init()

    addChild(sprite)
    name = "player"
  }
}
```

Here you define a `Player` class. When using Swift, the file in which you put your classes doesn't really matter, but I prefer to keep them organized like this, with a single class in a file with the same name.

`Player` extends `SKNode` and contains a single `SKSpriteNode` property named `sprite`. You're using a separate sprite rather than extending `SKSpriteNode` directly, because at the time of writing this chapter, Sprite Kit's physics break if you flip a node's scale values. You're going to be doing that later, so this is a preemptive workaround.

Inside init(), you create sprite's texture using an SKTextureAtlas, just as you've created the other sprites in this chapter. You're hard-coding the atlas name because you know all of Pest Control's player images are in the atlas named characters.

If you wanted to use more than one atlas, you could easily add an initializer that includes an atlas name parameter. You might want to do something like that if your player character wears different costumes in different levels, for example.

After calling super.init(), you add sprite as a child of the player and then you name the object player. This will make it easy to find using Sprite Kit's node-searching features, as you'll do a bit later.

Now go back to **GameScene.swift** to add your player to the scene.

First, add this property to provide convenient access to the Player object:

```
var player: Player!
```

Once again, you'll keep the scene's configuration code organized by adding a new method to create your characters. Add this method:

```
func createCharacters() {
  player = Player()
  player.zPosition = 50
  player.position = CGPoint(x: 300, y: 300)
  worldNode.addChild(player)
}
```

This creates a Player at a set position on the map. Later, you'll learn how to define a custom spawn point and you'll add more types of characters (like the bugs) to the map.

Notice you set player's zPosition to 50. When you set up the project, you set the scene's ignoresSiblingOrder property to true in GameViewController. That means you need to set a zPosition for your nodes to ensure they appear properly.

Thus far, you've only added a background to your scene, so it was fine to use the default zPosition of zero. However, you want Arnold to appear in front of the scenery, so you need to set his zPosition to a value greater than zero. Using 50 gives you plenty of room if you ever want to place sprites between Arnold and the background. Spoiler alert: You're going to want to place sprites between Arnold and the background.

Finally, add the following lines to didMoveToView(), just after your call to createWorld():

```
createCharacters()
centerViewOn(player.position)
```

This simply calls your new method to create the player and then uses the
`centerViewOn()` method you created earlier to make sure you can see your hero.

Build and run. Tough guy? Check. Camera centered on said tough guy? Not so much.

There's a subtle problem here. You create Arnold and center on him in
`didMoveToView()`. However, it turns out that Sprite Kit calls this method *before* the
view resizes the scene to match its size. That means the bounds `centerViewOn()`
performs its checks against are incorrect at this point.

There are a couple of ways you could handle this, but the easiest is to make sure you
create your scene using the correct size in the first place.

Inside **GameViewController.swift**, change the line that creates the scene from this:

```
let scene = GameScene(size: CGSize(width: 1024, height: 768))
```

To this:

```
let scene = GameScene(size: view.bounds.size)
```

Now your scene will start with the same size as the view, which is the size it was going to
end up with anyway, after the view resized it. (Remember, you set `scaleMode` to
`ResizeFill`, which tells Sprite Kit to resize the scene to match the view's size.)

Build and run. Now Arnold is the center of attention, just the way he likes it.

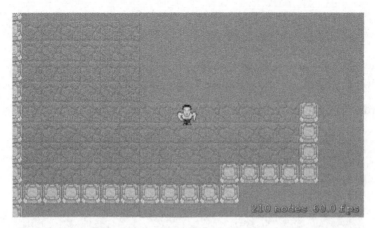

Stoic heroes are great and all, but it sure would be cool if this guy could move.

Physics-based motion

In Pest Control, your hero is obsessed with one thing: crushing bugs. Tapping the screen will send the hero running determinedly in the tap's direction. Nothing will deter him. If he hits something, he'll either smash right through it or bounce off and continue running in a new direction.

To create this behavior, you'll use Sprite Kit's physics engine. You've already read a lot about physics in earlier chapters, so I won't explain every detail here.

Open **Player.swift** and add the following code to the end of init():

```
// 1
var minDiam = min(sprite.size.width, sprite.size.height)
minDiam = max(minDiam-16.0, 4.0)
let physicsBody = SKPhysicsBody(circleOfRadius: minDiam/2.0)
// 2
physicsBody.usesPreciseCollisionDetection = true
// 3
physicsBody.allowsRotation = false
physicsBody.restitution = 1
physicsBody.friction = 0
physicsBody.linearDamping = 0
// 4
self.physicsBody = physicsBody
```

The above code adds a physics body to the player sprite, configured as follows:

1. It uses a circle that's a bit smaller than the sprite to provide more visually satisfying collision behavior.

2. It enables precise collision detection. Your hero moves fast, and you want the physics engine to keep up.

3. You want your hero to run forever, and you don't want him to tip over while he's doing it. These lines create that behavior by disabling the body's rotation, friction and linear damping properties, and setting restitution to 1. For a refresher on what these properties mean, check out Chapter 9, "Beginning Physics."

4. Finally, you set the player's `physicsBody` to the `SKPhysicsBody` you just created. You didn't *need* to create a temporary local `SKPhysicsBody`, but if you had worked directly with the player's `physicsBody` property, you would have needed to type `physicsBody!` everywhere you accessed it. Either solution works, but I prefer the look of this one.

Users will always want to see Arnold as he runs around, so open **GameScene.swift** and add this method:

```
override func didSimulatePhysics() {
  centerViewOn(player.position)
}
```

Remember from Chapter 11, "Advanced Physics," that this is the method that gets called after the physics engine has updated the positions of each node based on the physics simulation. Therefore, it is the perfect spot to center the view to the (newly updated) position of Arnold.

Build, run, and watch as Arnold makes a mad dash to the bottom of the map and then runs right off the screen. Hmm. Got somewhere to be, Arnold?

Come on, Arnold. If you run away now, what will you to do when the giant bugs show up?

Help your hero look more heroic by turning off gravity. To do so, add this line to **GameScene.swift** at the end of createWorld():

```
self.physicsWorld.gravity = CGVector.zeroVector
```

Run again, and you'll see that Arnold stands still. Actually, he won't budge, as if he's frozen with fear. Let's make him move again, but this time, where *you* want him to go.

Much like you did when building Zombie Conga, you're going to provide a target position, which the player's sprite will then run toward and beyond.

Open **Player.swift** and add the following method:

```
func moveToward(target: CGPoint) {
  let targetVector = (target - position).normalized() * 300.0
  physicsBody?.velocity = CGVector(point: targetVector)
}
```

This math should look familiar if you've completed the minigames up to this point. It simply sets the sprite's velocity to a vector pointing at target with a length of 300. Remember, the length is interpreted as a speed, so the larger this number, the faster he goes!

Open **GameScene.swift** and replace the line that calls centerViewOn() in touchesBegan(withEvent:) with the following:

```
player.moveToward(touch.locationInNode(worldNode))
```

This simply tells the player sprite to move toward the location of the user's tap.

Build and run. Arnold goes back to running right off the screen, but at least he does it in the direction you tell him to go. Tap the screen again, and you'll eventually see him run back into view, only to run away once more. I suppose that's progress.

It looks like Arnold needs a little encouragement to stick around. Much as you've done in some of this book's other minigames, you'll define a world boundary into which he'll collide. Basically, you're going to trap Arnold in a box. But *trapping* sounds so ugly. Let's say you're going to *convince* him to stay.

First, you need to define a physics category. To keep things organized, you'll create a new file to store any special types, like this one.

Go to **File\New\File...**, choose the **iOS\Source\Swift File** template and click **Next**. Name your file **Types**, be sure the **PestControl** target is checked and click **Create**.

Open **Types.swift** and replace its contents with the following:

```
struct PhysicsCategory {
  static let None     : UInt32 = 0
  static let All      : UInt32 = UInt32.max
  static let Boundary : UInt32 = 0b1        // 1
}
```

This defines a category for the edge of the world, called `Boundary`, as well as values that indicate no category and all categories. You won't need `None` and `All` just yet, but it's nice to see them here for comparison.

You'll add more physics category values later, but this will do for now.

Inside **GameScene.swift**, define a world boundary at the end of `createWorld()`:

```
let bounds = SKNode()
bounds.physicsBody =
  SKPhysicsBody(edgeLoopFromRect:
    CGRect(x: 0, y: 0,
           width: backgroundLayer.layerSize.width,
```

```
                    height: backgroundLayer.layerSize.height))
    bounds.physicsBody!.categoryBitMask = PhysicsCategory.Boundary
    bounds.physicsBody!.friction = 0
    worldNode.addChild(bounds)
```

Notice how this adds the physics boundary to a new node that is then added to
worldNode. That's because you're moving worldNode and you need the physics
boundary to move with it.

The player sprite is already set to collide with everything, so build and run. Tap the
screen, and watch that guy bounce around the map.

Moving the camera, revisited

Currently, the game centers its view on Arnold, keeping perfect pace with him as he runs
around the map, stopping only when necessary to ensure the user never sees anything
beyond your tile grid's boundaries. That works fine, and for some games that's exactly
what you'll want.

However, consider the poor camera operator who has to keep up with Arnold, lugging
around all that heavy equipment while desparately trying to keep Arnold perfectly
centered in the frame. That's hard work, and it may be a little much to expect anyone to
keep up with someone as fit as Arnold. More importantly, it's hard for your users to
appreciate the scenery if the world moves by so quickly; sometimes, it's downright
unpleasant.

It would be more realistic, and more pleasing to the eye, if the view lagged behind
Arnold ever so slightly, giving your users the feeling that Arnold moves so fast, it's
difficult for the game to keep up with him.

This effect is quite easy to implement. First, you'll refactor the code slightly. Create the following new method in **GameScene.swift**, which contains almost the same code that's currently in `centerViewOn()`, except instead of setting `worldNode`'s position, it simply returns the new position:

```
func getCenterPointWithTarget(target: CGPoint) -> CGPoint {
  let x = target.x.clamped(
    size.width / 2,
    backgroundLayer.layerSize.width - size.width / 2)
  let y = target.y.clamped(
    size.height / 2,
    backgroundLayer.layerSize.height - size.height / 2)

  return CGPoint(x: -x, y: -y)
}
```

And change `centerViewOn()`'s contents, replacing everything in it with the following single line:

```
worldNode.position = getCenterPointWithTarget(centerOn)
```

This simply sets `worldNode.position` using `getCenterPointWithTarget()`, which should result in exactly the same behavior you had before. After all, you're still executing the same code; you've just moved it to a different method.

The scene currently keeps itself centered over Arnold in `didSumulatePhysics()`, so that's the method you need to change. Replace its code with the following:

```
let target = getCenterPointWithTarget(player.position)
worldNode.position += (target - worldNode.position) * 0.1
```

This method calculates the target position using the `getCenterPointWithTarget()` method you just added, but rather than set `worldNode`'s position to this value, it does some math to calculate a different position to use. This math moves the camera from its current position *toward* the target position, but only 10% of the way there. This 10% is what makes the camera appear to lag behind Arnold, because it's always trying to catch up to where he is but never quite gets there. (Actually, if he were to stay put, the camera *would* eventually catch up to him due to the limited precision with which you can position sprites on a display.)

> **Note:** If you're curious about the math in `didSimulatePhysics()`, consider this: If the distance between the positions of Arnold and the `worldNode` is 100 points, then the math moves `worldNode` by 10% of that, or by 10 points.

The next time `didSimulatePhysics()` runs, assuming Arnold hasn't moved, the distance is now only 90 points and the camera moves 9 points closer to him. The distance shrinks to 81 points the next time, moving the camera 8.1 points. The camera keeps getting closer, but it gradually slows down, which makes the movement look smooth.

Run the app, and notice how much more natural the motion seems. It's now easier for your players to discern details in your levels, which is good when so much of your app development time will be spent designing those levels.

You can also see a side effect of this code when the level first loads. Instead of being centered on Arnold, the camera starts someplace else and pans over to him. It's a cool effect, but depending on where you position Arnold's spawn point—which you'll be doing as one of this chapter's challenges—it may not look good.

If it doesn't look good, you may need to adjust the code. For example, you'll be adding game states in Chapter 17, "Saving and Loading Games," after which point it would be easy to change `didSimulatePhysics()` to only move `worldNode` when the game is in an appropriate state.

This simple trick can make your apps appear much more polished. You'll learn more of these sorts of techniques in Chapters 18 and 19, "Juice Up Your Game, Parts 1 and 2."

In the next chapter, you'll add collisions with other things, like the walls and water. But for now, you've got a guy trapped in a box. Wouldn't it be fun to fill it with giant bugs? Whoa, this chapter just got creepy.

Challenges

Here are two short challenges to get you more familiar with the process of editing your level files to create different types of objects and behavior. First, you'll add some bugs, and then you'll add the ability to specify Arnold's spawn point in the level file.

As always, if you get stuck, you can find solutions in the resources for this chapter—but give it your best shot first!

Challenge 1: Bring on the bugs

A giant-bug invasion without giant bugs is not the kind of giant-bug invasion you're going for, am I right? Here's your chance to fix that.

Look inside the **Levels** folder you imported, and you'll find a file called **level-1-bugs.txt**. Here are its first few lines:

```
characters
32x32
................................
.........b....................
...b..............b...........
```

This file is formatted exactly like level-1-background.txt, so it can be turned into a `TileMapLayer` using `tileMapLayerFromFileNamed()`. It includes an atlas name and a tile size at the beginning, followed by a grid of characters. In the grid, each **b** represents a bug and each period (**.**) represents empty space. The periods make it possible to see the area covered by the grid.

Your challenge is to create a new `Bug` class, similar to your `Player` class, and then populate the world with bugs based on this file. Here are some detailed hints for how to do this:

1. Create a new `Bug` class that derives from `SKNode`. It should contain a child `SKSpriteNode` and just two methods: `init?(coder:)`, so it compiles, and `init()`. This method should be very similar to `Player`'s `init()`, except:

    a. Use the sprite named **bug_ft1**;

    b. Set the `name` property to "bug"; and

    c. Don't add in any of the code related to the `physicsBody` yet—you'll make the bug move in the next chapter.

2. Inside **TileMapLayer.swift**, edit `nodeForCode()` to return `nil` for a "." character and `Bug()` for a "b" character. You can return the new `Bug` object directly from the `case` statement or assign it to the `tile` variable. Either way, the bugs will use Sprite Kit's default blend mode that supports transparency.

3. Inside **GameScene.swift**, add a new implicitly unwrapped `TileMapLayer` property named `bugLayer`. Then, add this code to the *beginning* of `createCharacters`:

```
bugLayer = tileMapLayerFromFileNamed("level-1-bugs.txt")
bugLayer.zPosition = 10
worldNode.addChild(bugLayer)
```

Notice that this code sets bugLayer's zPosition to 10. I chose this number arbitrarily but not completely without reason. The value needs to be greater than zero to ensure the bugs appear above the map, but it should also be less than Arnold's zPosition of 50 to ensure the bugs don't walk all over him.

Build and run. Now your app is filled with bugs—but not the coding kind, I hope! :]

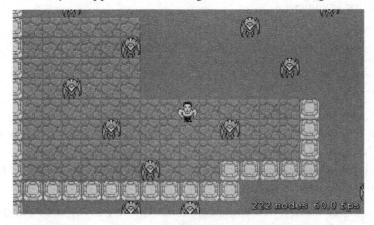

Note: I know I snuck it into a challenge, but the code you just wrote demonstrates a major benefit of using textures from SKTextureAtlas. Every time you request a texture using the same name, you receive the exact same object in memory.

In fact, if you implemented Bug like you did Player, then each Bug instance creates an SKTextureAtlas inside its init(). It turns out that multiple SKTextureAtlas objects created with the same atlas name all return references to the same texture object. That means no matter how many wall tiles, grass tiles or bugs you create, you'll never create more than one SKTexture object to reference each of their textures.

Now you may be asking yourself, "Don't SKSpriteNodes that reference the same image share their texture data, too?"

Yes, it's true that Sprite Kit stores the actual *texture* data only once, which is a significant performance feature of Sprite Kit. But each time they're called, SKSpriteNode(imageNamed:) and SKTexture(imageNamed:) create unique objects in memory to access their texture data.

> If you're creating many copies of the same sprite, as is common in a tile-based game (reusing image assets is one of the biggest benefits of tile-based games, right?), the memory savings you get by creating fewer objects is measurable. And that *can* improve performance.

Challenge 2: Player spawn, revisited

Even though hard-coding the player's spawn point is easier than doing it for a bunch of bugs, it's still not a very good idea. For one thing, you probably want to place the player in relation to where you put the bugs. You don't want Arnold spawning on top of a bug, do you?

Inside **level-1-bugs.txt**, there is a single p character. You can leave it like that, or you can change that p to a period and then change any other *single* character you like to a p. That will be where you'll spawn the player. From a gameplay standpoint, it's probably best to choose a spot away from any bugs.

Your challenge is to add support for this new character to `TileMapLayer`, just like you did for the others. Here are some detailed hints for how to do this:

1. Open **TileMapLayer.swift** and edit `nodeForCode()` to return a new `Player` object for a "p" character, the same way you created the `Bug` objects in the previous challenge.

2. Open **GameScene.swift** and find `createCharacters()`. Replace the line that creates `player` with two new lines of code: one that finds the child of `bugLayer` named "player" and assigns that node to `player`, and one that removes the player node from its parent (you want it as a child of `worldNode`, not `bugLayer`). Finally, remove the line that sets `player`'s position.

Build and run. Now the player will appear in whatever position you put the p in the file.

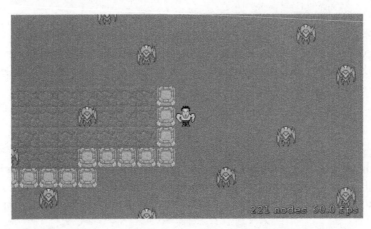

Pop quiz, hotshot. You're surrounded by giant bugs. They aren't moving, but you don't like that look in their eyes. What do you do? What do you do?

Actually, just head to the next chapter to find out!

Chapter 15: More Tile Maps

By Christopher LaPollo

So far, you have a world filled with giant bugs and a hero rampaging around wondering why he can't do anything about it. You're missing one critical element: collisions!

In this chapter, you'll continue investigating tile maps in Sprite Kit by adding physics-based collisions between Arnold and the bugs, as well as between Arnold and certain tiles on the map.

In addition, you'll add code to make the bugs move about randomly while avoiding certain types of tiles, and you'll animate your characters based on which direction they're facing. By the time you're done this chapter, you will have developed Pest Control's core logic.

> **Note:** This chapter begins where the previous chapter's Challenge 2 left off. If you were unable to complete the challenges or skipped ahead from an earlier chapter, don't worry—you can simply open **PestControl-Starter** from this chapter's resources to begin in the right place.

Physics-based collision detection

After finishing the challenges from the last chapter, you're probably itching to kill something. Well, so is Arnold. Wait. We *are* talking about bugs, here, right?

Arnold already uses physics to move around, so you'll use physics to detect collisions with the bugs, as well.

First, you need to define new physics categories for the player and the bugs, so add these to the `PhysicsCategory` type in **Types.swift**:

```
static let Player    : UInt32 = 0b10      // 2
static let Bug       : UInt32 = 0b100     // 4
```

Open **Player.swift** and add the following lines with the other `physicsBody` setup at the end of `init()`:

```
physicsBody.categoryBitMask = PhysicsCategory.Player
physicsBody.contactTestBitMask = PhysicsCategory.All
```

You assign the player's physics category to `PhysicsCategory.Player` so it will be easy to identify this object during collisions. You set the player's `contactTestBitMask` such that it generates contact notifications if the player touches anything. There won't be any physics bodies in Pest Control that can escape his wrath.

Now you need to set up the `Bug`'s physics properties.

In **Bug.swift**, add the following lines to the end of `init()`:

```
var radius = min(sprite.size.width, sprite.size.height) / 2
physicsBody = SKPhysicsBody(circleOfRadius: radius)
physicsBody!.categoryBitMask = PhysicsCategory.Bug
physicsBody!.collisionBitMask = PhysicsCategory.None
```

This code is simpler than the player's setup, because the bug won't use the physics engine for movement. You just create a circular physics body, assign the bug's physics category and set its collision bit mask so that the bug isn't moved by the physics engine when it collides with something else. However, the physics engine will notify you when the bug hits the player, since you set `contactTestBitMask` on the player appropriately.

Finally, whenever Arnold collides with a bug, you need to remove the bug from the scene. Open **GameScene.swift** and modify the line that declares `GameScene` so it looks like the following:

```
class GameScene: SKScene, SKPhysicsContactDelegate {
```

As you learned earlier in the book, this states that `GameScene` conforms to the `SKPhysicsContactDelegate` protocol, and as such, can register to receive callbacks when physics bodies contact each other.

Register for contact notifications by adding this line at the end of `createWorld()`:

```
physicsWorld.contactDelegate = self
```

Finally, add the following method to process contacts when they occur, along with a private array used by this method:

```
private var bugsToRemove: [Bug] = []

func didBeginContact(contact:SKPhysicsContact) {
  let other =
    (contact.bodyA.categoryBitMask == PhysicsCategory.Player ?
     contact.bodyB : contact.bodyA)

  switch other.categoryBitMask {
  case PhysicsCategory.Bug:
    bugsToRemove.append(other.node as! Bug)
  default:
    break;
  }
}
```

The way you've configured the physics bodies in Pest Control, your program will only call this method when the player contacts another body. That is, two bugs touching will not generate an event.

This method finds which of the two bodies is *not* the player (the other body) and checks its physics category. If it's a bug, the method adds it to the private array property bugsToRemove.

You know you want to remove the bugs, but Sprite Kit sometimes produces errors if you modify the physics simulation while it's processing. Just to make sure you don't run into any such problem, you're going to remove the objects *after* you know the physics simulation is done with them.

Add the following to didSimulatePhysics():

```
if !bugsToRemove.isEmpty {
  for bug in bugsToRemove {
    bug.removeFromParent()
  }
  bugsToRemove.removeAll()
}
```

This loops through any bugs you stored back in didBeginContact() and removes them from the scene. It then clears out bugsToRemove so you don't try removing the same bugs again.

Build and run. Tap the screen, and watch as Arnold gets his first taste of dead bug. Crunchy!

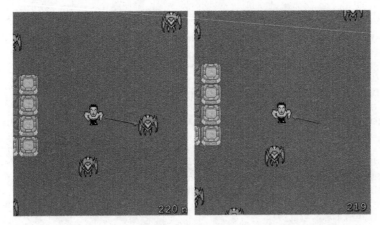

Unfortunately, Arnold doesn't smash right through the bugs as you had planned. Instead, he bounces off of them. That's because the Player object's physicsBody still uses the default collisionBitMask, which allows collisions with any type of object to affect the player's motion.

For now, you only want Arnold's motion to be affected by the world's boundary. Open **Player.swift** and add the following line with the other physicsBody setup in init():

```
physicsBody.collisionBitMask = PhysicsCategory.Boundary
```

Run the app again and now, Arnold plows right through bugs like a hot knife through… bugs! But for their part, the bugs just sit there; it almost seems mean to squash them. Let's make them move around a bit so they at least have a fighting chance.

Moving sprites with actions

The player sprite uses the physics engine to run around the map, but to move the bugs from one tile to another, you'll use actions instead of physics. That will give the bugs more purpose, plus it will let you explore some other tile-related issues.

When it's time for a bug to leave its current tile, it needs to answer a few questions. Where is it now? Where does it want to go? Is the desired position even a valid location? You'll add a few more methods to TileMapLayer to help it answer these questions.

Open **TileMapLayer.swift** and add the following methods:

```
func isValidTileCoord(coord: CGPoint) -> Bool {
  return (
```

```
    coord.x >= 0 &&
    coord.y >= 0 &&
    coord.x < gridSize.width &&
    coord.y < gridSize.height)
}

func coordForPoint(point: CGPoint) -> CGPoint {
  return CGPoint(x: Int(point.x / tileSize.width),
    y:Int((point.y - layerSize.height) / -tileSize.height))
}

func pointForCoord(coord: CGPoint) -> CGPoint {
  return positionForRow(Int(coord.y), col: Int(coord.x))
}
```

These methods are straightforward helper methods that you'll use to convert between grid coordinates and (x,y) positions in your map.

- isValidTileCoord(): checks tile coordinates against the layer's grid size to ensure they are within the range of possible grid coordinates.

- coordForPoint(): returns the grid coordinates (row,column) for the given (x,y) position in the layer. It's basically the reverse of the positionForRow(col:) that you wrote in the previous chapter.

- pointForCoord(): returns the (x,y) position at the center of the given grid coordinates, using positionForRow(col:) to find the position. Notice how the coord parameter is in (column,row) order. This keeps it in line with the other ways you interact with the layer, such as (x,y) positions and (width,height) measurements.

With those methods in place, you can add some brains to your bugs to make them walk.

Open **Bug.swift** and put the logic for picking tiles and moving between them inside walk(), like so:

```
func walk() {
  // 1
  let tileLayer = parent as! TileMapLayer
  // 2
  let tileCoord = tileLayer.coordForPoint(position)
  let randomX = CGFloat(Int.random(min: -1, max: 1))
  let randomY = CGFloat(Int.random(min: -1, max: 1))
  let randomCoord = CGPoint(x: tileCoord.x + randomX,
                            y: tileCoord.y + randomY)
  // 3
  var didMove = false
  if tileLayer.isValidTileCoord(randomCoord) {
```

```
    // 4
    didMove = true
    let randomPos = tileLayer.pointForCoord(randomCoord)
    let moveToPos = SKAction.sequence([
      SKAction.moveTo(randomPos, duration: 1),
      SKAction.runBlock(walk)])
    runAction(moveToPos)
  }
  // 5
  if !didMove {
    let pause = SKAction.waitForDuration(0.25, withRange: 0.15)
    let retry = SKAction.runBlock(walk)
    runAction(SKAction.sequence([pause, retry]))
  }
}
```

There's a fair bit of code here, so let's go over it carefully, one section at a time.

1. This line casts the bug's parent to type `TileMapLayer`. It's important that you only add `Bug` objects directly to `TileMapLayers`. Otherwise, your app will crash when it attempts to cast `parent` to type `TileMapLayer`.

2. You then use one of `TileMapLayer`'s new helper methods, `coordForPoint()`, to find the bug's current location within the tile grid. Using that cell as a starting point, you choose random coordinates from one of the eight surrounding tiles.

3. Next, you call `isValidTileCoord()` on the layer to make sure the random tile you chose is valid. That is, you make sure it's actually on the map. If the bug was already on the edge of the map when you asked, you may have chosen a position off the map.

4. If the random tile location you chose is valid, you find the new tile's (x,y) position using `pointForCoord()`, create a sequence action to move the bug to the new location and then call `walk()` when it gets there. This creates a cycle that looks like so: call `walk()`, choose a tile, move to the tile and repeat. It keeps the bug walking continuously from tile to tile.

5. Finally, if you didn't move the bug because the randomly chosen tile was invalid, you run an action that waits between 0.10 and 0.40 seconds and then calls `walk()` again. In these cases, the bug will remain in its current tile a bit longer before it continues on its way.

Now that you've implemented have `walk()`, you need to start each bug walking. At first, you might think to call `walk()` from within `init()`, but there's a problem with that: To move around, the bug needs access to its tile map parent. However, a node's `parent` is always `nil` inside its initializer. Even if you provide access to the tile map, it may be useless if the map is not yet fully initialized. For example, if the bug decides where to walk based on the types of tiles around it, it can't start walking until those tiles are set up.

The solution is to add a new method—call it `start()`—that your scene calls after all the nodes have been added.

Still inside **Bug.swift**, add this method:

```
func start() {
  walk()
}
```

`start()` simply calls `walk()` to get the bug walking. You define a `start()` method instead of having the scene access `walk()` directly so subclasses can perform additional setup before walking. (You'll be extending `Bug` in one of this chapter's challenges.)

Open **GameScene.swift** and add the following at the end of `createCharacters()` to get your bugs moving:

```
bugLayer.enumerateChildNodesWithName(
  "bug",
  usingBlock: { node, _ in
    if let bug = node as? Bug {
      bug.start()
    }
})
```

Build and run, and watch your bugs, well, run.

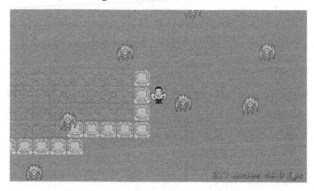

Now the bugs are moving, but they're doing it right over the walls! Between the bugs climbing over everything and Arnold bouncing around wherever he wants, it seems no one respects your boundaries. Or at least, the boundaries you've set up in the map. It's time to take care of that.

Collisions with tiles, two ways

When you have tiles that represent solid or otherwise impassible objects, you want the characters in your game to behave accordingly. In this section, you'll see two different methods to keep characters from moving through solid tiles. The player will use physics-based collision detection, while the bugs will query tile properties to decide where to walk.

Physics-based tile collisions

You want the player to bounce off walls (for now—in Chapter 19, "Juice Up Your Game, Part 2," you'll give him the ability to smash right through them!), and you probably don't want him to walk on water. Or maybe you'll want to add that as a power-up after you've finished going through the book?

To accomplish this, you need some additional physics settings. Open **Types.swift** and add the following categories for walls and water to the `PhysicsCategory` type:

```
static let Wall      : UInt32 = 0b1000    // 8
static let Water     : UInt32 = 0b10000   // 16
```

Then, go to **Player.swift** and add the new categories to the player's `collisionBitMask`, so that it looks like this:

```
physicsBody.collisionBitMask = PhysicsCategory.Boundary |
   PhysicsCategory.Wall | PhysicsCategory.Water
```

Now, the player wants to bounce off wall and water tiles as well as the world's boundary. However, the wall and water tiles need physics bodies for this to work.

Open **TileMapLayer.swift**, where you'll modify the nodes returned for walls and water.

Add the following code to the "x" `case` of the `switch` statement in `nodeForCode()`:

```
if let t = tile as? SKSpriteNode {
  t.physicsBody = SKPhysicsBody(rectangleOfSize: t.size)
  t.physicsBody!.categoryBitMask = PhysicsCategory.Wall
  t.physicsBody!.dynamic = false
  t.physicsBody!.friction = 0
}
```

This creates a physics body the same size as the tile. It sets its dynamic property to `false` because the wall won't move, and sets its friction to `0` so the player doesn't slow down when he hits the wall.

Now do the same for water tiles by adding the following to the "w" `case`:

```
if let t = tile as? SKSpriteNode {
  t.physicsBody = SKPhysicsBody(rectangleOfSize: t.size)
  t.physicsBody!.categoryBitMask = PhysicsCategory.Water
  t.physicsBody!.dynamic = false
  t.physicsBody!.friction = 0
}
```

Build and run. Tap the screen, and watch Arnold run around bouncing off walls and water just like he should.

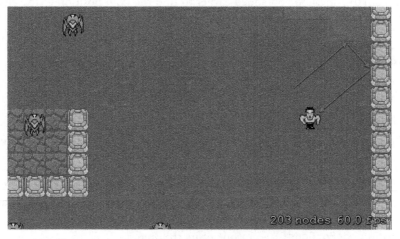

Now that Arnold obeys the rules, it doesn't seem fair that the bugs are walking through walls like your stones are made of nothing more than flat pixels! Let's fix that.

Property-based tile avoidance

Instead of moving the bugs using physics, you're using Sprite Kit actions to move the bugs between tiles, so you'll use the tiles' properties to determine where a bug can walk. Basically, the bugs will check if the way is clear before trying to move.

For the bugs to be able to do this, `TileMapLayer` needs to provide access to its tiles by position. It would be convenient to access tiles using either their grid coordinates (row,column) or their (x,y) positions.

Open **TileMapLayer.swift** and implement the following new methods:

```
func tileAtCoord(coord: CGPoint) -> SKNode? {
  return tileAtPoint(pointForCoord(coord))
}

func tileAtPoint(point: CGPoint) -> SKNode? {
  var node : SKNode? = nodeAtPoint(point)
  while node != nil && node !== self && node?.parent !== self {
    node = node?.parent
  }
  return node?.parent === self ? node : nil
}
```

tileAtCoord()'s implementation is straightforward. It simply uses the pointForCoord() method you added earlier to find the (x,y) position of the given grid location, and then uses tileAtPoint() to find the tile.

tileAtPoint()'s implementation may look needlessly complicated, but it's not so bad. It uses SKNode's nodeAtPoint() method to find the node at the given position, and then checks to make sure this TileMapLayer is the discovered node's parent. If it isn't, the code walks up the parent chain until it finds a node whose parent *is* this object.

Why do all that? Sometimes, nodeForCode()returns nodes with children, such as the player and bug nodes, both of which store their sprites as child nodes. In the future, you may also want to return nodes that contain multiple sprites.

When multiple nodes overlap, as shown in the following image of a tree on some grass, nodeAtPoint() returns the node on top. That's usually what you want when handling touches, for example, but in this case, you want to find the *bottom* sprite—the one you returned from nodeForCode()—not one of its children.

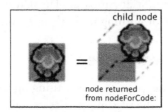

child node

=

node returned
from nodeForCode:

Now that TileMapLayer provides access to its tiles, your bugs need to check for tiles they can't traverse, but the bugs don't even know about the layer that contains the walls. As far as they're concerned, the world contains nothing but themselves. Is there anything worse than a narcissistic bug?

The scene itself is a good place to provide this access. You'll add a method that returns whether or not a map location has certain properties, such as `PhysicsCategory.Wall`.

Open **GameScene.swift** and add the following two methods to query tile properties:

```
func tileAtCoord(coord: CGPoint,
                 hasAnyProps props: UInt32) -> Bool {
  return tileAtPoint(backgroundLayer.pointForCoord(coord),
                     hasAnyProps: props)
}

func tileAtPoint(point: CGPoint,
                 hasAnyProps props: UInt32) -> Bool {
  var tile = backgroundLayer.tileAtPoint(point)

  if let categoryMask = tile?.physicsBody?.categoryBitMask {
    return categoryMask & props != 0
  }
  return false
}
```

These are two variations of the same method: Each will find a tile *in the scene's background layer*, either by point or grid location, and return `true` if the tile has a `physicsBody` with any of the given `props` bits set in its `categoryBitMask`.

Since you know the map tiles are in `backgroundLayer`, you find the tile at that location in `backgroundLayer` using the `tileAtPoint()` method you just added. You then compare the tile's physics category to the bits in `props`. The methods return `true` if any bit is set in both `props` and in `tile`'s `physicsBody`'s `categoryBitMask`, or `false` otherwise.

The background layer might return `nil` if you provided an invalid location, and the physics body won't be present on some tiles, such as grass. Those two possibilities are why the `if` check uses all those question marks to ensure the app doesn't crash in those cases.

> **Note:** To reduce the size of this chapter, the only properties you'll test for are the categories assigned to the physics body. In your own app, you could use the node's `userData` dictionary or some other mechanism to store other types of properties.

There's one last thing to do, and these bugs will finally know their places. In **Bug.swift**, replace the following line in `walk`:

```
if tileLayer.isValidTileCoord(randomCoord) {
```

With these lines:

```
let gameScene = scene as! GameScene
if tileLayer.isValidTileCoord(randomCoord) &&
  !gameScene.tileAtCoord(randomCoord,
    hasAnyProps: PhysicsCategory.Wall | PhysicsCategory.Water) {
```

This changes the bug logic so that now, they will only walk onto valid tiles that are not currently occupied by a wall or water.

Build and run. Finally, your walls are doing their jobs.

OK, you've got a level made of tiles and filled with bugs. You've got a hero with an almost disturbing need to crush those bugs. Life is good. But wouldn't things be better if they were a bit more... animated?

> **Note:** This next section is to add polish, have fun and practice the material you've learned so far in this book—it has little to do with tile maps. If you'd like to stay focused on tile map material, feel free to skip ahead to the Challenges section. You can pick up the finished project there, and we have some fun challenges in store for you!
>
> But if you'd like some extra practice animating sprites in a semi-tricky use case— making objects animate differently based on the direction they're facing—read on!

Animating sprites

In Pest Control, both Arnold and the bugs will animate. There will be some similarity in how you implement these animations, so you'll create a class that contains stuff both the bugs and Arnold can use. Then, you'll refactor `Player` and `Bug` so they subclass this new class.

Go to **File\New\File...**, choose the **iOS\Source\Swift File** template and click **Next**. Name your file **AnimatingSprite**, be sure the **PestControl** target is checked and click **Create**.

Open **AnimatingSprite.swift** and replace its contents with the following:

```swift
import SpriteKit

class AnimatingSprite : SKSpriteNode {

  var facingForwardAnim : SKAction?
  var facingBackAnim : SKAction?
  var facingSideAnim : SKAction?

  required init?(coder aDecoder: NSCoder) {
    fatalError("NSCoding not supported")
  }

  init(texture: SKTexture) {
    super.init(texture: texture, color: nil,
               size: texture.size())
  }
}
```

You'll use this class to replace the sprites in `Player` and `Bug`. The properties you add here each hold an `SKAction` for animating the sprite while facing in one of four directions: forward, back or to the left or right sides.

Add the following helper method, which both `Player` and `Bug` will use to create the animations they'll store in those properties:

```swift
class func createAnimWithPrefix(prefix: String,
                                suffix: String) -> SKAction {
  let atlas = SKTextureAtlas(named: "characters")

  let textures = [atlas.textureNamed("\(prefix)_\(suffix)1"),
                  atlas.textureNamed("\(prefix)_\(suffix)2")]
```

```
    textures[0].filteringMode = .Nearest
    textures[1].filteringMode = .Nearest

    return SKAction.repeatActionForever(
      SKAction.animateWithTextures(textures, timePerFrame:0.20))
}
```

The above code creates an animation action using textures from the atlas named `characters`. It generates the texture names using a specific format, described next, and then sets the `filteringMode` on those textures to account for the app's pixel art.

The image file names should be formatted as follows: **prefix_direction#**, where **direction** is one of **ft**, **bk** or **lt**, for front, back and left, and **#** is the animation frame number, starting at 1. Notice there is no option for the direction right. You'll see later how you use the same image for both directions.

As you can see, each animation in Pest Control consists of just two frames, but for more fluid animations, you'd want to include additional frames. If anything related to the `SKAction` code above seems unfamiliar to you, revisit Chapter 3, "Actions."

With that helper method in place, it's time to refactor `Player` and `Bug` to use it.

Player animations, part 1

In this section, you'll modify `Player` to support animation. Later, you'll implement logic to control those animations.

Inside **Player.swift**, change the line inside `init()` that initializes `sprite` so that it looks like this:

```
sprite = AnimatingSprite(texture: texture)
```

This simply creates an `AnimatingSprite` instead of a regular `SKSpriteNode`.

To access the methods from the `AnimatingSprite` class, change the line that declares the `sprite` property so that it's now an `AnimatingSprite`, like this:

```
let sprite : AnimatingSprite
```

Finally, add the following code at the end of `init()` to set up Arnold's animations:

```
sprite.facingForwardAnim =
  AnimatingSprite.createAnimWithPrefix("player", suffix: "ft")
sprite.facingBackAnim =
  AnimatingSprite.createAnimWithPrefix("player", suffix: "bk")
```

```
sprite.facingSideAnim =
  AnimatingSprite.createAnimWithPrefix("player", suffix: "lt")
```

Here you create Arnold's three animations using the
`createAnimWithPrefix(suffix:)` method you defined in `AnimatingSprite`. This
will make animations from frames named `player_ft1` and `player_ft2`, `player_bk1`
and `player_bk2`, and `player_lt1` and `player_lt2`.

To test the animations, temporarily add the following line at the end of `init()`:

```
sprite.runAction(sprite.facingForwardAnim)
```

Build and run. Your hero starts running in place. So that's how he stays so fit!

If you'd like to see the other two animations, modify the line you just added and run
again, using `facingBackAnim` and then `facingSideAnim`. When you're done, remove
that line completely.

Bug animations, part 1

Just as you did with `Player`, you'll first modify `Bug` to support animation. Later, you'll
implement logic to control those animations.

First, you'll make some of the same changes to `Bug` that you made to `Player`. Inside
Bug.swift, change the line inside `init()` that initializes `sprite` so that it looks like this:

```
sprite = AnimatingSprite(texture: texture)
```

Then, change the line that declares the `sprite` property so it's now an
`AnimatingSprite`, like this:

```
let sprite : AnimatingSprite
```

With `sprite`'s type changed, you now need to assign the sprite's animations, but you'll
do it a bit differently than you did in `Player`.

There are a lot of bugs running around your scenes. If the bugs created their animations
the same way the player does, each one would have an identical set of three actions. But

as you learned in Chapter 3, "Actions," actions can be shared amongst any number of nodes. So in an effort to conserve memory at runtime, your bugs will access actions in static variables shared by all the bugs. Awfully considerate bugs, aren't they?

To help your bug's share, add the following code *inside* the Bug class:

```
struct Animations {
  static let facingForwardAnim : SKAction =
    AnimatingSprite.createAnimWithPrefix("bug", suffix: "ft")
  static let facingBackAnim : SKAction =
    AnimatingSprite.createAnimWithPrefix("bug", suffix: "bk")
  static let facingSideAnim : SKAction =
    AnimatingSprite.createAnimWithPrefix("bug", suffix: "lt")
}
```

This struct contains three static constants that define the three animation actions all bugs will share. Ideally, these would be class-level constants inside Bug, but Swift does not currently allow you to create class constants. (You *can* create class-level computed properties, but getting the same result with those would be more cumbersome than this solution.)

Finally, add the following code at the end of init() to set up the animations:

```
sprite.facingForwardAnim = Animations.facingForwardAnim
sprite.facingBackAnim = Animations.facingBackAnim
sprite.facingSideAnim = Animations.facingSideAnim
```

These lines use the animations from the `Animations` struct. Because `Animations` declares these properties as `static`, the same `SKAction` objects are shared amongst all the bugs.

To test the animations, temporarily add the following line in init, after the ones you just added:

```
sprite.runAction(sprite.facingForwardAnim)
```

Build and run. Your bugs are on the march!

As with the player, if you'd like to see the other two animations, modify the line you just added and run again, using `facingBackAnim` and then `facingSideAnim`. When you're done, remove that line completely.

Changing directions

You need the ability to get and set the direction the sprite faces. For example, when a sprite is moving toward the bottom of the screen, you want to make sure it's animating with the `facingForwardAnim` action. Let's add one last property to access the direction the sprite is currently facing.

Open **AnimatingSprite.swift** and add the following enumeration inside the `AnimatingSprite` class:

```
enum SpriteDirection {
  case Forward, Back, Left, Right
}
```

This type defines the four different directions the sprite can face.

Add the following property to the `AnimatingSprite` class:

```
// 1
var facingDirection: SpriteDirection = .Forward {
  // 2
  didSet {
    // 3
    switch facingDirection {
      case .Forward:
        runAction(facingForwardAnim)
      case .Back:
        runAction(facingBackAnim)
      case .Left:
        runAction(facingSideAnim)
      case .Right:
        runAction(facingSideAnim)
    }
    // 4
    if facingDirection == .Right && xScale > 0 ||
       facingDirection != .Right && xScale < 0 {
      xScale *= -1
    }
  }
}
```

This property definition is a bit fancier than the others you've written, so it's worth taking a moment to understand it:

1. Here you declare `facingDirection`, a property of type `SpriteDirection` with an initial value of `Forward`.

2. You're taking advantage of Swift's observable properties by defining a `didSet` clause, which automatically gets called whenever you set `facingDirection`'s value.

3. Inside `didSet`, a `switch` statement choses and runs the animation action that matches the direction the sprite currently faces.

4. Remember how you only provided left-facing images? If you set the sprite's `xScale` to a negative value, it renders flipped about the y-axis. The checks here ensure this method flips the image if the sprite isn't already facing the correct direction. Flipping images like this is a great trick to get more use out of image assets.

Now that you can manipulate the direction the sprites face, it's time to complete this portion of Pest Control.

Player animations, part 2

You already added animation support to `Player`. In this section, you'll make sure Arnold always looks where he's going.

In **Player.swift**, add this method:

```
func faceCurrentDirection() {
  let dir = physicsBody!.velocity
  if abs(dir.dy) > abs(dir.dx) {
    sprite.facingDirection = dir.dy < 0 ? .Forward : .Back
  }
  else {
    sprite.facingDirection = dir.dx > 0 ? .Right : .Left
  }
}
```

This method checks the player's velocity to see if it's more vertical than horizontal. If so, the method chooses to make the sprite face either forward or backward, based on which direction the player is headed. If the player's movement is primarily horizontal, the method chooses to make the sprite face either to the right or to the left. Remember from the previous section that setting the sprite's `facingDirection` also runs the correct animation for the given direction.

Set the player sprite's direction by calling this new method at the end of `moveToward()`, like so:

```
faceCurrentDirection()
```

Now, every time you tell the hero to start running, he should face the appropriate direction.

Build and run. Things should look good each time you tap the screen, but Arnold's animation doesn't change direction when he bounces off of things. What now?

You're adjusting the player's direction inside `moveToward()`, which you call only when the user taps the screen. But you should also adjust the direction the sprite faces when it bounces off of something. Fortunately, the scene already registered to receive contact notifications, so you can handle it there.

Open **GameScene.swift** and add this method:

```
func didEndContact(contact:SKPhysicsContact) {
  // 1
  let other =
    (contact.bodyA.categoryBitMask == PhysicsCategory.Player ?
    contact.bodyB : contact.bodyA)

  // 2
  if other.categoryBitMask &
    player.physicsBody!.collisionBitMask != 0 {
      // 3
      player.faceCurrentDirection()
  }
}
```

The physics engine will call `didEndContact()` when the player ceases to touch a physics object it had been touching. Here's what your implementation of `didEndContact()` does:

1. You know that the player is one of the objects involved in the callback, so here you find the other object.

2. This compares the object's physics category with the player's `collisionBitMask`—if it gets a non-zero value, it means this collision was with something solid enough to cause the player to change direction.

3. You call `faceCurrentDirection()`. That method will use the player's current velocity to ensure the player sprite is facing in the correct direction.

> **Note:** Instead of calling `faceCurrentDirection()`, you could have called `moveToward()` here, passing in the sum of the player's current position and its velocity. However, that would require extra processing, first to do that sum, and then for `moveToward()` to calculate the player's new velocity, which would end up being the same as its current velocity anyway. It's more efficient to call `faceCurrentDirection()` directly.

Build and run. Arnold should be running around *and* looking where he's going.

With `Player` complete (for this chapter, anyway), let's finish up the bugs.

Bug animations, part 2

Now that Arnold looks where he's going, it's only fair that the bugs do the same. `Bug` already chooses a direction to move in `walk()`. Now it needs a method that chooses which direction to face based on which direction the bug is moving. However, because `bug` isn't using the physics engine as `Player` does, the logic here will be a little different.

Open **Bug.swift** and add the following method for choosing a direction to face:

```
func faceDirection(dir:CGVector) {
  // 1
  if dir.dy != 0 && dir.dx != 0 {
    // 2
    sprite.facingDirection = dir.dy < 0 ? .Back : .Forward
    zRotation = dir.dy < 0 ? π / 4.0 : −π / 4.0
    if dir.dx > 0 {
      zRotation *= −1
    }
  }
  else {
    // 3
    zRotation = 0
    // 4
    switch dir {
      case _ where dir.dx > 0:
        sprite.facingDirection = .Right
      case _ where dir.dx < 0:
        sprite.facingDirection = .Left
      case _ where dir.dy < 0:
        sprite.facingDirection = .Back
      case _ where dir.dy > 0:
        sprite.facingDirection = .Forward
      default:
        break;
    }
  }
}
```

There's a lot going on here, so let's go over it one section at a time:

1. dir will represent the relative direction from the bug's current tile, in grid coordinates. That is, its x- and y-components will each be one of 0, 1 or -1. This first if statement determines whether or not the new tile is located diagonally from the current tile.

2. For diagonal motion, you choose the appropriate facing direction, but then you rotate the sprite to add a bit more visual interest. The rotation values used here are based on the direction the image faces in the original image files.

3. If the movement direction is *not* diagonal, you set the rotation to zero. Without that line, bugs that had been rotated for diagonal movement would remain rotated if they began moving horizontally or vertically.

4. This switch statement figures out if the movement is horizontal (dx < 0 or dx > 0) or vertical (dy < 0 or dy > 0). It chooses the correct direction to face based on what it finds.

Calling `faceDirection()` sets the sprite's `facingDirection` property. Remember, setting that property also runs the correct animation for the given direction.

Add the following line to `walk()`, just after the line that runs the `moveToPos` action:

```
faceDirection(CGVector(dx: randomX, dy: randomY))
```

This uses the `randomX` and `randomY` offset values you calculated earlier in the method. Unlike `Player`'s use of its velocity, this method calculates the bug's facing direction using tile grid offsets from the current position.

Build and run. Take a moment. You just got a lot done.

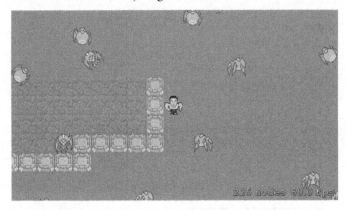

In this chapter and the last, you laid the groundwork for a fun game, but you also witnessed a lot of what you'll need to build any number of your own games in the future.

The next few chapters describe easier ways to make your maps, as well as guide you through adding gameplay features like timers, support for multiple levels, winning and losing, and autosaving progress. Then, in Chapters 18 and 19, you'll learn how you can take Pest Control or any other game to an amazing new level.

Before you move on, try the following challenges to add some cool new features on your own.

Challenges

If you've made it this far into the book, I'm convinced you can tackle some more advanced challenges—so this time, we've ramped up the difficulty level a notch. Do you think you have what it takes to make Arnold proud?

CHALLENGE ACCEPTED

Of course, if you have any trouble, you can find solutions to these challenges in the resources for this chapter.

Challenge 1: Breakables

The background tiles you've created so far have been single images, sometimes with a physics body attached, but tiles don't have to be so simple. For example, what if you planted a few trees in your level?

Sure, you could add support for a new character that returns a sprite that looks like a tree, just as you made the other tiles. But this is supposed to be a challenge, so let's take this opportunity to explore the notion of interactive tiles.

For example, instead of plain trees, you could have trees that your player can smash to potentially reveal hidden objects in your game, just like you may have seen in games from the *Super Mario Bros.* or *Legend of Zelda* series.

For this challenge, you won't go as far as creating hidden pickups, but you *will* create trees that Arnold can smash, leaving behind nothing but a stump. Later, in Chapter 18, "Juice Up Your Game, Part 1," you'll see how to make this destruction even more satisfying.

Take a look at the following hints and then give it a try.

You'll need a new PhysicsCategory value: call it Breakable. Be sure to modify Bug's walk() method so it avoids breakables—no one wants bugs crawling all over their trees.

By the way, you're using the term "breakable" instead of "tree" because the class you're about to write will be generic. The only thing that will make these objects trees instead of rocks or crates will be the images you use to render them.

Create a new class named `Breakable` that extends `SKNode` and includes the following initializer method:

```
init(wholeTexture: SKTexture, brokenTexture: SKTexture) {
  // Your code here
}
```

Here are some tips to help you implement `init(wholeTexture:brokenTexture:)`:

1. Create an `SKSpriteNode` property named `sprite` and initialize it using `wholeTexture`. Add `sprite` as a child of the `Breakable` node so that this texture appears before Arnold smashes it.

2. Create a property named `brokenTexture` and use it to store the `brokenTexture` value passed into `init(wholeTexture:brokenTexture:)`. You'll use this image to display debris left behind after a collision.

3. Add a physics body of type `Breakable`. Make it a static (not dynamic) rectangle that is 80% of the size of the sprite.

When Arnold collides with a `Breakable`, he should break it. Add the following method to the `Breakable` interface:

```
func smashBreakable() {
  // Your code here
}
```

Implement `smashBreakable()` to do the following:

1. Remove the node's physics body. Doing this means once the breakable has been smashed, the player will no longer collide with it, and the bugs will consider that space empty.

2. Replace `sprite`'s texture with `brokenTexture`. This gets rid of the pre-smashed image, which in this case is the full tree, and displays the post-smash wreckage, which in this case is the tree stump. Be sure to set `sprite`'s `size` equal to `brokenTexture.size()` after setting the texture, because Sprite Kit sometimes warps your textures if you don't do that.

Back in **GameScene.swift**, check for collisions with `Breakable` objects in `didBeginContact()`. When the player hits one, call `smashBreakable()` on it, but be sure to call `smashBreakable()` on the physics body's node—not on the physics body itself.

You'll need to modify `TileMapLayer` to return `Breakables` when appropriate. Add a `case` statement for 't' that returns a `Breakable` using the images **tree.png** and **tree-stump.png**. Look at the `case` statements for the bugs or player if you need help.

Finally, the trees should sit on a layer above the background layer, just as you put the bugs on their own layer. This will require several changes in **GameScene.swift**:

1. Add a new property called `breakableLayer` of type `TileMapLayer?`.

2. Then, add a new method called `createBreakables()` that returns an optional new `TileMapLayer` created from the file **level-2-breakables.txt**. This file looks just like the other level data files you've used, except with "t" characters to indicate tree positions.

3. Initialize `breakableLayer` at the *end* of `createWorld()` by assigning it the result returned from `createBreakables()`, and then add `breakableLayer` as a child of `worldNode`. Before adding it to `worldNode`, make sure `breakableLayer` is not `nil`, and remember to set `breakableLayer`'s `zPosition` to a value greater than zero, but lower than `bugLayer`'s `zPosition` of 10.

4. Finally, you need to make sure the scene checks these objects in addition to the background tiles when checking for properties, otherwise your bugs will walk all over them. Replace the first line of `tileAtPoint(hasAnyProps:)` with the following code, which finds the tile by looking for breakables first, only retrieving a background tile if no tile can be found in the breakable layer:

```
var tile = breakableLayer?.tileAtPoint(point)
if tile == nil {
  tile = backgroundLayer.tileAtPoint(point)
}
```

If you got it working, congratulations! Now you can plant trees to improve Arnold's environment, and then revel in their destruction. You've got issues.

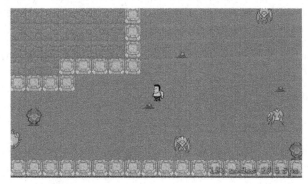

Challenge 2: Other enemies

Most games have more than one type of enemy. This challenge will show how you can add another type of bug with just a few tweaks to existing code.

Instead of bugs that meekly disappear when the player hits them, your task is to create a bug that is impervious to collisions. Rather than disappear when hit, this new bug will simply bounce a short distance away, sending the player off in a new direction, as well.

Of course, it wouldn't be fair if there were *no* way to kill these new bugs. Instead of smashing them, you'll make it so they drown when bounced into water. That big, strong exoskeleton isn't helping you now, is it, Mr. Sinky?

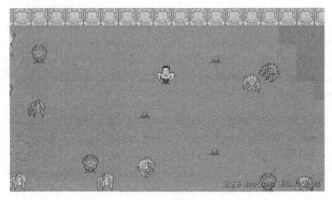

Completing this challenge will require quite a bit of what you've learned in this book. Here are a few tips to help you with it:

This new bug will be red and die in water, so create a new class named `FireBug` that extends `Bug`.

You'll need a new `PhysicsCategory` value: call it `FireBug`. This will let you perform different logic when the player collides with these versus regular bugs. Remember, you want the player to bounce off the `FireBugs`, so be sure to modify `Player`'s collision bit mask to include `PhysicsCategory.FireBug`.

Put `FireBug`'s initialization code in a method named `init()`. Inside `init()`, do the following:

1. Call `super.init()`.

2. Set the physics category to `PhysicsCategory.FireBug`.

3. Set the collision bit mask so the firebugs collide with the player, walls, breakables and the world boundary.

4. Set the linear and angular damping values to **1**. That will keep the firebugs from sliding too far when they get bumped.

5. Set the sprite's `color` to red. Remember, in Sprite Kit, you should use `SKColor` values.

6. Adjust the sprite's `colorBlendFactor` to `0.45`. I chose this value through experimentation and it produces a nicely colored bug.

Add the following methods to `FireBug`:

```
func kickBug() {
  // Your code here
}

func resumeAfterKick() {
  // Your code here
}
```

Implement `kickBug()` to do the following:

1. Remove all running actions. You could remove just the action that walks the bug between tiles. However, there are a few more steps involved in doing that.

2. Run an action that waits for one second before calling a new method called `resumeAfterKick()`.

Implement `resumeAfterKick()` to do the following:

1. Set the physics body's velocity to (0,0). That will bring the bug to a complete stop just in case it's still sliding a bit.

2. Then, query the scene to see if the firebug currently sits on top of a water tile. If it does, run the following code:

```
let drown = SKAction.group(
  [SKAction.rotateByAngle(4.0*π, duration:1),
   SKAction.scaleTo(0, duration:1)])
runAction(
  SKAction.sequence([drown,SKAction.removeFromParent()]))
```

This creates a simple action that makes the bug look like it's getting sucked into a whirlpool and then removes the bug from the scene.

If the bug is not on a water tile, you should make it resume walking by calling `walk()`.

Once you have all of that complete (it's a lot, I know), inside **GameScene.swift**, add a check for collisions with FireBug objects in didBeginContact(). When the player hits a firebug, call kickBug() on it.

Finally, you'll need to modify TileMapLayer to return FireBugs when appropriate. Add a case statement for 'f' that returns a FireBug. Look at the other case statements if you need help.

You can test your code by adding some fs to your bug layer file. Or, change createCharacters() in **GameScene.swift** to use **level-2-bugs.txt**. Build and run, and you should have firebugs!

That one was tough. If you got it working without looking at the completed project, nice job! If not, don't be discouraged; we both know those guys who said they got it without looking are liars. :]

Just look through the completed project and try to make sure you know what's going on, because you'll work with both Breakable and FireBug again in Chapters 18 and 19, "Juice Up Your Game, Parts 1 and 2."

Chapter 16: Imported Tile Maps

By Christopher LaPollo

Over the previous two chapters, you built the foundation of Pest Control, a game about a man, some giant bugs and the smashing of said bugs. To those of you who worked through those chapters, welcome back! We had some good times, didn't we? Yeah, we did.

For those of you who didn't follow the earlier chapters, don't worry—so long as you understand the basics of tile maps, you can complete this chapter on its own. You just might not laugh at our inside jokes.

In the last two chapters, you created tile maps using rows of characters in text files. While that's a good technique to know, it does have a few drawbacks, such as:

- **It's error prone.** A single misplaced newline or incorrect letter and your map breaks, and sometimes, these errors are difficult to find. For instance, if your bug layer doesn't have the same dimensions as your background layer, your bugs will check the wrong tiles when choosing a destination, potentially causing them to walk where they're not wanted. That's what bugs normally do, but these are *your* bugs.

- **You can't *really* see what the level looks like without loading it into the game**, or creating a tool for your designers so they can load levels without the game. For example, consider this line from a map:

```
@"xooooooooooooooooox"
```

Although you can kind of imagine the end result (and don't get excited; Sprite Kit doesn't have a crush on you), something nice and visual like this is a big improvement.

- **It's difficult to see the relationships between items when editing different layers.** Are you placing a bug right on top of a wall? You can either spend time squinting at character grids trying to compare positions of letters in different files, or you can build levels through trial and error, repeatedly loading levels to test how they look.

For example, try to line up this line from the background layer:

```
X==============X000000000000000X
```

With this line from the bug layer:

```
.....b.....b....p...............
```

While trying to line up characters is fun, for sure, is this the most efficient use of your time?

- **If you want an artist or designer to create your levels, it's easier to let them use a GUI.** Those people just don't appreciate numbers and letters as much as we programmer-types do.

In this chapter, you'll see how to alleviate these problems using Tiled, an open-source application that lets you build tile maps using a GUI. Tiled saves its maps in a file format known as Tile Map XML, or TMX. You'll learn how to load TMX files into Pest Control, which will make it much easier for you to create new levels.

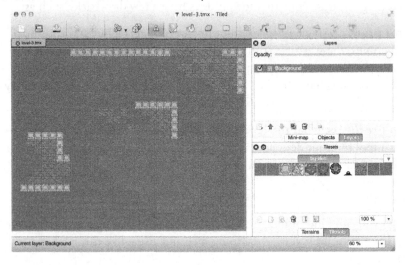

Oh, and to those of you who already know about Tiled and are joining us just because you want to learn how to get your precious TMX files into Sprite Kit, welcome! The rest of us will try not to judge you too harshly for skipping ahead. (Spoiler alert: We try, but we fail. Consider yourself judged.)

> **Note:** This chapter begins where the previous chapter's Challenge 2 left off. If you were unable to complete the challenges or skipped ahead from an earlier chapter, don't worry—you can simply open **PestControl-Starter** from this chapter's resources to begin in the right place.

> **Note:** If you already know how to use Tiled, you can skip various sections throughout this chapter that cover using that software to create a level, as the project already includes a sample TMX file you can use to complete the tutorial.
>
> However, you *need to read the section* titled "Tilesets" because in it, you will import some required assets, as well as learn the best way to create your own texture atlases for use with both Sprite Kit and Tiled. From there, you'll be directed to the next required section.
>
> Now go forth and choose your own adventure!

Introduction to Tiled

Tiled is a popular, open-source tile map editor that you can download for free at http://www.mapeditor.org.

The core functionality of Tiled is to paint tiles visually onto a map. The program supports multiple layers and different tile sets. Tiled also includes some cool features you'll learn about in this chapter, such as tile properties and object layers.

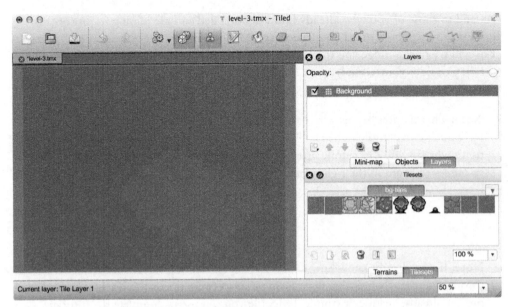

Tiled has an easy-to-use interface and saves map data in an XML format that you can read in your game. In this chapter, you'll use Tiled to create your maps, and then you'll add a third-party library to read the files that Tiled exports.

To create a map for Pest Control in Tiled, you first need to set up your tile images in a particular manner that Tiled supports. Let's get started!

Tilesets

Tiled allows you to access tiles from what it calls *tilesets*. I don't know why they spell it "tileset" instead of "tile set," but they do, so I'll do the same. Tiled also lets you place images in your maps that do not come from such a tileset, but you won't be using that feature here.

A tileset is simply a single image file, such as a PNG file, made up of a grid of smaller images and, optionally, some fixed amount of space between them. It's like the image portion of a texture atlas, but one whose images must all be the same size, arranged in a grid and not rotated.

> **Note:** Texture atlases also include a PLIST file that describes the contents of the image file, but Tiled doesn't need one because of the assumptions it can make about the uniformity of the layout of the images.

Here is the tileset you'll use in Pest Control:

In the next section, you'll create a texture atlas that includes the above image. If you already know how to do this or just want to skim through, you can skip ahead to the section titled "Importing texture atlases into Xcode," where you'll find instructions for using a prebuilt texture atlas.

Using TexturePacker to create tilesets

Unfortunately, the Texture Atlas tool that comes built-in with Xcode doesn't have enough configuration options to generate a texture atlas in the grid-based format that Tiled expects. So unless you enjoy doing a ton of copying and pasting in Photoshop, you'll have to turn to a third-party tool to help you out.

The good news is, there's a well-known, dependable tool for this called TexturePacker. You may already know you can use TexturePacker to create sprite sheets (aka packed texture files or texture atlases) for use with platforms like cocos2d, Unity and even HTML. It just so happens TexturePacker supports creating Sprite Kit texture atlases, too!

You'll be able to access this TexturePacker-generated texture atlas exactly the same way you've been accessing the atlases created for you by Xcode. You'll be able to create SKSpriteNodes using image names, get SKTextures from an SKTextureAtlas object... the works. This will come in handy a bit later.

This section is not meant to be a thorough tutorial on TexturePacker—there are many of those available on the Internet and I encourage you to explore the software on your own. The point of this section is simply to show you an easy way to create a texture atlas suitable for use in both Tiled and Sprite Kit.

If you don't already have TexturePacker, download it here:

• http://www.codeandweb.com/texturepacker

Unfortunately, generating Sprite Kit atlases requires the pro version of TexturePacker, but you can try it free for one week.

Open TexturePacker and it will prompt you to select a framework for a new project. Select **SpriteKit** and click **Create project**.

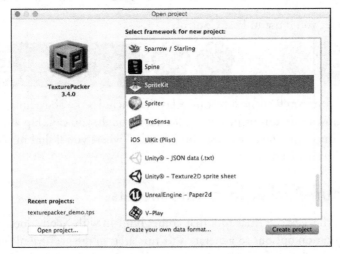

Take a look at the interface. If you don't see the three sections shown in the following image, then open the **View** menu and select **Settings left, sprites right**.

Inside the **Texture** section, choose **RGBA5551** for **Image format**, as shown:

Settings		
Data		show advanced
Data Format	SpriteKit	
Atlas bundle		
Header file		
Texture		show advanced
Texture format	PNG (.png)	
Png Opt Level		none
Pixel format	RGBA5551	
Dithering	FloydSteinbergAlpha	

Note: Setting the image format is actually optional—the default settings will work just fine. However, when creating texture atlases, you'll often want to tailor your settings to get the best image quality using the least amount of disk space. Since Pest Control's tiles have very few colors and pixels that are either fully opaque or fully transparent, you can choose this image format to produce a smaller file, as well as reduce memory usage by 50%!

Just remember, this setting won't work for all of your art—check the TexturePacker documentation for more information on the available formats. You'll also learn more about image quality and performance in Chapter 26, "Performance: Texture Atlases."

Next, click the **Folder** button to the right of the **Atlas bundle** field (still in the **Output** section) and choose a location to save the texture atlas. *Do not pick anywhere within your project folders*, because that will cause errors when you follow the import instructions in the next section. Name your atlas **tmx-bg-tiles** and click **Save**.

Now click **Add Sprites** in the toolbar at the top of the interface. In the dialog that appears, navigate to the **scenery.atlas** directory within your project hierarchy. Select all of the image files and click **Open**.

The center of TexturePacker's interface shows you what the packed texture would look like if you published it with the current settings (you can zoom in with the silder at the bottom). The right side of the interface shows the sprites that are part of the atlas, and the lower-right displays the size of the image that TexturePacker will produce.

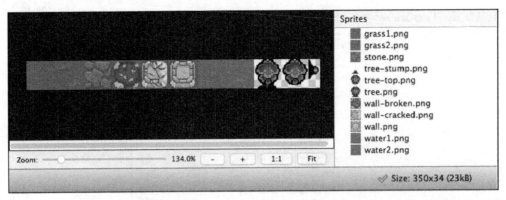

If you were *not* planning to use the texture atlas with Tiled, then you could publish at this point, as the default settings in the current version of TexturePacker produce a very tightly packed texture. In this case, it produced a texture of 350x34 pixels.

However, because you *are* going to use Tiled, you have to change a couple more settings. Tiled requires that all tile images within the grid are the same size. If they aren't, you'll get strange drawing behavior. Also, as mentioned earlier, Tiled expects tiles not to be rotated, but by default, TexturePacker rotates tiles when appropriate to pack images as tightly as possible, as you can see with the tree stump image.

To fix these issues, inside the **Layout** section click **show advanced** to bring up the full list of options. Then **uncheck Allow rotation**, and below in the **Sprites** section choose **None** for **Trim mode**, as shown below:

This keeps TexturePacker from trimming transparent space around the edges of tiles, which is important to make sure each tile retains its native size in the atlas. Notice that the tree stump image is no longer rotated and it has more transparent space around it.

These extra transparent pixels are one price you pay for using Tiled—if you have many tiles containing lots of transparent pixels, your texture atlases may be larger than they would be if you were using a non-TMX solution, such as the tile maps you implemented in the previous two chapters. However, for a small tileset like this, it makes very little difference.

One more thing: Still inside the **Sprites** section of the **Settings** on the left, click **show advanced** to reveal the full settings, and ensure the **Extrude** value is set to the default value of **1**, as shown in the following image:

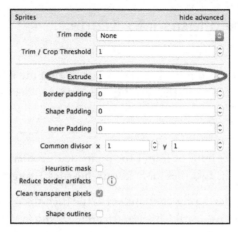

This setting extends the edges of each sprite in the texture atlas by one pixel, effectively making them larger than their 32x32 pixel size. In this case, they will be 34x34 pixels.

Without these extra pixels, Sprite Kit sometimes renders gaps between tiles due to occasional rounding errors. Extruding your tiles like this allows Sprite Kit to render appropriately-colored pixels if it accidentally grabs a little more than 32x32 pixels.

The final version of your atlas looks like this:

As shown in the above image, your tiles have grown a bit, and some of them look a little strange. Most obviously, the tree tile seems to have grown some extra pixels on top.

In general, tiles that include transparent pixels run the risk of looking the worst when extruded. They'll look fine when you see them in Pest Control, but keep in mind that for sprites with lots of transparency, especially those that make up character animations, it's advisable to include a margin of at least one transparent pixel. Otherwise, the extra extruded pixels might appear as display anomalies in your game.

Click **Publish sprite sheet** in the toolbar at the top of the interface and TexturePacker will write your texture atlas to the location you specified in the **Atlas bundle** field.

You should now have a directory named **tmx-bg-tiles.atlasc** that contains two files, named **tmx-bg-tiles.1.png** and **tmx-bg-tiles.plist**. In the next section, you'll add these to your project in Xcode.

Importing texture atlases into Xcode

> **Note:** If you skipped ahead to this section, you can find the texture atlas
> generated in the last section in the **tmx-bg-tiles.atlasc** folder of this chapter's
> resources.

At this point, you've either built or found the premade directory named **tmx-bg-tiles.atlasc**, which contains two files, named **tmx-bg-tiles.1.png** and **tmx-bg-tiles.plist**.

The image file **tmx-bg-tiles.1.png** contains every tile used to create Pest Control's maps, some of which you won't use until Chapters 18 and 19, "Juice Up Your Game, Parts 1 and 2." Sprite Kit uses **tmx-bg-tiles.plist** to find specific images within **tmx-bg-tiles.1.png**. Together, these two files form the texture atlas named **tmx-bg-tiles**.

The one special thing about adding this texture atlas to your project is that you need a *folder reference* in Xcode, not a standard group.

If you haven't done so already, open the PestControl project in Xcode. Highlight the **PestControl/Resources/Levels** group in the project navigator on the left, and then either right-click or go to the **File** menu and choose **Add Files to "PestControl"...**.

Select the **tmx-bg-tiles.atlasc** folder, either the one you made or the one from the project resources, and make sure **Copy items if needed** and the **PestControl** target are both selected. Finally, choose **Create folder references** and click **Add**. This is different from what you usually choose when importing:

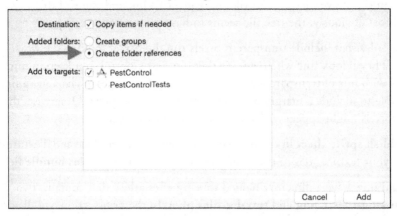

If everything went correctly, your **tmx-bg-tiles.atlasc** folder should look like this in the project navigator:

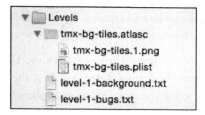

If the icon next to **tmx-bg-tiles.atlasc** is not blue like in the image above (and is yellow instead), this means you selected **Create groups** instead of **Create folder references**. To fix this, you should delete the tmx-bg-tiles.atlasc folder and try again. Be sure to choose **Move to Trash** when prompted during the delete operation.

My apologies to any readers viewing a black and white image above, but just use your imagination—pretend that one shade of gray is yellow and that other shade of gray is blue. No, you've got them backwards. Come on, you're not even trying!

> **Note:** You imported this folder into the **Levels** group for an important reason. At the time of writing, the class you'll be using to load TMX files requires those TMX files to only reference images from their same directory or from a subdirectory of that directory. The **Levels** group seemed like the best place for the TMX file, so the image had to be in this folder or in a descendent of this folder.

So, you have your tiles all lined up neatly in a grid and you've imported your texture atlas into Xcode. Next stop: Tiled town.

Creating maps in Tiled

> **Note:** If you're already familiar with making maps in Tiled and just want to know how to load TMX files into Sprite Kit, you can skip ahead to "Importing your maps." The starter project contains a TMX file named **level-3-sample.tmx** that you can use to allow you to focus on the code.

Now that you've created your tileset, you can finally start to create your map in Tiled.

Creating maps in Tiled is a straightforward affair. You define the size of the map and its tiles, load in your tilesets and start painting. In this chapter, you won't cover much more than the basics—just what's necessary to create a level for Pest Control—but I encourage you to explore Tiled on your own to see what you can do with some of its other features.

To install Tiled, go to http://www.mapeditor.org, click the **Download** button and then choose your preferred OS from the **Latest Release** area at the top of the page. After your download completes, double-click the disk image and follow any instructions provided.

Configuring your map

Create a new map by choosing **File\New…**. Set its **Orientation** to **Orthogonal**, its **Layer format** to **Base64 (zlib compressed)**, its **Map size** to **32 tiles** wide by **24 tiles** tall and its **Tile size** to **32 x 32 pixels**, as shown below:

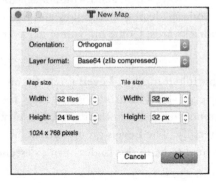

Click **OK**. Before you continue, go to **File\Save As…**, name your file **level-3.tmx** and save it inside your project's **Resources/Levels** folder.

> **Note:** For your app to work properly throughout this tutorial, you must configure your map exactly as described above. Certain steps in this tutorial mix TMX-based tiles with non-TMX tiles, and if you use different values here, those steps will not work correctly.
>
> After you've completed the chapter and the full TMX solution is in place, you can freely create maps with different sizes, but if you want to change the tile size, you'll need to supply your own graphics. You've been warned.

Maps in Tiled are comprised of layers similar to those used in Photoshop and most other image-editing programs. This means you don't need to try to cram all of your data into a grid that's only a single tile deep. You can instead, for example, create a background layer for your grass and water, with a layer above it for decorations like trees. In fact, that is exactly what you're about to do.

New maps in Tiled always start with a single layer named **Tile Layer 1**. You can see it, along with any other layers you make, in the **Layers** pane. Double-click **Tile Layer 1** in the **Layers** pane and rename it to **Background**, as shown below:

> **Note:** If you don't see the panes as shown above, toggle them on in the **View** menu. Be sure to show at least **Tilesets**, **Layers** and **Objects**, as you'll need each of those in this chapter.

You've completed your initial map setup. The next step is to add your tilesets.

Adding tilesets

As mentioned earlier, a tileset is an image that contains multiple smaller images, each of which you can place into your map any number of times. Think of it as a palette you use to paint your map.

Pest Control has only a single tileset, but Tiled allows you to use multiple tilesets in a map. In fact, you can use multiple tilesets within the same layer of a map. But it's best to group your tiles into sets based on their expected use together in a scene, because Sprite Kit's performance decreases as the number of tilesets it simultaneously needs to access increases.

Create a new tileset by choosing **Map\New Tileset...**. Name it **bg-tiles**, click **Browse...** and locate **tmx-bg-tiles.1.png** in your project's **Resources/Levels/tmx-bg-tiles.atlasc** directory. Be sure **Tile width** and **height** are both **32 px**, and **Drawing Offset X** and **Y** are both **0 px**. Finally, set **Margin** to **1px** and **Spacing** to **2px**.

Your dialog should look like the one below. Click **OK**.

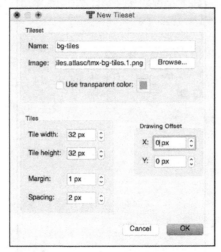

The margin and spacing settings above may seem odd, but they are necessary to account for the extruded tiles you added to your images. Here is what each of these settings means:

- **Margin** indicates how many pixels Tiled should skip (for both width and height) before reading the first tile. The margin setting of 1 accounts for the single extruded pixel along the top edge of the tiles in the top row and the single extruded pixel along the left edge of the tiles in the left column.

- **Spacing** indicates how many pixels Tiled should skip (for both width and height) to get from one tile to the next. The 2-pixel spacing accounts for the single extruded pixel in each of the two tiles on either side of that gap.

That wasn't so bad, and **bg-tiles** is now available for you to use, visible in the **Tilesets** tab:

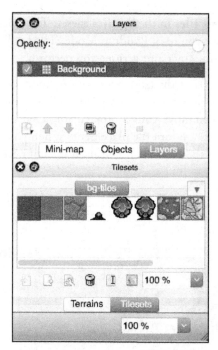

Your tiles are loaded, so it's time to start putting them into place.

Placing tiles

Tiled's shining attribute is the ease with which it lets you create maps using controls similar to any standard paint program. In this chapter, you'll use a few different techniques to make your level. To begin, you'll create a randomized field of grass with just five clicks.

Random fills

1. Click the **Random Mode** button in the toolbar, which looks like a pair of dice. Using this mode, you select multiple tiles and let Tiled randomly choose which one to use to paint.

2. Click the **Bucket Fill Tool** button in the toolbar, which looks like a paint bucket. (You can also press the letter F shortcut key.) This lets you modify any contiguous group of identical tiles with a single click.

3. **Shift+click** the **two grass tiles** in the **bg-tiles** tileset. This counts as two of those five clicks I mentioned. Since you're in Random Mode, Tiled will randomly choose between these two tiles for any paint actions you perform.

4. Move your mouse cursor over the large map area. As soon as the cursor enters this area, you'll see a preview of the map if you were to click. Notice that the background continues to change as you move your mouse cursor. That's because Tiled is constantly reevaluating its random tile placement. When you like the general look of the background, **click** in the map. Don't worry if it's not perfect—you'll learn how to fix it next.

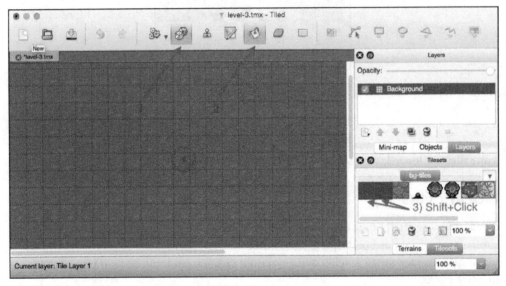

You may not like certain things about the way Tiled distributed the grass tiles. Perhaps there's too much tall grass, or maybe you just don't like a few specific clumps. There are a couple of easy ways to fix that.

Hover your mouse cursor over any part of the map and you'll see a preview of what it would look like if you clicked on that spot. Because you're still using the Bucket Fill Tool, Tiled highlights not only the tile you hover over, but also every identical tile that touches that tile, as shown in the next image:

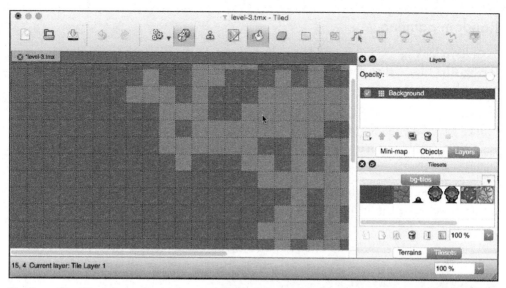

You're still in Random Mode, so the tiles you see previewed within the highlighted area will change as you move your cursor within it. Clicking the mouse button commits the changes you see to the area.

Continue to make adjustments until you think your lawn is almost perfect. At that point, it's time to do some spot weeding.

Single Tiles

To replace individual tiles, you use the Stamp Brush.

Click the **Random Mode** button again to toggle it **off**, and then click the **Stamp Brush** in the toolbar, which looks like a rubber stamp. You can also enable the Stamp Brush by pressing the letter **B** shortcut key.

Now click one or the other grass tile in your tileset so only one is selected, and then click in the map to place the selected tile in that spot on the grid. You can also click and drag if you'd like to paint a larger area with the chosen tile, and you can continue to paint with that tile until you choose a different one in this or another tileset.

Once you're tired of watching grass grow, move on to the next section to get your feet wet with… oh, forget it. Next, you'll paint some water tiles.

Random painting

Your lawn looks great, but it could use a little water. **Shift+click** the **two water tiles** in the **bg-tiles** tileset, then choose **Random Mode** and the **Stamp Brush** (if it isn't already selected).

Use your mouse cursor to click and/or click-drag in the map to create a small pond. Notice how the Random Mode option works with the Stamp Brush as well as the Bucket Fill Tool, so you can repeatedly paint over the same area and see it change slightly each time.

Tweak the appearance of the water using the same techniques you used with the grass, until you've created an inviting pond, similar to the one shown below:

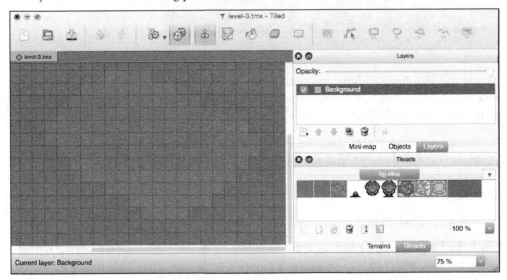

Wow, computer graphics have come a long way, don't you think? But I assure you that if you try to jump in for a swim, it will likely end in damage to your monitor, embarrassment and potentially, bodily harm. You've been warned.

Finishing touches

Use the **Stamp Brush** to finish up the background layer, adding solid walls and stone floor tiles wherever you see fit. Don't use the other tiles at this point, as you'll use those later for specific things. Here's what I made:

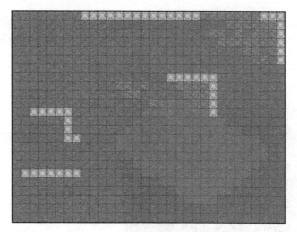

You've got a lovely field of grass, a cool, refreshing pond, and some oddly placed walls that look a bit like old ruins. Now you need to add some trees for shade.

Adding layers

One of the benefits of using Tiled over the text files you used in the previous chapters is that you can see all of your layers simultaneously. In this section, you'll add a separate layer for your trees.

Choose **Layer\Add Tile Layer,** which creates a new layer named **Tile Layer 2**. By default, the name field will have keyboard focus, so you should be able to simply start typing to change its name, but if not, double-click **Tile Layer 2** in the **Layers** pane and rename it to **Breakables**, as shown below:

With the **Breakables** layer selected, choose the **tree tile** that shows an entire tree, not just the top or the stump. Using the **Stamp Brush** (with Random Mode turned off), add several trees to the **Breakables** layer.

You may find it useful to turn on **View\Highlight Current Layer**. This dims the Background layer to indicate that it is not the active layer, as shown below:

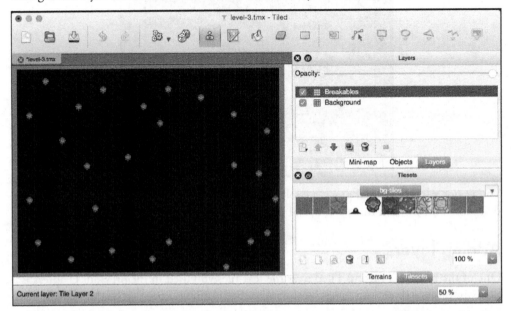

This is useful because it's easy to forget which layer you're working on within Tiled and accidentally draw to the wrong layer. With the dimming option, the layer you're in is clear at a glance.

If you don't like where you planted a tree, use the **Eraser** tool to remove it.

Once you've made a level you think Arnold would be happy to call home, move on to the next section to learn how you can pass data to your app by attaching it to your tiles.

Adding tile properties

One of Tiled's coolest features is that it lets you assign properties to your tiles. You can also assign properties to things like layers and tilesets, but for your purposes right now, tile properties will suffice.

You'll use properties to indicate tile types to your app, so that you'll be able to query your tiles to find out whether or not they are walls, for example. But properties are just arbitrary key-value pairs, so you can use to store any metadata you like.

You could use properties to store specific physics settings to make ice tiles more slippery than stone tiles; a class name to tell your app what type of object to instantiate; point values for your scoring system; item names to define pickups; or even just notes for yourself to keep track of things while working in Tiled, like how you planned to use a specific tile. The list is endless.

Right-click on the **wall image** in the **bg-tiles** tileset and choose **Tile Properties…**. In the dialog that appears, double-click in the **Name** column where it reads **<new property>** and enter **wall** as the new property's name. Then, double-click in the **Value** column next to **wall** and enter **1** as the value. Click **OK**.

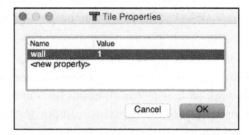

The value you set for a property will depend on the way you intend to use the property. In this case, the code you write is simply going to check if a property named wall is present on a tile, so the actual value you set here doesn't matter.

Now follow those steps again to add a property named **tree** to the tree tile containing the entire tree (not just the tree top or tree stump).

OK, you've seeded grass, planted trees, erected walls, paved floors and even dug a pond. You must be tired. It's time to take a break and see how it all looks in Sprite Kit.

Importing your maps

First, you need to add your TMX file to the Xcode project. If you skipped the previous section and didn't build **level-3.tmx** yourself, then ignore the next paragraph because your project already includes the TMX file you'll be using.

Select the **PestControl/Resources/Levels** group in the project navigator and either right-click or open the **File** menu, then choose **Add Files to "PestControl"…**. Choose the TMX file you just made, which should be named **level-3.tmx** and should be right there in the Levels folder. Make sure **PestControl** is checked in the **Add to targets** section of the dialog and click **Add**.

Now you've got a TMX file in your app's bundle, but what can you do with it? At the time of writing, Sprite Kit does not have built-in support for TMX files. However, the open-source community has created its own solutions. You can find different options online, but the one you'll use in Pest Control is called `JSTileMap`.

JSTileMap: An open-source TMX solution for Sprite Kit

`JSTileMap` is a custom subclass of `SKNode` that renders TMX files in Sprite Kit. It parses a TMX file and instantiates various objects to model the contents of the file, such as `TMXLayer`s for each tile layer, `TMXTilesetInfo` objects for each tileset and `SKSpriteNode`s for each tile. `JSTileMap` is a work in progress, so these things may change in the future.

Jeremy Stone started the `JSTileMap` project. JS—get it? He based his original implementation on the TMX parsing code from the open-source cocos2d-iPhone project. He continues to work on it, with contributions from myself and other members of the community, making it more Sprite Kit-centric, improving performance and adding support for features not included in the cocos2d version. For more information on `JSTileMap`, to download the latest version or to contribute code, go here:

- https://github.com/slycrel/JSTileMap

> **Note:** Because an open-source project like `JSTileMap` can change quickly and often, you're not going to download the latest code to follow along with this chapter. Instead, we've included a folder in this chapter's resources named **JSTileMap** that includes a version of the code that we know works at the time of this writing. Of course, after going through the chapter, you are encouraged to download the latest version of `JSTileMap` to use in your own apps.
>
> Also note that this chapter won't be covering the inner workings of `JSTileMap` and its supporting classes, so you should take a look at the source code if you want a detailed understanding of how it works.

Find the **JSTileMap** folder in this chapter's resources. Inside Xcode, choose **File\Add Files to "PestControl"…** and select the **JSTileMap** folder. Be sure **Copy items if needed**, **Create groups** and the **PestControl** target are all checked, and then click **Add**.

Your app would fail to build if you tried right now, because part of what you just imported is a compression utility named `LFCGzipUtility`, which requires you to link your app with an additional library. This compression utility is required because Tiled compresses the map data to make TMX files smaller.

Choose the **PestControl** project in the project navigator and then choose the **PestControl** target. Inside the **General** tab, click the **+** button in the section labeled **Linked Frameworks and Libraries**, as shown below:

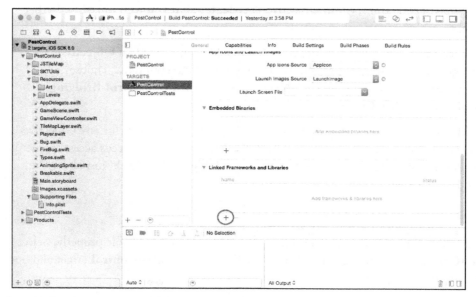

Select the library named **libz.dylib** and click **Add**.

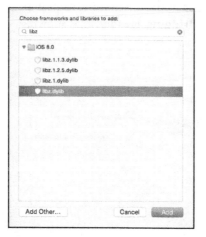

Build your project to make sure everything compiles OK. With JSTileMap and libz added to your app, you're now ready to write some code. Almost.

Making Swift play nicely with Objective-C

Believe it or not, at the time of writing, `JSTileMap` and its supporting classes are still written in Objective-C! I know, right? What year is it, anyway, the first half of 2014?

Fortunately, you can access Objective-C code from within your Swift code. You can access Swift code from within Objective-C code, too, but you won't need to do that here.

To access your Objective-C code, you need to add what's called an **Objective-C Bridging Header** to your project. To do so, go to **File\New\File…**, choose **iOS\Source\Header File** and click **Next**. Name the file **PestControl-Bridging-Header.h** and click **Create**.

Inside the Objective-C Bridging Header, you need to add imports for any Objective-C files you want to access from your Swift code. Pest Control only needs access to one file, so add the following statement to **PestControl-Bridging-Header.h**, just above the `#endif` statement:

```
#import "JSTileMap.h"
```

There is one more setting you need to make for Xcode to use this file properly. Select **PestControl** in the project navigator on the left, select the **PestControl** target and open the **Build Settings** tab.

Inside the search field, type **bridging** to find the row for **Objective-C Bridging Header**. Double-click on the right side of the row to reveal a popup field and type **PestControl/PestControl-Bridging-Header.h**, as shown:

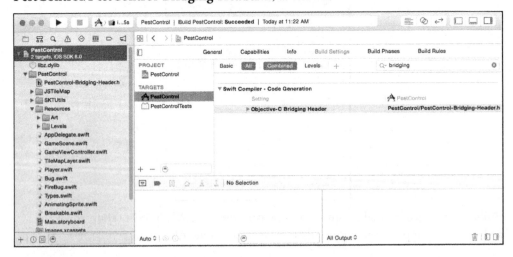

It's important to note that this field requires the path to the file, relative to your project.

Build your project to ensure everything still compiles.

Rendering TMX maps in Sprite Kit

To support TMX files along with the text files you used in the previous two chapters, you'll create a subclass of `TileMapLayer`. This will let you leverage all the code you've already written, so you won't have to write much new code to add TMX support. However, if you were only supporting TMX files, it might make more sense to replace `TileMapLayer` instead.

Go to **File\New\File…**, choose the **iOS\Source\Swift File** template and click **Next**. Name your file **TmxTileMapLayer**, make sure the **PestControl** target is checked and click **Create**.

Open **TmxTileMapLayer.swift** and replace its contents with the following:

```
class TmxTileMapLayer : TileMapLayer {

  var layer: TMXLayer

  required init?(coder aDecoder: NSCoder) {
    fatalError("NSCoding not supported")
  }

  init(tmxLayer: TMXLayer) {
    layer = tmxLayer
    super.init(tileSize: tmxLayer.mapTileSize,
               gridSize: tmxLayer.layerInfo.layerGridSize,
               layerSize: CGSize(width: tmxLayer.layerWidth,
                                 height: tmxLayer.layerHeight))
  }

}
```

You add a single property—`layer`—that holds a `TMXLayer` object. `TMXLayer` is a class declared in JSTileMap.h that gives you access to an individual layer defined in a TMX file. For some games, you won't need this access, because a single `JSTileMap` object can display all of its layers simultaneously. In the case of Pest Control, however, you'll create a single `TmxTileMapLayer` per TMX layer to fit your current `TileMapLayer`-based implementation.

After storing the `TMXLayer` passed into `init(tmxLayer:)`, you call `init(tileSize:gridSize:layerSize:)` with the relevant size-related data from the `TMXLayer`.

Later in this chapter, you'll need to override just one method from `TileMapLayer`. Can you guess which one? No, not that one! Actually, maybe that one. I don't really know because I can't hear you. You *do* know how books work, don't you?

For now, you're ready to load your TMX file into your scene. Inside **GameScene.swift**, add this property to `GameScene`:

```
var tileMap: JSTileMap?
```

This property holds a reference to an optional `JSTileMap`, which is an `SKNode` that you'll create from a TMX file. You're allowing it to be `nil` so that you can still support the text file approach from the previous chapters. Now you've got options!

To create your `JSTileMap`, you need to load a level from a TMX file. In the next chapter, you'll refactor your level-loading code to support multiple levels, but for now, you'll continue to hard-code things.

Comment out the contents of `createScenery()` and add the lines below in their place. Readers who did not work through the sections to create **level-3.tmx** should load the map named **level-3-sample.tmx**, instead.

```
tileMap = JSTileMap(named: "level-3.tmx")
return
  TmxTileMapLayer(tmxLayer: tileMap!.layerNamed("Background"))
```

You first initialize `tileMap` with a TMX file. Because `JSTileMap` extends `SKNode`, you could (and will, soon) add it to your scene and it would render the map it contains. That really couldn't be any easier. But you also return a new `TmxTileMapLayer` backed by the TMX file's `Background` layer.

Remember, your app initializes `backgroundLayer` with the return value from `createScenery()`, so the `TmxTileMapLayer` you return here is what you'll access when you interact with `backgroundLayer`. For example, when your scene checks for valid tile positions or queries tile properties, it will be using this object—and hence, data from your TMX file—to do so.

Inside `createWorld()`, add the following lines *after* the line that creates `worldNode`, but *before* the line that adds `backgroundLayer` as a child of `worldNode`:

```
if tileMap != nil {
```

```
    worldNode.addChild(tileMap!)
  }
```

This simply makes sure `tileMap` exists before adding it to `worldNode`, which will display the TMX file's contents in the scene.

Build and run. Remember when you were creating Pest Control and you had to keep iterating over it to get exactly the behavior you wanted? Well, all that work seems to have gone out the window: You've got trees all over the place, only some of which get smashed when Arnold runs through them, and Arnold and the bugs are once again running around wherever they want. It's a sprite mutiny!

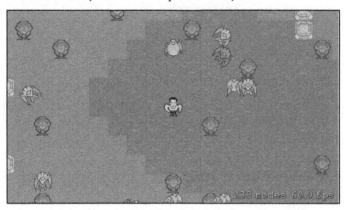

While this behavior is undesirable, it's perfectly reasonable based on the code you've written so far. First of all, you are rendering two sets of trees. Remember, your TMX file now contains a layer with tree sprites, but your app is also still loading trees from the text file, just as it did before. You'll fix this problem a bit later.

The other problem is that your background tiles are no longer rendered from `backgroundLayer` as they had been when loading from text files. Instead, you create `tileMap` and add *it* in `createWorld()`. Yes, you initialize `backgroundLayer` from the layer named `Background` inside your TMX file, and you add it as a child of `worldNode()`, but remember that `TmxTileMapLayer`'s `init(tmxLayer:)` calls `init(tileSize:gridSize:layerSize:)`.

Why is that important? Because that initializer in `TileMapLayer` *never creates any tiles*. No walls, no water, no nothing. Instead, `backgroundLayer` only acts as a pass-through object that lets you ask things like, "How big are its tiles?" or, "What are the dimensions of the background layer's grid?"

It looks like you have a few more things to do to get TMX files working properly in Pest Control. First, you'll reinforce those flimsy walls with some sturdy physics bodies.

Adding physics bodies

When you created **level-3.tmx**, you added a property named **wall** to the wall tile. (If you're running with **level-3-sample.tmx**, the `wall` property was defined for you.) Now you're going to use that property to determine where in your scene to add physics bodies of type `PhysicsCategory.Wall`.

Inside **TmxTileMapLayer.swift**, add the following method to `TmxTileMapLayer` to process the layer's tiles. You could add any custom tile-based setup here, but for now, you'll just process wall tiles:

```
func createNodesFromLayer(layer: TMXLayer) {
  let map = layer.map
  // 1
  for w in 0..<Int(gridSize.width) {
    for h in 0..<Int(gridSize.height) {
      let coord = CGPoint(x: w, y: h)
      // 2
      let tileGid = layer.layerInfo.tileGidAtCoord(coord)
      if tileGid == 0 {
        continue
      }
      // 3
      if let properties = map.propertiesForGid(tileGid) {
        if properties["wall"] != nil {
          // 4
          let tile = layer.tileAtCoord(coord)
          tile.physicsBody =
            SKPhysicsBody(rectangleOfSize: tile.size)
          tile.physicsBody!.categoryBitMask =
            PhysicsCategory.Wall
          tile.physicsBody!.dynamic = false
          tile.physicsBody!.friction = 0
        }
      }
    }
  }
}
```

The above code does the following:

1. It loops through all the cell locations in the layer.

2. At each location, it finds the global identifier for that cell's tile. TMX files reference specific tile types by unique global identifiers, or GIDs, where a value of zero means there is no tile at that location. If there is no tile, the code skips to the next cell location. This isn't absolutely necessary, but it's more efficient than running through

the remaining logic for a non-existent tile. For more information about the TMX format, consult its documentation here: https://github.com/bjorn/tiled/wiki/TMX-Map-Format

3. For each tile, the code checks for the existence of the **wall** property. As was mentioned when you added the property in Tiled, this code doesn't check the value, just whether or not the key exists.

4. Whenever this method finds a tile with the **wall** property, it attaches a physics body to that tile, just like the ones you made in `TileMapLayer`. Note that the code adds the physics body to a sprite that's in the `JSTileMap`, not the `TmxTileMapLayer`—the `TmxTileMapLayer` still contains no sprites of its own.

Don't worry about the water tiles for now; you'll handle those later using a different technique.

Now call this method at the end of `init(tmxLayer:)`:

```
createNodesFromLayer(tmxLayer)
```

Build and run. Arnold's back to banging his head into walls, just the way he likes it, but those bugs still don't seem to care where they walk.

Recall from the previous chapter that the bugs don't use physics for collisions. Instead, they query the scene to find out if it's safe to travel on a tile. And how does the scene determine that? It checks the properties of tiles in `breakableLayer` and `backgroundLayer`. However, you just saw that `backgroundLayer` no longer *has* any tiles.

And this brings us to that method you need override from `TileMapLayer`. The one you guessed earlier, remember? Or was that someone else? Speak up, please. Ha! Just kidding—still a book.

Add this method to **TmxTileMapLayer.swift**:

```
override func tileAtPoint(point: CGPoint) -> SKNode? {
  let tile = super.tileAtPoint(point)
  return tile ?? layer.tileAt(point)
}
```

This does two things. First, it checks for a tile using the method's `super` implementation from `TileMapLayer`, which looks for tiles that are children of this object. If there happens to be a tile there—and there sometimes will be before you're done with this chapter—the method returns it. But if there isn't a tile in this layer node, then this method asks the `TMXLayer` object `layer` for a tile at this position. This bridges the gap between the `TileMapLayer` logic and the `JSTileMap`. Now your layer object can access your walls and their physics bodies, even though they actually exist inside the `JSTileMap`.

Build and run, and now your bugs are back to avoiding walls. However, they still walk on water and half the trees—the half defined in the TMX layer:

Adding breakables

It's time to get rid of the old trees and add proper support for the trees from the TMX file.

Open **GameScene.swift** and replace the contents of `createBreakables()` with the following:

```
if tileMap != nil {
  let breakables = tileMap!.layerNamed("Breakables")
  return breakables != nil ?
    TmxTileMapLayer(tmxLayer: breakables) : nil
}
else {
  return tileMapLayerFromFileNamed("level-2-breakables.txt")
}
```

If `tileMap` is present, the above code checks for a layer named `Breakables`. If such a layer exists, the method returns a `TmxTileMapLayer` created from it, or `nil` otherwise. However, if `tileMap` is `nil`, the code falls into the `else` clause and executes your old logic.

Run now, and you'll see that all the old trees have disappeared.

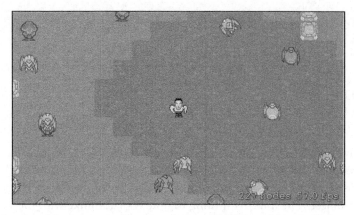

Unfortunately, the old trees were the ones that worked! Arnold and the bugs both happily pass right over the remaining trees as if there's nothing there.

You'll handle trees a bit differently than you did walls. Instead of modifying the tiles directly in the `JSTileMap`, you'll remove those tiles and add `Breakable` objects to the `TmxTileMapLayer` in their place.

Modifying tile maps at runtime

Sometimes, you'll want to modify your map at runtime. For example, you might have player pickups, destructible elements or scenery changes that occur based on in-game events. In this section, you'll get a taste of how to accomplish this sort of thing by removing tiles from the `JSTileMap` and adding `Breakable`s to your `TmxTileMapLayer`. In the process, you'll learn how to create sprites using the same tileset images referenced by the TMX file.

Open **TmxTileMapLayer.swift** and add the following line at the top of `createNodesFromLayer()`:

```
let atlas = SKTextureAtlas(named: "tmx-bg-tiles")
```

This gives you access to a texture atlas backed by exactly the same image this layer uses in the TMX file. Now you can create sprites knowing you're using the same images you saw when you were working in Tiled. Yes, this is a bit of hard-coding trickery that won't work if your TMX file uses multiple atlases. But don't worry—you'll see how you could correct for that in a moment.

To handle tree tiles, add this `else if` clause after the `if` block that handles wall tiles inside `createNodesFromLayer()`:

```
else if properties["tree"] != nil {
  let tile =
    Breakable(wholeTexture: atlas.textureNamed("tree"),
              brokenTexture: atlas.textureNamed("tree-stump"))
  tile.position = pointForCoord(coord)
  addChild(tile)
  layer.removeTileAtCoord(coord)
}
```

The code above checks for any tile that has the **tree** property—remember, it's in a loop inside `createNodesFromLayer()`. When it finds one, it creates a `Breakable` object and places it inside this `TmxTileMapLayer` object. Finally, it removes the tile it found from the `TMXLayer` object. The important thing to note is that, unlike with the walls, the tree sprite the game displays to the user is now in the `TmxTileMapLayer`, not the `JSTileMap`.

If you didn't want to hard-code the texture atlas name used in this method, then you could use the code below to find the name of the texture atlas containing a specific tile GID:

```
let info = map.tilesetInfoForGid(tileGid)
let textureFileName = info.sourceImage.lastPathComponent
let atlasName =
  textureFileName.stringByDeletingPathExtension.
    stringByDeletingPathExtension
```

This code will only work if you didn't use any periods in your texture atlas names. First, the code finds the tileset used by the current tile (as a `TMXTilesetInfo` reference), and then strips the path and unnecessary text from the file name, resulting in the atlas name.

You would then get the atlas using `atlasName` and proceed as before, but you'd have to do that once for each tile. Technically, you could cache references to the atlases by tile type. However, for the purposes of Pest Control, none of this is necessary.

Run again, and help Arnold prune some branches. Not too much, mind you—just take a little off the top.

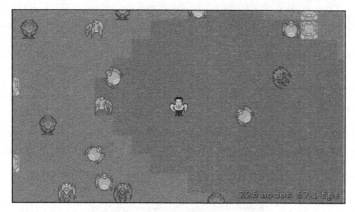

Also notice that once again, the bugs avoid your trees. How'd that happen? While it may look like Arnold invested in some bug repellent, this is the result of code you wrote a few steps ago.

Remember when you implemented `tileAtPoint()` in `TmxTileMapLayer` to check for tiles in the `TmxTileMapLayer` node before checking the `TMXLayer` object? The `Breakables` are now stored in the `TmxTileMapLayer`, and as such, `tileAtPoint()` returns them when appropriate. Since Pest Control calls this method when the bugs are planning their movements, they now correctly identify the trees as impassable tiles.

With your background and the trees both coming from the TMX file, it's time to turn your attention to Arnold and the bugs.

Defining spawn points

Right now, you've got parts of the level loading from a TMX file and parts of it loading from the text files you were using in the previous chapters, but you really want to store all the level data in a single TMX file. In this section, you'll add to the file the starting positions, or spawn points, for the player and all the bugs. To do that, you'll use a different type of layer called an **object layer**.

> **Note:** If you aren't following along in Tiled, you can skip ahead to "Accessing TMX data layers in Sprite Kit," where you'll see how to use data in an object layer to spawn the player and the bugs.

Adding data layers in Tiled

In much the same way you made the Breakables tile layer, you'll make a new layer to store character spawn points. However, instead of adding tiles to this layer, you'll just store metadata used by your app to create the appropriate objects. To accomplish this, you'll create what is called an object layer.

Open **level-3.tmx** in Tiled and choose **Layer\Add Object Layer**, which creates a new layer named **Object Layer 1**. Rename **Object Layer 1** to **Bugs**, as shown below:

Select the **Insert Rectangle** tool (shortcut **R**) from the toolbar, and with the Bugs layer selected, click someplace on the map where you'd like a bug to spawn. That will create a small square at that position, as shown below:

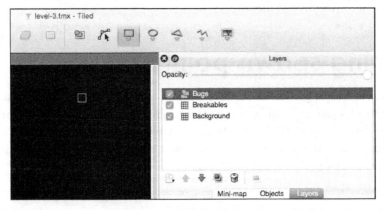

Now do more of that until you have a nice field of squares, making sure you position each square where it makes sense to spawn a bug:

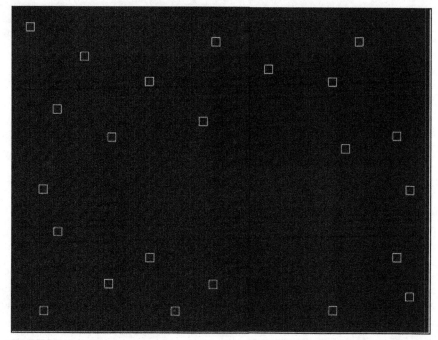

Each of these squares defines a bug's spawn point that you'll need to process in your code. To make that easier, you'll name each square. Click the **Objects** tab and expand the **Bugs** layer, which will show you the name and type for every object it currently contains. Because you haven't assigned any names or types, your list will look like the one below:

Double-click in the **Name** column to the right of one of the checkmarks and then enter the name **bug**. Do that for every object in the **Bugs** layer, which should result in something similar to the following:

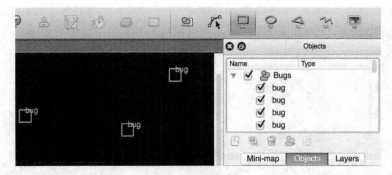

Notice how each object in the map view also displays its name.

In your original implementation, you also defined Arnold's spawn point in the bug data file, and you'll do the same thing here. To make Arnold's point easier to see, you'll define it using a different shape.

Select the **Insert Ellipse** tool (shortcut **C**) from the toolbar, and with the **Bugs** layer selected, click the spot on the map where you'd like Arnold to appear. That will create a small circle at that position. Inside the **Objects** list, name that object **player**, as shown below:

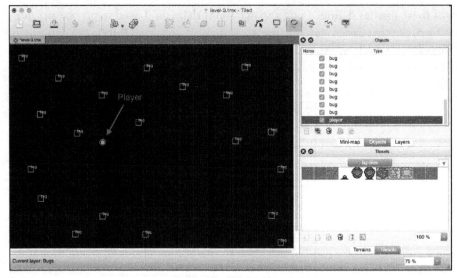

It's hard to see it, but the circle is displaying the object's name on the map just like the squares are. The circle's name is truncated, though, because the object is so small. If you had created a larger object, you'd see the name.

You're done for now, so save your map in Tiled.

You've defined all your spawn points and you can see at a glance exactly how your level is arranged. Now you need to use this spawn data in your app.

Accessing TMX data layers in Sprite Kit

JSTileMap creates TMXLayers for each tile layer in a TMX file, and you've already added support for those inside TmxTileMapLayer. But object layers are accessed via TMXObjectGroup objects, not TMXLayers, so you'll need to support those differently.

Open **TmxTileMapLayer.swift**. Much like the way you handled tiles with different properties in createNodesFromLayer(), you'll add support for objects with different names in a new method called createNodesFromGroup(). For now, add this implementation to handle spawning the player character:

```
func createNodesFromGroup(group:TMXObjectGroup) {
  if let playerObj = group.objectNamed("player") {
    let player = Player()
    let x = playerObj["x"] as? NSNumber
    let y = playerObj["y"] as? NSNumber

    player.position = CGPoint(x: CGFloat(x!), y: CGFloat(y!))
    addChild(player)
  }
}
```

This simply asks the group for the object named **player**. In the current version of the library, TMXObjectGroup returns objects as dictionaries of data. If one is found named **player**, then this method creates a new Player object, sets its position using the x- and y-values stored in the playerObj dictionary and adds it to the layer. But where did those position values come from?

Tiled defined those keys and values for you when you placed the object in the Bugs layer. This dictionary contains other data, too, which will vary depending on the object type, and it would contain any user-defined properties added to the object in Tiled.

> **Note:** The code to extract the x- and y-values looks a bit involved because Swift requires you to handle the possibility that the playerObj dictionary might return a nil value. Likewise, the compiler isn't sure if the value will be an NSNumber, so you perform a conditional cast. Finally, as of this writing, Swift has a problem dealing with Float objects in 64-bit environments, so you need to cast x and y to CGFloats before creating the position.

Now, add the following initializer so you can create a `TmxTileMapLayer` from a `TMXObjectGroup` instead of a `TMXLayer`:

```
init(tmxObjectGroup:TMXObjectGroup,
     tileSize:CGSize, gridSize: CGSize) {
  layer = TMXLayer()
  super.init(
    tileSize: tileSize, gridSize: gridSize,
    layerSize:CGSize(width: tileSize.width * gridSize.width,
                     height: tileSize.height * gridSize.height))

  createNodesFromGroup(tmxObjectGroup)
}
```

This method is similar to `init(tmxLayer:)`, except it doesn't need a layer, so it just creates a default one to make the compiler happy—and it calls `createNodesFromGroup()` instead of `createNodesFromLayer()`.

Unlike `TMXLayer`, `TMXObjectGroup` has no concept of tile or grid sizes, but for your purposes, you still want to interact with the `TmxTileMapLayer` object in terms of tiles and cells. For these reasons, this initializer requires you to pass in the tile and grid sizes, and it uses those when calling `super.init(tileSize:gridSize:layerSize:)`.

Next, you need to replace the current bug layer with a `TmxTileMapLayer`. To do so, you need to modify `createCharacters()` inside **GameScene.swift**. Replace its first line (the one that creates `bugLayer`) with the following code:

```
if tileMap != nil {
  bugLayer = TmxTileMapLayer(
    tmxObjectGroup: tileMap!.groupNamed("Bugs"),
    tileSize: tileMap!.tileSize,
    gridSize: backgroundLayer.gridSize)
} else {
  bugLayer = tileMapLayerFromFileNamed("level-2-bugs.txt")
}
```

Run the app. Arnold appears right where you put him and the bugs are nowhere to be seen. Just how Arnold likes it.

The bugs are gone because you're now loading the bugs from the TMX file's Bugs group, but you only added support in createNodesFromGroup() for the object named player.

To remedy this, open **TmxTileMapLayer.swift** and add this inside createNodesFromGroup():

```
if let bugs = group.objectsNamed("bug") as? [[String:AnyObject]]
{
  for bugObj in bugs {
    let x = bugObj["x"] as? NSNumber
    let y = bugObj["y"] as? NSNumber

    let bug = Bug()
    bug.position = CGPoint(x: CGFloat(x!), y: CGFloat(y!))
    addChild(bug)
  }
}
```

This is similar to the code you used to add the player. Run again, and the bugs are back in town!

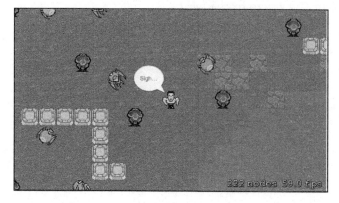

Your app is rendering a map from a TMX file. Your player and bugs are spawning where they should and colliding properly with the walls and trees. There's just one thing left to fix: water tiles.

You could handle water tiles the same way you did the walls, but instead you'll use a more efficient approach: another object layer.

Object layers for collisions areas

Previously, you created separate physics bodies for each wall tile. This works and in such small levels, it performs fine. But as the number of physics bodies in a scene increases, performance eventually suffers. To improve performance, you'll use object layers to define larger, more efficient physics bodies.

> **Note:** If you aren't following along in Tiled, you can skip ahead to "Using TMX object layers for collision areas in Sprite Kit," where you'll see how to use object layers to define physics objects.

Defining collision areas in Tiled

Open **level-3.tmx** in Tiled. Choose **Layer\Add Object Layer** and name the new layer **CollisionAreas**. With the **CollisionAreas** layer selected, choose **Insert Rectangle** (shortcut **R**) in the toolbar and find some water on your map.

Click and hold down the mouse button over the upper-left corner of a water tile, then drag the mouse cursor down and to the right to draw the largest rectangle you can that contains only water tiles. Don't worry if the rectangle doesn't line up perfectly with your tiles—you'll see an easy way to fix that next.

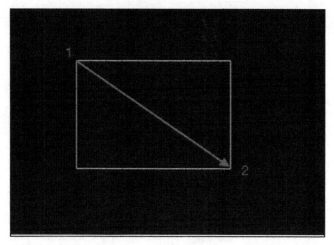

You now have a single large rectangle covering several water tiles, but it probably isn't covering them perfectly. To fix this, choose the **Objects** tab and expand **CollisionAreas** to see all the objects it contains. Select the single unnamed object in **CollisionAreas**, and then click the **Object Properties** button, as shown below:

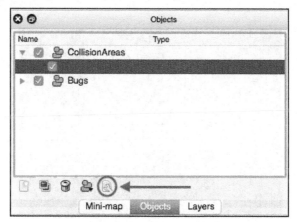

This brings up a dialog in which you can name your object and set its properties. You're most interested in the **X**, **Y**, **Width** and **Height** properties. You want to change each value to a whole number. In general, if you kept the rectangle smaller than the area of water tiles its meant to cover, you'll adjust the **X**- and **Y**-values **down** to the next whole number and then adjust the **Width** and **Height** values **up** to the next whole number. See the following example:

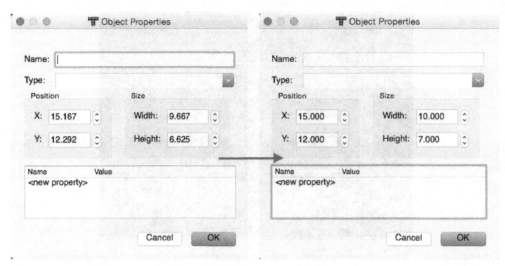

Of course, if any of your rectangle's edges are beyond the boundary of the area of water you meant to cover, you'll have to adjust these properties differently. But in general, it's pretty easy to line them up. After making the above adjustments, here's what this rectangle looks like:

Now repeat this process and continue to make rectangles, covering as much of the water as you can with as few rectangles as possible. Don't bother running algorithms trying to come up with the most efficient coverage that uses the fewest possible rectangles—the idea is simply to use fewer rectangles than you would if you created a separate one for each tile, which is essentially the path you took when creating the physics bodies for the walls.

Name each of these rectangles **water**. Here is one possible set of rectangles that covers the water tiles in this map:

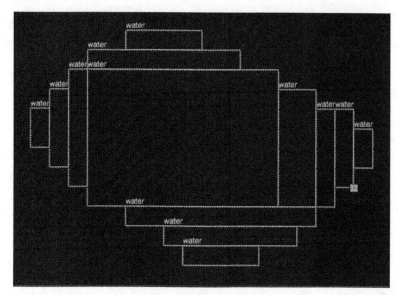

Tiled also lets you create polygons with arbitrary vertices, so you could create a single polygon that encompasses all of the water tiles in the above image. However, Sprite Kit currently imposes a vertex limit on physics bodies, so you'd have to do extra work in code to break the large polygon into multiple smaller ones anyway. The technique shown here is much simpler to understand and implement and still provides a large savings over using a separate physics body per tile.

Using TMX object layers for collision areas in Sprite Kit

You *could* create a new `TmxTileMapLayer` for the group named `CollisionAreas`, much as you did for the `Bugs` group, but recall that your app logic already checks `backgroundLayer` when testing for water tiles. To reuse as much code as possible between the TMX and non-TMX versions, and because `backgroundLayer` is already created from the `Background` tile layer, you'll simply add your collision areas to `backgroundLayer`.

This time, open **GameScene.swift** and add the following new method:

```
func createCollisionAreas() {
  // 1
  let group = tileMap!.groupNamed("CollisionAreas")
  if group == nil {
    return
  }
  // 2
```

```
    if let waterObjects =
      group.objectsNamed("water") as? [[String:AnyObject]]
    {
      for waterObj in waterObjects {
        let tmpX = waterObj["x"] as? NSNumber
        let tmpY = waterObj["y"] as? NSNumber
        // 3
        var tmpW = waterObj["width"] as? NSNumber
        if tmpW == nil {
          tmpW = (waterObj["width"] as? NSString)?.floatValue
        }
        var tmpH = waterObj["height"] as? NSNumber
        if tmpH == nil {
          tmpH = (waterObj["height"] as? NSString)?.floatValue
        }
        // 4
        if tmpX == nil || tmpY == nil ||
          tmpW == nil || tmpH == nil {
          continue
        }
        let x = CGFloat(tmpX!)
        let y = CGFloat(tmpY!)
        let w = CGFloat(tmpW!)
        let h = CGFloat(tmpH!)
        // 5
        let water = SKSpriteNode(color: SKColor.redColor(),
                                 size:CGSize(width: w, height: h))
        water.name = "water"
        water.position = CGPoint(x: x + w/2, y: y + h/2)
        water.physicsBody = SKPhysicsBody(
          rectangleOfSize: CGSize(width: w, height: h))

        water.physicsBody!.categoryBitMask = PhysicsCategory.Water
        water.physicsBody!.dynamic = false
        water.physicsBody!.friction = 0

        backgroundLayer.addChild(water)
      }
    }
  }
```

This method isn't as complicated as it looks. Here's what it does:

1. It first gets the group named **CollisionAreas** from the tile map. If there is no such group, the method simply returns.

2. Then it gets the objects named **water** and loops through them, much like the way createNodesFromGroup() in TmxTileMapLayer handles objects named **bug**.

3. After getting the x- and y-values from the `waterObj` dictionary, it gets values for `width` and `height`, too. These are two values Tiled adds automatically for rectangle objects. `JSTileMap` currently stores their values as strings instead of numbers, but that may change later—this bit of code handles either possible data type.

4. Because each of the variables holds an optional value, this section checks to make sure they are all present. If so, it unwraps all the values and converts them to `CGFloats` to keep the rest of the code clean.

5. The code then creates a red sprite using the position and dimensions you just read from the TMX file. You're just using the red color for debugging. Finally, the code creates a physics body with the same properties as the water tiles you've made in the past and adds it to `backgroundLayer`.

Add the following code at the end of `createWorld()`:

```
if tileMap != nil {
   createCollisionAreas()
}
```

Once again, to support the older data files you have from the previous chapters, you ensure `tileMap` exists before proceeding. If it does exist, you call your new method to create collision areas.

Build and run the app. Now that the water looks like hot lava, no one wants to touch it!

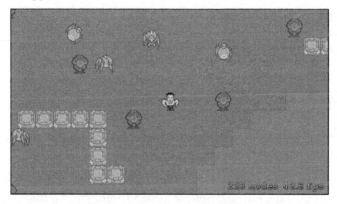

The red color helps you see that your objects were indeed created in the proper locations. Now that you've verified it's working correctly, add the following line in `createCollisionAreas()`, right before the line that adds the water to the background layer:

```
water.hidden = true
```

Run once more, and your water looks like water again, but now Arnold bounces off of it and the bugs avoid it. I guess no one in this game can swim.

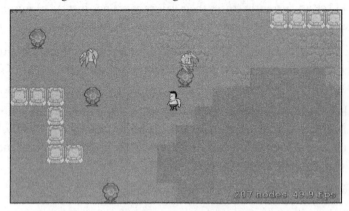

In this chapter, you added TMX support for almost every aspect of a Pest Control level. You'll take care of the one remaining item—the firebugs—as this chapter's single challenge. Afterward, spend some time with Tiled, create your own tilesets and see what you can make.

`JSTileMap` already supports more features of the TMX file format than you used in this chapter, and the plan is to support them all. However, there are other options available, so look into them and let us know on the forums which solution you end up preferring!

In the next chapter, you'll add various gameplay elements to Pest Control, like UI elements, progression through multiple levels and win/lose states. Plus, you'll use Sprite Kit's `NSCoding` support to implement autosaving.

Challenge: Spawning firebugs

The last chapter had larger-than-average challenges, so let's keep it simple this time around.

You already support spawn points for the player and the regular bugs—now you'll add them for the firebugs. To do so, add objects named **firebug** to the **Bugs** layer in **level-3.tmx**. Then, modify `createNodesFromGroup()` in **TmxTileMapLayer.swift** to get all the objects named **firebug** and create a `FireBug` for each of them. Take another look at the way you create the regular bugs if you need any hints.

If you still need help, you can find the solution in the resources for this chapter, but Arnold will know if you didn't try your best!

Chapter 17: Saving and Loading Games

By Christopher LaPollo

Players come and players go. That's never been truer than it is with mobile games, where play sessions for even the most successful games can be on the order of just a few seconds or minutes. If you don't want everyone who ever tries your game to walk away angry, chances are you need to save their game state between sessions.

There are various ways you can save game data: using plain text files, property files or binary files; storing data locally, in iCloud, on your own server or maybe even using one of various other services, like Dropbox. Given all of these possibilities, it doesn't make much sense to try to show you *the* way to save game state.

However, one of the most exciting features of Sprite Kit, at least from a tool developer's standpoint, is that users can archive any of its nodes and later make new objects from those archives. That means you can do a lot of fun things, such as create a level editor that uses Sprite Kit to let you see, modify and even test game levels, and then save those levels as SKNodes to use directly in your game.

Making something like a level editor would be a great application of Sprite Kit's archiving feature. In fact, the Scene Editor introduced in Xcode 6 relies on this technique. We don't have enough room in the book to cover building something that involved, but we also don't want to ignore archiving entirely. Therefore, this chapter will show you how to implement a nice, little autosave feature for Pest Control by saving the actual Sprite Kit scene to disk!

This chapter's first section, "Making a game out of pest control," covers implementing Pest Control's remaining gameplay features, like winning and losing and transitioning between multiple levels. As such, it doesn't relate directly to the chapter's topic, saving and loading games. However, without this additional logic, there isn't much to save or load. After all, it's hard to save a player's progress in a game if there's no way to make progress in the game, right?

> **Note:** This chapter begins where the previous chapter's Challenge left off. If you were unable to complete the challenge or skipped ahead from an earlier chapter, don't worry—you can simply open **PestControl-Starter** from this chapter's resources to begin in the right place.

> **Note:** If you're not interested in the details of creating Pest Control's remaining gameplay features, you can skip ahead to "Saving and loading Sprite Kit data." There, you'll find a starter project that picks up from that point, allowing you to focus on saving and loading.

Making a game out of pest control

Running and using muscles for smashing bugs. That strange sentence fragment came out of nowhere and feels incomplete, right?

Well, Pest Control is currently just like that. The user loads the app and suddenly, there are bugs moving around and a guy in the middle of the screen. You haven't indicated what's expected of your player, and once they figure out how to move Arnold and then begin killing bugs, the "game" never ends. Eventually, all the bugs are gone and Arnold is left roaming around the screen, forced to live out a solitary, empty existence for the rest of his days, pining for the very things he once sought to destroy.

Doesn't that make you want to cry? No? You, sir or madam, are a monster. Yes? Well then, stop it, crybaby. Arnold doesn't want your tears; he wants some direction in life. He wants to win.

You've got sprites that respond to player taps and to collisions with each other, but that doesn't mean you've got a game. Your players will want to decide when to start a level, will want ways to succeed or fail and will want to progress through multiple different levels. Let's begin at the beginning.

Starting the game

Right now, Pest Control just starts. The game appears and the bugs are wandering around and there's no indication of what your user should do. That's not very helpful. In this section, you'll add some instructions for your users and you'll modify the scene so that nothing starts moving until the player starts playing.

You'll create a new type to define the possible game states, which will allow you to perform different logic based on simple if checks at key points in your game. Inside **Types.swift**, define the following type:

```
enum GameState {
  case StartingLevel
  case Playing
}
```

You'll add more values later, but for now, these two let you differentiate between starting a level, when the app is still waiting for the player's first input, and playing the game, when Arnold is busy with his smashing spree.

Open **GameScene.swift** and add this property to store the game's current state:

```
var gameState = GameState.StartingLevel
```

You initialize gameState to StartingLevel so the scene will start in this state.

Now add this helper method, which will set up the initial user interface:

```
func createUserInterface() {
  let startMsg = SKLabelNode(fontNamed: "Chalkduster")
  startMsg.name = "msgLabel"
  startMsg.text = "Tap Screen to Run!"
```

```
   startMsg.fontSize = 32
   startMsg.position = CGPoint(x: 0, y: 20)
   startMsg.zPosition = 100
   addChild(startMsg)
}
```

This simply adds a label to the scene instructing the user to tap the screen to begin running. You named the label `msgLabel` because you'll want to find it later to use for other messages.

Call this method after the call to `centerViewOn()` inside `didMoveToView()`:

```
createUserInterface()
```

Build and run. You'll see the app runs just as it did before, but now it's got a high-tech user interface obscuring your view. So… helpful, right?

With instructions on the screen, the user knows what to do. That's good. But the instructions never go away—that's less good. Since you already handle touches in `touchesBegan(withEvent:)`, that's a good place to get rid of the label. It's also where you'll update the game state when the user starts playing.

Replace `touchesBegan(withEvent:)` with the following:

```
override func touchesBegan(touches: Set<NSObject>,
                           withEvent event: UIEvent) {
  switch gameState {
    case .StartingLevel:
      childNodeWithName("msgLabel")!.hidden = true
      gameState = .Playing

      fallthrough
```

```
    case .Playing:
      let touch = touches.first as! UITouch
      player.moveToward(touch.locationInNode(worldNode))
  }
}
```

This method handles touches based on the current value of `gameState`. If the state is `StartingLevel`, the method hides `msgLabel`, updates the game state to `Playing` and then falls through to the next `case`, where it moves `player`. If the state is `Playing`, the method simply moves `player`.

> **Note:** The first `case` in `touchesBegan(withEvent:)` includes a `fallthrough` statement so that the user's first tap starts Arnold running. If you don't like that behavior, remove the `fallthrough` statement.

Build and run now, and the message disappears as soon as you tap the screen. But there's still one issue: The bugs are moving around even before the player has a chance to start playing. If you waited long enough, there's a chance that all the bugs would walk right into Arnold! Not very sporting.

To keep your sprites from running their `SKActions`—and hence, keep your bugs from moving—you need to pause the scene. Add the following at the end of `didMoveToView()`:

```
if gameState == .StartingLevel {
  paused = true
}
```

This simply checks the game state after the scene is fully initialized, and pauses the scene if necessary.

Build and run again, and now no one is moving. At all. Ever.

The problem is that you paused the scene at start up, but you never un-paused it when the user started playing. To do so, add the following line to `touchesBegan(withEvent:)`, inside the case that handles `StartingLevel`, just *before* the `fallthrough` statement:

```
paused = false
```

Build and run, and *run*. Now things stay put until the player taps the screen, at which point the bugs start walking and Arnold darts off in the direction of the tap. Your player is in control and it's time to give them a goal.

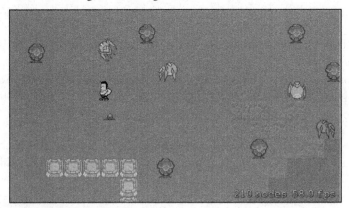

Winning the game

The win condition for Pest Control is pretty simple: kill all the bugs. You already have a separate node—bugLayer—which contains all the bugs, so all you have to do is check it to find out when all the bugs are gone.

You *could* maintain a separate counter to keep track of the bugs, updating it every time Arnold collides with a bug, and that may even be the most efficient way to do it. However, if you went that route, you'd also have to add logic in multiple places to update the counter for each type of enemy in the game.

More importantly, you're here to get more practice with Sprite Kit, so you'll query bugLayer directly rather than maintain a separate counter.

Still in **GameScene.swift**, implement update() as shown below:

```
override func update(currentTime: CFTimeInterval) {
  if bugLayer.childNodeWithName("bug") == nil {
    println("Who's the big winner? You are!")
  }
}
```

This simply searches bugLayer for the first object named bug that it can find. Every bug (including the firebugs) is named bug, so if childNodeWithName() returns nil, the bugs are gone and the player has cleared the level.

Build and run, and kill all those bugs! As soon as Arnold runs through the last one, you should see this statement appear repeatedly in the console:

```
Who's the big winner? You are!
```

> **Note**: Is killing all those bugs too much work? Your project includes a file named **level-3-bug-cheat.tmx**. This is the level you created in the previous chapter but with only a single regular bug and a single firebug. If you would like to speed up your testing, temporarily change the first line of `createScenery()` in **GameScene.swift** so it loads this file.

Now that you know the game properly recognizes its win state, you need to replace that console log with a notification to the player.

Add this new method that will handle notifying the player of both wins and losses:

```
func endLevelWithSuccess(won: Bool) {
  // 1
  let label = childNodeWithName("msgLabel") as! SKLabelNode
  label.text = won ? "You Win!!!" : "Too Slow!!!"
  label.hidden = false
  // 2
  let nextLevel = SKLabelNode(fontNamed: "Chalkduster")
  nextLevel.text = "Next Level?"
  nextLevel.name = "nextLevelLabel"
  nextLevel.fontSize = 28
  nextLevel.horizontalAlignmentMode = won ? .Center : .Left
  nextLevel.position =
    won ? CGPoint(x: 0, y: -40) : CGPoint(x: 20, y: -40)
  nextLevel.zPosition = 100
  addChild(nextLevel)
  // 3
  player.physicsBody!.linearDamping = 1
}
```

The above code does the following:

1. It displays `msgLabel` with an appropriate win/loss message based on the value you pass in for `won`.

2. It displays a new label named `nextLevelLabel` that gives the player the option of moving to the next level. Later, you'll find this object by name and process touch events that occur over it, effectively making it a button. Note that the code positions

this label differently based on whether this was a win or a loss, because later, you'll add an item next to it in the case of a loss.

3. This line is simply a nicety. Setting the player's `linearDamping` to 1 will cause Arnold to skid to a halt. It looks better than having him continue to bounce around in the background while you have UI elements for your user to read.

With that method in place, replace the `println` statement in `update()` with the following call:

```
endLevelWithSuccess(true)
```

Build and run. Kill all the bugs, and this time Arnold slows to a stop—of course, he continues to run in place, to stay fit—and you see your messages:

Unfortunately, even after squashing all those giant bugs, there is still one bug lurking in your code and it's wreaking havoc on your frame rate.

As you probably know by now, Sprite Kit calls `update()` once per frame, ideally 60 times per second. However, your scene's `update()` checks the bug count and calls `endLevelWithSuccess()` if the count is zero. That makes sense the first time you call it, but what about the next 59 times that second? And so on.

Calling `endLevelWithSuccess()` over and over is bad for multiple reasons. First, it's inefficient—once the app knows you've cleared the level, it shouldn't keep checking. But more importantly, `endLevelWithSuccess()` adds a new label to the scene. Even though you only see "Next Level?" on the screen once, your app is actually adding a new label in the exact same place every time you call that method, ideally 60 times per second.

Of course, as the node count goes up, Sprite Kit cannot maintain that ideal of 60 FPS, so you see the frame rate drop. In the screenshot above, there are 691 nodes (way up from the 220+ nodes that are usually in the scene while playing) and Sprite Kit is rendering at a sluggish six frames per second. As time passes, that frame rate just keeps getting lower.

The best way to fix this problem is to consider the time when the app is displaying these messages as a new game state, and then perform different processing in update() based on the game's current state.

Add the following new value to GameState inside **Types.swift**. You will use it to indicate when the game is showing a menu between levels:

```
case InLevelMenu
```

Note that, even though you are showing a sort of menu in the StartingLevel state, these are still unique states because you want to handle touches differently in each case.

Also, you may be confused by all this talk of levels, because Pest Control only has one level at the moment. Don't worry—you'll remedy that in the next section.

Now that you've added the InLevelMenu value to GameState, Xcode starts giving you an error. It claims that the switch statement in touchesBegan(withEvent:), inside **GameScene.swift**, must be exhaustive. You can fix that for now by adding the following case statement:

```
case .InLevelMenu:
    println("TODO: Handle InLevelMenu touches")
```

At the end of endLevelWithSuccess(), add the following line to update the game state:

```
gameState = .InLevelMenu
```

This updates the game state to indicate a menu is onscreen, but it inadvertently fixes another bug you had, as well. Before adding this code, if you tapped the screen after you won, Arnold would try to move again. His linearDamping value was still 1 and your frame rate was dropping to ridiculously low values, so he never got very far. But now, when you tap the screen while the menu is visible, Arnold completely ignores the touch event.

Finally, add these lines at the beginning of `update()`:

```
if gameState != .Playing {
  return
}
```

This simply ensures the bulk of `update()` only executes when the player is actually playing. Run again, and the app's performance is back to normal.

When the player has killed all the bugs, you present a hearty message of congratulations and an inviting `Next Level` button. Unfortunately, you don't have multiple levels. It's time to do something about that.

Multiple levels

In Pest Control, you currently hard-code the level to load. That's great for testing, but it's not a good long-term solution. In this section, you'll give your players the ability to progress through multiple levels, while giving Arnold a world that he can never truly rid of all its pests.

Before you can load levels, you need levels to load. The **Resources\Levels** group project includes a file named **Levels.plist** that defines the app's levels and looks like this:

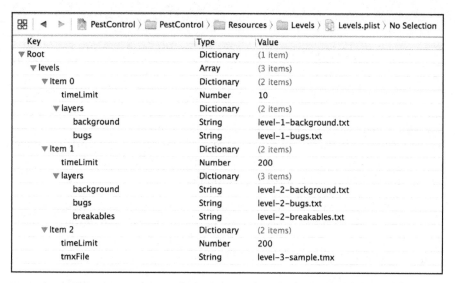

The `Root` dictionary contains a single array stored with the key `levels`. Each item in the `levels` array is a dictionary defining a single level. The game will progress through them in order (i.e., `Item 0`, `Item 1`, `Item 2` and so on) and loop back to the beginning after the final level.

Each level dictionary contains two keys:

1. `timeLimit` specifies the number of seconds the player has to complete a level. You'll use this when you implement a loss state in the next section.

2. One of the following:

    a. `layers` is a dictionary containing the file names that define the layers in your tile map. It is only present for levels defined using the non-TMX file approach from Chapters 14 and 15.

    b. `tmxFile`, on the other hand, is only present for levels defined using TMX files. It contains the name of the TMX file that defines the level.

You'll change `GameScene` to load the current level's configuration from **Levels.plist**. Add the following property in **GameScene.swift** to keep track of the scene's current level:

```
var currentLevel = 0
```

Add the following code at the *beginning* of `didMoveToView()`:

```
let config = NSDictionary(contentsOfFile:
```

```
    NSBundle.mainBundle().pathForResource("Levels",
                                          ofType: "plist")!)!
let levels = config["levels"] as! [[String:AnyObject]]
if currentLevel >= levels.count {
  currentLevel = 0
}
```

This loads the contents of **Level.plist** into `config` and then loads the array named
"Levels" into `levels`. It also resets `currentLevel` to zero if it is currently too high for
the number of levels available—remember that array indices start at zero, so a value
equal to the number of available levels is still too high.

Resetting `currentLevel` to zero will make the game loop back to the first level when a
user completes the last level, but you could make your game do something else at this
point, such as congratulate your player for completing the game and encourage them to
play again to beat their highest score or to make an In-App Purchase.

As you can see in **Levels.plist**, and as you learned in the previous chapter, your scene
needs to load levels stored in TMX files differently from those stored using plain text
files.

Begin by adding this code immediately after the lines you just added:

```
let levelData = levels[currentLevel]
if let tmxFile = levelData["tmxFile"] as? String {
  tileMap = JSTileMap(named: tmxFile)
}
```

This simply creates `tileMap` if `levelData` contains the key `tmxFile`. Throughout the
rest of `GameScene`, wherever there's a place that requires different logic for TMX vs.
non-TMX levels, you'll add a check for `tileMap`—if it's present, you'll perform TMX
logic; otherwise, you'll execute non-TMX logic.

Now you'll refactor `createScenery()`, `createWorld()`, `createCharacters()` and
`createBreakables()` to each take a `Dictionary` parameter, and you'll pass the
`levelData` dictionary to each of these methods.

Note: Once you make the next change, the project will no longer compile
successfully until you reach the next build and run step.

Start by replacing `createScenery()` with the following:

```
func createScenery(
  levelData: [String:AnyObject]) -> TileMapLayer?
{
  if tileMap != nil {
    return TmxTileMapLayer(
      tmxLayer: tileMap!.layerNamed("Background"))
  }
  else {
    let layerFiles: AnyObject? = levelData["layers"]
    if let dict = layerFiles as? [String:String] {
      return tileMapLayerFromFileNamed(dict["background"]!)
    }
  }
  return nil
}
```

With these changes, `createScenery()` now uses the data supplied in `levelData` to create `backgroundLayer`. Notice that `levelData` goes unused if `tileMap` exists—that's because you know you named the background layer "Background" when you created the TMX file. However, you could have stored the TMX layer names in `levelData` if you didn't want to hard-code their names in this class.

Now change the top of `createWorld()`, including its signature and the creation of `backgroundLayer`, so that it uses the level data dictionary:

```
func createWorld(levelData: [String:AnyObject]) {
  backgroundLayer = createScenery(levelData)
  // Remainder of the method unchanged...
}
```

Modify the signature for `createBreakables()` to take a level data dictionary, like this:

```
func createBreakables(
  levelData: [String:AnyObject]) -> TileMapLayer?
```

And replace its current `else` statement with the following:

```
else {
  let layerFiles: AnyObject? = levelData["layers"]
  if let dict = layerFiles as? [String:String] {
    if let layer = dict["breakables"] {
      return tileMapLayerFromFileNamed(layer)
    }
  }
}
return nil
```

This simply replaces the logic for loading breakables from a hard-coded file name with logic to find the file name in the level data dictionary. Remember, if `layerFiles` doesn't include a value for the key `breakables`, `tileMapLayerFromFileNamed()` will return `nil`. You also had to add a return statement at the end of the method because it's no longer guaranteed to return a value from the `if-else` statement.

Change the call to `createBreakables()` in `createWorld()` to pass it the level data dictionary, like this:

```
breakableLayer = createBreakables(levelData)
```

You have one more method signature to change. Modify `createCharacters()` to take a level data dictionary, like this:

```
func createCharacters(levelData: [String:AnyObject])
```

Also inside `createCharacters()`, find the following line:

```
bugLayer = tileMapLayerFromFileNamed("level-2-bugs.txt")
```

And replace it with these lines:

```
let layerFiles: AnyObject? = levelData["layers"]
if let dict = layerFiles as? [String:String] {
  bugLayer = tileMapLayerFromFileNamed(dict["bugs"]!)
}
```

This code initializes `bugLayer` with code similar to what you wrote in `createScenery()` and `createBreakables()`. Notice that it assumes an entry named "bugs" exists in the dictionary, unlike the way `createBreakables()` works with or without a "breakables" entry.

Now, fix the errors Xcode is complaining about by changing the calls to `createWorld()` and `createCharacters()` in `didMoveToView()`, passing in `levelData` so the code looks like this:

```
createWorld(levelData)
createCharacters(levelData)
```

Build and run. The app launches and uses `currentLevel`'s default value of zero to show the level defined in `Item 0` of **Levels.plist**.

Now that you can clear a screen and define multiple levels, you can go back and make that **Next Level** button do something.

First, add the following initializer that lets you specify a level to load:

```
init(size: CGSize, level: Int) {
  currentLevel = level
  super.init(size: size)
}
```

This initializes `currentLevel` to the specified level. Remember that you're performing a bounds check in `didMoveToView()`, so there's nothing more to do here.

Inside the `switch` statement in `touchesBegan(withEvent:)`, replace the `InLevelMenu` case with the following:

```
case .InLevelMenu:
  let touch = touches.first as! UITouch
  let loc = touch.locationInNode(self)

  if let node = childNodeWithName("nextLevelLabel") {
    if node.containsPoint(loc) {
      let newScene = GameScene(size:size, level: currentLevel+1)
      view!.presentScene(newScene,
        transition: SKTransition.flipVerticalWithDuration(0.5))
      break
    }
  }
}
```

The above code simply checks if the user touched the **Next Level?** label by finding the touch's location in the scene's coordinate space and then asking the label if it contains that point. If so, it creates a new `GameScene` object initialized to the level after the current one and asks this scene's view to transition to the new scene. Essentially, it replaces the current scene with a new one.

Build and run. Kill all the bugs in the first level, tap **Next Level?** and watch as the next level transitions into view.

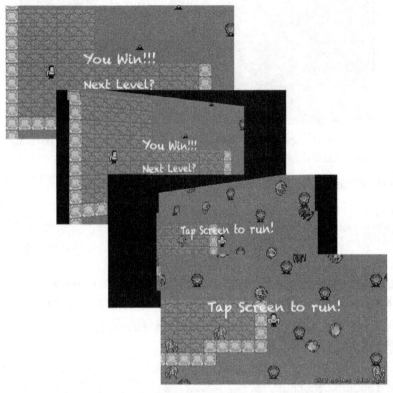

Neat! Except, there's a problem. (Why are you always causing problems?) Remember earlier in this chapter when you changed didMoveToView() to pause the scene until the user starts playing? Well, when the new level appears, the bugs are already moving, which means the scene isn't paused.

Here's what's happening. First, you create the new scene and ask the view to present it using a transition. Sprite Kit then calls didMoveToView(), in which you pause the scene. After that, Sprite Kit performs the visual transition to the new scene. At this point, what you see from the first scene is just an image, *not* a running scene. However, in order to perform the transition, Sprite Kit un-pauses the scene!

To fix this, you have to do something that may seem a bit strange. Add the following at the beginning of update():

```
if gameState == .StartingLevel && !paused {
  paused = true
}
```

Surprisingly enough, Sprite Kit continues to call `update()` in your scene even while the scene is paused. The only effect that pausing has on a scene is to stop its nodes from executing `SKActions`. Unfortunately, there's no way to know when the view transition animation completes, so you can't just pause the scene after that, either.

Instead, what you do is pause the scene every time `update()` executes while the game state is `StartingLevel`. You add an additional check so it only attempts to pause the scene if the scene isn't already paused. This probably isn't necessary, because the `paused` property setter most likely performs such a check internally, but I think checking here makes it clearer what the code is trying to accomplish.

Run Pest Control again and clear the first level. When you move on to the next level, the bugs will not move until you tap the screen to start.

With multiple levels and a way to clear them, the game is starting to shape up. However, there's still nothing at stake for Arnold or the user. "Failure is not an option" may sound cool when you're setting off on a mission to save the world, but it doesn't always make for a challenging game.

Time limits and losing

As you saw in the previous section, each level defined in **Levels.plist** includes a key named `timeLimit`, which specifies the maximum number of seconds the user is allowed to spend attempting to clear that level.

> **Note:** I chose the time limit values in the file to point out specific things in parts of this chapter, but in your own games, be careful when choosing values for time limits. You want them short enough to be challenging but not so short as to make beating them impossible.

You'll display the remaining time onscreen and make it count down to zero to give Arnold a sense of urgency. To start, add the following properties to **GameScene.swift**:

```
var levelTimeLimit = 0.0
var timerLabel: SKLabelNode!
```

You'll store the current level's time limit in levelTimeLimit and compare the amount of time spent playing a level against this value to determine when the player has lost. You'll display timerLabel onscreen as the user plays the game, counting down from levelTimeLimit to zero. This will give your players useful information and also add a bit of tension as they watch time running out.

Store the current level's time limit in didMoveToView(), right *before* the call to createUserInterface():

```
levelTimeLimit =
  (levelData["timeLimit"] as! NSNumber).doubleValue
```

At the end of createUserInterface(), use the following familiar-looking code to create timerLabel and add it in the upper-right of the display:

```
timerLabel = SKLabelNode(fontNamed: "Chalkduster")
timerLabel.text =
  String(format: "Time Remaining: %2.2f", levelTimeLimit)
timerLabel.fontSize = 18
timerLabel.horizontalAlignmentMode = .Left
if UIDevice.currentDevice().userInterfaceIdiom == .Pad {
  // different placement on iPad
  timerLabel.position = CGPoint(x: 200, y: size.height / 2 - 60)
} else {
  timerLabel.position = CGPoint(x: 0, y: size.height / 2 - 30)
}
timerLabel.zPosition = 100
addChild(timerLabel)
```

Run the app, and you'll see you have 10 seconds to kill those bugs. I hope you're better at this game than I am.

Now that you know what the label looks like, hide it until the player taps to start the level. Add the following line to the end of `createUserInterface()`:

```
timerLabel.hidden = true
```

Then, show the timer when the user taps to start. Add this line to the `StartingLevel` case in `touchesBegan(withEvent:)`, just *above* the `fallthrough` statement:

```
timerLabel.hidden = false
```

Run again. The timer readout won't appear until Arnold starts running.

A timer that never changes isn't very useful, so you need to make it count down to zero. Add the following new properties:

```
var currentTime = 0.0
var startTime = 0.0
var elapsedTime = 0.0
```

You'll use these three variables in conjunction with `levelTimeLimit` to handle Pest Control's timekeeping, as follows:

1. `currentTime` stores the `currentTime` value passed into `update()`, so you can access it from outside of that method.

2. `startTime` is the value of `currentTime` at the moment the player tapped the screen to start a level.

3. `elapsedTime` is calculated from `currentTime` and `startTime`, and you will use it to determine when the player has exceeded the time limit specified in `levelTimeLimit`.

Don't worry if you don't fully understand how you'll use each of these fields—it will become clear over the next few steps.

When the user taps the screen to start playing the level, you'll store the current time in `startTime`. Add this line to the `StartingLevel` case in `touchesBegan(withEvent:)`, just *above* the `fallthrough` statement:

```
startTime = currentTime
```

That was easy. But maybe you've noticed that you haven't yet set a value for `currentTime`. When Sprite Kit calls `update()`, it passes in a `currentTime` value. Because Sprite Kit calls `update()` once every frame, `currentTime` is constantly changing.

Add the following line at the top of update() to store the most recent time:

```
self.currentTime = currentTime
```

It's important that this is the first line in update() because there is a conditional return statement later in the method that will execute prior to the user tapping the screen. If you put this line anywhere in the method after that return statement, the code you added in touchesBegan(withEvent:) will initialize startTime with an incorrect time.

Each time update() executes, you can calculate the amount of time the user has spent on this level by subtracting the start time from the current time. Add the following line to update(), just *before* the if statement that checks bugLayer for a node named bug:

```
elapsedTime = currentTime - startTime
```

You store the time spent playing this level in elapsedTime. For now, you'll only use this value in the current method, but you store it in an instance variable because later, you'll need it outside of this method, too.

At the end of update(), you currently have an if statement that checks for a win condition, like this:

```
if bugLayer.childNodeWithName("bug") == nil {
  endLevelWithSuccess(true)
}
```

Replace that code with the following:

```
if elapsedTime >= levelTimeLimit {
  endLevelWithSuccess(false)
} else if bugLayer.childNodeWithName("bug") == nil {
  endLevelWithSuccess(true)
} else {
  timerLabel.text = String(format: "Time Remaining: %2.2f",
                           (levelTimeLimit - elapsedTime))
}
```

The first if statement you add checks if Arnold's time has run out by comparing the elapsed time to the level's time limit. If time has run out, you call endLevelWithSuccess(), passing in false. You change the existing if statement into an else if to handle the win condition, and you add an else statement that updates the onscreen timer display. The timer display should count down to show the player how much time is left, rather than count up to show how much time has elapsed, so you display the time limit minus the elapsed time.

Build and run. Because the time limit for this level is only 10 seconds, you've got an excellent chance of failing.

In the screenshot above, you can see two issues. The first is that the **Next Level?** button isn't centered, but that's by design and you'll handle it later.

The second issue is that the readout *sometimes* claims there are two hundredths of a second left, even while it claims you were too slow. A bit presumptuous, don't you think? What if you were just toying with the bugs, lulling them into feeling safe by waiting until the last possible moment before making a heroic push to win right at the end?

The problem here is that you update the label only *after* you check for wins and losses, which means the final value displayed in the readout is incorrect. The easiest solution is to move the label update logic to earlier in the method, but then you'd have to worry about showing a negative value for time remaining, because there's no guarantee the frame won't continue to update after time has expired.

First, remove the final `else` statement in `update()`. Then, add the following code just after the line that updates `elapsedTime`:

```
var timeRemaining = levelTimeLimit - elapsedTime
if timeRemaining < 0 {
  timeRemaining = 0
}
timerLabel.text =
  String(format: "Time Remaining: %2.2f", timeRemaining)
```

This simply calculates the remaining time, ensures it isn't less than zero and then updates the label text.

Run again, and this time, lose like you mean it!

Now that you've got the countdown timer working and players can win and lose, it would be nice if players who failed to clear a level could try again. Remember when you added the **Next Level?** button earlier and you moved it to the right to make room for another UI element? Today is the day you've been planning for! That is to say, now would be a good time to add a **Try Again?** button.

Add the following code inside endLevelWithSuccess():

```
if !won {
  let tryAgain = SKLabelNode(fontNamed: "Chalkduster")
  tryAgain.text = "Try Again?"
  tryAgain.name = "retryLabel"
  tryAgain.fontSize = 28
  tryAgain.horizontalAlignmentMode = .Right
  tryAgain.position = CGPoint(x: -20, y: -40)
  tryAgain.zPosition = 100
  addChild(tryAgain)
}
```

When the player fails to clear a level, this code adds a label named retryLabel that reads **Try Again?**. Just as with the **Next Level?** label, you want to handle touch events over the label so that it functions as a button.

Inside touchesBegan(withEvent:), add this if statement at the end of the InLevelMenu case statement:

```
if let node = childNodeWithName("retryLabel") {
  if node.containsPoint(loc) {
    let newScene = GameScene(size:size, level: currentLevel)
```

```
    view.presentScene(newScene,
      transition: SKTransition.flipVerticalWithDuration(0.5))
  }
}
```

The above code simply checks to see if the user touched the **Try Again?** label. If so, it creates a new GameScene object initialized to the current level and asks this scene's view to transition to the new scene. Essentially, it replaces the current scene with an identical one, but one that's initialized to its start state.

Build and run, and lose all over again. You'll get the options to try again or to move on to the next level. Try each button to see how they work:

At this point, you've implemented all of Pest Control's gameplay features. Arnold and the bugs wait patiently for your player to start a level; Arnold runs around smashing bugs; the bugs run around wondering why this guy is smashing them; a timer counts down to make your players anxious; players can beat, retry or skip a level; and you congratulate or chastise them as appropriate.

Now that players can progress through the game, you're ready to start saving and loading that progress.

Saving and loading state

> **Note:** If you skipped ahead to this part of the chapter and did not go through the steps to add the remaining gameplay features to Pest Control, start here using the **PestControl-WithGameLogic** project in this chapter's resources.

The previous part of the chapter focused on getting Pest Control's final gameplay elements in place. In this part, you'll implement autosave using Sprite Kit's archiving support.

To implement autosave, you'll simply write the entire scene to disk, and then later, you'll present the saved scene to the user. That is, you'll archive a single object—the scene currently in the view—and that will, in turn, archive all of the scene's child nodes and their actions. Then, when loading from the autosave file, you'll initialize a new scene from the archived one and present it to the user. Well, it's almost as easy as that, anyway.

> **Note:** As mentioned earlier in this chapter, this is only one of many ways to save your game's data. For example, you could take a far simpler approach and record the level number the player is in, and make them restart at the beginning of that level upon loading a saved game.
>
> In this chapter, you are learning about archiving the entire scene because it's one of the most unique and generally helpful features of Sprite Kit, and it's useful to know about even if you choose an alternate method of saving and loading data in your game.

To save the scene and all of its child nodes, the first thing you need to do is make sure everything *can* be saved.

Encoding and decoding with NSCoding

To archive an object, it must conform to the `NSCoding` protocol. `NSCoding` includes the two methods required to support encoding and decoding an object—`encodeWithCoder()` and `init?(coder:)`—and you use encoding and decoding to archive objects to disk. Your class's implementation of these methods can also encode and decode primitive data types and some `structs`, such as `int`, `double` and `CGSize`, but other class objects to be archived must be `NSCoding`-compliant.

Fortunately, `SKNode` and all of its subclasses, such as `SKScene` and `SKSpriteNode`, along with `SKAction`, all conform to the `NSCoding` protocol. If you create a subclass of an `SKNode` or one of its subclasses, you *may* need to add custom `NSCoding` support, as well.

Basic encoding/decoding

As a general rule, any class that has its own instance variables and/or properties needs to implement the methods from the `NSCoding` protocol, because those instance variables will receive default values when restored from an archive, and those default values probably won't match the values at the time the object was encoded.

For many classes, encoding is a straightforward matter of passing each of its instance variables to one of the various encoding methods on an `NSCoder`, which encapsulates the encoding and decoding logic into simple method calls. Decoding is simply the reverse of encoding, where you initialize each variable with a call to one of an `NSCoder`'s various decoding methods. Sometimes, though, you need to do more work.

You'll start by adding `NSCoding` support to `TileMapLayer`, a class that requires the least effort, and eventually handle `GameScene`, which will entail dealing with a few complications.

Open **TileMapLayer.swift** and add the following method:

```
override func encodeWithCoder(aCoder: NSCoder) {
  // 1
  super.encodeWithCoder(aCoder)
  // 2
  aCoder.encodeCGSize(tileSize, forKey: "TML-TileSize")
  aCoder.encodeCGSize(gridSize, forKey: "TML-GridSize")
  aCoder.encodeCGSize(layerSize, forKey: "TML-LayerSize")
  // 3
  if atlas != nil {
    aCoder.encodeObject(atlas!, forKey: "TML-Atlas")
  }
}
```

As you can see, implementing `encodeWithCoder()` is a straightforward affair.

1. When extending Sprite Kit classes, you always need to call `super.encodeWithEncoder()` to ensure superclasses encode their data, too. It doesn't necessarily need to be the method's first line—indeed, you'll see an example later where it must not be—but you do need to call it.

2. You encode each of `TileMapLayer`'s properties using the appropriate `NSCoder` methods. For example, `atlas` is an instance of `SKTextureAtlas`. Because `SKTextureAtlas` is `NSCoding`-compliant, you encode it using `encodeObject(forKey:)`. The key you use here, `TML-Atlas`, I chose arbitrarily but with the intent that its name would clearly indicate the value it references. I added the `TML-` prefix to make it obvious which class added the key—`TileMapLayer`—and to reduce the likelihood of reusing a key used by one of `TileMapLayer`'s ancestor classes.

3. Because `atlas` stores an optional value, you test for a non-`nil` value before unwrapping and encoding it.

And that's all it takes to encode a `TileMapLayer`.

`TileMapLayer`'s encoding logic is about as basic as it comes, as will be its decoding logic. Replace the stub implementation of `init?(coder:)` with the following:

```
required init?(coder aDecoder: NSCoder) {
  // 1
  tileSize = aDecoder.decodeCGSizeForKey("TML-TileSize")
  gridSize = aDecoder.decodeCGSizeForKey("TML-GridSize")
  layerSize = aDecoder.decodeCGSizeForKey("TML-LayerSize")
  // 2
  atlas =
    aDecoder.decodeObjectForKey("TML-Atlas") as? SKTextureAtlas
  // 3
  super.init(coder: aDecoder)
}
```

As you can see, `init?(coder:)` is a special, failable initializer method that reverses the work you did in `encodeWithCoder()`. A failable method, indicated by `init?` instead of `init`, can result in a `nil` object.

1. For each key-value pair you encoded in `encodeWithCoder()`, you decode it here using the same key and assign the decoded value directly to the instance variable. You can perform any additional initialization you'd like in `init?(coder:)`, but `TileMapLayer` requires none.

2. When decoding an object, you need to cast it to the correct type. For `atlas` you use a conditional cast to `SKTextureAtlas` because the object may not exist in the archive. In that case, `decodeObjectForKey()` will return `nil` and if you don't cast it conditionally, your app will crash.

3. `Init?(coder:)` functions much like any other initializer method and as such, you need to assign values to any properties that require them, and then you must call a

designated initializer in the class's superclass. In this case, you want to call `super.init(coder:)`.

With those two methods added, you can now safely archive `TileMapLayer` objects. But you still have a few other classes to handle before you can archive an entire scene.

Note: While `NSCoding` isn't very complicated, it's worth reading up on it to understand it fully. For more information, take a look at this tutorial:

http://www.raywenderlich.com/1914/nscoding-tutorial-for-ios-how-to-save-your-app-data

Or this one:

http://nshipster.com/nscoding/

Or at this excellent write up:

http://www.mikeash.com/pyblog/friday-qa-2010-08-12-implementing-nscoding.html

---

`AnimatingSprite` has a unique property to handle, so you'll take care of that next. Inside **AnimatingSprite.swift**, add the following method:

```
override func encodeWithCoder(aCoder: NSCoder) {
  super.encodeWithCoder(aCoder)

  aCoder.encodeObject(facingForwardAnim!,
                      forKey: "AS-ForwardAnim")
  aCoder.encodeObject(facingBackAnim!,
                      forKey: "AS-BackAnim")
  aCoder.encodeObject(facingSideAnim!,
                      forKey: "AS-SideAnim")

  // TODO: Handle facingDirection
}
```

This begins just as you'd expect, by calling `super.encodeWithCoder()` and then encoding the object's animation properties. But then, rather than encode `facingDirection`, it ends with a comment that reads "TODO: Handle facingDirection".

You didn't encode the facing direction because it's a `SpriteDirection` enumeration value, but there is currently no way to encode enumerations that don't have a raw data type. Fortunately, you can remedy this with a simple change.

Still inside **AnimatingSprite.swift**, change the declaration of `SpriteDirection` so that it has a raw type of `Int`, like this:

```
enum SpriteDirection : Int {
```

Now you can encode these values because you know their type. Add the following line to the end of `encodeWithCoder()`:

```
aCoder.encodeInteger(
  facingDirection.rawValue, forKey: "AS-Direction")
```

That takes care of encoding an `AnimatingSprite` object. Now replace the stub implementation of `init?(coder:)` with the following:

```
required init?(coder aDecoder: NSCoder) {
  super.init(coder: aDecoder)

  facingForwardAnim =
    aDecoder.decodeObjectForKey("AS-ForwardAnim") as? SKAction
  facingBackAnim =
    aDecoder.decodeObjectForKey("AS-BackAnim") as? SKAction
  facingSideAnim =
    aDecoder.decodeObjectForKey("AS-SideAnim") as? SKAction
  facingDirection =
    AnimatingSprite.SpriteDirection(rawValue:
      aDecoder.decodeIntegerForKey("AS-Direction"))!
}
```

This is a straightforward reversal of the encoding process. It first calls `super.init(coder:)`. After that, it reads from the archive each of the properties you wrote out and sets them on the object.

Notice how you use `SpriteDirection(rawValue:)` to create the correct enumeration value when decoding `facingDirection`. All enumerations with a raw type automatically include an `init(rawValue:)` method used to create instances from an appropriate value. You can override that method if you need to perform special processing.

Surprise exercise!

In Pest Control, there are seven classes that require `encodeWithCoder()` and custom `init?(coder:)` implementations. You already took care of two—`TileMapLayer` and `AnimatingSprite`. The others are `Player`, `Bug`, `TmxTileMapLayer`, `Breakable` and `GameScene`.

`GameScene` will be more complicated than the others, so you'll cover it in detail in the next section. For now, as an exercise, try adding `encodeWithCoder()` and `init?(coder:)` to `Player`, `Bug`, `TmxTileMapLayer` and `Breakable` yourself.

Remember to encode every property in each of these classes. When you're done, check your implementation against what follows below, but don't worry if you used different keys than the ones you see here—all that matters with key names is that they match between the encode and decode operations.

In **Player.swift**:

```
override func encodeWithCoder(aCoder: NSCoder) {
  super.encodeWithCoder(aCoder)
  aCoder.encodeObject(sprite, forKey: "Player-Sprite")
}

required init?(coder aDecoder: NSCoder) {
  sprite =
    aDecoder.decodeObjectForKey("Player-Sprite")
      as! AnimatingSprite
  super.init(coder: aDecoder)
}
```

In **Bug.swift**:

```
override func encodeWithCoder(aCoder: NSCoder) {
  super.encodeWithCoder(aCoder)
  aCoder.encodeObject(sprite, forKey: "Bug-Sprite")
}

required init?(coder aDecoder: NSCoder) {
  sprite = aDecoder.decodeObjectForKey("Bug-Sprite")
    as! AnimatingSprite
  super.init(coder: aDecoder)
}
```

These implementations are mostly the same as those for `Player`, but it's important to point out something here. Recall that the `AnimatingSprite`'s used by the `Bug` objects all store references to the same three static animations. You might be concerned that each Bug archives its sprite property, which in turn archives the sprite's animations. However, NSCoding only archives each shared object once and stores references to already stored objects each successive time you attempt to archive them. This keeps the size of archives containing many cross-references from growing out of control.

In **TmxTileMapLayer.swift**:

```
override func encodeWithCoder(aCoder: NSCoder) {
  super.encodeWithCoder(aCoder)
  aCoder.encodeObject(layer, forKey: "TmxTML-Layer")
}

required init?(coder aDecoder: NSCoder) {
  layer =
    aDecoder.decodeObjectForKey("TmxTML-Layer") as! TMXLayer
  super.init(coder: aDecoder)
}
```

In **Breakable.swift**:

```
override func encodeWithCoder(aCoder: NSCoder) {
  super.encodeWithCoder(aCoder)
  aCoder.encodeObject(sprite, forKey: "Breakable-Sprite")
  aCoder.encodeObject(brokenTexture, forKey: "Breakable-Broken")
}

required init?(coder aDecoder: NSCoder) {
  sprite = aDecoder.decodeObjectForKey("Breakable-Sprite")
    as! SKSpriteNode
  brokenTexture =
    aDecoder.decodeObjectForKey("Breakable-Broken") as!
SKTexture
  super.init(coder: aDecoder)
}
```

I hope you were able to come up with similar implementations on your own. If not, that's OK—you'll get more practice now as you tackle encoding and decoding GameScene, a class that requires more complex encoding/decoding logic than what you've seen so far.

Encoding/decoding complex objects

Each of the classes for which you've added NSCoding support so far has required nothing more than the most basic encoding or decoding of data. Unfortunately, that won't always be the case.

For GameScene, you'll have to do a bit more work. First, GameScene is using the GameState enumeration. You need to give it a raw type, just as you did earlier with SpriteDirection.

Open **Types.swift** and change the declaration of GameState so it has a raw type of Int, like this:

```
enum GameState : Int {
```

Now open **GameScene.swift** and add the following method:

```
override func encodeWithCoder(aCoder: NSCoder) {
  aCoder.encodeObject(worldNode, forKey: "GS-WorldNode")
  aCoder.encodeObject(player, forKey: "GS-Player")
  aCoder.encodeObject(
    backgroundLayer, forKey: "GS-BackgroundLayer")
  aCoder.encodeObject(bugLayer, forKey: "GS-BugLayer")
  if breakableLayer != nil {
    aCoder.encodeObject(
      breakableLayer!, forKey: "GS-BreakableLayer")
  }
  if tileMap != nil {
    aCoder.encodeObject(tileMap!, forKey: "GS-TmxTileMap")
  }

  aCoder.encodeInteger(
    gameState.rawValue, forKey: "GS-GameState")
  aCoder.encodeInteger(currentLevel, forKey:"GS-Level")
  aCoder.encodeDouble(
    levelTimeLimit, forKey: "GS-LevelTimeLimit")
  aCoder.encodeObject(timerLabel, forKey: "GS-TimerLabel")

  aCoder.encodeDouble(elapsedTime, forKey: "GS-ElapsedTime")

  super.encodeWithCoder(aCoder)
}
```

This method is not yet complete, but here's what you have so far:

1. It ends with a familiar call to super.encodeWithCoder(), after encoding *most* of GameScene's instance variables. Here, you once again take advantage of an important aspect of the NSCoder class: The fact that NSCoder includes each object in the archive only once and then later, during the decoding process, NSCoder will ensure all requests for that object reference the same item. In this case, calling super.encodeWithCoder() encodes all of the scene's child nodes as well, but then you archive specific child nodes again, like worldNode, player and

backgroundLayer—not to mention that `player` is a child of `worldNode`, so it's actually archived three times.

2. Notice you archive `elapsedTime` but not `currentTime` or `startTime`. That's because the current and start times are absolute values that only make sense during a specific run of the game. Instead, you'll rely on the code you already have in `update()` to continuously update `currentTime`, and you'll add code later to initialize `startTime`.

Now that most of the encoding is complete, replace the stub implementation of `init?(coder:)` with the following:

```
required init?(coder aDecoder: NSCoder) {
  worldNode =
    aDecoder.decodeObjectForKey("GS-WorldNode") as! SKNode
  player = aDecoder.decodeObjectForKey("GS-Player") as! Player
  backgroundLayer =
    aDecoder.decodeObjectForKey("GS-BackgroundLayer")
      as! TileMapLayer
  bugLayer =
    aDecoder.decodeObjectForKey("GS-BugLayer") as! TileMapLayer

  breakableLayer =
    aDecoder.decodeObjectForKey("GS-BreakableLayer")
      as? TileMapLayer
  tileMap =
    aDecoder.decodeObjectForKey("GS-TmxTileMap") as? JSTileMap

  gameState = GameState(rawValue:
    aDecoder.decodeIntegerForKey("GS-GameState"))!
  currentLevel = aDecoder.decodeIntegerForKey("GS-Level")
  levelTimeLimit =
    aDecoder.decodeDoubleForKey("GS-LevelTimeLimit")
  timerLabel =
    aDecoder.decodeObjectForKey("GS-TimerLabel") as! SKLabelNode

  elapsedTime = aDecoder.decodeDoubleForKey("GS-ElapsedTime")

  super.init(coder: aDecoder)
}
```

The above code simply decodes each item you encoded in `encodeWithCoder()` and sets the appropriate variables, just as you did before. Notice how you perform conditional casts for the optional values. This is important if you don't want your apps to crash.

This implementation won't be good enough to make the game work, but it is enough to begin testing—at which point, you'll find the problems.

Archiving and restoring scenes

To implement Pest Control's autosave feature, you'll automatically save the state of the scene whenever the user switches away from the game to another app. Then, whenever the user returns to the game, if there is a saved game available, you'll ask the user if they'd like to continue playing from that point or restart on the same level.

To begin, open **AppDelegate.swift** and import the Sprite Kit framework at the top of the file:

```
import SpriteKit
```

iOS calls `applicationWillResignActive()` when the app is about to become inactive. The first thing you should do, if nothing else, is pause the scene. Otherwise, your app may continue to execute actions even when the user thinks it's not running.

Add the following inside `applicationWillResignActive()`:

```
if let view = window?.rootViewController?.view as? SKView {
  view.scene?.paused = true
}
```

The way you've written Pest Control, you know its window contains a view controller whose view is an `SKView`. The above code simply attempts to get the app's view as an `SKView` and pauses the scene it is currently presenting. You've set up Pest Control so these conditional checks will always succeed.

Now un-pause the scene in `applicationDidBecomeActive()`:

```
if let view = window?.rootViewController?.view as? SKView {
  view.scene?.paused = true
}
```

This code simply gets the current scene and un-pauses it. There are quite a few question marks in those two lines of code because of all the conditional properties involved.

Before you can create a save game file, you need to pick a folder in which to store it. Apple recommends putting data like this—things you want backed up but that you don't want accessible to the user via iTunes—inside the **Private Documents** folder in the app's **Library** folder. Add this helper method, which returns a path to that folder:

```
class func getPrivateDocsDir() -> String {
  let paths =
    NSSearchPathForDirectoriesInDomains(.LibraryDirectory,
                                        .UserDomainMask, true)
```

```
let documentsDirectory =
  paths[0].stringByAppendingPathComponent("Private Documents")

var error: NSError?

NSFileManager.defaultManager().createDirectoryAtPath(
  documentsDirectory, withIntermediateDirectories: true,
  attributes: nil, error: &error)

return documentsDirectory
}
```

The above code returns the path to the **Private Documents** folder in the app's **Library** folder, creating it if it cannot be found.

With that helper logic in place, you can finally archive your scene. Replace the contents of applicationDidEnterBackground() with the following code:

```
// 1
if let view = window?.rootViewController?.view as? SKView {
  // 2
  let documentsDirectory = AppDelegate.getPrivateDocsDir()
  let filePath =
    documentsDirectory.stringByAppendingPathComponent(
      "autosaved-scene")
  // 3
  let data = NSMutableData()
  let archiver =
    NSKeyedArchiver(forWritingWithMutableData: data)
  // 4
  archiver.encodeObject(view.scene,
                        forKey: "AppDelegateSceneKey")
  archiver.finishEncoding()
  data.writeToFile(filePath, atomically: true)
}
```

This logic archives the scene whenever the app moves into the background on the device. Specifically:

1. It gets the scene from the app's current view.

2. It finds the path to a file named **autosaved-scene**, which is where you'll store the archive.

3. Here, it creates an NSKeyedArchiver backed by an NSMutableData object. You'll use these two objects to encode the data and write it to disk.

4. Using the archiver, the logic encodes the scene and writes it to disk. Calling `encodeObject(forKey:)` runs the scene's `encodeWithCoder()` method on itself, as well as on any of its children.

That's all it takes to archive your scene to disk. Now you need to load an archived scene and display it in the view. Replace the contents of `applicationDidBecomeActive()` with the following:

```
if let view = window?.rootViewController?.view as? SKView {
  let dataPath =
AppDelegate.getPrivateDocsDir().stringByAppendingPathComponent(
    "autosaved-scene")
  // 1
  if let codedData = NSData(contentsOfFile: dataPath) {
    // 2
    let unarchiver =
      NSKeyedUnarchiver(forReadingWithData: codedData)
    let scene =
      unarchiver.decodeObjectForKey("AppDelegateSceneKey")
        as? GameScene
    unarchiver.finishDecoding()
    if scene != nil {
      // 3
      view.presentScene(scene)
      // 4
      view.scene?.paused = false
    }
  }
}
```

This is mostly the same as what you did in `applicationDidEnterBackground()`, except here, you use an `NSKeyedUnarchiver` to unarchive a scene instead of archiving it. The following items are of interest:

1. Here the method instantiates an `NSData` object, but then checks to see if it is `nil` since it is optional.

2. The method then attempts to create a `GameScene` object from the archived data.

3. This line presents the unarchived scene in the view.

4. The last line of the method ensures the scene is not paused.

It's been awhile since you've run the app. In the next section, you'll test what you've written so far, and then fix all the mistakes I made you make.

Issues with archiving

To test the autosave feature, first remove Pest Control from your device or simulator to ensure you are starting fresh. Run Pest Control and then press the **Home** button on the device or Simulator (**Shift-Command-H**). *Be sure you are playing the first level when you do this.*

You should see a bunch of messages in the console, like this one:

```
PestControl[5738:70b] SKAction: Run block actions can not be
properly encoded, Objective-C blocks do not support NSCoding.
```

With Pest Control in the background on your device or the Simulator, tap the app's icon to bring it back into the foreground. At that point, you'll see a bunch more messages in the console, like this one:

```
PestControl[5738:70b] SKAction: Run block actions can not be
properly decoded, Objective-C blocks do not support NSCoding.
```

The messages are pretty clear—you cannot encode or decode SKActions that run Objective-C blocks. You might not recall writing any Objective-C blocks, but let's be honest; you're getting forgetful in your old age. Also, you *didn't* write any Objective-C blocks, so there's that.

The text of this message is probably old, but the meaning is basically the same: In this case, it is complaining about you trying to archive SKActions running Swift closures. Specifically, Bug runs just such an action. No wonder Arnold likes to smash these things.

If you had been writing Objective-C code, you could have avoided using blocks by instead calling a selector. Unfortunately, in Swift, functions and blocks are both closures. As such, there is no performSelector:onTarget: method in Swift like there is in Objective-C. This gives you two options:

1. **Mix your Swift with Objective-C.** You can call methods on Objective-C classes in your project, so you could rewrite some of these classes as Objective-C classes and then call performSelector:onTarget:. That's a bit drastic for this problem, but it's good to know you have the option if you ever need it.

2. **Remove the actions when you archive them**. Apple actually recommends against archiving SKActions, so this is the approach you'll take.

Open **Bug.m** and add the following line at the beginning of encodeWithCoder(), *before* the call to super.encodeWithCoder():

```
removeAllActions()
```

This simply removes the actions running on the bugs prior to encoding them. This will work here because you'll be able to add code to run the actions again later. However, if you had a game where you archived a node at times other than when you were closing the app, you would have to do extra work to make sure you didn't mess up the current play session.

Remove Pest Control from your device or the Simulator. This is an important step, because you don't want the app to try to load the old save file that you know had problems.

Now run Pest Control again. While playing the game's first level, press the **Home** button on the device or Simulator (**Shift-Command-H**). Once again, be sure you are playing the first level when you do this.

This time, pressing the Home button doesn't produce any messages in the console, and tapping Pest Control's icon to bring the app back into the foreground produces no messages, either.

There's another bug lurking among these, er, bugs, but it can wait. The following image shows something more important you need to deal with. See if you can spot it:

That text is a bit hard to read. Also, is that Arnold's twin brother running around up there?

Now take a look at this image, which shows a game after saving and loading the game a few times:

Whoa. It's a good thing Arnold's brother showed up—he's going to need help dealing with all those bugs!

As you can see, in the first screenshot above, there are 436 nodes, and in the second, there are a whopping 1313! It seems every time you load the archive, you're adding the archived nodes and an entire new scene. Then you archive all *those* nodes the next time you pause the game, only to add *another* new set of nodes to that!

The problem arises because you create your scene's nodes inside `didMoveToView()`. However, when unarchiving a scene, you are calling `init?(coder:)`, which already adds all the necessary nodes. To fix the situation, add the following code to the beginning of `didMoveToView()` inside **GameScene.swift**:

```
if worldNode != nil {
  return
}
```

Now remove Pest Control from your device or Simulator and then build and run. This time, when you pause the game and then come back to it, things look a bit better:

By now, you've probably noticed that no matter how much time is remaining when you save the game, the app claims you've run out of time when you start playing again. This issue will take a bit of work to fix, so before worrying about that, you're going to fix a couple of easier problems.

Tap **Next Level?** to move on to the next level, then press the **Home** button to move Pest Control into the background. Tap the Pest Control icon to bring the app back into the foreground and… crash?

Your app should crash with a message like this in the Console:

```
fatal error: NSCoding not supported: file
/Users/rwenderlich/Desktop/Chapter 17 - Saving and Loading
Games/PestControl/PestControl/FireBug.swift, line 14
```

It seems like you never implemented init?(coder:) in FireBug. So open **FireBug.swift** and replace the stub version of init?(coder:) with the following:

```
required init?(coder aDecoder: NSCoder) {
  super.init(coder: aDecoder)
}
```

Now when you run Pest Control, it loads fine.

There's one more little problem to fix. Tap **Next Level?** to move on to the next level, then press the **Home** button to put Pest Control into the background. Tap the Pest Control icon to bring the app back into the foreground and… hot lava?

You defined this level with a TMX file, and as such, it had some special processing. You may remember those red tiles from the previous chapter. You only put them there to define physics boundaries and they are supposed to be hidden, but Sprite Kit doesn't seem to have gotten the message.

To fix this, add the following code to the end of init?(coder:) in **GameScene.swift**:

```
if tileMap != nil {
  backgroundLayer.enumerateChildNodesWithName(
    "water", usingBlock: { node, _ in
      node.hidden = true
  })
}
```

This code checks to see if there's a `tileMap` present, which would indicate that the level was loaded from a TMX file. If so, it finds every node named **water** in `backgroundLayer` and hides it. It's important to only do this for TMX files, because you do *not* want to hide water tiles in any other case. Now when you run, water looks like water again, see?

Note: If you see a screen full of gibberish graphics at this step, it just means Sprite Kit lost its mind. Actually, it's more of an Xcode issue. Your console probably has an error like this one:

SKTexture: Error loading image resource: "/Users/rwenderlich/Library/Developer/CoreSimulator/Devices/00682CD8-C7A6-4EF0-8F07-9B29E2D3A4B4/data/Containers/Bundle/Application/06275CAB-D1C8-45C2-A23E-56830804334B/PestControl.app/tmx-bg-tiles.atlasc/tmx-bg-tiles.1.png"

If you check, that directly doesn't exist. It seems that Xcode sometimes recreates your working directory, but it still seems to be looking in the old location for the atlas file. This may be related to data stored in the archive, but it really doesn't matter. To fix the issue, just remove Pest Control from your device or Simulator and then run it again. (I've also corrected this error by tapping the screen where the **Next Level?** label should be. Doing so transitioned to the next level with the graphics looking normal again.)

One way or the other, get yourself back to the third level. Press the **Home** button to save your game state and then tap the Pest Control icon to bring the app back into the foreground. Your water should look plenty wet again.

Archiving SKActions

Before moving on, it's important to know one thing about SKActions: They don't play well with NSCoding. You've already seen how you can't archive block actions, but SKActions in general don't retain their state when archived. That is, if you archive a node that is currently running an action and you later create a new node from that archive, it will have a copy of that SKAction on it that will immediately start executing *from the beginning* rather than where it left off.

According to Apple, this behavior is as expected and by design, but it certainly does mess things up if you don't account for it, so let's discuss the problem briefly so you know when you might need to work around it.

Consider the node in the following diagram, which was at position (0,0) when it started running an action to move to (200,200) over two seconds. If you archived such a node after it had been running its action for one second, and later created a new node from that archive, the new node would appear at the position it occupied when archived— let's say (100,100)—and then immediately begin running an action to move from its current position to (200,200) *over two seconds*. But since the position of the node is now where you would have expected it to be after one second, it only needs to cover half the expected distance over those two seconds, meaning it will move at half the speed.

Node travels half the TOTAL distance in 1s, then archived

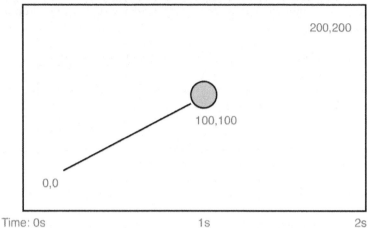

Time: 0s   1s   2s

When unarchived, node travels half the REMAINING distance in 1s

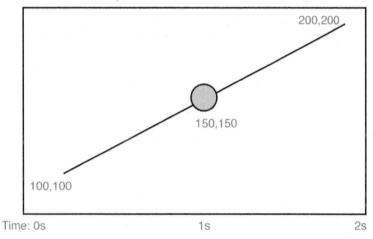

Time: 0s   1s   2s

This means that any running actions with durations, which are most of them, will have different speeds/rates of change when unarchived.

In addition, any action defined by a relative change, such as moveByX:y:duration:, will cause problems, sometimes completely breaking your game.

For example, consider the node in the following diagram, which was at position (0,0) when it started running an action to move by 100 points along the x-axis over two seconds. If you archived that action after one second, a new node created from that archive would appear at the position it occupied when it was archived and immediately begin to move *100 points along the x-axis* over two seconds. But since it was already about 50 points away from where it started the original action, it will end up moving 50 points too far.

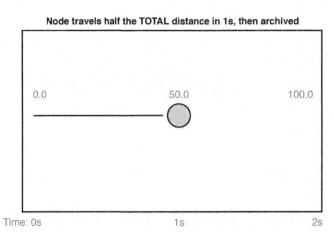

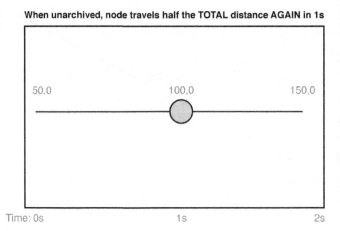

As you can see, you can't archive nodes that are running just any action and assume Sprite Kit will decode your scene in the same state it was in when you encoded it.

> **Note:** It seems Apple only wants developers to archive Sprite Kit nodes to support things like level editors. Level editors can most likely get away with not archiving in-progress actions, because a level editor usually doesn't have running actions, but is instead concerned with layout and game data issues.

In Pest Control, you've already run into one problem archiving actions for the bugs. In that case, you simply removed their actions when you archived them. That solution may not be feasible for your own game, so you may need to do some complicated pre- and post-processing during the encoding/decoding process to account for node state. And in some cases, because SKAction doesn't expose any of the information you would need to make this easy, it may be impossible without instead writing your own actions.

In the upcoming two chapters, you'll add more actions to Pest Control, and some of them do sometimes cause anomalies when restored from a save game file.

Continuing play from a restored archive

When the app finds an autosave file, it should ask the user whether to continue playing from the point of the save or to restart the current level. To do so, you'll add a new game state that displays the options, and you'll load games into this state if they were saved in-progress.

First, open **GameScene.swift** and add this method to display the options to the user:

```swift
func showReloadMenu() {
  let label = childNodeWithName("msgLabel") as SKLabelNode
  label.text = "Found a Save File"
  hidden = false

  if childNodeWithName("continueLabel") as? SKLabelNode == nil {
    let continueLabel = SKLabelNode(fontNamed: "Chalkduster")
    continueLabel.text = "Continue?"
    continueLabel.name = "continueLabel"
    continueLabel.fontSize = 28
    continueLabel.horizontalAlignmentMode = .Right
    continueLabel.position = CGPoint(x: -20, y: -40)
    continueLabel.zPosition = 100
    addChild(continueLabel)

    let restartLabel = SKLabelNode(fontNamed: "Chalkduster")
    restartLabel.text = "Restart Level?"
    restartLabel.name = "restartLabel"
    restartLabel.fontSize = 28
    restartLabel.horizontalAlignmentMode = .Left
    restartLabel.position = CGPoint(x: 20, y: -40)
    restartLabel.zPosition = 100
    addChild(restartLabel)
  }
}
```

This looks like a lot of code, but it just adds labels to the screen the same way you did for winning and losing. There is one important thing to note, though: Instead of automatically creating the labels, the code first checks the scene for a node named `continueLabel` and only creates the labels if it isn't there.

The reason for this check relates to how you're going to use this method. In the next step, you'll call this method when restoring from a saved game. But what if the player had paused the game—and hence created a save file—while they were looking at this menu? If that were to happen, you would restore the labels as part of the decoding process. If this method were to then add new ones, it would cause problems for you later. (By the way, you only check for one of the two labels, because if one is there, the other one is, too.)

Add the following new `GameState` value in **Types.swift**, which you'll use to indicate when the game should display this menu:

```
case InReloadMenu
```

Now head back to **GameScene.swift** and add the following case to the `switch` statement in `touchesBegan(withEvent:)`:

```
case .InReloadMenu:
  break;
```

You'll make that case do something later, but for now, you just need to keep the compiler happy.

Now call the new method at the appropriate times by adding this `switch` statement to the end of `init?(coder:)`:

```
switch gameState {
  case .InReloadMenu, .Playing:
    gameState = .InReloadMenu
    showReloadMenu()
  default:
    break
}
```

This `switch` statement calls `showReloadMenu()` if the game had been saved in either the playing state or the reload menu state itself. For all other states, the app restores itself into that state directly. If you think about it, there are only two other states, which occur at the beginning and end of a level, respectively. There is no reason to show the reload menu in those cases because they already have their own interface elements onscreen.

Build and run to see the new menu.

> **Note:** If you see the usual `Tap Screen to Run!` message, it means you either
> don't have an archive or you had paused the game while that message was
> showing. Tap the screen to start Arnold running and then pause the game to
> archive the scene. You should now see the above menu when you launch the app.

Besides the new labels, there are two other things you should notice. The first is that the
Time Remaining value is correct. We like it when things work. The other is that Arnold
and the bugs are running around even though the player is staring at a menu screen!
That one needs to be fixed.

Replace the first `if` statement in `update()` with the following:

```
if gameState == .StartingLevel || gameState == .InReloadMenu &&
    !paused {
```

You were already pausing the game when it loads a new level, but now you pause it while
you're displaying this new menu, too.

Build and run again, and you'll see the game is properly paused when displaying the
reload options screen. Of course, the player can't do anything, because the labels still
don't handle touch events. To rectify the situation, replace the `case` for `InReloadMenu`
in `touchesBegan(withEvent:)` with the following:

```
case .InReloadMenu:
  let touch = touches.first as! UITouch
  let loc = touch.locationInNode(self)
  var node: SKNode? = nodeAtPoint(loc)
```

```
    if node!.name != nil && node!.name == "restartLabel" {
      let newScene = GameScene(size: size, level: currentLevel)
      view!.presentScene(
        newScene,
        transition: SKTransition.flipVerticalWithDuration(0.5))
    } else if node!.name != nil && node!.name == "continueLabel" {
      node!.removeFromParent()
      node = childNodeWithName("restartLabel")
      node?.removeFromParent()
      childNodeWithName("msgLabel")?.hidden = true

      gameState = .Playing
      paused = false
    }
```

Just as you handle touches while in the `InLevelMenu` state, you check to see if one of the labels contains the touch event. If the user tapped **Restart Level?**, you transition to a newly initialized scene for the same level—the same thing you do when the user taps **Try Again?** after failing to clear a level. But if the user tapped **Continue?**, then you remove the two buttons from the scene, hide the `msgLabel` node, update the game state and un-pause the scene.

Build, run and tap **Continue?**. Aw, too slow.

The previous section mentioned the time values weren't saved properly, with a promise that this section would fix it.

First, an explanation of the cause:

The app archives and restores `elapsedTime` and `levelTimeLimit`, but not `startTime` and `currentTime`. As mentioned earlier, that's because those two values only make sense in relation to the current run. That is, if you were to start a level, play for 10 seconds, pause the game and then resume playing 30 minutes later, `startTime` would be 30 minutes and 10 seconds ago. In `update()`, you use `startTime` to calculate the amount of time spent playing this level, which means the app will think the player has been playing for an awfully long time. If players are having *that* much trouble finding the last bug, you may want to consider adding some sort of radar-type feature to your app.

To solve this problem, you didn't archive the start or current times. However, whenever a value is not set in `init?(coder:)`, it automatically receives a default value, which for variables of type `Double` is zero. As far as your app is concerned, Arnold has been looking for those bugs since the beginning of time!

The fix is simple—you need to initialize `startTime` to a time that makes sense for the current play session. To do so, add the following line to the `InReloadMenu` case in `touchesBegan(withEvent:)`, inside the `else if` block that handles touches for the node named `continueLabel`:

```
startTime = currentTime - elapsedTime
```

This initializes `startTime` by calculating what time the player *would* have started, had they started `elapsedTime` seconds before right now.

Build and run, and this time, when you tap **Continue?**, you'll see the game hasn't immediately declared you a loser. That's mighty kind of it. However, the bugs are all walking in place now!

The chapter foreshadowed this problem earlier, back when you archived the bugs and had to remove their actions. The problem is just that: You remove the actions from the bugs when you archive them, but you never add any new actions when you unarchive them.

To put a little pep in the step of your bugs, add the following code inside `init?(coder:)`, *before* the `switch` statement:

```
bugLayer.enumerateChildNodesWithName(
  "bug",
  usingBlock: { node, _ in
    let bug = node as! Bug
    bug.start()
})
```

This loops through the bugs in the newly unarchived scene and calls `start()` on each one, mimicking what you do in `createCharacters()` when you initially fill your scene with bugs.

Build and run, and you're really, really done! The game's countdown timer, Arnold and the bugs all pick up where they left off when they were archived and you're right back in the action. After all that, a few minutes of senseless bug destruction may be just what you need.

For this chapter's challenge, you'll implement high-score tracking. After that, Pest Control's gameplay features will be complete. In the next two chapters, you'll learn how to trick out your game with audio and visual effects that will turn the basic gameplay of Pest Control—or any other game you make—into something even more fun than a field full of bugs!

Challenge: High scores

Ready to see if you've mastered saving and loading your games? Try out this challenge!

As always, you can find a solution in this chapter's resources, but first aim to do it yourself.

As its name implies, Chapter 24, "Game Center Leaderboards," shows you how to set up leaderboards in Game Center. That's a cool way to track high scores, but for some additional practice with archiving, try tracking a player's high score locally in the save game file.

Every SKNode includes a userData property, which is a dictionary that lets you add any data you'd like to a node. Since you're already archiving the entire scene anyway, GameScene's userData is a convenient place to store high scores.

> **Note:** In a real app, you'll probably want to store things like high scores in a separate file or by using something like Game Center. The solution described here is simply to show how you can archive user data along with the scene. This could be used to associate extra data with objects in a level editor, for example.

Begin by initializing the userData property of the first scene you create (inside **GameViewController.swift**) with an empty NSMutableDictionary (userData is nil by default). Then, add an entry to the dictionary with the key bestTimes and another empty mutable dictionary as the value.

Next, modify endLevelWithSuccess(): in **GameScene.swift** so that each time the user *successfully* clears a level, it does the following:

1. It gets the dictionary stored with the key bestTimes in the scene's userData.

2. It then checks for a saved high score, using the current level as a key into the dictionary. In a real app, you'd probably want something more robust, like a unique level ID, so that you could reorder levels without breaking your users' high scores, but that's overkill for Pest Control.

3. If there isn't a high saved score or if elapsedTime is less than the saved value, update the saved score.

4. Update the msgLabel node to tell the player about the new high score.

There are three places in **GameScene.m** where you create a new scene and present it in the view. In each of these places, you need to pass the current scene's userData to the new scene. To do so, add a line like the following before presenting the scene in the view:

```
newScene.userData = userData
```

That's it! Play a level and beat it. The first time you do, you should see the message you added for new high scores.

The high score will persist across game loads since **SKNode** automatically persists its **userData** property.

When you get tired of trying to beat your best time, move on to the next chapter to start juicing up Pest Control.

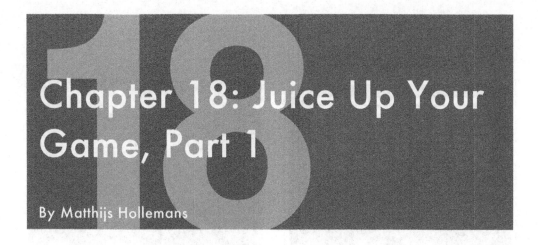

Chapter 18: Juice Up Your Game, Part 1

By Matthijs Hollemans

Pop quiz: What's the difference between a good game and a *great* game? Why does one game delight its players while another is greeted with indifference? Why do some games have raving fans? And what is this magical potion named "polish" that you're supposed to sprinkle on your games to make them awesome?

The answer is all in the details.

Great games are filled to the brim with droves of details that are often so subtle that you might not even consciously notice them while you're playing. And it gives you great pleasure when you finally *do* notice them. Polishing a game means paying attention to these details. Don't stop developing once your game reaches a playable state and rush it to the App Store. Push your game further. Spice it up!

"Juice," the topic of this chapter and the next, is a special type of polish that is easy to add and serves to bring joy to the game. When a game is *juicy*, it feels alive—every interaction between the player and the game world results in a visually stimulating response.

For example, when two objects collide, you shouldn't just see it happen on the screen— that collision should look so convincing that you can almost *feel* it in your body. Playing a juicy game is a visceral experience.

No Juice

With Juice

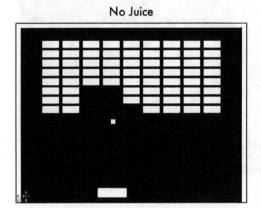

The great thing about juice is that you don't need to invest in a doubly large art budget or hire expensive consultants who used to work for Pixar. Instead, you can use simple animation effects—such as scaling, rotation and movement—to manipulate your sprites. This is wonderful news for programmers like you and me!

On their own, none of these effects are terribly exciting, but put together, every interaction with the game world results in a cascade of visual feedback that keeps players coming back for more. That is what we mean by making your games *juicy*.

In this chapter, you'll take the game from the previous chapter, **Pest Control**, and juice it up by adding a myriad of details to it. It's a good game as it is, but now you will make it totally awesome.

Don't misunderstand: You're not going to change the rules of the game. All you will do in these chapters is add special effects to make the game more appealing to see and experience. And you can apply these same effects to your own games!

> **Note:** This chapter begins where the previous chapter's challenge left off. If you were unable to complete the challenge or skipped ahead from an earlier chapter, don't worry—you can simply open **PestControl-Starter** from this chapter's resources to begin in the right place.

Getting started

First, you're going to need some new resources for this project. Open the latest Pest Control project, right click your **Resources\Art** folder and select **Add Files to**

PestControl. Browse to the resources for this chapter, and select the **Art\Particles** and **Art\Sounds** folders, and click **Add**. Make sure that **Copy items if needed** is checked, and the **PestControl** target is checked.

You'll also need some new new level files that were especially designed to show off the special effects from this chapter. Following a similar process, add all the files from the **Levels** folder in the resources for this chapter into the **Levels** group in your project.

Next, set up your game to use these new level files. Go to **GameScene.swift** and in didMoveToView(), change the following line to load the level data from **JuicyLevels.plist** instead of Levels.plist:

```
let config = NSDictionary(contentsOfFile:
  NSBundle.mainBundle().pathForResource("JuicyLevels",
                                    ofType: "plist")!)!
```

Delete your old build from the Simulator or device so that any save file you may currently have is not loaded on the next run. Now you're ready to rock!

Run the game in its current state, and you'll find that it works well enough—all the gameplay rules are functioning as they should—but it lacks excitement.

For example, when you catch a bug, it simply disappears from the screen. One moment it's there, the next it's gone. As players, we want to see something more gratifying as a reward for catching that bug. Big explosions always work well!

Note that the project already includes a special effect: When you push a red firebug into the water, it appears to drown. This is thanks to a combination of two SKActions: a rotation action to make the bug spin and a scaling action to shrink it at the same time—see resumeAfterKick() in **FireBug.swift**.

Together, these two actions make it look like the firebug gets sucked into a deadly vortex! Give it a try. Run the game, and try to push a firebug into the water.

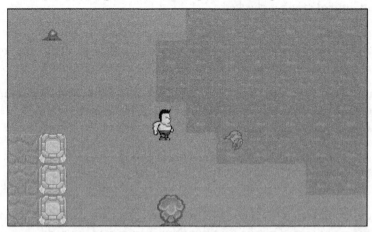

That is exactly the sort of enhancement you'll be making throughout this chapter and the next, until the entire game feels more alive—and is double the fun to play!

Three steps to juice your game

Juicing up your game is like performing a magic trick. The results may look impressive to an unsuspecting audience, but it's really just sleight of hand. Fortunately, you don't need to go to Hogwarts and study for years to become a special effects wizard.

The rest of this chapter and next will show you some special effects you can use in your game. But before you begin adding effects willy-nilly, you need to know where to apply them. If you add them arbitrarily or without consideration, your game runs the risk of feeling confusing and distracting for players.

The good news is, you just need to follow a simple algorithm. Without further ado, here are our "Three Steps to Juice Your Game":

1. **List the actors**. First, make a list of all the objects that play a role in your game— often called the *actors*. For example, two of your actors are Arnold and a tree.

2. **List the interactions**. Second, make a list of the interactions that exist between the actors. For example, one interaction is Arnold colliding with a tree to chop it down. An object can also perform interactions with itself, like moving or changing state.

3. **Add effects to interactions**. Finally, add as many effects to these interactions as you can. This is what makes the player feel like they're really making magic as they play.

For example, what if, instead of making the tree immediately switch from its normal, full appearance to a stump, you applied a series of actions to make the tree top appear to bounce off, as if the hero is chopping it down?

Simple enough, right? Let's give the steps 1 and 2 a try with Pest Control—then in this chapter and the next, you will repeatedly apply step 3.

First, what actors are there in Pest Control? Here is my list:

- **The hero**, making his living as an exterminator. You call him Arnold.

- **Normal bugs**. The antagonists of this story. The hero has to squash them all to win the game.

- **Firebugs**. These cannot be squashed, but must be shoved into water.

- **Trees**. Just for decoration. They break when the hero runs over them.

- **Walls**. These tiles block the hero's movement, as is usually the case with walls, but he can bounce off of them to his advantage.

- **Water**. Like walls, but with a different look.

- **Background**. This includes the grass and stone floor tiles. These serve no real purpose in the game, other than to make it look more interesting.

- **The screen itself**. The game world is the container of all the other actors. The hero can also bounce off the edges of the screen.

- **Gameplay rules**. Certain gameplay rules might cause interesting things to happen. For example, in Pest Control, if the player destroys all the bugs, she wins the game.

- **The player**. Yes, the player is an actor in the game, too—and with the most important role, one might argue! In this game, the hero is the player's avatar.

Second, now that you've identified the gameplay actors, what interactions exist between them? Here is a partial list:

- Hero interacts with tree (i.e., hero chops down tree).

- Hero interacts with normal bug (i.e., hero destroys bug).

- Hero interacts with firebug (i.e., hero kicks bug).

- Firebug interacts with water (i.e., fire bug is destroyed).

- Hero interacts with wall or water (i.e., hero bounces off wall or water).

- Player interacts with screen (i.e., player taps screen).

- Hero interacts with game world (i.e., hero performs an action like moving or changing direction).

- Bug interacts with game world (i.e., bug performs an action like moving or spawning).

- Game rule interacts with game rule (i.e., win or lose conditions are satisfied).

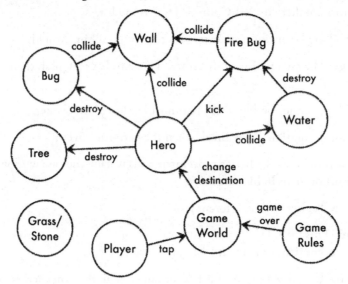

All of these interactions are opportunities for juice, like ripe fruit hanging from a tree, just waiting for you to pluck and squeeze. But what effects should you use?

Five basic special effects

In this chapter, you'll start out with five basic special effects. To use them, you just need to know SKActions, and you've had plenty of practice with those already in this book.

Here are the five basic effects you can apply to sprite nodes:

1. **Movement** changes a node's position.

2. **Scaling** changes a node's size.

3. **Rotation** changes a node's angle.

4. **Alpha** changes a node's translucency.

5. **Texture** changes a sprite node's image.

All of these effects can be temporary or permanent, immediate or animated, performed by themselves or—and this is where the magic happens—in combination with other effects. When you add a bunch of these effects together, they can make the entire screen jump and bounce. That's when things get juicy!

You've already seen in previous chapters how easy it is to make an object move or rotate using an SKAction. That's the wonderful thing about these effects: They are incredibly simple to program, so adding them to your games is a quick win. Although I have to warn you: Once you start adding special effects, it's hard to stop!

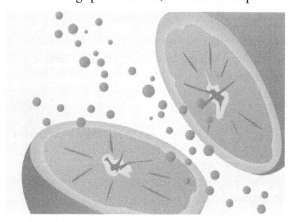

Four effects to fell a tree

You're going to start by applying four of the five basic special effects to the "hero collides with tree" interaction.

This is because smashing things is a lot of fun. You usually get into trouble for it in the real world, but luckily in games, you can get away with it. Pest Control already lets you run over trees, after which they are reduced to poor little tree stumps. This is an excellent opportunity to add some cool animations.

Currently, the tree-smashing code looks like this, in **Breakable.swift**:

```
func smashBreakable() {
  physicsBody = nil
  sprite.texture = brokenTexture
  sprite.size = brokenTexture.size()
}
```

The tree tiles are instances of the `Breakable` class, which is an `SKNode` with a child `SKSpriteNode` and some extra stuff. The `Breakable` tile starts out displaying one texture, which is the normal, unbroken tree, but it also has a variable named `brokenTexture` that references a different texture, which is the tree stump.

In `smashBreakable()`, you simply replace the sprite's current texture, the solid tree, with the `brokenTexture`, the tree stump. This is satisfyingly simple to code, but not to watch. Your players want to see something more spectacular!

In this section, you will add a new "treetop" sprite and make it tumble down the screen, so it looks like the hero is chopping down trees! That Arnold: He's an exterminator and a lumberjack all in one.

Pest Control's **scenery.atlas** folder already contains an image named **tree-top.png**. To use this new image in the `Breakable` class, you have to rewrite it slightly. First, add a new property to **Breakable.swift**:

```
let flyAwayTexture: SKTexture
```

Then, change the name of `init(wholeTexture:brokenTexture:)` to include a new parameter, `flyAwayTexture`:

```
init(wholeTexture: SKTexture, brokenTexture: SKTexture,
     flyAwayTexture: SKTexture) {
```

Add the following line inside the method, just after the code that sets up `self.brokenTexture`:

```
self.flyAwayTexture = flyAwayTexture
```

This simply stores the value from the new `flyAwayTexture` parameter into the `flyAwayTexture` property.

Since you added a new property, you need to update `Breakable`'s `NSCoding` support. Otherwise, these effects won't work properly after continuing from a saved level.

Add this line to `encodeWithCoder()` to encode `flyAwayTexture`:

```
aCoder.encodeObject(flyAwayTexture, forKey: "Breakable-FlyAway")
```

And add this line to `init?(coder:)` to decode it:

```
flyAwayTexture =
  aDecoder.decodeObjectForKey("Breakable-FlyAway") as! SKTexture
```

Finally, in **TileMapLayer.swift**'s nodeForCode(), modify the case "t" statement so it calls the new initializer:

```
case "t":
  return
    Breakable(wholeTexture: atlas!.textureNamed("tree"),
             brokenTexture: atlas!.textureNamed("tree-stump"),
             flyAwayTexture: atlas!.textureNamed("tree-top"))
```

Likewise, you need to change createNodesFromLayer() in **TmxTileMapLayer.swift** so it uses the new initializer. Replace the line that creates the Breakable with the following:

```
let tile =
  Breakable(wholeTexture: atlas.textureNamed("tree"),
           brokenTexture: atlas.textureNamed("tree-stump"),
           flyAwayTexture: atlas.textureNamed("tree-top"))
```

Build the app to see if everything compiles again without errors. Phew! That was a bit of work, but now you have everything set up to add some toppling trees to the game.

This diagram illustrates what you're going to implement:

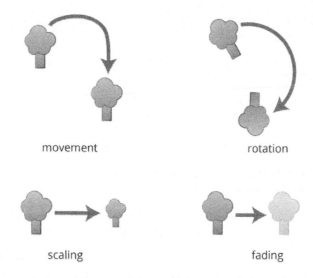

You will be combining four different effects (that's juicy!):

1. **Movement.** You will push the tree upward slightly and then make it fall down the screen.

2. **Rotation**. You'll rotate the tree by a random amount so it appears to topple over.

3. **Scaling**. To make the tree "pop," you'll first scale it up so it appears bigger for a moment, and then scale it down with an animation.

4. **Alpha**. As the scaling animation makes the tree smaller, you'll also lower the tree's alpha component so it becomes more and more transparent, until finally, the sprite is no longer visible.

Alone, none of these effects are spectacular, but together, they make for an very impressive animation.

Instead of adding these effects all at once, you'll add them one by one so you can see how to build up a complex effect. You'll begin with movement.

Effect 1: Movement

Hop on over to **Breakable.swift** and add the following to smashBreakable():

```
// 1
let topNode = SKSpriteNode(texture: flyAwayTexture)
addChild(topNode)
// 2
let upAction = SKAction.moveByX(0, y: 30, duration: 0.2)
upAction.timingMode = .EaseOut

let downAction = SKAction.moveByX(0, y: -300, duration: 0.8)
downAction.timingMode = .EaseIn
// 3
topNode.runAction(SKAction.sequence(
  [upAction, downAction, SKAction.removeFromParent()]))
```

The first part of this method remains the same as before, but in addition:

1. You add a new child node for the treetop image, topNode. This is the node that you're going to make fly off the screen.

2. You create two actions, the first to move the sprite 30 points up in 0.2 seconds and the second to move the sprite 300 points down in 0.8 seconds.

3. This runs the above actions in sequence: First, the treetop sprite flies slightly upward, so it looks like it was pushed up by the hero, then it falls down the screen, and finally—after about one second—the code removes the sprite from the scene altogether. If you're no longer using a node, you can improve performance and save memory by removing it.

Run the game, and smash through a tree to see what this looks like:

  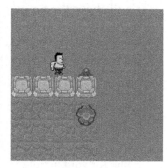

That already looks great, but you can take this even further by adding some horizontal movement to the treetop. Add the following lines to the bottom of `smashBreakable()`:

```
let direction = CGFloat.randomSign()
let horzAction = SKAction.moveByX(100 * direction, y: 0,
                                  duration: 1.0)
topNode.runAction(horzAction)
```

`randomSign()` is one of the `CGFloat` extensions provided by `SKTUtils`. It randomly returns either 1 or -1. That's very handy for situations like this: A value of 1 means the treetop flies to the right (the positive x-direction) while -1 means it flies to the left (negative direction). As a result, this `SKAction` makes the treetop fly 100 points in a random horizontal direction.

Notice you're running this as a separate action, so it's independent of the vertical movement that you added earlier. Sprite Kit combines the effects of these two different actions behind the scenes, making it look like the treetop flies in a neat curve.

Run the game to see it in action:

 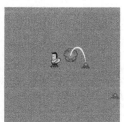  

It's all about the timing:

Look carefully at the SKActions in smashBreakable() and notice the following two lines:

```
upAction.timingMode = .EaseOut
downAction.timingMode = .EaseIn
```

Timing is arguably one of the most important aspects of the special effects you're adding in this chapter. SKAction lets you choose one of four possible timing modes for your actions. These are defined in the SKActionTimingMode enumeration.

The default is .Linear movement, which looks totally unrealistic. If you comment out the above two lines, then the treetop will appear to fly like this:

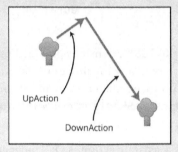

But by using .EaseOut for the upward push and .EaseIn for the downward phase, the flight path of the treetop becomes a lot more realistic:

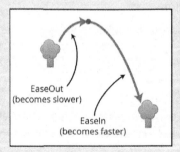

Unfortunately, SKAction only lets you choose between these two very basic timing modes. Later on in this chapter, you'll learn to do much crazier things with timing and unlock its full potential.

This concludes the first effect, movement. It looks pretty sweet by itself, but you've only used one trick from a full bag. When it comes to special effects, it's good to always ask yourself, "How far can I take this? What other fun stuff can I add?"

Effect 2: Rotation

The movement effect was by far the most complicated, because it combined two vertical stages—up and down—with a horizontal movement. Rotation is much simpler. Add the following lines to the bottom of smashBreakable():

```
let rotateAction = SKAction.rotateByAngle(
  -π + CGFloat.random()*2*π, duration: 1.0)
topNode.runAction(rotateAction)
```

This tells the treetop sprite to rotate by a random angle between -π and +π (-180 and +180 degrees) over the span of one second. You use the CGFloat.random() function from SKTUtils to get a random number between 0.0 and 1.0.

That's all you have to do to make the treetop tumble as it falls. Run the app to try it out:

Effect 3: Scaling

Messing with the scale of objects is equally simple but very effective. In fact, if you add only one of the five basic special effects to your game, make it scaling—it goes a long way toward making your game super juicy!

Obviously, in the real world, most objects don't become larger or smaller when you interact with them, but this is the virtual world and you can do as you please.

Add these lines to the bottom of `smashBreakable()`:

```
topNode.xScale = 1.5
topNode.yScale = 1.5

let scaleAction = SKAction.scaleTo(0.4, duration: 1.0)
scaleAction.timingMode = .EaseOut
topNode.runAction(scaleAction)
```

This first sets the scale of the treetop sprite to 150% so that it immediately becomes a lot bigger, then it slowly scales it down to only 40% of its original size, as the treetop tumbles down the screen.

Run the app and smash some trees:

Feels nice, doesn't it?

Notice the use of the `timingMode` property here. `EaseOut` will make the sprite shrink quickly at first, but then it slows down the degree of scaling. This looks better to me than linear animation. Feel free to experiment with the other timing modes, `.Linear`, `.EaseIn` and the combination of ease-in and ease-out, `.EaseInEaseOut`. The differences are subtle but noticeable.

Effect 4: Alpha

The final effect you'll apply to the treetop is a simple fadeout by modifying the alpha. For objects that need to disappear from the screen, it's always a good idea to apply a fadeout to make the effect less jarring.

Put these lines at the bottom of `smashBreakable()`:

```
topNode.runAction(SKAction.sequence([
  SKAction.waitForDuration(0.6),
  SKAction.fadeOutWithDuration(0.4)]))
```

This performs a fadeout action after 0.6 seconds. Notice that all the effects you've added so far each last for 1.0 second. That's no coincidence! They all need to work together as a well-orchestrated whole, or the combined effect won't look as polished.

Run the app and watch those trees fade into oblivion:

How cool is that? Simply by adding four of the five basic special effects to `smashBreakable()`, you now have trees that are irresistible to smash! When I'm playing this game, I can't keep myself from running into those trees just to see them get chopped up.

Five effects to smash a wall

The "hero collides with wall" interaction is one of the most important in the game; it's pure destruction, waiting to happen! Currently, Arnold simply bounces off the wall, but there is a wealth of potential here for special effects.

Before you continue reading, I'd like you to make a list of the things you could do to the wall sprite, as well as to the player sprite, when they collide. Go ahead—give it a shot. Remember the five basic animations that you can apply to any node.

Ready? Good. Compare your list to the one I made below. I'm sure we have some effects in common. This is what I came up with:

1. **Scaling (the wall).** Scale the wall up and then down again. You can apply this trick to any of your nodes in any interaction and it will look good, so this is a no-brainer.

2. **Movement.** Move the wall in the direction of the collision with a bouncing animation. This is totally unrealistic, of course (unless the hero is Arnold), but it does reinforce the idea of the collision.

3. **Scaling (the hero).** The wall isn't the only thing that should change. It takes two to tango, so the collision should also have some effect on the hero. Squashing is scaling with different horizontal and vertical amounts, so that the player sprite will look flattened—which is exactly what happens to a cartoon character when it bumps into something larger or heavier than itself.

4. **Scaling (other objects).** By putting a tiny scale effect on the actors that aren't directly involved in the collision, like the bugs, you can strengthen the illusion that the hero smacked into the wall.

5. **Texture.** When the hero hits the wall, it would be cool to replace the wall's texture with an image of a cracked wall. Letting players deform the terrain of your games in fun and unexpected ways is an excellent opportunity to generate delight.

You will add the first three of these effects now and add the final two as challenges. By the time you're done, you'll have experience using all five of the basic effects in Pest Control—many of them in several different ways. Let's get cracking!

Effect 1: Scaling (the wall)

No, I'm not talking about climbing here! Instead, you will scale the size of the wall up and back down again.

To keep the code clean, you'll put each special effect into its own method. Start by adding this new method to **GameScene.swift**:

```
func scaleWall(node: SKNode) {
  node.xScale = 1.2
  node.yScale = 1.2

  let action = SKAction.scaleTo(1.0, duration: 1.2)
  action.timingMode = .EaseOut
  node.runAction(action, withKey: "scaling")
}
```

You've seen this before. It sets the scale of the wall's sprite node to 120% and then scales it back down to 100% with an animation. You use ease-out timing to make the effect more natural.

You'll call `scaleWall()` from a new method named `wallHitEffects()`. Implement it as shown below:

```
func wallHitEffects(node: SKNode) {
  // 1
  if node.physicsBody!.categoryBitMask &
    PhysicsCategory.Boundary != 0 {
    // TODO: you will add code here later
  } else {
    // 2
    node.zPosition += 1
    node.runAction(SKAction.afterDelay(1.2, runBlock: {
      node.zPosition -= 1
    }))
    // 3
    scaleWall(node)
  }
}
```

Some notes on how this works:

1. There is a special situation you need to deal with here. There is a special node that surrounds the game world with the physics category `Boundary`. This node is not represented by any sprite on the screen, so you only want to perform some of the animations on that node. Scaling it won't make any sense, for example.

2. You need to bring the wall sprite in front of any other nodes so that during the animation, it doesn't get (partially) hidden behind any of the other tiles on the background layer. The drawing order is determined by the node's `zPosition`. You temporarily bump that up and restore it again when the special effects are over. `SKAction.afterDelay(runBlock:)` is a helper method from `SKTUtils`.

3. You call `scaleWall()`. You'll add more effects here later.

Collisions are detected inside **GameScene.swift** by `didBeginContact()`. Add this snippet inside the `switch` statement:

```
case PhysicsCategory.Boundary, PhysicsCategory.Wall,
        PhysicsCategory.Water:
    wallHitEffects(other.node!)
```

This simply adds another case that checks whether the collision was with the world boundary or a wall tile (or a water tile, which you'll treat the same for many of the effects) and then calls `wallHitEffects()`.

Run the app to see how it works.

Note that you can make the effect more pronounced by increasing the scale factor from 1.2 to some higher number. But be careful—too much scaling will destroy the illusion.

Interlude: Tweening for pros

Before you add the rest of the effects to the wall, let's take a moment to improve what you already have through the power of something called **tweening**.

The current scaling effect works, but to be honest, it doesn't give me shivers down my spine. The wall scales up and then neatly shrinks down again. Yawn… I want it to shake and crumble, like a bulldozer or an earthquake has hit it!

This is Arnold we're talking about here—have you seen his muscles? That wall needs to take some real damage!

```
Arnold
SMASH
wall!!!
```

If you've used other gaming toolkits such as cocos2d or Unity, then you may have come across so-called tweening or **easing** actions. These are special functions that alter the way time is perceived by the animation. The SKAction's timingMode is an example of that, but unfortunately, it only supports the most basic of these timing functions.

Why limit yourself to plain ease-in and ease-out when you can choose from among so much more timing goodness?

Here's a little preview:

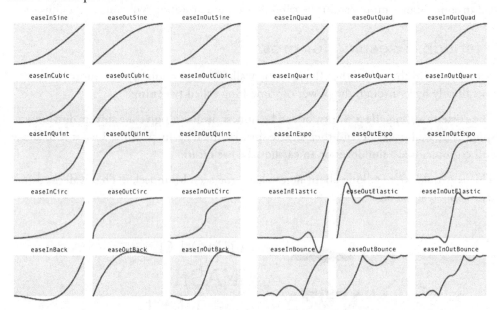

This is an overview of what are known as the Robert Penner easing equations. These are common in many other gaming and animation toolkits, but alas, not in Sprite Kit. (Image by Zeh Fernando from his open-source project Tweener.)

Since Sprite Kit doesn't support anything but the most basic timing functions, you'll have to use some tricks to get this working. The `SKTUtils` folder you added in Chapter 13 contains helper code to make this possible: **SKTEffects.swift** and **SKTTimingFunctions.swift**. These source files contain a way for you to do complex tweening using Sprite Kit, even though Sprite Kit doesn't support this out-of-the-box.

Here's how these helper classes and methods work:

1. **Create an SKTEffect.** An SKTEffect is kind of like an action—for example, there is an SKTScaleEffect, an SKTRotateEffect and so on.

2. **Set timing function.** SKTEffects allow you to set your own timing function (unlike SKAction). I've created a bunch of timing functions you can use, such as "bounce ease-in," "smoothstep" and many more.

3. **Convert to action**. After you create an SKTEffect, you convert it into an action with a handy extension of SKAction called actionWithEffect().

4. **Run the action.** Once you have the SKAction, simply run it as usual.

Let's put SKTEffects into action. Replace scaleWall() with the following:

```
func scaleWall(node: SKNode) {
  if node.actionForKey("scaling") == nil {
    // 1
    let oldScale = CGPoint(x: node.xScale, y: node.yScale)
    let newScale = oldScale * 1.2
    // 2
    let scaleEffect = SKTScaleEffect(node: node, duration: 1.2,
      startScale: newScale, endScale: oldScale)
    // 3
    scaleEffect.timingFunction = SKTCreateShakeFunction(4)
    // 4
    let action = SKAction.actionWithEffect(scaleEffect)
    // 5
    node.runAction(action, withKey: "scaling")
  }
}
```

Let's take this step by step:

1. Calculate a new scale but also remember the old scale. The SKTEffects code uses a CGPoint object to describe the scale, unlike Sprite Kit itself, which uses two separate float variables, xScale and yScale. The new scale is 120% larger than the old scale, because you multiply the x and y fields of the CGPoint by 1.2.

2. Create a new SKTScaleEffect that describes the scaling operation. You need to pass in a reference to the affected node, a duration in seconds and the starting and ending values for the scale size, respectively.

3. This is where the magic happens. SKTCreateShakeFunction() creates a fancy timing function that simulates a shaking effect. More about this in a minute.

4. You cannot apply an `SKTScaleEffect` object directly to a node, so you need to wrap it in an `SKAction`. `actionWithEffect()` comes from an extension that is provided by `SKTEffects`; it isn't a standard `SKAction` method.

5. You give the action the key name "scaling" when you add it to the node. If there's already one of these effects active on the node—which might happen if the player bumps into the wall twice in a row—then you don't want to start another animation.

Run the app to see how this works.

Wow, that's pretty sweet. The wall not only scales up, but now as it scales down, its size bounces a few times.

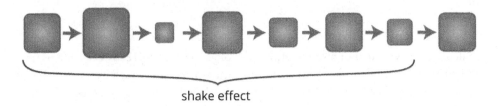

shake effect

To better see this, change the scale factor in `scaleWall()` from 1.2 to 3.0:

```
let newScale = oldScale * 3.0
```

You may notice a strange black effect—don't worry about that now; we'll discuss it in a bit.

Also feel free to play with the parameter to `SKTCreateShakeFunction()`. That value represents the number of oscillations in the animation. If you set it to 1, then the animation is very similar to the basic ease-out that you saw before. But if you set it larger, for example to 10, then wowza! The wall will bounce up and down 10 times.

```
scaleEffect.timingFunction = SKTCreateShakeFunction(10)
```

Run the game to try it out. Also, you may want to increase the duration of the animation to something like 3 seconds or more so you can see the shake motion a bit better.

This is not your grandmother's ease-out; this is mayhem!

Welcome to the power of timing functions. `SKTScaleEffect` does the same thing as a regular `SKAction` for scaling—it simply animates the node's `xScale` and `yScale` properties—except it lets you change the timing of the animation using one of these timing functions. While the start and end values of the animation are the same as before, what happens in the meantime is totally determined by the timing function—and this can be as wild as you can imagine it.

Note that `SKTEffect` contains many other types of timing functions beyond the shake function. You'll use some of the others in this chapter and the next, but I encourage you to look through SKTTimingFunctions.swift and experiment on your own, as well.

There's one ugly thing here, mentioned before: You can see a black gap behind the wall tile when it's scaled down because there is now nothing drawn in the background.

The black background color of the scene is showing through. You can fix this easily. Still in **GameScene.swift**, add the following line as the first thing in `createWorld()`:

```
backgroundColor = SKColorWithRGB(89, 133, 39)
```

This makes the background color of the scene green instead of black, so the gap won't be so noticeable.

Now set the scale factor, duration and number of oscillations back to their old values in scaleWall(): 1.2 for scale, 1.2 seconds for duration and 4 for the shakiness. Try it out:

Effect 2: Movement

There's still more you can do to the wall. Don't worry; it can take the abuse!

Besides tinting and scaling the wall, you can also temporarily move it out of the way, as if Arnold managed to push it aside during the collision. The combination of these three effects will make for a very convincing collision animation!

This brings up an interesting question, though: The wall needs to move in the direction of the hero's movement against the wall. In other words, if the hero hits the wall from above, the wall needs to move downward. Conversely, a collision with the bottom of the wall needs to send the wall moving up. So you need a way to determine: Which side of the wall did the hero hit?

First, add an enumeration type that can describe these sides to **Types.swift**:

```
enum Side: Int {
   case Right = 0
   case Left = 2
   case Top = 1
   case Bottom = 3
}
```

This is from the perspective of the player, so `Side.Right` describes a collision on the hero sprite's right side.

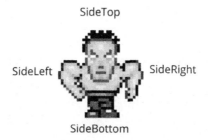

Add the following method to **GameScene.swift**:

```
func sideForCollisionWithNode(node: SKNode) -> Side {
   let diff = node.position - player.position
   let angle = diff.angle

   if angle > -π/4 && angle <= π/4 {
      return .Right
   } else if angle > π/4 && angle <= 3*π/4 {
      return .Top
   } else if angle <= -π/4 && angle > -3*π/4 {
      return .Bottom
   } else {
      return .Left
   }
}
```

This determines the angle between the player sprite and another node (in this case, the one it collided with) and then uses that angle to determine which side the collision was on. Remember that angles in Sprite Kit are always in radians, so you'll have to do some mental math to make the conversion. $\pi/4$ is the same as 45 degrees.

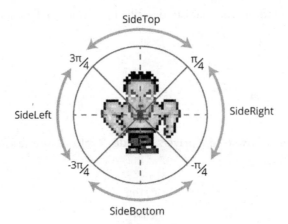

Now add this new method that will move a node appropriately based on a `Side` value:

```
func moveWall(node: SKNode, onSide side: Side) {
  if node.actionForKey("moving") == nil {
    // 1
    let offsets = [
      CGPoint(x:  4.0, y:  0.0 ),
      CGPoint(x:  0.0, y:  4.0 ),
      CGPoint(x: -4.0, y:  0.0 ),
      CGPoint(x:  0.0, y: -4.0 ),
    ]
    // 2
    let oldPosition = node.position
    let offset = offsets[side.rawValue]
    let newPosition = node.position + offset
    // 3
    let moveEffect = SKTMoveEffect(node: node, duration: 0.6,
      startPosition: newPosition, endPosition: oldPosition)
    // 4
    moveEffect.timingFunction = SKTTimingFunctionBackEaseOut
    // 5
    let action = SKAction.actionWithEffect(moveEffect)
    node.runAction(action, withKey: "moving")
  }
}
```

This is similar to the `scaleWall()` method you've just seen, except now you're using an `SKTMoveEffect` instead of an `SKTScaleEffect`.

1. The `offsets` array is a so-called **look-up table**. It describes how much you will add to the wall's current position. There is one entry in the array for each possible side. So if `side` is `Right`, which has value 0, then you use the first offset from the look-up

table (4.0, 0.0). In other words, you shift the wall 4 points to the right, and likewise for the other sides.

2. You find the offset for the current side and add it to the wall node's current position to obtain the new position.

3. You create an SKTMoveEffect for the wall node. It will immediately place the wall on its new position, 4 points shifted toward the direction of the collision's impact, and then move it back to its original position over the span of 0.6 seconds.

4. You set the timing function for the animation. Unlike the scaling effect, this doesn't use the shake timing but something called **back ease-out**. It's a subtle effect that makes the node overshoot its target a little bit.

5. You create an SKAction for this effect and add it under the name "moving" so that only one movement action at a time can be active on the wall node.

Now all that's left to do is find the direction of collision and call moveWall(onSide:). Add the following line at the top of wallHitEffects().

```
let side = sideForCollisionWithNode(node)
```

This determines which side of the hero had the collision.

Then add the following line in wallHitEffects(), just after the call to scaleWall():

```
moveWall(node, onSide: side)
```

This tells the wall node to move out of the way.

That should do the trick. Run the game, and watch those walls bounce:

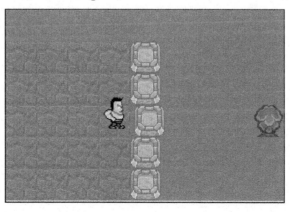

Now running into a wall is most definitely fun. Notice that these same effects also apply to the water tiles, although the green background behind them is less than ideal. It's a totally different sprite, but the animations don't care what the sprite looks like. Give them an SKNode and they will happily twist and pull it out of shape.

> **Note:** There are now two effects on the wall, scale and movement, each of which would be pretty simple on its own. But working together, these effects make bumping into the wall look very cool. To study each effect in detail, comment out the other and play with the various parameters. Maybe you like the scaling effect better if it's longer or shorter, or maybe the wall should move a bit further when it gets pushed. Experimentation is the name of the game!

Effect 3: Scaling (the hero)

There's one more effect for you to try before you set out on your own, and it has to do with cartoons.

I'm sure you watched cartoons when you were a kid (maybe you still do!). Remember how cartoons tend to exaggerate movement? This is actually a scale effect, but one where the x-scale is more or less than the y-scale.

The technical term for this is **squash and stretch**, and it's considered one of the basic principles of animation. Without it, moving objects seem stiff and lifeless.

This is what Arnold would look like if he jumped from a tall building, with squash and stretch applied:

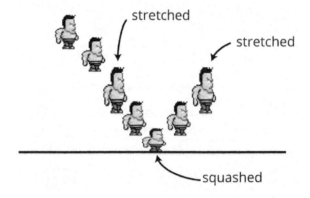

Squash happens when an object collides with something; **stretch** happens when an object accelerates. In this section, you'll add both to the most important actor in this game: Arnold.

First the stretch

Right now, when you tap in the game world, the hero simply changes direction and runs toward the location of your tap. This is a prime opportunity for some juice.

Add the following methods to **GameScene.swift**:

```
func tapEffectsForTouchAtLocation(location: CGPoint) {
  stretchPlayerWhenMoved()
}

func stretchPlayerWhenMoved() {
  let oldScale = CGPoint(x: player.sprite.xScale,
                         y: player.sprite.yScale)
  let newScale = oldScale * 1.4

  let scaleEffect = SKTScaleEffect(node: player.sprite,
    duration: 0.2, startScale: newScale, endScale: oldScale)

  scaleEffect.timingFunction = SKTTimingFunctionSmoothstep

  player.sprite.runAction(
    SKAction.actionWithEffect(scaleEffect))
}
```

`tapEffectsForTouchAtLocation()` is where you'll add all of the effects that happen when the player taps the screen. Right now, there's only one effect, but in the next chapter, you'll add several others—juicy games come from adding as many effects as you can get away with!

The real work happens in `stretchPlayerWhenMoved()`. There shouldn't be any surprises for you here. The `SKTScaleEffect` scales the hero up and then down again. The only new thing is `SKTTimingFunctionSmoothStep`, which is a special version of ease-in/ease-out. I like the way that looks for this effect.

> **Note:** You're adding the scale effect to `player.sprite`, not directly to `player`. Recall that `Player` is a regular `SKNode` that has a physics body; the actual sprite is a child node. It's best to add juice animations to the sprite, not to the node with

the physics body. When you start scaling the physics body rapidly up and down, weird things are bound to happen to the game's physics.

You need to call tapEffectsForTouchAtLocation() when a tap happens, which is in touchesBegan(withEvent:). Add the following lines to the Playing case statement, replacing the call to moveToward() on player:

```
let loc = touch.locationInNode(worldNode)
tapEffectsForTouchAtLocation(loc)
player.moveToward(loc)
```

Run the app, and now Arnold should briefly scale up whenever you tap the screen:

Simply scaling up the player sprite for a bit makes Arnold seem more alive.

Note: Granted, this isn't technically a stretch. The player sprite simply expands by the same amount in all directions. If this were a true stretch, the sprite would only scale up along its axis of acceleration. However, in this game, the hero doesn't ever accelerate—the dude is already running all the time! For this particular game, it's easier to uniformly scale up the sprite for a fraction of a second. You have to admit that it still looks good, even though it's only a basic scaling effect. What just a few lines of code can do to polish your game!

Then the squash

Exaggeration is the secret to convincing cartoon animation, but it also works well in video games. When the hero collides with a wall, you're going to squash his sprite to drive home the idea that there was a collision:

Add the following method to **GameScene.swift**:

```
func squashPlayerForSide(side: Side) {
  if player.sprite.actionForKey("squash") != nil {
    return
  }
  let oldScale = CGPoint(x: player.sprite.xScale,
                         y: player.sprite.yScale)
  var newScale = oldScale
  let scaleFactor: CGFloat = 1.6

  if side == Side.Top || side == Side.Bottom {
    newScale.x *= scaleFactor
    newScale.y /= scaleFactor
  } else {
    newScale.x /= scaleFactor
    newScale.y *= scaleFactor
  }

  let scaleEffect = SKTScaleEffect(node: player.sprite,
    duration: 0.2, startScale:newScale, endScale: oldScale)

  scaleEffect.timingFunction = SKTTimingFunctionQuadraticEaseOut

  player.sprite.runAction(
    SKAction.actionWithEffect(scaleEffect), withKey: "squash")
}
```

By now, you should be familiar with this sort of thing. First, you calculate the starting and ending values, and then you create the `SKTScaleEffect`, set a timing function and finally, run the action. The only new thing here is the method of calculating the amount of squash, which depends upon which side of the player sprite hit the wall.

It's important with these squashing and stretching effects that, no matter how much you scale the object, the total volume of the object appears to remain the same. That means if you're scaling the sprite up in the vertical direction, then you need to scale the sprite down in the horizontal direction to compensate:

Unconvincing
(volume appears
to become less)

Convincing
(volume stays
the same)

Call this new method at the top of `wallHitEffects()`, just after you set the `side` value:

```
squashPlayerForSide(side)
```

This applies the squashing effect not only for the wall and water tiles, but also for the edges of the screen.

Try it out!

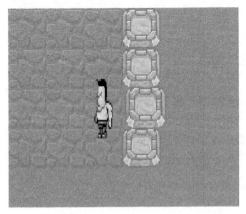

You may have noticed something odd at the edges of the screen. When you bump into a screen edge where there is no wall, the player sprite seems to squash the wrong way around. That's because `sideForCollisionWithNode()` calculates the angle between the player sprite and the node it collided with by first subtracting their positions and then performing some trigonometry.

But the screen edge is represented by a special "edge loop" node that is as big as the entire world. The position of this special node is at the center of the world layer. The calculations in `sideForCollisionWithNode()` don't make any sense for this world-bounds node, so you'll have to fix this method to make an exception. Modify the method as follows:

```
func sideForCollisionWithNode(node: SKNode) -> Side {
  // Did the player hit the screen bounds?
  if node.physicsBody!.categoryBitMask &
                              PhysicsCategory.Boundary != 0 {
    if player.position.x < 20 {
      return .Left
    } else if player.position.y < 20 {
      return .Bottom
    } else if player.position.x > size.width - 20 {
      return .Right
    } else {
      return .Top
    }
  } else {  // The player hit a regular node
    // put original contents of this method here
  }
}
```

Run the game again, and verify that bumping into the screen edges now gives you the right kind of squash effect. And not butternut squash, either. I told you the scaling effect was good for a lot of stuff!

At this point, you've used three out of the five special effects to juice up the wall smash. The remaining two are left as challenges for you!

Challenges

This chapter has three challenges. The first two challenges are about adding the remaining two basic special effects to the "hero interacts with wall" interaction. Don't worry—you'll get step-by-step hints along the way, as usual.

The final challenge is a bit more difficult, so it's optional. Your goal will be to juice up the "hero interacts with bug" interaction using your own creativity along with what you've learned in this chapter. I won't provide you detailed hints for this one, since your ideas and solutions may be different than mine!

As always, if you get stuck, you can find the solutions in the resources for this chapter—but give it your best shot first!

Challenge 1: Scaling (other objects)

The next special effect to add to your "hero interacts with wall" interaction is movement for objects other than the wall and hero.

Imagine if you were to slam yourself into the wall of your room, right now—don't actually do this though! If you were to hit the wall hard enough, then I'm sure other items in your room would shake from the impact. If you were Arnold, the whole house would tremble!

Your challenge is to make all of the bugs on the screen shake like jelly when the hero collides with the wall. You'll use the scale effect, since it will give the illusion of bouncing movement. Here are some hints for how to accomplish this:

- Add a new method to **GameScene.swift** called `bugJelly()` that takes no parameters. It should enumerate through all of the child nodes in `bugLayer` that have the name "bug". For each of these, it should scale the bug's sprite from 1.2 to 1.0.

- You should use the helper class `SKTScaleEffect` and `SKAction` category method `actionWithEffect()` to accomplish this, since that will allow you to use a custom timing function. I suggest using the "elastic ease-out" timing function.

- Call this method from `wallHitEffects()`, outside of the if/else statement so that it applies when Arnold hits the edges of the screen, as well, not just when he hits a wall.

When you're done, run the game and slam into some walls. You should see the bugs quiver whenever there's a collision:

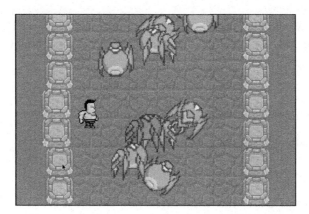

The effect is subtle, as it should be, but if you want to make it more extreme, try the following:

- Set the start scale to 1.5

- Set the duration to 3.0

- Set the timing function for a slightly bouncier result:

```
scaleEffect.timingFunction = SKTTimingFunctionBounceEaseOut
```

Challenge 2: Texture changing

One very effective way to make your games more delightful is to let the player deform the terrain. That's already what happens with the trees— you've seen how much fun it is to kick them over, even though it has no real bearing on gameplay mechanics. Such effects make it even more obvious to the player that they're interacting with the game world.

Your challenge is to add the last of the five basic effects that you can apply to a Sprite Kit node: changing the texture of a sprite. When the player sprite bumps into a wall, you will temporarily replace the wall image with a cracked version. After a couple of seconds, you'll put the original image back.

Here are some hints for how to accomplish this:

- Add a new method to **GameScene.swift** called `crackWall()` that takes an `SKSpriteNode` as a parameter (because wall tiles are sprite nodes).

- Check if the physics body for the node has the `Wall` category in its bitmask—you don't want to apply this effect to the water tiles.

- If it does, run an action to switch the node's texture to "wall-cracked", then back to "wall" after 2.0 seconds. These textures come from the `backgroundLayer`'s atlas.

- You may find it useful to use `SKAction.animateWithTextures(timePerFrame:)` to do this.

- You may find it useful to add this method to **TileMapLayer.swift**:

```
func textureNamed(name: String) -> SKTexture {
  return atlas!.textureNamed(name)
}
```

- Call the new `crackWall()` method from `wallHitEffects()`, just after the call to `moveWall()`:

```
crackWall(node as! SKSpriteNode)
```

Now run the app and crack some walls with Arnold's thick skull:

I bet now that you see those cracks, you're starting to wish you could bust straight through the walls! Don't worry—you'll get a "crack" at that in the challenges for the next chapter!

Challenge 3: Crush those bugs! [Optional]

So far, you've added special effects to the "hero interacts with wall" and the "hero interacts with tree" interactions. However, there's one major interaction that has escaped your attention so far: "hero interacts with bug"!

When you collide with a bug, it simply disappears (or gets kicked, in the case of a firebug), which is a bit of a letdown. You want to feel good about getting rid of this pest!

This is an optional challenge for the most hardcore of developers. Your goal is to use the knowledge you've gained so far in this book to add juice to the "hero interacts with bug" and "hero interacts with firebug" interactions.

To get started, add a method to **GameScene.swift** that looks like this:

```
func bugHitEffects(bug: Bug) {
  // 1
  bug.physicsBody = nil
  bug.removeAllActions()
  bug.sprite.removeAllActions()
  // 2
  let duration = 1.3
  bug.runAction(SKAction.removeFromParentAfterDelay(duration))

  // 3: Create and run special effects here!
}
```

This method is intended to be called after a collision between the player sprite and a normal orange bug. Step by step, this is what it does:

1. Since the bug sprite is now dead, it should no longer take part in any of the collision detection. To that end, you set its `physicsBody` property to `nil`. You also remove all the actions so the bug stops moving.

2. It's useful to declare a constant for the duration of the animation. Often, you want to tweak these times and by having just a single constant to modify, you can save yourself some work. All the animation effects that follow will use this same `duration` value. You also start a new action here that removes the bug sprite from the scene after 1.3 seconds.

3. Here you'll add more code to perform special effects on the bug. You might want to pull each special effect into a helper method to keep your code nice and clean.

You should also add a method named `fireBugHitEffects()` that runs some juicy actions when Arnold hits a firebug. Be sure you don't remove the firebug's physics body or remove the firebug from the scene—you're already handling that sort of stuff elsewhere.

You need to call `bugHitEffects()` from somewhere. For regular bugs, the obvious place is from `didSimulatePhysics()`, also in **GameScene.swift**, which handles removing the bugs. The following line is currently inside a `for` loop in that method:

```
bug.removeFromParent()
```

Replace that line with:

```
bugHitEffects(bug)
```

For firebugs, you should add a call to `fireBugHitEffects()` inside `didBeginContact()`, right before you call `kickBug()`.

Now it's time for you to fill up `bugHitEffects()` and `fireBugHitEffects()` with special effects. This is where your creativity comes into play!

Remember the five basic special effects you've learned about in this chapter:

1. **Movement** changes a node's position.

2. **Scaling** changes a node's size.

3. **Rotation** changes a node's angle.

4. **Alpha** changes a node's translucency.

5. **Texture** changes a sprite node's image.

How could these be useful when the hero interacts with the bugs?

Come up with your own ideas and try them out—and make it as cool as you can! After you're done, you can check out the solutions to this chapter to see what I came up with.

Here's one final hint for inspiration, in the form of a picture:

Have fun, and make it juicy!

Chapter 19: Juice Up Your Game, Part 2

By Matthijs Hollemans

In the previous chapter, you learned the secret to making a game juicy: add as many special effects as you can get away with for each interaction between game actors. You then learned about five basic special effects and applied them to your game to make chopping trees, smashing walls and squashing bugs super juicy—and super fun!

In this chapter, you'll add a whole set tricks to your repertoire. Specifically, you'll learn eight new types of special effects:

1. Tinting: Color nodes differently to indicate status effects.

2. Flashing: Make nodes flash quickly to draw the player's attention.

3. Screen Shake: Make the entire screen shake to punctuate an impact!

4. Screen Zoom: To really wow your audience, give your players a double-take.

5. Color Glitch: Make the screen flash to indicate something really shocking.

6. Particle Effects: A game can never have enough particles—learn why!

7. Shape Effects: Use shapes as quick but effective indicators.

8. Sound Effects: Last but not least, sound can make a huge difference in a game—especially when applied with fun in mind.

By the time you're done with this chapter, you'll have a huge set of tools in your kit, and you'll be ready to apply these in your own games to take them to the next level. Let's get started!

> **Note:** This chapter begins where the last chapter's Challenge 3 left off. If you were unable to complete the challenges or skipped ahead from an earlier chapter, don't worry—you can simply open **PestControl-Starter** from this chapter's resources to begin in the right place.

Custom timing functions

Before you begin learning the eight new special effects, I want to show you a little more about the cool things you can do with timing functions.

As an example, let's take the "hero interacts with bug" case that you were working with in the previous chapter's Challenge 3. It would be fun to make the dead bug bounce up and down a few times in addition to whatever other animations you added. Something like this:

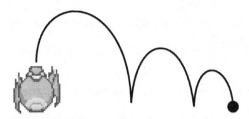

Given what you've seen in this chapter and the last, how would you go about programming this sort of effect? The naïve way would be to make a sequence of SKActions that move the bug up and down several times, using ease-out and ease-in to make smooth curves. That is certainly possible, but it's also a lot of work. Adding special effects is fun, but you're looking for quick gains with little effort here. If it takes you days to program a special effect, it may not be worth the trouble.

So instead of a sequence of movement animations, you're simply going to have a single movement action. You'll achieve the bouncing through the use of a timing function.

As you learned in the previous chapter, Sprite Kit comes with only basic timing functions by default, and it provides no built-in way to create your own. However, I created the SKTEffects and SKTTimingFunctions helper code that make it possible to do just that.

In the last chapter, you used these helper classes to apply a "shake" timing function when Arnold crashes into a wall, and an "elastic ease-in/out" when making the bugs shake like jelly. This time, rather than use these pre-created timing functions, you'll learn how to create a custom timing function of your own.

Here's all the code you need. Add it to **GameScene.swift**:

```swift
func bounceBug(bug: Bug, duration: NSTimeInterval) {
  let oldPosition = bug.position
  let upPosition = oldPosition + CGPoint(x: 0, y: 80)

  let upEffect = SKTMoveEffect(node: bug, duration:1.2,
    startPosition: oldPosition, endPosition: upPosition)

  upEffect.timingFunction = { t in
    pow(2, -3 * t) * fabs(sin(t * π * 3))
  }

  let upAction = SKAction.actionWithEffect(upEffect)
  bug.runAction(upAction)
}
```

As you can see, it only takes one line of code to define a timing function to create a bounce effect.

But how does it work? The timing functions used by SKTEffects are in the form of a closure that takes a CGFloat parameter, t, representing the normal animation time, a value from 0 to 1. The closure returns a new float with the modified time value.

First, you use an SKTMoveEffect to move the bug between its current position and 80 points higher. The timing function determines the exact shape of that movement. With a linear timing function, the sprite would simply slide from the start position to the end position, but here it's a little more involved.

The formula for the bouncing timing function is:

$$t_{new} = 2^{-3t} \cdot abs(sin(t \cdot 3\pi))$$

If your math is a little rusty, it will help to plot this using the Grapher app. In Finder, go to **Applications/Utilities** and launch **Grapher**. Choose **2D Graph**, **Default** as the template, and click **Choose**.

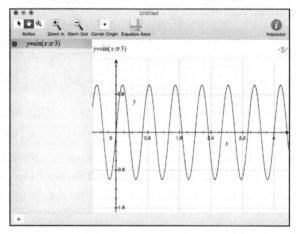

Type the following formula and then press return to plot it:

$$y = sin(x * pi * 3)$$

Grapher will automatically replace "pi" with the π symbol, and draw a basic sine wave. Because this is a timing function, the only important region is between $x = 0$ and $x = 1$, so zoom in on that:

Click the **+** button at the bottom of the window and choose **New Equation** from the popup menu. This lets you enter a second equation that gets plotted on top of the first, so you can easily see the difference.

Enter:

$$y = abs(sin(x * pi * 3))$$

This takes the absolute value of the sine wave, flipping the negative part to make it positive. Already, it looks like a basic bouncing motion:

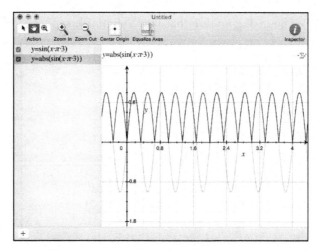

However, the amount of bouncing should diminish over time, just like it would for a bouncing ball. You can make that happen by multiplying the sine wave by something else. In this case, that something else will be an exponent. Add a new equation and enter:

$$y = 2\text{^-}3x$$

Typing the caret symbol creates the exponent. The plot now looks like this:

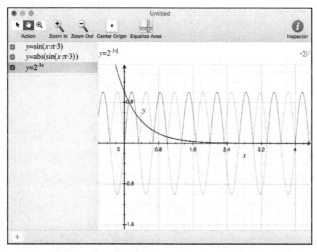

You can see that this creates a curve that grows smaller over time. To apply it to the sine wave, you just multiply the two formulas. Add a new equation and type:

$$y = 2\text{^-}3x * abs(sin(x * pi * 3))$$

(Make sure you press the down arrow key after *-3x* to move out of the exponent part.)

And there you go—a bouncing motion that slowly diminishes:

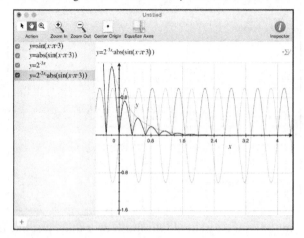

All that's left is calling the new `bounceBug(duration:)` method from the bottom of `bugHitEffects()`. This method comes from the previous chapter's Challenge 3, so if you skipped that challenge, please use the starter project for this chapter.

Add this line to the bottom of `bugHitEffects()`:

```
bounceBug(bug, duration: duration)
```

And you're ready to bounce. Run the game to try it out!

Take a little time—no pun intended!—to experiment with the timing function. For example, to add more bounces, change the 3 inside the *sin()* to a larger number.

Tinting

Now for a new type of effect: tinting!

As you learned when you turned the cats into green zombies the third challenge in Chapter 3, "Actions," you can set the color of a sprite to something other than the default value (white). This is called tinting, and it works by Sprite Kit multiplying the color value of each of the sprite's pixels by a tint color.

This one's so simple, it doesn't even require a method of its own. Just add these two lines to the bottom of `bugHitEffects()`:

```
bug.sprite.color = SKColorWithRGB(128, 128, 128)
bug.sprite.colorBlendFactor = 1.0
```

This blends the texture of the bug sprite with a medium gray color to make it darker. There's no need to make this an animation—just set the new color, and you're done.

It's useful for gameplay purposes to change the color of the dead bugs, because that makes it clear these sprites are no longer participating in the game. Besides, it looks cool!

See for yourself:

It's pretty obvious which of these bugs just got whacked.

> **Note:** Because the tint color is *multiplied* by the original color to get the final result, if you set the color of a sprite to blue, the end result won't necessarily be blue—it depends on the original color.

Because of this, if you want to dynamically set a sprite's color, it's convenient to make the source color of the sprite white, like the cat in Zombie Conga. If you want parts of your sprite to be different colors, you can also split your sprite into different parts, each of which you tint to a different color.

For more information, see the Beat 'Em Up Game Starter Kit available at raywenderlich.com.

Flashing

Remember from Chapter 12, "Crop, Video, and Shape Nodes", that Sprite Kit has a cool type of node called the `SKCropNode` that's quite useful for making special effects. A crop node can have child nodes like any other node, but it doesn't just draw them onscreen—it filters out some of the pixels based on a "mask" you set. A mask is an image that is filled where you want the image to be drawn, and transparent otherwise.

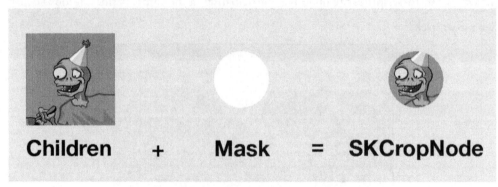

That is an excellent way to make a flashing effect. When Arnold runs over a bug, you will turn the bug completely white for a fraction of a second.

Note that you can't use tinting to achieve this, because tinting works via multiplying colors, and a color multiplied by white is the same color.

Without a crop node, you would have to make white versions of all the animation frames for all the bug sprites, which would add a lot to the size of your texture atlas and would be a bit of a pain. But with a crop node, the flash effect is easy-peasy.

Below is the complete flashing code. Add it to **GameScene.swift**:

```
func flashBug(bug: Bug, mask: SKNode) {
  // 1
  let cropNode = SKCropNode()
  cropNode.maskNode = mask
  cropNode.zPosition = bug.zPosition + 1
  // 2
  let whiteNode =
    SKSpriteNode(color: SKColor.whiteColor(),
                 size: CGSize(width: 50, height: 50))
  cropNode.addChild(whiteNode)
  // 3
  cropNode.runAction(SKAction.sequence([
    SKAction.fadeInWithDuration(0.05),
    SKAction.fadeOutWithDuration(0.3)]))
  bug.addChild(cropNode)
}
```

Here's what it does:

1. You create the SKCropNode and set its mask. The mask will be a copy of the bug sprite, as you will see momentarily. You set the zPosition of cropNode to one higher than the bug's so that the crop node appears above the bug sprite.

2. You create a new sprite node that's completely white. In Sprite Kit, if you create an SKSpriteNode without a texture, it will become a rectangle with a solid color. That's handy for debugging, but it's also useful here. You add the white node as a child node to the crop node.

3. You quickly fade in the crop node and then fade it out again. This creates the flashing effect.

Now call this new method from bugHitEffects():

```
let maskNode = SKSpriteNode(texture: bug.sprite.texture)
flashBug(bug, mask: maskNode)
```

Remember that here, bug refers to the SKNode on which you're performing all the effects and that bug.sprite is the original SKSpriteNode with the bug image. You create a copy of that bug image to use as the mask for the crop node.

Here's how it works: The white sprite gets masked by the bug image, leaving you with a bug that looks completely white.

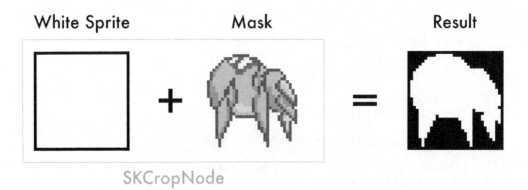

White Sprite   Mask   Result

SKCropNode

Run the game, and crush some bugs:

Any bugs you stomp will flash white, bounce up and down, and then fade to their darker tint color before they disappear completely. What a juicy exit!

The screen shake

It's time to introduce effect number eight to your collection, one that is probably my favorite: the *screen shake*.

So far, you've applied all your effects to individual gameplay objects: the player sprite, the bugs, the wall sprites and so on. But you can also consider the game world as a whole as an object—one to which you can apply effects!

The screen shake is an excellent example. As its name implies, the screen shake effect makes the whole screen shake up and down!

Given the nature of this game, where Arnold is running continuously, the beauty of the screen shake is hard to appreciate. It works best with a screen that doesn't already move so much. So first, you'll tweak the code a little just to see what the screen shake does, and after that, you'll add it to the game for real.

To test the screen shake effect, comment out the current `.Playing` case in `touchesBegan(withEvent:)` and temporarily replace it with the following:

```
case .Playing:
  let amount = CGPoint(x: CGFloat.random() * 20,
                       y: CGFloat.random() * 20)

  let action = SKAction.screenShakeWithNode(worldNode,
    amount: amount, oscillations: 10, duration: 3.0)

  worldNode.runAction(action)
```

Now any time you tap the screen, it no longer makes Arnold move, but it does perform a screen shake.

Build and run, and tap the screen. How cool is that! Imagine the impact of this when you combine it with a wall collision. Not only will the wall sprite bounce up and down—the entire game world will shake at its foundations!

I encourage you to play with the parameters of this screen shake effect for a moment. See what happens when you increase or decrease the number of oscillations or the duration of the animation. For example, try 20 oscillations and 2.0 seconds' duration. Boinggg!

OK, if you're done playing, then remove the above lines of code and uncomment out the original `.Playing` case so that Arnold is free to run once more.

> **Note:** If you're curious, the screen shake effect is implemented in **SKAction+SpecialEffects.swift** in an extension on SKAction that adds the method `screenShakeWithNode(amount:oscillations:duration:)`.
>
> Performing a screen shake is as easy as calling this method to create the action object and then running the action on the `worldNode`. The code that actually performs the screen shake is surprisingly simple. You can see this for yourself in the source code for the extension:

```
public class func screenShakeWithNode(node: SKNode,
  amount: CGPoint, oscillations: Int,
  duration: NSTimeInterval) -> SKAction! {

  let oldPosition = node.position
  let newPosition = oldPosition + amount

  let effect = SKTMoveEffect(node: node, duration: duration,
    startPosition: newPosition, endPosition: oldPosition)

  effect.timingFunction = SKTCreateShakeFunction(oscillations)

  return SKAction.actionWithEffect(effect)
}
```

This is all stuff you've seen before. It creates an SKTMoveEffect and then gives it a shake function for the timing. The main trick is that you apply this effect to the worldNode, which contains all the other nodes in the game world, so all the game objects move up and down by the same amount, which makes it appear that the whole screen is shaking.

Hero meets wall

You will now run a screen shake when the player bumps into a wall. Add the following method to **GameScene.swift**:

```
func screenShakeForSide(side: Side, power: CGFloat) {
  let offsets = [
    CGPoint(x:  1.0, y:  0.0 ),
    CGPoint(x:  0.0, y:  1.0 ),
    CGPoint(x: -1.0, y:  0.0 ),
    CGPoint(x:  0.0, y: -1.0 ),
  ]

  let amount = offsets[side.rawValue] * power
  let action = SKAction.screenShakeWithNode(worldNode,
    amount: amount, oscillations: 3, duration: 1.0)
  worldNode.runAction(action)
}
```

Remember that when a player collides with a wall, it's always on one side, which is represented by a value from the Side enum. This side determines the direction of the screen shake. If Arnold slams into a wall on his left, then the screen also shakes to the left. That will make the force of the impact seem a lot bigger.

The `power` parameter determines how far the screen will shake. The number of oscillations is 3 (how many times the screen shakes up and down) and the duration is one second. You want this effect to be subtle. In this game, the hero is running all the time already, so the screen is constantly in motion. You don't want to add a huge screen shake on top of that or you'll end up giving your players motion sickness!

Change `wallHitEffects()` to make it shake. Replace the comment that reads, "TODO: you will add code here later", with the following line:

```
screenShakeForSide(side, power: 20)
```

Then, add the following line to the `else` statement, just after the call to `crackWall()`:

```
screenShakeForSide(side, power: 8)
```

Note that this calls the screen shake method in two spots with different values for `power`, once for when Arnold hits a wall sprite and once for when he hits the edge of the screen. When the hero bumps into the screen edge, it's OK to make the shake more pronounced—the camera stops moving at the screen edges, so there's no motion in that direction already.

Give it a try! It's a bit hard to tell from a static screenshot, but on the left, you can see a gap between the background tiles and the edge of the screen. That's the screen shake in action (but trust me, it's much better when you run the app).

Notice how this screen shake effect, even though it's quite subtle, changes the entire feel of the game. It really does make it seem like Arnold is now slamming into those walls.

You can almost feel it in your own body as you play. Ouch! Powerful stuff, this screen shake.

Hero meets bug

The screen shake feels so cool, I'm a little bummed now whenever my guy steps on a bug. There is no visceral feedback from that. Whereas the wall collision gives the illusion of resistance, stepping on a bug feels comparatively weak. There's only one remedy: Add a screen shake on the bugs!

Add the following code to the bottom of bugHitEffects():

```
worldNode.runAction(
  SKAction.screenShakeWithNode(worldNode,
    amount: CGPoint(x: 0, y: -12), oscillations: 3,
      duration: 1.0))
```

This creates a screen shake action that moves the screen up by the slightest amount, 12 points. That makes it feel like Arnold has to stomp down hard on those bugs to squash them. I love this effect! As a player, I'm no longer controlling pixels on a screen; I feel like I'm interacting with real objects in a real world. The game has come alive! It's just a delight to run over these bugs. If only pest control was this much fun in the real world. :]

The screen zoom

What about the firebugs—shall you add a screen shake there, too? Nah, I've got something special in mind for them: the *screen zoom!*

The screen shake effect applies the shaky timing to an SKTMoveEffect, but there's no reason you can't do the same thing with a scale effect. That will really make it seem like running into a firebug is a bad idea!

Add the following lines to fireBugHitEffects(). (This method is from Challenge 3 in the last chapter; if you don't have it, refer to the starter project for this chapter.)

```
worldNode.runAction(
  SKAction.screenZoomWithNode(worldNode,
    amount: CGPoint(x: 1.05, y: 1.05), oscillations: 6,
      duration: 2.0))
```

This code applies only a little bit of scaling (105%) to the world node, but you don't want to go too extreme with this effect, anyway.

I dare you to run into a firebug now! Again, the screenshots don't do it justice. You have to see this to believe it.

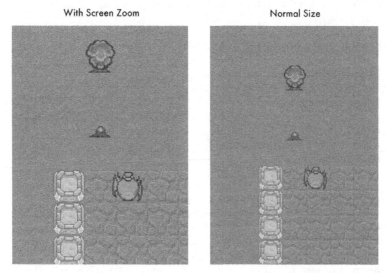

As a rule of thumb, any time you have a large impact between actors in your games, consider using a screen shake effect, and if it's a *really* dramatic impact, consider using a screen zoom effect.

> **Note:** The screen zoom code also lives in **SKAction+SpecialEffects.swift** and is very similar to the screen shake, except it uses an SKTScaleEffect instead of a move effect.

The color glitch

There's one more thing you'll add to firebug collisions and that's an effect known as the *color glitch*. It rapidly displays flashing colors for a fraction of a second, emulating color glitches that sometimes occurred in old arcade games.

This effect is a bit extreme, so you should apply it with caution. You don't want to use it all the time and risk your players collapsing from seizures. Firebug collisions don't happen very often—or at least they shouldn't!—so that's a reasonable place to add the color glitch.

The `SKTEffects` code comes with a handy method that runs a color glitch on an `SKScene`. You run it on the scene because the scene has a `backgroundColor` property, while regular nodes don't. However, there's a small problem: The scene isn't visible in this game because of the tile map. There are tiles everywhere. So in order to perform the color glitch effect, you need to temporarily remove these background tiles to let the scene's color show through.

Add the following method to **GameScene.swift**:

```
func colorGlitch() {
  // 1
  let backgroundNodes =
    (backgroundLayer.children as! [SKNode]).filter({node in
      node.name == "background"})
  for node in backgroundNodes {
    node.hidden = true
  }
  // 2
  let glitchAction = SKAction.colorGlitchWithScene(self,
    originalColor: SKColorWithRGB(89, 133, 39), duration: 0.1)
  // 3
  let restoreAction = SKAction.runBlock {
    for node in backgroundNodes {
      node.hidden = false
    }
  }
  runAction(SKAction.sequence([glitchAction, restoreAction]))
}
```

This looks a little scary, but it's actually quite simple:

1. You look at all child nodes of the background layer with the name "background" and hide them. For this game, you'll only remove unimportant tiles such as the grass and the stones, while leaving the walls and water visible.

2. You run the color glitch action. It lasts for only 0.1 seconds. When the action is done, you restore the scene's original background color.

3. After the color glitch action completes, you look at the background nodes again and un-hide them. The trees and grass only disappear for a moment while the color glitch is happening and then come back when it's over.

Call this new `colorGlitch()` method from within `fireBugHitEffects()`:

```
colorGlitch()
```

There's one more thing you need to do and that is tell the game which nodes are considered background nodes. Open **TileMapLayer.swift** and go to `nodeForCode()`. Add the following line to both the `case "o"` and `case "="` clauses, just after the lines creating the grass or stone tiles:

```
tile!.name = "background"
```

Great, that should do the trick. Now whenever you bump into a firebug, the screen will flash with random colors:

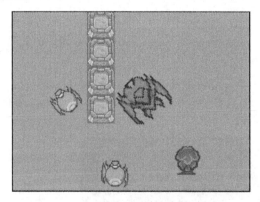

Particle effects

It's now time to introduce special effect number 11, arguably one of the most powerful of all: particle effects!

There exists an unspoken rule among game developers everywhere that no game is complete unless it has particle effects. You can use particles to create effects such as explosions, fire, smoke and flying debris, and they are simply wonderful for juicing up your game. You can't have too many of them.

> **Note:** This chapter assumes you already have some experience with particle systems. If you're unsure exactly what particle systems are or how they work, then check out Chapter 8, "Particle Systems," which discusses the subject in great detail.

I created some particle effects for you for this chapter, and you've already added them to your project.

Recall that a particle effect consists of a texture image and a number of configuration parameters that determine how the individual particles propagate. The texture image is a PNG file and the parameters are stored in an SKS file, which stands for "Sprite Kit Something-or-other." :]

To put such a particle effect inside your game, you use a special type of node, an SKEmitterNode. This node reads the configuration from the SKS file and then begins emitting particles onto your scene.

Tree leaves

To get started with particle effects in Pest Control, how about making the tree drop its leaves when you smash it?

The effect for this is in **TreeSmash.sks** and it uses a leaf image (**Leaf.png**) as its texture. To see the particle effect, click on the SKS file in the project navigator (under **Resources/Art/Particles**):

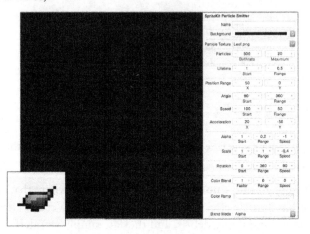

> **Note:** Unfortunately, the particle editor in Xcode 6.1 has a few bugs. If you just see a green dot but no particles, change the Maximum field to 0 and then back to 20. That somehow makes the particles appear properly.

Open **Breakable.swift**, which is the class that represents the trees. Recall from the previous chapter that the Breakable class has a method, smashBreakable(), that gets called when the player fells a tree. Add the following lines to the bottom of that method:

```
let emitter = SKEmitterNode(fileNamed: "TreeSmash")
emitter.particleTexture!.filteringMode = .Nearest
emitter.targetNode = parent
emitter.runAction(SKAction.removeFromParentAfterDelay(1.0))
addChild(emitter)
```

This loads the **TreeSmash.sks** effect into an SKEmitterNode. The filtering mode is set to Nearest to make sure the leaf image remains pixelated when scaled up for Retina.

The emitter node runs for 1.0 seconds and is then removed from the scene, so the particle effect is only visible for a second. It's a good idea to remove an emitter node from the scene when you no longer need it, or eventually it will slow your game to a crawl. (That advice goes for all types of nodes, by the way—not just particle emitters.)

Try it out. Now when you smack a tree, it sheds its leaves:

Sweet!

> **Note:** To keep the code short, you hard-coded this effect into `Breakable`. But `Breakable` is really meant to be a generic class that you could extend for multiple types of breakable objects. In a real app, you should either add an emitter parameter to the initializer, or subclass `Breakable` to put this logic in something like a `Tree` class.

Wall stones

If the trees can drop leaves, then there must also be something you can do about wall collisions. How about showing a short particle burst at the point of impact? The effect is **PlayerHitWall.sks** and it uses the **Rock.png** particle.

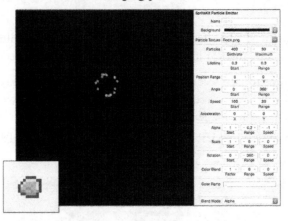

Add the following method to **GameScene.swift**:

```
func showParticlesForWall(node: SKNode, onSide side: Side) {
  var position = player.position
  switch side {
    case .Right:
      position.x =
        node.position.x - backgroundLayer.tileSize.width/2
    case .Left:
      position.x =
        node.position.x + backgroundLayer.tileSize.width/2
    case .Top:
      position.y =
        node.position.y - backgroundLayer.tileSize.height/2
    case .Bottom:
      position.y =
        node.position.y + backgroundLayer.tileSize.height/2
```

```
    }

    let emitter = SKEmitterNode(fileNamed: "PlayerHitWall")
    emitter.particleTexture!.filteringMode = .Nearest
    emitter.position = position
    emitter.zPosition = node.zPosition + 1

    emitter.runAction(SKAction.removeFromParentAfterDelay(1.0))
    backgroundLayer.addChild(emitter)
}
```

The code for creating and running the emitter node is the same as before, but this method also needs to calculate exactly where to place the emitter. It should go on the side of the wall where the collision took place.

Finally, call this new method from `wallHitEffects()`. Add it inside the `else` clause, just below the call for the screen shake:

```
showParticlesForWall(node, onSide: side)
```

Try it out. You'll now see stones fly away from the wall at the point of impact:

Water drops

There is one odd thing, though. If you bump into a water tile, you also get flying stones. It would make more sense if these were water drops, instead.

The resources for this project don't include a new particle system for water collisions. Instead, they contain an alternate texture image. You can simply load the particle effect for the wall collision and replace its texture image to make the particles look like water drops.

Add the following lines to showParticlesForWall(onSide:), immediately above the line that sets the filteringMode on the texture:

```
if node.physicsBody!.categoryBitMask &
   PhysicsCategory.Water != 0 {
   emitter.particleTexture = SKTexture(imageNamed: "WaterDrop")
}
```

After you've created the SKEmitterNode, you can still change its properties. These lines simply assign a different texture image to the emitter.

That should do it. Run the app, and bump into a water tile. Instead of stone particles, you'll now see a shower of water drops:

It's the same particle effect—just a different image!

Motion trail

Pest Control is shaping up nicely—or should I say, "juicily." It already feels a lot more polished than the bare-bones game you started with, but I do think Arnold could be even more awesome. After all, he's the hero of the game and heroes always have that little bit extra.

One easy trick is to give the hero a motion trail, which follows behind the sprite and shows the path the hero has just run along. Even better, a motion trail gives the player the impression of moving extra fast.

You'll use particles to make the motion trail. The project already includes a particle system named **PlayerTrail.sks** that draws stars, which is where you'll start.

Go to **Player.swift** and add a new property for the emitter node:

```
let emitter: SKEmitterNode
```

Add the following line to init(), just below the line that initializes sprite:

```
emitter = SKEmitterNode(fileNamed: "PlayerTrail")
```

Because you're adding a new property, you also need to update your archiving methods. In init?(coder:), add the following line before calling super.init(coder:):

```
emitter = aDecoder.decodeObjectForKey("Player-Emitter")
                     as! SKEmitterNode
```

And add this line in encodeWithCoder():

```
aCoder.encodeObject(emitter, forKey: "Player-Emitter")
```

Also add the following method:

```
func start() {
  emitter.particleTexture!.filteringMode = .Nearest
  emitter.targetNode = parent
  emitter.zPosition = zPosition - 1
  addChild(emitter)
}
```

This creates the emitter and sets its targetNode to the hero's parent, which is the world node. This way, the emitter will follow the hero wherever it goes, but the actual star particles stay put once they've been emitted, causing the trail effect.

Finally, go to **GameScene.swift** and call this new method from the touch handler, touchesBegan(withEvent:), just above the fallthrough statement inside the StartingLevel case:

```
player.start()
```

Run the game, and you'll see a big trail of stars following Arnold wherever he travels:

Particles are pretty easy to use and they can add a lot of polish to your game, provided you use them properly. Feel free to tweak the configuration parameters for these effects in Xcode's particle editor. They're a lot of fun to play with!

> **Public Safety Warning:** There is a high risk that you may get carried away and waste of lot time playing with these particles. :]

Shape effects

Now for special effect #12: shape effects.

Sometimes, you'll want to draw a simple shape to indicate an event in your game. As you learned in Chapter 12, "Crop, Video, and Shape Nodes," an SKShapeNode is perfect for that!

There's one interaction that you've mostly ignored so far: the user tapping on the screen. Right now when that happens, Arnold scales up for a brief moment, but he usually isn't anywhere near where the user tapped, so let's add a cool little animation to highlight the tap location.

Add the following method to **GameScene.swift**:

```
func showTapAtLocation(point: CGPoint) {
  // 1
  let path = UIBezierPath(ovalInRect:
    CGRect(x: -3, y: -3, width: 6, height: 6))
  // 2
  let shapeNode = SKShapeNode()
  shapeNode.path = path.CGPath
  shapeNode.position = point
  shapeNode.strokeColor = SKColorWithRGBA(255, 255, 255, 196)
  shapeNode.lineWidth = 1
  shapeNode.antialiased = false
  shapeNode.zPosition = 90
  worldNode.addChild(shapeNode)
  // 3
  let duration = 0.6
  let scaleAction = SKAction.scaleTo(6.0, duration: duration)
  scaleAction.timingMode = .EaseOut
  shapeNode.runAction(SKAction.sequence(
                   [scaleAction, SKAction.removeFromParent()]))
  // 4
```

```
    let fadeAction = SKAction.fadeOutWithDuration(duration)
    fadeAction.timingMode = .EaseOut
    shapeNode.runAction(fadeAction)
}
```

Let's go through this step by step:

1. You create a `UIBezierPath` object that describes a circle with a 6-point diameter. You'll place the center of this circle at the tap position.

2. You create a new `SKShapeNode` with the Bézier path as its shape. You position this shape node at the tap location and add it to the `worldNode`.

3. You define an action that scales up the shape node to six times its size and then removes it from the scene again.

4. While the shape node is scaling up, you also fade it out at the same time.

Call this new method at the end of `tapEffectsForTouchAtLocation()`:

```
showTapAtLocation(location)
```

Run the app, and you'll now see a small, animated circle anywhere you tap:

Sound effects

There's one final special effect to add to your bag of tricks: sound effects.

So far, all the effects you've dealt with have been visual, but sound is just as important. In fact, the quality of the sound effects can make or break your game. If your sound effects are annoying, then people will simply stop playing your game. But if they're amazing, then you've created an experience people will remember.

Creating compelling sound effects is a job for a good sound designer and is outside the scope of this chapter. Fortunately, playing those effects in a game is easy, and in this section, you'll find out how.

The resources for your project already include a folder named **Sounds** with pre-made sound effects. Take a listen-through to check them out.

It's important to preload your sound effects. Because sound files can take a while to load, you don't want the game to freeze up in the heat of the action. To do this, add the following constant declarations to **GameScene.swift**:

```swift
let hitWallSound = SKAction.playSoundFileNamed(
  "HitWall.mp3", waitForCompletion: false)
let hitWaterSound = SKAction.playSoundFileNamed(
  "HitWater.mp3", waitForCompletion: false)
let hitTreeSound = SKAction.playSoundFileNamed(
  "HitTree.mp3", waitForCompletion: false)
let hitFireBugSound = SKAction.playSoundFileNamed(
  "HitFireBug.mp3", waitForCompletion: false)
let playerMoveSound = SKAction.playSoundFileNamed(
  "PlayerMove.mp3", waitForCompletion: false)
let tickTockSound = SKAction.playSoundFileNamed(
  "TickTock.mp3", waitForCompletion: true)
let winSound = SKAction.playSoundFileNamed(
  "Win.mp3", waitForCompletion: false)
let loseSound = SKAction.playSoundFileNamed(
  "Lose.mp3", waitForCompletion: false)
var killBugSounds = [SKAction]()
```

Here, you create the actions to play each sound effect. You just create them once and then reuse these same actions over and over.

Pay close attention: Unlike the other sounds, `tickTockSound` passes `true` for its `waitForCompletion` argument. You'll learn why a bit later.

The sound for killing a bug is not one sound effect, but twelve different sounds rising in pitch. You'll load those in `didMoveToView()`. Add the following lines to the bottom of that method:

```swift
for i in 1...12 {
  killBugSounds.append(SKAction.playSoundFileNamed(
    "KillBug-\(i).mp3", waitForCompletion: false))
}
```

Now it's simply a matter of running these actions from the right places. Let's take them one by one.

Add the following lines to the bottom of `wallHitEffects()`:

```
if node.physicsBody!.categoryBitMask
                          & PhysicsCategory.Water != 0 {
  runAction(hitWaterSound)
} else {
  runAction(hitWallSound)
}
```

This plays the "wall hit" sound when the collision was with a wall tile, or the "water hit" sound when it was with a water tile.

Inside `didBeginContact()`, directly under the line that calls `smashBreakable()`, add this:

```
runAction(hitTreeSound)
```

Add this line to the bottom of `fireBugHitEffects()`:

```
runAction(hitFireBugSound)
```

And add this to the bottom of `tapEffectsForTouchAtLocation()`:

```
player.runAction(playerMoveSound)
```

That takes care of the basic sound effects. Let's also add some funky music. Add this line to `didMoveToView()` to start the music:

```
SKTAudio.sharedInstance().playBackgroundMusic("Music.mp3")
```

Finally, add these lines to the bottom of `endLevelWithSuccess()` to stop the music and play a sound effect based on whether the player won or lost:

```
SKTAudio.sharedInstance().pauseBackgroundMusic()
runAction(won ? winSound : loseSound)
```

Great, give that a try! When you run the app, you should hear a variety of sound effects.

> **Note:** If the app jumps into the debugger when you run it, make sure you disable the Exception Breakpoint if you have it enabled. For some reason, loading the sound effects triggers a harmless exception deep within Sprite Kit.

Making combos

Almost every interaction has a sound effect now, except for crushing orange bugs. For that, you're going to do something special.

Often, games are more fun if you can score *combos*. For example, if you kill one bug and then another quickly after that, you score extra points. This game doesn't have a score counter, but you can still make use of combos for the special effects.

Look at the sound files in the project, and you'll see there isn't just one "kill bug" sound—there are twelve, each one slightly higher in pitch than the one before. These will comprise the player's reward for making a combo. The more bugs the player kills in a short time, the higher the pitch will rise.

First, add an import for the QuartzCore framework at the top of **GameScene.swift**. You need this for the `CACurrentMediaTime()` function you'll call in a moment.

```
import QuartzCore
```

The combo logic requires a couple of new properties; add them to `GameScene`:

```
var lastComboTime: CFTimeInterval = 0
var comboCounter = 0
```

Add this bit of logic to the top of `bugHitEffects()`:

```
let now = CACurrentMediaTime()
if now - lastComboTime < 0.5 {
  ++comboCounter
} else {
  comboCounter = 0
}
lastComboTime = now
```

The `lastComboTime` instance variable keeps track of the last time the player crushed an orange bug. If the player crushes a new bug and it's been less than half a second since the last time, then it counts as a combo and the value of `comboCounter` goes up. But if it's been longer than half a second, `comboCounter` is reset to 0 again, which means no combo was made.

Add the following line to the bottom of `bugHitEffects()`:

```
bug.runAction(killBugSounds[min(11, comboCounter)])
```

This plays the corresponding sound effect from the `killBugSounds` array. If no combo was made, it picks the first sound effect (the lowest tone), but if `comboCounter` is greater than 0, it picks one of the higher-pitched sounds. The `min()` function makes sure the counter doesn't go over 11, which is the index of the highest sound. It won't often happen that a player kills 12 bugs within half a second of each other, but a little defensive programming never hurt anyone.

> **Note:** You aren't archiving `lastComboTime` and `comboCounter`. Each time the app loads a save file, the combo count will reset. It's not so bad if combos reset when the player pauses the game.

Run the app, and try to make some combos!

You're not limited to using the combo counter for sound effects. For example, you can use it to increase the size of a bug as it explodes. The larger the player's combo, the bigger the sprite will become.

In `scaleBug(duration:)`, replace the line that sets the `scaleFactor` with:

```
let scaleFactor = 1.5 + CGFloat(comboCounter) * 0.25
```

Now the scale factor is no longer fixed at 150% but increases 25% for every combo the player makes.

Try it out:

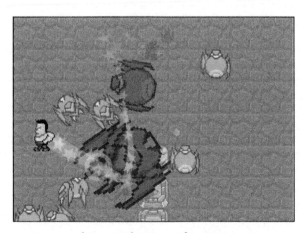

Scaling things up even greater than usual is a terrific, eye-popping way to visualize combos.

Running out of time

This is a time-based game—you need to catch all the bugs before the clock reaches zero—but there's currently no feedback when the player's time is close to running out, other than the count on the clock. You can make things more exciting by adding a sound effect when the player gets dangerously low on time. You want to get the player's adrenaline pumping!

The project includes a sound effect that mimics a ticking clock. You'll play this sound effect when the player has only a few seconds left.

Add a new property to **GameScene.swift**:

```
var tickTockPlaying = false
```

In `update()`, add the following code after the line that sets the text on the `timerLabel`:

```
if timeRemaining < 10 && timeRemaining > 0 && !tickTockPlaying {
  tickTockPlaying = true
  runAction(tickTockSound, withKey: "tickTock")
}
```

This starts the tick-tock sound playing when there are only 10 seconds left in the game.

To test this, open **JuicyLevels.plist** (under **Resources/Levels**) and change the **timeLimit** field to something like 15 seconds, so you don't have to wait for several minutes before you hear this sound:

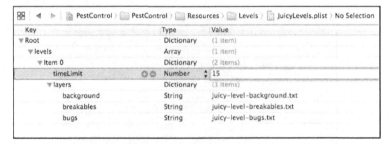

Run the game. Now tell me that hearing this clock tick down doesn't make you anxious to hurry up!

Note: There's one problem with this effect, and it relates to archiving.

`tickTockPlaying` doesn't need to be archived the way you've done for other variables, because you want the game to always load with `tickTockPlaying` equal to `false`. If the player chooses to continue with their current level, `update()` will reset `tickTockPlaying` appropriately based on the remaining time.

However, when you archive `GameScene`, any running actions are also archived. That means the `tickTockSound` action may be playing as soon as the player opens the app. To fix this, you need to remove the action when you create the archive. Add the following line to `encodeWithCoder()` in **GameScene.swift**, just before calling `super`:

```
removeActionForKey("tickTock")
```

This is why you initialized the `tickTockSound` `SKAction` by passing `true` as its `waitForCompletion` argument. Sound actions that don't wait for completion are considered instantaneous, which means they aren't considered to be running at all! If you had passed `false` when creating `tickTockSound` and then tried calling `actionForKey()` here instead of `removeActionForKey()`, you would find there's no action running with that key, even though you might hear the sound playing.

The above line should fix most of the problem, but there's one more issue: The sound file plays for ten seconds, but when you continue a level that was already in the final seconds, that sound continues to play past when the actual time ran out. To fix this, you need to stop the sound when the time runs out. Simply add the same line again, now at the top of `endLevelWithSuccess()`:

```
removeActionForKey("tickTock")
```

Unfortunately, as of the time of writing, there is a bug in Sprite Kit where sounds don't always stop playing when their actions are removed, even if they were created like `tickTockSound`. But some day, when that bug is fixed, this solution should keep your players from going crazy wondering what is that mysterious ticking noise they hear.

Guess what… you're done!

If you've been counting, then you know you've added about 30 special effects to this project. And it shows! Just for fun, play the original starter project again to see the difference. That game looks very static and stiff in comparison, doesn't it?

Remember that you didn't change any of the gameplay rules. You only added a ton of special effects. And most of these effects didn't take a lot of programming at all.

When you're ready to juice up your game, remember to apply the three steps from the previous chapter:

1. List the actors.

2. List the interactions.

3. Add effects to interactions.

Here is the full list of effects you tried out in these chapters:

1. Movement	**8. Screen Shake**
2. Scaling	**9. Screen Zoom**
3. Rotation	**10. Color Glitch**
4. Alpha	**11. Particle Effects**
5. Texture	**12. Shape Effects**
6. Tinting	**13. Sound Effects**
7. Flashing	

This is only the beginning! I encourage you to experiment with your own types of effects. Remember, the goal is to provide feedback to the player that their actions matter. Your players will love you for it!

> **Note:** A lot of the techniques used in this chapter are based on a fun talk by Martin Jonasson and Petri Purho. They show how to take a bland breakout game and turn it into a spectacular display of mayhem by applying the exact same sort of animations you've seen here. I strongly recommend that you check out the video of their presentation on YouTube for some inspiration: http://bit.ly/juice-it

And with that, you've reached the end of this chapter—but the juice isn't over yet! We have two final challenges for you to add the finishing touches to Pest Control.

Challenges

This time, you have two challenges. In the first, you'll add a gratuitous bug squish effect to the game, and for the grand finale, you'll let Arnold bust straight through the walls, just like he does in his dreams.

As always, if you get stuck, you can find the solutions in the resources for this chapter—but give it your best shot first!

Challenge 1: Bug guts for breakfast

In this chapter, you added several types of particle systems to the game: tree leaves, wall stones, water drops and a motion trail.

Is there anywhere else you can put particles to good use? But of course! What about when the hero crushes a bug? I don't mind seeing some bug goo fly across the screen, do you?

Your challenge is to add a particle effect when the player collides with a bug, using the particle effect **BugSplatter.sks** and the texture image **Splat.png**.

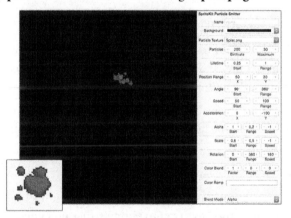

This works in exactly the same way as the other particle effects. If you've done it once, you can do it again. Here are a few hints for how to accomplish this:

- Create a new method in **GameScene.swift** called `showParticlesForBug()` that takes a `Bug` object as an argument. It should create a `SKEmitterNode` using "BugSplatter", position it at the node's position, add it as a child of the background layer and remove it from its parent after 0.4 seconds.

- Then, call this method at the bottom of bugHitEffects():

```
showParticlesForBug(bug)
```

Run the game, and get ready to get dirty:

Now that's some juice!

Challenge 2: Smashing through walls

This is a fun one! When Arnold bangs into a wall, you currently show a cracked version of the wall texture on that tile, and after a second or two, the wall magically heals itself by returning to the original texture.

What if Arnold were to hit the wall again within that two-second interval? Your challenge is to make the wall tile fall apart and disappear in this event, making Arnold appear to bust straight through!

Here are some hints for how to accomplish this:

- Define a new collision detection category for the wall when it's in its temporary cracked state. Add this to the PhysicsCategory struct in **Types.swift**:

```
static let CrackedWall : UInt32 = 0b10000000    // 128
```

- In **GameScene.swift** inside crackWall(), when the wall's physics body has the Wall category, set the category mask to CrackedWall instead. Also, run an action that sets the category back to the regular Wall category after 2 seconds. Give this action a key of "restoreCrack". Finally, set the animate action (created earlier) to have a key of "crackAnim".

- Still inside `crackWall()`, add an `else` case that checks if the wall's physics body has the `CrackedWall` category. In this case, remove the "crackAnim" and "restoreCrack" actions, set the wall texture to "wall-broken" from the background layer's atlas, and set the category and collision bitmask of the wall's physics body to `None`.

- Edit `didBeginContact()` to add `CrackedWall` to the case that calls `wallHitEffects()`.

Build and run, and you should be able to smash straight through the walls:

If you've made it this far, you've accomplished a lot—you've made Arnold the master of bugs, and yourself the master of juice! We hope to see many juicy games from you in the future.

Challenge 3: Make the game run on OS X

Your final challenge is to port Pest Control to the Mac. You've already learned how to make Sprite Kit apps work on OS X in Chapter 6, so refer back to that chapter if you get stuck. Here are some hints:

- You need a new target for the OS X version of the game, named **PestControlMac**.

- It's a good idea to put all the shared code and resources into a new **Shared** group. The only things that are not shared between the iOS and OS X versions are the storyboard and launch file, the AppDelegate.swift and GameViewController.swift source files, and Info.plist.

- All the files from the Shared group should be added to the PestControlMac target (you don't need to add the .h files).

- The PestControlMac target should also link with libz.dylib.

- The PestControlMac target should not use the GameScene.swift and Images.xcassets from the template but the shared ones. You can also remove GameScene.sks.

- The OS X icons should be added to the asset catalog. You can find the icon images in the Resources folder for this chapter.

- You need to tell PestControlMac to use an Objective-C bridging header so it can see the `JSTileMap` class. In the **Target Settings** screen, under **Build Settings**, click on **All** and search for **Objective-C Bridging Header**. Give this field the value: **PestControl/PestControl-Bridging-Header.h**

- Place the `touchesBegan()` method in **GameScene.swift** into an `#if os(iOS)` block and add a `mouseDown()` method to handle clicks on OS X. You'll have to move the logic from `touchesBegan()` into one or more methods that work independently of `UITouch` (on iOS) and `NSEvent` (on OS X).

- In `createUserInterface()`, the `UIDevice` class is used. That class does not exist on OS X. Use an `#if os(iOS)` block to change that logic between iOS and OS X.

- In `showTapAtLocation()`, use `NSBezierPath` instead of `UIBezierPath`. You also need to add the file **NSBezierPath+CGPath.swift** from this chapter's resources to the PestControlMac target. This adds a new method `quartzPath()` that turns the `NSBezierPath` into a `CGPath` object.

- In **TileMapLayer.swift**, use `#if os(iOS)` to replace `decodeCGSizeForKey()` and `encodeCGSizeForKey()` with `decodeSizeForKey()` and `encodeSizeForKey()`, respectively. So drop the "CG" from the method name. The OS X methods return `NSSize` values, but these are just an alias for `CGSize`.

- Add the following line to the very top of **JSTileMap.m**, so that it will build in OS X mode inside the PestControlMac target:

```
#define TARGET_OSX (TARGET_OS_IPHONE == 0)
```

- Change **AppDelegate.swift** so that it doesn't load the scene from GameScene.sks but instantiates it programmatically, just like GameViewController.swift does it. A scene size of 800 by 600 points looks just right.

- If the PestControlMacTests target gives you a compile error, simply delete that target from the Project Settings screen.

- If you get the error "+[SKEmitterNode nodeWithFileNamed:]: unrecognized selector" when you run the game, add the file **SKEmitterNode+Extras.swift** to both the Mac and iOS targets and replace all calls to `SKEmitterNode(fileNamed: . . .)` with `SKEmitterNode.emitterNamed(. . .)`.

It's quite a few steps, but now you've got PestControl running on the Mac!

Section V: Other Game APIs

In this section, you'll learn about some APIs other than Sprite Kit that are good to know when making games for iOS. In particular, you will learn how to make user interfaces with UIKit; control movement with the accelerometer; and expand your OS X skills.

In the process, you will create a top-down racing game called Circuit Racer, where you take the role of an elite racecar driver out to set a world record. It would be no problem if it weren't for the debris on the track!

Chapter 20: UIKit

Chapter 21: Accelerometer

Chapter 22: More OS X

Chapter 20: UIKit

By Marin Todorov

If you've made your way through the entire book up to this point, you've created four minigames: Zombie Conga, XBlaster, Cat Nap and Pest Control. In the process, you've learned a ton about making Sprite Kit games—from sprites to actions to nodes to physics to tile maps, and much else in between.

But there's more to making games than the Sprite Kit APIs themselves. One of the advantages of Sprite Kit is that it's easy to integrate the rest of the frameworks in the iOS ecosystem that you may have learned about in our *iOS Apprentice* and *iOS by Tutorials* series. For example, you can use other iOS APIs in your game to make remote calls to web services, save data to iCloud and make in-app purchases.

In this chapter, you'll learn how to integrate one of these frameworks into your Sprite Kit games: a user interface library called UIKit.

The games you've created so far have all used Xcode's built-in Sprite Kit template, which provides you with a simple starter project made up of a storyboard with just one view controller to display a Sprite Kit view on the screen. This way, your Sprite Kit scene is displayed as soon as the app launches, so players can immediately begin enjoying your game.

That's a great starting point, but for most games, you want to provide some sort of menu first, so the player can do things like load saved games (as you can see in the screenshot to the lower left), select game difficulty, choose a level to play (as you can see in the screenshot to the lower right), and more.

You'll also need a GUI *inside* your game for in-game controls (as you can see in the screenshot to the lower left), the head-up display (HUD), in-game menus (as you can see in the screenshot to the lower right) and more.

You could make user interfaces like this in Sprite Kit using sprites and a ton of custom code, but this would be reinventing the wheel. Apple already has a library called UIKit that's chock full of controls you can use in your apps, such as buttons, table views and scroll views.

If you've made any iPhone apps in the past, then you've probably used UIKit before. The goal of this chapter isn't to teach you UIKit, as plenty of tutorials and books already do that quite well. Rather, this chapter will show you how to integrate UIKit into your Sprite Kit games.

> **Note:** If you're completely new to UIKit, don't worry—you can still follow along with this chapter. However, you might want to go through our *iOS Apprentice* or *iOS by Tutorials* series if you'd like to learn more about what you can do with UIKit.

Throughout this and the next few chapters, you'll create the fifth and final minigame in this book: **Circuit Racer**. Here's what it will look like when you're finished:

In Circuit Racer, players take the role of an elite racecar driver out to set a world record. It would be no problem if it weren't for the debris on the track!

You'll build this game across the next six chapters, in stages:

1. **Chapter 20, UIKit**: You are here! You'll get started by integrating UIKit with Sprite Kit to create view controllers for your game's different screens, as well as use standard iOS controls within your main game scene itself, such via an onscreen joypad.

2. **Chapter 21, Accelerometer**: You'll use the device's built-in accelerometer to move your sprites around the screen.

3. **Chapter 22, More OS X**: You'll port the game to work on OS X. This will be a bit more complicated than the previous games since this game has a UIKit interface you'll need to port as well.

> **Note**: The gameplay idea behind Circuit Racer originates from one of the examples included with the AndEngine game engine. The code you'll develop will be completely different from that of the AndEngine game, but we still think it's appropriate to give them credit.

There's a lot to cover, so let's get started!

Getting started

> **Note**: The first part of this chapter covers building the initial implementation of Circuit Racer, which is a review of material already covered in this book.
>
> If you think you have a strong handle on the material so far and would rather jump straight to UIKit integration, you can skip ahead to the section called "UIKit game controls." We'll have a starter project waiting for you there!

Start Xcode and select **File\New\Project...** from the main menu. Select the **iOS\Application\Game** template and click **Next**.

Enter **CircuitRacer** for the Product Name, select **Swift** as Language, **Sprite Kit** as Game Technology, choose **Universal** for Devices and click **Next**. Choose somewhere on your hard drive to save your project and click **Create**. At this point, Xcode will generate the standard Sprite Kit starter project for you.

On the **General Project properties** screen (open by default when you create a new project), make sure only **Landscape Left** is selected so your game will start in landscape mode instead of portrait mode. You're only supporting Landscape Left rather than both landscape orientations because you'll be adding accelerometer support in the next chapter, and it will be easier to support just one device orientation.

```
Device Orientation  ☐ Portrait
                    ☐ Upside Down
                    ☑ Landscape Left
                    ☐ Landscape Right
```

You also need to modify this in one more spot. Open **Supporting Files\Info.plist**, and find the **Supported interface orientations (iPad)** entry. Delete the entries for **Portrait (bottom home button)**, **Portrait (top home button)**, and **Landscape (right home button)** you see there, so that only the landscape left option remains.

Open the assets folder for this chapter and drag and drop the folder called **Resources** onto Xcode's project file list, making sure **Copy items if needed** is checked. These are all the assets you'll need throughout the Circuit Racer chapters:

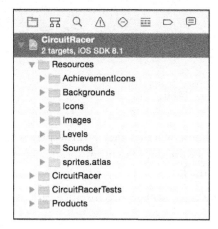

As with previous games in this book, you have your sprite images inside the folder sprite.atlas (so that Xcode will automatically create a texture atlas for you), screen backgrounds in Backgrounds and level configuration files in Levels. Peek inside these folders if you want to see all the coolness coming your way!

One last step: For polish, let's give the game an icon. Open **Images.xassets** and select the **AppIcon** entry. Then in the Art for this chapter that you've already copied over, drag all the relevant files from the **Icons/iOS** folder into the area on the right. You should see the following when you're done:

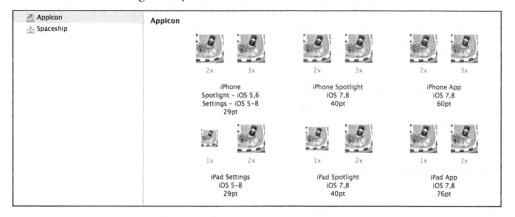

Initializing the scene

It's time to begin coding. The completed mini-game will feature several different tracks and cars, so you need to define a few constants. Open **GameScene.swift,** delete all of the existing methods inside the class and add the following at the top of the file, outside of the class:

```
enum CarType: Int {
  case Yellow, Blue, Red
}

enum LevelType: Int {
  case Easy, Medium, Hard
}
```

The player will be able to choose whether they want to play with a yellow, blue or red car, each of which will have a different maximum speed, and they will also be able to choose the difficulty of the track.

Next, inside the GameScene class, declare two instance variables to store the scene settings:

```
var carType: CarType!
var levelType: LevelType!
```

> **Note:** carType and levelType won't be initialized until the player has selected a car and a level. As Swift enforces initialization of non-optional variables, it makes sense for these to be optionals. However, as you'll always have the carType and levelType variables set before using them in the game, you've used the ! to declare these as implicitly unwrapped optionals. This makes the variables a lot easier to access, and the only thing you have to do in your code is ensure they're not accessed before they've been initialized.

Next, add the following didMoveToView(view:) implementation, as well as a method that you'll call as soon as the scene appears onscreen. This new method is going to perform all of your initialization.

```
override func didMoveToView(view: SKView) {
  initializeGame()
}

private func initializeGame() {

}
```

You'll fill out initializeGame() quite soon.

Configuring the levels

Now that your scene is in shape, it's time to clean up your view controller. Open **GameViewController.swift** and scroll to `viewDidLoad()`. Before presenting the scene, you need to configure which track and car to display. Add the following lines of code just before you present the scene:

```
scene.levelType = LevelType.Easy
scene.carType = CarType.Yellow
```

In `viewDidLoad()`, as usual, you grab a reference to your `SKView`, create an instance of your scene and present it onscreen. For now, you have the car and level types hard-coded, but later in the chapter, you'll allow the player to choose.

Here are the level details you'll load from **LevelDetails.plist**:

Key	Type	Value
▼ Root	Array	(3 items)
▼ Item 0	Dictionary	(2 items)
time	Number	15
laps	Number	2
▼ Item 1	Dictionary	(2 items)
time	Number	25
laps	Number	5
▼ Item 2	Dictionary	(2 items)
time	Number	35
laps	Number	10

As you can see, for each increase in track difficulty, the player has less time to do the required number of laps. To load the level configuration, open **GameScene.swift** and add the following private instance variables:

```
private var timeInSeconds = 0
private var numberOfLaps = 0
```

You'll use these to store the level settings. Now add this new method:

```
private func loadLevel() {
  let filePath = NSBundle.mainBundle().pathForResource(
    "LevelDetails", ofType: "plist")!

  let levels = NSArray(contentsOfFile: filePath)!

  let levelData = levels[levelType.rawValue] as! NSDictionary

  timeInSeconds = levelData["time"] as! Int
```

```
    numberOfLaps = levelData["laps"] as! Int
}
```

This method loads LevelDetails.plist. Then, it fetches the time and laps keys from the first, second or third elements in the PLIST file, depending on levelType's value.

Now add another auxiliary method that sets the correct track background image based on the level type set for the scene:

```
private func loadTrackTexture() {
    let track = self.childNodeWithName("track") as! SKSpriteNode
    track.texture = SKTexture(imageNamed:
        "track_\(levelType.rawValue + 1)")
}
```

You fetch the track node and set its texture. At present, this code always sets *track_0.png* as the texture for the track node.

There is but one problem: You don't have a sprite on the scene to show the track's background. If only all problems in life were this easy to fix.

Open **GameScene.sks** and set the scene size as follows:

Width	Height
2048	1536

Next drag a single Color Sprite object onto the empty scene. Adjust its properties as shown below:

Texture	Name	X-Position	Y-Position	Width	Height
track_1.png	track	1024	768	2048	1536

You pre-set the texture of the track node in Scene Editor so you can position the rest of the game objects relative to the track onscreen. Since all tracks have the same general layout, game objects' positions will work for all levels. You only need to set the correct track texture from code.

With your level ready to go, open **GameScene.swift** and add this code to initializeGame() to load the level details and show the level background, depending on the level configuration:

```
loadLevel()
loadTrackTexture()
```

Game on! Build and run. Woot!

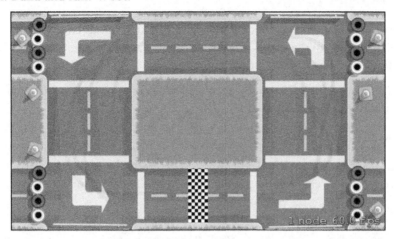

You can barely see the track fence on an iPhone screen, but if you run the project on an iPad simulator, you'll see the background stretching nicely beyond the area of the track where the player can actually race:

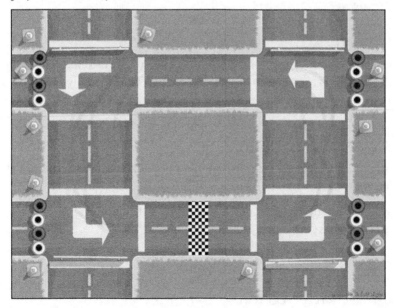

Just like in previous games, you're going to restrict the gameplay of Circuit Racer to a core "playable area" that is visible across all devices, so it's no problem that you can see extra room on the iPad.

A little physics review

Let's start this chapter section, which is a review of what you learned about physics in Sprite Kit, by setting up the level's playable area (same as you've done for the rest of the games in this book) as well as the track boundaries.

First, turn on physics visualization by opening **GameViewController.swift** and adding the following line to viewDidLoad():

```
skView.showsPhysics = true
```

Next, open **GameScene.swift** and add a method to create the physics bodies for your game objects. Start by creating the physics body for the inner boundary of the track:

```
private func setupPhysicsBodies() {
  let innerBoundary = SKNode()
  innerBoundary.position = childNodeWithName("track")!.position
  addChild(innerBoundary)

  innerBoundary.physicsBody = SKPhysicsBody(rectangleOfSize:
    CGSizeMake(720, 480))
  innerBoundary.physicsBody!.dynamic = false
}
```

You create a new SKNode. There's no texture associated with this node, as the boundary is part of the track's texture already. You are adding this node simply for its physics body. You position the boundary in the center of the track and add it to the scene.

Then, you create a new body of 720x480 points for innerBoundary, and since it's never going to move around, you set its dynamic property to false.

Good job so far! However, the track has an outer boundary, as well—you can clearly see the fence around it. The cars should not be able to drive through this fence.

This sounds like a job for an edge loop body. Append the following to setupPhysicsBodies():

```
let trackFrame = CGRectInset(
  self.childNodeWithName("track")!.frame, 200, 0)

let maxAspectRatio: CGFloat = 3.0/2.0 // iPhone 4
let maxAspectRatioHeight = trackFrame.size.width /
  maxAspectRatio
let playableMarginY: CGFloat = (trackFrame.size.height –
  maxAspectRatioHeight)/2
```

```
let playableMarginX: CGFloat = (frame.size.width -
  trackFrame.size.width)/2

let playableRect = CGRect(x: playableMarginX,
  y: playableMarginY,
  width: trackFrame.size.width,
  height: trackFrame.size.height-playableMarginY*2)

physicsBody = SKPhysicsBody(edgeLoopFromRect: playableRect)
```

You are already familiar with this code from previous scenes. It detects the current playable area from the scene size.

You start by subtracting 200 points from the left and right sides of the track node (look at the image, and you'll see the sides are cut off by fence) and then, based on the iPhone 4's screen dimensions, you detect the current playable area.

You use the `playableRect` to create an edge loop body for your scene, and you're done! Now you just need to call `setupPhysicsBodies()` to see the bodies onscreen. Add this to the end of `initializeGame()`:

```
setupPhysicsBodies()
```

Build and run the game:

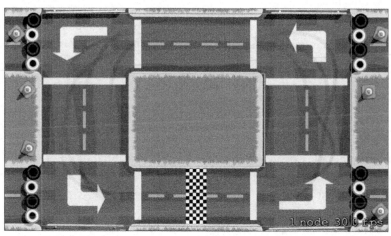

Now you can see the inner boundary (in green) and outer boundary (in blue) on the screen.

Next, add the rest of the game objects to the scene. Open **GameScene.sks** and add these three Color Sprites:

Texture	Name	Position	Body Type	Category Mask	Collision Mask	W	H
car_2.png	car	848, 442	Alpha Mask	1	2	200	120
box.png	box_1	1722, 762	Bounding Rectangle	2	1	176	176
box.png	box_2	314, 748	Bounding Rectangle	2	1	176	176

You are adding the car at the starting line, as well as two crates that will serve as track obstacles.

There's an extra step you need to take to configure your car sprite. In Circuit Racer, you'll update the car's orientation manually; therefore, you need to instruct Sprite Kit to leave that to you.

Select the car sprite and in the Assistant Editor, find the checkbox called **Allows Rotation** and uncheck it.

Now, just as you did for the track image, you'll update the car node texture based on the current scene configuration. Open **GameScene.swift** and add this method:

```
private func loadCarTexture() {
  let car = self.childNodeWithName("car") as! SKSpriteNode
  car.texture = SKTexture(imageNamed:
    "car_\(carType.rawValue + 1)")
}
```

This method fetches the existing car sprite as a local constant and uses it to set the correct image for the car. For now, you'll see only the yellow car, but you'll change that later on in this chapter.

Add a call to `loadCarTexture()` at the end of `initializeGame()`:

```
loadCarTexture()
```

Run the project, and you'll see your newly added game objects:

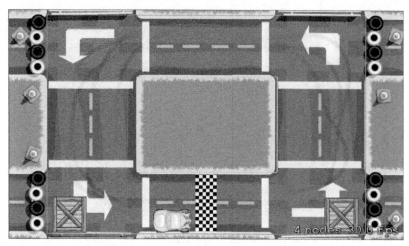

Hmm, that's not right! All the objects fall down to the bottom of the screen.

This happens because by default, Sprite Kit sets a gravity simulation for your game scene. But this is a top-down game, so you don't need gravity! Let's turn it off for good.

Back in **GameScene.sks**, without selecting anything, the following scene properties will appear in the Assistant Editor:

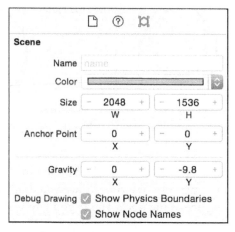

Notice that Sprite Kit sets a default gravity vector of (0, -9,8). To disable the gravity, just set the gravity to (0, 0) and run the project again:

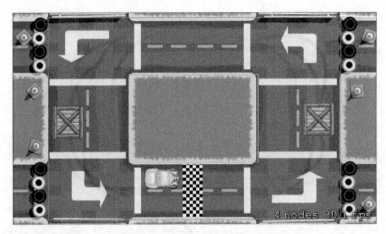

Now you'll see the yellow car positioned at the start line and ready to race!

Speaking of racing cars, you're going to use physics bodies to detect collisions and contacts with the track fence and track obstacles. Of course, having completed Cat Nap, you're already a master of contacts and collisions.

For now, though, you're going to finish configuring the crates and then move on to the game's UI.

Open **GameScene.sks** and select the two crates by holding the Cmd key on your keyboard while clicking the crates one at a time. Since you don't want collisions with cars to send the crates flying across the track, you're going to make the crates extraordinarily heavy.

Set the **Mass** property for both nodes to **10:**

Then, open **GameScene.swift** and add these two instance variables to your GameScene class:

```
private var box1: SKSpriteNode!, box2: SKSpriteNode!
```

As you did for the other objects, add a relevant helper method:

```
private func loadObstacles() {
   box1 = self.childNodeWithName("box_1") as! SKSpriteNode
   box2 = self.childNodeWithName("box_2") as! SKSpriteNode
}
```

Finally, add a call to loadObstacles() at the end of intializeGame():

```
loadObstacles()
```

Build and run. What an outrage! Somebody could crash into those boxes! Well, if your car could move, that is.

Your first taste of the user interface

Before you get to drive your car, there's one step left.

Although you'll create much of this game's user interface from UIKit controls, there's one aspect of UIs that Sprite Kit can do well, as you may remember from your old friend XBlaster—drawing labels.

So as the last step of the game setup, you'll add two labels in the center of the screen to show the player how much time she has left and how many laps remain.

Switch back to **GameScene.sks** in Scene Editor and add two Label objects to the scene. Adjust the labels' properties to be like so:

Name	Position	Text	Font
laps_label	982, 824	Laps:	Chalkduster 112.0
time_left_label	958, 664	Time:	Chalkduster 112.0

> **Note**: In the fonts panel the maximum size is 100 points. Just click the text field and enter 112 instead of dragging the font size slider.

These two labels will display in-game info at the center of the screen. You'll need to access the labels from code, so open **GameScene.swift** and add these two private instance variables to the class:

```
private var laps: SKLabelNode!, time: SKLabelNode!
```

Then add this new method:

```
private func addLabels() {
  laps = self.childNodeWithName("laps_label") as! SKLabelNode
  time = self.childNodeWithName("time_left_label") as!
    SKLabelNode

  laps.text = "Laps: \(numberOfLaps)"
  time.text = "Time: \(timeInSeconds)"
}
```

Inside addLabels(), you connect the two label nodes and set up their initial text. The laps label node displays the laps to go, as specified by LevelDetails.plist according to the track's difficulty, and time shows the time left to finish the laps remaining. You position both labels in the center of the track, within the inner boundary area.

Call this new method at the end of initializeGame():

```
addLabels()
```

That's it for the basic game setup! It was a long stretch, no doubt... but for your trouble, build and run one last time, and you'll see the labels onscreen:

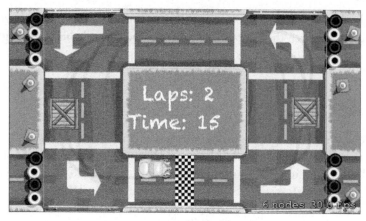

Now let's turn your attention to UIKit, beginning with making the car move!

UIKit game controls

> **Note**: If you skipped the last section of the chapter, open the project **CircuitRacer-SkippedSetup** from the chapter's assets folder to continue from here.

In this section, you'll implement a classic joypad control in Circuit Racer that the player will use to control the car. You'll create the joypad as a normal UIView and add it on top of the game scene. Then, you'll make your scene read the knob position to change the car's velocity.

Here's how the joypad will look when you're finished:

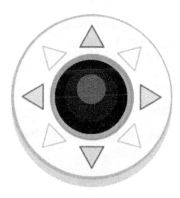

You probably already know how to use one of these from playing games on your iPhone or iPod touch. You touch the knob in the center of the control and then drag it around to control a hero, a car or a gun inside the game. It's quite easy to make a joypad, so let's get to it!

Adding the joypad

As you've done for several other games in this book, you'll integrate the SKTUtils library into this game. You can find SKTUtils in the root folder for this book. Drag the entire **SKTUtils** folder into the project navigator in Xcode. Make sure **Copy items if needed** and the **CircuitRacer** target are both checked, and click **Finish**.

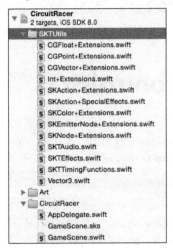

Next, from Xcode's menu, select **File/New/File...** and as a template, select the **iOS/Source/Cocoa Touch Class**. Enter **AnalogControl** as the class name and make it a subclass of **UIView**. Remember to make sure **Swift** is selected as the Language. Click **Next** and make sure the new class is included in your **CircuitRacer** target and create the file.

Switch to **AnalogControl.swift** and add a couple of constants to the AnalogControl class:

```
let baseCenter: CGPoint
let knobImageView: UIImageView
```

In this chunk of code, you add two instance variables that you'll need soon—the building blocks of the completed joypad:

• knobImageView is for the joypad knob image onscreen.

- **baseCenter** will store the "neutral" position of the control—that is, the center of the control's frame.

You'll immediately see an error in the editor—Xcode complains that you have constants that are not initialized in the custom class `init`. Hold your horses Xcode; not everything can be done at once!

Let's add substance to `initWithFrame(frame:)` to get something more than an error message and an empty transparent view onscreen. Add a new `init` method with the following code:

```
override init(frame viewFrame: CGRect) {

  //1
  baseCenter = CGPoint(x: viewFrame.size.width/2,
    y: viewFrame.size.height/2)

  //2
  knobImageView = UIImageView(image: UIImage(named: "knob"))
  knobImageView.frame.size.width /= 2
  knobImageView.frame.size.height /= 2
  knobImageView.center = baseCenter

  super.init(frame: viewFrame)

  //3
  userInteractionEnabled = true

  //4
  let baseImageView = UIImageView(frame: bounds)
  baseImageView.image = UIImage(named: "base")
  addSubview(baseImageView)

  //5
  addSubview(knobImageView)

  //6
  assert(CGRectContainsRect(bounds, knobImageView.bounds),
      "Analog control should be larger than the knob in size")
}
```

Let's go over this section by section:

1. You calculate the center of the control's frame—this will be the neutral position for the knob.

2. You create an image view out of knob.png and position it neutrally. Also you adjust the size of the knob image so its exactly half of the width and height of the whole view. This is the proper size of the knob when visible on screen.

3. After calling the superclass' init(frame:), you instruct the view to handle touches by setting userInteractionEnabled to true.

4. Then, you create an image view out of base.png and make it fit the control's frame.

5. You add the knob image to the view.

6. Finally, you check if the control's bounding box contains the entire knob, just to make sure the knob fits the base image. This check will always pass for the assets you have for Circuit Racer, but if you reuse this class for your own games, the check might save you some debugging time.

Also, add this required initializer to make the compiler happy:

```
required init(coder aDecoder: NSCoder) {
    fatalError("NSCoding not supported")
}
```

Xcode is finally happy and the class is ready to show a nice joypad control on screen.

Displaying the joypad

Now it's time to step back for a moment and think about where and how to display the joypad on the screen. This is a UIKit view control, and therefore, you can't add it to GameScene. You'll have to add it to your GameViewController's view, instead.

Open **GameViewController.swift** and add this instance variable to the class:

```
private var analogControl: AnalogControl!
```

Now you only need to display the view on the screen, so add this at the bottom of the if statement in viewDidLoad(), taking care to put the code *inside* the if statement:

```
let padSide: CGFloat = view.frame.size.height / 2.5
let padPadding: CGFloat = view.frame.size.height / 32

analogControl = AnalogControl(frame: CGRectMake(padPadding,
    skView.frame.size.height - padPadding - padSide,
    padSide, padSide))

view.addSubview(analogControl)
```

You set the bottom-left corner of the screen, where joypads usually reside, as the origin of the control. You make the control grow or shrink based on the current screen size, putting yourself on a path to having Circuit Racer run on iPad and OS X, too. For reference, on an iPhone screen, the size of the control would be 256x256 points.

The following diagram shows you how you use the padPadding and padSide constants to create the frame. Remember, in UIKit (0, 0) represents the top-left of the screen rather than the bottom-left in Sprite Kit, so to get the y-coordinate, you have to subtract padPadding from the height of the screen.

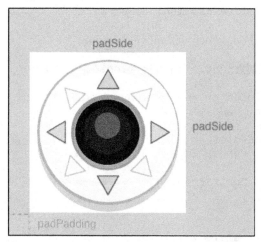

Build and run the project to see your first UIKit game control onscreen:

Seeing that pad, don't you just want to grab it and drive the car around the track? If you try that, you'll see that instead of leaping forward, the car stays still.

Wiring up the joypad

The main task of the analog control is to expose the position of the knob to other classes in the game. Therefore, you need a new property on the `AnalogControl` class to do that. Open **AnalogControl.swift** and add a new variable to the class:

```
private var relativePosition: CGPoint!
```

Add the following method, which will move the knob:

```
func updateKnobWithPosition(position:CGPoint) {
  //1
  var positionToCenter = position - baseCenter
  var direction: CGPoint

  if positionToCenter == CGPointZero {
    direction = CGPointZero
  } else {
    direction = positionToCenter.normalized()
  }

  //2
  let radius = frame.size.width/2
  var length = positionToCenter.length()

  //3
  if length > radius {
    length = radius
    positionToCenter = direction * radius
  }
}
```

Let's go over this section by section:

1. You subtract the position of the touch from the center of the joypad image. This gives you a relative offset for the touch location. You also get the direction of the offset by normalizing the vector, as you learned to do in Chapter 2, "Manual Movement."

2. This joypad is circular, so you don't want the knob to move further outside of the radius of the joypad image. Here, you calculate the radius and the length of the relative offset.

3. If the length is greater than the radius, then you make a vector that points in the same direction but has the length of the radius, instead. You do this by multiplying the normal vector (which has a length of 1) by the radius, as you also learned in Chapter 2.

You're not finished with this method just yet. Continue by adding this code to the bottom of `updateKnobWithPosition(position:)`:

```
let relPosition = CGPoint(x: direction.x * (length/radius),
    y: direction.y * (length/radius))
```

This converts the direction into a vector of length (length/radius)—in other words, the closer the knob is to the edge of the circle, the closer the length will be to 1. This will be helpful when moving the car later.

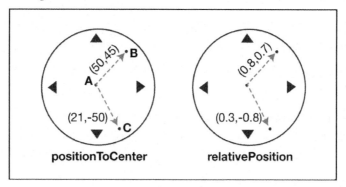

You need to update the control with the calculated position, so add at the end of the method:

```
knobImageView.center = baseCenter + positionToCenter
relativePosition = relPosition
```

`SKTUtils` really shines when used for tasks that involve a lot of geometry, like the one above. Notice how you simply use the + operator to add one point (`baseCenter`) to another point (`positionToCenter`).

The last step is to implement the standard `UIView` touch-handling callbacks so the player will be able to drag the knob around. Add these new methods to `AnalogControl`:

```
override func touchesBegan(touches: Set<NSObject>,
    withEvent event: UIEvent) {

    let touchLocation = (touches.first! as!
UITouch).locationInView(self)
```

```
        updateKnobWithPosition(touchLocation)
    }

    override func touchesMoved(touches: Set<NSObject>,
      withEvent event: UIEvent) {

        let touchLocation = (touches.first! as!
    UITouch).locationInView(self)
        updateKnobWithPosition(touchLocation)
    }

    override func touchesEnded(touches: Set<NSObject>,
      withEvent event: UIEvent) {

        updateKnobWithPosition(baseCenter)
    }

    override func touchesCancelled(touches: Set<NSObject>,
      withEvent event: UIEvent) {

        updateKnobWithPosition(baseCenter)
    }
```

When the player touches the screen and drags, you call
updateKnobWithPosition(position:) with the position of the touch. When the
touch ends, you call updateKnobWithPosition(position:) with baseCenter, which
sets the knob back to its neutral position.

Believe it or not, that's all. Run the game again, and fool around with the joypad.

At least one thing in this game is moving!

Using physics for positioning

Now that you have the car direction vector, you want to be able to move that car around the track. Luckily, that's going to be very easy to implement. A physics body's velocity is also a vector, so all you need to do is take the `relativePosition` of `AnalogControl` and set the current velocity of your car's body.

Using delegation

To connect your UIKit control to your Sprite Kit scene, you're going to make your scene a delegate of the control. This is the easiest and fastest way to connect those two classes and make them exchange data.

Another approach would be to use key-value-observing. You might want to go the observing route if there were other classes in addition to the scene class that were interested in the current joypad position.

Switch to **AnalogControl.swift** and just above the class declaration; add a new protocol for the control's delegate class:

```
protocol AnalogControlPositionChange {
  func analogControlPositionChanged(
    analogControl: AnalogControl, position: CGPoint)
}
```

Add a variable to `AnalogControl` to store the class's delegate:

```
var delegate: AnalogControlPositionChange?
```

The joypad's delegate will have to implement a single method, which will receive the current position of the knob. Easy and simple.

Back in **GameScene.swift**, make `GameScene` conform to this new protocol:

```
class GameScene: SKScene, AnalogControlPositionChange {
```

Xcode immediately lets you know that you didn't implement the protocol method, so let's add a simple stub to the class:

```
func analogControlPositionChanged(analogControl: AnalogControl,
  position: CGPoint) {

}
```

Finally, open **GameViewController.swift** and add the following to `viewDidLoad()`, inside the body of the `if` statement:

```
analogControl.delegate = scene
```

This sets up the communication between the control and the scene quite nicely.

Translating direction vectors into movement

Next, you'll translate the joypad's direction vector to a velocity vector that will move the car. You'll need to define the maximum speed of the car and then multiply `relativePosition` vector by that speed—that will give you the car's momentous velocity. For example, a direction vector of (0.67, 0.45) will set the car's velocity to (167.5, 112.5) for a car with a maximum speed of 250:

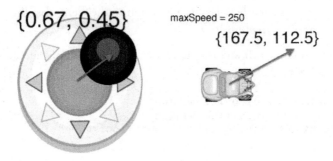

In **GameScene.swift**, add the code that will determine the car's maximum speed based on the car type. First, add an instance variable to store the maximum speed:

```
private var maxSpeed = 0
```

And add this line at the end of `initializeGame()`:

```
maxSpeed = 500 * (2 + carType.rawValue)
```

This line at the end of `initializeGame()` will set `maxSpeed` to either 1000, 1500 or 2000, depending on the car type. The value of `carType` is 0, 1 or 2—you can look it up at the top of the source code.

Now that you can calculate the car's velocity based on the joypad's `relativePosition` and the car's maximum speed, the only thing left to do is move the car when the player moves the knob. Replace your `analogControlPositionChanged(analogControl:, position:)` stub with the following code:

```swift
func analogControlPositionChanged(analogControl: AnalogControl,
  position: CGPoint)  {

  let car = self.childNodeWithName("car") as! SKSpriteNode

  car.physicsBody!.velocity = CGVector(
    dx: position.x * CGFloat(maxSpeed),
    dy: -position.y * CGFloat(maxSpeed))
}
```

This fancy new method takes in a reference to the analog control and sets the car's velocity to the `relativePosition` vector multiplied by `maxSpeed`.

Note that you negate the y-axis. Can you guess why?

I hope you nailed it: The coordinate systems of UIKit and Sprite Kit differ. In UIKit, the y-coordinate increases toward the bottom of the screen, while in Sprite Kit, it increases toward the top of the screen.

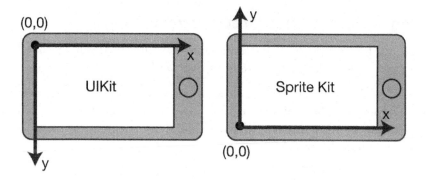

There's one remaining step. You still don't call the delegate method from your `AnalogControl` class. Open **AnalogControl.swift** and add this at the bottom of `updateKnobWithPosition(position:)`:

```swift
delegate?.analogControlPositionChanged(self,
  position: relativePosition)
```

It's that easy—you just call `analogControlPositionChanged(analogControl:, position:)` on the delegate and pass in the relative position of the knob.

With that, you've connecting all the dots on your game controls treasure map! Build, run and enjoy.

At this point, you can control the car via the onscreen joypad and you can also test those track boundaries and crash into the obstacles.

Rotating sprites using a direction vector

Let's make one final touch—the car doesn't take those turns very well. By the time it gets to the other side of the track, it's running backwards!

In Chapter 11, "Advanced Physics," you used a constraint to make sure the rope is always oriented toward the hook in Cat Nap's Level 3. In Circuit Racer, you have a similar problem, but you don't have a reference point or node to use for the constraint, so you need a different approach.

Luckily, when you have the direction vector, it's quite easy to set the car sprite's `zRotation` so it will always face the direction of movement.

In **GameScene.swift**, scroll down and add the following at the end of `analogControlPositionChanged(_:, position:)`:

```
if position != CGPointZero {
  car.zRotation = CGPoint(x: position.x, y: -position.y).angle
}
```

First, you check if the knob is in the neutral position. If so, you don't change the car's orientation. Otherwise, you get an angle out of the `relativePosition` vector (with inverted y-axis) and simply set the result as the car's `zRotation`.

Build and run. Now the car rotates as you steer it toward the finish line. Sweet!

I hope you're getting more and more accustomed to using the functions found in SKTUtils—as you've seen, they can greatly simplify your coding tasks.

In this section, you learned how to add UIKit controls to your game and how to communicate between UIKit and Sprite Kit classes. Your next big task is to monitor the car's progress on the track and decrease the number of laps remaining with each completed revolution. In other words, it's gameplay time!

Implementing the gameplay

In Circuit Racer, you need to know when the user successfully completes a lap. Unfortunately, it's not as simple as tracking when the car crosses the finish line—if it were, a clever player could make the car go back and forth across the finish line to win in no time!

So to determine when the user actually completes a lap, you'll divide the track into four sections and decrease the laps remaining only if the car has passed through all four sections of the track. To do this, you'll need to calculate the angle between the car sprite and the center of the track:

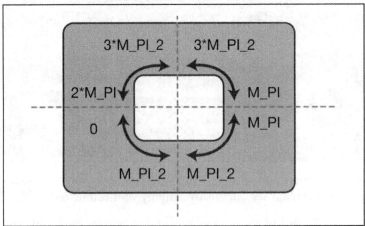

Your car starts at angle M_PI_2 (90 degrees) and when it passes M_PI (180 degrees), that means it's reached the next quadrant. Every time the car reaches the next target angle, you need to set a new target by adding M_PI_2. When the target angle is greater than 2*M_PI (on the left side of the scheme above), you need to set it back to M_PI_2, the starting car point. Finally, each time the car passes through the M_PI_2 angle (the starting point), you need to decrease the number of laps remaining. That's the entire game logic, right there!

Tracking the car

Let's put this into code. You'll take care of the car tracking in the game loop. Add these variables to the class in **GameScene.swift**:

```
private var trackCenter = CGPoint.zeroPoint
private var nextProgressAngle = M_PI
```

At the end of initializeGame(), initialize trackCenter to the track's position—that is, the center of the screen:

```
trackCenter = childNodeWithName("track")!.position
```

Then, add the following update(currentTime:) method:

```
override func update(currentTime: CFTimeInterval) {
```

```
    let carPosition = childNodeWithName("car")!.position
    let vector = carPosition - trackCenter
    let progressAngle = Double(vector.angle) + M_PI
}
```

Let's go over each line in turn:

1. First, you fetch the current car position.

2. You then subtract `trackCenter` from `car.position`.

3. Finally, you use `angle` on the resulting vector `CGPoint` to get the angle for the subtraction result. Since `angle` returns values between −M_PI and M_PI, you add another M_PI to the result so you have only positive values for `progressAngle`. That makes calculations much easier.

Look at the last scheme on the previous page and you'll see how `progressAngle` is tied to the calculations you're going to make to track the car's progress through the four quadrants. Speaking of which, add this chunk of code at the end of `update(currentTime:)` to do your tracking:

```
//1
if progressAngle > nextProgressAngle
  && (progressAngle - nextProgressAngle) < M_PI_4 {

  //2
  nextProgressAngle += M_PI_2

  //3
  if nextProgressAngle >= (2 * M_PI) {
    nextProgressAngle = 0
  }

  //4
  if fabs(nextProgressAngle - M_PI) < Double(FLT_EPSILON) {
    //lap completed!
  }
}
```

Let's go over this one section at a time:

1. In the `if` condition, you check whether the current angle is greater than the next target, but you're only interested if the current angle is greater by just a bit: M_PI_4. This prevents the player from cheating by going backward.

2. When the `if` condition is met, you increase the next target by M_PI_2, which is equal to one quadrant in the scheme above.

3. Then, you check if the next target is greater than 2*M_PI and if so, you reset the target to 0.

4. Finally, you check if the next target angle equals M_PI. If it does, that means the car just passed through the finish line and is heading to the right side of the screen.

    Many programmers don't realize that they can't reliably compare two float variables by using ==, so mind the equality condition to compare nextProgressAngle and M_PI.

    You can read more about comparing float numbers here:

    http://www.mikeash.com/pyblog/friday-qa-2011-01-04-practical-floating-point.html

Finally, replace the **//lap completed!** placeholder with this:

```
numberOfLaps -= 1
laps.text = "Laps: \(numberOfLaps)"
```

That will take one lap off the lap count and update the UI accordingly.

Build and run, and give the game a try – every time you pass through the finish line, you'll see the number of laps decrease.

That was easier than expected.

Gratuitous sound effects

Hey, completing a lap is fun! Let's spice it up a bit with some sound effects.

First, add these four instance variables to the GameScene in **GameScene.swift** for all the sounds you'll eventually use in Circuit Racer (all declared on a single line):

```
private var boxSoundAction: SKAction!, hornSoundAction:
SKAction!, lapSoundAction: SKAction!, nitroSoundAction:
SKAction!
```

Then, initialize them at the end of initializeGame():

```
boxSoundAction = SKAction.playSoundFileNamed("box.wav",
  waitForCompletion: false)
hornSoundAction = SKAction.playSoundFileNamed("horn.wav",
  waitForCompletion: false)
lapSoundAction = SKAction.playSoundFileNamed("lap.wav",
  waitForCompletion: false)
nitroSoundAction = SKAction.playSoundFileNamed("nitro.wav",
  waitForCompletion: false)
```

Finally, add this line after setting the laps.text in update(currentTime:):

```
runAction(lapSoundAction)
```

Build, run, and complete a lap—vroom, vroom!

Tracking time

To finish up this game, you need to keep track of time. In Circuit Racer, a player only has a certain number of seconds to complete all the laps before she loses!

Make the following changes to **GameScene.swift** to add the game timer. First, add a private instance variable:

```
private var previousTimeInterval: CFTimeInterval = 0
```

This new instance variable will store the last time `update:` ran, which you need to calculate the delta time between runs of the game loop. You have used this technique in several other games in this book.

Insert the following code **at the top** of `update(currentTime:)`:

```
if previousTimeInterval == 0 {
  previousTimeInterval = currentTime
}

if paused {
  previousTimeInterval = currentTime
  return
}

if currentTime - previousTimeInterval > 1 {
  timeInSeconds -= Int(currentTime - previousTimeInterval)
  previousTimeInterval = currentTime
  if timeInSeconds >= 0 {
    time.text = "Time: \(timeInSeconds)"
  }
}
```

Here you handle three cases via three `if` statements:

1. If `previousTimeInterval` hasn't been initialized, simply save the current time, running `update(currentTime:)` for the first time.

2. If the scene is paused, don't decrease the player's remaining time. It may seem strange, but the app continues to call `update(currentTime:)` even while your scene is paused, as discussed in Chapter 17, "Saving and Loading Games."

3. Finally, if the delta time since the previous time check is more than a second, update `timeInSeconds` and `previousTimeInterval` to the current values and then update the UI with the new amount of time remaining.

That should get your timer ticking. Give it a try!

Implementing a UIKit callback

Since your `GameViewController` is now taking care of the scene flow, whenever the game reaches either a win or a lose state, you would like your `GameScene` class to pass the ball back to the view controller.

Open **GameScene.swift** and declare a new custom closure property in `GameScene`:

```
typealias GameOverBlock = (didWin: Bool) -> Void
var gameOverBlock: GameOverBlock?
```

`GameViewController` will pass a block to be executed upon game finish to the scene class. The block takes in one Boolean parameter so that the closure knows whether the player won or lost.

Add at the end of `update(_:)`:

```
if timeInSeconds < 0 || numberOfLaps == 0 {
  paused = true

  if let block = gameOverBlock {
    block(didWin: numberOfLaps == 0)
  }
}
```

The code easily detects a game over state by checking whether the player is out of time or out of laps. You pause the scene in both cases, and then simply invoke the game over block, passing `true` to the block if the player completed all laps and `false` in any other case. Easy-peasy!

Now open **GameViewController.m** to add the game over code. First, add this method, which shows a game over message to the user:

```
func gameOverWithWin(didWin: Bool) {

  let alert = UIAlertController(title: didWin ? "You won!": "You
lost", message: "Game Over", preferredStyle: .Alert)
  presentViewController(alert, animated: true, completion: nil)

}
```

Here, you present a simple alert view to display whether the player has won or lost. In your own games, this might be a good opportunity to present a new view controller or run some kind of animation.

Now scroll up to `viewDidLoad()` and add this code right after the line `view.addSubview(analogControl)`:

```
scene.gameOverBlock = {(didWin) in
  self.gameOverWithWin(didWin)
}
```

You create a weak copy of your view controller in order to use it inside the block you're going to pass to the scene. Then, you set a simple block to `scene.gameOverBlock` that calls `gameOverWithWin(didWin:)` on your `GameViewController` class.

That's all there is to it—you've implemented the complete game logic. Give the game a try and finish all the laps:

Note there's currently no way to dismiss this alert or continue the game; you'll add that later on in this chapter.

In this section, you've learned how to pass the ball between Sprite Kit and the UIKit parts of your game. Next, you'll look at integrating UIKit into your game flow on an even bigger scale!

Navigating between screens

As things stand, you don't have any navigation in your project. Well, it's time to add some. Like most classic racing games, Circuit Racer is designed to present the user with car and level selection screens when the game starts, and your next task is to implement them.

Adding a new view controller

The car selection screen will be the first screen the user sees upon starting the app. Open **Main.storyboard**, grab a new view controller and drop it onto the empty space in the storyboard:

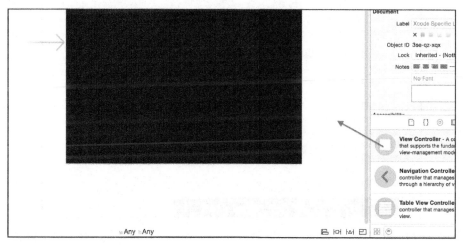

With the new view controller selected, open the Attributes Inspector, set the orientation to **Landscape** and tick the box that says **Is Initial View Controller**.

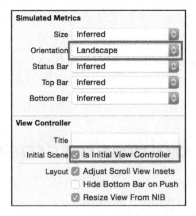

As the first order of business, drag an image view and hold it a bit before dropping it onto the view, so it can resize itself to the view's frame:

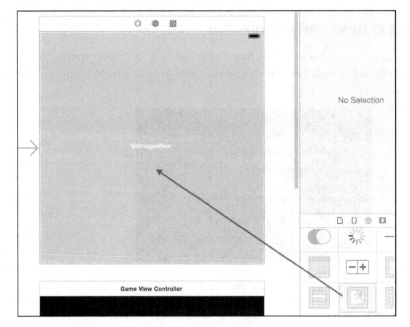

With the `UIImageView` selected, in the Attributes Inspector enter **bg-select-car.png** into the Image field. The screen background should show up.

To make sure the background stretches correctly on screens of different sizes, you need to pin the image view to the edges of the controller's view.

Select the image view and bring up the alignment constraints menu (you need to click on the square-ish tie-fighter button):

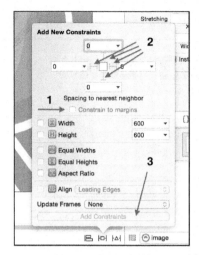

First **uncheck Constrain to margins**, then click the four dashed lines to pin the image view to the four sides of its container view. This will make the image view grow or shrink, depending on the size of the screen (accept the automatically proposed margins).

To create the constraints, click the button at the bottom of the dialogue, which now says **Add 4 Constraints**.

Finally, with the image view still selected, look at the Attributes Inspector and choose **Aspect Fill** for Mode to make the background image stretch proportionally up or down.

At this point, build and run the project on both an iPhone simulator and an iPad simulator to verify that the background fits well on each:

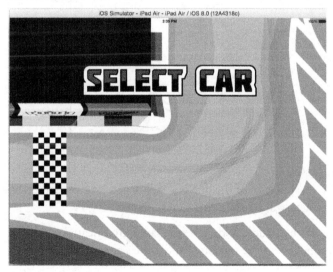

Next, add three buttons to the view controller, like so:

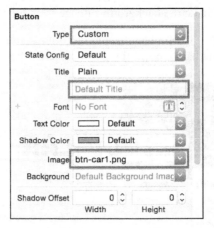

Select the button on the left and change the properties as follows: select **Custom** as the type, then delete the default button title and enter **btn-car1.png** for the image. Finally, enter **0** for the tag:

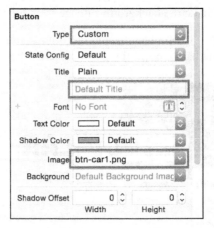

Change the button size to 121 x 169 – this is just a reference size to allow you to design the storyboard, the actual size of the buttons will depend on the screen size and will be set by constraints. You will set the constraint in a second.

Select the button in the middle and make the same modifications, but for the image enter **btn-car2.png** and for the **tag** enter **1**. Set the size to 121 x 169.

For the button on the right, again make the same modifications, but for the image enter **btn-car3.png** and for the tag enter **2**. Set the size to 121 x 169.

So far, you should have a layout like this:

Now you need to create a number of constraints to make sure the buttons resize and reposition properly on differently sized screens.

Setting constraints on the blue car button

Select the button with the blue car. Hold the **Ctrl** key on your keyboard and **drag** within the button itself, like so:

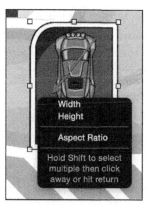

When you do that, a small popup menu appears. From it, select **Aspect Ratio**. This creates a constraint that will preserve the aspect ratio of the button across screen sizes. This doesn't mean that the button will have the same width and height, but it means the ration between them will be preserved. You can see that by looking at the constraints next to the button:

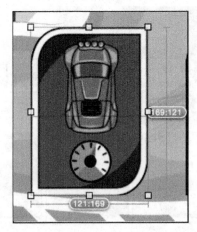

Next, hold **Ctrl** again and **drag** with your mouse from the button to the background image. From the resulting popup menu, choose **Center X**. This will center the button horizontally in its superview.

Hold **Ctrl** once more and **drag** from the button to the background image. This time, choose **Center Y** from the resulting popup menu. This will center the button vertically in its superview.

The final constraint to add will scale the button proportionally to the screen size. Hold the **Ctrl** key a final time and **drag** with your mouse from the button to the background and choose **Equal Heights**.

This final constraint will make the button as high as the view, which isn't exactly what you wanted. Let's edit the constraint. Select the button and in the Assistant Editor (the sidebar on your right), select the size and position tab:

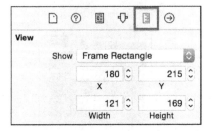

Look down in this panel and find the list of all the constraints currently set for the button:

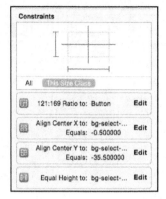

Double-click the one called **Equal Height to...** and you'll see the details of the constraint equation, which you can edit:

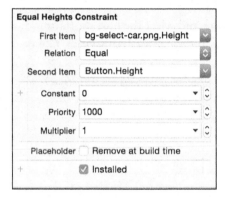

In this case, Xcode always sets the image view as the first item and the button as the second, so your first move is to click on First Item and choose **Reverse First and Second Item**.

Since the button height should be equal to the reference view height, the Multiplier is **1**. You actually want the button height to always be 50% of its superview, so change Multiplier to **0.5**.

Now build and run the project to see the state of your menu so far.

It should look something like this:

The blue car button is nicely centered horizontally and with correct size. This is great! But it could be a little bit higher, as there's too much empty space between the **Select Car** screen title and the button.

Go back to Interface Builder and select the blue car button. From the list of constraints already set for this button, double-click **Align Center Y to...**:

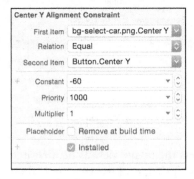

Make sure the background image is the first item so that you get the correct offset on screen.

As you can see, Xcode hard-coded the value -60 for the button's y-position constraint. Since you're creating a universal game, constants are never a good idea for UI positioning.

> **Note:** Depending where you dropped the button on your scene, you may see a value other than -60. If you got exactly -60, congrats—you have a sharp eye and a steady hand!

So what is the difference between using the constant and the multiplayer? In the case when you want to center a view in its superview on the Y axis you essentially set your constraint like so:

```
View.center.y = view.superview.center.y
```

If you want to offset the view just a little bit to the top you can use the constraint constant like so:

```
View.center.y = view.superview.center.y − 60
```

This will position the view always at the center of it superview and then 60 upwards. But since you have a universal device UI it's best to use the multiplayer – this is a value you would like to multiply your reference by. Like so:

```
View.center.y = view.superview.center.y * 0.5
```

This way if your superview center is (100, 200) your view will be automatically position at half on the Y axis – say (100, 100).

Since you want to offset the buttons a bit off the scene center, but by the same relative amount on each screen size you will use the multiplayer. Edit the constraint equation to set **0** for Constant and **0.8** for Multiplier. These values will position the button nicely and leave a bit of space both on top and bottom, like so:

You've finished with the first button! Now—there are only two more left!

Setting constraints on the yellow car button

Hold **Ctrl** and **drag** with the mouse within the yellow car button; choose **Aspect Ratio** from the menu.

Hold **Ctrl** and **drag** with the mouse from the yellow car button to the blue car button; choose **Top** from the menu. This will align the two buttons vertically.

Hold **Ctrl** and **drag** with the mouse from the yellow car button to the blue car button; choose **Equal Heights** from the menu. This will make the yellow car button as high as the blue car button.

Hold **Ctrl** and **drag** from the yellow car button to the background image; from the menu, choose **Center X**. Now re-select the yellow car button and in the Assistant Editor, double-click the constraint called **Align Center X.** Reverse the first and second items if necessary so that the button is the first item. Edit the constraint equation to set **0** for Constant and **0.45** for Multiplier. This will put the button in its place!

Setting constraints on the red car button

Positioning the final button is quite similar to the last one. Try to create the constraints from the table below, remembering to hold **Ctrl** while dragging:

	Drag from	Drag to	Menu option
Constraint 1	Red car button	Red car button	**Aspect Ratio**
Constraint 2	Red car button	Blue car button	**Top**
Constraint 3	Red car button	Blue car button	**Equal Heights**
Constraint 4	Red car button	Background image	**Center X**

For the final touch, select the red car button and in the Assistant Editor, double-click the constraint called **Align Center X to**. Reverse the first and second item if necessary, so that the button is the first item. Edit the constraint equation to set **0** for Constant and **1.55** for Multiplier.

Build and run to see how everything looks:

Try running the screen on the iPad simulator, as well. Since you used no constants whatsoever for positioning, everything aligns just fine:

The provided assets make this screen look great! Setting this screen up visually was a lot of work, but very rewarding, no?

In case you're curious, the dials below the cars indicate the speed of each car—remember, you made each car progressively faster.

Adding additional view controllers

The first screen of the game is ready, but you need yet more screens. To get proper navigation between those screens, you need to use a navigation controller.

To do this, first select the view controller you just created by clicking on it in the dock:

Then from Xcode's main menu, select **Editor/Embed In/Navigation Controller**. That should create a new navigation controller in the storyboard and also make it the initial controller that loads when the application starts.

With the new navigation controller still selected in the storyboard, open the Attributes Inspector and set **None** for Top Bar (this will both remove the bar in Interface Builder and will uncheck the checkbox **Shows Navigation Bar** to hide the bar at runtime). This last bit is important because otherwise, you'll see a navigation bar item over your game scene.

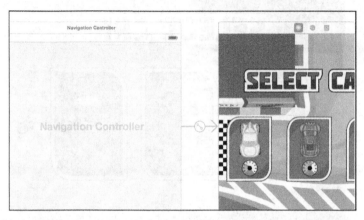

Now let's add the level selection screen, which from the user's point of view will be a difficulty selection screen.

Start by dragging a new view controller onto an empty space in your storyboard.

Just as before, drag in a UIImageView, let it grow until it resizes to take up all the space in the view and then in the Attributes Inspector, set **bg-select-difficulty.png** as the image:

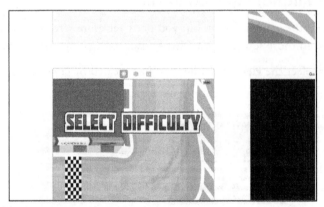

Remember to make the background image fill the screen. Select the image view and pin it to the four sides of its superview:

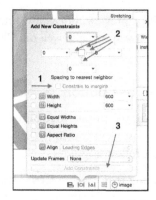

Select the image view once again and select **Aspect Fill** for Mode in the Assistant Editor.

Now, let's add buttons for the three difficulty levels. Just as for the previous screen, drag three UIButton instances one by one. But this time, arrange them in a **vertical** stack with equal spacing (not horizontal).

Select the top button and make the following adjustments in the Attributes Inspector: set **Custom** as the type, delete the prefilled title, enter **btn-easy.png** as the image and enter **0** as the tag. Adjust the button size to 301 x 55 – again, this is just a reference size so the button appears nicely in Interface Builder.

For the middle button, set the type to **Custom**, delete the prefilled title, enter **btn-medium.png** for the image and enter **1** as the tag. Set the size to 301 x 55.

Finally, for the bottom button, set the type to **Custom**, delete the prefilled title, enter **btn-hard.png** as the image and enter **2** as the tag. Adjust the button size to 301 x 55.

Align the buttons again, and you should end up with something like this:

That's nice for an Interface Builder preview, but you would like to also set constraints for these three buttons so they show up equally well on iPhone, iPhone6, iPad, and (later on) OS X.

Setting constraints on the Easy button

There are number of constraints to set on the three buttons, but it's all an iteration of what you've already done for the last view controller, so you should have no problem using this table and the ones that follow as guides.

	Ctrl+Drag from	Ctrl+Drag to	Menu option
Constraint 1	Easy button	Easy button	**Aspect Ratio**
Constraint 2	Easy button	Background image	**Center X**
Constraint 3	Easy button	Background image	**Center Y**
Constraint 4	Easy button	Background image	**Equal Widths**

There are a few things to adjust in the default constraint equations.

For the constraint **Align Center Y**, make sure the button is the first item in the equation then set Constant to **0** and Multiplier to **0.85**.

For the constraint **Equal Width, once again make sure that the** button is the first item then set Constant to **0** and Multiplier to **0.6**.

These constraints should resize and position the button just under the Select Difficulty title. You won't be able to preview this in the Simulator yet, since the navigation isn't working, so continue setting up the rest of the screen.

Setting constraints on the Medium button

	Ctrl+Drag from	Ctrl+Drag to	Menu option
Constraint 1	Medium button	Medium button	**Aspect Ratio**
Constraint 2	Medium button	Easy button	**Center X**
Constraint 3	Medium button	Easy button	**Equal widths**
Constraint 4	Medium button	Background image	**Center Y**

For the constraint **Align Center Y**, make sure the button is the first item in the equation then set Constant to **0** and Multiplier to **1.29**.

The four constraints above, when set correctly, will position the Medium button at the center of the screen. No additional changes to the default constraints are required, so you can move on to the last button for this screen.

Setting constraints on the Hard button

	Ctrl+Drag from	Ctrl+Drag to	Menu option
Constraint 1	Hard button	Hard button	**Aspect Ratio**
Constraint 2	Hard button	Medium button	**Center X**
Constraint 3	Hard button	Medium button	**Equal widths**
Constraint 4	Hard button	Background image	**Center Y**

For the constraint **Align Center Y**, set Constant to **0** and Multiplier to **1.73**. Make sure the button is the first item in the equation.

The buttons will stack nicely on top of each other and resize for different screens so that the layout consistently looks like so:

Setting up a back button

Since the difficulty selection screen will be the second screen seen by the user, you need one extra button: a back button that will let the player return to the car selection screen. Drag in another UIButton, set its type to **Custom**, delete its title and enter **btn-back.png** for the image.

Move the button to the bottom-left corner:

Create the constraints to pin the button to its current position. Pin it only to the left and bottom sides of its superview:

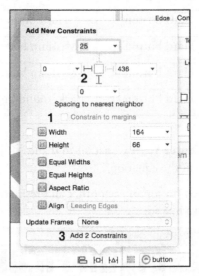

Again just be sure you positioned the button in the bottom left corner in Interface Builder and then accept the automatically proposed left and bottom margins for the constraint.

Set the following additional constraints for this last button:

	Ctrl+Drag from	Ctrl+Drag to	Menu option
Constraint 1	Back button	Back button	**Aspect Ratio**
Constraint 2	Back button	Background image	**Equal Widths**

For the constraint **Equal Width to,** set Constant to **0** and Multiplier to **0.15**.

Let's test to make sure you have the constraints set up correctly. Select your view controller by clicking the button on the top:

And click **Is Initial View Controller** to temporarily make it the first view controller that appears. Build and run, and the buttons should appear in nice spots on both iPhone and iPad:

Once you've verified it's working, select the navigation controller in Interface Builder and tick the checkbox **Is Initial Controller**.

Great! Your storyboard is complete and it should look much like this, though don't worry if your controllers aren't perfectly aligned.

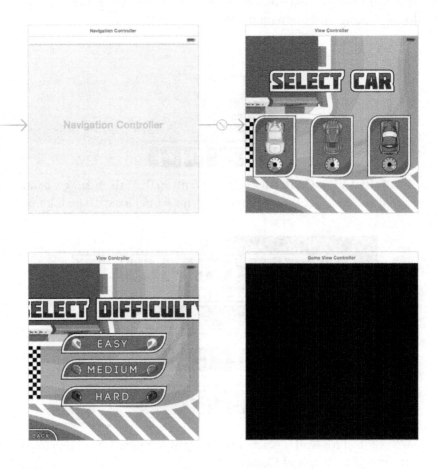

Implementing the navigation

Now, let's add the code required for the navigation to work. As you've probably already guessed, the tags of the buttons correspond with the car and level types. You simply have to pass this info from screen to screen so that the user first selects a car, then a track and finally, the screen with the appropriate game shows up.

For this to work, you need two custom view controller classes. In Xcode's main menu, select **File\New\File…**, select the **Cocoa Touch class** template and click **Next**. Enter **SelectCarViewController** for Class and **UIViewController** for Subclass of. Ensure that the **Also create XIB file** option is **unchecked** and select **Swift** as Language. Click **Next**. Finally, make sure the **CircuitRacer** target is checked and click **Create**.

Repeat these steps one more time, but call the new file **SelectLevelViewController**.

Now, you need to connect your storyboard view controllers to your new custom classes. Open **Main.storyboard** again and zoom in on the car selection screen. Select the view controller object and switch to the **Identity Inspector** panel (third from left to right); then, for both the Custom Class and the Storyboard ID, enter **SelectCarViewController**:

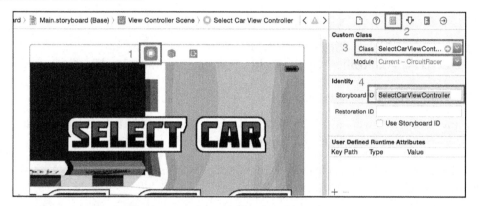

Now zoom in on the level selection view controller, select it, switch again to the Identity Inspection panel and for both the Custom Class and Storyboard ID, enter **SelectLevelViewController**.

Select the original view controller that Xcode created for you—the one currently showing a black window—and enter **GameViewController** as the Storyboard ID.

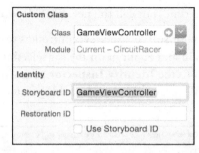

That takes care of configuring the controllers' identities. Next, open
SelectLevelViewController.swift and add a new variable inside the class:

```
var carType: CarType!
```

The previous screen will set this instance variable to store the selected car type. Speaking
of which, switch to **SelectCarViewController.swift** and add this method:

```
@IBAction func carButtonPressed(sender: UIButton) {
  SKTAudio.sharedInstance().playSoundEffect("button_press.wav")

  let levelViewController =
self.storyboard!.instantiateViewControllerWithIdentifier("Select
LevelViewController") as! SelectLevelViewController

  levelViewController.carType = CarType(rawValue: sender.tag)!
  navigationController!.pushViewController(levelViewController,
    animated: true)
}
```

You define a new `@IBAction` called `carButtonPressed(sender:)`, which plays an
audio jingle and then fetches the next screen's view controller from the storyboard. You
set `SelectLevelViewController`'s `carType` property and then push it to the screen.

Since the method doesn't use a hard-coded value for the car type but rather fetches the
tag of the pressed button, you're going to use this single method for all three buttons.

Open **Main.storyboard** one more time and select the first button in the **Select Car
View Controller**. Then, while pressing **Ctrl** on your keyboard, **drag** with your mouse
from the button to the view controller, like so:

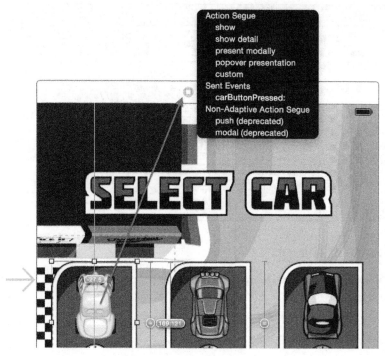

From the popup menu, select **carButtonPressed:** to connect the button to the action. Repeat exactly the same procedure for the other two buttons.

Before you take a look at this screen, let's add a touch of excitement to the game menu by playing some wild racing tunes! Open **SelectCarViewController.swift** and add a new method:

```
override func viewDidAppear(animated: Bool) {
  super.viewDidAppear(animated)

SKTAudio.sharedInstance().playBackgroundMusic("circuitracer.mp3"
)
}
```

This tune should get the players in the mood for a race.

Build and run the project, and enjoy the music while you click away on the car buttons to verify that any of them will take you to the next scene. None of the buttons on the difficulty selection screen work yet though – it's time to do that now!

Getting back in the game

Open **GameViewController.swift** and add these two properties so that it can receive the player's game selections:

```
var carType: CarType!
var levelType: LevelType!
```

To finish up with `GameViewController`, find the line where you pre-set the car and level types (this was for testing purposes only, remember?):

```
scene.levelType = LevelType.Easy
scene.carType = CarType.Yellow
```

Replace this code with the values you'll be getting from the previous screen:

```
scene.levelType = levelType
scene.carType = carType
```

Do you see how everything's falling together to make this whole navigation thing work? I hope so. :]

Open **SelectLevelViewController.swift** one more time and add these methods:

```
@IBAction func backButtonPressed(sender: UIButton) {
  navigationController!.popViewControllerAnimated(true)
  SKTAudio.sharedInstance().playSoundEffect("button_press.wav")
}

@IBAction func levelButtonPressed(sender: UIButton) {
```

```
    SKTAudio.sharedInstance().playSoundEffect("button_press.wav")

    let levelType = LevelType(rawValue: sender.tag)

    let gameViewController =
  self.storyboard!.instantiateViewControllerWithIdentifier("GameVi
  ewController") as! GameViewController

    gameViewController.carType = carType
    gameViewController.levelType = levelType

    navigationController!.pushViewController(gameViewController,
      animated: true)
}
```

Here you define the action for the back button: It simply pops out the current view controller and plays a sound effect.

For the level/difficulty button, you play the same jingle, fetch the next view controller from the storyboard, configure it and push it onto the screen.

To connect these actions, first open **Main.storyboard** and select the **Select Level View Controller**. Just as you did in the car selection view controller, hold down the **Ctrl** key, **drag** with your mouse from the back button to the view controller and select backButtonPressed: from the popup menu.

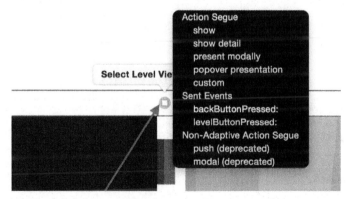

Then **Ctrl-drag** from each of the difficulty buttons to the view controller and select levelButtonPressed: to connect all of them to this action.

Build and run the game, and see how it all fits together!

Everything works, except the gameplay gets stuck at the point where you finish a game. Now that you have menus, you can simply pop the gameplay view controller from the navigation stack when the player finishes a game and return to the game's GUI.

To quickly implement this, open **GameViewController.swift** and add the following new method:

```
func goBack(alert: UIAlertController) {
  alert.dismissViewControllerAnimated(true, completion: {
self.navigationController!.popToRootViewControllerAnimated(false
)
  return
  })
}
```

And add these lines at the end of `gameOverWithWin(didWin:)`:

```
let delayInSeconds = 3.0
let popTime = dispatch_time(DISPATCH_TIME_NOW,
  Int64(delayInSeconds) * Int64(NSEC_PER_SEC))

dispatch_after(popTime, dispatch_get_main_queue(),  {
  self.goBack(alert)
})
```

The new `goBack` method hides the alert box and pops all view controllers back to the car selection screen. You simply call this method with a 3-second delay at the end of `gameOverWithWin(didWin:)`.

Build and run the game once more, and after you complete a level, win or lose, you'll see that you're transported right back to the car selection, where you can try a different set of wheels.

Excellent! You've wrapped up the UIKit integration part of this book and now have the know-how to extend your Sprite Kit games in many exciting ways with in-game HUDs and UIs, custom level selectors and anything else you can build with UIKit!

Challenges

You've achieved a lot in this chapter, but you can bring the project up one more notch! Solving this challenge requires you to apply what you've learned and make use of your UIKit skills in a new way.

As always, if you get stuck, you can find the solutions in the resources for this chapter— but give it your best shot first!

Challenge 1: In-game menu

Like most games, Circuit Racer needs an in-game menu. In this challenge, you'll add a pause button over the game scene and show a menu when a user taps the button.

Follow these simple instructions to implement this on your own:

1. Add a button on top of your game scene in `GameViewController` in your storyboard. Use the image **btn-pause.png** to fit it in the top-right corner.

2. Size and position the new button via constraints much as you did for the back button. Hint: The button will look good if its width is 12% of the screen's width.

3. Create a new `@IBAction` method in `GameViewController` called `showInGameMenu(sender: AnyObject!)` and connect the pause button to it.

4. Make `showInGameMenu(sender:)` show an alert with two buttons, one that says **Go to menu** and the another that says **Resume level**.

5. To stop the level timer, set `paused` of the scene class to `true` when you show the in-game menu. Hint: from your view controller you can directly access the currently visible scene like so: `let scene = (self.view as SKView).scene!`

6. Don't forget to un-pause the scene, no matter which button the user presses. If the user presses **Go to menu**, simply call `gameOverWithWin(didWin:)` and pass

`false`—this will end the game (with the "you lose" alert) and bring the player back to the the car selection screen.

If you implement all the steps, you should end up with an in-game menu like this:

Besides learning about UIKit in this chapter, you reviewed a lot of what you already knew about Sprite Kit and should be feeling quite proficient.

Now you have the opportunity and the confidence to take on more advanced topics, starting with the next chapter—where you'll learn to control your Circuit Racer car via the built-in accelerometer!

Chapter 21:
Accelerometer

By Marin Todorov

Apple's inclusion of the accelerometer was one big factor contributing to the early success of the iPhone and iPod touch as gaming devices. Mobile gamers could play in a totally new and different way—by tilting the device, they could change the point of view of the game, move the hero or alter the game's gravity.

The accelerometer is a hardware component built into the iPhone that measures the acceleration over time caused either by gravity or by the movement of the device. It allows you, as a developer, to track the device's position in space and determine whether it is moving or still.

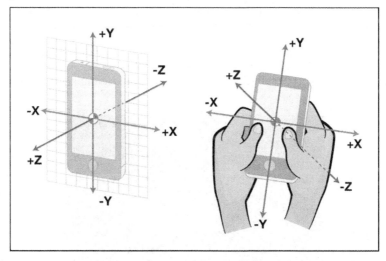

As a developer, you can use the accelerometer to simplify a game's controls. It's feels more "natural" to tilt the device in the desired direction to move an element within the game than it is to tap one button or another. This is the sort of feature that will draw casual gamers to your app—those who want to be able to play a game when they feel like it without thinking too much about the details.

Look at Doodle Jump, one of the early successes in the App Store. With its accelerometer-driven game controls, it's so incredibly simple to play that almost anyone can pick it up and get started right away. That's what casual gaming is all about!

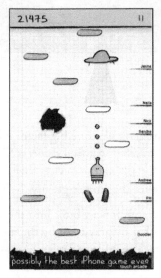

The topic of using the iPhone's accelerometer as game controller is quite appropriate to the game you developed in the last chapter: Circuit Racer. The accelerometer is the perfect controller for a racing game, because steering with buttons isn't much fun. Just look at some of the racing games in the App Store, such as *Asphalt 7* and *Need For Speed: Undercover*. They demonstrate that the accelerometer and driving are made for each other:

In this chapter, you'll learn how to read data from the accelerometer and use this data to control sprite movement, so your players can drive in Circuit Racer simply by tilting their iPhones.

> **Note:** This chapter begins where the previous chapter's Challenge 1 left off. If you were unable to complete the challenges or skipped ahead from an earlier chapter, don't worry—you can simply open **CircuitRacer-Starter** from this chapter's resources to begin in the right place.

Getting acceleration data

Run Circuit Racer and have a look at the way the game is set up. Players move through car type and level selection screens before reaching the main game scene, where they use an onscreen joypad to control the car:

By the end of this chapter, the onscreen joypad will be history. You'll be able to move the car solely by tilting the device.

> **Note**: To follow through this chapter, you'll have to test the game *on the device*, because there's no way to simulate the accelerometer while running the game in the iOS Simulator on your computer.

In iOS, a framework called **Core Motion** takes care of connecting hardware sensors like the accelerometer to your app. You normally "subscribe" to updates from the sensors in one or more of your classes and can then read their measurements.

> **Note:** Core Motion gives you access to the readings of three different sensors. The first is the accelerometer. You will learn a ton about it while working through this chapter.
>
> The second is the gyroscope, a sensor measuring the device's orientation in space. You would use its readings if you were to create an airplane fighting game or a virtual reality game where you will need to read the precise orientation of the device in space.
>
> The third is the magnetometer, which assists in measuring magnetic fields. This last one is useful when you want to detect Earth true north in map applications and some other niche applications (like detecting if you are nearby a giant audio speaker.)
>
> Accessing data from these three sensors works in much the same way, so once you're comfortable using the accelerometer, you can easily take on the gyroscope and magnetometer on your own.
>
> If you're interested in using more of the device's sensors with the Core Motion framework, have a look at Apple's documentation here:
> https://developer.apple.com/library/ios/documentation/CoreMotion/Reference/CoreMotion_Reference/_index.html

The accelerometer uses extra energy to fetch the acceleration data, so your device battery will drain a little faster when the accelerometer is on. It is therefore important to only subscribe to accelerometer data when you *need* it—that is, when the game scene is actually displayed onscreen.

Turning the accelerometer on and off

It's once again time to switch into coding mode! Open **GameViewController.swift** to make a few changes. First, add the following line just under the existing `import` statements:

```
import CoreMotion
```

Add this private instance variable:

```
private let motionManager = CMMotionManager()
```

`CMMotionManager` is the class that gives you access to the accelerometer data. Here, you declare a new instance variable named `motionManager` to get a hold of your manager instance.

Add this at the end of the `if` block in `viewDidLoad()`, right after the code that sets the `gameOverBlock`:

```
motionManager.accelerometerUpdateInterval = 0.05
motionManager.startAccelerometerUpdates()
```

Here, you set the `accelerometerUpdateInterval` to 0.05, meaning that the manager will read the accelerometer about 20 times per second. You then tell the Core Motion motion manager to begin reading acceleration data.

Updating the acceleration data 20 times per second might seem like a lot at first sight, but since games are all about responsiveness, it could just as well be too few readings! Of course, it's true that you don't want to over-read the accelerometer—after all, these readings consume non-trivial amounts of energy.

The right frequency of accelerometer updates will vary from game to game. For your own games, I encourage you to experiment with different intervals until you find the one that best suits your gameplay.

Now be a good iOS citizen and turn off the accelerometer as soon as the view is about to go off-screen. Add a `deinit`:

```
deinit {
  motionManager.stopAccelerometerUpdates()
}
```

This way, as soon as the view controller is deallocated, it will also stop the motion manager updates. How nice of you!

Getting the data

"But what are those updates and where can I find them?" you might be wondering.

Never fear—CMMotionManager has a property called accelerometerData that the motion manager updates constantly with the current accelerometer reading. It's up to you to read this property repeatedly and adjust your game accordingly.

The game loop update in GameScene seems like the right place to do this, so open **GameScene.swift** and get cracking.

Import Core Motion to give GameScene access to CCMotionManager, like this:

```
import CoreMotion
```

And add this variable to the class:

```
var motionManager : CMMotionManager!
```

This instance variable will hold a reference to GameViewController's motionManager.

Go back to **GameViewController.m** and at the end of viewDidLoad(), where you create the motion manager instance, add this line:

```
scene.motionManager = motionManager
```

Now your scene can access the accelerometer readings. I'm sure you're aching to see some output already, so let's take a peek at the accelerometer data.

Open **GameScene.swift** and add this to the end of update(currentTime:):

```
if motionManager.accelerometerData != nil {
    println("accelerometer
[\(motionManager.accelerometerData.acceleration.x),
\(motionManager.accelerometerData.acceleration.y),
\(motionManager.accelerometerData.acceleration.z)]")
}
```

The accelerometerData is a Swift optional, and therefore, you need to check that you have valid data before attempting to display it. It will take a moment for the accelerometer data to begin updating.

Now run the game again, and remember to run the game on your device. Navigate to the game screen by choosing a car and a track, and move your device around. As you do so, take a look at Xcode's output console:

```
adjust(  night  )
lection
         accelerometer [0.0377197265625, -0.0057373046875, -1.02604675292969]
         accelerometer [0.0224609375, -0.0077056884765625, -1.00056457519531]
         accelerometer [0.0224609375, -0.0077056884765625, -1.00056457519531]
         accelerometer [0.0224609375, -0.0077056884765625, -1.00056457519531]
         accelerometer [0.0206298828125, -0.0009918212890625, -1.00942993164062]
         accelerometer [0.0206298828125, -0.0009918212890625, -1.00942993164062]
         accelerometer [0.01959228515625, -0.0058135986328125, -0.996658325195312]
         accelerometer [0.01959228515625, -0.0058135986328125, -0.996658325195312]
         accelerometer [0.01959228515625, -0.0058135986328125, -0.996658325195312]
         accelerometer [0.0330810546875, -0.0085601806640625, -1.03683471679688]
```

Oh, my! It definitely works, but what does it mean?

Interpreting the data

The three coordinates on each line of the console output denote the device's rotation along the x-, y- and z-axes, respectively. The rotation values for each axis range between -1 and 1.

When your device lies on a flat surface (like a kitchen table) that's the neutral position on its x and y axes – in other words the accelerometer gives a reading of 0 along those two axes. Notice that the reading is not a flat zero – it always flickers up and down around the zero; the accelerometer is a very sensitive sensor and picks up even the smallest vibrations from your environment.

But, what's the kitchen table to do with detecting rotation? you might ask. Well when you do not actually move the device, the accelerometer picks up the acceleration produced by Earth's gravity so it will actually show readings oriented towards Earth.

As for the z axis - its neutral position is when the device stands on its long side. For Circuit Racer, as the game supports only Landscape Left orientation, that's the side of the iPhone with the sim card tray. So if you let the iPhone stand on its side it'll give you a reading of zero on the z axis.

For example, look at the diagram on the next page to see how the x-axis works. The big arrow shows you how to rotate the device for the accelerometer to report acceleration around x.

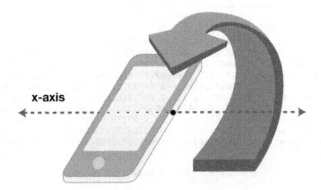

x-axis

The next diagram shows how the three axes work together. Note that unlike the x- and y-axes, which are on the same plane as the screen's surface, the z-axis occupies a perpendicular plane, intersecting the screen only through the screen's center point.

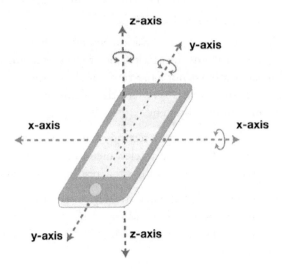

Now lay your device flat on a table and rotate it around one axis at a time while you watch the output console.

If you do this carefully, you'll see only one data component at a time change from 0 to 1, back to 0 and then to -1 as you rotate the device. This is a great way to understand how the accelerometer works.

All right, you now have the data and a basic understanding of what it represents—it's time to make use of it.

Working with device orientation

> **Note:** The accelerometer code you're going to write in this chapter is based on a piece of code Alex Okafor wrote in a blog post called, "Lessons Learned in Tilt Controls." The post summarizes what Alex learned while making *Tilt to Live*, a particularly great game released in the early days of the App Store that is heavily dependent on accelerometer controls. You can read the full post here:
>
> http://www.paradeofrain.com/2010/07/lessons-learned-in-tilt-controls/

The biggest difficultly when working with the accelerometer isn't fetching the current device orientation, but rather interpreting what the player *meant* by tilting the device to its current orientation. To be able to make that interpretation, you first have to define a starting orientation.

Let's visualize the problem by again considering only the x-axis. Run the Circuit Racer game, navigate to the gameplay screen and then lay the device flat on a table. Look at the output console in Xcode. You should see a lot of readings of about `0.00` for the x-axis, like so:

```
oduct(row, right, on)
lection
        accelerometer [0.0077197265625, −0.0057373046875, −1.02604675292969]
        accelerometer [0.0224609375, −0.0077056884765625, −1.00056457519531]
        accelerometer [0.0224609375, −0.0077056884765625, −1.00056457519531]
        accelerometer [0.0224609375, −0.0077056884765625, −1.00056457519531]
        accelerometer [0.0206298828125, −0.0009918212890625, −1.00942993164062]
        accelerometer [0.0206298828125, −0.0009918212890625, −1.00942993164062]
        accelerometer [0.01959228515625, −0.0058135986328125, −0.996658325195312]
        accelerometer [0.01959228515625, −0.0058135986328125, −0.996658325195312]
        accelerometer [0.01959228515625, −0.0058135986328125, −0.996658325195312]
        accelerometer [0.0330810546875, −0.0085601806640625, −1.03683471679688]
```

As you can see, the accelerometer's *neutral* position for the x-axis is when the device is horizontally flat, such as it is on a table.

Now rotate the device slightly around its x-axis (refer to the diagrams in the last section) and monitor the output:

```
accelerometer [0.49041748046875, -0.0057373046875, -0.896408081054688]
accelerometer [0.49041748046875, -0.0057373046875, -0.896408081054688]
accelerometer [0.49041748046875, -0.0057373046875, -0.896408081054688]
accelerometer [0.481033325195312, -0.0095062255859375, -0.905227661132812]
accelerometer [0.481033325195312, -0.0095062255859375, -0.905227661132812]
accelerometer [0.45269775390625, -0.0132904052734375, -0.905288696289062]
accelerometer [0.45269775390625, -0.0132904052734375, -0.905288696289062]
accelerometer [0.45269775390625, -0.0132904052734375, -0.905288696289062]
accelerometer [0.505325317382812, -0.009674072265625, -0.862014770507812]
accelerometer [0.505325317382812, -0.009674072265625, -0.862014770507812]
```

The x-component increases and decreases in value, just as expected.

Now think of all the times you played an iPhone game while having your device flat on a table. That's right—it probably happened around zero times! Most of the time, you hold your device at an angle—whatever feels comfortable to you.

This raises a difficult question: What position/orientation of the device would your typical player consider *neutral*? That is, what's the device orientation from which they will most likely try to control your game? Probably, it's not from a tabletop.

The answer is, the neutral position varies from person to person. You won't have a one-fits-all solution. Still, you can aim to satisfy most people, or even better, you can have several predefined positions for your player to choose from, like so:

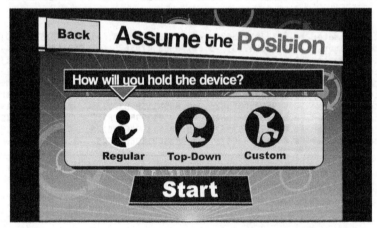

This is a screenshot from the original *Tilt to Live* game. For this chapter, you'll make your neutral position the same as the **Regular** position depicted above. Let's go!

> **Note:** While you're only going to implement one neutral position for Circuit Racer, *Tilt to Live*'s solution is quite smart, and you should consider using it for your own games. Provide one or two default positions as well as a custom option, and let the player select which they prefer. If they select the custom option, simply save the readings from the accelerometer and make that position the neutral one.
>
> In any case, implementing accelerometer-based game controls isn't a trivial task. Plan to test your game with a number of people and consider their specific feedback as you strive for the perfect game controls.

Using accelerometer data

Now that you know more about how the accelerometer works and you understand the implications of device tilts, you can proceed with using the accelerometer data to move the car.

Getting the accelerometer vector

The game loop seems like a good place to move the car based on the accelerometer data, but it would be better to handle it in a separate method—it will get messy inside `update(currentTime:)` if you do everything there.

In **GameScene.swift**, add the following method:

```
func moveCarFromAcceleration() {

  var accel2D = CGPoint.zeroPoint

  if motionManager.accelerometerData == nil {
    println("no acceleration data yet")
    return
  }

  var raw = Vector3(
    x: CGFloat(motionManager.accelerometerData.acceleration.x),
    y: CGFloat(motionManager.accelerometerData.acceleration.y),
    z: CGFloat(motionManager.accelerometerData.acceleration.z))

}
```

Call this new method at the end of `update(currentTime:)`:

```
moveCarFromAcceleration()
```

Now you're back to coding! You introduce a new method called
`moveCarFromAcceleration()`, which you call from the game loop.

First, you declare a variable called `accel2D`, which will hold the car's acceleration vector.

Next, you check that you actually have accelerometer data, as discussed above.

Then as the first order of real business, you create a three-dimensional vector called `raw`
where you store the raw accelerometer data.

Defining the neutral orientation

Now comes the tricky part—defining the device's neutral position. Add these as class
constants to `GameScene`:

```
private let ay = Vector3(x: 0.63, y: 0.0, z: -0.92)
private let az = Vector3(x: 0.0, y: 1.0, z: 0.0)
private let ax = Vector3.crossProduct(Vector3(x: 0.0, y: 1.0, z:
0.0),
   right: Vector3(x: 0.63, y: 0.0, z: -0.92)).normalized()
```

Let's discuss these vectors one by one.

Imagine that each of these three vectors defines the origin and the direction of an axis in
space, together describing a whole three-dimensional coordinate system.

You define ay as (-0.63, 0, -0.92). This is an approximate reading of the iPhone's
accelerometer when you hold the device with two hands in front of you so that you're
looking at the screen comfortably. This is, as you've seen, the most-used gaming
position.

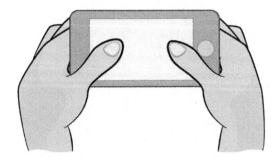

You define the az vector as `(0, 1, 0)`. This is an auxiliary vector you need to build upon your ay vector and define a plane. You're going somewhere with this, so don't worry!

Now your ay and az vectors define a rectangle that looks approximately like so:

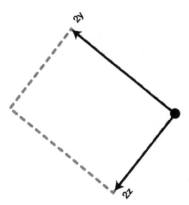

When you add a third vector to the two above, one that is both perpendicular to ay and az, you'll get three perpendicular vectors that together define a slightly tilted coordinate system in 3D space.

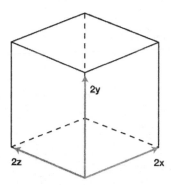

This will be your neutral coordinate system.

To make this a bit clearer, consider two coordinate systems. The first is aligned to the horizon and is the expected neutral position if the device is lying on a table. You could define it by using the three unit vectors: `(1, 0, 0)`, `(0, 0, 1)`, and `(0, 1, 0)`. The diagram below shows a cube that uses these three vectors as sides:

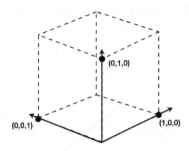

The second coordinate system is the one you just defined by ax, ay and az, starting with ay, which is the vector reading of the accelerometer when people hold the device "normally." It looks like this:

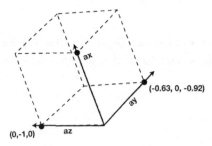

As you can see, this second coordinate system is simply the first one rotated in space based on the new, "neutral" ay. You'll use this rotated coordinate system as a starting point for reading the accelerometer.

Losing a dimension: Getting from 3D to 2D

So far, you have your 3D accelerometer data and you have your tilted 3D space coordinate system. However, your car moves only in 2D—the plane defined by the screen. In this section, you'll translate the 3D position of the accelerometer to a 2D vector, which you'll use later to set the car's velocity vector.

Let's take a look at the basic idea. Imagine you have a cube floating just above a small table. On top of the table, there's a desk lamp. The shadow of the cube on the table is the 2D projection of the 3D cube. That wasn't so difficult, was it?

To do the same thing in code, you'll "project" the 3D acceleration vector over the plane defined by (az, ax). Add this piece of code to `moveCarFromAcceleration()`:

```
accel2D.x = Vector3.dotProduct(raw, right: az)
accel2D.y = Vector3.dotProduct(raw, right: ax)
accel2D.normalize()
```

You project the 3D `raw` vector over the `az` vector and get a scalar, which will be the x-component of your 2D vector. You do the same over the `ax` vector to get the y-component of your 2D vector.

At the end, you normalize the `accel2D` vector so that its values aren't too big or too small. Now the vector is perfect to use to determine direction, velocity, force and so on—in fact, it's similar to the 2D vector you get from the joypad you developed in the last chapter.

Controlling for accelerometer "noise"

The accelerometer is a very "noisy" input device. It produces tons of data consisting of many small updates—usually it's more than you want!

It can be very annoying for the player if the game's hero or vehicle jumps around when the device is unintentionally tilted just a tiny bit. That's why you're going to implement an accelerometer **dead zone**. ☠

Since your 2D acceleration vector is normalized, the values of its components range from -1 to 1. Therefore, preventing the car from moving when the acceleration on the x- or y-axis is less than 0.15 should give the player a nice comfort zone.

The darker area in the image below represents the dead zone, in which you will not move the car:

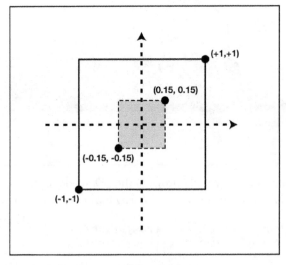

First, define a class constant for the size of the dead zone:

```
private let steerDeadZone = CGFloat(0.15)
```

Then, this simple piece of code should take care of the matter—add it to `moveCarFromAcceleration()`:

```
if abs(accel2D.x) < steerDeadZone {
  accel2D.x = 0
}

if abs(accel2D.y) < steerDeadZone {
  accel2D.y = 0
}
```

You define the dead zone as `steerDeadZone`, and then you check if any of the x- and y-coordinate values are less than the dead zone cap. In that case, you set the car's acceleration on that axis to zero.

You are almost there! Now you simply need to set the car body's velocity and let the physics simulation do the rest. Add this to `moveCarFromAcceleration()`:

```
let maxAccelerationPerSecond = maxSpeed
let car = childNodeWithName("car") as! SKSpriteNode
car.physicsBody!.velocity = CGVector(
  dx: accel2D.x * CGFloat(maxAccelerationPerSecond),
```

```
    dy: accel2D.y * CGFloat(maxAccelerationPerSecond))
```

You multiply `accel2D` (the normalized direction vector) by the maximum speed per second and set the result as the body's velocity.

That's it! Give the game a try. You should be able to control the car by tilting the device:

In fact, you can now control the car via both the joypad and the accelerometer—it's your call!

Filtering out even more accelerometer noise

If you play with the car for a while, you'll see its movement can be a little jittery, especially if you suddenly tilt the device to an extreme angle.

To prevent sudden changes of pace, you'll use another trick that's common when working with the accelerometer: a low pass filter.

The low pass filter will "smooth" the changes in the car's velocity by damping the deltas on each coordinate.

Here's a visual representation of the effect of the low pass filter, taken from Apple's own accelerometer demo app:

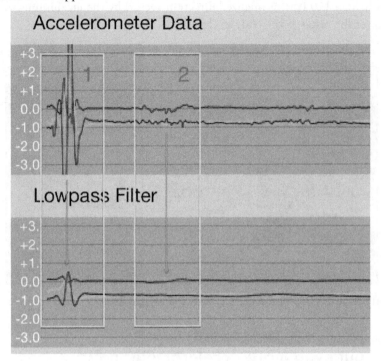

The graph represents the three coordinates of the acceleration vector. The top graph is the raw data, and below that are the filtered values.

In region 1, you see accelerometer data from when I shook the device. In this case, the filter smoothens the shock and prevents axis changes from -1.0 to 1.0 and back.

In region 2, you see data from when I casually held the device. As the top graph shows, the accelerometer picks up even the smallest shakings of my hand and therefore produces updates that will make the car's movement jittery. The low pass filter cuts out these very small changes, so the car stands calmly ready to go.

> **Note:** You can find Apple's accelerometer demo app at the link below.
>
> https://developer.apple.com/library/ios/samplecode/AccelerometerGraph/Introduction/Intro.html

Add a constant and a variable to the `GameScene` class. These will help you filter out the input noise:

```
private let blend = CGFloat(0.2)
private var lastVector = Vector3(x: 0, y: 0, z: 0)
```

Then, add a new method that will take a raw 3D vector and output the result of the low pass filter:

```
func lowPassWithVector(var vector: Vector3) -> Vector3 {

    vector.x = vector.x * blend + lastVector.x * (1.0 - blend)
    vector.y = vector.y * blend + lastVector.y * (1.0 - blend)
    vector.z = vector.z * blend + lastVector.z * (1.0 - blend)

    lastVector = vector
    return vector
}
```

This method always keeps the last accelerometer data vector in the variable `lastVector` and uses it to dampen the changes on each coordinate of the new accelerometer data, passed in as the `vector` parameter.

You can use this method as-is in your games, but try playing with the value of `blend` to see the effect it has on acceleration.

Now for the last bit: passing the accelerometer vector through your new low pass filter method. Back in `moveCarFromAcceleration()`, add the following immediately after you declare your `raw` variable:

```
raw = lowPassWithVector(raw)
```

Run the game now, and the car's movement should look smoother. As a side effect, the low pass filter introduces inertia to the car's movement, and that's also really cool.

But the car still needs another tune-up. I'm sure you've noticed that, when you tilt the device, the car doesn't rotate in the direction of movement as it does when you use the joypad. Let's fix that before wrapping things up.

Rotation dampening

As I said earlier, the accelerometer produces quite a noisy set of input data. The acceleration can often jump around its neutral position, even with the dead zone you have in place, so you don't want to immediately rotate the car to any direction indicated by the accelerometer.

You're going to dampen the car's orientation so it doesn't jump straight to the new direction of acceleration, but instead responds with a bit of a delay. The car will rotate as the accelerometer instructs, but over time rather than instantly.

Add this code to the bottom of moveCarFromAcceleration() to implement the rotation:

```
//1
if accel2D.x != 0 || accel2D.y != 0 {

  //2
  let orientationFromVelocity = CGPoint(
    x: car.physicsBody!.velocity.dx,
    y: car.physicsBody!.velocity.dy).angle

  var angleDelta = CGFloat(0.0)

  //3
  if abs(orientationFromVelocity - car.zRotation) > 1 {
    //prevent wild rotation
    angleDelta = orientationFromVelocity - car.zRotation
  } else {
    //blend rotation
    let blendFactor = CGFloat(0.25)
    angleDelta = (orientationFromVelocity - car.zRotation) *
      blendFactor

    angleDelta = shortestAngleBetween(car.zRotation,
      car.zRotation + angleDelta)
  }

  //4
  car.zRotation += angleDelta
}
```

Here's what you're doing, step by step:

1. First, you check if the accelerometer data is in the dead zone. If it is, you don't rotate the car at all, as it's not moving on the track.

2. You get the angle from the acceleration vector and put it into orientationFromVelocity. You also declare the angle by which you will, in the end, rotate the car—angleDelta.

3. This next block is a tricky one. If the car needs to rotate from an angle of 175 degrees to an angle of 185 degrees, that means the value of zRotation needs to change from 3.05 radians to -3.05 radians.

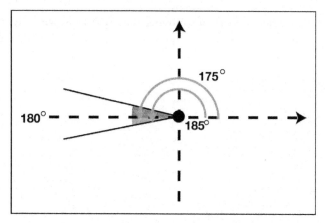

Therefore, if you apply damping to the rotation, it won't go over the 180-degree border, but it will rotate the car backwards, in the clockwise direction. It will rotate the long way around, and that's not what you want at all.

The quickest and best solution is to check whether the difference between the target and current angles is more than a whole radian, and if so, simply set `angleDelta` straight to the new rotation value:

```
angleDelta = (orientationFromVelocity-car.zRotation)
```

This introduces a small jump in the car's rotation over the 180-degree margin, but it looks good and you don't have to worry about it.

On the other hand, if the new rotation isn't going through the 180-degree margin, you want to apply damping to the rotation animation. First, you fetch the difference between the target and current angles and take a small "step" in that direction:

```
angleDelta = (orientationFromVelocity - car.zRotation) *
blendFactor
```

For example, for a difference of 10 degrees, you get a resulting step of 2.5 degrees after multiplying by `blendFactor`, which you set to 0.25. This way, the rotation will be smooth with no big, sudden jumps.

Finally, to make sure you're working with normalized angle values, you call `shortestAngleBetween` and overwrite what you had so far in `angleDelta` with the result.

4. The last line of your code adjusts the car's current rotation by `angleDelta` (finally!).

There you have it—smooth rotation, in the flesh! Ahem, I mean, in the code.

Build and run the game, and experience moving the car around with tilt control like it's absolutely real! Except, of course, that it doesn't turn into a smashed ruin when you hit the track walls.

As a final touch, open **GameViewController.m** and delete or comment out this entire section of `viewDidLoad()` to remove the joypad:

```
// let padSide: CGFloat = view.frame.size.height / 2.5
// let padPadding: CGFloat = view.frame.size.height / 32

// analogControl = AnalogControl(frame: CGRectMake(padPadding,
//   skView.frame.size.height - padPadding - padSide,
//   padSide, padSide))
// analogControl.delegate = scene

// view.addSubview(analogControl)
```

> **Note**: Check if there's any other lines of code where you refer to `analogControl` inside `viewDidLoad()`. If yes – comment them as well.

What can I say? You now have a fully functional, accelerometer-controlled minigame. Even more exciting, you've reached the next level of iOS sorcery—you are becoming a master of acceleration!

Challenges

Challenge 1: Detect your neutral position

You still have the code that logs the current accelerometer reading to the output console. Monitor the output and find your own "comfort zone." Hold the device in what feels like a neutral position for you, and take note of the values of x, y and z.

When you have the neutral values, copy them over to the code and try the game again. Does steering the car feel more natural? Remember that what's natural for you is not necessarily natural for everyone.

Now try playing the game in several different positions, such as while lying in bed or sitting in a comfy chair. Again take note of the neutral values for x, y and z. You get pretty different values for each position, right?

Try using each set of values for your neutral device orientation and see which one you'd use in your own games.

There is no solution provided for this challenge, because it depends on what feels natural for you.

Chapter 22: More OS X

By Marin Todorov

In Chapter 6, "OS X," you learned how to port your iOS Sprite Kit game to OS X, and you also may have gotten some extra practice in some challenges. This is easy to do when you use Sprite Kit, because Sprite Kit is truly multi-platform.

However, as you learned in the previous two chapters, there's more to most games than a single scene. There are menu screens, onscreen controls, device-specific capabilities, and all kinds of other stuff that Sprite Kit doesn't handle for you.

Since UIKit is available only on iOS, everything you learned in Chapter 20, "UIKit," is only applicable to the iPhone/iPad versions of your games. Luckily, building an OS X app for the Mac isn't that different from building an iOS app. Instead of UIKit, you'll be using a framework called Cocoa, but the patterns are quite similar.

The purpose of this chapter is to introduce you to OS X-specific development techniques so that you can use your Sprite Kit skills to create games for the Mac. You'll continue to work on Circuit Racer until you have a functional OS X port of the game.

By the end of **this chapter,** you'll have learned many common OS X development techniques: creating Cocoa projects, using storyboards, handling mouse and keyboard input, creating games that run in full-screen mode and more!

> **Note:** This chapter begins where the previous chapter's challenge left off. If you were unable to complete the challenge or skipped ahead from an earlier chapter, don't worry—you can simply open **CircuitRacer-Starter** from this chapter's Resources folder to begin in the right place.

Creating a Cocoa target

In previous chapters, you've used Xcode's default template to add an OS X target to your game. This template includes a single .xib file, which simply features a full-window SKView to display your game scene.

To mimic the navigation functionality you introduced to Circuit Racer in Chapter 20, you'll have to go beyond the default Sprite Kit OS X setup.

In Xcode, select the **CircuitRacer** project in the project navigator and at the bottom of the panel on the right, under the Targets list, click the plus sign (+) to add a new target.

Select **OS X/Application/Cocoa Application** (instead of Game as you did before) and click **Next**.

Enter **CircuitRacer OSX** as the Product Name and make sure **Swift** is selected as the Language. Also make sure **Use Storyboards** is **checked**. All other checkboxes must be unchecked.

Click **Finish**, and you'll see your new OS X target in the Targets list.

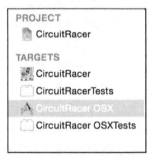

As you can see, your new target features the default OS X application icon rather than your custom Circuit Racer icon, so let's first take care of this issue and add the custom icon to the project.

Open the **Circuit Racer OSX** file group in the project navigator and find
Images.xcassets. Rename it to **ImagesOSX.xcassets**. This way, it will be easier to
distinguish it from the iOS assets catalogues in your project.

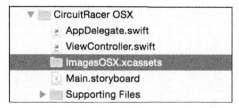

Now select the OS X target from the Targets list again and find the **App Icons** section.
You should now see an option called **ImagesOSX/AppIcon**—select it.

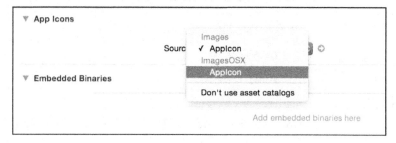

Open the OS X image assets catalogue. By default, Xcode created an empty **AppIcon**
group. Select that group and have a look at the icon sizes you need for OS X:

You need a bunch of different sizes. Lucky for you, in this chapter's **Art** folder, you'll
find a subfolder called **OS X Icons** containing all the required icon sizes. Drag them into
the **AppIcon** group as you did for the other minigame projects.

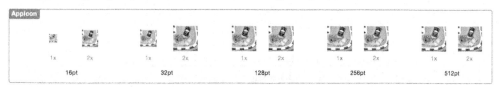

While you're at it, also drag the **Art/OSX Images** folder into your project to add the
extra images you'll need for the Mac version of Circuit Racer. Ensure you add these
images to your new **CircuitRacer OSX** target:

That's that, but that's not all. :]

Select the Mac target of your game as the default one to run:

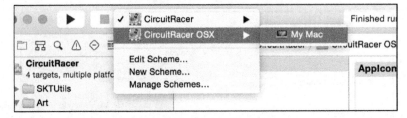

Start the project, and you won't see the game you developed so far, but an empty window.

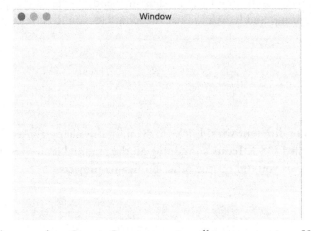

Don't worry! The complete Circuit Racer game is still in your project. You simply need to take care of some UI formalities before showing the game scene and getting the player behind the wheel.

Assembling your storyboard

In the project navigator, select **Main.storyboard** in the CircuitRacer OSX group to peek into the default storyboard that Xcode created.

In many ways, OS X storyboards are quite similar to the iOS storyboards that you've gotten to know and love in the previous chapters. First of all, the storyboard contains a **menu** object:

> **Note:** If the menu is not visible by default, select the Application object in the storyboard object list to see the menu appear.

This is the menu that will display at the top of the Mac's screen whenever your application is active. You can connect the menu items to @IBAction methods in your classes just as you can with any normal button by holding Ctrl and dragging with your mouse.

You also have a **window** object.

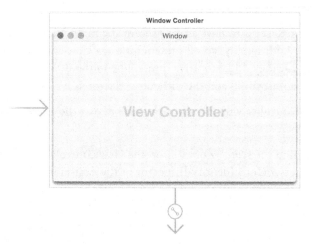

This represents a window in your application. Unlike in iOS, where apps usually have only one window, on OS X, your app can have multiple windows on- or off-screen.

See the arrow pointing to the window from the left? That indicates this is the default window to open when the app starts.

The window is connected to a view controller (much like the view controllers on iOS) via a segue representing a relationship:

The target view controller provides the window's content, and can be seen at the bottom of the storyboard:

This view controller plays an identical role as in iOS: it manages a view and provides you with the events like `viewDidLoad`, `viewDidAppear`, `viewDidDisappear` and so forth.

Your plan for Circuit Racer is to have an `SKView` in the main window to show your existing game scene. Additionally, you'll present an extra view controller to allow players to select the type of car they'd like to drive, much like in the iOS version. In the challenge for this chapter, you'll add the difficulty selector as well.

The select car view controller will also allow the user to exit the game or choose a full-screen game experience.

Let's start by presenting the scene. Zoom in on the view controller in the storyboard and select its view. Then, switch to Identity Inspector in the Assistant Editor and change the view's class to **SKView**.

To present your game scene in the `SKView`, you need to load the .sks file you've already designed. This time, however, you haven't told Xcode you're making a game, so you need to add the code to load .sks files and present them onscreen.

Luckily, you can just copy that code from your iOS target. Open **GameViewController.swift** from your iOS version of Circuit Racer and find the `SKNode` extension code at the top.

```
extension SKNode {
  // more here...
}
```

Copy the complete extension block and paste it into the **ViewController.swift** file of your **OSX target**. The code doesn't use any iOS-specific APIs, so it should work just fine. You do, however, need to make a few changes to get things rolling.

After you paste the code, Xcode will complain that it doesn't recognize `SKNode`. As you've probably already guessed, the remedy for this little issue is to import Sprite Kit at the top of **ViewController.swift**:

```
import SpriteKit
```

Next, Xcode will tell you that `GameScene` is not declared. Well, you actually do have a `GameScene` class, but currently GameScene.swift only belongs to your iOS target. Open **GameScene.swift** and in the Assistant Editor, check the **OS X target** checkbox:

Target Membership	Hide
☑ 🎮 CircuitRacer	
☐ 🧱 CircuitRacerTests	
☑ 🎮 CircuitRacer OSX	
☐ 🧱 CircuitRacer OSXTests	

This will make the `GameScene` class available in your OS X target.

Do the same for **GameScene.sks**—open the file and check the OS X target, so you can use the scene file in your Mac game.

Now is also a good time to include other resources and source code files you want to share between your iOS and OS X targets.

Begin by selecting all files in **SKTUtils**:

Check the **CircuitRacer OSX** target checkbox in the Assistant Editor, just like you did for GameScene.swift.

Do the same for all the files in **Art/Backgrounds, Art/Images, Art/Levels** and **Art/Sounds.** Finally, add **sprites.atlas**, as well. As it's a single file, you simply need to select the blue folder called **sprites.atlas** and check the **CircuitRacer OS X** target once to include all of the textures inside.

This should resolve several of the errors Xcode was complaining about, but there are still few things left to fix. Open **GameScene.swift** and find the line that declares the GameScene class:

```
class GameScene: SKScene, AnalogControlPositionChange {
```

The offending code is the `AnalogControlPositionChange` protocol. Since both `AnalogControl` and `AnalogControlPositionChange` won't play any substantial role in your OS X game, you can just mock them to make Xcode happy, which you'll do in a moment.

You also need to mock the `CMMotionManager` class, which provides you input from the accelerometer censor on iOS. Under OS X, you don't need to import Core Motion at all. Replace `import CoreMotion` at the top of the file with the following:

```
#if os(iOS)
  import CoreMotion
#endif

#if os(OSX)
  class CMMotionManager {}
  class AnalogControl {}
  protocol AnalogControlPositionChange {}
#endif
```

That's all you need to do here—your OS X view controller doesn't display a joypad, so your scene will never need to handle input from one, nor will it receive any accelerometer input. Later on in this chapter, you will add alternative code to move the car via the mouse or keyboard.

Next, tell the compiler that all the code dealing with the input from the accelerometer has to be compiled only for iOS. Open **GameScene.swift** and find `moveCarFromAcceleration()`. Right after `var accel2D = CGPoint.zeroPoint`, add:

```
#if os(iOS)
```

Then, scroll down and find the line `let maxAccelerationPerSecond = maxSpeed`. Just **above that line** (i.e., before that line in the code), close the compilation condition:

```
#endif
```

The chunk of code you enclosed in an `#if` statement deals with `CMMotionManager` and that class exists only on iOS, so you naturally want this piece of code only in your iOS target.

If you still have the code in `update()` that prints out the accelerometer data, you'll need to delete that as well.

Now all the code compiles again—congratulations!

Presenting the scene

Open **ViewController.swift** from your OS X file group and add two variables to the `ViewController` class—you'll need them to present the game scene:

```
@IBOutlet var skView: SKView!
var scene: GameScene!
```

You don't strictly need a separate `skView` variable to access the controller's view, but defining it specifically as an `SKView!` data type will save you the effort of casting it every time you want to reference it in your code. You also declare a `scene` variable where you'll store a reference to your game scene.

Open the OS X group's **Main.storyboard** and connect your view controller's view to the new outlet—hold **Ctrl** and **drag** with your mouse from your view controller object to the view, and from the popup menu, select **skView**.

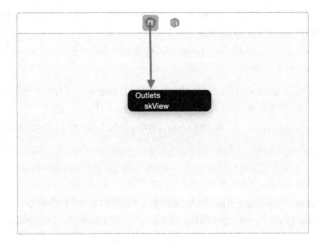

Next, add a method to present the scene. In **ViewController.swift**, add
`presentGame()`:

```
func presentGame() {
  scene = GameScene.unarchiveFromFile("GameScene") as! GameScene
  scene.scaleMode = .AspectFill

  scene.carType = CarType.Yellow
  scene.levelType = LevelType.Easy

  skView!.ignoresSiblingOrder = true
  skView!.showsFPS = true
  skView!.showsNodeCount = true

  skView!.presentScene(scene)

}
```

The code is almost identical to the equivalent method in your iOS target.

First, you load GameScene.sks to set up the game's general layout. Then, you make the
scene scale properly and configure the debug information you want to see onscreen.

You hard-code the yellow car and the easy track as the default choices for the time being.
Remember: You're still trying to get *anything* to show up in your window! You'll fix this
code later on.

Finally, you call `presentScene(scene:)` on your view. Piece of cake!

Now, override `viewWillAppear()` so it calls your new method and, as a bonus, plays
Circuit Racer's background tune:

```
override func viewWillAppear() {
  super.viewWillAppear()

  presentGame()

  SKTAudio.sharedInstance().playBackgroundMusic(
    "circuitracer.mp3")
}
```

Build and run, and check out the result:

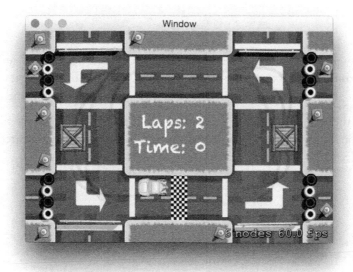

That's Circuit Racer running as a Mac app!

Constraining window size

Next, let's look at window size constraints. Notice that you can resize the window while Circuit Racer is running. Most games don't allow the player to resize the window, as it avoids strange situations like a window with a long width, but a short height.

Open **Main.storyboard** and select the application's window. To do that, you need to click on the window storyboard object somewhere close to where it says **View Controller**:

This will show the window properties in the Assistant Editor. Select the Size Inspector tab (fourth from the right) to set the default window size and position. You can also set the maximum and minimum sizes to which the user can manually resize the window.

At the top of the panel, fill in **1024** for Width and **768** for Height. Set the same dimensions for Minimum Size: click the **Minimum Size checkbox** and enter **1024 x 768**.

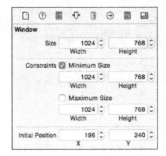

Now to finish the window setup, switch to the Attributes Inspector tab (fourth from the left) and enter **Circuit Racer OSX** as the window's title.

Just to make sure there aren't conflicts while sizing the window – select the view in the view controller and also set its size to 1024 x 768:

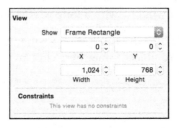

Build and run. The game will launch in a 1024 x 768 window.

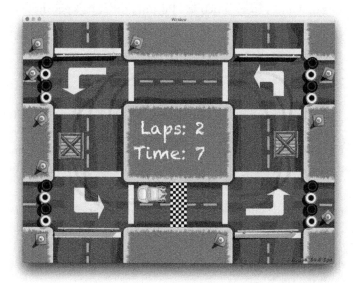

Since the window is rather large let's make it appear centered on screen. Back in
Main.storyboard select the window again and open the Size Inspector. There is a
control, which visualizes how the window will appear when the app launches:

Change the selection in the two drop down menus to **Center Horizontally** and **Center
Vertically**. This will center the window when the app launches.

To prevent OSX from remembering the last position the app window appeared on (and
therefore force it to the screen center every time it appears) switch to the Identity Tab
and uncheck **Restorable**.

Now, I'm sure you've noticed that you can't move the car in any way, even though the game timer counts down just fine, which is a bit unfair. So, let's get those engines roaring again!

Controls in OS X

As you already know from previous chapters, input in OS X is handled differently than in iOS. If your game features single touch controls, it's pretty easy to port that input to OS X—you can capture the mouse clicks in a similar fashion to how you handle single touches. But other control methods that are suitable for iOS gaming may not port to your desktop.

Take the two input methods you developed for Circuit Racer: At first, you created a joypad control, which is handy when you play on a phone because the pad appears onscreen and you interact directly with it via touches. Later, you removed the joypad in favor of using the built-in accelerometer, which allowed the player to have even more fun driving around the track.

Neither of these control methods is suitable for a desktop game. You need to develop a completely new way to control the car on the track.

In this next section, you're going to develop two different input control methods to further explore the Cocoa APIs.

Following the mouse

The first input method you'll implement for your OS X game will be mouse-driven. The car will drive toward the mouse cursor, rotating correctly as it goes. The player will therefore be able to navigate successfully around the track by moving the mouse.

You'll see that you can do this by just adding few code chunks!

Select **File/New/File...** from Xcode's main menu, then select **OS X/Source/Swift file** and click **Next**. Save the new file in your project's folder and call it **GameScene+OSXControls.swift**.

All of your OS X navigation code will go in this new extension of GameScene, since GameScene.swift is becoming quite lengthy.

When the editor opens **GameScene+OSXControls.swift**, make sure it's *not* included in your iOS target:

Target Membership
☐ 🖼 CircuitRacer
☐ ▢ CircuitRacerTests
☑ 🖼 CircuitRacer OSX
☐ ▢ CircuitRacer OSXTests

Now, import the Cocoa framework, since you'll use some built-in Cocoa classes in this file:

```
import Cocoa
```

Next, add this chunk of code to the file:

```
//1
private var currentMouseDown = CGPoint.zeroPoint

extension GameScene {
  //2
  func accelWithCarOrientationToMouse() -> CGPoint {
    //3
    if currentMouseDown == CGPoint.zeroPoint {
      return CGPoint.zeroPoint
    }

    //4
    let accel = currentMouseDown -
childNodeWithName("car")!.position
    return accel.normalized()
  }
}
```

The code looks simple enough, but what does it do?

1. You declare a new global variable called `currentMouseDown`, which is where you'll store the location of the mouse pointer. `currentMouseDown` has a default value of `CGPoint.zeroPoint`, and you're only going to update it if the player drags the mouse while pressing the mouse button.

2. Then, in an extension to `GameScene`, you add a new method, `accelWithCarOrientationToMouse()`, which will provide your `GameScene` with an acceleration vector for the car based on the car's current position and the position of the mouse.

3. If the player isn't pressing the mouse button (and therefore `currentMouseDown` has its default value of `CGPoint.zeroPoint`), the function simply returns `CGPoint.zeroPoint` as the current car acceleration—that is, the car doesn't move.

4. Finally, you subtract the car's current position from the mouse position and normalize the resulting vector. This vector indicates the direction the car should move. This is quite similar to your input from the joypad and the accelerometer, so it should be relatively easy to tap into the existing code and add the new input method for OS X.

You're still missing the code to update currentMouseDown with the latest mouse coordinates. Override these NSResponder methods to react on mouse events. Add these methods inside the class extension:

```
override func mouseDown(event: NSEvent) {
  currentMouseDown = event.locationInNode(self)
}
override func mouseDragged(event: NSEvent) {
  currentMouseDown = event.locationInNode(self)
}
override func mouseUp(event: NSEvent) {
  currentMouseDown = CGPoint.zeroPoint
}
```

When the player presses the mouse button and drags the mouse while holding the button down, you update currentMouseDown. Whenever the player releases the mouse button, you reset currentMouseDown to its default value, and this will stop the car from moving.

Switch to **GameScene.swift** and find the function called moveCarFromAcceleration(). Right after the iOS check #endif, append this code:

```
#if os(OSX)
  accel2D = accelWithCarOrientationToMouse()
#endif
```

You get the car acceleration vector from accelWithCarOrientationToMouse(), the method you added earlier to your OS X target.

You've reached the magic moment. Build, run, and fool around on the track!

Everything will work just fine now. Whenever you press the left mouse button and hold or drag, the car will drive toward your mouse pointer. Move the mouse around to navigate the track.

Sweet! You can play your game on OS X and you know something about handling mouse events. Now, you'll explore a totally different control mechanism: keyboard events!

Arrow keys are key

Car racing games on OS X usually use the arrow keys as input. You accelerate/decelerate with the up and down arrow keys and steer with left and right. Let's apply these controls to Circuit Racer.

It would be fair of you to point out that the iOS version of the game has no controls for acceleration! Implementing keyboard steering will require major design changes. The car will need to accelerate and decelerate over time when the player presses the up/down arrow keys, rather than go immediately from stationary to full speed, and vice-versa. The car will also have to rotate in a way that looks realistic when the player uses the left and right arrow keys.

You're going to track both acceleration and rotation values for the car, and change them as the player holds down the corresponding keys. Start by opening **GameScene+OSXControls.swift** and adding this code outside of the class extension, just under where you declare currentMouseDown:

```
//1
enum SteeringDirection {
  case None, Left, Right
}

//2
enum Acceleration {
  case None, Accelerate, Break
}

//3
private var accelerationStatus: Acceleration = .None
private var steeringStatus: SteeringDirection = .None

//4
private var acceleration: CGFloat = 0
private var steering: CGFloat = 0
```

Let's look in detail at the code you've just written:

1. First you add SteeringDirection, which declares three cases: the player is holding the left arrow key, the right arrow key or neither of them.

2. Similarly, the Acceleration enumeration declares three states: the player is pressing the up arrow key, the down arrow key or neither of those.

3. accelerationStatus and steeringStatus are the variables that will help you track whether the player is currently accelerating, breaking, turning left or turning right.

4. Finally, the acceleration and steering variables will keep track of the current acceleration and rotation values of the car.

You need to handle two different events: when the player presses a key and when the player releases a key. When the player releases a key, you'll simply set the appropriate status variable to .None. That sounds easy enough, so let's implement it first.

Add this new method to the extension of GameScene:

```
//1
override func keyUp(event: NSEvent) {

  //2
  if event.modifierFlags & .NumericPadKeyMask ==
.NumericPadKeyMask  {

    //3
```

```
    for keyChar in
      event.charactersIgnoringModifiers!.unicodeScalars {
      //handle keys
    }

  }

}
```

Much like with the mouse events, NSResponder (from which SKScene is inherited) handles events coming from the keyboard. keyDown(event:) fires when a user presses a key and keyUp(event:) fires when a user releases a key.

To help you understand this, let's consider the code you just added:

1. First, you override NSResponder's default keyUp(event:) implementation. The NSEvent parameter that this method receives provides information about the particular key being pressed and whether there were any additional conditions—for example, whether the Shift or Ctrl keys were pressed at the same time.

2. You check for these additional conditions by exploring event.modifierFlags. This is a bitmask value, since several conditions can be present at the same time—for example, the user can hold both Cmd and Ctrl keys. On the current Mac keyboard, only the arrow keys have the numeric pad bit set, so this is what you check for first.

3. You call event.charactersIgnoringModifiers() to get all the event's key characters. Finally, to fetch the characters' codes, you call unicodeScalars(), which returns an array of code values so you can loop over them.

That isn't too complex, right? When you add a switch to react to different keys, it's going to make even more sense.

In place of //handle keys in the code you just entered, add the following:

```
switch UInt32(keyChar) {
case 0xF700: //up key
  accelerationStatus = .None

case 0xF701: //down key
  accelerationStatus = .None

case 0xF702: //left key
  steeringStatus = .None

case 0xF703: //right key
  steeringStatus = .None
```

```
default:
  break

}
```

Here, you add a case for each of the four key codes representing the up, down, left and right arrow keys, respectively. Letting go of the up or down keys will reset the acceleration status variable. Letting go of the left or right keys will reset the steering status. If the event concerns any other key, you pass by calling `break`.

You've probably already guessed that the method to handle key presses is going to be very similar, but instead of setting the statuses to `.None`, it will assign unique values depending on which key was pressed.

Add `keyDown(event:)`:

```swift
override func keyDown(event: NSEvent) {

  if event.modifierFlags & .NumericPadKeyMask ==
.NumericPadKeyMask  {
    for keyChar in
      event.charactersIgnoringModifiers!.unicodeScalars {

      switch UInt32(keyChar) {
      case 0xF700: //up key
        accelerationStatus = .Accelerate

      case 0xF701: //down key
        accelerationStatus = .Break

      case 0xF702: //left key
        steeringStatus = .Left

      case 0xF703: //right key
        steeringStatus = .Right

      default:
        break

      }
    }
  }
}
```

This new method is almost identical to the last, except it sets `.Accelerating`, `.Break`, `.Left` and `.Right` for the corresponding arrow keys.

Let's pause to consider how driving is going to work via the keyboard, since it's a bit different from the two steering mechanisms you implemented for iOS.

You will track the car's speed in the variable `acceleration`, keeping the value between 0 (the car is stationary) and 0.65 (a decent maximum value for the game). While the player is pressing the up or down keys, you'll increase or decrease that value:

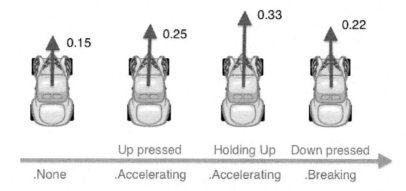

In the diagram above, you can see that the car's speed increases (up to the maximum) as long as the player is pressing the up arrow key. The speed begins decreasing when the player presses the down arrow key. To make the gameplay a bit more realistic, you'll also make the car slowly decelerate when the player isn't pressing any keys.

You already have a vector, which sets the car's forward movement. The rest you can handle by simply rotating this vector left or right, depending on the current orientation of the car:

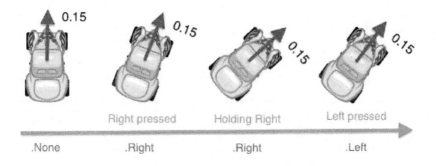

By combining the current forward vector and the current rotation of the car, you'll produce almost the same acceleration vector you used in the previous input methods, making it easy to integrate into your current game scene code.

Add the initial version of the method that will return the car's acceleration vector, depending on the keyboard input:

```
func accelWithCurrentCarRotation() -> CGPoint {

  switch accelerationStatus {
  case .Accelerate:
    acceleration += 0.01
  case .Break:
    acceleration -= 0.02
  case .None:
    acceleration -= acceleration/10
  }

}
```

Much like `accelWithCarOrientationToMouse()`, the method doesn't take in any parameters and returns a `CGPoint`. Ignore, for the moment, the error Xcode is showing you. Right now, you are not returning a `CGPoint` from this method, but that is coming very soon.

In this new method, you simply either increase or decrease the current `acceleration` value depending on the acceleration status. If the player is pressing neither the up nor the down arrow key, you decrease the car's speed slightly to simulate the physical inertia of the car.

So far, so good. Next, you need to set bounds on the resulting acceleration. Add to the method:

```
if abs(acceleration) < 0.01 {
  acceleration = 0
} else {
  acceleration.clamp(0, 0.65)
}
```

If the car's speed is nearing zero, you kill the acceleration, because otherwise the car will continue to move slowly forward, pixel by pixel, forever. You also clamp the value to anywhere between 0 and 0.65.

Next, build a forward acceleration vector based on the acceleration you just calculated. Add the following code at the bottom of the method:

```
let nominalAcceleration = CGPoint(x: acceleration, y: 0)
```

This way, your car can move forward faster or slower, but can never turn around. Now it's time to take care of the car's rotation by modifying the rotation delta according to the rotation status. Still in the same method, add the following:

```
switch steeringStatus {
case .Left:
  steering += 0.05
case .Right:
  steering -= 0.05
case .None:
  steering -= steering/5
}
```

Just as before, you either increase or decrease the value based on the current rotation status. In the same way you set bounds for the acceleration, do so for the steering by adding this code:

```
if abs(steering) < 0.05 {
  steering = 0
} else {
  steering.clamp(-0.33, 0.33)
}
```

This restricts the turning circle of the car. If rotation delta is too small, you reset it to zero so the car goes on moving straight forward. Otherwise, you clamp the rotation delta to the range between -0.33 and 0.33. Negative values turn the car to the left, 0 keeps it straight and positive values turn it to the right.

There isn't much left for the steering logic. You need to calculate the rotation angle by adding the rotation delta to the car's current rotation angle:

```
let rotation = childNodeWithName("car")!.zRotation + steering
```

`rotation` contains the angle to which you need to orientate the car. You need to turn this angle into a vector (by using an `SKTUtils` function) and multiply it by the acceleration to get a true acceleration vector, so add the following code:

```
let accel = CGPoint(angle: rotation) * acceleration
```

`CGPoint(angle:)` gives you a normalized vector pointing to the direction of `angle` and you simply multiply that result by the current car `acceleration` to get the properly-oriented acceleration vector.

Finally, add this code to return that vector:

```
return accel
```

It's time to wrap up and test the new input method! Open **GameScene.swift** and find the line you added earlier for the mouse control: `accel2D = accelWithCarOrientationToMouse()`. For the time being, you won't need the mouse-based input, so comment out that line and add the following line, still within the `#if os(OSX)` check:

```
//accel2D = accelWithCarOrientationToMouse()
accel2D = accelWithCurrentCarRotation()
```

You are good to go! Build and run the game. This time, you can make the car go forward by pressing and holding the up arrow key. Steer by pressing left and right. If you're about to crash, you can hold the down arrow key to quickly stop the car. Neat!

Now that you have a good base of code for handling keyboard events, you are welcome to fine-tune the steering mechanism. Adjust some of the magic numbers to get a better (or worse) driving experience, as you see fit!

This concludes the section of the chapter on handling input in OS X. Next, it's time to bring more cars into the game.

More Cocoa UI

Currently, the OS X version of Circuit Racer is missing two very important features of the iOS version. Your players cannot play more than once, and they also cannot choose between the available cars or difficulty.

Since UI and navigation are handled outside of Sprite Kit—you used UIKit for these purposes in the previous chapters—you can't get this functionality out-of-the-box on OS X. In this next part of the chapter, you'll learn how to design and present additional view OS X controllers with Cocoa controls in your game.

Most OS X games begin by showing you a configuration window where you can select various game options before starting the game itself. You're going to implement something similar for Circuit Racer.

In the CircuitRacer OS X group, open **Main.storyboard** and drag in a view controller:

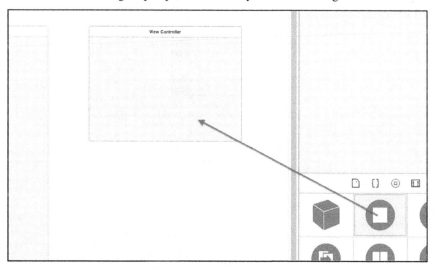

Select the view and set a Width of **640** and a Height of **460**. You might need to zoom in on the view controller to be able to select its view.

Ctrl-drag from the blue button on top of your game view controller to your new view controller, like so:

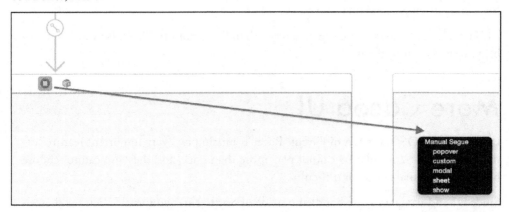

Choose **sheet** from the popup menu to create a modal segue to your new view controller. The **sheet** option allows you to modally present the view controller as a little panel that falls down from the top of the application's window. I'm sure you've seen this happen a million times in Mac apps.

Now select the segue object:

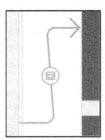

Back in Attributes Inspector, set the Identifier to **selectCarSegue**. This way, you can invoke it from code by using its name.

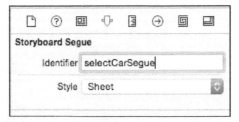

Great work so far! Let's now go on with designing the car selector UI. Zoom in on the new view controller if you need to, then drag and drop an image view:

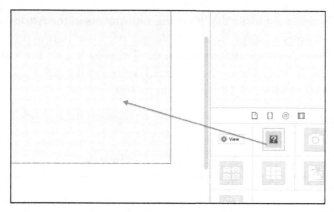

Set the frame of the new image view to X: **0**, Y: **0**, Width: **640** and Height: **460** so that it fills the parent view. Switch to the Attributes Inspector, and as the Image, enter **select-car-osx**. This should set you up with a nice background for the view controller:

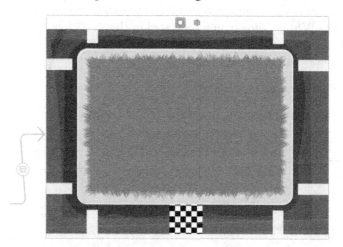

Next, drag and drop three default push buttons and align them horizontally, like so:

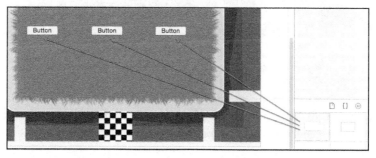

Select all three buttons and make the following adjustments in the Attributes Inspector: set Type to **Momentary Change** (to disable default effects on button press), uncheck the **Bordered** checkbox, delete the default text in the **Title** box and set **btn-car1** as the Image. Then, with the three buttons still selected, switch to the Size Inspector and set the frame to Y: **116**, Width to **121** and Height to **169**.

There are a few more attributes left. Make these changes on the individual buttons, one by one:

	X	Image	Tag
Left button	110	btn-car1	0
Center button	254	btn-car2	1
Right button	398	btn-car3	2

Next, drag a label onto the scene and adjust its properties like so: set Title to **Select your car**, Text Color to **White Color** (you might need to choose **Other...** to get a color picker) and Alignment to **Center**. In the Size Inspector, set X to **142**, Y to **308**, Width to **356** and Height to **70**.

Set the font to **Chalkduster** at **36 points** height.

Following the instructions correctly should produce a familiar interface:

You will present this dialogue and let the player choose a car. Clicking one of the buttons will set the scene's carType property and start the game.

However, there's something else you have to take care of first. Switch to
ViewController.swift and add one more line to `presentGame()`:

```
scene.paused = true
```

This will pause the game until the player selects which car they want to drive. You don't
want the timer to continue counting while the player is choosing a car.

Now you can present the car selector. Perform the segue at the end of `presentGame()`:

```
performSegueWithIdentifier("selectCarSegue", sender: self)
```

Build and run, and as soon as you do, you'll see the scene window present a modal sheet
that instructs you to choose a car:

Hooray! You've just learned how to present view controllers onscreen in OS X.

> **Note:** You'll need to press the stop button in Xcode to kill the game. You can't
> quit an app in any other way if it currently displays a modal dialogue.

Now you need to modify the scene a bit so that it shows an empty track until the player
has selected a car. Open **GameScene.swift** and replace `didMoveToView()` with this new
implementation:

```
override func didMoveToView(view: SKView) {
```

```
    let bg = SKSpriteNode(imageNamed: "bg-main-menu")
    bg.position = CGPointMake(size.width/2, size.height/2)
    bg.name = "bg"
    bg.zPosition = 100
    addChild(bg)
}
```

Instead of starting the scene right away, you create an image sprite showing the empty game track and show it, instead. You'll remove this placeholder image as soon as the game starts. At the top of `initializeGame()`, insert:

```
childNodeWithName("bg")?.removeFromParent()
```

Now that you are no longer calling `initializeGame()` from `didMoveToView()`, you need to call it manually on your iOS build. Before you do that you will need to change `initializeGame()` to be a public method. Remove the **private** modifier in front of that method declaration to allow other classes to call it:

```
public func initializeGame() {
```

Open **GameViewController.swift** and add this line right after the call to `presentScene()`:

```
scene.initializeGame()
```

Build and run again on OS X, and this time, you'll see the game configuration scene on its own background:

All right! You're making excellent progress. Let's keep the tempo up and finish the car selector window sheet.

Go back to **Main.storyboard** and drop a push button near the bottom-left corner of the car select view controller. Set its title to **Exit Game** and leave its default properties as they are (resize the button a bit if the text doesn't fit).

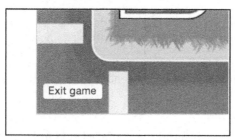

As mentioned above, you need a special **Exit game** button because your car selector is presented as a modal sheet, and while you present a modal sheet the player cannot close the application via the usual application menu option.

Now let's add some code for your car selector view controller. Select **File/New/File...** from Xcode's main menu, then select **OS X/Source/Swift File** and click **Next**. Save the file as **SelectCarViewControllerOSX.swift** and make sure that only your OS X target is checked in the save dialogue:

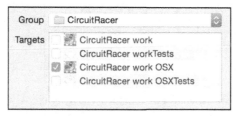

Let's start by adding the bare bones of the class:

```
import Cocoa

class SelectCarViewControllerOSX: NSViewController {

  var didSelectCarHandler: ((Int, Int)->())?
  var closeAppHandler: (()->())?

}
```

You will be using UI classes, so you import the Cocoa framework first. Then you declare a new subclass of NSViewController with two class instance variables.

`didSelectCarHandler` is a closure variable that will get called when the player selects a car. It takes two parameters—the first will be the selected car type, and the second you will use a bit later. `closeAppHandler` will be called when the player clicks on your **Exit game** button.

Add the implementation of these methods to the class:

```
@IBAction func actionSelectCar(sender: NSButton) {
  didSelectCarHandler?(sender.tag, 0)
}

@IBAction func actionCloseApp(sender: NSButton) {
  closeAppHandler?()
}
```

When the player clicks on a car button, `actionSelectCar(sender:)` invokes the stored closure and passes over the button tag—0 for the yellow car, 1 for the blue car, etc. When the player clicks on **Exit game,** `actionCloseApp()` simply invokes whatever closure you set for `closeAppHandler`.

That's all the coding for the moment; you need to connect the button events in Interface Builder and you'll be good to go. Open **Main.storyboard** and select the car selector view controller object:

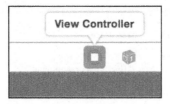

Switch to the Identity Inspector, and as Custom Class, enter **SelectCarViewControllerOSX**:

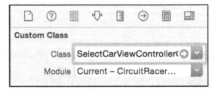

Now hold the **Ctrl** key on your keyboard and **drag** with the mouse from the **Exit game** button to the view controller object at the top of the view controller in your storyboard:

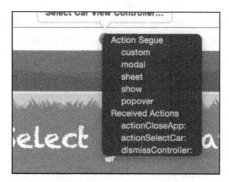

From the popup menu, select **actionCloseApp:**. Then repeat the same procedure for each of the car buttons, but connect them to the **actionSelectCar:** method.

This finishes up the car selector. Now you need to hook it up to your view controller.

You'll tap into the segue's presentation event to configure its target view controller. You already know how to do that from the iOS version of the game and the process isn't any different under OS X.

Open **ViewController.swift** and add a prepareForSegue(segue:, sender:) method:

```
override func prepareForSegue(segue: NSStoryboardSegue,
  sender: AnyObject!) {

  if (segue.identifier == "selectCarSegue") {

    let scvc = segue.destinationController as!
      SelectCarViewControllerOSX

    scvc.closeAppHandler = {
      self.dismissViewController(scvc)
      NSApplication.sharedApplication().terminate(self)
    }

  }
}
```

First, you check for the name of the modal sheet presentation segue. It's true that you have only one segue right now, but it's a good practice, since you're might want to add more segues later on.

Then, you fetch segue.destinationController, which is the view controller about to be presented, and you cast it to an instance of SelectCarViewControllerOSX so that you can access its variables.

You set the `closeAppHandler` closure with code that simply dismisses the sheet view controller and then you call `terminate()` on the shared instance of `NSApplication`. This nicely closes the modal sheet and quits the game.

Now you can also add the car selection closure. Add at the end of (but still inside) the segue identifier `if` block:

```
scvc.didSelectCarHandler = {carTypeInt, fullScreen in

  self.dismissViewController(scvc)

  self.scene.carType = CarType(rawValue: carTypeInt)!
  self.scene.levelType = LevelType.Medium
  self.scene.initializeGame()
  self.scene.paused = false
}
```

This just about wraps up the navigation code. First, you dismiss the modal car selector sheet, and then, you set the scene's car type from the car button tag that was passed to the closure. You always load the medium difficulty track (to keep things simple, you won't be adding the select difficulty screen in this chapter).

Finally, you call `initializeGame()` on the scene so that it loads the level data and builds up the scene. You un-pause the scene, and it all comes together!

Build and run the game, and play with any of the available cars:

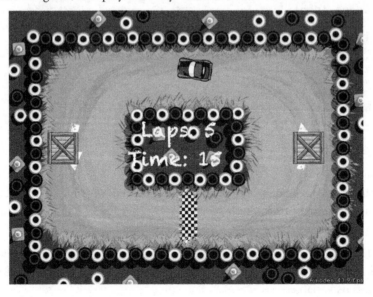

The only navigation bit remaining is to provide a way to restart the game once the player completes a track race. This is easy to do—I hope you still remember that the scene class has a closure variable called `gameOverBlock`, which gets called whenever the race ends.

Switch to **ViewController.swift** and just under `skView!.presentScene(scene)`, add this:

```
scene.gameOverBlock = {(didWin) in

    let alert = NSAlert()
    alert.addButtonWithTitle("Close")
    alert.messageText =  "Game over"
    alert.informativeText = didWin ? "You won!": "You lost..."
    alert.runModal()

    self.presentGame()
}
```

The code to present an alert box in OS X is a little more verbose compared to the iOS equivalent, but the principle is the same. You set the alert's title (`messageText`) and the alert's body text (`informativeText`), and add a button to close it.

`runModal()` displays the alert on top of the application window and prevents the player from interacting with anything else until they close the alert box.

Finally, you call `presentGame()`. In the background, under the alert box, you simply reload the complete scene from GameScene.sks and show the car selector again. Whenever the player closes the alert box, the game is ready for another race!

Build and run, and now you can race again after winning or losing the first race:

As soon as you click the Close button, the window's contents are updated and you see the car selector again. However, you'll soon notice that when you play for a second or third time, the car starts by itself before you even touch the up arrow key.

This is because you use global module variables to track the acceleration and rotation states of the car, so that when you reload the scene, it still sees the acceleration status from the last level. No problem—you simply need to reset those variables whenever you present the game scene onscreen.

Open **GameScene+OSXControls.swift** and add a new method to the class extension:

```
func resetControls() {
  accelerationStatus = .None
  steeringStatus = .None
  acceleration = 0.0
  steering = 0.0
}
```

Switch to **ViewController.swift** and add a call to this new method at the end of presentGame():

```
scene.resetControls()
```

This should fix the acceleration bug you were experiencing. Give the game another try!

Full-screen gameplay

For the last topic of this chapter, you'll implement a full-screen mode for your OS X Circuit Racer game.

Some players will prefer to play full-screen and some will favor the window mode. It's best if your game offers both. The Sprite Kit Circuit Racer code already supports different scene sizes, so resizing the app window is not a problem. You only need to handle the Cocoa UI and provide a way for the user to switch to full-screen.

Let's go through the process step by step. First, you'll add a checkbox to the car selection view controller. Open **Main.storyboard** and drop a checkbox near the bottom-right corner of the car selection view controller. Set its title to **Full Screen** and change its default State to **Off**:

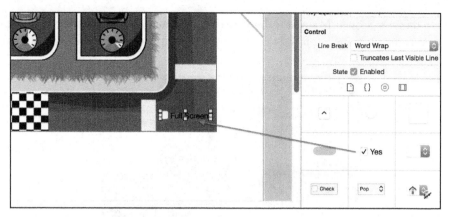

Next, you need to connect the button and its action. Open
SelectCarViewControllerOSX.swift in the editor and add this to the class body:

```
var fullScreenPreselectedState = 0

@IBOutlet var fullScreenButton: NSButton!

override func viewWillAppear() {
  super.viewWillAppear()
  fullScreenButton.state = fullScreenPreselectedState
}
```

First, you declare a variable to store the player's last choice, for convenience. In other
words, once the player chooses to play in full-screen mode and completes a race, they'll
see the car selector sheet again, and the checkbox will still be checked.

Then, you create an outlet so you can access the current state of the checkbox. Note that
a number of controls in Cocoa, including the checkbox, are just different types of
`NSButton`, so your outlet is also of type `NSButton`.

Finally, right before displaying the car selector sheet onscreen in `viewWillAppear()`,
you set the selection state of the checkbox to whatever has been set to
`fullScreenPreselectedState`. The default value for this variable is `0`, which gives
you an unchecked checkbox.

Remember that second argument on `didSelectCarHandler`? It's going to take the state
of the checkbox. So, in `actionSelectCar(sender:)`, replace the second argument of
the call to `didSelectCarHandler` (hard-coded to `0` at the moment) with
`fullScreenButton.state`, as shown here:

```
didSelectCarHandler?(sender.tag, fullScreenButton.state)
```

To wrap things up, open **Main.storyboard**, and while holding the **Ctrl** key, **drag** from your view controller object (on the top of the storyboard view controller window) to the checkbox:

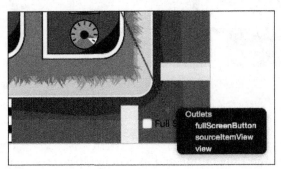

From the popup menu, select **fullScreenButton** to connect your outlet to the checkbox in your storyboard.

Go on by adding the code that toggles your game window to full-screen mode and back. Open **ViewController.swift** and add a variable to track the last selected mode:

```
var fullScreenState: Int = 0
```

You keep track of what the user chose when starting the game so you know whether you need to toggle Full Screen again when the race finishes. Find:

```
let scvc = segue.destinationController as
  SelectCarViewControllerOSX
```

And add this under that line:

```
scvc.fullScreenPreselectedState = self.fullScreenState
```

This presets the Full Screen checkbox state with the user's last choice when presenting the car selector sheet.

Now it's time for the real thing. Find the line where you set `scvc.didSelectCarHandler`, and just under `self.dismissViewController(stvc)`, add the following:

```
self.fullScreenState = fullScreen

if self.fullScreenState>0 {
  NSApplication.sharedApplication().windows[0].toggleFullScreen(
  self)
}
```

First, you store the current mode selection and then, you fetch the current window—it's the first object in the windows array—and call `toggleFullScreen()` on it.

This should put the window to Full Screen when the game starts if the user has selected that mode. Now you need to put your game in a normal window (if needed) when the user finishes the race and wants to select another car.

Add the same chunk of code to toggle between modes at the beginning of `presentGame()`:

```
if self.fullScreenState>0 {
  NSApplication.sharedApplication().windows[0].toggleFullScreen(
    self)
}
```

The code is complete. The UI is ready. There's one final step—to configure your application's window for Full Screen mode. Open **Main.storyboard** and click on your window:

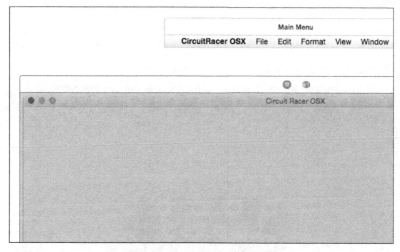

In the Attributes Inspector, you'll find a drop-box called **Full Screen**. Set the value of this drop-box to **Primary Window**.

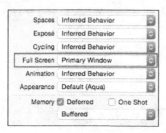

Run the game, and on the car selection screen, check the Full Screen checkbox:

Then select your car, and enjoy full-screen gameplay:

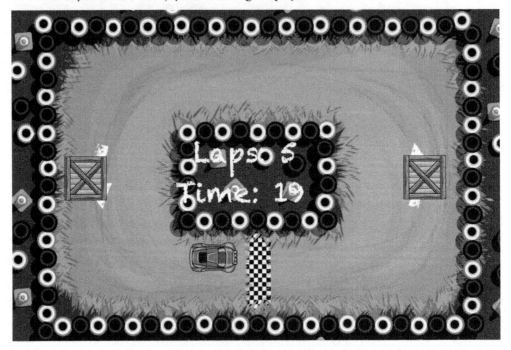

OS X recap

In this chapter, you got acquainted with a number of OS X development techniques. While porting Circuit Racer to Mac, you learned how to:

• Create a Cocoa target, which can include an application menu, a storyboard and more.

• Design OS X storyboards featuring view controllers and segues.

• Share Sprite Kit code between your iOS and OS X targets, but implement the UI with UIKit and Cocoa separately.

• Handle mouse events and keyboard input.

• Tap into full-screen gameplay.

I hope this chapter has shown you that Cocoa APIs aren't much different from UIKit, after all. By now, you have enough of an understanding of Cocoa to explore OS X integration even further on your own. For starters, give the chapter's challenge a try—it will put what you've learned to the test and give you all the confidence you need to bring your own games to life on OS X!

Challenges

Your challenge for this chapter will complete your porting of Circuit Racer from iOS to OS X. No doubt you've noticed I've left one important game element unaddressed!

As always, if you get stuck, you can find the solutions in the resources for this chapter— but give it your best shot first!

Challenge 1: Build a level selector

Right now, the OS X version of Circuit Racer incorporates only one level, the medium difficulty track. Use everything you learned in this chapter about Cocoa and OS X to create a level selection dialogue. Your level selector should use the same assets and basic layout as the one you built for iOS in Chapter 20.

The rough outline of the steps you need to take to re- create the track selector are as follows:

- Lay out a view controller in your storyboard with the 3 difficulty buttons (remember to set their tags to 0, 1, and 2 respectively). The correct size of the buttons is 301 x 55 points.

- Add an **Exit Game** button and a **Full Screen** checkbox in exactly the same way you did for the car selector dialogue.

- Create a segue from your view controller to the level selector view and call it **selectLevelSegue**.

- Create a custom `NSViewController` sub- class called `SelectLevelViewControllerOSX`, set it as the class for the view controller in Interface Builder.

- Copy over the class variables from `SelectCarViewControllerOSX` to `SelectLevelViewControllerOSX`: `didSelectLevelHandler` (it's originally called didSelectCarHandler – change the name to reflect the new class' purpose), `closeAppHandler`, `fullScreenPreselectedState`, and `fullScreenButton` .

- Copy over the `actionCloseApp(sender:)` and `viewWillAppear(animated:)` methods.

- Connect `fullScreenButton` to the checkbox in Interface Builder, connect the action of Exit Button to `actionCloseApp(sender:)`.

- Create an `actionSelectLevel(sender:)` method after how `actionSelectCar(sender:)` works in `SelectCarViewControllerOSX`.

- Connect all three level difficulty buttons to `actionSelectLevel(sender:)` – don't forget to set the tags 0, 1, and 2 to the buttons.

- When all dialogues are set you will need to change the logic as well – look in **ViewController.swift** and change the `didSelectCarHandler` of the car dialogue to open the level selector when the player selects a car:

```
scvc.didSelectCarHandler = {carTypeInt, fullScreen in
  self.dismissViewController(scvc)

  self.fullScreenState = fullScreen
  self.scene.carType = CarType(rawValue: carTypeInt)!

  self.performSegueWithIdentifier("selectLevelSegue",
    sender: self)
}
```

- Finally you will need to start the game when the player selects a track and also implement again the code to switch to Full Screen mode:

```
if (segue.identifier == "selectLevelSegue") {

  let scvc = segue.destinationController as!
SelectLevelViewControllerOSX

  scvc.fullScreenPreselectedState = self.fullScreenState

  scvc.closeAppHandler = {
    self.dismissViewController(scvc)
    NSApplication.sharedApplication().terminate(self)
  }

  scvc.didSelectLevelHandler = {levelTypeInt, fullScreen in

    self.dismissViewController(scvc)

    self.fullScreenState = fullScreen

    if self.fullScreenState>0 {
      NSApplication.sharedApplication()
        .windows[0].toggleFullScreen(self)
    }

    self.scene.levelType = LevelType(rawValue: levelTypeInt)!
```

```
        self.scene.initializeGame()
        self.scene.paused = false
    }
}
```

This should pretty much be all you have to do to complete this challenge. Now you have full featured game navigation and game configuration dialogues for Circuit Racer on OSX.

Section VI: Bonus Chapters

To thank you for purchasing this book, we've included some bonus chapters for you!

The first three chapters show you how to add Game Center leaderboards, achievements, and multiplayer support into your game. The next two chapters are about getting the most performance out of your game, and the final chapter is about learning how to get great art for your game – whether you hire someone or take the do-it-yourself approach.

These bonus chapters come as an optional PDF download, which you can download for free here:

• http://www.raywenderlich.com/store/ios-games-by-tutorials/bonus-chapters

Chapter 23: Game Center Achievements

Chapter 24: Game Center Leaderboards

Chapter 25: Game Center Multiplayer

Chapter 26: Performance: Texture Atlases

Chapter 27: Performance: Tips and Tricks

Chapter 28: Making Art for Programmers

Conclusion

We hope that you have enjoyed your adventure through this book. If you followed along the entire way, you have made five complete iOS games with Sprite Kit from scratch – spanning everything from zombies to cats to badasses named Arnold. You now have all the knowledge it takes to make a hit game, so why not go for it?

Come up with a great idea, prototype a game, get people to play it, watch them for feedback and keep iterating and polishing your game based on all you have learned. Be sure to set aside time in your schedule to add juice to your game, and make sure you have killer art and sound effects, following the advice in the book.

We can't wait to see what you come up with! Be sure to stop by our forums and share your progress at http://www.raywenderlich.com/forums.

You might also be interested to know that we have a monthly blog post where we review games written by fellow readers like you. If you'd like to be considered for this column, please visit this page after you release your game: http://www.raywenderlich.com/reviews

We have one final question for you: Did we succeed in our goal to write the best book on game programming you've ever read? Please email us anytime at ray@raywenderlich.com to let us know either way.

Thank you again for purchasing this book. Your continued support is what makes the tutorials, books and other things we do at raywenderlich.com possible. We truly appreciate it.

Best of luck in all your iOS adventures,

> — Tom, Mike, Jake, Ali, Matthijs, Chris, B.C., Vinnie, Rod, Marin, Ray and Vicki
>
> (the raywenderlich.com Tutorial Team and friends!)

CPSIA information can be obtained at www.ICGtesting.com
Printed in the USA
LVOW03s1715150615

442538LV00011B/440/P